T0268123

PENGUIN CLASSICS

BRAHMANDA PURANA: VOLUME 1

Bibek Debroy is a renowned economist, scholar and translator. He has worked in universities, research institutes, industry and for the government. He has widely published books, papers and articles on economics. As a translator, he is best known for his magnificent rendition of the Mahabharata in ten volumes, the three-volume translation of the Valmiki Ramayana and the *Shiva Purana*, along with the *Harivamsha, Bhagavata Purana, Markandeya Purana, Brahma Purana* and *Vishnu Purana*, published to wide acclaim by Penguin Classics. He is also the author of *Sarama and Her Children*, which splices his interest in Hinduism with his love for dogs.

PRAISE FOR *SHIVA PURANA*

'Bibek Debroy's translation of the *Shiva Purana* is written in an easy-to-understand language, with copious footnotes, and marked by scrupulous attention to consistency in the use of terms. The greater use of Sanskrit terms that do not have an exact or reasonably accurate translation in English is eased for the reader through the use of explanatory footnotes'—News18

PRAISE FOR *THE BHAGAVATA PURANA*

'An exhaustive but accessible translation of a crucial mythological text'—*Indian Express*

'The beauty of recounting these stories lies in the manner in which the cosmic significance and the temporal implications are intermingled. Debroy's easy translation makes that experience even more sublime'—*Business Standard*

'The Puranas are 18 volumes with more than four lakh *shloka*s, and all in Sanskrit—the language of our ancestors and the sages, which only a few can speak and read today and only a handful have the mastery to translate. Bibek Debroy is one such master translator, who wears the twin title of economist and Sanskrit scholar, doing equal justice to both'—*Outlook*

PRAISE FOR THE *MARKANDEYA PURANA*

'[The] *Markandeya Purana* is a marvellous amalgam of mythology and metaphysics that unfolds a series of conversations in which sage Markandeya is asked to answer some deeper questions raised by the events in the Mahabharata'—*Indian Express*

'Bibek Debroy's translation of the *Markandeya Purana* presents the English reader with an opportunity to read the unabridged version in English. As he writes in the introduction, "*But all said and done, there is no substitute to reading these texts in the original Sanskrit.*" If you cannot read the original in Sanskrit, this is perhaps the next best thing'—Abhinav Agarwal

PRAISE FOR *VISHNU PURANA*

'Bibek Debroy's unabridged translation brings his trademark felicity of prose. Copious footnotes, numbering over a thousand, and scrupulous attention to keeping this a translation and not an interpretation, make this a much-needed and valuable text'—Firstpost

'Like the others, this *Purana* captures ancient and medieval stories, and concepts of Hinduism in a range and complexity that no other Sanskrit texts offer . . . or the *Vishnu Purana* ends on a sombre note, but not without offering hope that those who chant Vishnu's name can still reclaim dharma'—*Business Standard*

'Immense credit to the translator for keeping the flow as light and engaging as the original may allow and for capturing and conveying intact the soul of the *Vishnu Purana* . . . In essence, this text functions as a concise encyclopaedia of perhaps the most evolved research and thought of the time and a 360-degree portrayal of Lord Vishnu in myriad forms aggregated from various oral or lost sources and tales . . . A treasure trove; a slow-paced perusal of the text is an eye-opener, an education in itself'—*New Indian Express*

PRAISE FOR *THE BRAHMA PURANA*

'In two volumes and over 1000 pages, Mr Debroy's translation of what is called the Adi Purana (or the original Purana) brings alive the many myths and legends surrounding Hindu gods, traditions, customs and ways of living'—*Business Standard*

BRAHMANDA PURANA

Volume 1

BIBEK DEBROY

PENGUIN BOOKS

An imprint of Penguin Random House

PENGUIN BOOKS

USA | Canada | UK | Ireland | Australia
New Zealand | India | South Africa | China | Singapore

Penguin Books is part of the Penguin Random House group of companies
whose addresses can be found at global.penguinrandomhouse.com

Published by Penguin Random House India Pvt. Ltd
4th Floor, Capital Tower 1, MG Road,
Gurugram 122 002, Haryana, India

Penguin
Random House
India

First published in Penguin Books by Penguin Random House India 2024

ISBN 9780143465287

Typeset in Sabon by Manipal Technologies Limited, Manipal
Printed at Gopsons Papres Pvt. Ltd., Noida

www.penguinbooksindia.com

MIX
Paper from
responsible sources
FSC® C191020

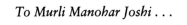

To Murli Manohar Joshi . . .

Contents

Contents

Introduction

The word 'Purana' means old, ancient. The Puranas are old texts, usually referred to in conjunction with Itihasa (the Ramayana and the Mahabharata).[1] Whether Itihasa originally meant only the Mahabharata, with the Ramayana being added to that expression later, is a proposition on which there has been some discussion. But that's not relevant to our purposes. In the Chandogya Upanishad, there is an instance of the sage Narada approaching the sage Sanatkumara for instruction. Asked about what he already knows, Narada says he knows Itihasa and Purana, the Fifth Veda.[2] In other words, Itihasa-Purana possessed an elevated status. This by no means implies that the word 'Purana', as used in these two Upanishads and other texts too, is to be understood in the sense of the word being applied to a set of texts known as the Puranas today. The Valmiki Ramayana is believed to have been composed by Valmiki and the Mahabharata by Krishna Dvaipayana Vedavyasa. After composing the Mahabharata, Krishna Dvaipayana Vedavyasa is believed to have composed the Puranas. The use of the word 'composed' immediately indicates that Itihasa-Purana are 'smriti' texts, with a human origin. They are not 'shruti' texts, with a divine origin. Composition does not mean these texts were rendered into writing. Instead, there was a process of oral transmission, with inevitable

---

[1] For example, *shloka*s 2.4.10, 4.1.2 and 4.5.11 of the Brihadaranyaka Upanishad use the two expressions together.

[2] Chandogya Upanishad, 7.1.2.

noise in the transmission and distribution process. Writing came much later.

F.E. Pargiter's book on the Puranas is still one of the best introductions to this corpus.[3] To explain the composition and transmission process, one can do no better than to quote him. 'The Vayu and Padma Puranas tell us how ancient genealogies, tales and ballads were preserved, namely, by the *sutas*,[4] and they describe the *suta*'s duty . . . The Vayu, Brahmanda and Visnu give an account, how the original Purana came into existence . . . Those three Puranas say—Krsna Dvaipayana divided the single Veda into four and arranged them, and so was called Vyasa. He entrusted them to his four disciples, one to each, namely Paila, Vaisampayana, Jaimini and Sumantu. Then with tales, anecdotes, songs and lore that had come down from the ages, he compiled a Purana and taught it and the Itihasa to his fifth disciple, the suta Romaharsana or Lomaharsana . . . After that he composed the Mahabharata. The epic itself implies that the Purana preceded it . . . As explained above, the *suta*s had from remote times preserved the genealogies of gods, rishis and kings, and traditions and ballads about celebrated men, that is, exactly the material—tales, songs and ancient lore—out of which the Purana was constructed. Whether or not Vyasa composed the original Purana or superintended its compilation, is immaterial for the present purpose . . . After the original Purana was composed, by Vyasa as is said, his disciple Romaharsana taught it to his son Ugrasravas, and Ugrasravas the sauti appears as the reciter in some of the present Puranas; and the sutas still retained the right to recite it for their livelihood. But, as stated above, Romaharsana taught it to his six disciples, at least five of whom were brahmans. It thus passed into the hands of brahmans, and their appropriation and development of it increased in the course of time, as the Purana grew into many Puranas, as Sanskrit learning became peculiarly the province of the brahmans, and as new and frankly sectarian Puranas were composed.' Pargiter cited reasons for his belief that the Mahabharata was composed

---

[3] *Ancient Indian Historical Tradition*, F.E. Pargiter, Oxford University Press, London, 1922.

[4] *Suta*s were bards, minstrels, raconteurs.

after the original Purana, though that runs contrary to the popular perception about the Mahabharata having been composed before the Puranas. That popular and linear perception is too simplistic since texts evolved in parallel, not necessarily sequentially.

In popular perception, Krishna Dvaipayana Vedavyasa composed the Mahabharata. He then composed the Puranas. Alternatively, he composed an original core Purana text, which has been lost, and others embellished it through additions. The adjective 'Purana', meaning 'old account' or 'old text', became a proper noun, signifying a specific text. To be classified as a Purana, a text has to possess five attributes—*pancha lakshana*. That is, five topics must be discussed— *sarga*, *pratisarga*, *vamsha*, *manvantara* and *vamshanucharita*. The clearest statement of this is in the *Matsya Purana*. Unlike the Ramayana and the Mahabharata, there is no Critical Edition of the Puranas.[5] Therefore, citing chapter and verse from a Purana text is somewhat more difficult, since verse, if not chapter, may vary from text to text. With that caveat, the relevant *shloka* (verse) should be in the fifty-third chapter of the *Matysa Purana*. *Sarga* means the original or primary creation. The converse of *sarga* is universal destruction and dissolution, or *pralaya*. That period of *sarga* lasts for one of Brahma's days, known as *kalpa*. When Brahma sleeps, during his night, there is universal destruction.

In measuring time, there is the notion of a *yuga* (era) and there are four *yugas*—*satya yuga* (also known as *krita yuga*), *treta yuga*, *dvapara yuga* and *kali yuga*. *Satya yuga* lasts for 4000 years, *treta yuga* for 3000 years, *dvapara yuga* for 2000 years and *kali yuga* for 1000 years. However, all these are not human years. The Gods have a different timescale and these are the years of the Gods. As one progressively moves from *satya yuga* to *kali yuga*, virtue (*dharma*) declines. But at the end of *kali yuga*, the cycle begins afresh, with *satya yuga*. An entire cycle, from *satya yuga* to *kali yuga*, is known

---

[5] The Critical Edition of the Valmiki Ramayana was brought out by the Baroda Oriental Institute, now part of the Maharaja Sayajirao University of Baroda. The Critical Edition of the Mahabharata was brought out by the Bhandarkar Oriental Research Institute, Pune. For a few Puranas, work on Critical Editions has started.

as a *mahayuga* (great era). However, a *mahayuga* is not just 10,000 years. There is a further complication. At the beginning and the end of every *yuga*, there are some additional years. These additional years are 400 for *satya yuga*, 300 for *treta yuga*, 200 for *dvapara yuga* and 100 for *kali yuga*. A *mahayuga* thus has 12,000 years, adding years both at the beginning and at the end. 1000 *mahayuga*s make up one *kalpa* (eon), a single day for Brahma. A *kalpa* is also divided into fourteen *manvantara*s, a *manvantara* being a period during which a Manu presides and rules over creation. Therefore, there are 71.4 *mahayuga*s in a *manvantara*. Our present *kalpa* is known as the Shveta Varaha Kalpa. Within that, six Manus have come and gone. Their names are: (1) Svayambhuva Manu, (2) Svarochisha Manu, (3) Uttama Manu, (4) Tapasa Manu, (5) Raivata Manu and (6) Chakshusha Manu. The present Manu is known as Vaivasvata Manu. Vivasvat, also written as Vivasvan, is the name of Surya, the sun God. Vaivasvata Manu has that name because he is Surya's son. Not only do Manus change from one *manvantara* to another, so do the Gods, the ruler of the Gods and the seven great sages, known as the *saptarshi*s (seven rishis). Indra is the title of the ruler of the Gods. It is not a proper name. The present Indra is Purandara. However, in a different *manvantara*, someone else will hold the title. In the present seventh *manvantara*, known as Vaivasvata *manvantara*, there will also be 71.4 *mahayuga*s. We are in the twenty-eighth of these. Since a different Vedavyasa performs the task of classifying and collating the Vedas in every *mahayuga*, Krishna Dvaipayana Vedavyasa is the twenty-eighth in that series. Just so that it is clear, Vedavyasa isn't a proper name. It is a title conferred on someone who collates and classifies the Vedas. There have been twenty-seven who have held the title of Vedavyasa before him and he is the twenty-eighth. His proper name is Krishna Dvaipayana; Krishna because he was dark and Dvaipayana because he was born on an island (*dvipa*). This gives us an idea of what the topic of *manvantara* is about. This still leaves *pratisarga*, *vamsha* and *vamshanucharita*. The two famous dynasties/lineages were the solar dynasty (*surya vamsha*) and the lunar dynasty (*chandra vamsha*), and all the famous kings belonged to one or the other of these two dynasties. *Vamshanucharita* is about these lineages and the conduct of these kings. There were the Gods and sages (*rishis*) too, not always born through a process of physical procreation. Their lineages are described under the heading of *vamsha*. Finally, within that cycle of primary creation and destruction, there are smaller and secondary cycles of creation and destruction. That's the domain of *pratisarga*. To a greater or lesser degree, all the Puranas cover these five topics, some more than the others. The Purana which strictly adheres to this five-topic classification is the *Vishnu Purana*.

There are many types of Puranas. Some are known as Sthala Puranas, describing the greatness and sanctity of a specific geographical place. Some are known as Upa-Puranas, minor Puranas. The listing of Upa-Puranas has regional variations and there is no countrywide consensus about the list of Upa-Puranas, though it is often accepted that there are eighteen. The Puranas we have in mind are known as Maha-Puranas, major Puranas. Henceforth, when we use the word Puranas, we mean Maha-Puranas. There is consensus that there are eighteen Maha-Puranas, though it is not obvious that these eighteen existed right from the beginning. The names are mentioned in several of these texts, including a *shloka* that follows the *shloka* cited from the *Matsya Purana*. Thus, the eighteen Puranas are: (1) *Agni* (15,400); (2) *Bhagavata* (18,000); (3) *Brahma* (10,000); (4) *Brahmanda* (12,000); (5) *Brahmavaivarta* (18,000); (6) *Garuda* (19,000); (7) *Kurma* (17,000); (8) *Linga* (11,000); (9) *Markandeya* (9000); (10) *Matsya* (14,000); (11) *Narada* (25,000); (12) *Padma* (55,000); (13) *Shiva* (24,000); (14) *Skanda* (81,100); (15) *Vamana* (10,000); (16) *Varaha* (24,000); (17) *Vayu* (24,000); and (18) *Vishnu* (23,000).

A few additional points about this list: first, the Harivamsha is sometimes loosely described as a Purana, but strictly speaking, it is not a Purana. It is more like an addendum to the Mahabharata. Second, *Bhavishya* (14,500) is sometimes mentioned, with *Vayu* excised from the list. However, the *Vayu Purana* exhibits many more Purana characteristics than the *Bhavishya Purana* does. There are references to a *Bhavishya Purana* that existed, but that may not necessarily be the *Bhavishya Purana* as we know it today. That's true of some other Puranas too. Texts have been completely restructured hundreds of years later. Third, it is not just a question of *Bhavishya Purana* and *Vayu Purana*. In the lists given in some Puranas, *Vayu* is part of the eighteen, but *Agni* is knocked out. In some others, *Narasimha* and *Vayu* are included, but *Brahmanda* and *Garuda* are knocked out. Fourth, when a list is given, the order also indicates some notion of priority or importance. Since that varies from text to text, our listing is simply alphabetical, according to the English alphabet. Fifth, when one uses the term *Bhagavata*, does one mean *Bhagavata Purana* or *Devi Bhagavata Purana*? The numbers within brackets indicate the number of *shloka*s each of these Puranas has or is believed to have. The range is from 9000 in *Markandeya* to a mammoth 81,100 in *Skanda*. The aggregate is a colossal 4,09,500 *shloka*s. To convey a rough idea of the order of magnitude, the Mahabharata has or is believed to have 1,00,000 *shloka*s. It's a bit difficult to convert a *shloka* into word counts in English, especially because Sanskrit words have a slightly different structure. However, as a very crude approximation, one *shloka* is roughly twenty words. Thus, 1,00,000 *shloka*s become two million words and 4,00,000 *shloka*s, four times the size of the Mahabharata, amounts to eight million words. There is a reason for using the expression 'is believed to have', as opposed to 'has'. Rendering into writing is of a later vintage; the initial process was one of oral transmission. In the process, many texts have been lost, or are retained in imperfect condition. This is true of texts in general and is also specifically true of Itihasa and Puranas. The Critical Edition of the Mahabharata, mentioned earlier, no longer possesses 1,00,000 *shloka*s. Including the Harivamsha, there are around 80,000 *shloka*s. The Critical Edition of the Mahabharata has, of course, deliberately excised some *shloka*s. For the Puranas, there is no counterpart of Critical Editions, though work has started on a few. However, whichever edition of the Puranas one chooses, the number of *shloka*s in that specific Purana will generally be smaller than the numbers given above. Either that number of *shloka*s did not originally exist, or they have been lost. This is the right place to mention that a reading of the Puranas assumes a basic degree of familiarity with the Valmiki Ramayana and the Mahabharata, more the latter than the former. Without that familiarity, one will often fail to appreciate the context completely. More than a passing familiarity with the Bhagavat Gita, strictly speaking, a part of the Mahabharata, helps.[6]

Other than the five attributes, the Puranas have a considerable amount of information on geography and even geological changes (changes in the courses of rivers) and astronomy. Therefore, those five attributes shouldn't suggest the Puranas have nothing more. They do, and they have therefore been described as encyclopedias. Bharatavarsha is vast and heterogeneous and each Purana may very well have originated in one particular part of the country. Accordingly, within that broad compass of an overall geographical description, the extent of geographical information varies from Purana to Purana. Some are more familiar with one part of the country than with another. Though not explicitly mentioned in the five attributes, the Puranas are also about pursuing *dharma, artha, kama* and *moksha*, the four objectives of human existence, and about the four *varna*s and the four *ashrama*s. The general understanding and practice of *dharma* is based much more on the Puranas than on the *Veda*s. Culture, notions of law, rituals, architecture and iconography are based on the Puranas. There is beautiful poetry too.

Perhaps one should mention that there are two ways in which these eighteen Puranas are classified. The trinity has Brahma as the creator, Vishnu as the preserver and Shiva as the destroyer. Therefore, Puranas where creation themes feature prominently are identified with Brahma (*Brahma, Brahmanda, Brahmavaivarta, Markandeya*). Puranas where Vishnu features prominently are identified as Vaishnava Puranas (*Bhagavata, Garuda, Kurma, Matysa, Narada, Padma, Vamana, Varaha, Vishnu*). Puranas where Shiva features prominently are identified as Shaiva Puranas (*Agni, Linga, Shiva, Skanda, Vayu*). While there is a grain of truth in this, Brahma, Vishnu and Shiva are all important and all three feature in

---

[6] The Bhagavat Gita translation was published in 2006 and reprinted in 2019, the translation of the Critical Edition of the Mahabharata in ten volumes between 2010 and 2014 (with a box set in 2015) and the translation of the Critical Edition of the Valmiki Ramayana in 2017. The translations are by Bibek Debroy, and in each case, the publisher is Penguin.

every Purana. Therefore, beyond the relative superiority of Vishnu vis-à-vis Shiva, the taxonomy probably doesn't serve much purpose. The second classification is even more tenuous and is based on the three *guna*s of *sattva* (purity), *rajas* (passion) and *tamas* (ignorance). For example, the Uttara Khanda of the Padma Purana has a few *shloka*s along these lines, recited by Shiva to Parvati. With a caveat similar to the one mentioned earlier, this should be in the 236th chapter of Uttara Khanda. According to this, the Puranas characterized by *sattva* are *Bhagavata, Garuda, Narada, Padma, Varaha* and *Vishnu*. Those characterized by *rajas* are *Bhavishya, Brahma, Brahmanda, Brahmavaivarta, Markandeya* and *Vamana*. Those characterized by *tamas* are *Agni, Kurma, Linga, Matysa, Skanda* and *Shiva*.

Within a specific Purana text, there are earlier sections, as well as later ones. That makes it difficult to date a Purana, except as a range. Across Purana texts, there are older Puranas, as well as later ones. Extremely speculatively, the dating will be something like the following. (1) *Agni* (800–1100 CE); (2) *Bhagavata* (500–1000 CE); (3) *Brahma* (700–1500 CE); (4) *Brahmanda* (400–600 CE); (5) *Brahmavaivarta* (700–1500 CE); (6) *Garuda* (800–1100 CE); (7) *Kurma* (600–900 CE); (8) *Linga* (500–1000 CE); (9) *Markandeya* (250–700 CE); (10) *Matsya* (200–500 CE); (11) *Narada* (900–1600 CE); (12) *Padma* (400–1600 CE); (13) *Shiva* (1000–1400 CE); (14) *Skanda* (600–1200 CE); (15) *Vamana* (450–900 CE); (16) *Varaha* (1000–1200 CE); (17) *Vayu* (350–550 CE); (18) *Vishnu* (300 BCE to 450 CE); and (19) *Bhavishya* (500–1900 CE). Reiterating once again that there is no great precision in these ranges, by this reckoning, the Vishnu Purana is the oldest and some parts of the Bhavishya Purana are as recent as the nineteenth century. To state the obvious, within the same Purana, there may be older sections and newer ones.

As mentioned earlier, there is no Critical Edition of the Puranas. Therefore, one has to choose the Sanskrit text one is going to translate from. If one is going to translate all the Puranas, it is preferable, though not essential, that one opts for a common source for all the Purana texts. In all the Purana translations, as a common source, I have used and will use, the ones brought out by Nag Publishers, with funding from the Ministry of Human Resource

Development. But Nag Publishers does not seem to have published
Brahmanda Purana. Hence, in contravention of this principle, I have
used a different source.[7] To the best of my knowledge, other than
this translation, there is only one other unabridged translation of
the *Brahmanda Purana* in English. G.V. Tagare was the translator,
published under the 'Ancient Indian Tradition and Mythology
Series'.[8] In the course of this translation, extensive comparisons have
been made with the Tagare translation. The Sanskrit texts used for
the two translations are similar but not always identical. However,
the differences are minor. More importantly, the discerning reader,
who compares the two, will find that we have sometimes differed in
interpreting words and sentences.

In the second half of the nineteenth century, the contribution of
Calcutta and Bengal towards preserving the Itihasa-Purana legacy
was remarkable. Consider the following: (1) Kaliprasanna Singha's
unabridged translation of the Mahabharata in Bengali; (2) the
Sanskrit and unabridged Bengali translation of the Burdwan edition
of the Mahabharata; (3) the unabridged Bengali translation of the
Mahabharata, published by Pratap Chandra Roy; (4) the unabridged
English translation of the Valmiki Ramayana by William Carey and
Joshua Marshman; (5) Hemachandra Bhattacharya's unabridged
translation of the Valmiki Ramayana in Bengali; (6) Ganga Prasad
Mukhopadhyaya's verse translation of the Valmiki Ramayana;
(7) Panchanan Tarkaratna's Sanskrit editions and Bengali
translations of Valmiki Ramayana, Adhyatma Ramayana and
several Puranas; (8) unabridged translations of the Mahabharata
in English by Kisari Mohan Ganguli and Manmatha Nath Dutt;
(9) Asiatic Society's[9] Bibliotheka Indica Sanskrit editions of *Agni
Purana, Brihad Dharma Purana, Brihad Naradiya Purana, Kurma
Purana, Varaha Purana and Vayu Purana*; and (10) F.E. Pargiter's
unabridged English translation of Markandeya Purana; and

[7] *Brahmanda Purana*, Krishnadas Academy, Varanasi, 1983.
[8] *The Brahmanda Purana*, translated and annotated by G.V. Tagare,
five volumes, Motilal Banarsidass Publishers, Delhi, 1983 to 1984.
[9] Asiatic Society went through several name changes, but it can simply
be called Asiatic Society.

(11) most important of all, Horace Hayman Wilson's translation
of the *Vishnu Purana*, in five volumes, between 1864 and 1870.[10]
Though Wilson's translation wasn't part of the Bibliotheka Indica
corpus, it was part of the same broad tradition. Wilson's work was
almost certainly the first unabridged translation of any Purana into
English and the scholarship was remarkable. An act of research and
scholarship still needs to be undertaken, cross-referencing names,
genealogies and incidents across Itihasa and Purana texts. Often,
when the same incident is narrated in different Purana texts, there
are differences in nuances and details. Since ours is a translation,
we have deliberately refrained from undertaking such an exercise.
But the Horace Hayman Wilson translation did seek to do that.
Before that work can be undertaken, the Purana corpus has to be
translated, meaning translation into English. More often than not,
practices of *dharma* are based on the Itihasa-Purana corpus. The
Purana project, published by Penguin, is part of that translation
endeavour. Translations of the *Bhagavata Purana*, *Markandeya
Purana*, *Brahma Purana*, *Vishnu Purana* and *Shiva Purana* have
already been published and *Brahmanda Purana* is the sixth.

As has been mentioned earlier, the composition of the *Brahmanda
Purana* is dated to between 400 and 600 CE. It is a relatively early
Purana. The *Brahmanda Purana* has a considerable degree of
overlap with the *Vayu Purana*, dated to between 350 and 550 CE.
R.C. Hazra's dissertation is still one of the best introductions to the
Purana corpus for all the Puranas.[11] This is what he had to say about
the *Brahmanda Purana*. 'From the facts that it has sometimes been
called "Vayaviya Brahmanda", that it also, like the Vayu Purana, is
said to have been proclaimed by Vayu, and that its chapters often
agree almost literally with those of the Vayu, F.E. Pargiter has rightly
said that originally these two Puranas were not separate. This view
of Pargiter seems to be supported by some of the verses quoted in

---

[10] *The Vishnu Purana, A System of Hindu Mythology and Tradition*,
Horace Hayman Wilson, Trubner & Company, London, 1864–1870.

[11] *Studies in the Puranic Records on Hindu Rites and Customs*, R.C.
Hazra, University of Dacca, 1940. This has since been reprinted several
times, by different publishers.

the Nibandhas from the "Vayu Purana" or "Vayaviya" but found only in the present Brahmanda . . . It is not known definitely when and why the same original Purana, which was named most probably after Vayu, came to have a second version with a different title. A comparison between the dynastic accounts given in the Vayu and Brahmanda shows that the separation took place after AD 325, and most probably, not earlier than AD 400.'

A quote from Wilson's preface[12] will add to what has already been said. Note that the version of *Brahmanda Purana* Hazra used did not possess the Lalita Mahatmya section. To quote Wilson, 'The first and largest portion, however, proved to be the same as the Vayu Purana, with a passage occasionally slightly varied . . . The second portion of this Brahmanda is not in any part of the Vayu; it is, probably current in the Dakhin as a Samita or Khanda . . . In illustration of the efficacy of this form of adoration, the main subject of the work is an account of the exploits of Lalita Devi, a form of Durga, and her destruction of the demon Bhandasura. Rules for her worship are also given, which are decidedly of a Sakta or Tantrika description; and this work cannot be admitted, therefore, to be part of a genuine Purana.' As one reads this translation, one will realize the abruptness with which the Lalita Mahatmya section is introduced and the abruptness with which it ends. Effectively, *Brahmanda Purana* does seem to end in the first part, with the second part more like an add-on. With its overlay of *tantra*, the translation of the Lalita Mahatmya section also proved to be relatively more difficult.

In all Puranas, there are chapters that are almost verbatim reproductions of sections from the Mahabharata, Harivamsha and other Puranas. One should not deduce that a specific Purana text has been copied from another since these various texts might have had a common origin. That apart, even when the *shloka*s seem to be virtually identical, there are interesting changes in words and nuances. This has a bearing on the Hazra and Wilson arguments. Today, given the texts we possess, it is impossible to unambiguously

---

[12] *Op.cit.*

establish the original text. There may very well have been an original proto-*Vayu Purana* and an original proto-*Brahmanda Purana*. Who can determine which preceded which? After all, each Purana evolved and was added to.

In terms of its present structure and attributes, the *Brahmanda Purana* displays all the characteristics of a Maha-Purana. It covers the five topics and is divided into four *pada*s or segments. The first section is known as *prakriya pada* and this section also summarizes the account. The other sections are *anushanga*, *upodghata* and *upasamhara*. *Prakriya pada* is the section on rites (*kriya*). *Anushanga* means something that is closely associated, a necessary consequence. *Upodghata* is commencement and *upasamhara* is conclusion. The first three, *prakriya pada*, *anushanga pada* and *upodghata parva* constitute the first part of *Brahmanda Purana*. *Upasamhara*, which includes Lalita Mahatmya, is the second part. The *Brahmanda Purana* is supposed to have 12,000 *shloka*s. As the table at the beginning of the translation indicates, this text possesses 13,674 *shloka*s, divided into 9498 *shloka*s for the first part and 4176 *shloka*s for the second part. There are 156 chapters, divided into 112 for the first part and forty-four for the second part. A word about the numbering we have followed for the chapters, such as Chapter 145-2(32). The first number is a consecutive numbering of chapters of the entire *Brahmanda Purana*, while the second number indicates the part, the first or the second as the case might be. The number within brackets indicates a consecutive numbering of chapters within that part. As with many Purana texts, the chapters have no headings. If there is a colophon, the chapter heading is based on the colophon. If there is no colophon, the chapter heading is based on what the chapter is about.

As with every Purana, there are layers within layers, and the account is not recited by a single person. The basic template is, of course, the standard one of Suta reciting the Purana to sages who have assembled for a sacrifice in Naimisha forest. But there is a core template that is behind this, that of Vayu reciting the Purana to Brahma. Through a line of transmission, this eventually reached Suta. In the second part, there is the narration by Hayagriva to Agastya.

When reading one Purana and comparing it to another, there is often the feeling that accounts are repetitive. This is partly true, but there is more to it than that. Even when the same incident is narrated, each Purana has its own twists and nuances. Other than the Lalita Mahatmya section, the *Brahmanda Purana* has, as its name implies, extensive sections on creation and dissolution, cosmology and geography, astronomy and measurements of time, funeral ceremonies and music. There is a detailed description of types of fires, types of ancestors and different kinds of beings. Plus there is an expansion of the Parashurama story, with rather unusually, Krishna and Radha brought into the story. This exemplifies the incremental value addition every Purana has.

In the translations of the Bhagavat Gita, the Mahabharata, the Harivamsha, the Valmiki Ramayana, the *Bhagavata Purana*, the *Markandeya Purana*, the *Brahma Purana*, the *Vishnu Purana* and the *Shiva Purana*,[13] we followed the principle of not using diacritical marks. The use of diacritical marks (effectively the international alphabet of Sanskrit transliteration) makes the pronunciation and rendering more accurate, but also tends to put off readers who are less academically inclined. Since diacritical marks are not being used, there is a challenge of rendering Sanskrit names in English. Sanskrit is a phonetic language and we have used that principle as a basis. Applied consistently, this means that words are rendered in ways that may seem unfamiliar. Hence, Gautama will appear as Goutama here. This is true of proper names, and, in a few rare cases, of geographical names. The absence of diacritical marks causes some minor problems. How does one distinguish Mahadeva Shiva from Parvati Shivaa? Often, the context will make the difference clear. If not, we have written Mahadeva as Shiva and Parvati as Shivaa. This is especially the case when names of feminine divinities might give rise to confusion. In translating, the attempt has been to provide a word-for-word translation, so that if one were to hold up

[13] *The Bhagavata Purana,* Volumes 1–3, Penguin Books, 2018. *The Markandeya Purana,* Penguin Books, 2019. *The Brahma Purana,* Volumes 1–2, Penguin Books 2021. *The Vishnu Purana,* Penguin Books, 2022. *The Shiva Purana,* Volumes 1–3, Penguin Books, 2023.

the Sanskrit text, there would be a perfect match. In the process, the English is not as smooth as it might have been, deliberately so. We have strictly adhered to whatever the text says, word for word.

The intention is to offer a translation, not an interpretation. That sounds like a simple principle to adopt, and for the most part, is easy to follow. However, there is a thin dividing line between translation and interpretation. In some instances, it is impossible to translate without bringing in a little bit of interpretation. Inevitably, interpretation is subjective. We have tried to minimize the problem by (a) reducing interpretation; (b) relegating interpretation to footnotes; and (c) when there are alternative interpretations, pointing this out to the reader through those footnotes. But all said and done, there is no substitute for reading these texts in the original Sanskrit.

Finally, the *Brahmanda Purana* is not an easy Purana to translate, read and understand, particularly the second part. That's often because the average reader is relatively unfamiliar with *mantra*, *mandala*, *tantra*, *yantra*, *chakra*, Shakti concepts (*iccha*, *jnana*, *kriya*), rituals and the theology (for want of a better word) of Devi's *dharma*. The thirty-six *tattva*s are different from the *tattva*s of *samkhya*, with many people being somewhat familiar with the latter. If this sounds esoteric, it is undoubtedly so. But a reading of *Brahmanda Purana* is also a convenient means of becoming exposed to these topics.

The Brahmanda Purana

	Chapter		Number of shlokas
Purva Bhaga (The first part)	1-1(1)	Preliminaries to the Purana	174
	2-1(2)	Account of Naimisha	48
	3-1(3)	Origin of Hiranyagarbha	38
	4-1(4)	Creation of the worlds	34
	5-1(5)	Creation of the worlds continued	141
	6-1(6)	*Kalpa*s and *manvantara*s	77
	7-1(7)	Description of knowledge about the worlds	195
	8-1(8)	Creation through mental powers	66
	9-1(9)	Rudra's creation	92
	10-1(10)	Mahadeva's glory	88
	11-1(11)	Creation of *rishi*s	45
	12-1(12)	Agni's collection	53
	13-1(13)	Description of time	151
	14-1(14)	Description of Priyavrata's lineage	75
	15-1(15)	Dimensions of the earth	80

	37-1(37)	Chakshusha creation	60
	38-1(38)	Description of the *manvantara*	33
	39-1(39)	Origin of *rishi*s	125
	40-1(40)	Prajapati's lineage	32
	41-1(41)	Svayambhu's three *guna*s	131
	42-1(42)	Curse on Jayas	37
	43-1(43)	Origin of Maruts	106
	44-1(44)	Danu's lineage	39
	45-1(45)	Kashyapa's descendants	479
	46-1(46)	Lineage of *rishi*s	102
	47-1(47)	Rites for ancestors	76
	48-1(48)	Rites for ancestors continued	120
	49-1(49)	Description of kindling	116
	50-1(50)	Continuation of *shraddha* rites	46
	51-1(51)	Description of sacred places	143
	52-1(52)	Norms for purification	117
	53-1(53)	Test of a *brahmana*	68
	54-1(54)	Praise of donations	59
	55-1(55)	Right *tithi*s for *shraddha*s	22
	56-1(56)	*Shraddha*s under specific *nakshatra*s	15
	57-1(57)	Testing a *brahmana*	74
	58-1(58)	Rites of a *shraddha*	23
	59-1(59)	Bhrigu and Parashurama	81
	60-1(60)	Parashurama's austerities	81
	61-1(61)	Parashurama's austerities continued	81

	86-1(86)	Sagara keeps his pledge	49
	87-1(87)	Sagara's conquest	66
	88-1(88)	Sagara visits Ourva's hermitage	58
	89-1(89)	Asamanja's exile	69
	90-1(90)	Release of the horse	43
	91-1(91)	Destruction of Sagara's sons	52
	92-1(92)	The horse is brought back	56
	93-1(93)	Amshuman obtains the kingdom	27
	94-1(94)	Descent of Ganga	57
	95-1(95)	Varuna visits Bhargava	75
	96-1(96)	Land reclaimed from the ocean	37
	97-1(97)	Origin of Vaivasvata	86
	98-1(98)	Vaivasvata Manu's creation	28
	99-1(99)	*Murchhana*s of *gandharva*s	53
	100-1(100)	Art of *gandharva*s	44
	101-1(101)	Ikshvaku's lineage	216
	102-1(102)	Nimi's lineage	24
	103-1(103)	Soma and Soumyas	50
	104-1(104)	Amavasu's lineage	90
	105-1(105)	Dhanvantari's origin	105
	106-1(106)	Yayati's story	107
	107-1(107)	Kartavirya's birth	57
	108-1(108)	Jyamagha's lineage	49
	109-1(109)	The Vrishni lineage	265
	110-1(110)	In conclusion, the praise	195
	111-1(111)	Vishnu's greatness	126
	112-1(112)	Description of lineages	278
Total in the first part	112		9,498

Lalita Mahatmya (the second part)			
	113-2(1)	Description of the deluge	243
	114-2(2)	Description of Shiva's city	316
	115-2(3)	Dissolution	113
	116-2(4)	The cycle of the cosmic egg	73
	117-2(5)	Agastya's journey and Janardana's manifestation	39
	118-2(6)	Nature of violence	73
	119-2(7)	Theft and drinking	79
	120-2(8)	Forbidden intercourse	61
	121-2(9)	Churning for *amrita*	82
	122-2(10)	Mohini's manifestation	90
	123-2(11)	Bhandasura's appearance	38
	124-2(12)	Lalitaa's manifestation	75
	125-2(13)	Lalitaa's praise	36
	126-2(14)	Manifestation of Kameshvara	29
	127-2(15)	Wedding festivities	59
	128-2(16)	Victory march with the soldiers	36
	129-2(17)	Advance of Dandanathaa and Shyamalaa	51
	130-2(18)	Lalitaa Parameshvari's victory march	19
	131-2(19)	Chakraraja and divinities on chariots	95
	132-2(20)	Divinities on Kirichakratha	106

	151-2(39)	Kamakshi's glory	121
	152-2(40)	Kamakshi's greatness	142
	153-2(41)	Worship of Kamakshi	83
	154-2(42)	*Mudra*s	19
	155-2(43)	*Diksha* and a *mantra*	88
	156-2(44)	*Dhyana* on Devi	151
Total in Lalita Mahatmya (the second part)	44		4,176
Total in Brahmanda Purana	156		13,674

Purva Bhaga (The first part)

Chapter 1-1(1) (Preliminaries to the Purana)[1]

Iprostrate myself before the one who is full of *sattva* at the time of creation, preservation and destruction. I bow down. I prostrate myself before Svayambhu, who has the three forms of *sattva*, *rajas* and *tamas*.[2] The victorious Bhagavan Hari holds up the worlds. He is Aja and the universe is his form. He is *nirguna*, but the *guna*s exist in his *atman*. Brahma is the creator of the worlds. He is omniscient and unvanquished. He is the lord of the past, the present and the future. Right now, he is the virtuous lord. The lord of the universe possesses unmatched *jnana*, non-attachment, powers and *dharma*.[3] The virtuous should serve these four objectives. Within them, humans constantly possess virtuous and wicked sentiments. Understanding these sentiments, without hesitation, Ishvara

---

[1] There are several typos and inconsistencies in this introductory chapter.

[2] Svayambhu means the one who is his own origin. It is applied to each of Brahma, Vishnu and Shiva. Here, it is clearly addressed to Vishnu. *Sattva*, *rajas* and *tamas* are the three respective *guna*s of purity, passion and darkness/ignorance. Aja means someone who is devoid of birth and *nirguna* means someone who is devoid of *guna*s.

[3] *Jnana* is knowledge. The words *jnana* and *vijnana* are often used synonymously and both words mean knowledge. When distinct meanings are intended, *jnana* signifies knowledge obtained from texts and *guru*s, while *vijnana* signifies knowledge obtained through inward contemplation and self-realization.

repeatedly engages them in *kriya*.[4] The creator of the world knows about the truth. He knows *yoga* and has resorted to *yoga*. Thus, he created all beings, mobile and immobile. I seek refuge with the virtuous lord who created the universe and is a witness to the worlds. That is because I wish to know about the account of the Purana. The Purana possesses all the truth about the worlds and is in conformity with the *Veda*s. Bhagavan Prajapati described it to Vasishtha. The illustrious *rishi* Vasishtha taught this sacred *jnana* about the truth, which is like *amrita*, to his grandson, Shakti's son, Parashara.[5] In ancient times, the illustrious *rishi* Parashara taught Jatukarnya this divine Purana, which is in conformity with the *Veda*s. Having specially understood this Purana, Jatukarnya bestowed this eternal and supreme knowledge about the *brahman* on Dvaipayana, who was in control of himself. These extremely wonderful prescriptions conveyed the truth about the worlds, and a delighted Dvaipayana bestowed it on five *shishya*s—Jaimini, Sumantu, Vaishampayana, Pailava as the fourth and Lomaharshana as the fifth.[6] This was done to explain this knowledge, which is full of many kinds of meanings and is in conformity with the *shruti* texts, to the worlds. Suta was humble, pure and full of *dharma*. Full of humility, Lomaharshana studied this wonderful account, the Purana. He was accomplished in wisdom and extremely devoted to *dharma*. He was questioned by the *rishi*s and by you.[7] Along with other sages, full of great devotion, he lowered his head in prostration before the sage Vasishtha and performed *pradakshina* around him.'[8]

'Having obtained the knowledge, he was content and went to Kurukshetra. The pure *rishi*s were engaged in performing a sacrifice there. Following the norms prescribed in the sacred texts, the

[4]   Deeds or rites.

[5]   Shakti was Vasishtha's son and Shakti's son was Parashara. Jatukarnya was the Vedavyasa of the twenty-seventh *dvapara yuga*.

[6]   Lomaharshana is also known as Romaharshana. The word means that the body-hair of listeners stood up. He is also known as Suta.

[7]   In these preliminaries, this 'you' remains unclear.

[8]   *Pradakshina* is more specific than a mere act of circumambulating. This circling or circumambulation has to be done in a specific way, so that the right side (*dakshina*) always faces what is being circled.

performers of the sacrifice humbly approached Romaharshana. He surpassed them in wisdom. At the time, seeing Romaharshana, all the *rishi*s were extremely happy and delighted in their minds. They honoured and worshipped him, offering him *padya* and *arghya*.[9] Taking the king's[10] permission, he greeted all the sages. Permitted by all the *rishi*s, he asked about their welfare. After all the sages, he approached the energy of the eternal *brahman*. When all those in the assembly granted him permission, he seated himself on the beautiful seat that had been spread out. The delighted sages were firm in their vows. When he was seated, as is proper, full of humility, they controlled themselves. All the *rishi*s surrounded the one who was great in his vows. Extremely happy, they addressed the son of a *suta*.[11] 'O immensely fortunate one! Welcome. O intelligent one! O one excellent in vows! O supreme sage! You are well and it is good fortune that we have been able to see you here. You are pure in your deeds and without you, this place would have been bereft of any essence. O Suta! You are the intelligent *shishya* of the great-souled sage, Vyasa. Because of your qualities as a *shishya*, he has always shown you his favours. O lord! You are accomplished in intelligence, and he has shown you the favour of revealing the truth to you. Having obtained this extensive *jnana*, all your doubts have been dispelled. O wise one! You should tell us everything that we ask you about. We wish to hear the divine Purana account, which is in conformity with the *shruti* texts. It is full of *dharma* and *artha*[12]

---

[9] A guest is offered *padya* (water to wash the feet), *achamaniya* (water to rinse the mouth), *asana* (a seat) and *arghya* (a gift).

[10] The king (*rajan*) should be interpreted symbolically here and probably refers to Indra or King Soma (the moon, or the *soma* plant). He took that permission in his mind.

[11] Lomaharshana was known as Suta and was also the son of a *suta*. The *suta*s were charioteers, as well as raconteurs of tales. *Magadha*s were minstrels and bards. So were *bandi*s. But *magadha*s seem to have also composed, while *bandi*s sang the compositions of others.

[12] The four *purushartha*s (objectives of human existence) are Dharma, *artha* (pursuit of wealth), *kama* (pursuit of sensual pleasures) and *moksha* (pursuit of emancipation). But here, *dharma* and *artha* can simply be taken as *dharma* and 'meaning'.

and you have heard it from Vyasa.' Addressed by the *rishi*s in this
way, Suta was filled with humility. Becoming even more humble,
the extremely wise one replied. 'My wisdom has resulted from my
service to the *rishi*.[13] This determination is also true that my task is
to serve. O supreme *dvija*s![14] That being the case, according to my
capacity, I will speak. You should ask me whatever you desire to
know about.' The words spoken by him were sweet. Hearing them,
the eyes of the sages were filled with tears of joy, and they replied to
Suta, 'You are especially skilled and you have directly seen Vyasa.
Therefore, you can make us understand the creation of the entire
world. We wish to know about the different lineages. Earlier, how
did Prajapati embark on this wonderful act of creation?' Honoured,
the great-souled Romaharshana was asked this. In the due order,
the excellent one described everything in detail.

Suta answered, 'O excellent *dvija*s! Pleased with me,
Dvaipayana described this account to me. O *brahmana*s! This is
sacred and I will narrate it in the due order. Earlier, when he was
asked by the great-souled sages in Naimisha, this is the Purana
Matarishvan spoke about.[15] This exhibits the five characteristics
required of a Purana—*sarga*, *pratisarga*, *vamsha*, *manvantara* and
vamshanucharita.[16] The first section is known as *prakriya pada*
and this section also summarizes the account. The other sections
are *anushanga*, *upodghata* and *upasamhara*.[17] I have thus briefly
described the four sections. Subsequently, in the due order, I will
describe them in detail. Among all the sacred texts, Brahma heard

---

[13] Vyasa.

[14] *Dvija* means twice born. It is often used for *brahmana*s but can also
be used for any of the first three *varna*s, who have a second birth when they
are invested with the sacred thread. When the text uses *dvija*, as opposed to
some other word for *brahmana*, we will retain *dvija*.

[15] Matarishvan is the wind-God, Vayu, who narrated *Vayu Purana* to
the assembled sages in Naimisha forest. This explains the overlap between
Vayu Purana and *Brahmanda Purana*.

[16] These terms have been explained in the Introduction.

[17] *Prakriya pada* is the section on rites (*kriya*). *Anushanga* means
something that is closely associated, a necessary consequence. *Upodghata*
is commencement and *upasamhara* is conclusion.

this Purana first. Thereafter, the *Vedas* emerged from his mouth, as did the *Vedangas*, the *dharmashastras*, *vratas* and *niyamas*.[18] The unmanifest cause is eternal and has existence and non-existence[19] in its *atman*. The determination to create was made, starting with Mahat and ending with Vishesha.[20] The golden egg and Brahma's excellent origin will be described. The egg had a sheath of water, and the water was covered by fire. The fire had a sheath of wind, and the wind was covered by space. This was covered by *bhutadi*,[21] and *bhutadi* was enveloped by Mahat. Mahat was covered by the unmanifest. The egg has been described as being located inside the elements. The origin of rivers and mountains can be read about here. All the *manvantaras* and *kalpas* are described.[22] There is a description of the tree that is the *brahman* and Brahma's birth is narrated. After this, there is a description of how Brahma created subjects. Brahma's birth is not manifest. However, his situation is described. There is a narration of the origin of the *kalpas* and the establishment of the universe. To raise the earth, Hari lay down in the water. There is a specific description of cities and other things, the divisions into *varnas* and *ashramas*.[23] The location of *nakshatras*, planets and *siddhas* is described, as is their movement,

[18] *Vedanga* means a branch of the *Vedas*, and these were six kinds of learning that were essential to understand the *Vedas*—*shiksha* (phonetics), *kalpa* (rituals), *vyakarana* (grammar), *nirukta* (etymology), *chhanda* (metre) and *jyotisha* (astronomy). The corpus of texts about *dharma* is known as *dharmashastras*. *Vratas* are vows and *niyamas* are rituals and restraints.

[19] *Sat* and *asat*. Alternatively, cause and effect.

[20] These are expressions that will be explained later. Mahat is the primordial principle, while Vishesha is the specific and the individual.

[21] The beginning of creation, meaning *ahamkara*.

[22] *Kalpa* is the duration of Brahma's day. At the end of Brahma's day, when it is Brahma's night, there is a secondary cycle of dissolution/ destruction. When night is over, the secondary cycle of creation begins afresh.

[23] As in the four *varnas*, brahmana, kshatriya, vaishya and shudra and the four *ashramas*, brahmacharya, garhasthya, vanaprastha and sannyasa.

extending for many *yojana*s.[24] For mortals who are auspicious in deeds, there is a description of places earmarked in heaven. Trees, herbs and creepers are described. There is a narration of the two paths followed by *deva*s and *rishi*s. There is a description of the creation and expansion of mango and other trees and of animals and humans. The derivation and assumption of the *kalpa*s is spoken about. Next, there is a description of the nine kinds of creation Brahma engaged in, using his intelligence. Thinking about the worlds, three of these resulted from his powers of the mind. Dharma and others originated from Brahma's body. In every *kalpa*, for the creation of subjects, these twelve are born again and again.[25] The period of *pratisandhi*, joining two *kalpa*s, is also described. When Brahma was shrouded only in *tamas*, Adharma[26] originated. When there was a lot of *sattva* in his body, Purusha[27] was created. Thereafter, through Shatarupa, he had two sons, Priyavrata and Uttanapada, and two auspicious daughters, Prasuti and Akriti.[28] Those who have cleansed themselves from sins are established in the three worlds and are praised. Following *dharma*, Ruchi Prajapati had twins through Akuti.[29] Through Prasuti, Daksha had auspicious daughters. Through Daksha's daughters, Shabda and others, the great-souled Dharma is described as having offspring that were full of *sattva* and flowed upwards, giving rise to happiness.[30] Through Himsa, Adharma had offspring that were full of *tamas*, possessing inauspicious qualities. There is a description of the creation of offspring by Bhrigu and other *rishi*s. Brahmarshi Vasishtha's *gotra*

---

[24] The *nakshatra*s aren't quite stars. They can be constellations too. There are twenty-seven *nakshatra*s. A *yojana* is a measure of distance, between eight and nine miles.

[25] This probably means the seven *saptarshi*s, Daksha and Sanaka, Sananda, Sanatana and Sanatkumara.

[26] The antithesis of Dharma.

[27] This seems to mean Svayambhuva Manu.

[28] Also known as Akuti.

[29] Ruchi Prajapati's wife, daughter of Svayambhuva Manu and Shatarupa.

[30] The name is usually given as Shraddha, not Shabda. Thirteen of Daksha's daughters were married to Dharma—Shraddha, Lakshmi, Dhriti, Tushti, Pushti, Medha, Kriya, Buddhi, Lajja, Vapu, Shanti, Siddhi and Kirti. Since these were superior offspring, they flowed upwards.

is narrated.[31] There is a description of Agni having offspring through Svaha. After this, there is a description of the two types of ancestors, born through Svadha. In connection with the lineage of ancestors, Maheshvara's cursing of Daksha and Sati's cursing of Bhrigu and other intelligent ones is narrated. To illustrate the taints of enmity and ward it off, Daksha's counter curse on Rudra, extraordinary in his deeds, is narrated. In connection with *manvantara*s, there is a description of time. There is a narration of the auspicious traits of Prajapati Kardama's daughter. There is a detailed account of Priyavrata's sons and their separate instatement in different *dvipa*s[32] and regions. In that way, Svayambhuva's[33] creation is described, along with *varsha*s, rivers and all their divisions. In the seven *dvipa*s, there are thousands of internal divisions. There is a detailed description of the circle around Jambu-*dvipa* and the ocean. The dimension is first cited, in *yojana*s, along with the mountains. The seven mountains, Himalaya, Hemakuta, Nishadha, Meru, Nila, Shveta and Shringi, are described. In *yojana*s, the distance between them, their diameters, heights and expanse are described. There is a narration of Bharata and the other *varsha*s, the rivers and the mountains, along with those who reside there. Creatures who can move and immobile entities are established there. Jambu-*dvipa* and other *dvipa*s are surrounded by seven oceans. After this, there is a description of the golden region of Lokaloka.[34] There are the dimensions of the worlds and the seven *dvipa*s on earth. Form and others are described, since they have been created, along with Prakriti. All of these are indications of the transformations of Pradhana. There is a brief narration of the movements and dimensions of the sun and the moon and especially that of the

---

[31] *Gotra* is the lineage/descent a person is born into. A *gotra* is traced to a specific *rishi* and marriage between individuals belonging to the same *gotra* is prohibited. In the hierarchy of sages, *brahmarshi* is superior to *maharshi* and *maharshi* is superior to *rishi*.

[32] Regions of the world, continents. *Varsha* is a further sub-division of a *dvipa*.

[33] Svayambhuva Manu's.

[34] Lokaloka can be interpreted in various ways, places where there is light versus places where there is darkness, populated places versus uninhabited regions, and so on.

earth. The current dimensions are expressed in *yojana*s. To the
north of Manasa, there are the sacred and auspicious summits of
Mahendra and the others. Above this, it is said that the sun moves
like a circle of fire. The characteristics of Nagavithi and Akshavithi
are described.[35] The orbits, the lines and the locations are given
in *yojana*s, the intervening period between light and darkness, the
day and the equinox. There is a description of the guardians of
the worlds, established in the four directions, and the respective
northern and southern paths followed by *deva*s and ancestors.
There is a description of householders who renounce, resorting to
sattva and *rajas*. There is also a narration of the worlds of Vishnu,
Dharma and others. There is a description of the sun, the moon,
the planets and the luminary bodies. According to capacity, they
sustain the auspicious and the inauspicious for subjects. It is recited
that Brahma himself created a habitation for the sun. As the day
diminishes, the illustrious one proceeds on this chariot, which is
populated by *deva*s, Adityas, *rishi*s, *gandharva*s, *apsara*s, *gramani*s,
*sarpa*s and *rakshasa*s.[36] The juices that exude from the chariot are
said to represent the essence of water. It is said that the waxing
and waning of the moon leads to the creation of *soma* juice. The
chariots of Surya and the others revolve around Dhruva.[37] It is said
that Dhruva is located on the tail of Shishumara. The habitations of
all those who have the forms of stars, *nakshatra*s, planets and *deva*s,

---

[35] Nagavithi is the Milky Way, the progress of the moon through the
signs of the zodiac (*rashi*). Akshavithi must refer to right ascension and
declination.

[36] *Gandharva*s are semi-divine species, they are celestial musicians.
*Apsara*s are celestial dancers. *Gramani* means leader. In this context, the
word can be interpreted as *yaksha*. *Sarpa*s are snakes. It is derived from
the word for creeping along. The word *sarpa* is often used as a synonym
for *naga/uraga/*pannaga. Throughout this translation, we will use the word
'snake' for *sarpa* and the word 'serpent' for *naga*. *Naga*s are a semi-divine
species.

[37] Surya is the sun and Dhruva is the Pole Star. Shishumara is the
Gangetic porpoise/dolphin. In the sky, it is a constellation, which can partly
be identified with Draco, the dragon. Dhruva is towards the rear end of
Shishumara.

auspicious in their deeds, are described here. The one thousand
rays of Surya; the flow of rain, cold and heat; the names, tasks and
movements of the different kinds of rays and the measurement and
movement of the planets, which depend on the sun, are narrated.
The measurement and origin of Mahat, which obtains its residence
from Pradhana, is described.'

'There is a description of the greatness of Pururava, Ila's son.
The greatness of the two types of ancestors and those who are dead
is narrated. The *parvas*[38] and conjunctions of *parvas* are described;
the movements of those who have gone to the world of heaven and
those who have proceeded downwards. There is a narration of the
great favours that are obtained from the two types of ancestors
through *shraddha* ceremonies.[39] There is a description of the
duration and characteristics of *yugas*, of *krita yuga*, of the decline
setting in with *treta* and getting worse with *dvapara* and of the
nature of *dharma* in *varnas* and *ashramas*. There is a description of
the fashioning of the *vajra* weapon, the conversation between the
rishis and Vasu,[40] Vasu's downfall and redemption and the nature
of sound, Pradhana and Manus beyond Svayambhuva Manu.
Austerities are praised and there is a description of the nature of all
the *yugas*, with *dvapara* and *kali* briefly described. The duration of
manvantaras is described in human years along with the
characteristics of all the *manvantaras*. Present, past and future
manvantaras and the characteristics of intervening periods between
manvantaras are described. Starting with Svayambhuva, the past
manvantaras are described. The progress of *rishis* and knowledge
about the progress of time is spoken about. There is a narration of
the number and dimensions of forts, means of subsistence on the
onset of a *yuga* and the birth and signs of *chakravartis*[41] in *treta
yuga*. The birth of Pramati and the diminishing of beings by one

[38] Sacred and auspicious days.
[39] Funeral ceremonies.
[40] Uparichara Vasu.
[41] *Chakravarti* is a universal emperor, literally, a king whose wheel
(*chakra*) travels everywhere on earth.

angula[42] in *kali yuga* is spoken about. There is an enumeration of the branches,[43] the importance of *shishya*s, and there is also a description of the seven kinds of *vakya*[44] and the *gotra*s of *rishi*s. All the signs are described for *brahmana*s and sons of *suta*s and the classification of the *Veda*s by the great-souled Vedavyasa. For the *manvantara*s, there is a description of *deva*s and lords of subjects, with the due order of *manvantaras* and knowledge about time. There is a recounting about sons of Daksha's daughter born through Brahma and others, and Savarni and other Manus who reside on the slopes of Meru. There is a description of offspring born through Dhruva, Uttanapada's son. There is a narration of the valiant offspring born through Chakshusha Manu's creation and how the lord, Vena's son,[45] went about milking the earth, with a special mention of the vessels, the milk and the calves. Brahma and others had milked the earth earlier. There is a description of how the intelligent Prajapati, Daksha, was born through the ten Prachetas and Marisha, with each contributing an equal part. The great Indras, past, present and future, are described. There are many accounts about the future, about Manus and others. The creation of Vaivasvata Manu is narrated in detail. The origin of Bhrigu and others from the sheaths of Brahma and others is narrated. Chakshusha Manu's creation of subjects was auspicious and distinguished. In Vaivasvata *manvantara*, there is a description of how Daksha created through meditation. Narada had a conversation with Daksha's extremely strong sons. The son born through Brahma's mental powers[46] destroyed them and was cursed. After this, Daksha created the famous daughters known as Vairinas.[47] As a result of the flow of the wind, the Maruts were born through the divine Diti. There is a description of the forty-nine categories of

---

[42] The length of a finger, a reference to shorter stature.
[43] Of knowledge, such as the *Veda*s.
[44] *Vakya* is speech and this is probably a reference to the seven kinds of grammatical cases.
[45] That is, Prithu.
[46] That is, Narada.
[47] They were born through his wife, Virini.

Maruts. They reside on the shoulders of Vayu,[48] and since they resided with Indra, they obtained the status of *deva*s. There is a detailed description of the origins of *daitya*s, *danava*s, *yaksha*s, *gandharva*s, *rakshasa*s, all *bhuta*s and *pishacha*s among the *yaksha*s, birds, creepers and *apsara*s.[49] There is a description of the origin of Vainateya and his instatement as a king.[50] The Bhrigus and the Angiras are spoken about in detail. The offspring of Kashyapa, Pulastya, the great-souled Atri and the sage Parashara are described in detail. There are three famous daughters who are established in the worlds.[51] After this, Iccha and Aditya are spoken about in detail.[52] Kinkuvit's conduct and his destruction by Dhruva is spoken about.[53] Brihadbala, Ikshvaku and the others are described briefly. There is a detailed description of Nishi and other kings, Palanduharana[54] and the offspring of King Yayati. After Krodha[55] has been spoken about, there is a detailed narration of Yadu's lineage and the Haihayas. There is a narration of the greatness of Jyamagha and his creation of subjects, and of Devavridha, Andhaka and the great-souled Dhrishta. There is a description of Animitra's lineage, the false accusation of the two Vishas,[56] the obtaining of the jewel by the two Vishas, the creation of offspring by the intelligent

[48] While Vayu is the wind-God, the Maruts are also Gods of the wind.
[49] As the antithesis of *sura*s, there are the demons, *asura*s. *Daitya*s and *danava*s are used as synonyms for *asura*s. *Daitya*s are the offspring of Diti and *danava*s are the offspring of Danu, both married to the sage Kashyapa. *Bhuta*s are demons, *pishacha*s are demons who survive on flesh.
[50] As the king of birds. Vainateya is Vinata's (who was married to Kashyapa) son, Garuda.
[51] Probably meaning Daksha's daughters—Aditi (mother of *aditya*s), Diti (mother of *daitya*s) and Danu (mother of *danava*s).
[52] Iccha is probably a typo for Ila. The sentence then means *chandra vamsha* and *surya vamsha*.
[53] Kinkuvit might mean Vikukshi, but his destruction had nothing to do with Dhruva.
[54] Literally, the one who has stolen an onion.
[55] This is probably a typo and should read Kroshtu, Yadu's son.
[56] Presumably referring to Krishna and Balarama being falsely accused of stealing the Syamantaka jewel.

Satrajit and *rajarshi*[57] Devamidha and the birth and conduct of the great-souled Shura. There is a narration of the wicked conduct of Kamsa and the birth of the infinitely energetic Vishnu through Vasudeva and Devaki, leading to the two lineages becoming one. After this, in connection with the creation by *rishis*, there is a description of subjects created by them. In ancient times, when there was a conflict between *devas* and *asuras*, in an attempt to protect Shakra from being killed, Vishnu killed a woman and was cursed by Bhrigu.[58] However, Bhrigu revived Shukra's divine mother. There were twelve battles between *devas* and *rishis*.[59] There is a narration of Narasimha and the others and it destroys sins. To worship Sthanu,[60] Shukra performed terrible austerities. To obtain a boon, he praised Sharva. Thereafter, the activities of *devas* and *asuras* are recounted. As a result of Shakra's goading, the great-souled Shukra was with Jayanti.[61] The intelligent Brihaspati assumed Shukra's form and deluded the *asuras*, whereupon, the immensely radiant Shukra cursed him. Vishnu's greatness and his birth is stated in words. The daughter's son, Turvasu, was Yadu's younger brother.[62] There is a description of Anu, Druhyu and the others, and their sons, who were kings. Those born in Anu's lineage were great-souled and excellent kings. Their wealth and energy were extensive and all of this is described. There is a narration of the hospitality extended by the seven *brahmana rishis* who resorted to *dharma* and the incident about the learned ones cursing Brihaspati. Hara's

[57] Royal sage.

[58] Vishnu killed Kavyamata, Bhrigu's wife, the mother of Shukracharya. Shakra is Indra.

[59] This should clearly be between *devas* and *danavas*.

[60] The immobile one, Shiva's name. Sharva is another of Shiva's names.

[61] The story is told in the *Matsya Purana*. To ensure the triumph of *asuras*, Shukracharya, the preceptor of *asuras*, prayed to Shiva. At the time, to distract him from his austerities, Indra/Shakra sent his daughter, Jayanti. We have amended the text, which has Brihaspati cursing Shukra.

[62] Shukracharya's daughter, Devayani, was married to Yayati and had two sons, Yadu and Turvasu. Yayati was also married to Sharmishtha, and her sons were Puru, Druhyu and Anu.

lineage is touched upon and Shantanu's valour is expressed in words. In the concluding section, there is an account of future kings. The categories of future lords are also described. When Bhoutya *manvantara* comes to an end and *kali yuga* is about to end, there is a description of destruction. There are said to be three types of dissolution—*naimittika, prakritika* and *atyantika*.[63] The withdrawal of the many kinds of beings is narrated. There is no rain and the sun is terrible, with the *samvartaka* fire.[64] The signs are mentioned in the *samkhya* texts.[65] There is special mention of the *brahman*. There is a description of the seven worlds, Bhuloka and the others.[66] The signs are described through *parardha*[67] and the other part. Using *yojana*s, there is a determination of the dimensions of Brahma's world. Rourava and the other hells are described, as meant for sinners. There is a determination of the consequences for all living beings. There is a narration of *samsara*,[68] all fixed by Brahma's secondary cycles of creation. Depending on whether one resorts to *dharma* or *adharma*, the upward or downward movement is spoken about. In every *kalpa*, there is a great destruction of beings and there are innumerable hardships. Even Brahma is not permanent. There is wickedness in pleasures and hardship in destruction. It is shown that, because of taints, non-attachment and emancipation are difficult to obtain. A being should cast aside the manifest and the unmanifest and seek refuge with the *brahman*. Since insight is clouded by the many, one withdraws from the pure. However, if

[63] *Naimittika* dissolution (*pralaya*) occurs at the end of Brahma's day, *prakritika* at the end of Brahma's life (when everything dissolves into Prakriti) and *atyantika* when the *jivatman* merges into the *paramatman*. In addition, *nitya pralaya* is the daily destruction of beings.

[64] The fire of destruction.

[65] *Samkhya* is one of the six schools of philosophy (*darshana*).

[66] There are fourteen worlds. The seven upper regions are Bhuloka, Bhuvarloka, Svarloka, Maharloka, Satyaloka, Tapoloka and Janaloka. The seven nether regions are Atala, Vitala, Sutala, Rasatala, Talatala, Mahatala and Patala.

[67] Brahma's life consists of two *parardha*s.

[68] The cycle of worldly birth, death and rebirth.

one is scared of the three kinds of miseries,[69] one seeks a form that is without blemish. When one obtains the bliss of the *brahman*, one is never frightened. Thereafter, as was the case earlier, the creation by another Brahma is described. There is a narration of the creation, transformations and dissolution of the universe. When beings follow *pravritti*, it bears fruits.[70] There is a description of the creation of different categories of *rishi*s and this destroys sins. Vasishtha originated and Shakti was born. Because of what Vishvamitra did, Soudasa gathered his bones.[71] There is a narration of lord Parashara's birth through Adrishyanti.[72] Through this father and the maiden,[73] the great sage, Vyasa, was born. There was the birth of his son, the intelligent Shuka. Hence, Parashara bore enmity towards *rishi* Vishvamitra. With a desire to kill Vishvamitra, Vasishtha gathered fire. However, the divinity Vidhatri[74] wished to do a good turn to the *brahmana* Vishvamitra. For the sake of a son, the intelligent lord, Girnaskandha, did this.[75] Having obtained the favours of Sharva, the illustrious lord, Vyasa, subsequently divided the single *Veda* into four parts. His disciples and sub-disciples created many branches of the *Veda*s. They were not distracted in applying these principles. When they saw Svayambhu, those sages, seeking *dharma*, specifically asked him about their desired sacred spot. The lord desired their welfare and replied, 'This wheel possesses an excellent nave. Its complexion and form are divine. It

[69] The three kinds of hardship relate to *adhidaivika* (destiny), *adhibhoutika* (nature) and *adhyatmika* (one's own nature).

[70] *Pravritti* is attachment to action and consequent fruits. *Nivritti* is detachment from fruits and renunciation of action.

[71] King Soudasa became a *rakshasa*. Instigated by Vishvamitra, he devoured Vasishtha's son, Shakti. In his form as a *rakshasa*, Soudasa was known as Kalmashapada.

[72] Adrishyanti was Shakti's wife and Parashara was the son of Shakti and Adrishyanti.

[73] Satyavati.

[74] The creator, Brahma.

[75] It is impossible to make sense of this. There is no one known as Girnaskandha. *Girna* means to swallow. Given the enmity between Vasishtha and Vishvamitra, the text says Vasishtha gathered some fire. Perhaps *skandha* is to be taken as fire and Brahma swallowed up this fire.

is auspicious and praiseworthy and has seven spokes. It is unmatched. As it descends, follow it attentively from the rear. There will be a place where the felly of the wheel will be shattered. This region should be regarded as sacred.'[76] This was the lord's answer. Stating this to all the *rishi*s, he disappeared. The sages performed a sacrifice in Naimisha. In Naimisha, they subsisted on barley and water from the Ganga. When Sharadvan[77] died there, the *rishi*s of Naimisha were filled with great compassion and revived him. Having removed all boundaries from the earth, they brought Krishna as the king. In the proper way, full of love, they displayed hospitality towards their king. When the cruel *asura* Svarbhanu came to the sacrifice, he abducted the king. When the king disappeared, all the sages followed him and saw that he had been protected by a *gandharva* in a habitation in Kalapagrama.[78] At this, the *rishi*s started the sacrifice again. Seeing that everything had turned golden, he had an argument with them. The sacrifice in Naimisha lasted twelve years. While they debated, Yadu was instated by them. Yadu's son and Ayu were born in that forest. When the sacrifice was over, they worshipped Vayu. Thus, a summary and parts of the Purana have been described. This is the order in which the Purana reveals itself. Even if it is mentioned briefly, it is seen to lead to great happiness. Thus, after having stated it briefly, I will now narrate it in detail. After conquering his senses, a person should study this first part properly. That will be like studying the entire Purana. There is no doubt about this. O *brahmana*s! There is knowledge in the four *Veda*s, the *Vedanga*s and the Upanishads. That knowledge of the *Veda*s must be enhanced through Itihasa and Purana. The *shruti* texts are scared of a person

[76] *Nemi* is the felly or rim of the wheel. Hence, the place came to be known as Naimisha.

[77] Meaning Goutama, or Goutama's son.

[78] The village (*grama*) of Kalapa has been speculatively located in various places, including near Badarikashrama. The last remaining kings of the solar and lunar dynasties are respectively Maru and Devapi. It is believed that they meditate and reside there, waiting for *kali yuga* to be over. The sentence probably implies that Svarbhanu stands for *kali yuga* and when this is over, all kings vanish.

with limited learning, fearing, "He will strike us." If one studies and practices this part, spoken by Svayambhu himself, one is not deluded and obtains the desired destination. Since this is what occurred in ancient times, this is described as Purana. If a person understands this derivation, he is freed from all sins. Therefore, listen to this summary. At the time of creation, Narayana creates everything in this Purana. When it is the time for destruction and he destroys, it doesn't remain.'[79]

Chapter 2-1(2) (Account of Naimisha)

The *rishi*s, stores of austerities, spoke to Suta again. 'Where did they, extraordinary in deeds, undertake that sacrifice? How long did it last for? What was done? How did Prabhanjana[80] narrate the Purana? Please tell us everything in detail. We have great curiosity.'

Thus urged, Suta answered in these auspicious words. 'Hear about how those patient ones performed that excellent sacrifice, about how long it lasted and about what was done. In ancient times, desiring to create the universe, he[81] himself participated in that extremely sacred sacrifice, which lasted for one thousand years. Thus, Brahma himself became the householder who was performing austerities. Ida was the wife. In the sacrifice of those great-souled ones, the intelligent and immensely energetic Mrityu acted as *shamitra*.[82] For one thousand years, the Gods resided there. As it revolved, the felly of the wheel of *dharma* shattered there. Because of this incident, it became famous as Naimisha and is worshipped by sages. That is the place where *siddha*s and *charanas*[83] frequent the sacred Gomati. In an instant, Gomati had a daughter

[79] The Purana also vanishes.
[80] Another name for Vayu.
[81] Brahma.
[82] Mrityu is Death, *shamitra* is the act of killing animals at a sacrifice.
[83] Celestial bards.

there, known as Rohini. The great-souled Vasishtha and Arundhati
had sons. Of these, the infinitely energetic Shakti was the eldest.
King Kalmashapada and Shakra met Shakti there. The enmity
between Vasishtha and Vishvamitra also originated there. Through
Adrishyanti, that is the place where the sage Parashara was born.
In *jnana*, that is the place where Vasishtha was surpassed.[84] Those
who know about the *brahman* thought of a mountain in Naimisha.
Those born in Naimisha are known as Naimishiyas.'

'The sacrifice undertaken by those intelligent ones lasted twelve
years. At the time, the valiant Pururava ruled over the earth. We have
heard that Pururava was not satisfied with the jewels he obtained
from the eighteen *dvipa*s in the oceans.[85] Urged by a messenger of
the *deva*s, Urvashi came to him. Having accepted him, Urvashi went
to the sacrifice with him. While he was the lord of men, the residents
of Naimisha performed the sacrifice. Through Pavaka, blazing in
his energy, Ganga conceived.[86] Unable to bear it, she deposited it
on the mountain, which turned into gold. The sacrificial arena of
those great-souled ones thus became golden. The divinity who is
the creator of the universe,[87] the one who thinks of the creation of
the worlds, himself went to the sacrifice of those infinitely energetic
ones. On a hunting expedition, Pururava came there along with Ida.
He saw that great wonder of a sacrificial arena that was golden. His
vijnana[88] was destroyed by avarice and he sought to seize it. The
residents of Naimisha were filled with great rage against the king.
The sages, devoted to austerities, were urged by *deva*s and became
angry. They used *kusha* grass, which turned into *vajra*s, to kill the

[84] By his grandson Parashara, while Parashara was still inside the
womb.

[85] Usually, the number of *dvipa*s is given as seven. Eighteen is clearly
obtained by adding some *varsha*s, such as the nine *varsha*s in Jambu-dvipa.

[86] Pavaka is the one who purifies, a name for Agni. This conception
was actually through Shiva's seed, which Agni temporarily bore. Eventually,
this led to the birth of Skanda.

[87] The word used is Vishvakarma, which clearly means Brahma here,
and not Vishvakarma, the architect of the gods.

[88] *Vijnana* is knowledge but is specifically used for knowledge obtained
through inward reflection and self-contemplation.

king. Struck by *kusha* grass, which turned into vajras, the king
gave up his body. Meanwhile, the king who is described as the
great-souled father of Nahusha and was Urvashi's son, fought
on earth.[89] This lord of the earth was devoted to *dharma*. This
excellent man was the foremost among those who performed
avabhritha.[90] Then, those who know about the *brahman* pacified
the king. For the sake of the earth, they thought of their own
forms as calves used to milk the earth. Those great-souled ones
observed *brahmacharya* and performed the sacrifice. In those
ancient times, the creator of the universe desired to create the
universe. The king was as radiant as Indra of the *deva*s and
was surrounded by *vaikhanasa*s,[91] *valakhilya*s,[92] who love their
friends, *marichipa*s,[93] sages who have no birth and sages who are
born and are as resplendent as the sun and the fire. There were
the ancestors, *deva*s, *apsara*s, *siddha*s, *gandharva*s, *uraga*s and
*charana*s and other residents of Bharata. Following the norms, all
the species, *gandharva*s and others, were worshipped. *Stotram*s[94]
were used from the sacred texts. Rites were used for household
divinities, fathers and grandfathers. Through all these rites, they
were remembered and worshipped. The *gandharva*s chanted
from the *Sama Veda* and large numbers of *apsara*s danced. The
sages chanted auspicious words, with wonderful *akshara*s and
*pada*s.[95] The learned chanted *mantra*s and performed *japa*.[96] They
debated and sought to defeat adversaries through arguments.
The *rishi*s were learned and knew about the meanings of words.

[89] Pururava's son was Ayu and Ayu's son was Nahusha. Presumably,
Ayu fought with other claimants to the throne.
[90] *Avabhritha* is the most important final component of a sacrifice,
characterized by the taking of a bath.
[91] Those who subsist on wild grain.
[92] 60,000 sages who were the sizes of thumbs. They preceded the sun's
chariot.
[93] Sages who subsist on the rays of the sun and the moon.
[94] Hymns of praise.
[95] *Akshara* is a syllable, *pada* is a sentence.
[96] *Japa* is silent chanting.

They were accomplished in *nyaya*.[97] No *brahma-rakshasa*[98] entered and caused harm. Using feathered and swift weapons, no *daitya*s destroyed the sacrifice. No poor person entered and there was no reason for *prayashchitta*.[99] Following the norms, power, wisdom, rites and *yoga* were used to obtain benedictions. In this way, the learned ones performed the sacrifice for twelve years. The sacrifice performed by the Naimishiya *rishi*s was like one performed by the wielder of the *vajra*.[100] Separately, brave and aged *ritvija*s performed *jyotishtoma* sacrifices.[101] When this was over, copious amounts of *dakshina* were offered by those who followed them.[102] O *brahmana*s! After the sacrifice was over, they asked the great lord, the divinity Vayu,[103] who is extensive in his *atman*, what you have asked me. Thus urged, for the sake of his own lineage,[104] the lord replied to them. He is a *deva* who is Svayambhu's *shishya*. He is controlled and directly witnesses everything. He possesses *anima* and the other powers[105] and his limbs are subtle. Through winds that blow sideways and rain, he sustains all the worlds and all mobile and immobile entities.

---

[97] *Nyaya* means good policy. But *nyaya* is also one of the six *darshana*s, with an emphasis on logic and epistemology.

[98] A *brahmana* who is born as a *rakshasa*.

[99] A rite of atonement, implying there was no deficiency in the sacrifice.

[100] That is, Indra.

[101] *Ritvija*s are officiating priests. Though the classification varied over time, there were four types of *ritvija*s. The *adhvaryu* chanted hymns from the *Yajur Veda*, the *hotri* chanted hymns from the *Rig Veda*, the *udgatri* chanted hymns from the *Sama Veda* and the *brahmana* chanted hymns from the *Atharva Veda*.

[102] *Dakshina* is the fee given by a *shishya* to a *guru* after the successful completion of studies, as well as a sacrificial fee.

[103] The text says Vasudeva. It should obviously read Vayudeva, and we have corrected the typo.

[104] In the sense of Brahma's lineage, Brahma being his preceptor.

[105] *Siddhi*s mean powers. Specifically, *yoga* leads to eight major *siddhi*s or powers. These are *anima* (becoming as small as one desires), *mahima* (as large as one desires), *laghima* (as light as one wants), *garima* (as heavy as one wants), *prapti* (obtaining what one wants), *prakamya* (travelling where one wants), *vashitvam* (powers to control creatures) and *ishitvam* (obtaining divine powers).

He bears the branches on his seven shoulders.[106] The forty-nine Maruts are stationed in his dominion. Through his circle of sons, the immensely strong one ensures that a sacrifice is performed. Through his energy, he sustains life in those with bodies. The five kinds of *prana*[107] follow their respective conducts and sustain. They fill all bodies and perform the act of sustenance. Wind originates from space and possesses two qualities, sound and touch. Those who are accomplished in the words used in the sacred texts have said that he is the *arani* of speech.[108] He seemed to delight all the sages in gentle words. O ones who know the Puranas! O ones with excellent minds! O ones who seek refuge in the Puranas! O *brahmana*s who are devoted to the Puranas! The lord described these accounts to them. O excellent *dvija*s! These accounts are exactly in accordance with what happened. They are about excellent incidents in the world of *rishi*s. Earlier, Brahma narrated this excellent *jnana*, in the form of the Purana. It is about *deva*s and *rishi*s and destroys all sins. In detail and in the due order, I will narrate it to you.'

Chapter 3-1(3) (Origin of Hiranyagarbha)

Suta said, 'Listen to their divine account. It destroys all sins. I will narrate this wonderful account. It is full of many meanings and is in conformity with the *shruti* texts. If a person nurtures and listens to this constantly, having cultivated his own lineage, he obtains greatness in the world of heaven. It enables one to

---

[106] A reference to seven types of wind.

[107] *Prana* is the breath of life or the life-force. *Prana* draws breath into the body, *apana* exhales it. *Vyana* distributes it through the body and *samana* assimilates it. *Udana* gives rise to sound.

[108] *Arani* stands for the two churning sticks used to kindle a fire, by rubbing them against each other. That is, Vayu gives rise to speech, through sound.

cross over the world and one has the five characteristics.[109] This is in accordance with what transpired and what has been heard. It enhances the deeds of the predecessors and I will narrate it for your understanding. All of them were auspicious in their deeds and their fame is permanent. Recounting this ensures wealth, fame, a long lifespan, heaven and the destruction of enemies. I prostrate myself before Svayambhu Hiranyagarbha. He is Purusha, Ishvara and Aja. He is the first and the greatest. He is the creator of subjects. It is from him that *kalpa* obtains its entire form. He is the purest among the pure. He is Brahma, who ordains the worlds. I will narrate the excellent creation of beings,[110] starting with Mahat and ending with Vishesha, with all the features and characteristics, with the five kinds of *pramana* and the six that bind, presided over by Purusha.[111] The cause is always unmanifest and has existence and non-existence within it.[112] Those who have thought about the *tattva*s have spoken of this as Purusha and Prakriti. It is devoid of smell, form or taste. It is devoid of sound or touch. This is the great element that is the origin of the universe. This is the supreme and eternal *brahman*. This is the unmanifest, who assumed a form in all beings. The *brahman* is without a beginning and without birth.

[109] The word Vishvatara and use of the word (*pancha*) causes problems in understanding and translating this sentence. In this context, bringing in *tantra* seems unwarranted. Were *tantra* to be brought in, Vishvatara would be taken to mean the goddess Tara, with her five aspects of green Tara, white Tara, yellow Tara, blue Tara and red Tara. With *tantra* avoided, liberties have been taken in translating the sentence.

[110] Known as *bhuta-sarga*.

[111] There is a reference to *samkhya*, but the allusion is unclear. *Pramana* means proof and four kinds of proof are easy to identify—*pratyaksha* (perception), *anumana* (inference), *upamana* (comparison) and *shabda* (testimony). In any listing of *pramana*s, these are standard. The fifth is impossible to identify unambiguously and might be *arthapatti* (postulation). Similarly, it is impossible to decide which six of *samkhya*'s *tattva*s (principles) are being singled out. Somewhat subjectively, it might be the three *guna*s, *sattva* (purity), *rajas* (passion) and *tamas* (darkness) and Mahat/*buddhi* (intelligence), *ahamkara* (ego) and *manas* (mind).

[112] *Sat* and *asat*. This can also be translated as cause and effect, with Pradhana as the cause and Prakriti as the effect.

It is subtle and possesses the three *gunas*. It is the origin and does
not belong to the present. It is impossible to comprehend and is
beyond existence and non-existence. Everything was full of *tamas*
and was pervaded by its *atman*. Since there was an equilibrium
between the *gunas*, everything was full of *tamas* and nothing was
manifest. At the time of creation, Pradhana was presided over by
kshetrajna.[113] With disequilibrium between the *gunas*, the *tattva* of
Mahat emerged. Mahat is subtle and initially, it is shrouded by what
is not manifest. Mahat has an excess of *sattva* and initially, it only
exhibited *sattva*. It should be known that Mahat is full of *sattva*.
That is the reason it alone is spoken of as the cause. There were
only the signs of Mahat and *kshetrajna* presided over it. Its two
functions are described as resolution and enterprise. It is beyond
notions of measurement. Desiring to create, it embarked on this
great creation. For the functioning of beings in the world, *dharma*
and other principles are the causes. The great-souled *brahman* is
present in the mind. Ishvara enables an entity to identify wicked
intelligence. Through his many rays, the lord controls the centres of
wisdom in all beings and attains his desired objective. The mind is
spoken of as the one who exists by dividing itself into two, the part
that enjoys and the part that saves.

Mahat gathers together all the *tattvas* and forms an aggregate.

But Mahat's body is conceived as transcending all the *gunas*
and *tattvas*. The mind is thought of as the one that divides itself
into parts. The *jivatman* is associated with enjoyment.[114] However,
the *brahman* is large and enables all the sentiments to seek a higher
refuge. It is spoken of as the *brahman* because it enables sentiments
to become lofty.[115] In this way, it exhibits its favours and enables all
embodied entities to fill up. Purusha understands all these separate
sentiments. Hence in ancient times, the *brahman* used Purusha as
the instrument to accomplish the task. Know that the *brahman* is
revered as *kshetrajna* and Devi Prakriti works through nature. The

---

[113] *Kshetra* is the physical body, *kshetrajna* is one who knows about
the *kshetra*, that is, the *atman*.

[114] In these sections, the text is obscure, and we have taken liberties.

[115] From a verbal root that means growing or increasing.

first embodied entity is spoken of as Purusha. Brahma existed at the beginning and is the original creator of beings. Hiranyagarbha,[116] with the four faces, manifested himself from the egg. In the original creation and in subsidiary cycles of creation, Brahma is revered as *kshetrajna*. He assumes the tasks and abandons them at the time of withdrawal.[117] He again assumes a body when the required amalgamation of time comes about. The great-souled one holds up the golden Meru. When the water has vanished, he is the one who takes away the five elements. The seven worlds are well-established in the egg. The earth is there, with its seven *dvipa*s, seven oceans, extremely large mountains and thousands of rivers. The worlds and the entire universe are inside it. The moon, the sun, the *nakshatra*s, the planets, the wind, Lokaloka and everything else is established inside the egg. On the outside, the water is surrounded by fire that is ten times the size. On the outside, fire is surrounded by wind that is ten times the size. On the outside, the wind is surrounded by space that is ten times the size. Similarly, space is enveloped everywhere by *bhutadi*. *Bhutadi* is enveloped by Mahat and Mahat is enveloped by Pradhana. In this way, the egg is shrouded by seven sheaths associated with Prakriti. Until they are destroyed, all these elements of Prakriti are willingly established there. They are established there at the time of creation and devour each other at the time of destruction. In this way, they sustain each other and devour each other. They support and are supported. They transform and are transformed. The unmanifest is spoken of as *kshetra* and the *brahman* is spoken of as *kshetrajna*. This is the nature of Prakrita creation and *kshetrajna* presides over this. This first creation did not result from resolution and manifested itself like lightning. A person who knows this birth of Hiranyagarbha knows the truth. There is no doubt that he obtains a long lifespan, fame and wisdom and is blessed.'

---

[116] The one with a golden womb, Brahma.
[117] Destruction/dissolution.

Chapter 4-1(4) (Creation of the worlds)

Suta said, 'When transformations were withdrawn and the manifest retreated within the *atman*, Pradhana and Purusha were established in a similar kind of *dharma*. They were similarly established, with *tamas* and *sattva gunas*. There was nothing excessive and they are described as following each other. Equilibrium between the *gunas* should be understood as dissolution, an excess is spoken of as creation. When there is an increase in *sattva*, that is certainly a case of preservation and the lotus is situated at the top. Just as water causes a seed to sprout, when *rajas* follows *tamas* and *sattva*, it is *rajas* that goads the function. When the *gunas* are established in a state of disequilibrium, they are associated with each other. It should be lovingly noted that the three[118] originate from an agitation in the *gunas*. They are eternal, supreme and hidden, present in the *atmans* of all those with bodies. *Sattva* is Vishnu, *rajas* is Brahma and *tamas* is Rudra Prajapati. Vishnu illuminates *rajas* and obtains the status as Brahma, the creator. For the wonderful task of creating the worlds, the greatly energetic one originates. Vishnu illuminates *tamas* and is established in the status as Kala.[119] Illuminating *sattva*, Vishnu is established in the role of preserver. These three exist in the worlds in this way and such are the three *gunas*. They are the three *Vedas* and they are the three Agnis.[120] They follow each other and are attached to each other. They follow each other's conduct and urge each other. They are united with each other and obtain sustenance from each other. They are not separated even for an instant and do not abandon each other. At the time of creation, when there is disequilibrium between the *gunas*, Pradhana functions. What cannot be seen is established first, with existence and non-existence in its *atman*.

---

[118] Brahma, Vishnu and Shiva.

[119] Kala means time, as well as the Destroyer. Here, it means Shiva Rudra.

[120] The three *Vedas* are *Rig Veda*, *Sama Veda* and *Yajur Veda*. The three fires (Agnis) are *ahavaniya*, *garhapatya* and *dakshinatya* (the fire that burns in a southern direction).

Brahma and *buddhi* originated simultaneously, as a couple, from the unmanifest *tamas*. This is known as Brahma, the *kshetrajna*. To accomplish the task, Brahma originated first, possessing both the task and the instrument. His energy was unmatched. He was intelligent and unmanifest. He was the one who caused illumination. For the sake of nurturing, he was the first to hold a body. He was unmatched in *jnana* and he was the virtuous lord of non-attachment. He was unmanifest and everything he desired was in his mind. The three *guna*s were under his control and his inclinations were favourable. In his status as Brahma, he has four faces. He is Kala Bhava, the Destroyer. He is Purusha, the one with one thousand heads.[121] Svayambhu has these three forms. When he is Brahma, he is only full of *rajas*. As Kala, he possesses *rajas* and *tamas*. As Purusha, he is full of *sattva*. Svayambhu is surrounded by *guna*s. As Brahma, he creates the worlds. At the time of destruction, he is Kala. As Purusha, he is indifferent. These are Svayambhu's three states. Brahma's eyes are like the petals of lotuses. Since the time of origin, Kala's complexion is like that of collyrium. In his form as the *paramatman*, Purusha has eyes like lotuses.[122] The lord of *yoga* creates one body, two bodies, three bodies and many bodies, and then takes them away again. In his own pastimes, he resorts to many kinds of forms, diverse features and acts. Since he exists in three forms in the world, he is spoken of as Triguna. Since he divides himself into four forms, he is spoken of as Chaturvyuha.[123] At the end of a *parardha*, he lies down and sleeps. The lord is the one who enjoys material objects. Since he always possesses the natural disposition of well-being, he is spoken of as the *atman*.[124] Since the lord goes everywhere and enters the body, he is *rishi*.[125]

[121] Meaning Vishnu.

[122] Pundarikaksha (with eyes like lotuses) is one of Vishnu's names.

[123] Vishnu has four manifestations (*vyuha*) as Vasudeva, Samkarshana, Pradyumna and Aniruddha.

[124] There are alternative etymological derivations of the word *atman*. One such means 'natural temperament'.

[125] Etymologically, *rishi* is usually derived from 'to see', but 'to go' is not grammatically incorrect.

Since he is the lord of everything, he is known as Sarva.[126]
Since he enters everywhere, he is Vishnu.[127] Since he devours
bhavas, he is Bhagavan.[128] Since there is no taint[129] in him, he
is Naga. Since he is supremely delighted, he is Parama. Since
he is a deva, he is remembered as OUM. Since he possesses
vijnana about everything, he is Sarvajna. Since everything flows
from him, he is Sarva. Since Brahma causes men to sleep, he
is described as Narayana.[130] He divides his atman into three
and functions as Sakala.[131] In three forms, he himself creates,
preserves and destroys. In the beginning, the lord manifested
himself as Hiranyagarbha. He was the first and was in control
of himself. He is said to be without origin and without birth.
Thus, the Puranas speak of him as Hiranyagarbha. In his form as
Kala, Svayambhu withdraws himself. He is foremost among the
varnas. Even if one tries for one hundred of Manu's years, one
is incapable of enumerating him. In the enumeration of kalpas,
there is said to be a parardha when Brahma withdraws himself.
When that period is over, there is another of equal duration when
he wakes up. For those who reside in households, thousands of
crores of years have passed since the advent of kalpas and there
are that many that still remain. Know that the kalpa presently
underway is Varaha kalpa. There was a first kalpa and this is the
current one.[132] Until one thousand mahayugas are over, lords of
men will protect.'

---

[126] Sarva means everything/everyone.

[127] The root vish means to enter or pervade.

[128] The word bhava can be translated in different ways, the simplest is
'state of being'. This derivation of Bhagavan is extremely contrived.

[129] Agas. Na+agas.

[130] After dissolution, Vishnu sleeps in the water (naara). The usual
derivation of Narayana is Naara + ayana (path/course). Here, it is based on
nara (men).

[131] One with parts.

[132] The Matsya Purana lists thirty kalpas. Shveta was the first and
Varaha is the twenty-sixth.

Chapter 5-1(5) (Creation of the Worlds Continued)

Shri Suta said, 'In the beginning, water was present everywhere on
earth. When everything was dissolved, the winds were pacified
and nothing could be discerned. All mobile and immobile entities
were destroyed and everything was reduced to a single ocean.
The lord Brahma was present, with one thousand eyes and one
thousand feet. In the form known as Narayana, Brahma lay down
on the waters and slept. He was Purusha with one thousand heads,
golden in complexion and beyond the senses. Since he possessed
sattva alone, he was restrained. He saw that the world was empty.
In this connection, a *shloka* is cited about Narayana. "Water
is known as *naara*. Water is spoken of as the offspring of *nara*.
Since his *ayana* was the water, he is spoken of as Narayana." He
remained in this way for one thousand *mahayuga*s, meditating on
the golden petals.[133] He did this so that he might be able to see the
status of Brahma. Manifesting himself, Brahma moved downwards
in the water, like a firefly during a monsoon night. He understood
that the earth was submerged inside that great mass of water and
focused on raising it. Earlier, at the beginning of *kalpa*s, in his
body as Oumkara, he possessed the eight parts.[134] In his mind, the
great-souled one thought of his divine form. Seeing that the earth
was submerged in water, he thought, "For the sake of raising the
earth from the water, what form shall I assume?" Appropriate for
sporting in the water, he thought of the Varaha form.[135] It was
invisible to all beings and could only be expressed in words that
meant the *brahman*. It was ten *yojana*s wide and one hundred
*yojana*s long. It resembled a dark cloud and its voice rumbled like
thunder. Its body resembled a gigantic mountain. Its tusks were
white, sharp and fierce. It resembled lightning and fire and was
infinitely energetic, like the sun. Its shoulders were thick and round

[133] Of the lotus.
[134] Oumkara is the utterance of OUM. The eight can be interpreted in
different ways. But it is simplest to take it in the sense of Ishvara's powers,
knowledge, strength, lordship, vigour, energy and so on.
[135] Boar.

and its stride resembled Vishnu's. The area around the hips was
thick and raised. It possessed the signs revered in a bull. The infinite
Hari assumed this unmatched form of Varaha. To raise the earth,
he entered Rasatala. His tusks were the completion of *diksha* and
ishti.[136] Oblations were his mouth. The fire was his tongue. The
darbha grass was his body hair. An immensely ascetic *brahmana*[137]
was his head. The *Veda*s were his shoulders. His smell was that of
oblations of *ghee*. *Havya* and *kavya* were his speed.[138] *Pragvamsha*[139]
was his body. The resplendent one was full of many kinds of *diksha*.
Dakshina was the *yogi*'s heart. The lord was full of *shraddha*[140] and
sattva. *Upakrama*[141] was his inclination. *Pravargya*[142] was the hair
that ornamented his chest. The different *chhandas*[143] constituted his
path. The secret Upanishads were his seat. *Maya*[144] was the wife
who was his aide. He was as tall as the summit of a mountain. The
night and day were his eyes. *Vedanga*s and *shruti* texts were his
ornaments. His fragrance was that of oblations of *ghee*. The *shruva*
was his snout.[145] His voice was the loud chanting of hymns from the
Sama Veda. He was full of the *dharma* of truth. He was illustrious
and honoured because of his valour and deeds. His nails were
prayashchitta. He was terrible and the sacrificial animal constituted

[136] This is a description of Yajna-Varaha, Vishnu's Varaha incarnation,
representing a sacrifice (*yajna*). Diksha is a process of initiation for a
sacrifice (or any auspicious task). Ishti is a sacrifice. A *yajna* and a *kratu*
are both sacrifices. However, the former is performed with a sacrificial post
and the latter without one. More specifically, the former is performed with
sacrificial animals and the latter without sacrificing animals.

[137] As in one of the four officiating priests, mentioned earlier.

[138] *Havya* is oblations offered to *deva*s, *kavya* is oblations offered to
ancestors.

[139] A sacrificial room where oblations are kept, facing the east.

[140] Faith.

[141] Ceremony before reading the *Veda*s.

[142] Ceremony before a *soma* sacrifice.

[143] Metres.

[144] The personified form of illusion. Any ceremony must be performed
with the wife.

[145] Both *shruk* and *shruva* are sacrificial ladles, *shruk* is like a bowl
with a handle, *shruva* resembles a spoon.

his thighs. He was the great sacrifice. The chants of the *udgatri* were his entrails. The oblations were his sign. Fruits and seeds were the great herbs. Lack of ego was the sacrificial altar.[146] *Soma* juice was his blood. Having become Yajna-Varaha, Prajapati entered the water again and found that the earth was covered with water.[147] He reached and laid out the existent and the non-existent as oblations. The waters of oceans were separately placed in oceans and the waters of rivers were separately placed in rivers. Having done this, he levelled the earth and placed mountains. The *samvartaka* fire had burnt everything down from the previous cycle of creation. All the mountains on earth had been destroyed by that fire. Everything that had existed had merged into that single ocean, agitated by the wind. Wherever this water was sprinkled, a new mountain originated. In this way, the worlds, the oceans and the mountains were spread out. In this way, at the beginning of every *kalpa*, the creator of the universe divides again and again. He repeatedly creates this earth, with its oceans, seven *dvipa*s and mountains, and the four worlds starting with Bhuloka, again and again.'[148]

'After having created the worlds, he embarked on the task of creating subjects. Bhagavan Svayambhu Brahma desired to create many kinds of subjects. At the beginning of the *kalpa*, he created them in the same forms, as had existed earlier. As he meditated on creation, along with *buddhi* and Pradhana, at the same time, darkness manifested itself. From the great-souled one, Avidya appeared and this had five components, known as—*tamas, moha, mahamoha, tamisra* and *andha-tamisra*.[149] As he proudly meditated, these were the five kinds of creation. There was darkness everywhere, like a seed and a creeper inside a pot. Inside and outside, it was devoid of

[146] We have corrected the typo of *vadyantara* to *vedyantara* (sacrificial altar).

[147] The text says fire, obviously a typo. The earth was submerged in water.

[148] The three higher worlds, Satyaloka, Tapoloka and Janaloka, are not destroyed in secondary cycles of destruction.

[149] *Avidya* is ignorance, the antithesis of knowledge. *Tamas* is ignorance, *moha* is delusion, *mahamoha* is great delusion, *tamisra* is darkness and *andha-tamisra* is blinding darkness.

illumination and consciousness. Thus, what is described as *mukhya sarga*[150] came about, consisting of trees and mountains. Since they were created with the use of intelligence, there were reasons for misery. Brahma saw the *mukhya sarga* that had evolved from him. He was unhappy and contemplated creation again. As he meditated on this, another *tiryaka-srota* creation resulted.[151] This is known as *tiryaka-srota* because it flows downwards and sideways. As a consequence of the large degree of *tamas*, all of them are described as beings characterized by a great lack of *jnana*. They originated, but not in the way they should have been. Though they lacked in *jnana*, they prided themselves on *jnana*. They were proud and full of *ahamkara*. This creation had twenty-eight different types.[152] There were eleven sense organs and nine kinds of *atman*. There were the eight, *taraka*s and others, and they are remembered because they destroyed powers.[153] All of them possessed inner illumination but were covered on the outside. It is said that beings in the three types[154] of *tiryaka-srota* were in control of their *atman*s. The creator of the universe created this second creation of *tiryaka-srota*. Having seen this, he thought about the creation he should undertake. As he meditated, a creation full of *sattva* resulted. This third creation was *urddhva-srota*[155] and was established upwards. Since this did not withdraw from an upward direction, it is described as *urddhva-srota*. They are full of a great deal of joy and happiness and are not covered, inside or outside. The subjects of *urddhva-srota* are illuminated, inside and

---

[150] Primary creation, consisting of immobile entities.

[151] One that flows downwards and diagonally, resulting in inferior species. A possible reference to the circulation not flowing upwards. These are entities that draw their nourishment from inside the body.

[152] Alternatively, this creation suffered from twenty-eight types of impediments. In this, and subsequent sentences, it is impossible to identify what the numbers precisely mean.

[153] Speculatively, it is possible *taraka* refers to *Citrullus colocynthis*, the gourd family of plants, also known as Indravaruni.

[154] Speculatively, animals, birds and reptiles.

[155] Literally, with an upward flow. *Urddha-srota* is interpreted as beings that draw their nourishment from outside the body. *Deva*s obtain their food from outside the body.

outside. The nine categories, Dhata and the others, are described as learned, satisfied in their *atman*s. The third creation of *urddhva-srota* is remembered as having consisted of all the *deva*s. At that time, the lord made the third creation of *urddhva-srota*, consisting of all the *deva*s. Brahma was pleased in his mind and did not think of anything else. However, thereafter, Ishvara wished to embark on another act of creation. He meditated on creation and then on the truth. Thus, *bhouta-sarga*, the creation known as *arvak-srota*,[156] came about. Since the flow was downwards, this was known as *arvak-srota*. These possessed a lot of illumination, but they were touched by *tamas* and had an excess of *rajas*. Therefore, they repeatedly act so that they repeatedly suffer from a lot of misery. However, humans are illuminated inside and outside and are *sadhaka*s.[157] If they are established with eight characteristics, they can also go to hell. But there are humans who attain *siddhi* and their *dharma* is no different from that of *gandharva*s. As a result of his favours, the fifth creation, *anugraha*, is established in four forms—*viparyaya, shakti, siddha* and *mukhya*.[158] Repeatedly, they are withdrawn, are born and exist. The sixth creation is said to be that of elements and beings. Creatures are known to display the conduct of eating and seizing. Brahma's first creation should be known as the creation of Mahat. The second creation involved the creation of *tanmatra*s[159] and is known as the creation of subtle elements. The third creation is known as *vaikarika* and involved the creation of the senses. These three resulted from resolution and are known as Prakrita *sarga*s. The fourth creation is described as *mukhya sarga*, the creation of immobile entities. The fifth creation is *tiryaka-srota*, involving the creation of inferior

[156] Literally, downward flow. This is interpreted as humans, because for humans, food flows downwards. This is also below heaven, hence, downwards.

[157] *Sadhya* is the attainable objective, *sadhana* is the means. *Sadhaka* is the person who is using the means to attain the objective. *Siddhi* is success in attaining the objective.

[158] *Anugraha* means favour/kindness, *viparyaya* is loss of consciousness/non-existence, *shakti* is energy/strength, *siddha* is success and *mukhya* means foremost.

[159] The *tanmatra*s are the subtle elements and senses.

species. The sixth creation is described as *urddhva-srota*, the creation of *deva*s. The seventh creation is *arvak-srota*, that of humans. The eighth creation is *anugraha* and it has elements of both *sattva* and *tamas*. The first three are known as Prakrita *sarga*s and the other five are Vaikrita.[160] The three Prakrita *sarga*s resulted before the use of resolution. When Brahma embarked on his task of creation, he used his resolution for the Vaikrita *sarga*s. As I describe all this in detail, listen. He is established in all beings in four forms—*viparyaya*, *shakti*, *buddhi* and *siddhi*. He is in immobile entities in the form of *viparyaya* and in inferior species in the form of *shakti*. He is in all humans in the form of *siddhi* and in *deva*s in the form of *pushti*.'[161]

'After this, Brahma used his mental powers to create sons who were like his own self. They were immensely energetic in their existence, *jnana* and non-attachment. As a result of their understanding, these three did not indulge in the expected conduct.[162] They did not create subjects and embarked on the process of subsidiary creation. As a result of their non-attachment, Brahma created other *sadhaka*s. He created *deva*s, who were proud of their status and obeyed Brahma's instructions. As a consequence of creation, different entities were established in different places. Listen. There were water, fire, earth, wind, space, heaven, the directions, oceans, rivers, *vanaspati*s, medicinal herbs, *vriksha*s, creepers, winding plants, *kashtha*, *kala*, *muhurta*, *sandhya*, night, day, fortnights, months, *ayana*s, years and *yuga*s.[163] They are proud

---

[160] The first three occurred naturally, from Prakriti. Vaikrita creations were deliberately created.

[161] *Pushti* means nourishment.

[162] There were actually four, not three, Sanaka, Sananda, Sanatana and Sanatkumara. In these sections, the text clearly has several typos and we have taken liberties. The expected conduct was that of creating, but they were not interested in that.

[163] There are many words for trees. *Vanaspati* is a large tree that grows in the forest. Specifically, it is a tree with fruit, but no visible flowers. *Vriksha*s have both flowers and fruit. *Sandhya* is dawn and dusk, when night meets day and day meets night. *Ayana* means movement. *Uttarayana* is the movement of the sun to the north of the equator, the period from the winter to the summer solstice. *Dakshinayana* is the movement of the sun to the south of the equator, the period from the summer to the winter solstice. *Kashtha*, *kala* and *muhurta* are different units for measuring time.

of their positions and are said to be established in their respective positions. After creating and establishing them in their positions, he created others—*deva*s and ancestors. Subjects flourished because of them. Using his mental powers, he created Bhrigu, Angiras, Marichi, Pulastya, Pulaha, Kratu, Daksha, Atri and Vasishtha. In the Purana, these nine are described as Brahma, because their selves were just like those of Brahma. They were *yogi*s devoted to the *brahman*. Brahma next created Rudra as a son, born from his rage. He created Sankalpa[164] and Dharma, who were like mountains before everyone else. Brahma created Vyavasaya,[165] which brings happiness to beings. Sankalpa was born from the resolution of the one whose birth is not manifest. Daksha was created from his *prana* and Marichi from his speech and his eyes. The *rishi* Bhrigu was created from the heart of the one who originated in water. Angiras was born from his head and Atri from his ears. Pulastya was born from his *udana* and Pulaha from his *vyana*. Vasishtha was born from his *samana* and Kratu was created from his *apana*. These twelve are described as the best among Brahma's sons.[166] Dharma and the others[167] are known as the first among Brahma's sons. The others who were created, Bhrigu and the others, did not expound about the *brahman*. These sons of Brahma are known as ancient householders. O *dvija*s! Along with Rudra, there were twelve who were born. Kratu and Sanatkumara were the two who held up their seed. In ancient times, these were the ones to originate first. Therefore, among everyone, they are the eldest. In this world, these two were ancient *sadhaka*s from the seventh *kalpa*, long over. Having given up their bodies, their energy makes them radiant in other worlds. Those two followed the *dharma* of that *yuga* and fixed their *jivatman*s on the *paramatman*. For the sake of subjects, those two immensely energetic ones followed *dharma* and *kama*. However, since the day he originated, the one known as

[164] Resolution.

[165] Enterprise/exertion.

[166] Bhrigu, Angiras, Marichi, Pulastya, Pulaha, Kratu, Daksha, Atri, Vasishtha, Rudra, Dharma and Sankalpa.

[167] From the next sentence, this seems to mean Dharma and Sankalpa.

Sanatkumara is spoken of as having remained a boy.[168] That is the reason he is known by that name. Those twelve lineages are divine and are full of *deva*s. They are ornamented by *maharshi*s who performed rites and had offspring. Brahma saw that those twelve, full of *sattva*, were born from his breath of life.'

'Thereafter, the lord created *asura*s, ancestors, *deva*s and humans. *Deva*s were born from his mouth and ancestors from his chest. Humans were created from his genitals and *asura*s from his posterior. Then Brahma created night and the *atman*s of humans from moonlight. The lord of *deva*s created ancestors from the nectar. After having created major *deva*s and *asura*s, he next created minor ones. From his mind, he created humans and ancestors who were as great as their forefathers. He created lightning, thunder, clouds and the rainbow, tinged with red. For success in sacrifices, he fashioned hymns from the *Rig Veda*, the *Yajur Veda* and the *Sama Veda*. From his greatness, superior and inferior beings originated. Brahma's creation of subjects included *deva*s, *rishi*s, ancestors and humans. He next created mobile and immobile entities, *yaksha*s, *pishacha*s, *gandharva*s and all the *apsara*s, men, *kinnara*s,[169] *rakshasa*s, birds, *pashu*s, *mriga*s,[170] *uraga*s, the perishable and the imperishable, both mobile and immobile. Prior to this, Svayambhu created *karma* for them. When they are created again and again, it is this that they undertake. The learned know that they are divided into three categories that they have been born into—violent and non-violent; mild and cruel; and those following the *dharma* of what should be done and those following the *adharma* of what should not be done. It is like this and not otherwise. They are in couples. However, those who possess *sattva* and are impartial in outlook say that they are engaged in their respective *karma* and those differences don't really exist. The great lord created the five elements and Prapancha

---

[168] That is, *kumara*.

[169] *Kinnara/kimpurusha* is a semi-divine species.

[170] *Pashu*s and *mriga*s are both animals. *Pashu*s are large animals, while *mriga*s are small animals, such as deer. There is an alternative difference. A *pashu* is a sacrificial animal (hence domestic animal), while *mriga* is an animal that is hunted (hence wild animal).

is made out of these.[171] He created the firmament, illuminated by
these five. The lord gave names to the *rishis* and *deva*s he created, to
those who were not born during the night.[172] Because of the reasons
mentioned, this is the way the creation of the worlds by Svayambhu
came about, starting with Mahat and ending with Vishesha. He
himself brought about these transformations in Prakriti. The world
is illuminated by the sun and the moon and is ornamented by
planets and *nakshatra*s. There are thousands of rivers, oceans and
mountains. There are many kinds of beautiful cities and flourishing
habitations. This is Brahma's forest[173] and the unmanifest Brahma,
who knows everything, wanders around in it. It was created from a
seed that is not manifest[174] and is established because of his favours.
Intelligence forms the trunk and branches and the senses are the
hollows in the tree. The great elements provide the illumination and
the objects of the senses are the leaves. *Dharma* and *adharma* are
the excellent flowers and happiness and misery are the fruits. This
is Brahma's eternal tree and provides life to all beings. Brahma's
forest is constituted by Brahma's tree. The unmanifest, the eternal
abode of existence and non-existence, is the cause. Those who
speak about the truth call this Pradhana, Prakriti or Maya. This
is described as Brahma's *anugraha* or *naimittika* creation. These
three creations, due to Prakriti, resulted from Brahma not having
resorted to his resolution. Six creations, *mukhya* and the others,
were the consequence of transformations and occurred with the use
of resolution. They resulted because of Brahma consciously taking
decisions. Hence, with Prakrita and Vaikrita,[175] there are nine cycles
of creation. They are connected to each other and the learned speak
of the cause. He is the one whose *atman* is unthinkable, the creator
of all beings. They say that the *Veda*s are his head, the firmament
is his navel and the sun and the moon are his eyes. The directions

[171] Prapancha means the visible universe. The word *pancha* means five.
[172] This probably means Brahma's night and refers to those *deva*s and
*rishi*s who are not destroyed during the secondary cycles of destruction.
[173] Brahmavana.
[174] Prakriti.
[175] Those that result from transformations (*vikriti*).

are his ears and it should be known that the earth represents his feet. *Brahmana*s originated from his mouth and *kshatriya*s from the front of the chest. *Vaishya*s were born from his thighs and *shudra*s from his feet. All the *varna*s originated from his body.'

'The unmanifest Narayana is beyond the egg, which is described as unmanifest. To create the worlds, Brahma himself originated from the egg. After remaining there for ten *kalpa*s, they go to Satyaloka again.[176] They reach Brahma's world and this is a world from which there is no return.[177] They do not possess lordship. But in other respects, such as prosperity, beauty and dominion, they are Brahma's equal. They remain there, full of happiness they have themselves brought. When he thinks about it, he himself expands on Prakriti's creations. When they have been cleansed, they are not associated with anything. This is like a state of sleeping, when there is understanding, without the exercise of intelligence. When they cleanse themselves in this way, *jnana* results. Unlike those who are merely energetic, they withdraw themselves from all manner of differences. For those who reside in Brahma's world, they can not only see many kinds of things, but also cause and effect. Since they are established in their own *dharma*, they withdraw from all transformations. They are auspicious in their *atman*s and unblemished, exhibiting the same signs as *siddha*s. Though Prakriti gives them instruments, they are established in their own *atman*s. When they are established in their *atman*s, they know the truth about Prakriti and do not see it functioning in many different ways.[178] They comprehend Purusha, the cause. Thereafter, creation starts afresh. Those who engage in *yoga* know about Prakriti and possess insight into the truth. They are emancipated and do not have to go through the process of return again. Since they are in Satyaloka and are not reborn, they are like flames that have been

---

[176] Satyaloka refers to Brahma's world. Satyaloka is not affected by secondary cycles of destruction (and creation). Because of a discontinuity in the text, it is not clear who 'they' refers to, probably to certain *rishi*s.

[177] No rebirth.

[178] These *shloka*s are very abrupt and cryptic, possibly with typos difficult to identify. Hence, the translation has taken liberties.

pacified. Those who go to those three higher worlds are filled with delight. Those who cannot reach Maharloka also go with them. Until the burning of the *kalpa* presents itself, they remain there, along with their disciples. At that time, there are *gandharvas* and others, *pishachas*, humans, *brahmanas* and others, animals, birds, immobile entities and reptiles who remain on the surface of the earth. These are destroyed by the one thousand rays of the sun. Each of the rays of the sun becomes seven rays and each of these becomes one hundred, burning down the three worlds. Mobile and immobile entities, rivers and all the mountains have already been dried up because of the lack of rain. They are scorched. All of them, mobile and immobile, *dharma* and *adharma*, are helpless and are burnt by the sun's rays. When it is the end of a *mahayuga*, their bodies are burnt and they are cleansed of their sins. When they are scorched and freed of their ultimate bonds, they are described as those who are auspicious. When night is over for Brahma, whose birth is not manifest, those entities are born again, in forms just like the ones they possessed earlier. Creation starts afresh and sons are born through Brahma's mental powers. Those who reside in the three worlds are distressed because the worlds are scorched by the seven rays of the sun. The earth is flooded by rain and becomes a desolate and single ocean. Oceans, clouds, water and land become like an immovable mass of water, as sharp as arrows. A large mass of water arrives and envelopes everything so that the earth is reduced to the state of an ocean. Water is known as *ambhas*, because it shines and its beauty is radiant.[179] Everything merges into it and merges into its radiance. The word verbal root "*tanoti*" means to extend. In every direction, everything on earth extends into its body. Therefore, this is known as *apas-tanu*.[180] The word "*shara*" is said to have many kinds of verbal roots. One meaning is to get shattered. When everything is reduced to a single ocean, the

---

[179] From the root word *abhati*, meaning splendor/light.

[180] *Tanu* means body. Literally, the text uses the word *apatanu*, but there is no such word. Hence, we have taken it as *apas-tanu*, meaning waterbody.

waters are not shattered. Hence, the water is known as Naara.[181] When Brahma's day comes to an end, his night extends for the same duration of one thousand *mahayuga*s and everything is full of water. All the fires on the surface of the earth are destroyed in that water. The wind is pacified. Everything is dark and no illumination exists in any direction. The lord, Brahma Purusha, alone exists and he desires to divide the worlds again. At that time, everything mobile and immobile is destroyed in that single ocean. Brahma, known as Narayana, sleeps on the waters then. He possesses one thousand eyes, one thousand feet and one thousand heads. He is Purusha, golden in complexion and beyond the reach of the senses. When there is an excess of *sattva*, he awakes and sees that the world is empty. The first *pada* of the Purana has thus been narrated.'[182]

Chapter 6-1(6) (*Kalpa*s and *manvantara*s)

Suta said, 'Hearing the description of the first *pada*, which was about Prakriti, Kapeya[183] was delighted in his mind. He praised and worshipped Suta and to hear more accounts, addressed him in these words. "O one who knows about *kalpa*s! Please tell me about the intervening period between *kalpa*s now, about the *kalpa* that has passed and the one that is going on now. You are accomplished. Therefore, I wish to hear about the intervening period between these two *kalpa*s." Suta, supreme among eloquent ones, was addressed in this way by Kapeya and started to narrate everything about the origin of the three worlds.'

Suta answered,[184] 'O ones excellent in vows! I will accurately describe the *kalpa* that is in the past, the *kalpa* in the future and

---

[181] This is an extremely dubious etymological derivation.

[182] Within Purva Bhaga, this concludes the *prakriya pada* segment.

[183] Meaning Shounaka, who was descended from the sage Kapi.

[184] The two Sutas in succession might cause confusion. In Naimisha, Suta recounted the Purana to Shounaka and other sages. Since Sutas belonged to a class, logically, it is possible for another Suta to narrate this entire conversation.

the intervening period between the two. O ones excellent in vows! I will tell you about the *manvantara*s in the *kalpa*s. The present auspicious *kalpa* is Varaha *kalpa*. The old *kalpa* that preceded this is over. Hear about the intervening period between that and the present *kalpa*. When one *kalpa* ends and another *kalpa* begins without an intervening period between the two, this can only be true of Janaloka and the others.[185] Otherwise, the intervening period separates one *kalpa* from another *kalpa* and at the end of a *kalpa*, all the subjects are always destroyed during this intervening period. Therefore, there is always an intervening period between one *kalpa* and another *kalpa*. Within a *manvantara*, there is an intervening period between two *yuga*s too. The *manvantara*s and *yuga*s exist simultaneously. In *prakriya pada*, the earlier *kalpa*s have been briefly mentioned. Every *kalpa* has a first half and a second half. As a *kalpa* proceeds, the second half of this *kalpa* will be followed by the first half of the next *kalpa*. In this way, there are two such halves. O *dvija*s! In the present *kalpa*, the first half is going on now. This is the first half and the one that will follow is known as the second half. This is a period of preservation and the period of withdrawal is said to occur later. Before the present *kalpa*, there was an old *kalpa* that preceded it that lasted for one thousand sets of four *yuga*s, along with the *manvantara*s. When that *kalpa* decayed, the time for burning arrived. At that time, *deva*s were astride their *vimana*s.[186] There were also *nakshatra*s, planets, stars, the sun and the moon. All these, performers of good deeds, numbered twenty-eight crore. In each of the fourteen *manvantara*s, the number is the same. Therefore, aggregating, the number is three hundred and ninety-two crore. In addition, in each *kalpa*, the number of *deva*s astride *vimana*s is described as an additional seventy thousand. Thus, in each of the fourteen *manvantara*s, in the firmament and in heaven, there are *deva*s, ancestors, *rishi*s, those who live on *amrita*, their followers, wives and sons. At that time, the Gods who are in the firmament are beyond the purview of *varna*s and *ashrama*s. When the time for the

---

[185] The intervening period is the secondary cycle of destruction and Satyaloka, Tapoloka and Janaloka are not subject to this.

[186] A *vimana* is a celestial vehicle. The word is also used for a palace or mansion.

submergence of material objects and creatures presented itself, the
Gods followed a conduct that was identical with all those who had
attained *sayujya*.[187] However, their *atman*s were overwhelmed and
subjugated by intelligence. Therefore, *deva*s who resided in the three
worlds became proud of this world. When the period of preservation
was over, the subsequent period arrived. When the end of the *kalpa*
arrived and the deluge was imminent, the *deva*s were anxious and
distressed and abandoned their respective positions. Full of anxiety,
they turned their minds towards Maharloka. Though their bodies
were in Maharloka, all of them possessed minds that were full of
a great deal of purification and they attained *siddhi*. Along with
them, others from that *kalpa*, *brahmana*s, *kshatriya*s, *vaishya*s and
others, also resided in Maharloka. Fourteen categories of *deva*s
reached Maharloka. However, since they were agitated, they turned
their minds towards Janaloka. In this way, the residents of that
kalpa progressively engaged in *yoga* and thousands of divine *yuga*s
passed. All of them possessed minds that were full of a great deal
of purification and they attained *siddhi*. After remaining there for
ten *kalpa*s, they went to Satyaloka again. They reached Brahma's
world, a destination from which there is no return. They became like
him in lordship over *vimana*s and prosperity. They were Brahma's
equal in beauty and dominion. While remaining there, they were
full of restraint and delight. They obtained the bliss of the *brahman*
and along with Brahma, were emancipated.[188] However, they were
themselves inevitably influenced by Prakriti. Influenced in this way
at that time, they were bound to honour and worship.'

'When a person is asleep, despite a lack of intelligence, there
is understanding.'

'Like that, when they are immersed in service, there is bliss.
Despite differences being withdrawn, differences remained
amongst those powerful ones. That is how, along with them,

---

[187] *Salokya* is the ability to reside with the Lord, *samipya* is proximity to
the Lord, *sarupya* is to be like the Lord in form and *sayujya* is identification
with the Lord. These are different grades of emancipation.

[188] These *shloka*s are terse and cryptic, probably reflecting typos and
errors. Hence, liberties have been taken.

tasks and instruments flourished. However, among the many
who resided in Brahma's world, there were some who possessed
insight about the truth. They withdrew from their rights and
remained established in their own *dharma*. They were pure in their
*atman*s and without blemish, equal in signs to *siddha*s. Though
established in their own *atman*s, Prakriti made them instruments.
In truth, Prakriti proclaimed itself to be different from Purusha
and evidently functioned in many different kinds of ways. When
creation started afresh, those who are emancipated and possess
insight about the truth, should know that this occurred because
of Prakriti's engagement as the cause. Those who are emancipated
in this way do not again follow the path of return. Like flames
that have been extinguished, they do not have origin again and
remain non-existent. Those great-souled ones proceed above the
three worlds. Along with them, there are others who do not reside
in Maharloka. When the scorching of the *kalpa* presents itself, they
become their disciples.'

'However, there are others—*gandharva*s and others, *pishacha*s
and humans, *brahmana*s and others, animals, birds, immobile
entities and reptiles. At that time, they reside on the surface of
the earth. The one with seven rays himself divides each of these
rays into one thousand and each of these becomes a separate
Ravi.[189] They gradually rise up and burn down the three worlds,
mobile and immobile objects, all the rivers and mountains. They
have already been dried because of the lack of rain and are now
scorched by the sun. Everything is scorched by the rays of the sun
and incapacitated—mobile and immobile objects and *dharma* and
adharma. In between two *mahayuga*s, their bodies are scorched and
cleansed of sin. However, they are freed from what is known as
scorching by the auspicious drops of rain. Entities attach themselves
to those that are similar in form. Brahma's birth is not manifest.
Having spent the night there, when creation starts afresh, they
become Brahma's sons, born through his mental powers. Residents
of the three worlds were completely burnt down by the rays of the

---

[189] Surya, the sun.

sun. But those worlds are populated again. The earth was flooded
with rain and became a desolate ocean. Water from the oceans
and clouds flooded everything on earth. The water was as fierce as
arrows and copious floods of water arrived and merged with the
water that was already there. Since everything on earth came to be
submerged, this came to be known as an ocean. Water is known as
ambhas, because it shines and its beauty is radiant. The root "*bha*"
signifies that it is radiant and spreads. The water is thought of as
enveloping everything equally. Hence, water is also thought of as
tanus,[190] since it covers everything on earth. The root "*tan*" means
to spread and therefore, it is known as *tanus*. The word "*shar*" has
many kinds of root meanings. But when there is a single ocean, the
water is not swiftly decayed. Therefore, water is known as *naara*.[191]
At the end of one thousand *mahayuga*s, Brahma's day is over.
Night lasts for an equal duration and everything is full of water.
The fires on the surface of the earth are extinguished by the water.
The winds are quietened. There is darkness and no illumination in
any direction. Everything is presided over by Brahma, the lord who
is Purusha. He again wishes to create and divide the worlds. At that
time, there is a single ocean and everything mobile and immobile has
been destroyed. Brahma becomes an entity with one thousand eyes,
one thousand feet and one thousand heads. He is Purusha, golden
in complexion and in control over his senses. In this connection,
a *shloka* is cited about Narayana. "Water is Naara and we have
heard that they are his body. Since he fills them and resides there, he
is known as Naarayana." The first Prajapati possessed an excellent
mind and one thousand heads, one thousand feet, one thousand
eyes, one thousand faces and one thousand arms. He performed
one thousand acts. He is spoken of as Purusha, full of the three.[192]
His complexion is like that of the sun. He is the protector of the
universe and is one. He is not manifest. He is the first and is Virat.

---

[190] *Tanus* means body and is grammatically derived as something
that stretches.

[191] *Naara* does mean water. But this is a contrived derivation, based on
something that does not weaken (*shar*).

[192] Brahma, Vishnu and Shiva.

He is the great-souled Purusha, Hiranyagarbha and is beyond the reach of the mind. At the beginning of the *kalpa*, he has an excess of *rajas*. Becoming Brahma, the lord creates. At the end of the *kalpa*, he possesses an excess of *tamas*. Becoming Kala, he devours it again. With an excess of *sattva*, he becomes Narayana and lies down in the water. He divides his *atman* into three and presides over the three worlds. He himself creates, witnesses and devours. At the end of one thousand cycles of four *yuga*s, everything mobile and immobile was destroyed in that single ocean. There was water everywhere. At that time, Brahma, known as Narayana, was himself radiant in the water. As a result of Brahma's powers, the four kinds of subjects[193] were enveloped in *tamas*. In Maharloka, the *maharshi*s perceived that Kala was asleep. At that time, the *maharshi*s mentioned were Bhrigu and the others.[194] When the *kalpa* was over, those eight *maharshi*s resorted to Satyaloka and others, beyond Maharloka. The etymological root "*rish*" is said to mean "to go". Since their spirit and movement were great, they are spoken of as *maharshi*s.[195] Residing in Maharloka, they saw that Kala was asleep. When the *kalpa* was over, the seven *maharshi*s, full of *sattva*, resided in what was beyond. In this way, Brahma remained for thousands of their nights and the *maharshi*s, conveyed by him, saw that Kala was asleep. At the beginning of the *kalpa*, Brahma conceived of fourteen extremely extensive worlds. That is the reason it is spoken of as a *kalpa*.[196] At the beginning of a *kalpa*, he repeatedly creates all the beings. In everything in the universe, the great divinity is both manifest and not manifest. The intervening period between the two *kalpa*s has thus been described. The present is an intervening period between the past and what will come. The previous *kalpa* has been described, accurately and briefly. I will now describe the present *kalpa*. Listen.'

[193] Born from wombs, born from eggs, plants and trees and born from sweat (worms and insects).

[194] Liberties have been taken in a couple of *shloka*s, since the meanings are not at all clear. Hence, it is not clear whether the number of *maharshi*s is seven or eight.

[195] *Maha + rish*.

[196] Based on a root that means imagine, fashion, make.

Chapter 7-1(7) (Description of knowledge about the worlds)

Suta said, 'Brahma spent a period equal to one thousand *mahayugas* as his night. When the night was over, he acted and was the cause behind creation. In that water, Brahma became the wind and moved around. In that dark ocean, everything mobile and immobile had been destroyed. Everything on the surface of the earth had been flooded in water. There were only some categories of beings, established in Satyaloka. At the time, he moved around, like fireflies during a monsoon night. As he swiftly moved around, as he willed, he turned his mind towards a mean of stabilization. As he searched for the earth, he got to know that the earth had been submerged inside the water. In that great darkness, he knew that he was incapable of raising the earth and remembered the divinity who had acted at the start of the former *kalpa*s. He created the true and supreme form of Varaha and entered the water. Prajapati sought for the earth, shrouded in water. He raised and placed it. He placed the water as it should be, that of the oceans in the oceans and that of the rivers in the rivers. He separated and levelled the earth and gathered the mountains. Those from the earlier cycle of creation had been burnt down by the *samvartaka* fire. As a result of that fire, all the mountains on earth had been destroyed. In that single ocean, the mountains had been scattered by the wind. They had become immobile in whichever place they had been deposited. Since the ridges had become immobile, they are known as *achala*s.[197] Since they have joints, they are known as *parvata*s. Since they were swallowed, they are known as *giri*s. Since they moved around, they are known as *shilochchaya*s. The lord raised the earth from inside the water. He created seven *dvipa*s and each *dvipa* was divided into seven *varsha*s. He levelled uneven parts and used rocks to fashion

---

[197] These are different names for mountains. *Achala* is something that does not move, *parvata* is something with joints (*parva*). The word *giri* is usually derived from something that is venerated, not something that is swallowed. Similarly, *shilochchaya* is usually derived as a collection of rocks (*shila*).

mountains. There are thus forty-nine *varsha*s in the *dvipa*s.[198] He placed that many mountains at the ends of the *varsha*s. At the beginning of creation,[199] they were naturally bright, not otherwise. Seven *dvipa*s and oceans surround each other. They are naturally established in this way, surrounding each other. Brahma created Bhuloka and the four worlds just as they had been earlier, along with the moon and the sun, the planets and all immobile entities. Brahma created the Gods of this *kalpa*, along with their places, water, fire, earth, wind, space, the firmament, heaven, the directions, oceans, rivers, all the mountains, the *atman*s of herbs, the *atman*s of trees and creepers, *lava*s, *kashtha*s, *kala*s and *muhurta*s,[200] *sandhya*s, night and day, fortnights, months, *ayana*s, years and *yuga*s. He separately created locations and those who take pride in the locations. After creating the *atman*s of the locations, he fashioned *yuga*s— the *yuga*s of *krita*, *treta*, *dvapara* and *tishya*.[201] At the beginning of the *kalpa*, he created subjects for the first *krita yuga*. I have already spoken to you about the subjects of the former *kalpa*. All those from that earlier *kalpa*, those who could not reach Tapoloka and remained on earth, were burnt down by the fire. When it was again time for creation, they returned and became visible.[202] For the sake of creating again, they remained there and became visible. Though they are stated to have accomplished the objectives of *dharma*, *artha*, *kama* and *moksha*, for the sake of having offspring, they remained there. In the due order, there were *deva*s, ancestors and humans. They were full of austerities and they were the ones who filled the locations first. Indeed, humans who have obtained *siddhi*

[198] 7X7 = 49. In standard descriptions, each *dvipa* is divided into nine *varsha*s.

[199] The text says *svarga* (heaven). We have changed this possible typo to *sarga* (creation), as that makes better sense.

[200] These are different units for measuring time, not always standardized. *Muhurta* is forty-eight minutes. *Nimesha* is the twinkling of an eye, a minute, and six *lava*s are equal to one *nimesha*. *Kala* is a small measure of time, but that measure is not consistently defined. In terms of astronomy, *kala* is 1/60th of a degree, that is, a minute. A *kashtha* is 1/30th of a *kala*.

[201] *Tishya yuga* is another name for *kali yuga*.

[202] That is, those who had not been emancipated.

become *brahmana*s. Since their *karma* was tainted by attachment and enmity, they went to heaven. They are known as *tadatmaka*s.[203] As a result of the fruits of their own *karma* remaining, they return in embodied form, from one *yuga* to another *yuga*. When the new *kalpa* arrives, people bound in this way are born in the worlds. One should understand that the cause is *karma*, which is formless. As a result of their own auspicious and inauspicious *karma*, people are born in the worlds. They assume many kinds of bodies, forms and species. In the mutual relationship, this starts with *deva*s and ends with immobile entities. Their names, forms and everything else depends on the nature of auspicious *karma*. In each *kalpa*, they are repeatedly born, with such names and forms.'

'After this, Brahma desired to embark on the task of subsidiary creation. Meditating on subjects, he meditated on the truth. Thus, one thousand couples emerged from his mouth. The people who originated in this way were extremely energetic and possessed an excess of *sattva*. He created another one thousand couples through his eyes. All of them possessed an excess of *rajas* and were radiant and intolerant. He next created another one thousand wicked couples from his arms. They possessed an excess of *rajas* and *tamas* and are described as being attached to households. As long as they were alive, they repeatedly gave birth through sexual intercourse. The offspring who were born were both deceitful and upright, but they were mortal. This is how lineages originated, despite physical bodies being given up. Since then, the origin in the *kalpa* has been through sexual intercourse. In *krita yuga*, birth of subjects was through mental meditation. At that time, it was pure and could occur through each of the five traits—sound and the others.[204] In that way, beloved offspring could also be created through thought. Those who were created in this way filled up the universe. They populated rivers, lakes, oceans and mountains. However, though they moved around, they obtained little satisfaction in that *yuga*.[205]

[203] Literally, that (the *brahman*) in the *atman*. Though they achieved this union and should have been liberated, their *karma* was still tainted.

[204] The five objects of the senses, sight, sound, smell, taste and touch.

[205] We have corrected a typo. The text says *yuddha* (battle) instead of *yuga*.

The earth was full of juices then. They fed on this and moved around. Wandering around as they willed, those subjects desired *siddhi* in their minds. In that *krita yuga*, their lifespans, happiness and beauty were identical. At the beginning of the *kalpa*, in that first *krita yuga*, there was no *dharma* or *adharma*. From one *yuga* to another *yuga*, they were accordingly born with their own respective entitlements. Enumerated in divine years, there were such four thousand cycles of *yuga*s. In that first *krita yuga*, the number of years at the beginning, and at the end is said to be four hundred. Thus, there were thousands of famous subjects. They did not suffer from impediments or the opposite pairs of sentiments.[206] Nor, among them, was there any order of progression. They resided in many habitations: in mountains and oceans. They were bereft of sorrow and possessed an excess of *sattva*. Those subjects were extremely happy. They always moved around as they were willing, and they were constantly in happy frames of mind. There were no animals or birds, nor any reptiles. Nothing caused anxiety and there was nothing horrible. Such was the nature of *dharma*. For subsistence, an infinite number of roots, fruits and flowers existed. That period was full of great joy, not too hot and not too cold. Everything they mentally desired was always obtained. As a result of their meditations, from the nether regions, they rose up from the earth.[207] These led to strength and good complexions, destroying old age and death. Even though their bodies did not go through *samskara*s,[208] youth was ever-lasting in those subjects. Even without

[206] Happiness and unhappiness, hot and cold and so on.

[207] The vegetation.

[208] *Samskara* means cleansing, specifically done at certain periods of life. There are thirteen *samskara*s or sacraments. The list varies a bit. But one list is *vivaha* (marriage), *garbhalambhana* (conception), *pumshavana* (engendering a male child), *simantonnayana* (parting the hair, performed in the fourth month of pregnancy), *jatakarma* (birth rites), *namakarana* (naming), *chudakarma* (tonsure), *annaprashana* (first solid food), *keshanta* (first shaving of the head), *upanayana* (sacred thread), *vidyarambha* (commencement of studies), *samavartana* (graduation) and *antyeshti* (funeral rites). After *samavartana*, one ceases to be a student and becomes (usually) a householder.

sexual intercourse, offspring resulted through mental conception. Their birth and beauty were identical. Their delight was identical. At that time, there was truthfulness, lack of avarice, contentment, joy and self-control. Among all of them, there was no special distinction in beauty, lifespans, skill of artisanship or effort. Without thinking about it, the subjects managed to sustain themselves. At that threshold of *krita yuga*, there was no inclination towards *karma*, good or bad. At that time, there were no arrangements for *varna*s and *ashrama*s, nor any taxes. Their relationships with each other were not based on desire or enmity. All of them were similar in beauty and lifespan. There was no superior or inferior. In *krita yuga*, there was general happiness and lack of misery. There was no gain or loss, friend or enemy, loved or hated. Their minds were such that they were not addicted towards material objects of this world. At that time, they did not cause violence to each other. Nor did they show each other favours. It is said that *jnana* is supreme in *krita yuga*, whereas in *treta yuga*, it is sacrifices. It is *pravritti* in *dvapara yuga* and fighting in *kali yuga*. It is *sattva* in *krita yuga*, *rajas* in *treta yuga*, *rajas* and *tamas* in *dvapara yuga* and *tamas* in *kali yuga*. This should be known as the way the *guna*s function. Hear about the duration of *krita yuga* and the intervening periods. *Krita yuga* has four thousand years. In divine years, the duration of intervening periods is eight hundred.[209] The duration in human years is four thousand.[210] As long as *krita yuga* was going on, there were no anxieties or calamities and this was true of the intervening period too. The *dharma* of the *yuga* was always followed until one-quarter of the intervening period was left. The intervening period progressed until only the last bit of the intervening period of the *yuga* remained. When only one quarter of the intervening period remained, the *dharma* of the intervening period merged into *krita yuga* and left no remnants.'

'When the intervening period of *krita yuga* was over, the subjects born through mental powers were destroyed. They obtained *siddhi*

---

[209] Four hundred at each end.
[210] This must obviously be divine years, not human years. There are errors in these sections. To make sense, we have taken some liberties.

in another *yuga*—in *treta yuga*, occurring after *krita yuga*. In the beginning, eight creations that resulted from the use of mental powers have been described. In due course, all of them obtained success and were destroyed. At the start of the *kalpa*, there is only one kind of mental *siddhi* in *krita yuga*. In all the *manvantaras*, there are divisions of the four *yuga*s. Success in *karma* is achieved by following the conduct designated for *varna*s and *ashrama*s. The intervening period of *krita yuga* is reduced by one-fourth.[211] In the three *yuga*s, the *sandhyamsha* portions progressively decline. Following the *dharma* of *yuga*s, austerities, learning, strength and lifespans also decline. O excellent *rishi*s! When *krita yuga* and its *amsha* is over, it is time for *treta yuga* and its constituent parts. When *krita*'s *amsha* was over, the seven virtuous ones,[212] who existed at the beginning of the *kalpa*, remained at the onset of *treta yuga*. Following the course of time, *siddhi* diminishes. It cannot but be otherwise. When one kind of *siddhi* is destroyed, another kind of *siddhi* originates. Parts of the water return to the clouds. The clouds thunder and lead to the showering of rain. Even when it rains once, success is obtained on the surface of the earth. Subjects originated and trees came to be designated as their homes. For them, every kind of enjoyment resulted from trees. At the onset of *treta yuga*, subjects obtained their subsistence from these. After a long period of time, they faced a catastrophe. Suddenly, sentiments of addiction towards intercourse developed. For women, menstruation lasted till the end of their lives. However, as a consequence of the power of the *yuga*, it wasn't like that at other times. Subsequently, the menstrual flow occurred every month. As a consequence, sexual intercourse also occurred at that time. As a result of their desire, sexual intercourse took place at that time of the month. If intercourse occurred at the wrong time, conception did not take place. However, as a result

---

[211] The intervening period is *sandhyamsha*. Sometimes, *sandhya* is used for the intervening period at the beginning and *sandhyamsha* for the intervening period at the end of a *yuga*. For *krita yuga*, this will be 400+400=800 years. In *treta*, this becomes 300+300=600 years. In *dvapara* it is 200+200=400 years and in *kali yuga*, it is 100+100=200 years.

[212] Probably the *saptarshi*s.

of their perverse sentiments, a calamity took place. All the trees, described as homes, were destroyed. When these were destroyed, they were bewildered and their senses were agitated. They started to meditate on *siddhi* and the truth. At this, the trees, described as homes, manifested themselves in front of them. These supplied garments, fruits and ornaments. There was fragrant honey in every cup, full of energetic juices, without any flies in it. At the onset of *treta yuga*, subjects subsisted on the basis of this. They were happy, well-nourished and successful, not suffering from any kind of fever. However, as time passed, the subjects were again overwhelmed with avarice. They used force to seize trees and the honey from them. When they were again overcome by avarice, as a result of their wicked conduct, the *kalpa-vriksha*s and the honey were sometimes destroyed.[213] Having come under the subjugation of time, only a little bit of the *siddhi* was left. As they subsisted on this, the opposite pair of sentiments increased. The cold, the wind and the heat were fierce and they suffered terribly.'

'Suffering from the opposite pair of sentiments, they created coverings for themselves. To counter the opposite pair of sentiments, they consciously created these habitations. Earlier, there was no desire to act to create these homes. In those ancient times, they acted to create these habitations and happily resided in them. They found habitations full of honey, in mountains and along rivers. They constructed fortifications in mountainous passages, where there was a supply of water. According to energy and desire, they created these habitations in plains and uneven terrain, so as to ward off the heat and the cold. They constructed hamlets and cities. Areas were divided into villages and cities. There were many other habitations, with differing lengths and widths. This was done according to their knowledge, measuring it out with their own *angula*s. Using this as a unit, other measurements were worked out. These are *angula*, *pradesha*, *hasta*, *kishku* and *dhanus*. Ten joints of *angula*s are described as a *pradesha*. The span from an extended thumb to an

---

[213] A *kalpa-vriksha* (or *kalpa-taru*) is a tree that grants whatever is wished for. The text has a typo, reading *prabhu* (lord) instead of *madhu* (honey). This has been corrected.

extended index finger is spoken of as *pradesha*. The span up to the
middle finger is described as *tala*, up to the extended ring finger
is known as *gokarna*. The span up to the extended little finger is
vitasti, also described as the distance of twelve *angula*s.[214] The span
of twenty-one *angula*s is said to be a *ratni*. Twenty-four *angula*s
amount to one *hasta*. One *kishku* is said to be two *ratni*s or forty-
two *angula*s. Four *hasta*s are one *dhanus*, also known as *danda* or
two *nalika*s. Two thousand *dhanus* amount to one *gavyuti*.[215] These
were the units of measurement they worked out. They thought
of eight thousand *dhanus* amounting to one *yojana*. In this way,
habitations were worked out, using *yojana*s as a measure. Among
the four types of *durga*s,[216] three are natural. The fourth type of
durga is artificial. I will describe the determination. There should
be elevated walls with entry-points, with moats on all sides. Every
gate should be beautiful, resembling an apartment in which young
girls are kept.[217] In the case of a *kumaripura*, it is best if the flow
of water in the moats measures at least two *hasta*s. However, a
flow of eight, nine or ten *hasta*s is excellent. There are indicated
lengths and breadths for all hamlets, cities and villages and the three
types of natural forts—in mountains, in water and in desert regions.
Artificial forts must have a diameter of half a *yojana* and a length
of one-eighth *yojana*. The length of a city must be twice the breadth
and a river must flow to the east. It must be divided into quarters
and sub-quarters and spread out like a fan. A city that is circular,
long, or shaped like a diamond, is not praised. A city constructed
such that it has quadrangles is divine and is praised. A dwelling-
house that is less than twenty-four *hasta*s is too short. The best
is more than one hundred and eight *hasta*s. Anything medium or

[214] There are differences in units, reflected in what is stated in the text.
One *pradesha* can be eight *angula*s, ten *angula*s or twelve *angula*s. *Vitasti*
is often described as twelve *angula*s.
[215] A *gavyuti* is the distance from which a cow's call can be heard. A
yojana is the distance travelled through a single yoking.
[216] *Durga* is a stronghold or fortification.
[217] *Kumaripura* means an apartment in which young girls are kept.
This is the way we have translated the word. However, *kumaripura* can
also be taken as an artificial or fresh fort.

short, which does not use wood, is praised. It is said that the chief
residence should have eight hundred *kishku*s. The diameter of a
hamlet should be half that of a city, but that of a village can be
more.[218] A hamlet must be at a distance of one *yojana* from a
city and a village must be at a distance of half a *yojana* from a
hamlet. The perimeter of a field must be four *dhanus* and the outer
boundary must be two *krosha*s.[219] Along the directions,[220] they
constructed roads that were twenty *dhanus* wide. The roads in the
villages were twenty *dhanus* wide and those along the boundaries
ten *dhanus* wide. They constructed a beautiful royal road that
was ten *dhanus* wide. Men, horses, chariots and elephants could
move along the road, without any obstructions. They constructed
branch roads that were four *dhanus* wide. The roads joining major
roads were three *dhanus* wide and minor roads were two *dhanus*
wide. Major village roads were four feet wide and the roads
between houses were three feet wide.[221] Firmer roads were one-
sixth more in width and in due order, footpaths are also described.
In every direction, there were coverings for passing excrement and
these were only one foot wide. When they had constructed these
places, they constructed houses and dwellings. They remembered
how, earlier, dwellings had been constructed on trees. Thinking
about this repeatedly, they started to construct similar ones. Using
their intelligence, they thought about how branches grew on trees.
Since they were constructed like branches, habitations are known
as *shala*s.[222] Thus, homes came to be known as *shala*s and are
renowned as branches. They are described as *shala*s to underline

[218] We have corrected the *pana* of the text to *grama*. *Grama* is a village,
kheta is a hamlet and *nagara/pura* is a city.

[219] *Krosha* is one-fourth of a *yojana*, the distance from which a shout
can be heard.

[220] North-South, East-West and so on.

[221] The typo in the text (*janghapatha*) has been corrected to *ghantapatha*
(major village road). *Pada* is a measure of distance and we have taken it as
one foot. We have translated *dhritimarga* as a firmer road.

[222] The word *shala* means branch, as well as house.

their importance as branches. The ones that ensured delight are
described as *prasada*s.'[223]

'However, the *kalpa-vriksha*s were destroyed, along with the
honey. Confronted with the opposite pair of sentiments, they started
to think about the means. The subjects who were created were
seen to suffer from sorrow and anxiety. At this time, in *treta yuga*,
another kind of *siddhi* appeared before them. Without their wishing
for it, there was another kind of rain and this yielded every kind
of success. The water from the rain was sweet. When this second
kind of rain appeared, there was a new means of subsistence. The
surface of the earth came into contact with the drops of water that
showered down. As a result of the contact between water and the
ground, herbs grew. Without being tilled and without being sown,
fourteen kinds of wild and village plants grew.[224] Seasonal flowers
and fruits, trees and creepers were born. At the beginning of *treta
yuga*, subjects were sustained on these herbs. However, in every
possible way, attachment and avarice again manifested themselves
among them. This was inevitable in *treta yuga* and they were
subjugated. Therefore, with as much strength as they possessed,
they seized the rivers, fields, mountains, trees, creepers and herbs.
I have earlier described to you those who obtained *siddhi* in their
*atman*s in *krita yuga*. From Janaloka, they were born in this world
as sons who originated through Brahma's mental powers. They
were tranquil and radiant, dedicated to *karma*. However, they
were born again in *treta yuga* and were miserable. In their earlier
births, they were known for their inauspicious and wicked deeds.
They became *brahmana*s, *kshatriya*s, *vaishya*s, *shudra*s and people
who were full of hatred. Some were powerful. Others were true in
conduct and non-violent. These were devoid of avarice. Conquering

[223] A *prasada* is a palace/mansion, or the upper part of one,
etymologically derived from something that pleases the mind.

[224] The list is usually given as *vrihi* (paddy), *yava* (barley), *masha* (*urad
dal*), *godhuma* (wheat), *chanaka* (chick-pea), *tila* (sesamum), *priyangu*
(camel's foot/long pepper), *kulatthaka* (*matar dal*), *shyamaka* (a kind of
grain), *nivara* (wild paddy), *jartila* (wild sesamum), *gavedhuka* (a species of
grass), *venuyava* (seed of cane) and *markataka* (a kind of grain).

their *atmans*, they lived according to the *smriti* texts. They spoke, without receiving, and their tasks were carried out by those who were weaker than them. Those who were limited in energy remained there, serving them. In this way, they depended on each other and sought refuge with each other. As a result of these taints, the herbs were soon extinguished. When they were seized, like sand in the fists, they were destroyed. As a result of the power of the *yuga*, they again tried to gather up the fourteen kinds of herbs from the village and the forest, the fruits, the flowers and the roots. However, when these were destroyed, the subjects were bewildered. Overwhelmed by hunger, all of them went to Svayambhu. At the beginning of *treta yuga*, they sought some means of subsistence. Bhagavan Svayambhu Brahma got to know what was in their minds. As a result of his vision, he could directly see and thought of a means for nourishment. He got to know that the herbs had been devoured by the earth. He made them grow again. Using Sumeru as a calf, he milked the earth. Like milk from cows, this led to seeds on the surface of the earth. The lord made the seeds instantly grow into seventeen kinds of herbs from the village and the forest, which ended with ripe fruits. These were *vrihi, yava, godhuma, chanaka, tila, priyangu, udara, koradushta, vamaka, masha, mudga, mashura, nivara, kulatthaka, harika* and *charaka*.[225] These are described as the seventeen types. These are spoken of as herbs from villages. Fourteen kinds of herbs are described as those that grow both in villages and forests— *shyamaka, nivara, jartila, gavedhuka, kuruvinda, venu, yava* and *tamatirkataka*.[226] At the beginning of *treta yuga*, these were the ones that originated first. All these fourteen kinds of plants, belonging to the village and the forest, grew without being tilled or being sown. There were trees, shrubs, creepers, winding plants, herbs, types of

---

[225] There are only sixteen names in the list. *Udara* is a grain with long stalks, *koradushta* (*kodrava*) is an inferior type of grain, there is no crop immediately identifiable as *vamaka*, *mudga* is *moong dal*, *mashura* is *masoor dal*, *harika* is *Paspalum frumentaceum* and *charaka* (also known as *parpata*) is a medicinal plant.

[226] There are only eight names. *Kuruvinda* is a type of barley, *venu* is bamboo, while *tamatirkataka* is probably a medicinal herb.

grass, roots, fruits and shoots. They seized these fruits and nourished themselves. Earlier, Svayambhu milked these seeds from the earth. They now grew as herbs, seasonal flowers and fruits. But there was a time when the herbs created earlier no longer grew. Therefore, he devised an occupation for them to sustain themselves.[227] For them, Bhagavan Svayambhu ensured that success in tasks would come about through their own hands. Since then, plants grew and ripened only when there was ploughing. In this way, Prajapati ensured that they would be successful in sustaining themselves. He established rules so that they would protect each other.'

'Among them, there were those who are stronger and these were the ones who seized. He established them as kshatriyas and gave them the task of protecting. "Everything created will worship you. You will speak the exact truth." These were the ones certainly established as brahmanas. There were others who were engaged in the task of protecting those who were weaker. Others were engaged in buying and selling and found a successful means of subsistence in agriculture. These were always spoken of as vaishyas. There were others engaged in serving others, running around here and there. They were limited in energy and valour and he spoke of them as shudras. In this way, Lord Brahma determined karma and dharma for them. In this way, he created and established the four varnas. However, the subjects were deluded again and did not follow dharma. Though they survived because of the dharma of varnas, they opposed each other. Lord Brahma knew and understood the truth about everything. He instructed that kshatriyas should use their strength to wield the rod of chastisement and that they should earn a living through fighting. Lord Brahma instructed that the tasks of brahmanas would be performing sacrifices, teaching, receiving and giving. He gave vaishyas the tasks of animal husbandry, trade and agriculture. He gave shudras the task of earning a living through artisanship. He again bestowed the general tasks of performing sacrifices, studying and donating on brahmanas, kshatriyas and vaishyas. These were the common tasks. In this way, he respectively

---

[227] Marking a transition from gathering to agriculture.

gave them tasks and means of subsistence for this world. In a different world, he also established higher worlds for them. For *dvija*s engaged in rites, that place is described as Prajapati's world. *Kshatriya*s who do not run away from battles have a place in Indra's world. *Vaishya*s who earn a living through their own appointed tasks obtain a place in the world of Marut. *Shudra*s engaged in servitude earn a place in the world of *gandharva*s. In different *varna*s, these are the places earmarked for virtuous ones who follow appropriate conduct. He established the four *varna*s and virtuous deeds for these. Scared of the rod, all the *varna*s remained established in their own *varna*s. After having established the *varna*s, he established the *ashram*s—*garhasthya*, *brahmacharya*, *vanaprastha* and the state of being a *yati*.[228] As was the case earlier, the lord established the four *ashrama*s. Among the four *varna*s, there were some who performed the appointed tasks. They resided in habitations, performed these tasks and enjoyed themselves. However, though Brahma established the *ashrama*s, there were those who deviated. Brahma spoke to them and instructed them about *dharma*, their places, self-control and rules. For the four *varna*s, the *ashrama* of *garhasthya* is the foremost. The other three *ashrama*s earn their sustenance through this. In the due order, I will speak about vows and rules. Briefly, for a householder, *dharma* accumulates through marriage, maintaining a fire, tending to guests, performing sacrifices, *shraddha* ceremonies[229] and rites and having offspring. A person in *brahmacharya* must have a staff, wear a girdle[230] and deer-skin, sleep on the ground, serve his *guru*, live through begging and strive for learning. A person in *vanaprastha* must wear barks, leaves and deer-skin, eat roots, fruits and plants, bathe at the time of the two *sandhya*s and offer oblations. Svayambhu spoke of ten characteristics of *dharma*[231]—begging for alms when the pestle is

---

[228] The state of being a *yati* (mendicant) is being used as a synonym for *sannyasa*. *Garhasthya* is the state of being a householder, *brahmacharya* the state of being a celibate student, while in *vanaprastha*, a person resorts to the forest.

[229] A funeral rite.

[230] Made of *munja* grass.

[231] For a person in *sannyasa*.

quiet;[232] lack of theft; purity; lack of distraction; refraining from intercourse; compassion towards beings; forgiveness; listening; serving the *guru*; and truthfulness as the tenth. Five of these are only for those who are not mendicants. The other five are for mendicants who also follow the vows of the *Vedas*. He also spoke about abodes for these and other radiant ones. There are eighty-eight thousand *rishis* who hold up their seed. Their place has been earmarked for those who reside with the *guru*.[233] For those in *vanaprastha*, it is said that their place is that of the *saptarshis*. Those in *garhasthya* have a place in Prajapati's world and those in *sannyasa* obtain Brahma's undelaying world. The place meant for *yogis* is not for those who have not conquered themselves. Brahma accordingly determined places for the different *ashramas*. There are thus these four modes, devised for those who follow *Devyani*.[234] The modes followed by those who pursue *pitriyana* are also four. In ancient times, in the first *manvantara*, Brahma, the one who ordained the worlds, created these paths. The sun is said to be the gate to *Devyani*. Similarly, the moon is spoken of as the gate to *Pitriani*. In this way, he divided the *varnas* and the *ashramas*. However, though they followed the *dharma* of the *varnas*, subjects did not flourish. Therefore, in the middle of *treat yuga*, using his own mental powers, he created other subjects. They were similar to him in bodies and like him in their atmans. In this way, when *treta yuga* reached its middle period, he used the powers of his mind and started to create subjects. The lord created subjects who possessed an excess of *sattva* and *rajas*. They were *sadhanas* who strove to achieve *dharma*, *artha*, *kama* and *moksha*. There were *devas*, ancestors, *rishis* and humans. Following *dharma* that was appropriate for the *yuga*, subjects flourished. When the time for creation presented itself, Svayambhu Brahma meditated and used the powers of his mind to create subjects with different kinds of energy. I have spoken to you about them earlier. These were the ones who resorted to Janaloka. In the past and

---

[232] That is, those in the house have already eaten.

[233] That is, those in *brahmacharya*.

[234] *Devayana* is the path followed by *devas*, while *pitriyana* is that followed by ancestors.

ancient *Kalpa*, there were *deva*s and subjects in this world. When he meditated on them, they manifested themselves and appeared before him. In the order of the *manvantara*s, there were those who were younger and those born first. These were famous lineages that he had thought of earlier. There were the accomplished. And there were the less accomplished, destroyed because of their inferiority. They suffered from the taint of the fruits of their own *karma*. As a result of these impediments, they were born again. Earlier, he had thought of lineages in this world. There were *deva*s, *asura*s, ancestors, *yaksha*s, *gandharva*s, humans, *rakshasa*s, *pishacha*s, animals, birds, reptiles, trees and insects from hell. There were many kinds of forms. Knowing what was in the minds of these subjects, he created their food too.'

Chapter 8-1(8) (Creation through mental powers)

Suta said, 'So as to create subjects through the powers of his mind, he meditated. Cause and effect were created from the intelligent one's body. *Kshetra* and *kshetrajna*s resulted. There were four categories—*deva*s, *asura*s, ancestors and humans. Desiring to create, he engaged his *atman*. As he engaged himself, *tamas* alone originated. Prajapati sought to meditate on the task of creation. As a result of this, the first sons who were born were *asura*s, born from the loins. *Asu* is described as the breath of life. That is the reason those who were born are known as *asura*s.[235] When *asura*s were born from his body, he cast aside that body. Night instantly originated from the body that was cast aside. Night consists of three *yama*s and thus possesses an excess of *tamas*.[236] Therefore, during the night, subjects are enveloped in darkness. After creating *asura*s, he assumed another body. This was unmanifest and possessed an excess of *sattva*. When the lord engaged himself with this body,

[235] The standard derivation is antithesis of *sura*.
[236] Day and night are divided into eight *yama*s, each *yama* is a period of three hours. The four *yama*s of the night are from 6 p.m. to 6 a.m.

he was indeed filled with delight. The radiant *deva*s originated
from his mouth. Since they were born from that radiance, they
are described as *deva*s.[237] The verbal root "*div*" means to play,
as well as to shine. *Deva*s were born from his shining body.
Having created *deva*s, he abandoned that radiant body. The day
originated from the body he cast aside. Therefore, rites are used to
worship *deva*s during the day. Having created *deva*s, he assumed
another body. This possessed an excess of *sattva* and he engaged
himself with this. The lord meditated on these sons, thinking of
them as fathers. Separate from day and night and representing the
intervening periods, ancestors resulted from this. Therefore, they
are the fathers of *deva*s and are described as possessing the state
of fatherhood. Having created ancestors, he cast aside that body.
Sandhya was instantly created from the body he abandoned. Thus,
it is said that day belongs to *deva*s and night belongs to *asura*s.
The body that is in between is that of the ancestors and it is the
greatest. Hence, when engaged in *yoga*, *deva*s, *asura*s, *rishi*s and
humans worship Usha, which is between the two.[238] Hence, *dvija*s
worship *sandhya*, which joins night and day. After this, Brahma
again assumed a different body. The lord created this through his
mental powers and this possessed an excess of *rajas*. Through the
powers of his mind, he gave birth to sons who were *praja*s.[239] Since
he thought of them, they are known as *manushya*s. Since they were
generated, they are spoken of as *praja*s. Having created *praja*s, he
again discarded that body. Moonlight was instantly generated from
the body he cast aside. Therefore, *praja*s are delighted when the
moonlight appears. The bodies abandoned by the great-souled one
immediately became night, day, *sandhya* and moonlight. Three
of these, moonlight, *sandhya* and day, only possess *sattva*. Night,

[237] The word *deva* means the radiant one.
[238] Usha is dawn or daybreak, before the sun rises.
[239] *Praja* means offspring or subject and is based on the root for
generation. *Manushya* means human. Here, the derivation is based on
manana (reflection).

which has three *yamas*,[240] only possesses *tamas*. *Deva*s were born when Brahma's face was content and radiant. As a result of being born during the day, *deva*s are strong during the day. From his loins and his breath of life, the lord created *asura*s during the night. As a result of being born at night, they are invincible at night. In this way, these four, moonlight, night, day and *sandhya*, became the causes for all men, *asura*s, *deva*s and ancestors, in past *manvantara*s and in future ones. The verbal root "*bha*" means to "spread and shine". Since it spreads and shines, water is known as *ambhas*.'

'After creating water, *deva*s, *danava*s, humans and ancestors, he created other subjects in the due order. Casting aside the moonlight, the lord assumed another body. This body possessed an excess of *rajas* and *tamas* and he united with this. In the darkness, he created other subjects who were overwhelmed by hunger. Thus created and suffering from hunger, these subjects got ready to seize the water. There were some who said, "We will protect these waters." These are described as *rakshasa*s.[241] They are afflicted by hunger and roam around in the night. There were others who said, "Let us destroy the waters and cause each other delight." As a result of this deed, they became *yaksha*s[242] and *guhyaka*s, cruel in deeds. The root word "*raksh*" means to protect and preserve, while the root word "*kshi*" means to destroy. Therefore, those who protected are known as *rakshasa*s and those who destroyed are described as *yaksha*s. On beholding this, the intelligent one was displeased and his hair withered. When the hair withered, it repeatedly rose and fell downwards. Hair fell from the head, slithered and crawled. Since this was hair, they are spoken of as *vyala*s. Since they dropped down, they are described as *ahi*s. Since they writhed, they are *pannaga*s and since they crawled, they are *sarpa*s.[243] They move around on earth, the sun, the moon and clouds. Since they originated from his

---

[240] The text states *niyamika*, that which controls. We have amended this to *triyamika* (with three *yamas*), as that makes better sense.

[241] From the root word for protect.

[242] From the root word for destroy.

[243] *Vyala*s, *ahi*s, *pannaga*s and *sarpa*s are synonyms for serpents/ snakes. The etymology given in the text is sometimes contrived.

anger, they have fire in their wombs and are extremely terrible. The rage entered the *sarpa*s and filled them with poison. Having created the *sarpa*s from his rage, he created *bhuta*s.[244] They were tawny in complexion and full of anger, feeding on flesh. Since they originated, they are known as *bhuta*s. Since they fed on flesh, they are *pishacha*s. While he was singing, *gandharva*s were born as his sons. The wise say that the verbal root "*dhay*" should be taken in the sense of "drinking". When they were born, they drank up his words. Hence, they are remembered as *gandharva*s. The lord created these eight divine species.[245] From his will, he created *chhanda*.[246] From his age, he created birds.[247] Having created birds, he created a large number of animals. Goats were created from his mouth and sheep were created from his chest. Cattle were created from Brahma's stomach. Horses, elephants, donkeys, *gavaya*s,[248] deer, camels, boar, dogs and other species were created from his flanks and his feet. Herbs, fruits, roots and others were created from his body-hair. In this way, he created five kinds of herbs that would be used for sacrifices. In ancient times, at the beginning of the *kalpa*, he did this when *treta yuga* commenced. Cows, goats, humans, sheep, horses, mules and donkeys—these seven are described as village animals. There are another seven that are forest animals—predatory beasts,[249] leopards, elephants, monkeys, birds as the fifth, aquatic animals as the sixth and reptiles as the seventh. Buffaloes, *gavaya*s, camels, those with cloven hooves, *sharabha*s,[250] elephants and monkeys as the seventh, these seven are also regarded as wild animals. From his first mouth,

[244] Loosely, *bhuta*s are malignant spirits and ghosts. The word *bhuta* means to come into being, explaining the derivation given. The word *pishita* means flesh, often human flesh.

[245] Presumably meaning *deva*s, *danava*s, ancestors, *rakshasa*s, *yaksha*s, *sarpa*s, *bhuta*s and *gandharva*s.

[246] *Chhanda* means metre. The word also means desire or will. From his will, he created metres and prosody.

[247] The word *vayas* means both age (stage of life) and bird.

[248] Wild oxen.

[249] More specifically, the word *shvapada* means tiger.

[250] Mythical eight-legged creature that feeds on lions. However, the word also means a young elephant or a camel.

he created the *gayatri* metre, the hymns of the *Rig Veda*, *trivitstoma*, *rathantara* and the *agnishtoma* sacrifice.[251] From the mouth that is to the south, he created the hymns of the *Yajur Veda*, the *trishtubh* metre, the fifteenth *stoma* and Brihatsaman.[252] From his mouth that is to the west, he created the hymns of the *Sama Veda*, the *jagati* metre, the seventeenth *stoma* and *vairupya* and *atiratra* sacrifices.[253] From his fourth mouth, he created the twenty-first *stoma*, the hymns of the *Atharva Veda*, the *aptoryama* sacrifice and the *anustup* and *vairaja* metres. After creating the extremely famous *deva*, known as Parjanya,[254] he created lightning, thunder, clouds and red-tinged rainbows. For success in sacrifices, he created the hymns of the *Rig Veda*, the *Yajur Veda* and the *Sama Veda*. Inferior and superior beings were born from his body. In this way, Prajapati Brahma embarked on the creation of *prajas*. He first created four of these—*devas*, *rishis*, ancestors and humans. After this, he created mobile and immobile entities. He created *yakshas*, *pishachas*, *gandharvas*, *apsaras*, humans, *kinnaras*, *rakshasas*, *pashus*, *mrigas*, *uragas*, the perishable and the imperishable, the mobile and the immobile. When they were created, they followed their earlier *karma*. When they were repeatedly created, they followed these. Thus, when they were created, they practised whatever appealed to them—violence or non-violence, cruelty or otherwise, *dharma* or *adharma*, truth or falsehood. He is the one who ordained the great elements and invoked bodies, suffering from the senses, for creatures. Some men say that human endeavour is supreme, others cite *karma*. Other *brahmanas* mention destiny. Others, who think about creatures, say that it is innate nature. Those who know say that there is no separate distinction between human endeavour, destiny and nature, in so far as fruits and conduct are concerned. Some say it is this and not that. Others say that it is both, or neither. Those who are

---

[251] *Stoma* is a hymn of praise, *trivitstoma* is when three (*tri*) of them are sung together. *Rathantara* is a hymn from the *Sama Veda*. This mouth is to the east.

[252] Brihatsaman means the hymn in *Rig Veda* 1.10.52.

[253] *Vairupya* and *atiratra* are components of *jyotishtoma* sacrifices.

[254] Indra, the God of rain.

impartial in insight speak of the *karma* of creatures. In this way, at the beginning, the great lord used the words of the *Veda*s to create creatures in many forms and the visible universe. At the end of the night, when they were born again, Aja gave names to *rishi*s and insight to *deva*s.'

Chapter 9-1(9) (Rudra's creation)

Suta said, 'Through the powers of his mind, the lord then created Rudra, Dharma, Manas, Ruchi and Akriti. They were agents. All of them were mighty-armed and were responsible for the preservation of subjects. When herbs decay, Rudra repeatedly re-establishes them. Once they have obtained the herbs, those who desire fruits worship the divinity properly. Hence, when herbs decay, sages worship the three-eyed one with three *kapala*s and he is spoken of as Tryambaka.[255] The three are described as the *gayatri*, *trishtubh* and *jagati* metres. I have spoken of the three mothers, the origins of trees. When the three come together and become one, the *purodasha* is permeated by their individual energy. Hence, these three means are spoken of as the three *kapala*s. The *purodasha* is Tryambaka and is spoken of as Tryambaka. Dharma nurtures all subjects and Manas is said to bestow *jnana* on them. Akriti provides beauty and form, while Ruchi is said to lead to faith. In this way, these are the ones who protect subjects. They are responsible for the preservation of subjects. In this way, he embarked on creation, so that the subjects might flourish. However, the created subjects did not flourish, whatever be the means. He used his intelligence to reflect on this and arrived at a determination. He saw that it was *tamas* alone moving around inside him. Having abandoned *sattva* and *rajas*, it was engaged in its own action. At this, the lord of the universe was sad and ensured purity. He cast aside *tamas* and

---

[255] Tryambaka, the one with three eyes, is Shiva's name. *Kapala* can be interpreted as skull, copper vessel, or cake (*purodasha*). A subsequent sentence suggests this should be taken in the sense of cake.

covered it with *rajas*. The expelled *tamas* gave birth to a couple. Since it had resorted to *adharma*, these were Himsa and Shoka.[256] Thus, enveloped by the covering, this couple was born. Bhagavan was delighted at this development. When he was pleased, a woman emerged from half of his body. She was extremely fortunate and caused joy to all beings. From Prakriti, he used his desire to create this extremely beautiful one. She was spoken of as Shatarupa and this is how she was repeatedly addressed. After this, as I have already told you in *prakriya pada*, in the middle of *treta yuga*, *praja*s originated from the great-souled one. But the *praja*s created by the intelligent one did not flourish. Therefore, using the powers of his mind, he created sons who were just like him. He created sons through his mental powers—Bhrigu, Angiras, Marichi, Pulastya, Pulaha, Kratu, Daksha, Atri and Vasishtha. The Puranas have determined that these were the nine. Since they were born from Brahma, they owed their origin to the *paramatman*. After this, Brahma again created Dharma, who brings pleasure to beings. He also created Prajapati Ruchi. These two were the eldest among the forefathers. The one whose origin is in the water gave birth to *rishi* Bhrigu from his heart. Brahma created Daksha from his *prana* and Marichi from his eyes. He created Rudra Nilalohita from his pride, Angiras from his head and Atri from his ears. Pulastya was created from his *udana* and Pulaha from his *vyana*. Vasishtha was created from his *samana* and Kratu from his *apana*. These twelve[257] are described as Brahma's sons, the first among *praja*s. Dharma is described as the first among *deva*s to be born. The others who were created, Bhrigu and the others, are described as *brahmarshi*s. They are ancient householders and they were the ones to first propound *dharma*. From one *kalpa* to another *kalpa*, these twelve repeatedly give birth to offspring. The lineages of these twelve are divine and possess the qualities of *deva*s. They performed rites and had offspring and the lineages were distinguished by *maharshi*s. The intelligent one created Dharma and the other *maharshi*s, but the subjects did not flourish. Therefore, he suffered from grief and was enveloped by *tamas*. When Brahma

---

[256] The personified forms of violence and grief, respectively.
[257] Adding Dharma, Ruchi and Rudra to the earlier list of nine.

was enveloped by *tamas*, other sons emerged and they were full
of *tamas*. Adharma has a perverse flow and Himsa has all that is
inauspicious. He was countered in this way and it was evident that
he was covered. Therefore, Brahma discarded his own radiant body.
He divided his body into two, and half of his body became a man.
A woman originated from the other half and she was Shatarupa.
This mother emerged from Prakriti and the lord created her from
his desire. She was established there, pervading the earth and the
firmament in her greatness. Earlier, she was part of Brahma's body
and she remained there, pervading the firmament. From half of his
body, the woman Shatarupa originated. For one hundred thousand
years, this Goddess performed extremely difficult austerities. She
then obtained the radiant and famous Purusha as her husband. This
Purusha is spoken of as the former Svayambhuva Manu. Seventy-
one *mahayuga*s are described as a *manvantara*. Purusha obtained
Shatarupa, who was not born from a womb, as his wife.[258] He
amused herself with her and therefore, she is spoken of as Rati. That
first union occurred at the beginning of the *kalpa*. Brahma created
Virat and Virat became Purusha. He is Samrat, with one hundred
different forms. He is described as Vairaja Manu. As Vairaja Manu,
Purusha embarked on the task of creating offspring.'

'Through Vairaja Purusha, Shatarupa had two valiant sons.
These two sons were Priyavrata and Uttanapada and they were
supreme among sons. She also had two extremely fortunate
daughters as twins and all these subjects originated from them.
Their names were the Goddess Akuti and the auspicious Prasuti.
The lord Svayambhuva bestowed Prasuti on Daksha and bestowed
Akuti on Prajapati Ruchi. Through Ruchi, the son born through
mental powers, Akuti gave birth to an auspicious couple. The twins
who were born were Yajna and Dakshina. Yajna and Dakshina
gave birth to twelve sons. In Svayambhuva *manvantara*, these were

---

[258] In this description of creation, Svayambhuva Manu is equated with
Purusha, Vairaja, Virat and Samrat. Prakriti is equated with Shatarupa and
Rati. Rati means pleasure, usually of the sexual kind. One should remember
that in different *kalpas*, the same entity may have different names, being
repeatedly born from one *kalpa* to another.

the *deva*s, known as Yamas. They were known as Yamas because they were the sons of the twins, Yajna and Dakshina.[259] There are said to be two categories descended from Brahma—Ajitas and Shukras.[260] The Yamas, described as residents of the firmament, circumambulated the former. Svayambhuva Manu's daughter, Prasuti, became the mother of the worlds. Through her, the lord Daksha had twenty-four daughters. All of them were extremely fortunate. All of them possessed eyes like lotuses. All of them were the wives of *yogi*s. All of them were the mothers of *yoga*. All of them spoke about the *brahman*. All of them were the mothers of the universe. The lord Dharma accepted thirteen of Daksha's daughters as his wives—Shraddha, Lakshmi, Dhriti, Tushti, Pushti, Medha, Kriya, Buddhi, Lajja, Vasu, Shanti, Siddhi and Kirti. Svayambhuva himself ordained that they would be gates.[261] There were another eleven daughters who were younger and they possessed beautiful eyes. They were Sati, Khyati, Sambhuti, Smriti, Priti, Kshama, Sannati, Anasuya, Urja, Svaha and Svadha. The other *maharshi*s accepted them. They were Rudra, Bhrigu, Marichi, Angiras, Pulaha, Kratu, Pulastya, Atri, Vasishtha, the ancestors and Agni. Sati was bestowed on Bhava[262] and Khyati on Bhrigu. He bestowed Sambhuti on Marichi and Smriti on Angiras. He bestowed Priti on Pulastya and Kshama on Pulaha. He bestowed Sannati on Kratu and Anasuya on Atri. He bestowed Urja on Vasishtha and Svaha on Agni. Svadha was bestowed on the ancestors. Now hear about their offspring. All of them were extremely fortunate. Across *manvantara*s, until the time of the deluge, their offspring followed them and obeyed them. Shraddha gave birth to Kama and Lakshmi's son is described as Darpa.[263] Dhriti's son was Niyama and Tushti's is said to be

---

[259] The word *yama* has several meanings. One meaning is, one of a pair, twin.

[260] Two categories of *deva*s.

[261] Probably because they were the embodied forms of faith, prosperity, fortitude, contentment, nourishment, intellect, rites, intelligence, modesty, riches, peace, success and fame respectively.

[262] Rudra/Shiva.

[263] *Kama* means desire and *darpa* means insolence.

Santosha.[264] Pushti's son was Labha and Medha's son was Shruta.[265] Kriya's sons are said to have been Dama and Shama.[266] Buddhi's two sons were Budha and Apramada.[267] Lajja's son was Vinaya and Vasu's son was Vyavasaya.[268] Shanti's son was Kshema and Siddhi's son was Sukha.[269] Kirti's son was Yasha.[270] These were the sons of Dharma. Through the Goddess Siddhi, Kama had Harsha[271] as a son. In this way, Dharma's sons, Sukha and the others, resulted in a creation full of *sattva*. Through Adharma, Himsa gave birth to Nikriti and Anrita.[272] Nikriti and Anrita gave birth to two pairs of twins—Bhaya and Naraka, and Maya and Vedana.[273] Through Maya, Maayaa gave birth to Mrityu,[274] who takes away beings. Through Rourava, Vedana gave birth to Duhkha.[275] Through Mrityu, Vyadhi gave birth to Jara, Shoka, Krodha and Asuya.[276] All of these are remembered as the signs of *adharma*, leading to greater and greater grief. All their wives and sons are described as those who are not destroyed. When Adharma was in control, a creation full of *tamas* resulted in this way.'

'Brahma instructed Nilalohita to have offspring. He meditated on his wife, Sati, and created offspring from himself. They were not superior or inferior to him. They were born through his mental powers and were just like him. There were thousands and thousands

[264] *Niyama* means control/rules and *santosha* means contentment.

[265] *Labha* means gain and *shruta* means learning.

[266] *Dama* means physical restraint, while *shama* means mental restraint.

[267] *Budha* means understanding, while *apramada* means lack of distraction.

[268] *Vinaya* means humility, while *vyavasaya* means enterprise.

[269] *Kshema* means welfare and *sukha* means happiness.

[270] Fame.

[271] Delight.

[272] *Nikrita* means dishonesty/deceit, while *anrita* means falsehood.

[273] *Bhaya* means fear, *naraka* means hell, *maya* means illusion and *vedana* means pain.

[274] Death.

[275] Misery.

[276] *Vyadhi* means disease, *jara* means old age, *shoka* means grief, *krodha* means anger and *asuya* means jealousy.

of them and they were clad in hides.[277] All of them were exactly
like him in beauty, energy, strength and learning. They were tawny
in complexion and possessed quivers. They had matted hair and
their complexion was blue-red. They were without tufts of hair
and hair. They could kill through their glances and held skulls.
They possessed gigantic and hideous forms. Their forms were such
that the universe was their form. They were archers and armoured,
on chariots with fenders. They possessed one thousand arms and
one hundred arms. They could travel through heaven, earth and
the firmament. Their heads were large, with eight fangs. They
possessed two tongues and three eyes. They ate food and flesh.
They drank *ghee* and *soma* juice. Their penises were extremely
large and their bodies were fierce. Their throats were blue. They
possessed quivers and armour. They were archers, with swords
and shields. Some were seated, while others ran. Some yawned,
while others stood. Some studied. Some performed *japa*. Others
engaged in *yoga* and *dhyana*. They blazed and showered. They
emitted light and smoke. Some possessed understanding, others
had a greater understanding. Some were like the *brahman*, others
had insight about the *brahman*. They possessed blue throats and
one thousand eyes. They roamed around everywhere on earth.
They were invisible to all beings. They were great *yogis*, full of
great energy. They cried and ran around. In this way, there were
thousands of them. Rudra created such excellent divinities who
could not be measured. On seeing this, Brahma said, "Do not
create such *prajas*. One should not create *prajas* who are superior
to one's own self, or like one's own self. O fortunate one! Create
other *prajas*, those who are vulnerable to death. *Prajas* who do
not suffer from death do not engage in *karma*." Thus addressed,
he replied, "I will not create *prajas* who suffer from old age and
death. O fortunate one! O lord! I will stand here. You create. I have
created these malformed ones, blue-red in complexion. There are
thousands and thousands and they have emerged from me. They

---

[277] Krittivasa, one of Shiva's names. Krittivasa means one whose
garment is a hide. *Kritti* specifically means the hide of an antelope, but in
Shiva's context, refers to the hide of an elephant.

will be immensely strong *deva*s, known by the name of Rudras. Rudranis[278] are famous on earth and in the firmament. Revered in the Shatarudriya,[279] they will perform sacrifices in this world. Along with all the other categories of *deva*s, they will be entitled to shares in sacrifices. There are *deva*s who are worshipped through the *chhanda*s. Until the *yuga*s are over, in all the *manvantara*s, they will remain and be worshipped along with them." The lord Brahma was addressed in this way by Mahadeva. Prajapati glanced towards the terrible one and replied, "O fortunate one! O lord! It shall be exactly as you have stated it." When Brahma agreed, everything occurred in that way. Since then, the divinity Sthanu did not create any *praja*s. Until the end of the deluge, he held up his seed. Since he said, "I will stand," the learned remember him as Sthanu.[280] *Jnana*, austerities, truth, prosperity, *dharma*, non-attachment and knowledge of the *atman*—all these exist in Shankara. In his energy, the divinity Mahadeva is said to surpass all *deva*s, *rishi*s and *asura*s. He surpasses *deva*s in prosperity and the great *asura*s in strength. He surpasses all the sages in *jnana* and is superior to everyone in *yoga*. Therefore, all *deva*s bow down to Mahadeva. After creating *praja*s who lacked in enterprise, he refrained from creation.'

Chapter 10-1(10) (Mahadeva's Glory)

'The *rishi*[281] said, "In this *kalpa*, you have not spoken about the origin of the great-souled Mahadeva Rudra, along with the *rishi*s."

'Suta replied, "I have briefly spoken about the original creation. I will now describe the names and bodies in detail. In past *kalpa*s,

[278] Rudrani is feminine of Rudra.

[279] Literally, *Shatarudriya* means one hundred Rudras and is a *mantra* to Rudra, from the *Yajur Veda*.

[280] The verbal root 'stha' means to stand. Shankara (the one who bestows auspiciousness) is one of Shiva's names.

[281] Since this is in the singular, this is Shounaka speaking.

through his wives, Mahadeva had many sons. Hear about them in this *kalpa*. At the beginning of the *kalpa*, the lord[282] meditated on sons who were exactly like him. At this, the boy Nilalohita appeared on his lap. The terrible one wept in a loud voice and seemed to burn everything down through his energy. He suddenly saw the boy, Nilalohita, crying. Brahma said, "O child! Why are you weeping?" He replied, "O grandfather! Give me a name first." He responded, "O divinity! Since you have cried, your name will be Rudra."[283] But he cried again. Brahma asked him, "O child! Why are you weeping?" He told Svayambhu, "Give me a second name." He responded, "O divinity! Your name will be Bhava." But he cried again. Brahma asked the one who was crying, "Why are you weeping?" Thus addressed, he answered again, "Give me a third name." He said, "O divinity! Your name will be Sharva." But he wept again. Brahma again asked the one who was crying, "Why are you weeping?" Thus addressed, he answered again, "Give me a fourth name." He said again, "O divinity! Your name will be Ishana." Thus addressed, he wept again. Brahma again asked the one who was crying, "Why are you weeping?" He replied to Svayambhu, "Give me a fifth name." He said, "You will be Pashupati." However, thus addressed, he wept again. Brahma again asked the one who was crying, "Why are you weeping?" Thus addressed, he answered, "Give me a sixth name." He said, "O divinity! Your name will be Bhima." But spoken to in this way, he wept again. Brahma again asked the one who was crying, "Why are you weeping?" Thus addressed, he answered, "Give me a seventh name." He said, "O divinity! Your name will be Ugra." Thus addressed, he wept again. He told the weeping child, "Do not cry." He again answered, "O lord! Give me an eighth name." When he was told that his name would be Mahadeva, he stopped. Having obtained these names from Brahma, Nilalohita said, "Please indicate the abodes for these names." At this, Svayambhu created abodes for these names—sun, water, earth, wind, fire,

---

[282] Meaning Brahma.
[283] The root '*rud*' means to cry/weep.

space, a *brahmana* consecrated through *diksha* and the moon.[284]
These were the eight bodies. One must make efforts to worship,
salute and show obeisance to these.

'Brahma spoke to the boy, Nilalohita, again. "O lord! In the
beginning, I said that your name will be Rudra. This is your first
name and your first body will be the sun." The energy from his eye
provides illumination. When this was said, it entered the sun and
the sun is known as Rudra. One should not look at the sun when it
is rising or setting. Since the sun is not permanently placed, but
permanently rises, a pure person, who desires a long lifespan, should
not glance at the sun. If *brahmana*s chant hymns from the *Rig*,
Sama and *Yajur Veda*s and worship the sun at the time of the two
*sandhya*s, when it rises and sets, they worship past and future
Rudras. When it rises, the sun is based on the *Rig Veda*. At midday,
it is based on the *Yajur Veda*. In the afternoon, it is based on the
Sama Veda and Rudra gradually enters it. The sun does not actually
rise or set. Externally, that seems to be the case. Whatever be the
situation, one must never pass urine in the direction of the sun. If
*dvija*s observe this, the divinity Rudra causes them no harm. After
this, Brahma spoke to the divinity, Nilalohita, again. "I have said
that your second name will be Bhava. Associated with this name,
your second body will be water." Thus addressed, the juices entered
this body and since they entered, water is described as Bhava.
Creatures originate from him and are conceived by him. Since he
conceives beings and leads to their existence, he is known as
Bhava.[285] Therefore, one must never release urine or excrement in
water. Nor should one spit while bathing in water or have intercourse
in it. Nor should one test waters, whether still or flowing. Sages
have described which bodies of water are pure and which are
impure. Water that has a foul colour, taste or smell and water that
is limited in quantity must always be avoided. Waters originated
from the ocean. Therefore, waters desire it. When they reach the

---

[284] The sun (Surya) for Rudra, water for Bhava, earth for Sharva, wind
for Ishana, fire for Pashupati, space for Bhima, an initiated *brahmana* for
Ugra and the moon for Mahadeva.

[285] From the root '*bhu*', meaning 'to become'.

ocean, waters become like *amrita* and are pure. Hence, one should restrict waters that desire the ocean. If a person treats water in this way, the divinity Bhava does not make him suffer. After this, Brahma spoke to the child, Nilalohita, again. "O lord! I said that your third name is Sharva. The body associated with this third name will be the earth." When this was said, whatever was firm in his body, known as the bones, entered the earth and the earth is spoken of as Sharva. Therefore, one should not pass urine or excrement on land that has been tilled. Nor should one do this in a place where there is shade,[286] along a road, or in one's own shadow. One must pass excrement after covering one's head and after covering the ground with grass. If one treats the earth in this way, Sharva does not cause the person any suffering. After this, Brahma spoke to the child, Nilalohita, again. "I said that your fourth name is Ishana. The body associated with this fourth name will be the wind." When this was said, the five kinds of breath of life that were in his body entered the wind. Therefore, the wind is known as Ishana. Hence, one should not censure the wind when it blows strongly. It is Ishvara. If a person conducts himself in this way and tends to the wind through sacrifices, the divinity Maheshana does not harm him. After this, Brahma again spoke to Ishvara, whose complexion was like that of smoke. "I said that your fifth name is Pashupati. The fifth body, associated with this fifth name, will be fire." When this was said, the energy in his body, known as Ushna,[287] entered the fire and fire is known as Pashupati. Agni is Pashupati and protects *pashus*.[288] Therefore, Agni is spoken of as Pashupati. Therefore, one should burn impure stuff in a fire, or use the fire to heat one's feet. One should not place fire under one's feet, or step over it. If a person acts in this way, the divinity Pashupati does not harm him. After this, Brahma spoke to the divinity who was white and tawny again. "O lord! I said that your sixth name is Bhima. Associated with this name, space will be your sixth body." When this was said, the hollows that existed in his body entered space.

[286] Shade from trees.
[287] Meaning hot.
[288] *Pashu*s are animals and Pashupati is the lord of *pashu*s.

This body of space is known as Bhima. Since space is named as a divinity, one should not pass urine or excrement, eat, drink, have sexual intercourse or fling away leftover food, without covering oneself. If a person acts in this way, the divinity Bhima does not harm him. After this, Brahma spoke to the mighty lord again. "O lord! I said that your seventh name is Ugra. The body associated with this name will be a *brahmana* who has taken *diksha*." When this was said, the consciousness in his body entered an initiated *brahmana* engaged in performing a *soma* sacrifice. Since that time, a *brahmana* who has taken *diksha* has been described as the divinity Ugra. Therefore, one should not abuse such a person, or say vulgar things about him. Those who abuse him take away his sins.[289] If a person acts in this way, the divinity Ugra does not harm him. After this, Brahma spoke to the divinity who was as resplendent as the sun again. "I said that your eighth name is Mahadeva. The body associated with this eighth name will be the moon." When this was said, the resolution in the lord's mind entered the moon and the moon is known as Mahadeva. Hence, Mahadeva is considered to be the moon. At the time of *amavasya*,[290] a *dvija* should not cut down trees, creepers and herbs. Mahadeva is spoken of as the moon and the large number of herbs represent his *atman*. If a person knows this about the lord and if a person always acts thus on *parva* days,[291] Mahadeva does not kill him. The sun protects subjects during the day and the moon does it at night. On these two nights, the sun and the moon are together. On the night of *amavasya*, one must always perform *yoga*. In these bodies and with these names, Rudra pervades everything. Surya wanders around alone and is spoken of as Rudra. It is because of Surya's illumination that subjects can see with their eyes. Rudra's *atman* is free. He is established there, drinking up the water with his rays. One eats and drinks because one desires food and drink. The body that arose from the water nourishes bodies in this way. This energy sustains subjects and is steady inside them. In

[289] And assume them.
[290] The night of the new moon.
[291] In general, a *parva* is an auspicious day for festivals. Here, it means *amavasya* and *purnima* (the night of the full moon).

the form of the earth, the virtuous body sustains subjects. It is present in the bodies of creatures and sustains their breath of life. Ishana is in the wind. This is the breath of life that sustains beings. Anything eaten and drunk is cooked inside the stomachs of creatures. The body known as Pashupati is the cook, the fire that does the cooking. There are spaces within bodies. The body known as Bhima is known as the wind that circulates there. Those who speak about the *brahman* exist because of the consciousness[292] of those who have taken *diksha*. This body is Ugra and those who have taken *diksha* are spoken of as Ugra. Resolution exists in the minds of *praja*s. In the form of the moon, this is established in the bodies of creatures. As a being is born again and again, it is generated again and again. At the right time, along with the ancestors, the learned drink this. The moon, with juices in it, is remembered as Mahadeva, with *amrita* in his *atman*. His first body is described as Rudra. His wife is Suvarchala, and her son is Shanaishchara.[293] His second body, in the form of water, is Bhava. His wife is remembered as Dhatri and her son is said to be Ushanas. The third body, in the form of the earth, is named Sharva. His wife is Vikeshi and her son is said to be Angaraka. The fourth name, with the wind as a body, is named Ishana. His wife is named Shivaa and her son is Manojava. Anila had two sons, Manojava and Avijnanagati. *Dvija*s say that the body in the fire is named Pashupati. His wife is said to be Svaha and her son is remembered as Skanda. The sixth body, in space, is named Bhima. The directions are said to be his wives and his son is said to be Svarga. The seventh body, Ugra, is said to be in the body of a *brahmana* who has taken *diksha*. His wife is said to be Diksha and her son is said to be Santana. The eighth great body of Mahadeva is remembered as the moon. His wife is Rohini, and her son is said to be Budha. The names and the bodies have thus been described.

[292] We have corrected a typo in the text, which says *vaitanya* (despondency) instead of *chaitanya* (consciousness).

[293] Shanaishchara is Saturn, Ushanas is Venus, Angaraka is Mars, Manojava is something/someone with the speed of thought, Anila is the wind, Avijnanagati means someone whose movement cannot be discerned, Svarga is heaven and Budha is Mercury.

He must be worshipped and shown obeisance in these names and bodies. Devotees should devoutly worship him in the sun, the water, the earth, the wind, the fire, space, in a *brahmana* who has taken *diksha* and in the moon. If a person knows of this divinity in these bodies and names, he has offspring and obtains *sayujya* with Ishvara Bhava. I have thus spoken to you about Bhima's secret fame. O *brahmanas*! Let there be welfare to bipeds. Let there be welfare for quadrupeds. The names and bodies of the divinity Mahadeva have thus been described. Now hear about Bhrigu's progeny.'

Chapter 11-1(11) (Creation of *rishis*)

Suta said, 'Bhrigu's wife, Khyati, gave birth to two lords who bestow happiness and unhappiness. They bestow the auspicious and the inauspicious on all those who have life. These were the two divinities, Dhatri and Vidhatri,[294] who roam around in the *manvantaras*. Their elder sister was the Goddess Shri,[295] who resides in the worlds. The beautiful one obtained the divinity Narayana as her husband. As Narayana's sons, she gave birth to Bala and Unmada.[296] Bala's son was Tejas and Unmada's son was Samshaya.[297] Through his mental powers, he had other sons who roam around in the firmament. They bear the *vimanas* of *devas* and those who are auspicious in deeds. In the *kalpa* known as Meru, Ayati and Niyati are known to have been the respective wives of Vidhatri and Dhatri. They had two sons who were firm in their vows—Prana and Mrikanda. They were eternal and were stores of the *brahman*. Through Manasvini, Mrikanda had Markandeya as a son. Through Dhumrapatni, Markandeya had Vedashira as a son. Vedashira's sons, through Pivari, are remembered as those who extended the lineage. These *rishis* are known as the

---

[294] Dhatri is the one who nurtures, and Vidhatri is the one who ordains.
[295] Lakshmi.
[296] *Bala* means strength and *unmada* means intoxication.
[297] *Tejas* means energy and *samshaya* means doubt.

Markandeyas, and they were accomplished in the *Veda*s. Through Pundarika, Dyutiman was born as the son of Prana. Dyutiman had two sons—Unnata and Svanavata. Through alliances with the Bhargavas, they had sons and grandsons. This was in the past Svayambhuva *manvantara*.'

'Now hear about Marichi's progeny. Through his wife Sambhuti, Prajapati Marichi had Purnamasa as a son. Hear about the daughters. They were Krishi, Vrishti, Tvisha and the auspicious Upachiti. Through Sarasvati, Purnamasa had two sons. They were Viraja, who was devoted to *dharma*, and Parvasha. Viraja's son was learned and famous, known by the name of Sudhama. Sudhama, the powerful son of Viraja and Gouri, had *dharma* in his soul. He resorted to the eastern direction and was a guardian of the world. The immensely illustrious Parvasha embarked on the task of calculating *parva*s. Through Parvashaa, Parvasha had two sons. They were Yajurdhama and the intelligent Stambhakashyapa. Their sons, Sannyasa and Nishchita, established this *gotra*.'

'Through his wife Smriti, Angiras had two sons and four daughters, who were auspicious and famous in the worlds. They were Sinivali, Kuhu, Raka and Anumati. The two sons were Bharatagni and Kirtiman. Through Sadvati, Agni[298] had Parjanya as a son. Marichi had a son known as Hiranyaroma Parjanya. Until the deluge, he was famous as a guardian of the world. Through Dhenuka, Kirtiman had two sons who were devoid of blemishes. They were Charishnu and Dhritimanta and they were among the excellent descendants of Angiras. In the past, their sons and grandsons numbered thousands.'

'Anusuya gave birth to five Atreyas who were devoid of blemishes. She had a daughter named Shruti, who was Shankhapada's mother. Shruti was the wife of Kardama Prajapati, Pulaha's son. The five Atreyas were Satyanetra, Havya, Apomurti and Shanaishchara, with Soma as the fifth. They belonged to the past Svayambhuva *manvantara*, along with the Yamadevas. These are described as the five Atreyas. Their sons and grandsons are described as the great-

---

[298] That is, Bharatagni.

souled Atreyas. In the past Svayambhuva *manvantara*, there were hundreds and thousands of them.'

'Danagni was the son of Priti, Pulastya's wife. In his past birth, in Svayambhuva *manvantara*, he was remembered as Agastya. Pulastya had three sons. The one in the middle was Devabahu and the other one was named Atri. Their younger sister was famous by the name of Sadvati. This auspicious one is remembered as Agni's[299] auspicious wife, Parjanya's mother. The intelligent Danagni was the son of *brahmarshi* Pulastya and Priti. Through his wife, Sujanghi, he had many sons. They were famous as the Poulastyas and are described as having existed in Svayambhuva *manvantara*.'

'Kshama bore the sons of Prajapati Pulaha.[300] They were as radiant as the three sacrificial fires[301] and their fame was established. These three were Kardama, Urvarivan and Sahishnu. There was the *rishi* Kanakapitha[302] and an auspicious daughter, Pivari. Kardama's wife was Shruti, Atri's daughter. She had a son named Shankhapada and a daughter, Kamya. The prosperous Shankhapada Prajapati was a guardian of the world. He established himself in the southern direction. Kamya was bestowed on Priyavrata. Through Kamya, Priyavrata had ten sons who were the equals of Svayambhuva Manu. He also had two daughters. The lineage of *kshatriyas* spread through these. The son, Kanakapitha, was famous under the name of Sahishnu. Through the slender-waisted Yashodhara, he had Kamadeva as a son.'

'Sannati bore auspicious sons to Kratu, and they were Kratu's equals. They did not have wives or sons and all of them held up their seed. They are famous as the *valakhilyas* and there were sixty thousands of them. They surround the sun and proceed ahead of Aruna.[303] Until the onset of the deluge, they accompany the sun.[304]

---

[299] Bharatagni's.

[300] The text says Pulastya. We have corrected it to Pulaha.

[301] *Ahavaniya, garhapatya* and *dakshinagni* (the fire that burns in a southern direction).

[302] Another name for Sahishnu.

[303] Aruna, Vinata's son and Garuda's brother, is described as the sun's charioteer.

[304] The word used in the text is Patanga. We have taken this as the sun.

Their younger sisters were Punya and Satyavati. They were the daughters-in-law of Parvasha, the son of Purnamasa.'

'Through Urja, Vasishtha had seven sons, known as the Vasishthas. Their elder sister was the slender-waisted Pundarika. She was Prana's beloved queen, Dyutiman's mother. The seven famous Vasishthas were younger than her. They were Raksha, Garta, Urddhabahu, Savana, Pavana, Sutapa and Shanku. All of them are famous as the *saptarshi*s.[305] Markandeya's illustrious daughter had beautiful limbs. She gave birth to Ratna, also known as Prajapati Ketuman. He was the king of the western direction. These are the names and *gotra*s of the great-souled Vasishthas. They existed in the past Svayambhuva *manvantara*. Now hear about Agni's offspring. The creation of the *rishi*s, and their associates, has been described. After this, I will speak about Agni's lineage in detail."

Chapter 12-1(12) (Agni's collection)

Suta said, 'In Svayambhuva *manvantara*, a son born through Brahma's mental powers is remembered as having occupied the position of Agni. Through Svaha, he had three sons. They are known as the fires Pavaka, Pavamana and Shuchi. Pavamana is known as the fire obtained through churning.[306] Pavaka is the fire in lightning. Shuchi is known as the fire in the sun. These were Svaha's three sons. Pavamana is the fire obtained through churning and Shuchi is the fire in the sun. Pavaka originates in lightning. These are their abodes. Kavyavahana is described as Pavamana's son. Havyavahana, Shuchi's son, is the fire of *deva*s, Kavyavahana is the fire of ancestors. Saharaksha is the son of Pavaka and Saharaksha is the fire of *asura*s. These three are fires that descended through the three sons of Agni. Their sons and grandsons number forty-nine. I will tell you about their names and separate divisions. The fire

[305] In the sky, the *saptarshi*s are the constellation Great Dipper, part of Ursa Major.
[306] By churning *arani*.

that is famous in the worlds is known as Brahma's first son. This
fire, Brahma's son and given by Brahma, is famous under the name
of Bharata. His son was Vaishvanara, who carried *havya* for one
hundred years. Earlier, Atharvan collected the Edhiti fire from the
ocean of Pushkara. This fire gathered by Atharvan is common in the
worlds.[307] Darpaha is said to have been the son of Atharvan. Bhrigu
was reborn as Atharvan and the fire is remembered as Atharvan.
Thus, the fire common in the worlds is known as *dakshinagni*,[308]
Atharvan's son. The wise remember Pavamana, Atharvan's son,
as the fire obtained through churning, and this is also known as
garhapatya. Agni is said to have had two sons, Shamsya and Shuka.
Shamsya is remembered as Havyavahana. The second son, Shuka,
is spoken of as the fire that is carried around. Shamsya had two
sons—Sabhya and Avasathya.[309] Shamsya Havyavahana desired
sixteen rivers. *Dvija*s remember Shamsya as the *ahavaniya* fire and
as the fire that was proud. The rivers were Kaveri, Krishnavena,
Narmada, Yamuna, Godavari, Vitasta, Chandrabhaga, Iravati,
Vipasha, Koushiki, Shatadru, Sarayu, Sita, Sarasvati, Hladini and
Pavana. He divided himself into sixteen parts. Having done this,
he established abodes for himself there. When the Krittikas moved
around, through these abodes, the Dhishnis were born.[310] There are
Viharaniya fires and there are Upastheya fires. Briefly, but accurately,
I will describe these. Listen. In the course of a *savana* sacrifice,[311]
it is recommended that there are sons who must be kept in a fixed

---

[307] Atharvan offered *soma* and brought fire down from heaven, starting
a system of worshipping the fire. The word Pushkara also means heaven.

[308] We have changed *dadhyan*, given in the text, to the more likely
dakshinagni.

[309] Since the text says Savya and Apasavya, there is a typo. We have
corrected this.

[310] Krittikas (the Pleiades) are the third *nakshatra* and the deity
associated with this *nakshatra* is Agni. Dhishni means abode. It also
means an altar for fire, placed at the side when a sacrifice was conducted.
Viharaniya fires were carried out, while Upastheya fires were kept in a
fixed place.

[311] A *savana* sacrifice is one where *soma* juice is extracted and drunk.
Savana also means the ceremonial conclusion of a sacrifice.

place, in the due order. These are Vibhu, Pravahana, Agnidhra and
other Dhishnis. In the due order, hear about the fires that have no
determined resting-place. Samradagni is one. The second, Krishanu,
is placed inside the altar. Dvijas place Samradagni in the eight
directions. Parishatpavamana[312] is the second fire that has no fixed
direction. Pratalka fire, also named Nabhas, is thought of in the
quadrangle, the level ground for the sacrifice. Using a sacrificial
vessel, havya that has not been covered must be deposited in the
fire. Ritudhama and Sujyoti are described as fires that exist in a fig
tree.[313] Vishvavyacha is described as the fire that is in the ocean,
Brahma's place. Vasurdhama, or Brahmajyoti, is spoken of as the
fire that is in Brahma's place. Ajaikapat is an Upastheya fire, as is
Shalasukhiyaka. Ahirbudhnya, remembered as the garhapatya fire,
is one with no fixed place. Dvijas remember all these sons of Shamsya
as Upastheya fires. I will now speak about the eight sons who are
Viharaniya fires. These are Vibhu, Pravahana, Agnidhra and other
Dhishnis.[314] In the course of a savana sacrifice, it is recommended
that there are sons who must be kept in a fixed place, in the due
order. The fire used by hotris is remembered as Havyavahana. The
second fire, which is a pacified one, is remembered as Prachetas.
After this, there is the Vaishadeva fire, described by brahmanas as
weak.[315] Ushiragni or Kavi is thought of as the fire for ritvijas.[316]
It is also thought of as the Avari, Vabhari or Vaishthiya fire. The
Avasphurja fire is spoken of as Vivasvan and Asthan. The eighth
fire, Sudhyu, is also known as Marjaliya.[317] Dvijas invoke these
Viharaniya fires on the day when soma juice is extracted.'

[312] The same as Krishanu.

[313] Udumbara.

[314] This is a repetition of what has already been said.

[315] We have taken the word shamsi (meaning weak) as an adjective, not
as a noun.

[316] We have taken pota as a type of ritvija. Otherwise, Potogni is
another name for the same fire.

[317] Some names, translated as synonyms, are probably independent
names of fires. Otherwise, one doesn't have eight names. The meanings of
these terse shlokas are not self-evident.

'There is a fire named Pavaka, which originated from the water as a womb. It is therefore described as a fire that had water as a source. This should be known as the fire that is used at the time of an *avabhritha* rite and it is worshipped along with Varuna. Pavaka's son is Hricchaya, the fire that caused digestion in the stomachs of men. Mrityuman is remembered as the learned son of the fire that is within the stomach. In this way, they arise from each other and there is a fire that scorches all beings in this world. This is described as the terrible Samvartaka fire, the son of Mrityuman.[318] It drinks water and resides in the ocean as the Vadavamukha fire.[319] The son of the fire that resides in the ocean is thought of as Saharaksha. Saharaksha's son is Kshama, and it burns down the houses of men. Kshama's son is Kravyad. This is the fire that consumes dead men. Thus, Pavaka's sons have been described. Shuchi is the fire in the sun and the *gandharvas* speak of it as Ayus. There is a fire that results when *arani* is churned. This fire exists in kindling and is carried around. This illustrious lord is named Ayus. Mahisha was the son of Ayus and the son of Mahisha was named Sahasa. Sahasa is remembered as the proud fire associated with a *paka-yajna*.[320] Sahasa's son was the immensely illustrious Adbhuta. The great fire, Vividhi, is described as the son of Adbhuta. This is the proud fire associated with a *prayashchitta* rite and it always consumes oblations that are offered into the fire. Vividhi's son was Arkka. The Arkka fire's sons were Anikavan, Vajasrik, Rakshoha, Yashtikrit, Surabhi, Vasu, Annada, Pravishta and Rukmarat. These fourteen[321] are described as the descendants of the Shuchi fire. These are described as the fires that are carried for sacrifices. In the past Svayambhuva *manvantara*, in the course of the original creation, these were the proud fires that existed, along with the

---

[318] The text says Manyuman, which we have changed to Mrityuman.

[319] Literally, with the face of a mare. This is the subterranean fire.

[320] This has been interpreted as the recommended modes for cooking food offered at sacrifices. However, *paka-yajna* also means a simple sacrifice undertaken at home and that seems to be a better meaning.

[321] Mahisha, Sahasa, Adbhuta, Vividhi, Arkka and Arkka's nine sons.

Yamas, the excellent Gods. Earlier, in the world, these were the
Havyavahanas who were proud of their places. In the sentient
and the non-sentient, they existed as Viharaniya fires. In the
former *manvantara*, they existed in sacrifices and in *kamya* and
naimittika karma.[322] Those fires and sacrifices have passed away,
along with the auspicious and great-souled *deva*s. They belonged
to the *manvantara* of the first Manu. I have thus spoken about
the abodes and about those who occupied those abodes. I have
also enumerated the characteristics of all the Jataveda fires in the
past and future *manvantara*s. All of them were ascetics and all of
them upheld the *brahman*. All of them are described as radiant.
There were the lords of subjects. Along with their names, forms
and needs, they should be known to have existed in all the seven
*manvantara*s, from Svarochisha to Savarni.[323] Fires existed along
with *deva*s known as Yamas. There are ones that exist now, and
future fires will exist along with future *deva*s. In the proper order,
the collection of fires has thus been described. In the due order
and in detail, I will now speak about the ancestors.'

Chapter 13-1(13) (Description of time)

Suta said, 'In the course of the former Svayambhuva *manvantara*,
when Brahma created sons, *asura*s, *deva*s and humans were born
from his body. Thinking of him as their father, the ancestors were
also born. Their creation has already been described. Briefly, hear
about it again. After creating *deva*s, *asura*s and humans, Brahma
honoured them. Those revered as ancestors were born from his

---

[322] Rites can be *nitya karma* (daily rites), *naimittika karma* (occasional
rites) and *kamya karma* (rites performed for a specific objective).

[323] The current *manvantara* is Vaivasvata. The former six are
Svayambhuva, Svarochisha, Uttama, Tamas, Raivata and Chakshusha. The
next one will be Savarni.

flanks. The six seasons, Madhu and the others, were born.[324] The *shruti* texts, the *Vedas*, say, "The seasons are ancestors and *devas*." This is true of all *manvantaras*, past and future. It was also true of the auspicious and former Svayambhuva *manvantara*. They are remembered under the names of Agnishvattas and Barhishads.[325] The Agnishvattas are remembered as those who were householders and did not perform sacrifices. These ancestors did not maintain sacrificial fires. There were ancestors who performed sacrifices and drank *soma*. Barhishads are remembered as ancestors who performed *agnihotra* sacrifices. The sacred texts have determined that seasons are *devas* and ancestors. Madhu and Madhava should be known as Rasas;[326] Shuchi and Shukra are the Shushmins;[327] Nabhas and Nabhasya[328] are cited as Jivas; Isha and Urja[329] are cited

---

[324] The six seasons (*ritus*) are *Vasanta* or spring (Chaitra and Vaishakha), *Grishma* or summer (Jyeshtha and Ashadha), *Varsha* or monsoon (Shravana and Bhadrapada), *Sharad* or early autumn (Ashvina and Kartika), *Hemanta* or late autumn (Margashirsha/Agrahayana and Pousha) and *Shishira* or winter (Magha and Phalguna). Chaitra is March-April, Vaishakha is April-May, Jyeshtha is May-June, Ashadha is June-July, Shravana is July-August, Proushtha (Proshthapada or Bhadrapada) is August-September, Ashvayuja (Ashvina) is September-October, Kartika is October-November, Margashirsha (Agrahayana) is November-December, Pousha is December-January, Magha is January-February and Phalguna is February-March. Madhu is another name for Vasanta, though it also means the month of Chaitra.

[325] There are different categories of ancestors, Agnishvatta, Barhishad, Soumya, Ajyapa, Havishmats and Kalinas. For example, Ajyapas accept oblations of *ghee* (clarified butter), Soumyas (Somapas) accept *soma*. While on earth, Agnishvattas did not perform fire sacrifices. Barhishads seated themselves on *barhi* grass. Havishmats accept oblations. *Kavya* stands for oblations to ancestors in general. Kavyavahas are those who convey such oblations.

[326] Madhu and Madhava are respectively Chaitra and Vaishakha. Rasa seems to be a name for a category of ancestors, though the word Rasa also means the Tushita *devas*.

[327] Shuchi and Shukra are respectively Jyeshtha and Ashadha. Shushmins are the radiant ones.

[328] Respectively Shravana and Bhadrapada.

[329] Respectively Ashvina and Kartika.

as Svadhavats; Saha and Sahasya[330] are mentioned as Ghoras; and Tapa and Tapasya,[331] the two months of Shishira, are said to be the Manyumats. The units of time, known as months, are established in the six seasons. For the sentient and the non-sentient, these are spoken of as the seasons. The seasons should be known as the proud sons of Brahma. It is held that months, fortnights and seasons occupy these positions. As the positions change, it should be known that those who take pride in these positions also change. In due order, the abodes and those who take pride in these abodes are said to be days, nights, months, seasons, *ayana*s and years. According to the time, these are the ones who are established in these abodes. These are the natures of their own selves. I will describe them. Listen. The units of time are *tithi, parva, sandhya, paksha,* regarded as the same as *arddha-masa, nimesha, kala, kashtha, muhurta, divasa* and *kshaya.*[332] Two *arddha-masa*s make up one *masa*, while two *masa*s constitute one *ritu*. There are three *ritu*s in one *ayana*. There are two *ayana*s—*uttarayana* and *dakshinayana*. Taken together, they amount to one *samvatsara*. These are the positions and those who occupy these positions. It should be known that there are six *ritu*s and that these are the sons of Nimi.[333] The five kinds of subjects[334] are said to exhibit the signs of *artava*s, the sons of the *ritu*s. Mobile and immobile objects are born through *artava*s. Therefore, *artava*s are described as fathers and *ritu*s as grandfathers. When they come together, Prajapati's *praja*s are born. Hence, *vatsara* is decribed as the great grandfather of *praja*s. Abodes, the nature of abodes and those who occupy those abodes have thus been described. Their

[330] Respectively Margashirsha and Pousha.
[331] Respectively Magha and Phalguna.
[332] *Tithi* is a lunar day, *paksha* is a fortnight, *arddha-masa* is half a month, *divasa* is day and *kshaya* (decay) is night. *Masa* means month, *ritu* means season. *Samvatsara* means year. *Vatsara* generally means year, but within that, there are variations, described later.
[333] Nimi was a famous king from the Ikshvaku lineage. As a result of a curse, he lost his physical body, but resides in all living beings as *nimesha*.
[334] Bipeds, quadrupeds, birds, reptiles and trees. *Artava* can be translated in different ways, seasonal change, menstrual cycle or a combination of seasons.

nature and essence are described in the same way. *Samvatsara* is described thus and is held to be Prajapati. The learned speak of Agni, *samvatsara*'s son, as *rita*.[335] Since *ritu*s originate from *rita*, they are said to be *ritu*s. This is how *masa*s and the six *ritu*s are known. There are said to be five *artava*s. Depending on the time, the five kinds of subjects, bipeds, quadruped, birds, reptiles and immobile entities, are described as resulting from *artava*s. Both *ritu* and *artava* are described as possessing the nature of fatherhood. Thus, *ritu*s and *artava*s are known as ancestors. This is because, depending on the time, all beings originate from them. Hence, we have heard that *artava*s are ancestors. Priding themselves on the time, they have remained in the *manvantara*s. They possess cause and effect and are established in their prosperity. As a result of being established in this way, they possess the pride of being associated with these positions.'

'The ancestors are of different kinds, Agnishvattas, Barhishads and so on. Through Svadha, the ancestors had two daughters who were famous in the worlds. They were Menaa and Dharani and those two held up this entire universe. Both of them spoke about the *brahman*. Both of them were *yogini*s.[336] For the sake of *dharma*, the ancestors bestowed their two auspicious daughters. Menaa is said to have been born through the mental powers of the ones known as Agnishvattas. Dharani is described as the daughter, born through mental powers, of the Barhishads. The ancestors known as Barhishads are remembered as those who drank *soma* juice. They bestowed the auspicious one, named Dharani, as a wife on Meru. The Agnishvattas bestowed Menaa as a wife on Himalaya. They are described as *upahuta*s.[337] Hear about the sons their daughters had. Through his wife Menaa, Himalaya had Mainaka as a son. She also had Ganga, the excellent river, as a daughter. She became the wife of the salty ocean. Mainaka's son was Krouncha and Krouncha-*dvipa* was named after him. Meru's wife, Dharani, gave

---

[335] The word *rita* means truth. But here, it can simply be taken in the sense of the luminous one.

[336] *Yogini* is the feminine of *yogi*.

[337] Those who performed *soma* sacrifices and drank *soma*.

birth to the son Mandara, full of divine herbs. She also had three
famous daughters. They are known as Vela and Niyati, with Ayati
as the third. Ayati became Dhatri's wife and Niyati is remembered
as the wife of Vidhatri. Their descendants, who existed during
Svayambhuva *manvantara*, have already been described. Through
the ocean, Vela gave birth to a single unblemished daughter.
This daughter of the ocean, named Savarna, became the wife of
the Prachinabarhis. Through Savarna, ten sons were born to the
Prachinabarhis. All of them were named the Prachetas. They were
accomplished in *dhanurveda*.[338] The lord Daksha, Svayambhu's
son, became their son. This happened because Tryambaka cursed
him during Chakshusha *manvantara*.'

Hearing this, Shamshapayani asked Suta, 'Consequent to
Bhava's[339] curse, how was Daksha born earlier, during Chakshusha
manvantara? We are asking you. Please tell us.' Thus invited and
addressed by Shamshapayani, Suta described Daksha's account and
the reason for Tryambaka's curse.

Suta continued, 'I have already said that Daksha had eight
daughters. He brought them to his own house and honoured them
in their father's house. Honoured in this way, all of them resided
in their father's house. The eldest among them was named Sati and
she was Tryambaka's wife. Since Daksha hated Rudra, he did not
invite this daughter. This was because Maheshvara never showed
any respect to Daksha. Established in his own energy, the son-in-
law disregarded the father-in-law. Sati got to know that all her
sisters had reached their father's house. Despite not being invited,
Sati went to her own father's house. The honour and respect the
father showed to Sati was inferior to what was shown to them. At
this, Devi was filled with rage and intolerance and spoke to her
father. "O lord! You showed me honour inferior to those shown
to those who are younger. O father! By slighting me in this way,
you have done something reprehensible. I am the eldest and the
best. Therefore, you should have honoured me." On being told this,
Daksha's eyes turned red. He replied, "These other daughters of

---

[338] Knowledge of fighting (with the bow).
[339] Shiva's.

mine deserve to be honoured. They are superior to you and better than you. O Sati! Compared to your husband, their husbands are also greatly respected by me. They are excellent ascetics, immersed in the *brahman*. They are great *yogis*, extremely devoted to *dharma*. All of them are superior in qualities to Tryambaka and more praiseworthy. My excellent sons-in-law are Vasishtha, Atri, Pulastya, Angiras, Pulaha, Kratu, Bhrigu and Marichi. Sharva always challenges me and dishonours me. Since Bhava is against me, I have not honoured you." With his intelligence deluded, Daksha spoke in this way. What he said brought about a curse on him and on the supreme *rishi*s. Enraged at what her father had said, Devi replied to him. "I am innocent in thoughts, words and deeds. Nevertheless, you have censured me. O father! Therefore, I am casting aside this body, which owes its origin to you." As a result of the disrespect, Sati was miserable and intolerant. Devi bowed down before Svayambhu and addressed him in these words. "Whether I am again born with a radiant body or not, whether I am not born, or whether I am born from a person full of *dharma*, following *dharma*, let me be the wife of the intelligent Tryambaka." Seated there, she fixed herself in *yoga*. She fixed her mind on meditation. The fire that rose from her *atman* was fanned by the wind that arose from her *atman*. The fire that arose from her limbs reduced her body to ashes. The wielder of the trident heard about Devi Sati's death. Bhagavan Shankara heard the nature of the conversation between the two of them and the lord became angry at Daksha and the *rishi*s. Rudra said, "Bhuloka is spoken of as the first among all the worlds. Following the instructions of Parameshthi, I always hold it up. All the radiant worlds exist because they are held up by this earth. Following his command, I have always held up this world. There are four *varna*s among *deva*s. However, they eat together. But I do not eat with them and am offered food separately. O Daksha! Because of me, the innocent Sati was dishonoured. All her other sisters, along with their husbands, were praised. Therefore, when Vaivasvata *manvantara* arrives, all these *maharshi*s, who have not been born from wombs, will be reborn when my second sacrifice takes place." Having told all of them this, he next cursed

Daksha. "In the *manvantara* of Chakshusha Manu, Brahma will offer oblations to Shukra. At the time, you will become a human king in the lineage of Chakshusha Manu. You will be the grandson of Prachinabarhi and the son of the Prachetas. Your name will be Daksha and you will be born as the son of Marisha, the daughter of the trees. O evil-minded one! When Vàivasvata *manvantara* arrives, you will be engaged in a task of *dharma* that is difficult to assail. Nonetheless, I will cause impediments in your path." Hearing this, Daksha also cursed Rudra. "Because of what I did, you caused harm to the *rishi*s. Therefore, when *dvija*s perform a sacrifice, they will not worship you, along with the Gods. O cruel one! In the course of a rite, you should not be offered oblations. Hence, if oblations are offered to you, they will touch water. Until the end of the *mahayuga*, they will have to leave heaven and reside here, in this world."[340] Therefore, he is not worshipped along with *deva*s, but is worshipped separately. Daksha was addressed in this way by the infinitely energetic Rudra. He gave up the body he obtained from Svayambhu and was born as a human. Knowing this, in all sacrifices, the householder Daksha did not worship the lord Ishvara, along with other *deva*s. When Vaivasvata *manvantara* arrived, Devi Sati was born as Uma, Menaa's daughter. Devi was born as the daughter of the king of the mountains. The one who was Devi Sati earlier, became Uma later. She is always Bhava's wife and Bhava never abandons her. Devi Aditi follows Kashyapa, Marichi's son. Shri always follows Narayana and Shachi always follows Maghavan.[341] Kirti always follows Vishnu, Usha follows Surya and Arundhati follows Vasishtha. These Goddesses never leave their husbands. As the *kalpa*s proceed, they return and are born along with them.[342] In this way, in Chakshusha *manvantara*, Daksha was born as the son of the Prachetas. He was thus born a second time as a king, the son of Marisha and the ten Prachetas. This happened as a consequence of the curse. This is what we

---

[340] If they offer oblations to Rudra, who should not be worshipped. Having done this, they must touch water to purify themselves.

[341] Indra. Indra's wife is Shachi.

[342] In that way, Sati does the same with Shiva.

have heard. Earlier, in the first *treta yuga* of Vaivasvata Manu, the seven *maharshi*s, Bhrigu and the others, were also born. A great sacrifice was held for *deva* Varuna and they obtained their bodies from him. In this way, there was enmity between Prajapati Daksha and the intelligent Tryambaka and this continued to follow them. Therefore, one must never allow enmity to perpetuate. Despite being born again, a creature does not let go of the auspicious and the inauspicious and the fame that occurred in a former birth. But a learned person should not act in this way. This is an account of what Daksha did earlier and what transpired. It is an account that cleanses sins. Earlier, you asked me to tell you about this. This was described to you in connection with the lineage of the ancestors.'

'After speaking about the lineage of ancestors in the due order, I will next speak about that of *deva*s. This happened at the beginning of *treta yuga*, in the former Svayambhuva *manvantara*. Earlier, *deva*s were known as Yamas and they were the sons of Yajna. They were the famous sons of Brahma. Since they were born from Aja, they were the Ajitas.[343] Born through the mental powers of Svayambhu, they were named the Shaktas. The categories of *deva*s are said to have been three.[344] In Svayambhu's creation, there were thirty-three who chanted the *chhanda*s. The twelve Yamas are described as the two *deva*s Yadu and Yayati, Vivadha, Trasata, Mati, Vibhasa, Kratu, Prayati, Vishruta, Dyuti, Vayavya and Samyama. The Ajitas were Asama, Ugradrishti, Sunaya, Shuchishrava, Kevala, Vishvarupa, Sudaksha, Madhupa, Turiya, Indrayuk, Yukta and Ugra. The twelve Shaktas[345] are described as Janima, Vishvadeva, Javishtha, Mitavan, Jara, Vibhu, Vibhava, Richika, Durdiha, Shruti, Grinana and Brihat. In the past Svayambhuva *manvantara*, these were the ones who drank *soma*. These categories were radiant, valiant and extremely strong. Their first Indra was the lord Vishvabhuk. At that time, the *asura*s were their descendants and relatives. Along with *deva*s and ancestors, *suparna*s, *yaksha*s, *gandharva*s, *pishacha*s,

[343] Aja means Brahma. Ajitas means the unvanquished ones.
[344] Yamas, Ajitas and Shaktas. These are categories. Within each category, there were several.
[345] Here, the text says Shukras.

*uraga*s and *rakshasa*s constituted the eight categories that belonged
to the *deva* species. In the past Svayambhuva *manvantara*, there
were thousands of their offspring. They possessed power and
beauty, long lifespans and strength. Since they are not relevant to
the present context, it is not necessary to speak about them in detail.
That creation by Svayambhuva should be understood in the present
context. In *praja*s, *deva*s, *rishi*s and ancestors, the past can be seen in
the present Vaivasvata *manvantara*. In Svayambhuva *manvantara*,
the seven *rishi*s were Bhrigu, Angiras, Marichi, Pulastya, Pulaha,
Kratu, Atri and Vasishtha.[346] Svayambhuva Manu's ten extremely
energetic sons were Agnidhra, Agnibahu, Medha, Medhatithi,
Vasu, Jyotishman, Dyutiman, Havya, Savana and Sattra. They
were greatly spirited and were as fleet as the wind. They were the
kings in that first *manvantara*. Along with them, there were *asura*s,
excellent *gandharva*s, *yaksha*s, *uraga*s, *rakshasa*s, *pishacha*s,
humans, *suparna*s and large numbers of *apsara*s. Even if one speaks
for one hundred years, one is incapable of describing them in the
proper order. There were many names. How can there be a limit to
the numbers in their lineages? These are described as the *praja*s who
existed in Svayambhuva *manvantara*. Because of the great passage
of time, through the progressive order of *ayana*s, years and *yuga*s,
this belongs to the past.'

The *rishi*s asked, 'Who is Bhagavan Kala, who takes away all
beings? What is his origin? What is his nature? What kind of *atman*
does he possess? What is his eye? What are described as his limbs
and body? What is his name? What is his *atman*? Please tell us the
true nature of all this.'

Suta answered, 'Hear about the nature of Kala. After hearing,
retain this. Surya is his source. *Nimesha* is his beginning. His eyes
are said to be the units of measurement. Night and day are his form
and the *nimesha*s are his limbs. His essence is *samvatsara*. His name
is Kalatmaka.[347] For the past, the present and the future, Kalatmaka

---

[346] The addition of Bhrigu gives us eight names, not seven. Usually, the
list of *saptarshi*s in Svayambhuva *manvantara* has the other seven names,
without Bhrigu.

[347] One who possesses *kalaa*s or digits.

is Prajapati. Understand this. Depending on the state of time, Kala is divided into five components—day, *arddha-masa*, *ritu*, *ayana* and *samvatsara*. Kala, described as *yuga*, is divided according to five measures—the first is *samvatsara*; the second is *parivatsara*; the third is *idvatsara*; the fourth is *anuvatsara*; and the fifth is *vatsara*. I will describe their nature. Understand. The fire that is sacred to Kratu is held to be *samvatsara*. Kala in the form of the fire of Surya, Aditi's son, is *parivatsara*. Soma, which bears the essence of water, has *shuklapaksha* and *krishnapaksha* movements in the sky. The Puranas have determined this movement to be *idvatsara*. There is the one who purifies the worlds in his forty-nine bodies. The wind that blows favourably in the worlds is *anuvatsara*. The fierce Rudra was born from Brahma's *ahamkara*. *Vatsara* is known to be reckoned according to Rudra Nilalohita.[348] I will describe the essential nature. Listen. Through the union of his limbs and sub-limbs, Kalatmaka is the great-grandfather. He is the origin of the *Rig Veda*, *Sama Veda* and *Yajur Veda* and the lord and master of the five. He is Agni, Yama, Kala, Sambhuti and Prajapati. As the origin of Surya, the learned speak of him as *samvatsara*. He is the origin of the divisions of time—months, seasons, *ayanas*, planets, *nakshatras*, cold, heat, rain, lifespans and *karma*. Bhaskara[349] is the origin of sub-divisions like days. He possesses these transformations and is pleased in his *atman*. He is the Prajapati who is Brahma's son. He is one, but he is not one. He is day, month, season and the grandfather. He is Aditya,

[348] According to astronomical traditions, of the five types of years, *samvatsara* is sacred to Agni, *parivatsara* is sacred to Surya, *idavatsara* is sacred to Chandra, *anuvatsara* is sacred to Prajapati and *vatsara* is sacred to Rudra. The forty-nine bodies is a reference to the forty-nine Maruts. The standard distinction is the following. *Samvatsara* is the solar year, *anuvatsara* is the lunar year, *parivatsara* seems to have been calculated on the basis of Jupiter's orbit and *vatsara* was calculated on the basis of the *nakshatras*. Since *idavatsara* occurred once every five years, it probably had an intercalary month. But the text suggests the solar year as *parivatsara* and the lunar year as *idvatsara*. Perhaps the best way to understand the text is to take it as a five-year cycle, with *samvatsara* as the first and *vatsara* as the fifth.

[349] Surya, the sun.

Savitar, Bhanu and Jivana[350] and is honoured by Brahma. For beings, Bhaskara is the cause behind origin and dissolution. The one who is proud of Tara should be known as the second, *parivatsara*.[351] Soma is the lord of all herbs and is the great-grandfather. He provides life to all beings and is the lord who ensures *yoga* and *kshema*.[352] Through his rays, he always glances at the universe and illuminates it. The one who causes the night is the origin of *tithis*, conjunctions of *parvas*, *purnima* and the day when the moon is invisible. With *amrita* in his *atman*, he is Prajapati. Therefore, among the ancestors, Soma is remembered as *idvatsara*. Among all living beings in the world, Vayu urges every kind of enterprise and *karma* through the five—*prana*, *apana*, *samana*, *vyana* and *udana*. He ensures the five senses, the mind, intelligence, memory and strength. He ensures that the cause of action and action function simultaneously, at the same time. Through his flows that come and go, he is in all *atmans* and is the lord of everyone. He exists and undertakes good turns through his forty-nine bodies. For all beings, he is the ordainer. Prabhanjana[353] is the one who always ensures what is beneficial. He is the origin of fire, water, earth, space, the sun and the moon. He is the Prajapati who is in the *atmans* of everything. He is the great grandfather who causes night and day. Vayu is *anuvatsara*. These four are Prajapatis and were born from the flanks. They are ancestors of all the worlds and are described as existing within all *atmans*. When Brahma meditated, Rudra originated from his face. One reads about him as *rishi*, *brahmana*, Mahadeva, the *atman* of all beings, the great grandfather, the lord of all beings and Pranava.[354] When his *atman* enters beings, the limbs and sub-limbs originate. Rudra shows favours, but also causes intoxication. He is spoken of as *vatsara*. Rudra is the sun, the moon, fire and wind. He is Kalatmaka, proud of his position in a *yuga*. The lord is always the cause of destruction. In his own energy, Bhagavan Rudra entered

[350] The one who bestows life.
[351] Brihaspati is Tara's husband. Hence, this does suggest a calculation based on Jupiter's orbit.
[352] *Yoga* is the acquisition of what is not possessed and *kshema* is the protection of what is possessed.
[353] Vayu.
[354] AUM/OUM.

this universe. He is the refuge, and his bodies and names provide the contact. Thus, through his energy, he shows favours to the worlds. He possesses the status of a *deva*, an ancestor, Kala and everything else. Hence, those who know this always worship Rudra. Bhagavan is the lord. As the lord of all *prajas*, he is Prajapati. He is the one who conceives all beings. Nilalohita is in all *atmans*. Again and again, Rudra revives herbs that decay. He is Prajapati, properly worshipped by all the *devas* who desire fruits. Using three *kapalas*, Bhagavan Tryambaka is worshipped when herbs decay. That is the reason he is known as Tryambaka. The three metres, *gayatri*, *trishtubh* and *jagati*, are known by the name of Tryambaka. The origin of trees is lovingly worshipped. The *purodasha* is described as the three *kapalas* and is worshipped using the means of the three metres. The three individual energies come together as one when they are uttered together. The *purodasha* is Tryambaka and he is spoken of as Tryambaka. The learned say that a *yuga* thus consists of five types of years. *Dvijas* speak of these five components. *Samvatsara*, which is one, is known to consist of the six *ritus*, described as Madhu and the others. The five *artavas* are the sons of the *ritus*. Creation has thus been described briefly. Kala has many kinds of measurements. It is unattached. But like the great force of a river, it rushes forward, taking away living beings. It is impossible to enumerate the dimensions of offspring. The number of sons and grandsons is many and infinite. Such are the lineages of lords of *prajas*. They were great and auspicious in deeds. If one chants their auspicious deeds, one obtains great success.'

Chapter 14-1(14) (Description of Priyavrata's lineage)

Suta said, 'In all the past and future *manvantaras*, those proud ones are born, similar in name and form. In that *manvantara*, *devas*, who were the lords, were of eight types. All the *rishis* and Manus were similar in purpose. The creation of *maharshis* has already been narrated. In the due order, I will now describe in detail

Svayambhuva Manu's lineage. Understand. Svayambhuva Manu
had ten grandsons who were similar to him. They inhabited the seven
*dvipa*s and each *varsha* on earth, the habitations, oceans and mines.
This occurred in the past Svayambhuva *manvantara*, in the first
treta yuga. Priyavrata's sons were the grandsons of Svayambhuva
Manu. They possessed offspring, spirit and austerities and populated
these. Kamya was the immensely fortunate daughter of Kardama
Prajapati. She is the one who gave birth to Priyavrata's valiant
sons. In addition to ten sons, she had two auspicious daughters,
Samrat and Kukshi. Their ten brothers were brave and similar to
Prajapati. They were Agnidhra, Agnibahu, Medha, Medhatithi,
Vasu, Jyotishman, Dyutiman, Havya, Savana and Sattra. Following
dharma, Priyavrata instated seven of them as kings in seven *dvipa*s.
Hear about the extremities of these *dvipa*s. The extremely strong
Agnidhra was made the lord of Jambu-*dvipa*. Medhatithi was made
the lord of Plaksha-*dvipa*. Vapushman[355] was instated as the king
of Shalmala-*dvipa*. The lord made Jyotishman the king of Kusha-
dvipa. He instated Dyutiman as the king of Krouncha-*dvipa*.
Priyavrata made Havya the lord of Shaka-*dvipa*. The lord made
Savana the lord of Pushkara-*dvipa*. In Pushkara-*dvipa*, Savana had
Mahavita and Dhataki as sons and these two were excellent sons.
In accordance with the name of that great-souled one, a *varsha* is
named Mahavita. The region known as Dhataki is said to have
been named after Dhataki. Havya, the lord of Shaka-*dvipa*, had
seven sons who ruled over that part. They were Jalada, Kumara,
Sukumara, Manivaka, Kusumottara, Modaka and Mahadruma as
the seventh.[356] After Jalada, the first *varsha* of Shaka-*dvipa* is said
to be Jalada and after Kumara, the second is described as Koumara.
After Sukumara, the third is named Sukumara. After Manivaka, the
fourth is named Maniva. The fifth *varsha*, Kusumottara, is named
after Kusumottara. After Modaka, the sixth *varsha* is described as
Modaka. After Mahadruma, the seventh is named Mahadruma.
In this way, the seven *varsha*s were named after them. Dyutiman,

---

[355] This is the same as Vasu.
[356] The text says Mahadruga. Since the name is given as Mahadruma
later, we have corrected the typo.

the lord of Krouncha-*dvipa*, had seven sons. They were Kushala, Manonuga, Ushna, Pavana, Andhakaraka, Muni and Dundubhi. These were the sons of Dyutiman. The auspicious sub-regions of Krouncha-*dvipa* were named after their names. The region known as Koushala became famous after the name of Kushala. The region of Manonuga is described after the name of Manonuga. The region of Ushna is named after Ushna and that of Pavana is named after Pavana. The region of Andhakara is described to have been named after Andhakaraka. The region of Mouni is named after Mouni and that of Dundubhi is said to have been named after Dundubhi. These were the seven radiant dominions of Krouncha-*dvipa*. Jyotishman, the lord of Kusha-*dvipa*, had seven extremely energetic sons. They were Udbhijja, Venuman, Vairatha, Lavana, Dhriti, Prabhakara as the sixth and Kapila is said to have been the seventh. The first *varsha* is named Udhbhijja. The second is named Venumandala. The third is named Vairathakara and the fourth is described as Lavana. The fifth *varsha* is named Dhritimat and the sixth *varsha* is named Prabhakara. After the name of Kapila, the seventh is said to have been named Kapila. In this way, the regions of Kusha-*dvipa* were named after their names. Vapushman had seven sons who became lords of Shalmala-*dvipa*. These regions were ornamented by subjects who followed the conduct of the *ashrama*s. They were Shveta, Harita, Jimuta, Rohita, Vaidyuta, Manasa and Suprabha as the seventh. The region of Shveta was named after Shveta and that of Suharita after Harita. Jimuta was named after Jimuta and Rohita after Rohita. Vaidyuta was named after Vaidyuta and Manasa after Manasa. Suprabha was named after Suprabha. In this way, these seven protected these regions. I will speak about Plaksha-*dvipa* now. I will speak about Jambu-*dvipa* later. Medhatithi had seven sons who were kings and lords of Plaksha-*dvipa*. The eldest was named Shantabhaya and the second is said to have been Shishira. Sukhodaya was the third and the fourth is said to have been Nanda. Shiva was the fifth among them and the sixth is said to have been Kshemaka. Dhruva was the seventh. These are known as the sons of Medhatithi. Seven *varsha*s were named after these seven names. Thus, there were regions of Shantabhaya, Shishira, Sukhodaya, Ananda, Shiva, Kshemaka and Dhruva. These seven regions, the *varsha*s, were similar to each other in dimensions. In the former Svayambhuva *manvantara*, they were inhabited by the sons of Medhatithi, who were the lords and masters of Plaksha-*dvipa*. They made the subjects of Plaksha-*dvipa* follow the conduct of the *varna*s and the *ashrama*s. Beginning with Plaksha-*dvipa* and ending with Shaka-*dvipa*, in these five, it should be known that *dharma* was segregated according to *varna*s and *ashrama*s.[357] In these five *dvipa*s, it is remembered that everyone generally obtained happiness, a long lifespan, beauty, strength and *dharma* eternally.'

'After Plaksha-*dvipa* has been described, hear about Jambu-*dvipa*. The extremely strong Agnidhra was the eldest son of Kamya and Priyavrata. He was instated as the lord and king of Jambu-*dvipa*. He had nine sons who were the equals of Prajapati. The eldest was known as Nabhi and Kimpurusha was younger to him. Harivarsha was the third and the fourth was Ilavrita. The fifth son was Ramya and the sixth is said to have been Hiranvan. Kuru was the seventh among them and Bhadrashva is said to have been the eighth. The ninth was Ketumala. Hear about their dominions. His father bestowed the southern *varsha*, known as Hima, on Nabhi. He gave Kimpurusha the *varsha* of Hemakuta. The *varsha* known as Naishadha was given to Harivarsha. Ilavrita was given the middle region of Sumeru. His father gave Ramya the *varsha* known as Nila. The father gave Hiranvan the region of Shveta, to the north. He gave Kuru the *varsha* that was to the north of Shringavan. He bestowed the *varsha* of Malyavan on Bhadrashva. The *varsha* of Gandhamadana was given to Ketumala. Thus, I have spoken about the division into nine *varsha*s. Agnidhra instated his sons in these *varsha*s in the due order. After this, with *dharma* in his soul, he engaged in austerities. In this way, the seven *dvipa*s were populated by Priyavrata's seven sons, grandsons of Svayambhuva Manu. When dissolution takes place repeatedly, these *varsha*s and the seven *dvipa*s are populated again and again by seven kings. Across *kalpa*s, this is the natural way in which *dvipa*s get inhabited. The following has been heard about the eight *varsha*s, Kimpurusha

---

[357] Jambu-*dvipa* comes later, but this leaves out Pushkara-*dvipa*.

and the others. *Siddhi* is naturally obtained there, and happiness is generally obtained without striving for it. There is no calamity there. Nor is there fear from old age or death. There is no *dharma* or *adharma* there. There is no one who is superior, middling or inferior. In none of those eight regions, is there anything like a *yuga*.'

'I will tell you about Nabhi's creation, in the region known as Hima. Listen. Through Merudevi, Nabhi had an extremely radiant son. He was Rishabha, supreme among kings. He was the forefather of all *kshatriyas*. Rishabha's son was the brave Bharata, the eldest among one hundred sons. Rishabha instated this son and embarked on the great journey.[358] He bestowed that southern *varsha*, known as Hima, on Bharata. Therefore, the learned know that this region is named Bharatavarsha. Bharata's learned son was named Sumati and he was devoted to *dharma*. Bharata instated him in that kingdom. After instating his son in the kingdom, the king entered the forest. Sumati's son, Tejas, was lord of subjects and conquered the enemies. The son of Tejas is said to have been the learned Indradyumna. Indradyumna's son, Parameshthi, was born after his death. Parameshthi's son was Pratihara and the lineage came to be known after his name. The intelligent and famous Pratiharti was born in this lineage. Pratiharti's son was Unneta and Unneta's son was Bhuma. Bhuma had a son named Udgitha and Udgitha's son was Prastavi. Prastavi's son was Vibhu and Vibhu's son was Prithu. Prithu's son was Nakta and Nakta's son was Gaya. Gaya's son was Nara and Nara's son was Virat. Virat's son was Mahavirya and Mahavirya's son was Dhiman. Dhiman's son was Mahan and Mahan's son was Bhouvana. Bhouvana's son was Tvashta and Tvashta's son was Viraja. Viraja's son was Raja and Raja's son was Shatajit. Shatajit had one hundred sons and all of them were kings. Vishvajyoti was foremost among them, and they ensured the prosperity of the subjects. They marked out Bharatavarsha, with its seven divisions. In earlier times, those born in this lineage, the Bharatis, enjoyed this land. There are seventy-one sets of *mahayugas*, consisting of *krita*, *treta* and the others. In

---

[358] Leading to renunciation and death.

the former Svayambhuva *manvantara* and in those that followed, there have been such past *mahayugas*, along with hundreds and thousands of kings. In this way, Svayambhuva's creation filled up the world with *rishi*s, *deva*s, ancestors, *gandharva*s, *rakshasa*s, *bhuta*s, *pishacha*s, humans, animals and birds. This is spoken of as their creation and the circulation of *mahayuga*s occurs alongside.'

Chapter 15-1(15) (Dimensions of the earth)

Suta said, 'In this way, Shamshapayani heard about the settlement of subjects. Controlling himself, he asked Suta about the dimensions of the earth. "How many *dvipa*s and oceans are there? How many mountains are there said to be? How many *varsha*s are there? How many rivers are there said to be? What are the dimensions of the great elements and the Lokaloka mountains? What is the nature of the transit and movement of the sun and the moon? Please describe all this to us in detail and accurately."'

Suta answered, 'I will tell you about the dimensions of the earth, the number of oceans and the details of *dvipa*s. There are thousands of sub-divisions within the seven *dvipa*s. I am incapable of describing them in the due order since the world is always full of these. I will speak in detail about the seven *dvipa*s, along with the sun, the moon and the planets. Humans speak about their dimensions and debate them. But they are actually incapable of being thought about and nothing is achieved through debates. Anything that is beyond Prakriti is said to be unthinkable. I will speak accurately about the nine *varsha*s of Jambu-*dvipa*. In terms of *yojana*s, understand the expanse and circumference. All around, its expanse is more than one hundred thousand *yojana*s. It is full of many countries and diverse auspicious cities. It is populated by *siddha*s and *charana*s. It is ornamented with beautiful mountains. The mountains are bound with every kind of mineral, originating from clumps of rocks. In every direction, there are rivers that flow from the mountains. Jambu-*dvipa* is large and beautiful. In every direction, there are large circles. It is surrounded by nine worlds and each of these has beings that have been created. Jambu-*dvipa* is surrounded, all around, by the salty ocean and its dimensions are the same as those of Jambu-*dvipa*. Starting from the east, there are six *varsha-parvata*s, with excellent ridges.[359] In both directions, they are submerged in the eastern and western ocean. Himalaya is generally covered with ice and Hemakuta is covered with gold. The great mountain of Nishadha is pleasant in all the seasons. Meru is said to be the best of the lot. It is golden in complexion, but also possesses four hues. The summit extends for thirty-two thousand *yojana*s. It is circular in shape and lofty on four sides. Possessing Prajapati's qualities, it has many hues along its sides. It arose from the umbilical cord of Brahma, whose birth is not manifest. On the east, it is white in complexion, reflecting the nature of being a *brahmana*. On the northern side, it is naturally red in complexion. Because of many reasons and deeper meanings, this reflects Meru's nature of being a *kshatriya*. The south is yellow in complexion and is said to reflect the nature of being a *vaishya*. Towards the west, it is marked like the wing of a black bee,[360] signifying its nature of being a *shudra*. These are described as the hues. It is said to be naturally circular and the dimensions and hues have been described. Nila is full of *vaidurya*,[361] while Shveta is white and full of gold. Shringavan has the complexion of a peacock's feathers and is full of gold. These are the kings among mountains, populated by *siddha*s and *charana*s. The distance between them is said to be nine thousand *yojana*s. In the midst of the great Meru, is the *varsha* named Ilavrita. In every direction, it extends for nine thousand *yojana*s. Like a fire without smoke, the great Meru is right in the middle. The southern part of Meru is like half of an altar and the other half is towards the north. Each of the six *varsha-parvata*s that exist in the *varsha*s is two thousand *yojana*s in length and height. Their expanse is described in accordance with that of Jambu-*dvipa*. The two mountains, Nila

---

[359] *Varsha-parvata*s, or *varshachala*s, are mountains that form boundaries between the *varsha*s.

[360] We have interpreted the word *bhringpatra* in this way, meaning, on this side, Meru is black/dark.

[361] Lapis lazuli or cat's eye.

and Nishadha, are each one hundred thousand *yojana*s long. The others, Shveta, Hemakuta, Himalaya and Shringavan, are shorter. The first two are ninety thousand *yojana*s long and the last two are eighty thousand *yojana*s long. Countries exist between them and there are seven *varsha*s.[362] They are surrounded by mountains with sudden precipices, making it difficult to cross them. Rivers divide the *varsha*s and it is difficult to travel from one *varsha* to another. Living beings reside there and they belong to every kind of species. This Haimavata *varsha* is famous by the name of Bharatavarsha. Beyond Himalaya, the *varsha* is known by the name of Kimpurusha *varsha*.[363] Beyond Hemakuta, the region is known as Hari *varsha*.[364] Meru and Ilavrita *varsha* are beyond Nishadha and Hari *varsha*.[365] Beyond Ilavrita is Nila and beyond that is the *varsha* known by the name of Ramyaka.[366] Shveta is beyond Ramyaka and beyond that is the *varsha* known by the name of Hiranmaya.[367] Shringavan is beyond Hiranmaya and beyond that is the *varsha* known as Kuru.[368] The two *varsha*s to the extreme north and south should be known to be stretched out like a bow. There are four that are stretched out straight. Ilavrita *varsha* is in the centre. The region that is below Nishadha is described as the southern half of the sacrificial altar. The region that is above Nila is described as the northern half of the sacrificial altar. There are three *varsha*s in the southern half of the sacrificial altar and three *varsha*s in the northern half of the

---

[362] Geographical descriptions aren't uniform across Puranas. Usually, Jambu-*dvipa* is stated to possess nine *varsha*s, not seven. The two missing from the list given here are Ketumala *varsha* and Bhadrashva *varsha*. But as we shall see, these are to the west and the east, not in the linear line.

[363] We are moving northwards and Himalaya separates Bharatavarsha from Kimpurusha *varsha*. In an obvious typo, the text says Hemakuta and we have corrected this to Himalaya.

[364] Hemakuta separates Kimpurusha *varsha* from Hari *varsha*.

[365] Nishadha separates Hari *varsha* from Ilavrita *varsha* and Mount Meru is in the centre of Ilavrita *varsha*.

[366] Nila separates Ilavrita *varsha* from Ramyaka *varsha*.

[367] Shveta separates Ramyaka *varsha* from Hiranmaya *varsha*.

[368] Shringavan separates Hiranmaya *varsha* from Kuru *varsha*. Kuru *varsha* is also known as Uttara Kuru.

sacrificial altar. It should be known that Meru is in the centre, in the middle of Ilavrita *varsha*, which is to the south of Nila and to the north of Nishadha.'

'From the north to the south, there is a large mountain that extends from Nila to Nishadha. This is named Malyavan and it has a width of one thousand *yojana*s. Its length is said to be thirty-four thousand *yojana*s. Mount Gandhamadana is said to be located to its west and its length and width are said to be the same as those of Malyavan. The golden mountain of Meru is located between two concentric circles. It is golden and also possesses four hues. It is lofty and has four sides. Sumeru is lustrous and is established like a radiant king. Its complexion is like that of the rising sun. It is like a fire without smoke. It rises for eighty-four thousand *yojana*s and penetrates the ground below for sixteen thousand *yojana*s. Its radius is also sixteen thousand *yojana*s. The summit is like a shallow dish and the diameter is thirty-two thousand *yojana*s. All around, the circumference is three times the diameter.[369] The circumference is always three times the diameter. Since the circumference is always three times the diameter, it is also described as forty-eight thousand *yojana*s, or sixty-four thousand *yojana*s along the four sides.[370] This mountain is extremely divine and is full of celestial herbs. Its beauty is auspicious and golden, and it is surrounded by all the worlds. All the large number of *deva*s, *gandharva*s, *uraga*s and *rakshasa*s, as well as large numbers of auspicious *apsara*s, can be seen on that king of mountains. That mountain is surrounded by the worlds,

[369] The approximate deduced value of Pi is 3.

[370] To make sense, we have resorted to some subjectivity in translating. Meru is always described to be in the shape of an inverted cone. With a diameter of 32,000 *yojana*s, the circumference will be 96,000 *yojana*s at the top and 48,000 *yojana*s in the middle. The radius is 16,000 *yojana*s at the top. At the top, the circle seems to be inscribed inside a large square, with four smaller sub-squares. The edge of the large square is 32,000 *yojana*s and the edges of each of the smaller squares are 16,000 *yojana*s. Each of the smaller squares thus has a perimeter of 64,000 *yojana*s. This is one possible way of understanding what is being described. This is about the top. Three-dimensionally, an inverted cone is inside an inverted symmetrical tetrahedron.

full of created beings. Four countries exist along the four sides.
These are Bhadrashva, Bharata, Ketumala to the west and Kuru
to the north.[371] These are populated by those who have performed
auspicious deeds. Along the side of Gandhamadana, there is the
region of Gandika.[372] It is always delightful and auspicious and is
pleasant in all the seasons. From the east to the west, it extends
for thirty-two thousand *yojana*s. The length is thirty-four thousand
*yojana*s. Those who are auspicious in their deeds reside in Ketumala.
All the men there are dark. They are immensely strong and extremely
spirited. All the women there are beautiful to behold and possess
complexions that are like the petals of lotuses. There is a divine and
large jackfruit tree there, possessing six kinds of taste.[373] Brahma's
son, Ishvara, is there. He possesses the speed of thought and goes
where he wills. He drinks the juice of the fruit and lives for ten
thousand years. Towards the east, along the side of Malyavan, there
is another region of Gandika. The length and breadth of this is the
same as that of the other Gandika. Those who dwell in Bhadrashva
are known to be always delighted in their minds. The forest of
Bhadrashala is there and it has a large Kalamra tree.[374] The men there
are fair. They are strong and full of great enterprise. The women
there are handsome and beautiful to behold, with complexions like
the petals of water lilies. Their radiance is like that of the moon.
Their complexions resemble that of the moon. Their faces are like
full moons. The limbs of the women there are as cool to the touch as
the moon. They possess the fragrance of lotuses. Not suffering from
any disease, the lifespan is ten thousand years. All of them drink the
juice of Kalamra and have perpetual youth. To the south of Shveta
and to the north of Nila, is the *varsha* named Ramanaka.[375] The
sparkling men who are born there are fond of sexual intercourse.
They do not suffer from old age, or physical and mental ailments.
All of them are fair, are beautiful to behold and possess noble

---

[371] Bhadrashva is to the west and Bharatavarsha to the south.
[372] Suggesting this is a country.
[373] Sweet, sour, salty, pungent, bitter and astringent.
[374] Literally, Kalamra would mean black mango.
[375] The same as Ramyaka.

birth. There is an extremely large red *nyagrodha* tree[376] there. They subsist by drinking the juice of the fruit. Those excellent men are always happy. They are extremely fortunate and survive for eleven thousand and five hundred years. To the south of Shringavan and north of Shveta, there is the *varsha* named Hairanvata.[377] The river Hairanvati is there. Men who are born there are extremely strong and extremely energetic. They are great-spirited and brave *yaksha*s, wealthy and handsome to behold. They are greatly energetic, and the duration of their lifespan is eleven thousand five hundred years. There is a large *lakucha* tree[378] in that *varsha* and it possesses six kinds of tastes. They drink the juice of the fruit and survive, not suffering from disease. Mount Shringavan has three large and lofty peaks. One of them is full of jewels and another is full of gold. The third is covered with gems everywhere and is decorated with houses. To the north of Shringavan and south of the ocean, there is the sacred *varsha* of Kuru, populated by *siddha*s. There, the trees are always full of flowers and fruit, and the fruit exudes honey. The fruit yields garments and ornaments. Some trees are extremely beautiful and yield everything that is desired. They exude excellent honey, possessing fragrance, colour and taste. There are other beautiful trees there, named *kshirin*s.[379] They always exude milk that possesses the six tastes and is like *amrita*. Everywhere, the ground is covered with jewels and fine golden sand. The region provides happiness in all the seasons. It sparkles and is devoid of mud and dust. The auspicious men who are born there are those who have been dislodged from the world of *deva*s. They are noble in birth and fair. All of them possess perpetual youth. The women are like *apsara*s and give birth to twins. They drink milk from the *kshirini* trees, which is like *amrita*. The twins are born instantly and grow up together. They are similar in conduct and beauty and love

---

[376] The Indian fig tree.
[377] Named after the river, the same as Hiranmaya *varsha*.
[378] The breadfruit tree.
[379] Literally, trees that exude milk.

each other. Like *chakravaka* birds,[380] they are devoted to each other and follow each other's *dharma*. They do not suffer from disease or grief and enjoy constant happiness. They are immensely valiant and live for fourteen thousand and five hundred years, not approaching the wives of others.'

Chapter 16-1(16) (Description of Bharata)

Suta said, 'Such was the creation of the auspicious Bharatavarsha. Those who know about the supreme truth witnessed this. What will I describe to you next?'

The *rishi* answered, 'This is Bharatavarsha, where the fourteen Manus, Svayambhuva and the others, were born, in the course of the creation of *praja*s. O excellent one! We wish to hear about this again. Please tell us.'

Suta continued, 'Hearing this, Romaharshana replied.'

Romaharshana said, 'I will describe to you the *praja*s in Bharatavarsha. This is a wonderful region in the centre, where the fruits of auspicious and inauspicious deeds are enjoyed. This is to the north of the ocean and to the south of the Himalaya. This is the *varsha* named Bharata and the *praja*s of this region are Bharati. Manu is known as Bharata because he nurtured the *praja*s.[381] This etymological root explains why the region is described as Bharatavarsha. Here, at the end, one attains heaven, *moksha*, or the middle region.[382] Indeed, for mortals, there is no other region that has been determined to be *karmabhumi*. Hear about the nine separate divisions of Bharatavarsha. They

---

[380] *Chakravaka* is the Brahminy duck. The male and the female are believed to be devoted to each other.

[381] The word *bharana* means to maintain, nourish or support. The region is known as Bharata because Manu maintained the subjects. Traditionally, Bharatavarsha is so named after the name of King Bharata.

[382] Bharatavarsha is described as *karmabhumi*, the destination depends on one's *karma*. With superior *karma*, one goes to heaven. With inferior *karma*, one goes to hell. With middling *karma*, one is reborn again, on earth.

are separated by oceans, and it should be known that it is impossible to traverse from one to the other. They are Indradvipa, Kasheruman, Tamravarna, Gabhastiman, Nagadvipa, Soumya, Gandharva, Varuna and this ninth region, which is surrounded by the ocean.[383] From the origin of Ganga to Kumari,[384] from the north to the south, the length of this region is one thousand *yojana*s. If one calculates diagonally, the northern part measures nine thousand *yojana*s. In every direction, the outer extremities of the region are populated by *Mlecchas*.[385] Kiratas dwell along the eastern border and Yavanas are said to reside along the western border.[386] *Brahmanas*, *kshatriyas*, *vaishyas* and *shudras* reside in the region that is in the middle. They are established there, subsisting through engaging in sacrifices, use of weapons and trade.[387] Their conduct vis-a-vis each other is based on the pursuit of *dharma*, *artha* and *kama* and the *varna*s are engaged in their respective tasks. The *ashrama*s and the five categories[388] have been conceived in this way. Their human pursuits seek to achieve heaven and emancipation. This ninth region is said to extend diagonally. A person who conquers all of it is described as an emperor. Indeed, this world is spoken of as Samrat and the firmament is described as Virat. The other world is spoken of as Svarat.[389] I will speak about these in detail again.'

[383] This ninth region is the narrow definition of Bharatavarsha. The text has a broader definition. There is speculation in geographical identification. Subject to that, Indradvipa (Indradyumna) has been identified as the Andamans, Kasheruman as Malaya, Tamravarna as Srilanka, Gabhastiman as Java, Nagadvipa as the Nicobar Islands, Soumya as Sumatra, Gandharva as the region beyond the river Sindhu (Indus) and Varuna as Borneo.

[384] Kanyakumari.

[385] *Mleccha* can loosely be translated as barbarian, but means someone who does not speak Sanskrit.

[386] Kiratas are hunters, Yavanas are identified as Ionians (Greeks).

[387] Respectively for *brahmanas*, *kshatriyas* and *vaishyas*.

[388] Including those who are outside the fourfold *varna* system.

[389] Samrat means emperor, Virat means large and Svarat means someone who has conquered the world of heaven. Here, Bhuloka is being referred to as Samrat, Bhuvarloka as Virat and Svarloka as Svarat.

'There are seven famous *kula-parvata*s,[390] with excellent ridges. These are Mahendra, Malaya, Sahya, Shuktiman, Mount Riksha, Vindhya and Pariyatra.[391] These are the seven *kula-parvata*s. Near these, there are thousands of other mountains. Some of them are weighty but are not known. They have many wonderful summits. There are Mandara,[392] best among mountains, Vaihara,[393] Durdura,[394] Kolahala,[395] Surasa,[396] Mainaka,[397] Vaidyuta,[398] Vatandhama,[399] Nagagiri,[400] Pandura-parvata,[401] Tungaprastha,[402] Krishnagiri,[403] Mount Godhana,[404] Pushpagiri,[405] Ujjayanta,[406] Mount Raivataka,[407] Shriparvata,[408] Chitrakuta and Mount Kutashaila.[409] There are other mountains that are not known. They are shorter and not too many live on them.'

'There are different countries and divisions populated by Aryas[410] and Mlecchas. They drink the waters of the rivers. There

[390] A *kula-parvata* is the principal range of a *varsha*. Each *varsha* is said to have seven *kula-parvata*s.

[391] Mahendra is part of the Eastern Ghats, Malaya is the southern part of the Western Ghats, while Sahya is the northern part. Shutiman, Riksha, Vindhya and Pariyatra belong to central India and are all different parts of what is referred to as the Vindhya range today.

[392] This will now be identified with the one in Bhagalpur.

[393] One of the five hills in Rajagriha, also known as Vaibhara.

[394] Alternatively, Dardura. This has been identified as the Nilgiris and the Deogarh peak of the Vindhyas. But it might also be in the Mayurbhanj district.

[395] Speculatively, the Brahmayoni hill, near Gaya.

[396] Unidentified, but clearly towards the west.

[397] The Shivalik range.

[398] Near Kailasa and Lake Manasa, source of the river Sarayu.

[399] An unidentified mountain, in all probability, a typo.

[400] Near Ramgarh in Jharkhand.

[401] The pale mountain, south of Meru.

[402] Probably to the west of Nishadha.

[403] The Karakoram range.

[404] Probably Garatha in the Western Ghats.

[405] In Kodagu in Karnataka.

[406] Girnar in Gujarat.

[407] Also part of Girnar.

[408] Shrishaila in Andhra Pradesh.

[409] This cannot be easily identified.

[410] Those who speak Sanskrit.

are rivers that originate from the feet of Himalaya—Ganga, Sindhu, Sarasvati, Shatadru, Chandrabhaga, Yamuna, Sarayu, Iravati, Vitasta, Vipasha, Devika,[411] Kuhu,[412] Gomati, Dhutapapa,[413] Bahuda,[414] Drishadvati, Koushiki, Tridiva, Nishthivi, Gandaki and Chakshurlohita.[415] The rivers said to flow from Pariyatra are Vedasmriti,[416] Vedavati,[417] the Vritraghni,[418] Sindhu,[419] Varnasha,[420] Nandana,[421] Sadanira,[422] Mahanadi, Para,[423] Charmanvati,[424] Nupa, Vidisha,[425] Vetravati,[426] Kshipra and Avanti. The following rivers, with auspicious waters that sparkle like jewels, flow from Rikshavan—Shona, Mahanada,[427] Narmada, Surasa, Kriya, Mandakini, Dasharna,[428] Chitrakuta, Tamasa,[429] Pippalashyena,[430] Karamoda,[431] Pishachika, Chitrotpala, Banjula,[432] Vastuvahini,[433]

[411] Probably a tributary of Iravati (Ravi).

[412] This might be River Kabul.

[413] We have translated Dhutapapa as a separate river. Dhutapapa means something that cleanses sins and this might be an adjective for Gomati, not a distinct river. As a separate river, Dhutapapa is probably the river Sharda (Kali/Mahakali).

[414] Probably Ramaganga. The text says Budbuda, but it should clearly be Bahuda.

[415] Lohitya (Brahmaputra).

[416] Banas.

[417] Berach.

[418] Banganga in Rajasthan.

[419] Probably meaning Kali Sindh, not Indus.

[420] The western part of Banas.

[421] Perhaps Sabarmati.

[422] Speculatively identified with Gandak or Rapti.

[423] Identified as the river Parbati. The text says Pasha, but we have changed it to Para.

[424] Chambal.

[425] Betwa.

[426] Also part of Betwa.

[427] That is, Mahanadi.

[428] Dhasan.

[429] The river Tons.

[430] This might be the river Parsuni.

[431] This sounds like Karmanasha, but the geography would be wrong.

[432] Read as Jambula, this might be Jamner.

[433] Perhaps Baghain.

Saneruja,[434] Shuktimati,[435] Mankuti, Tridiva and Kratu. The
auspicious rivers, with sacred waters, that flow from the feet of the
Vindhyas are Tapi,[436] Payoshni,[437] Nirvindhya,[438] Sripa, the river
Nishadha,[439] the auspicious Veni, Vaitarani,[440] Kshipra,[441] Vala,
Kumudvati,[442] Toya,[443] Mahagouri,[444] Durga and Vanashila. Rivers
that flow in a southern direction emerge from the feet of Sahya—
Godavari, Bhimarathi,[445] Krishna, Venya, Banjula,[446] Tungabhadra,
Suprayoga,[447] Bahya[448] and Kaveri. Auspicious rivers, with cool
waters, flow from Malaya—Kritamala,[449] Tamraparni, Pushpaja[450]
and Utpalvati.[451] The following rivers are described as the daughters
of Mahendra—Trisama,[452] Rishikulya, Banjula, Tridiva,[453] Abala,
Langulini[454] and Vamshadhara. The rivers that flow from Shuktiman
are said to be Rishikulya, Kumari,[455] Mandaga,[456] Mandagamini,[457]

[434] Read as Sumeruja, this could refer to Sonar/Bearma, tributaries of
Ken.
[435] Ken.
[436] Tapti. The word Vindhya was then used in a wider geographical
sense.
[437] Identified with Purna, or part of Tapti.
[438] Speculatively identified as a tributary of Warda.
[439] Probably the Kali Sindh.
[440] Probably the one in Odisha.
[441] This is different from the Kshipra mentioned earlier.
[442] Speculatively, Suvarnarekha.
[443] That is, Karatoya.
[444] Probably Brahmani in Odisha.
[445] The river Bhima.
[446] Manjira.
[447] Vedavati.
[448] Varada.
[449] Vaigai.
[450] Pambar.
[451] Periyar.
[452] Probably three tributaries of Rishikulya, like Baghua, Dhanei and
Badanadi.
[453] Distinct from the earlier Tridiva.
[454] The river Nagavali/Langulya.
[455] Probably Suktel.
[456] River Mand.
[457] Probably meaning Mahanadi.

Kripa[458] and Palashini.[459] All these rivers, which flow towards the ocean, are like Sarasvati and Ganga. They are mothers of the universe and all of them are said to remove sins from the world. All of them possess hundreds and thousands of tributaries.'

'The countries that have developed along the banks of the rivers in the central region are generally described to be Kurus, Panchalas, Shalvas, Madreyas, Jangalas, Shurasenas, Bhadrakaras, Bodhas, Patachcharas, Matsyas, Kushalyas, Soushalyas, Kuntalas, Kashis, Koshalas, Godhas, Bhadras, Kalingas, Magadhas and Utkalas. River Godavari flows to the north of Sahya. Among all the regions on earth, this is the most pleasant. The city of Govardhana was constructed by Rama there.[460] There were divine trees and celestial herbs loved by Rama. To bring him pleasure, the sage Bharadvaja planted them there. Thus, the region around that excellent city became beautiful. Bahlikas, Vatadhanas, Abhiras, Kalatoyakas, Aparantas, Suhmas, Panchalas,[461] Charmamandalas, Gandharas, Yavanas, Sindhu-Souvira-Mandalas, Chinas, Tusharas, Pallavas,[462] Girigahvaras,[463] Shakas, Bhadras, Kulindas, Paradas, Vindhyachulikas, Abhishahas, Ulutas, Kekayas, Dashamalikas, lineages of *brahmanas*, *kshatriyas*, *vaishyas* and *shudras*, Kambojas, Daradas, Barbaras, Angalouhikas, Atris, Bharadvajas, Prasthalas, Dasherakas, Lamakas, Talashalas, Bhushikas and Ijikas—these are spoken of as the northern countries. Now hear about the countries to the east. Angas, Vangas, Cholabhadras, categories of Kiratas, Tomaras, Hamsabhangas, Kashmiras, Tanganas, Jhillikas, Ahukas, Hunadarvas, Andhravakas, Mudgarakas, Antargiris, Bahirgiris, Plavangus, Maladas, Malavartikas, Samantaras, Pravrisheyas, Bhargavas, Goparthivas, Pragjyotishas, Pundras, Videhas, Tamraliptakas, Mallas and Magadhagonardas—these are described

---

[458] Arpa.

[459] Jonk.

[460] Meaning, built by Balarama. This is identified as the village of Govardhana in Nashik district.

[461] This is repeated. There are other repetitions too.

[462] That is, Pahlavas.

[463] Those who dwelt in caves in mountains.

as the countries to the east. There are other countries and the residents of Dakshinapatha.[464] These are Pandyas, Keralas, Cholas, Kulyas, Setukas, Mushikas, Kshapanas, Vanavasikas,[465] Maharashtras, Mahishikas, all the Kalingas, Abhiras, Aishikas, Atavyas, Saravas, Pulindas, Vindhyamouliyas, Vaidarbhas, Dandakas, Pourikas, Moulikas, Ashmakas, Bhogavardhanas, Konkanas, Kantalas, Andhras, Kulindas, Angaras and Marishas—these are the countries to the south. Now hear about the western regions. Suryarakas, Kalivanas, Durgalas, Kuntalas, Pouleyas, Kiratas, Rupakas, Tapakas, Karitis, all the Karandharas, Nasikas, others who lived in the Narmada region, Kacchas, Samaheyas, Sarasvatas, Kacchipas, Surashtras, Anartas and Arbudas—these are the ones from the western region. Now hear about those who reside in the Vindhyas—Maladas, Karushas, Mekalas, Utkalas, the excellent Dasharnas, Bhojas, Kishkindhakas, Toshalas, Koshalas, Traipuras, Vaidishas, Tuhundas, Barbaras, Shatpuras, Naishadas, Anupas, Tundikeras, Vitihotras and Avantis. All these countries belong to those who reside on the slopes of the Vindhyas. I will now speak about countries that are on mountains—Nihiras, Hamsamargas, Kupathas, Tanganas, Shakas, Apapravaranas, Urnas, Darvas, Huhukas, Trigartas, Mandalas, Kiratas and Tamaras. The *rishis* have said that there are four *yuga*s in Bharatavarsha—*krita*, *treta yuga*, *dvapara* and *tishya*.[466] I will narrate their creation, in detail, later.'

Chapter 17-1(17) (Description of Kimpurusha and other *varshas*)

The *rishis* said, 'You have spoken about Bharata. Please tell us now, about the nature of Kimpurusha *varsha* and Hari *varsha*.'

---

[464] *Dakshinapatha* means the southern route, but is a term also applied to the southern region.

[465] Those who reside in the forest.

[466] *Tishya* is another name for *kali*.

Suta replied, 'O *brahmanas*! Listen attentively to what you wish
to hear about. There is a clump of *plaksha* trees in Kimpurusha
and it resembles the extremely great Nandana.[467] It is said that the
lifespan in Kimpurusha is ten thousand years. The men are golden
in complexion and the women are like *apsaras*. They are bereft of
disease and sorrow and are always pleased in their minds. Humans
who are born there possess complexions that are like molten gold.
In Kimpurusha *varsha*, there is a sacred and auspicious tree that
exudes honey. All those in Kimpurusha drink the excellent juice
from this. It is said that Hari *varsha* is beyond Kimpurusha. Humans
who are born there possess a great complexion that is like that of
silver. All of them have been dislodged from the world of *deva*s and
all of them are similar to *deva*s. All the men in Hari *varsha* drink the
auspicious juice of sugarcane. Not suffering from any disease, they
live in Hari *varsha* for eleven thousand years and all of them are
delighted in their minds. They do not suffer from old age, and they
do not die suddenly. I have spoken about the *varsha* in the middle,
named Ilavrita. The sun does not scorch there, and humans do not
decay. The illumination from the sun, the moon and the *nakshatra*s
is not shrouded. Humans who are born there have complexions
like lotuses. Their radiance is like that of lotuses and their eyes are
like lotuses. They possess the fragrance of lotuses. Their bodies do
not sweat and are fragrant. They are spirited and eat the fruit of
the *jambu* tree.[468] They enjoy themselves and enjoy the fruits of
their virtuous deeds. They have been dislodged from the world of
*deva*s and their splendid garments are made out of silver. Those
excellent men live for thirteen thousand years. That is the duration
of the lifespan in Ilavrita *varsha*, which extends all around Meru
for nine thousand *yojana*s. The length of the perimeter is thirty-six
thousand *yojana*s. It is in the shape of a square and is established
like a shallow vessel. Mount Gandhamadana is at a distance of nine
thousand *yojana*s from Meru to the west. From Nila to Nishadha,
from the north to the south, its length is thirty-four thousand

---

[467] *Plaksha* is the Indian fig tree. Nandana is Indra's divine pleasure
garden.

[468] The rose apple.

*yojana*s. From the surface of the earth, its elevation is forty thousand
*yojana*s. It penetrates one thousand *yojana*s into the ground and its
width is of the same magnitude. Mount Malyavan is to the east
and its dimensions have already been described.[469] Nila is to the
north and Nishadha is to the south.[470] With its own dimensions,
the great Meru is located between them. All these mountains are as
wide as the extent to which they are submerged in the ground. The
length of these mountains[471] is said to be one hundred thousand
*yojana*s. Like the ocean circles the earth, there are four mountains
that surround Meru on four sides.[472] Their lengths decline. Ilavrita
is in the form of a quadrilateral and is divided down the middle by
a river that is full of *jambu* juice, the river's complexion resembling
that of collyrium. To the south of Meru and to the north of
Nishadha, there is a great and eternal *jambu* tree, known by the
name of Sudarshana. It always bears flowers and fruit and *siddha*s
and *charana*s resort to it. Jambu-*dvipa* is so named after the name
of the tree. The height of this great-souled king among trees is one
thousand and one hundred *yojana*s. In every direction, it touches
the sky. *Rishi*s who know about the truth have enumerated that the
size of the fruit is eight hundred and sixty-one *aratni*s.[473] When they
fall on the ground, the fruits make a loud sound. The juice of the
jambu fruit flows in the form of a river. Circling Meru, it enters the
ground at the root of the *jambu* tree. Those in Ilavrita always drink
the *jambu* juice happily. Since they drink the juice of the *jambu*
fruit, they do not suffer from old age. They do not suffer from
hunger or exhaustion. They are attentive and do not suffer from
death. A gold known as *jambunada* results[474] and this is used to
make ornaments for *deva*s. It is produced in this radiant form and

---

[469] To the east of Meru. Malyavan's dimensions are the same as those
of Gandhamadana.

[470] The text states the wrong directions and we have corrected it.

[471] Nila and Nishadha.

[472] Mandara and Gandhamadana are two. The other two are usually
stated as Vipula and Suparshva. As one moves away from Meru, the lengths
of the mountains diminish.

[473] *Aratni* is the length of an elbow, that is, a cubit.

[474] From the river.

resembles *indragopa*.[475] The auspicious juice of fruits is exuded from all the trees and as this sparkling juice flows, the gold used for *deva* ornaments results. As a result of Ishvara's favours, urine, excrement and dead bodies are swallowed up by the earth in every direction and cannot be seen. It is said that all the *rakshasas*, *pishacha*s and *yaksha*s reside in the Himalayas. It is known that *gandharva*s and large numbers of *apsara*s dwell in Hemakuta. All the *naga*s, Shesha, Vasuki and Takshaka, live on Nishadha. The thirty-three groups of Gods have the right to perform sacrifices on the great Meru. Nila is full of *vaidurya* and *siddha*s and unblemished *brahmarshi*s live there. *Daitya*s and *danava*s are said to live on Mount Shveta. The ancestors move around on the excellent mountain of Shringavan. Different beings live and move around in the nine *varsha*s, these divisions having been certainly determined. Many kinds of growth and development are seen, human and divine. The numbers cannot be enumerated. Those who possess faith, believe.'

Chapter 18-1(18) (Description of Jambu-dvipa)

Suta said, 'In the centre of the slopes of the Himalayas, there is the mountain named Kailasa. Along with the *rakshasa*s, the prosperous Kubera reside there. The king and lord of Alaka[476] find pleasure there, with the *apsara*s as followers. From the feet of Kailasa, there originates a lake named Manda, full of water lilies and sacred, auspicious and cool waters. It resembles the ocean. The auspicious and divine river, Mandakini flows from there. There is a great forest along its banks. This is the divine forest of Nandana. Mount Kailasa is divine and possesses all the herbs. It is wonderful and is full of jewels and minerals. To the north-east of this powerful mountain, there is a mountain named Chandraprabha. It is extremely white and resembles a jewel. There is a great and divine lake near its

[475] A reddish insect, sometimes identified with a firefly, also known as *shakragopa*.
[476] Alaka or Alakapuri is Kubera's capital.

BRAHMANDA PURANA: VOLUME I

feet, named Svacchoda. The divine river, named Svacchodaa, flows
from there. Along its banks, there is the auspicious, great and divine
forest of Chaitraratha. Manibhadra resides on that mountain, along
with his followers. He is the ruthless general of the *yaksha*s and is
surrounded by *guhyaka*s. Passing through the centre of the earth's
circle, the sacred Mandakini and River Svacchodaa enter the large
ocean. Mount Kailasa has auspicious living beings and herbs. It is
divine and wonderful, covered with red arsenic. To its south-east,
there is the great mountain Suryaprabha, red in colour and with
a golden summit. There is a great and divine lake, named Lohita,
at its feet. The great and sacred river, Louhitya, flows from there.
There is the great forest of Devaranya along its banks and it is
devoid of sorrows. The self-controlled *yaksha*, Manidhara, resides
on that mountain. He is surrounded by amiable *guhyaka*s who are
extremely devoted to *dharma*. Along the southern flank of Kailasa,
there is a mountain that is full of herbs and cruel creatures. This
is Anjana, with three peaks, and it originated from Vritra's body.
Near that, there is the extremely great mountain of Vaidyuta, full
of every kind of mineral. The sacred lake of Manasa, frequented
by *siddha*s, is at is feet. The sacred Sarayu, famous in the world,
flows from there. There is a divine forest along its banks, and
it is famous under the name Vaibhraja. Praheti's self-controlled
son, Kubera's follower, resides there.[477] This is the infinitely
valiant *rakshasa*, Brahmapeta. He is surrounded by hundreds of
*yatudhana*s,[478] who roam around in the sky. Mount Kailasa is full
of herbs and auspicious beings. On its western side, there is Aruna,
the best among the mountains. It is auspicious and is full of gold
and minerals. This handsome mountain is loved by Bhava and
resembles a cloud. It is covered with sparkling cloud and heaps
of rocks. Mount Munjavan is extremely divine and great. It is
marked with gold and is difficult to cross. Through hundreds of

[477] Praheti was the father of *rakshasa*s and Heti was the father
of *yaksha*s.
[478] Demons.

golden peaks, it seems to etch on the sky. Girisha,[479] with eyes
that resemble smoke, resides on that mountain. The lake known as
Shailoda flows from its feet. The sacred river, named Shiloda, flows
from there. Between the rivers Chakshu and Sita, it enters the salty
ocean. There is a divine forest along its banks, famous as Surabhi.
To the left and north of Kailasa, there is a mountain named Goura.
It is best among mountains and is full of beings, herbs and yellow
orpiment. Next to that is the divine and extremely large mountain
Hiranyashringa, full of jewels.'

'There is the beautiful, auspicious and greatly divine lake at its
feet. It is named Bindusara. For the sake of Ganga, *rajarshi* King
Bhagiratha resided there for many years. "Immersed in the Ganga,
my ancestors will go to heaven."[480] Having decided this, he fixed
his mind on Shiva. The Goddess, with the three flows, was first
established there. Originating from the feet of Soma,[481] she divides
herself into seven flows. Golden sacrificial posts, studded with
gems, are strewn around there. Shakra and all the Gods performed
a sacrifice there and obtained success. In the night sky, the radiant
Milky Way is seen amidst the circle of *nakshatras*. That is the
Goddess with the three flows. The divine river flowed through
heaven and the firmament and descended on Bhava's head, where
she was held up by the *maya* of his *yoga*. She became angry because
of this and some drops fell on the ground. These drops formed a
lake, known as Bindusara.[482] In this way, when she was restrained
by Bhava, the Goddess smiled. She thought in her mind that she
would fling Shankara down. "I will penetrate and enter the nether
regions, bearing Shankara along with my flow." He understood the
cruel intentions of the Goddess. Therefore, he made up his mind to
make the Goddess disappear within his limbs. Understanding this,

[479] Girisha means lord of the mountains and is one of Shiva's names.
Here, it is possibly being used for one of the Rudras.
[480] King Bhagiratha brought down Ganga so that his ancestors (the
sons of Sagara) might be saved. Ganga has three flows—in heaven, on earth
and in the nether regions.
[481] Indicating a mountain named Soma.
[482] Literally, lake formed with drops (*bindu*) of water.

Shankara was enraged and concealed the river. As she descended
with force on the ground, he confined her within his head. At this
time, he saw the king in front of him. He was emaciated, reduced to
only veins. His senses were suffering from hunger.[483] "For the sake
of the river, this one has already satisfied me." He restrained his
rage and made up his mind to grant him a boon. Hearing Brahma's
words, he had held up the celestial river, confining her with his own
energy. Since Bhagiratha had satisfied him with fierce austerities,
he now released the river. Released in this way, she flowed in seven
streams—three towards the east and three towards the west. Thus,
River Ganga flowed through seven streams. Nalini, Hradini and
Pavani are the ones that flow towards the east. Sita, Chakshu and
Sindhu are the ones that flow in a western direction. The seventh
followed Bhagiratha towards the south. That is the reason she is
known as Bhagirathi, and she entered the salty ocean. These seven
sanctify the region of the Himalayas. Originating from the auspicious
Lake Bindusara, the river flows in these seven streams. She flows
through many countries, generally populated by Mlecchas. Flowing
through all these, she reaches the regions where Vasava showers—
Shilindhras, Kuntalas, Chinas, Barbaras, Yavanas, Andhrakas,
Pushkaras, Kulindas and Ancholadvicharas. Dividing herself into
three in the region known as Simhavan, Sita flows into the western
ocean. Chakshu flows through the regions of Chinamarus, Talas,
Masamulikas, Bhadras, Tusharas, Lamyakas, Bahlavas, Paratas and
Khashas and enters the ocean. Sindhu flows through the regions of
Daradas, Kashmiras, Gandharas, Rourasas, Kuhas, Shivashailas,
Indrapadas, Vasatis, Visarjamas, Saindhavas, Randhrakarakas,
Shamathas, Abhiras, Rohakas, Shunamukhas and Urddhvamarus.
Ganga sanctifies *gandharva*s, *kinnara*s, *yaksha*s, *rakshasa*s,
*vidyadhara*s, *uraga*s, Kalapagramakas, Paradas, Tadganas, Khashas,
Kiratas, Pulindas, Kurus, Bharatas, Panchalas, Kashis, Matysas,
Magadhas, Angas, Suhmottaras, Vangas, Tamraliptas and other
auspicious regions. Obstructed by the Vindhyas, she then enters the
salty ocean. The sacred Hradini flows in an eastern direction. She
floods the banks of Naishadhas, Trigartakas, Dhivaras, Rishikas,

---

[483] As a result of Bhagiratha's austerities.

Nilamukhas, Kekaras, Oushtakarnas, Kiratas, Kalodaras, Vivarnas, Kumaras and Svarnabhumikas. Covering the lands up to the ocean in the eastern direction, she then disappears. In that way, Pavani also flows in an eastern direction, flooding the regions of Supathas, Lake Indradyumna, Kharapathas and Vetrashankupathas. Flowing through the centre of the region of Janaki and Kuthapravaranas, she enters the salty ocean in Indradvipa. Nalini rapidly flows in an eastern direction, sanctifying the regions of Tomaras, Hamsamargas and Haihayas. As she flows through the eastern region, she penetrates many mountains. She reaches Karnapravaranas and the adjacent Shvamukhas. She passes through sandy deserts and mountains and the region of Vidyadharas. Through ranges of mountains, she then enters the salty ocean. The rivers have hundreds and thousands of tributaries. All of them pass through the region where Vasava showers down. On the banks of Vasvoukasa, there is a fragrant and famous forest. Kubera's learned and self-controlled son resides on the golden summit. He is extremely great and extremely valiant. Infinite in energy, he performs sacrifices. He is surrounded by learned *brahma-rakshasas*. Kubera is said to have four followers, who are his equals. This should be known as the prosperity of those who reside on the mountain. In pursuit of *dharma*, *artha* and *kama*, each possesses double the qualities of the one who precedes. The lake known as Varchovan is on the slopes of Hemakuta. The rivers Manasvini and Jyotishmati originate there. They flow on either side and merge into the eastern and western oceans. On the excellent mountain of Nishadha, there is a lake named Vishnupada. The rivers Gandharvi and Nakuli originate there. The large lake, Chandraprabha, originates from the side of Meru. The sacred river, Jambu, originates there and the gold known as *jambunada* is found there. Lake Payoda is on Nila. It sparkles and is full of lotuses. The rivers Pundarika and Payodaa originate from there. It is certain that the sacred Sarayu flows from Shveta. The rivers Jyotsna and Mrigakama originate from Manasa. In the land of Kuru, there is a lake known by the name of Rudrakanta. It was created by Bhava and is full of lotuses, fish and birds. There are twelve other famous lakes there, full of lotuses, fish and birds. These lakes are known under the name of Jaya and they resemble oceans. The two rivers, Shanta and Madhvi, originate from there. The divinity does not shower down in the region of Kimpurusha. Excellent rivers flow from water that emerges from the ground. The extremely large mountains, Rishabha, Dundubhi and Dhumra, extend towards the east. They possess excellent ridges and rivers originating from there, head towards the salty ocean. The extremely large mountains, Chandra, Kaka and Drona, extend towards the north. They have heaps of rocks and towards the north, they are submerged in the large ocean. Somaka, Varaha and Narada are large mountains. They extend in the western direction and enter the salty ocean. The extremely large mountains, Chakra, Balahaka and Mainaka, extend in the direction of the Southern Ocean. In between Chakra and Mainaka, in the southern direction, there is a fire named *samvartaka*, which drinks up the water. This resides in the ocean and is named Ourva and *vadavamukha*.[484] Earlier, the great Indra severed the wings of mountains. Scared, these twelve mountains[485] entered the salty ocean. In the white moon, the mark of a dark hare can be seen.[486] The nine divisions of Bharatavarsha have been described. Anything seen here is seen in other places too. Progressively, the regions rival each other in lack of disease, duration of lifespans and pursuit of *dharma*, *artha* and *kama*. These sacred regions are full of beings. Many kinds of species dwell in these regions. In this way, the earth holds up the world, which is located in the universe.'

Chapter 19-1(19) (Description of Plaksha-*dvipa* and other *dvipas*)

Suta said, 'I will speak about the expanse of Plaksha-*dvipa* accurately. O excellent *dvijas*! Listen to the truth. Its dimensions

---

[484] This is the subterranean fire, in the shape of a mare's head (*vadavamukha*), named after the sage Ourva.

[485] Three in each of the four directions. Earlier, mountains possessed wings. These were sliced off by Indra.

[486] This does not belong.

are double those of Jambu-*dvipa*. In every direction, its perimeter is double that of Jambu-*dvipa*. The salty ocean is surrounded by this *dvipa*. There are sacred countries there and the people do not die for a long time. There is no fear of famine there. How can there be fear of old age and death? There are seven sacred mountains there and these are adorned with jewels. They are stores of gems. I will speak about their names and those of rivers. In Plaksha-*dvipa* and the other five *dvipa*s,[487] there are seven *varsha-parvata*s each. They are long and straight and extend in every direction. I will speak about the seven in Plaksha-*dvipa* and they are extremely firm. The first mountain is Gomedaka and it resembles a cloud. After its name, the region around it is named Gomeda. The second mountain is Chandra, and it possesses all the herbs. For the sake of immortality, the two Ashvins collected herbs from here. The third mountain, named Narada, has heaps of rocks and is impossible to cross. Earlier, the sages Narada and Parvata were born on this mountain. The fourth mountain is named Dundubhi. Earlier, the *asura* Dundubhi could die as he willed. He loved to swing from ropes on a silk-cotton tree and this is how the Gods killed him.[488] The mountain is named after him. The fifth mountain is named Somaka. Earlier, *deva*s collected *amrita* from there. For the sake of his mother, Garuda also brought it. The sixth of the seven mountains is named Sumanas. It was on this mountain that Hiranyaksha was killed by the boar.[489] The seventh mountain is Vaibhraja. It is large and radiant, sparkling like crystal. Since its rays shine, it is known as Vaibhraja.[490] In the due order, I will mention the names of the *varsha*s there. Gomeda is the first *varsha*, named Shantabhaya.[491] The *varsha* around Chandra is named Shishira, while that around Narada is Sukhodaya. The *varsha* around Dundubhi is Ananda, while that around Somaka is known as Shiva. Kshemaka is the

---

[487] Since Jambu-*dvipa* has already been described.
[488] Dundubhi is mentioned in Valmiki Ramayana as a demon killed by Vali. There is no mention there of a *shalmali* (silk-cotton) tree.
[489] By Vishnu in his *varaha avatara*.
[490] *Bhraja* means shining.
[491] Where fears have been pacified.

varsha around Sumanas, while Dhruva is the one around Vaibhraja.
In these, *deva*s, *gandharva*s and *siddha*s are seen to roam around
and sport, along with *charana*s. There are rivers in the seven
*varsha*s and they flow towards the oceans. O stores of austerities!
I will tell you the names of the seven Gangas. They are Anutapta,
Sukhi, Vipasha, Tridiva, Kramu, Amritaa and Sukrita. These are
the seven excellent rivers. Thousands of other rivers flow into them.
They have plenty of water and flow towards the part where Vasava
showers down. The people who live in these countries happily drink
water from the rivers. They are the auspicious Shantabhayas, the
delighted Shishiras, the Shivas, the Anandas, the Sukhodayas, the
Kshemakas and the Dhruvas. The *praja*s who reside there follow the
conduct of the *varna*s and the *ashrama*s. All of them are extremely
strong. The *praja*s are such that their bodies are devoid of disease.
They do not ascend, nor do they descend. The nature of the four
*yuga*s, *krita* and the others, never exists there. A period like that
of *treta yuga* always exists there. This should be known to be the
nature of Plaksha-*dvipa* and the other five *dvipa*s. The time in these
regions is known to be commensurate with the place. Humans live
there for five thousand years. They are handsome, with excellent
garments. They are strong and do not suffer from ailments. They
possess happiness, lifespans, strength, beauty, freedom from disease
and *dharma*. It should be known that it is like this, from Plaksha-
dvipa to Shaka-*dvipa*. Plaksha-*dvipa* is large and prosperous, full of
grain and wealth. There are divine herbs and fruits and every kind
of herb and tree. It is populated by thousands of animals, from the
village and from the forest. O excellent *dvija*s! In the centre of a
number of *jambu* trees, there is a gigantic *plaksha* tree. The region
is named after the name of the tree. In the centre of the country,
that tree is worshipped. Plaksha-*dvipa* is surrounded by an ocean of
sugarcane juice. Its length and breadth are double those of Plaksha-
dvipa. This is described to be the location of Plaksha-*dvipa*. In the
due order, I have briefly described this to you.'

'Now hear about Shalmala-*dvipa*. I will speak about the third
excellent *dvipa* of Shalmala. Shalmala-*dvipa* surrounds the ocean of
sugarcane juice, which is double the dimensions of Plaksha-*dvipa*.
It should be known that there are seven mountains there and they

yield jewels. There are seven rivers in the *varsha*s, and they are stores of gems. The first mountain is named Kumuda, and it resembles the sun. The summits are covered with minerals everywhere and there are heaps of rocks. The second mountain there is known by the name of Uttama. It is full of yellow orpiment and the peaks rise up and cover the sky. The third mountain there is known by the name of Balahaka. It is full of natural collyrium, and the peaks rise and cover the sky. The fourth mountain is Drona and it possesses the great herbs of *vishalyakarani* and *mritasanjivini*.[492] The fifth extremely large mountain is Kanka. It is always full of flowers and fruits and is covered by trees and creepers. The sixth mountain there is Mahisha, and it resembles a cloud. The fire that owes its origin to water, named Mahisha, resides there. The seventh mountain there is known by the name of Kakudma. There are many jewels there and Vasava protects it himself. Taking the *praja*s with him, he approaches Prajapati in the proper way. These are the seven mountains in Shalmala-*dvipa* and they are adorned with jewels. I will speak about the seven auspicious *varsha*s. The *varsha* around Kumuda is known as Shveta and that around Uttama as Lohita. The *varsha* around Balahaka is known as Jimuta and that around Drona as Harita. The *varsha* around Kanka is named Vaidyuta and that around Mahisha is known as Manasa. The one around Kakudma is named Suprada. These are the seven *varsha*s around the seven mountains. Now understand about the rivers. They are Jyoti, Shanti, Tushtaa, Chandraa, Shukraa, Vimochani and Nivritti as the seventh. These are described as the rivers in each *varsha*. There are hundreds and thousands of others that are near them. No human is capable of enumerating their number. This is described to be the location of Shamala-*dvipa*. In the midst of a number of *plaksha* trees, there is a gigantic *shalmali* tree, with a large trunk. The region is named after the tree. Shalmala-*dvipa* is surrounded by an ocean of liquor and in every direction, the dimensions of this are said to be the same as those of Shalmala-*dvipa*. O ones who know about *dharma*! Now hear about the *praja*s in the northern *dvipa*s. I will describe them accurately, as I have heard. Understand.'

---

[492] Respectively, those that cure wounds (stakes) and revive the dead.

'I will briefly speak about Kusha-*dvipa*, which is the fourth. In every direction, Kusha-*dvipa* surrounds the ocean of liquor, which has dimensions that are double those of Shalmala-*dvipa*. There are seven mountains there. I will describe them. Listen. The first mountain in Kusha-*dvipa* is known as Vidruma. The second mountain in that *dvipa* is Hemparvata. The third mountain is Dyutiman and it resembles a cloud. The fourth mountain is named Pushpavan and the fifth is Kusheshaya. The sixth is named Harigiri and the seventh is said to be Mandara. The word "*manda*" means water and it has this name because it shattered the water.[493] Their internal diameter is double the distance between them. The first *varsha* is Udbhida and the second is Venumandala. The third is Rathakara and the fourth is said to be Lavana. The fifth *varsha* is Dhritimat and the sixth *varsha* is Prabhakara. The seventh is named Kapila. In all these *varsha*s, *deva*s and *gandharva*s purify them and are lords of the worlds and of *praja*s. They can be seen everywhere, roaming around and sporting. There are no bandits there, nor any *mleccha*s. Almost all the people are fair and die in the due order.[494] There are seven rivers there—Dhutapapa, Shivaa, Pavitra, Santati, Vidyut, Dambha and Mahi. There are hundreds and thousands of others, not that well-known. All of them proceed to the region where Vasava showers down. Externally, Kusha-*dvipa* is surrounded by an ocean of ghee. It should be known that its dimensions are the same as those of Kusha-*dvipa*. It is said that Kusha-*dvipa* is located in this way.'

'After this, I will speak about the dimensions of Krouncha-*dvipa*. Its dimensions are said to be double those of Kusha-*dvipa*. The ocean of *ghee* is in contact with Krouncha-*dvipa*. In that *dvipa*, the first mountain is Krouncha, the best among the mountains. The next mountain in Krouncha is Vamanaka and after Vamanaka, there is Andhakaraka. Beyond Andhakaraka, there is a mountain named Divavrit. After Divavrit, there is the supreme mountain of Dvivida. After Dvivida, there is the great mountain of Pundarika.

---

[493] *Manda* doesn't quite mean water, though it is an adjective that can be used to describe some types of water, or the froth.

[494] That is, the young do not die before the old.

The mountain beyond Pundarika is said to be Dundubhisvana. These seven mountains in Krouncha-*dvipa* are full of jewels. They are full of many flowers and fruit and are covered with trees and creepers. They extend for double the size of the preceding one and extend delight. I will mention the names of the *varsha*s there. Understand. Next to Krouncha is the country of Kushala. Next to Vamanaka is the country of Manonuga. Beyond Manonuga, there is said to be the third *varsha* of Ushna. Beyond Ushna, there is Pivara and beyond Pivara, there is Andhakara. The learned describe the region beyond Andhakara as Munidesha. The region of Dundubhisvana is said to be beyond Munidesha. It is full of *siddha*s and *charana*s, and the people are generally said to be fair. In these *varsha*s, there are said to be seven auspicious rivers—Gouri, Kumudvati, Sandhya, Ratri, Manojava, Khyati and Pundarikaa. These are said to be the seven kinds of Ganga there. There are thousands of other rivers that are near them and approach them. All of them are large and full of a great deal of water. In every direction, Krouncha-*dvipa* is surrounded by an ocean of curds. It is handsome and its dimensions are the same as those of Krouncha-dvipa. Thus, I have briefly described Plaksha-*dvipa* and the others. Even if one tries for one hundred divine years, one is incapable of describing the natural features of all these *dvipa*s in progressive detail, or the creation and destruction of prajas in them.'

'I will speak about Shaka-*dvipa*, as it has been certainly determined. I will describe it factually. Listen to the facts. Its dimensions are double those of Krouncha-*dvipa*. It is established there, surrounding the ocean of curds. There are auspicious countries there and people die after a long period of time. There is no famine. How can there be fear from old age or disease? There are seven sparkling mountains there, embellished with jewels. The rivers there are stores of gems. Hear about their names. The first mountain, full of *deva*s, *rishi*s and *gandharva*s, is said to be Meru. The mountain named Udaya is golden and extends towards the east. For the sake of rain, clouds go there and are created there. On its other side, there is the extremely large mountain, Jaladhara. From there, Vasava always obtains excellent waters. During the monsoon, he accordingly showers down on subjects. To the north, there is the mountain of

Raivataka. Following the rules established by the grandfather, the *nakshatra* Revati is always established there, in the sky. Beyond this, there is an extremely large mountain, named Shyama. Indeed, because of its shadow, it is said that the *prajas* here formerly became dark. To its west, there is a large and silvery mountain, described as Asta. To its west, there is Ambika's extremely large mountain of Durgashaila. Beyond Ambika's mountain, there is the beautiful mountain of Kesari, which possesses all the herbs. From this mountain, Prajapati Vayu obtains *kesara*.[495] The first *varsha* is near Udaya and is remembered as Jalada. The second, near Jaladhara, is said to be Sukumara. The *varsha* near Raivataka is Koumara and that near Shyama is Manivaka. The auspicious *varsha* near Asta is known as Kusumottara. The *varsha* near Ambika's mountain is Modaka and that near Kesara is Mahadruma. The dimensions of the *dvipa*, the length and the breadth, are commensurate with those of Krouncha-*dvipa*. There is a large and famous tree, named Shaka, and it is like a standard. It is followed and worshipped by many followers. There are sacred countries, populated by the four *varnas*. There are the seven Gangas, extremely sacred rivers—Sukumari, Kumari, Nalini, Venuka, Ikshu, Venuka[496] and Gabhasti as the seventh. There are other rivers, with auspicious waters. They are sacred and bear cool water. There are said to be thousands in the place where Vasava showers down. It is impossible to enumerate the names and dimensions of these excellent and sacred rivers. O Shamshapayana![497] People in those countries always happily drink the water from these rivers. This *dvipa* is vast and is established like a wheel. It is covered with rivers and water and with mountains that are like clouds. These possess all the wonderful minerals and are adorned with jewels and coral. There are many cities and flourishing countries. In every direction, there are trees full of flowers and fruit. There is grain and wealth. From every side, it is surrounded by an

---

[495] Kesara can be interpreted as the filament (from flowers), Vayu's hair, or saffron.

[496] The name is repeated. In other Puranas, it is given as Dhenuka.

[497] The name is sometimes given as Shamshapayani and sometimes as Shamshapayana.

ocean of milk. On all sides, its dimensions are the same as those of Shaka-*dvipa*. Such are the countries. The mountains are sacred, and the rivers are auspicious. The seven *varsha*s are said to follow the *varna*s and *ashrama*s. They never deviate from *varna*s and *ashrama*s and there is no mixture of *varna*s. Since there is no deviation from *dharma*, the *praja*s enjoy ultimate happiness. There is no greed or deception among them. How can there be envy or jealousy? They do not suffer from any calamities and time takes its own natural and supreme course. Taxes are not imposed on them. There is no punishment and there is no one to be punished. They know about *dharma* and follow their own *dharma*, protecting each other. I am capable of saying only this much about that *dvipa*. This is what has been heard about the residents of Shaka-*dvipa*.'

'I will speak about the seventh *dvipa* of Pushkara. Understand. From the outside, Pushkara-*dvipa* surrounds the ocean of milk. On every side, its dimensions are double those of Shaka-*dvipa*. In Puskhara, there is only one large and prosperous mountain. It is marvellous and full of jewels. With heaps of rocks, the summits rise up. This wonderful and large mountain is located on the eastern side of the *dvipa*. Its extensive circle extends for twenty-five thousand *yojana*s. It rises thirty-four thousand *yojana*s up, from the surface of the ground. This mountain, Manasottara, covers half of the *dvipa*. Like a moon that has just risen, it is established along the shores of the ocean. On the western half of the *dvipa*, there is the mountain of Manasa, which holds up the earth. It rises up for a height of fifty thousand *yojana*s and on all sides, its circumference is of the same magnitude. Actually, there is only one mountain, great in substance. But it is so located that it seems to be divided into two. In every direction, the *dvipa* is surrounded by an ocean of fresh water. On all sides, the dimensions of this are as large as those of Pushkara-*dvipa*. There are said to be two sacred and auspicious countries in that *dvipa*. They are on both sides of Manasa's circle. The *varsha* of Mahavita is outside Manasa. The one that is inside is known as Dhatakikhanda. There, humans live for ten thousand years. They do not suffer from disease and enjoy an excess of happiness. They obtain *siddhi* in their minds. In those two *varsha*s, it is said that people are identical in lifespans and beauty. There is no one who is superior or inferior. They are equal in beauty and conduct. There are no bandits or oppressors. There is no envy, jealousy or fear. There is no imprisonment or punishment. There is no greed or seizure of possessions. There is no truth or falsehood. There is no *dharma* or *adharma*. There are no *varna*s or *ashrama*s, no activities for subsistence, no animal husbandry. There are no trade routes. The three kinds of knowledge,[498] policies for criminal justice, servitude and artisanship—none of these exist in the two *varsha*s in Pushkara. There is no rain and there are no rivers. There is no heat or cold. Water does not rise through the earth and there are no waterfalls in mountains. The time there is similar to that in Uttara Kuru. In all the seasons, the people there are extremely happy. They do not suffer from the onset of old age. This is the way it is in Mahavita and Dhatakikhanda. In the due order, everything ordained for Pushkara has been described. Pushkara is surrounded by an ocean of sweet water. The dimensions and circumference of this are the same as those of Pushkara. In this way, the seven *dvipa*s are surrounded by seven oceans. The ocean that immediately follows a *dvipa* has the same dimensions as the *dvipa*. Thus, the dimensions of *dvipa*s and oceans should be known to increase vis-à-vis each other. An ocean is known as *samudra* because it has a plentiful supply of water.[499] Since four types of *praja*s enter a region and reside there, a region is known as *varsha*. It brings them happiness. The root "*rish*" means to sport, and the root "*vrish*" means to increase their strength.[500] Since it gives them success in obtaining success for sexual intercourse, it is known as *varsha*.'

'During *shukla paksha*, the moon waxes and always fills up the ocean. When the moon decays and sets in the sky, it also diminishes a lot. When it fills up, the ocean is naturally filled up in this way. Like that, when it diminishes, it withdraws into itself. When brought into contact with a fire, the water inside a pot is

[498] The three *Veda*s.

[499] *Samudra* means ocean and *samudreka* means abundant, plentiful.

[500] Etymologically, the word *varsha* is being traced to four roots—'*vish*' (enter), *vas* (reside), *rish* (sport) and *vrish* (strengthen). Sometimes, alternative derivations are possible.

seen to increase. In that way, the water in the great ocean naturally increases. Though the water seems to increase or diminish, there is actually neither an excess nor a deficit. This occurs during *shukla paksha* and *krishna paksha*, when the moon rises and sets. The increase and decrease in the ocean follow the waxing and waning of the moon, which occur to the extent of five hundred and ten *angula*s.[501] During *parva* days,[502] the increase and decrease in waters in the ocean can be seen. *Dvipa*s are surrounded by water on all sides and are known as *dvipa*s because they have water on both sides.[503] Since it is the resting place for water, an ocean is known as "*udadhi*".[504] If it has no ridges, a mountain is called "*giri*". If it has ridges, a mountain is called "*parvata*".[505] Mount Gomeda in Plaksha-*dvipa* is known as *parvata*. Those who are extremely great in their vows worship a *shalmali* tree in Shalmala-*dvipa*. Kusha-*dvipa* is said to be named after a clump of *kusha* grass. Mount Krouncha is in the centre of the country of Krouncha-*dvipa*. Shaka-*dvipa* is said to have been named after the name of a *shaka* tree.[506] A *nyagrodha* tree is worshipped in Pushkara-*dvipa*. The great divinity, Brahma, the lord of the three worlds, is worshipped there. Along with Sadhyas, Prajapati Brahma resides there. The thirty-three *devas*[507] and *maharshi*s worship him there. The supreme among *devas* is worshipped by *devas* there. There are many kinds of jewels in Jambu-*dvipa*. The nature of *praja*s in all the *dvipa*s follows a due order—in *brahmacharya*, truthfulness, self-control, lack of disease and duration of lifespan, these are double in the succeeding one, compared to the preceding one. There are two *varsha*s in Pushkara-*dvipa* that have been spoken about. Whether the *praja*s there are

[501] Both *kala* (digit) and *angula* (length) were used in astronomical measurements, the moon's diameter consisting of 16 *kala*s. *Angula* was not used consistently. Therefore, the *angula* to *kala* conversion in the text is not obvious.

[502] *Purnima* and *amavasya*.

[503] Based on the roots for 'two' and 'water'.

[504] From *udaka* (water).

[505] *Giri* is a single mountain, while *parvata* is a range.

[506] The word *shaka* is used in a generic sense. But it also means teak.

[507] Twelve Adityas, eleven Rudras, eight Vasus and the two Ashvins.

dumb or learned, Svayambhu protects them. The divinity Brahma, lord of three worlds, also raises his rod of chastisement. He is Vishnu's adviser. The divinity is the father and the grandfather. The subjects there always enjoy the extremely energetic food with the six kinds of taste. This presents itself on its own, without any effort being made. The two halves of Pushkara-*dvipa* are surrounded by a great ocean of fresh water, which surrounds it from every side.'

'Beyond this, a great world can be seen. This is golden and is double in size.[508] Everywhere, the ground consists of a single slab of rock. On its other side, there is a mountain that is circular at the ends. It is partly illuminated and partly not illuminated. This is known as Lokaloka.[509] There is light on this side and darkness on the other side. Its height is said to be ten thousand *yojana*s. Its expanse is also that much, and it extends over the earth, as it wills. Where there is light, worldly activities take place. Where there is a lack of light, it is other worldly. All the worlds exist in the half that possesses light. The regions without light exist outside. Outside, there is a lack of light everywhere, by as much of an expanse as there is light inside. The worlds inside are surrounded by water and it surrounds the water. The world without light is established there, surrounded by the cosmic egg. The worlds and the earth, with its seven *dvipa*s, are inside the egg. This accumulation of worlds consists of Bhuloka, Bhuvarloka, Svarloka, Maharloka, Janaloka, Tapoloka and Satyaloka. This is all that is known about the worlds and about what is beyond. When *shukla paksha* starts, the moon appears in the western direction, as if it is seated on a pot. The body of the cosmic egg is like that. It should be known that there are thousands of such cosmic eggs, established above, below and sideways. The unmanifest *atman* is the cause. There are seven that evolve from Prakriti and hold everything up.[510] Each is ten times the

[508] Compared to the ocean of fresh water.

[509] The mountain that separates the region illuminated by the sun from the region not illuminated by the sun.

[510] There are the seven shells/sheaths of the cosmic egg, water, fire, wind, space, *bhutadi* and Mahat. *Bhutadi* is the origin of the elements/creatures, that is, *ahamkara*.

size of the preceding one and they support each other. They support each other and evolve from each other. All around the cosmic egg, there is a dense ocean. It is established there, surrounded on all sides by this mass that is a dense ocean. That globe, with the dense mass of water, is supported, above, below and sideways, by fire on every side. Externally, on every side, it is a globe, resembling a ball of iron. On the outside, this is in turn supported by a dense mass of wind. Similarly, that dense mass of wind is indeed supported by a dense mass of space. *Bhutadi* supports space and is in turn supported by Mahat. Mahat is supported by the infinite and the unmanifest. It is infinite and not manifest. It is subtle in ten different kinds of ways.[511] It is infinite, but it is a form of the *atman* that has not been cleansed. It is without a beginning and an end. Compared to the supreme, it is not permanent. It is not terrible. It is without support and without disease. It is remote, many thousands of *yojana*s away. It is not covered. It is full of darkness, without any light. It has no boundaries and cannot be determined. *Deva*s do not know it and it is devoid of any conduct. This is known as the end of darkness. Beyond space, it lacks any radiance. Its boundaries are infinite. This is the great divinity's abode. The Gods cannot reach that spot and the *shruti* texts speak of it as the divine region. It is established there, following the rules set by the great lord of *deva*s. The learned speak of regions that are below the sun and the moon as the worlds. There is no doubt that these are described as the worlds of the universe. There are seven netherworlds, Atala and the others and there are seven worlds above Atala. O *dvija*s! With its seven layers, Vayu resides in Brahma's abode.[512] From Patala to the firmament, it only possesses five of these flows. These are the dimensions of the world, the ocean that is *samsara*. There are many species that originate and roam around here. They are without a beginning and without an end. This world is wonderful

---

[511] It is difficult to pin down the number ten.

[512] Proceeding upwards from Bhuvarloka, Vayu has seven courses, a succeeding one flowing above the preceding one. As mentioned in Shanti Parva of the Mahabharata, these are *pravaha, avaha, udvaha, samvaha, vivaha, parivaha* and *paravaha*.

and is caused by Prakriti, established in the *brahman*. This divine
creation has many dimensions and is beyond the senses. Even the
immensely fortunate *siddha*s cannot ascertain it. O excellent *dvija*s!
Earth, water, fire, wind, space, darkness, the mind, the body and
the infinite do not have a decay or a transformation. They do not
possess an end. Everything is infinite. That is what is read in texts
on *jnana*. When describing the names, I have spoken about him.
When all names are described, he is spoken of as Padmanabha.
He goes everywhere and is worshipped everywhere—the earth, the
surface of the ground, sky, wind and fire. There is no doubt that
he exists in all the oceans and directions. It should be known that
the immensely radiant one exists in darkness too. Janardana is the
great *yogi* and has divided his limbs into many parts. He is the lord
of all the worlds. The lord is worshipped in all the worlds in many
ways. In this way, the worlds support each other. They support
and are supported. They are transformations of the one who has
no transformations. The earth and the others are transformations
and are confined by each other. They are superior to each other and
enter each other. Since they have been created from each other, they
approach each other and obtain stability. In the beginning, there
was no Vishesha. They became Vishesha because they qualified
each other. The elements, earth and the others are restricted by the
three *guna*s from beginning to end. Because of this essence in the
accumulation, they are circumscribed and are Vishesha. The subtle
elements are not restricted by any limits and cannot be conceived.
Beyond the gross elements, there are the radiant subtle elements,
which support them.[513] Like a smaller vessel that is inside a larger
vessel, all the gross elements are circumscribed by space. Since
they support each other, each is smaller than the one it is inside.
It is thus held that all the gross elements are restricted by being
inside space. The other four are larger than each other and superior
to each other. An element exists as long as its origin is said to
exist. Just as threads are woven into each other, it is held that the
elements are inside each other. Something known as an element,
which is the effect, does not exist if the cause is non-existent. All

---

[513] We have taken liberties in this sentence.

these differences, which are like effects, are limited. Differences like Mahat and the others are said to be the causes. O *dvijas*! I have thus spoken accurately about the locations of the seven *dvipa*s and the oceans and the expanse and enumeration of the globes. I have also indicated the form of the universe, which is a transformation of Pradhana. Bhagavan pervades everything in the universe. In this way, the seven categories of elements[514] enter each other. I am capable of speaking only this much about the locations. This is all that can be heard about the location of earth and the others. These seven manifestations of Prakriti support each other. I am not interested in enumerating their dimensions. The manifestations of Prakriti are innumerable, above, below and sideways. The stars are established in the circle of the firmament. The circle of the earth is below and restricted by this. O ones with discrimination! After this, I will speak about what is above the earth.'[515]

Chapter 20-1(20) (Description of the nether regions)

Suta said, 'I will speak about the dimensions of what is below and what is above. Understand. Earth, wind, space, water and fire as the fifth—the ingredients of these are infinite. Hence, they are described as pervasive. The earth is the mother of all beings and sustains all creatures. It is full of many countries, diverse cities and habitations. There are many large and small rivers and mountains, full of many kinds of species. The Goddess Earth is extremely extensive and is sung about as infinite. Water should also be known as infinite. It exists in large and smaller rivers, oceans, smaller waterbodies, in mountains, in the air and inside the ground. In that way, fire pervades all the worlds. One reads about it as being infinite. It is pervasive and everything originates from it. Space is also

---

[514] Probably referring to the five elements, mind and intelligence.

[515] However, what follows is about the nether regions.

described as something that cannot be marked out. It is beautiful and provides many refuges. One reads about wind, which originates from space, as being infinite. Water exists within earth, and the earth is established on water. Earth is above water, and space is above earth. In this way, it is held that anything evolved from the elements is infinite. The growth of the earth occurs because earth, water and space progressively support each other.'

'This is also said to be the situation in the seven nether regions. The land in the nether regions extends for eleven thousand *yojana*s. The virtuous ones have enumerated that each is more extensive than the preceding one. The first is named Atala and the next is Sutala. After that is Talatala, followed by Vitala, which is known to be extremely extensive. Below that is the region named Mahatala.[516] After this is Rasatala. Below all these, there is the seventh region, described as Patala. The ground in the first region is described as consisting of black earth. The ground in the second is pale, while that in the third consists of blue earth. In the fourth, it consists of yellow soil. The ground in the fifth is full of gravel. The sixth is known to be covered with rocks, while the seventh is said to be golden.'

'In the first region of Atala, there exists the famous residence of Namuchi, Indra among *asura*s and Indra's enemy. There also exist the residence of Mahanada; Shankukarna's city; Kabandha's residence; Nishkulada's city, which is full of delighted people; the *rakshasa* Bhima's residence; Shuladanta's abode; those of Lohitakshas and Kalingas; Shvapada's city; the city of the great-souled Dhananjaya, Indra among *naga*s; Kaliya *naga*'s city and that of Koushika. In this way, there are thousands of cities of *naga*s, *danava*s and *rakshasa*s. It should be known that there is no doubt that the ground in the first region of Atala consists of black soil.'

'O *brahmana*s! In the second region of Sutala, there exist the city of Mahajambha, the foremost Indra of *daitya*s and *rakshasa*s; the residences of Hayagriva, Krishna and Nikumbha; that of the *daitya* known as Shankha; Gomukha's city; the residences of the *rakshasa*s Nila, Megha and Kathana; Kukupada's abode; the

---

[516] The text says Tala, which we have amended to Mahatala. Similarly, we have adjusted for other errors in names in the text.

residence of Mahoshnisha that of Kambala *naga* Ashvatara's city and the city of the great-souled Takshaka, Kadru's son. In this way, there are thousands of cities of *naga*s, *danava*s and *rakshasa*s. O *brahmana*s! There is no doubt that the ground in the second region of Sutala is pale.'

'In the third, famous as Talatala, there exists the residence of the great-souled Prahlada; the city of Anuhrada; the city of Agnimukha; the city of Taraka; the city of Trishiras; Shishumara's city; the city of Tripura; the city of *daitya* Puranjana, full of well-nourished and happy people; the abode known to belong to *rakshasa* Chyavana; the city of Kumbhila, Indra among *rakshasa*s; that of Khara; the city of the cruel Viradha, who emits fire from his mouth; the abode of *naga* Hemaka; that of Panduraka; Maninaga's city; Kapila's abode; that of Nandaka, lord of *uraga*s and Vishalaksha's residence. In this way, there are thousands of cities of *naga*s, *danava*s and *rakshasa*s. O *brahmana*s! There is no doubt that the ground in the third region of Talatala has blue soil.'

'In the fourth region, there is the residence of the great-souled Kalanemi, lion among *daitya*s; Gajakarna's city; Kunjara'a city; the extremely large city of Sumali, Indra among *rakshasa*s; the residences of Munja, Lokanatha and Vrikavakra and the city of Vainateya, which extends for many *yojana*s and is full of many birds. All this exists in the fourth region of Vitala.'

'The fifth region extends for many *yojana*s, and the ground is covered with gravel. There exists the city of the intelligent Virochana, lion among *daitya*s; the residences of Vaidyuta, Agnijihva and Hiranyaksha; the city of the intelligent Vidyujjihva, Indra among *rakshasa*s; the city of Sahamegha; that of Malin, Indra among *rakshasa*s and the residences of Kirmira *naga*, Svastika and Jaya. In this way, there are thousands of cities of *naga*s, *danava*s and *rakshasa*s. It should be known that in the fifth region of Mahatala, the ground is always covered with gravel.'

'In the sixth region of Rasatala, there exists the excellent city of Kesari, lord of *daitya*s; those of Suparvan and Puloman; Mahisha's city and the city of the great-souled Surosha, Indra among *rakshasa*s. Shatashirsha, Surama's son, happily resides there. The prosperous king of *naga*s, named Vasuki, the great Indra's friend, also lives there. In this way, there are thousands of cities of *naga*s, *danava*s and *rakshasa*s. It should be known that the ground in the sixth region of Rasatala is famous because it is covered with rocks.'

'The last region, after all the others, is the seventh and is known as Patala. Bali's city exists there and is full of delighted men and women. It is full of *asura*s, venomous serpents and delighted enemies of *deva*s. The great city of *daitya* Muchukunda is also there. There are great cities, full of many of Diti's sons. In that way, there are thousands and prosperous cities of *naga*s, *daitya*s and *danava*s. There are many such great cities. The place is full of many flourishing residences of *rakshasa*s. O Indras among *brahmana*s! Where Patala ends, the extensive region extends for many *yojana*s. The extremely radiant, Shesha Ananta, king of all the *naga*s, resides there. He is great-souled and does not suffer from old age or death. His eyes are like red lotuses. His body is as white as a washed conch-shell. He is attired in blue garments and is extremely strong. His form is large and radiant. The strong one wears many colourful garlands. He possesses a single coil, but the lord is radiant with one thousand shining hoods that resemble golden peaks. He blazes in his garland of tongues and his flickering tongues emit sparks of fire. With a net of flames flung all around, he seems to resemble Kailasa. The two thousand eyes blaze, coppery-red like the rising sun. But his body is fair and pleasant, with a complexion like that of the moon or the *kunda* flower.[517] The garland of his eyes shines, like a garland of rising suns above the summit of Mount Shveta. His lofty body is cruel, as he lies down on his couch. He resembles an extensive mountain with one thousand peaks, covering the earth. He is worshipped by great-souled ones, great and extremely prosperous *naga*s, who are great in their wisdom. The immensely energetic one is the lord of all the great *naga*s. Following the rules established by Vishnu, he is there, at the boundary. The nature of the seven nether regions has been described. They are always inhabited by *deva*s, *asura*s, great *naga*s and *rakshasa*s. Beyond this, there is a region that lacks illumination, one that virtuous ones and *siddha*s cannot travel to. Even if they wish to, *deva*s do not know about

[517] Jasmine.

what is there. O excellent *dvija*s! There is no doubt that *rishi*s have described the greatness of the earth, water, fire, wind and space in this way. After this, I will speak about the movements of the sun and the moon.'

Chapter 21-1(21) (The solar circle)

Suta said, 'The sun and the moon are elevated through their discs and illumination. They revolve in their radiance. The light covers the expanse of the earth, with its seven *dvipa*s and oceans, on the inside, but not on the outside. Light from the sun and the moon cover one part of the rotation,[518] not the other. The expanse of the earth's rotation is said to be the firmament. As it revolves, the sun illuminates the three worlds. The root "*av*" means to shine and protect. Since the sun does this, it is known as Ravi. After this, I will speak about the sun and the moon's measures. This *varsha* is known as Mahi because it is great and revered.[519] In *yojana*s, Bharatavarsha's diameter is the same as that of Bhaskara's disc. Understand. Bhaskara's diameter is nine thousand *yojana*s. The circumference is three times the diameter.[520] The moon's diameter is twice that of the sun. I will now speak about the earth's dimensions, in *yojana*s. The expanse of the earth's globe has seven *dvipa*s and oceans. The dimensions of this world have been enumerated in the Puranas. I will describe this, along with the names of divinities who take pride in their positions. In the past, there were divinities who took pride, and they are comparable to those who take pride now. I will speak about the forms and names of the past *deva*s on earth, through the current ones. All of these are now located in the firmament. The earth's expanse is described as fifty crore *yojana*s. Half of this extends upwards, till the position where

---

[518] That part which, while rotating, faces the sun and the moon.

[519] The earth is known as Mahi, from the root of greatness and reverence.

[520] With a Pi value of 3.

Meru is. This half of the earth's expanse is described in terms of
yojanas. From Meru's centre, the extent of the earth's radius is one
crore, one hundred and eighty-nine thousand and fifty thousand
yojanas. Reckoned in yojanas, the earth's circumference is stated
to be eleven crores and thirty-seven lakhs.[521] This is described as
the dimensions of the earth's globe. The magnitude of the earth's
orbit is said to be the same as the extent to which stars exist in the
firmament. The extent of the earth's revolution is said to be the
same as the firmament. The earth is described as the place where the
seven dvipas are located. It is such that the spheres are progressively
inside each other. In the due order, a succeeding sphere encircles the
previous one. This has been laid down as the establishment of all
the worlds and creatures reside within them. These are described
to be the dimensions of the vessel that is the cosmic egg. The earth,
with its seven dvipas, and the worlds, exist within this egg. They are
Bhuloka, Bhuvarloka, Svarloka as the third, Maharloka, Janaloka,
Tapoloka and Satyaloka as the seventh. These are the seven worlds,
arranged in the form of an umbrella. Each of these is supported by
its own individual and subtle covering.[522] The nature is such that,
externally, each covering is ten times the size of what it covers. They
support each other and are filled up by Vishesha. Everywhere around
this egg, there is a dense ocean. Earth's entire globe is supported by
a dense mass of water. The dense mass of water is supported by
a dense mass of fire. Above, below and sideways, externally, the
dense mass of fire is established such that it is supported by a dense
mass of wind. The dense mass of space is supported by the great
space. All around, space is supported by the great bhutadi. Bhutadi
is surrounded by Mahat and Mahat is surrounded by infinite and
immutable Pradhana.'

'In the due order, I will speak about the cities of the guardians
of the worlds. The dimensions, qualities and movements of the
luminary bodies are as follows. To the east of Meru and above

---

[521] This is inconsistent with what has been said about the radius. There
is a typo in one or the other.

[522] The coverings of the five elements, followed by those of ahamkara,
Mahat and Pradhana.

Manasa, there is the great Indra's city, polished with gold. This is the abode of prosperity. To the south of Meru and above Manasa, Vaivasvata Yama resides, in the city of Samyamana. To the west of Meru and above Manasa, there is a beautiful city named Sukha, belonging to the intelligent Varuna. Varuna, lord of aquatic creatures, dwells in the city named Sukha. To the north of Meru and above Manasa, there is Soma's city of Vibhavari, the equal of the great Mahendra's city. To establish *dharma* and protect the worlds, the guardians of the worlds are established in the four directions, on the slopes of Manasottara. In the four quarters, understand Surya's movement during *dakshinayana*, beyond the guardians of the worlds. During his southern movement, Surya dashes forward, like an arrow that has been released. As he moves, the circle of luminary bodies always follows him. When Bhaskara is in the middle of Amaravati,[523] he is seen to rise in Vaivasvata's Samyamana. It will be midnight in Sukha and the sun will set in Vibhavari. Like that, when Ravi is in the middle of Vaivasvata's Samyamana, he will be seen to rise in Varuna's Sukha. It will be midnight in Vibhavari, and he will set in the great Indra's city. When it is afternoon in the south-east, it is forenoon for those in the south-west. When it is the second half of the night for those in the north-west, it is the earlier part of the night for those who are in the north-east. In this way, the worlds in the northern regions are illuminated. When Aryama[524] is in the middle of Varuna's Sukha, Vibhavasu will rise in Soma's city of Vibhavari. It will be midnight in Amaravati and the sun will set in Yama's city. When Divakara is in the middle in Soma's city of Vibhavari, Surya will be seen to rise in the great Indra's Amaravati. It will be midnight in Samyamana and the sun will set in Varuna's city. Like a circle of fire, Bhaskara moves swiftly. As Ravi revolves and moves, he moves across the revolving *nakshatras*. In this way, when the sun moves south, he traverses the four directions. He repeatedly rises and sets. With his rays, in the forenoon, afternoon and midday, he heats two abodes of the *devas*. Ravi rises and his heat increases till midday. After this,

[523] Indra's city.
[524] Surya. Vibhavasu is another name for Surya, as is Divakara.

his rays diminish, until he sets. The eastern and western directions are remembered as those where he respectively rises and sets. When he heats in front, he also does this at the back and along the sides. When Surya is seen, that is described as the period of sunrise. When he moves and vanishes, that is described as a period of sunset. Meru is to the north of all the worlds and Lokaloka is to the south of all the worlds. Arka[525] is far away and is covered by the earth's horizon. Therefore, his rays disappear, and he cannot be seen during the night. The sight of planets, *nakshatras*, the moon and the sun must be understood in this way. The measure of their rising and setting must also be known thus. Fire and water have a white shadow. Earth has a dark shadow. Since Arka is far away, when he rises, he possesses no rays. There is a red tinge because of the lack of rays and because of this redness, there is no heat. Whenever Surya is seen above the horizon, he is seen one hundred thousand *yojanas* above that line. When Surya's rays diminish and Bhaskara gradually moves towards setting, his rays enter the fire. Therefore, at night, he can only be seen from a distance. When Surya rises again, the heat from the fire enters him. Thus, united with fire, Surya heats during the day. Illumination and heat represent the energy of Surya and fire. They enter each other and illuminate night and day. In the northern part of the earth, as well as the southern part, when Surya rises, night enters water. Therefore, since night enters water, water is cool during the day. When Surya sets, day enters the water. Hence, since day enters it, water is warm during the night. This is the due order in the northern and the southern half of the earth. Depending on whether Arka rises or sets, night and day enter the water. When Surya's illumination exists, it is spoken of as day. When there is darkness, it is spoken of as night. That is the way both are defined, and night is the period when Surya is not present. Bhaskara traverses through the centre of the sky. It covers parts of the earth in a single *muhurta*. Understand the duration of a *muhurta* in this world, measured in *yojanas*. It is said to be a complete one hundred and eighty-one thousand *yojanas*. That is understood to be

---

[525] Surya.

the movement of Surya in the course of one *muhurta*. In the quarters, that is also the movement when it moves south. In the course of the movement, it covers the first, the central and the final quarters. In the course of *dakshinayana*, it traverses the centre of the sky. *Vishuva* occurs within Mount Manasottara.[526] Understand the quarters when it moves in a southern direction. In *yojana*s, the sun's orbit is one crore and forty-five hundred thousand. This is said to be the distance traversed in the course of a day and a night. Withdrawing from the south, Ravi is based in *vishuva*. It then moves northwards, towards the ocean of milk. In *yojana*s, understand the distance between the two *vishuva* points. The orbit between the two *vishuva* points is said to be three crores and eighty-one thousand *yojana*s. When Chitrabhanu[527] is in the *nakshtra*s of Shravana and Uttarashadha, it moves north of the sixth region of Shaka-dvipa. O *dvija*s! Nagavithi is the *vithi* towards the north and Ajavithi that towards the south.[528] The three, Mula, Purvashada and Uttarashada, represent Ajavithi. The three, Ashvini, Krittika and Bharani, represent Nagavithi. The lengths of the northern and southern orbits are eight hundred thousand, four hundred and thirty-three *yojana*s. Thus, the distance between the two-quarter points has been described in *yojana*s. I will next speak about the distance between the northern and southern quarters and the two longitudinal

---

[526] *Sankranti* is the movement of the sun from one sign of the zodiac (*rashi*) to another. Thus, there are twelve of these. The entry of Surya into Capricorn, with the movement from *dakshinayana* to *uttarayana*, is known as *makara sankranti*, while its entry into Cancer, with the movement from *uttarayana* to *dakshinayana*, is known as *karka sankranti*. The entry into Gemini, Virgo, Sagittarius and Pisces are known as *shadashiti*. The entry into Taurus, Leo, Scorpio and Aquarius are known as *vishnupada*. The entry into Aries and Libra is known as *vishuva sankranti*.

[527] Or Bhanu, one of Surya's names.

[528] There are twenty-seven lunar mansions or *nakshatra*s, twenty-eight if Abhijit is included. Since some *nakshatra*s are constellations, *nakshatra* should not really be translated as star. *Vithi* means three *nakshatra*s taken together. *Ajavithi* means the three *nakshatra*s that indicate *dakshinayana*— Mula, Purvashada and Uttarashada, when the sun rises above these. *Nagavithi* means the three *nakshatra*s that indicate *uttarayana*—Ashvini, Krittika and Bharani (Yamya), when the sun rises above these three.

lines, enumerated in *yojana*s.[529] Understand the external and internal distance between these two lines and the two quarterly points is seven million,[530] one hundred and seventy-five thousand *yojana*s. During *uttarayana*, the sun moves along the inner circle. In the due order, during *dakshinayana*, it moves along the outer circle. There are one hundred and eighty-three divisions of the sky[531] in the north. In the south too, Vibhavasu moves through that number of divisions. In *yojana*s, understand the length of a *mandala*. In *yojana*s, this is collectively said to amount to seventeen thousand, two hundred and twenty-one *yojana*s. This is the length of a *mandala*, measured in *yojana*s. The diameter of a *mandala* is laid down diagonally. Every day, Surya traverses these *mandala*s in the due order. The outer rim of a potter's wheel revolves faster. Like that, during the southern transit, Surya moves faster. Hence, it traverses this excellent earth over a shorter period of time. A day consists of twelve *muhurta*s.[532] During *dakshinayana*, Surya moves rapidly and covers thirteen and a half *nakshtra*s in twelve *muhurta*s. Ravi covers that number of *nakshatra*s in the eighteen *muhurta*s of the night. The inside of a potter's wheel moves slowly. Like that, during *uttarayana*, Surya moves with slower vigour. Therefore, over a longer period of time, it traverses a shorter distance on earth. When it is *uttarayana*, there are eighteen *muhurta*s in a day. With this slower vigour, Ravi covers thirteen and a half *nakshtra*s over this period of time. Like that, it covers that number of *nakshatra*s in a night of twelve *muhurta*s. The centre or nave of a potter's wheel moves even more slowly. Dhruva[533] moves like that lump of clay in the centre. Day and night are said to consist of thirty *muhurta*s and

---

[529] The two longitudinal lines probably mean 0⁰ longitude and 180⁰ longitude. The astrological terms are difficult to translate and may not have been rendered completely accurately. In addition, the measures in *yojana*s are also not very clear.

[530] We have read *viyuta* as *niyuta*.

[531] *Mandala*s.

[532] Twenty-four hours have thirty *muhurta*s. Therefore, a day actually has fifteen *muhurta*s. This means the twelve *muhurta*s from sunrise to sunset, shorter during *dakshinayana*.

[533] The Pole Star.

Dhruva rotates during this period. In a circle, Dhruva rotates between the two quarterly points. This is just like the rotation of the centre of a potter's wheel. It should be known that Dhruva rotates in a fixed spot. Between the two quarterly points, it rotates in a circle. Depending on whether it is night or day, Surya moves slowly, or fast. During *uttarayana*, Surya's movement is slow during the day and swift during the night. During *dakshinayana*, Surya's movement is swift during the day and slow during the night. In this way, depending on the movement, night and day are divided. The transit is both regular and irregular.'

'The guardians of the worlds are established in the four directions of Lokaloka. Swiftly, Agastya[534] moves over them. During night and day, with differences in speed, he moves to the south of Nagavithi and north of Lokaloka. Beyond Vaishvanara's path,[535] he is the one who extends the worlds. As long as Surya shines from the back, there is illumination in front, at the back, and along the sides of Lokaloka. The mountain rises up for ten thousand *yojana*s. All around it, there are parts with illumination and parts without light. *Nakshatra*s, the moon, the sun, the planets and a large number of stars provide illumination on the inside of Mount Lokaloka. The worlds exist up to this point. Everything beyond is without light. There is illumination in the worlds on one side of Lokaloka and darkness in what is beyond Lokaloka. Surya separates light from darkness and the intervening region is known as *sandhya*. It is thus that *sandhya* is spoken of as *vyushti* and *usha*.[536] In that way, *brahmana*s remember *vyushti* as day and *usha* as night. At the time of *sandhya*, *rakshasa*s wished to devour Surya's fire. Urged by Prajapati, these evil-souled ones were cursed. Even when they died, their bodies would be imperishable. Three crore such *rakshasa*s are famous under the name of Mandehas. Every day, when the one with the one thousand rays rises and heats, those evil-souled ones pray and desire to devour Surya. Thereafter, there is an extremely terrible battle between them and Surya. At this,

---

[534] In this context, the star Canopus.

[535] Vaishvanara usually means Agni. But here, it means Surya.

[536] *Vyushti* means dawn. *Usha* means both early morning/dawn and twilight/night.

Brahma, *deva*s and excellent *brahmana*s worship and perform the *sandhya* rites. They always sprinkle water, invoked with the *gayatri mantra*, along with the sound of Oumkara *brahman*.[537] His radiance is ignited and with his fierce rays, Bhaskara provides illumination. In this way, he again becomes extremely energetic and immensely strong and valiant. He rises one hundred thousand *yojana*s above. The illustrious one swiftly proceeds, along with his rays, protected by the *brahmana*s and the *valakhilya* sages supporting his rays.'

'Fifteen *nimesha*s are one *kashtha*. Thirty *kashtha*s are reckoned as one *kalaa*. One *muhurta* consists of thirty *kalaa*s. There are thirty *muhurta*s in one day and night. Using these divisions, there is a progressive increase and decrease in the duration of a day. *Sandhya* is said to amount to one *muhurta* and is said to represent the increase or decrease. After the sun rises above the horizon, a period of three *muhurta*s is described as morning.[538] This is one-fifth of a day. The three *muhurta*s after morning constitute *samgava*. The three *muhurta*s after *samgava* constitute midday. Those who are learned about the divisions of time describe the duration of three *muhurta*s after midday as afternoon. The three *muhurta*s post the afternoon are known as evening. There are fifteen *muhurta*s in a day. At the equinoctial points, the day is said to consist of fifteen *muhurta*s. Depending on whether it is *dakshinayana* or *uttarayana*, there is an increase or decrease. In the former, night devours day. In the latter, day devours night. The equinoctial points are in the middle of autumn and the middle of spring. At these times, the moon has an equal number of *kalaa*s in day and night. Fifteen days are said to amount to one *paksha*. Two *paksha*s amount to one *masa*[539] and two solar *masa*s are one *ritu*. Three *ritu*s amount to one *ayana* and there are two *ayana*s in a solar year. *Nimesha* is also known as *vidyuta* and there are fifteen such in a *kashtha*. Thirty *kashtha*s constitute one *kalaa*. There are one hundred and sixty *matra*s in a *kashtha*. There are also said to be

---

[537] The first line of the *gayatri* (*savitri*) *mantra* is—*oum bhuh bhuvah svah*.
[538] Morning is *pratah*. *Samgava* is forenoon. Literally, it is the period when cows come together to be milked. Midday is *madhyahna*, afternoon is *aparahna*, evening is *sayahna*.
[539] Month. *Ritu* is season.

forty-five *matra*s in a *kashtha*.[540] Eighty-five *matra*s are also said to constitute a *kalaa* and there are said to be four thousand and eight hundred *vidyuta*s in a *kashtha*. It has not been certainly determined whether there are seventy or ninety *matra*s in a *kalaa*. There are also said to be four hundred and two *vidyuta*s in a *kashtha*. The best measurement of time should be known as that based on *nadika*.[541] Using four kinds of measurement, five kinds of years, *samvatsara* and the others have been conceived. For all kinds of measurements of time, the notion of *yuga* is fixed. *Samvatsara* is the first, while *parivatsara* is the second. *Idavatsara* is the third and *anuvatsara* is the fourth. The fifth is *vatsara*. When these durations of time are taken together, there is *yuga*. A solar year is complete when there are three hundred and sixty days, with some additional days.[542] In an *ayana*, Bhaskara rises one hundred and eighty times. There are three *ritu*s in an *ayana* and two *ayana*s in a solar year. Bhaskara's year lasts for three hundred and sixty-five days. A solar month lasts for thirty days and nights. One *ritu* is thought of as consisting of sixty-one days and nights.[543] The duration of Chitrabhanu's *ayana* is thought to consist of one hundred and eighty-three days. It should be known that the Puranas have determined there are four kinds of years—solar, lunar, *savana* and that based on *nakshatras*.[544] The mountain named Shringavan is to the north of Shveta. It has three peaks, which seem to touch the sky. The mountain is said to have received this name

[540] In other words, *matra* should be taken to mean any unit of measurement, instead of a specific unit of measurement, explaining the inconsistency. Sometimes, *nimesha* is equated with *matra*, but this need not always be the case. Sometimes, but not invariably, *nimesha* is also equated with *vidyuta*. The text isn't very clear, and we have expanded a bit, subjectively.

[541] *Nadika* also varies, but is sometimes taken to be equal to *ghatika*, or half a *muhurta*.

[542] There are typos in the text, which we have tried to correct. With thirty days in a month.

[543] That is, the solar year consists of 366 days.

[544] *Vatsara* is the one based on *nakshatra*s and is the sidereal year. *Savana* is related to a sacrifice and can be interpreted in different ways here. Since a solar year has already been mentioned, the word can be taken in the sense of the correct solar year, that is, with the intercalary month taken into consideration.

because of the summits.[545] Its diameter and circumference are equally
glorified. The eastern peak and the central peak are golden. The peak
to the south is silvery and sparkles like crystal. The excellent northern
peak is full of jewels everywhere.[546] Because of these three deep peaks,
the mountain is famous as Shringavan. Between autumn and spring,
Arka moves at a medium speed and reaches above the eastern peak.
In this way, the dispeller of darkness makes night and day equal.[547]
Divine green horses are yoked to his great chariot. They are radiant
and seem to be smeared with rays that are like red lotuses. Bhaskara's
rise then occurs towards the end of Mesha, or the end of Tula.[548]
Both day and night are then said to last for fifteen *muhurtas*. When
Surya enters the first quarter of Krittika, it should be known that the
moon enters the fourth part of Vishakha. When Surya enters the third
quarter of Vishakha, it should be known that the moon is located at
the top of Krittika. *Maharshis* say that these times should be known
as *vishuva*. *Vishuva* is determined by Surya and time is reckoned
by considering the position of the moon. When it is *vishuva*, the
durations of day and night are equal. At the time of *vishuva*, offerings
must be rendered to the ancestors. In particular, gifts must be given
to *brahmanas*, since they are the mouths of *devas*. Specific times are
*unamasa, adhimasa, kalaa, kastha, muhurta, pournamasi, amavasya,
sinivali, kuhu, raka* and *anumati*.[549] The months of *uttarayana* are

[545] *Shringa* means peak. Shringavan is one with peaks.
[546] This makes it four peaks. So, in addition to the central peak, there
are three peaks, to the east, the north and the south.
[547] The reference being to the vernal/spring equinox.
[548] Mesha *rashi* is Aries and Tula *rashi* is Libra. There is a complication
because of the precession of the equinoxes. But otherwise, the end of Mesha
means the *nakshatra* Bharani and the end of Tula means the *nakshatra*
Vishakha. But for use of the word 'end', this means *vishuva sankranti*. Of
course, 'end' can be either end, in which case, the *nakshatras* would be
Ashvini and Chitra. These are the respective indicated points for the vernal
equinox and the autumn equinox.
[549] *Unamasa* is a month that falls short of thirty days, *adhimasa* is an
intercalary month, *pournamasi* is the same as *purnima*, *sinivali* is the day
preceding the night of the new moon, *kuhu* is the night of the new moon,
raka is the night of the full moon and *anumati* is the fourteenth night of
shukla paksha.

Tapas, Tapasya, Madhu, Madhava, Shukra and Shuchi.[550] The months of *dakshinayana* are known as Nabhas, Nabhasya, Ishu, Urja, Sahas and Sahasya.[551] The five kinds of years are Brahma's sons and are known as *artava*s. The *ritu*s are known in this way and they are said to be *artava*s because they originate from *ritu*s. The *parva* of *amavasya* is known as one that has the *ritu*s as its face. Therefore, for the welfare of *deva*s and ancestors, one should always know about *vishuva*. If a man knows about *parva*s, he is not confused about what should be done for *deva*s and ancestors. *Vishuva* travels everywhere and subjects should not forget about it.'

'Lokaloka is known as that because that is the point up to which the worlds exist. The guardians of the worlds are established in the middle of the region with illumination and the region without illumination. Until the onset of the deluge, four great-souled ones are established there. They are Sudhama, Vairaja, Kardama, Shankhapa, Hiranyaroma, Parjanya, Ketuman and Rajasa.[552] They are devoid of the opposite pair of sentiments and devoid of pride. They are without boundaries and do not receive anything. In four directions, the guardians of the worlds are established on Lokaloka. North of Agastya and south of Ajavithi, is the path of the ancestors, *pitriyana*. This is beyond the sun's[553] path. Sages who perform *agnihotra* sacrifices and have offspring are established there. They are established along the path of the ancestors and ensure that the worlds continue. This southern path is for those who desire that the worlds should commence. They are *ritvija*s and perform acts of benediction so that creation starts. In every *yuga*, they again establish *dharma*, when it has deviated. They adhere to the boundaries set by the *shruti* texts and torment themselves through austerities. In this world, predecessors are born in the homes of descendants. When

[550] Older names for the months of Magha, Phalguna, Chaitra, Vaishakha, Jyeshtha and Ashadha.
[551] Older names for the months of Shravana, Bhadrapada, Ashvina, Kartika, Margashirsha and Pousha.
[552] Because of the sub-directions, eight have been named.
[553] Vaishvanara's.

the predecessors die, descendants are born. Conducting themselves
in this way, they remain until the onset of the deluge. There are
such eighty-eight thousand *rishi*s who are householders. As long
as the moon and stars exist, they are established on a path that
is to the south of the sun. There are these numbers who perform
rites and frequent cremation grounds.[554] For the sake of starting
creation, they follow worldly conduct. They indulge in desires
and hatred and engage in sexual intercourse. Caused by desire,
they indulge in material objects. These are the reasons why,
despite being *siddha*s, they frequent cremation grounds. Seeking
offspring, these sages are born in *dvapara yuga*. There is a path
that is to the north of Nagavithi, to the south of the group of
*saptarshi*s and to the north of the sun's path. This is known as
devayana. The *siddha*s who reside there are without blemish and
follow *brahmacharya*. They hate offspring and have conquered
death. There are eighty-eight thousand such *rishi*s who hold up
their seed. Until the onset of the deluge, they are established on
that northern path. Even when they come into contact with the
worlds, they avoid sexual intercourse. They withdraw from desire
and hatred and have nothing to do with the creation of beings.
They are disassociated from desire and devoid of taints associated
with sound and sight. Because of these reasons, they are *siddha*s
who are immortal. They enjoy this immortality until the onset
of the deluge. To establish the three worlds, they approach their
wives again.[555] There are others who have performed good deeds
and wicked ones, like performing horse sacrifices or killing
foetuses. Though they hold up their seed, when the deluge arrives,
they decay. To the north of the *rishi*s, the region is known by
Dhruva's name. This is a radiant and divine third firmament,
Vishnu's abode. This is Vishnu's supreme destination and a
person who goes there does not grieve. *Sadhaka*s of the worlds,
like Dharma and Dhruva, inhabit that region.'

[554] In the sense of dying.
[555] Probably after the deluge.

Chapter 22-1(22) (Description of divine planets)

Suta said, 'All the *manvantara*s in the course of Svayambhuva's creation have been described. In the due order, I will describe the future ones.'

Hearing this, the sages asked Romaharshana about the movements of the sun, the moon and all the planets.

The *rishi*s asked, 'How do the luminary bodies move around in the circle of the firmament? The arrangements are such that they do not get mixed up. Do they revolve on their own or does anyone make them do this? O excellent one! We wish to know this. Please tell us.'

Suta replied, 'This confounds beings. I will tell you. Understand. Although this can be directly seen, *prajas* are confounded. Dhruva, Uttanapada's son, is like the central pivot of the firmament, located in Shishumara.[556] In the four directions, the sun, the moon and the planets always revolve around him. As he rotates, like a wheel, the *nakshatra*s also follow. It is as if Dhruva's mind makes the group of luminary bodies, the sun, the moon, the stars, the *nakshatra*s and the planets revolve around him. Arrays of winds bind them to Dhruva. Everything is ensured by Dhruva—their conjunction and separation, the duration of movement, rising and setting, their falling, *dakshinayana* and *uttarayana*, *vishuva* and the hues of the planets. Everything is ensured by Dhruva—rain, heat, cold, night, *sandhya*, day and the auspicious and inauspicious for *prajas*. When Dhruva is established, Surya gathers water up and showers it down. The sun's blazing rays are like the fire of destruction. O *brahmanas*! As he revolves, Surya illuminates the worlds with his rays. In every direction, his net of rays is united with the wind. O excellent *dvijas*! He takes away water from the entire world. The moon spreads all the water that is drunk up by the sun. Water is showered down on the world through channels that are connected to the wind. The water exuded by the moon resides in the food. Obstructed by

---

[556] Literally, *shishumara* means dolphin/porpoise. These are circumpolar stellar bodies in the shape of a dolphin. Shishumara's tail corresponds to the constellation Draco, the dragon.

the wind, clouds release water on earth. In this way, the water is gathered up and falls. The water circulates in this way and is not destroyed. This universal *maya* has been devised for the sustenance of the worlds. The three worlds, with their mobile and immobile entities, are pervaded by this *maya*. Prajapati, the lord of the universe, possessing one thousand eyes, has done this for the sake of the worlds. He is the creator of all the worlds. The powerful Vishnu is the sun. The water that exudes from the moon is the water in all the worlds. Everything in the world is based on the flow from the moon. This is described as the truth. The sun exudes heat, the moon exudes coolness. Together, the vigour of heat and cold sustain the world. The flow from the moon is in the sacred River Ganga, full of pure water. O excellent *dvijas*! Bhadrasoma[557] is foremost among the great rivers. The waters in the bodies of all creatures follow her. When waters in mobile and immobile entities are scorched, they become vapour and emerge in all directions. Clouds result from this and there is said to be a place that is full of clouds. Through the energy of his rays, Arka receives water from all entities. United with the wind, those rays receive water from the oceans. This is like *amrita* and gives life to crops. As time changes and Divakara revolves, his rays convey water to white and dark clouds. Urged by the wind, water falls from the clouds. For the welfare of all beings, in every direction, it unites with the wind. In this way, it rains down for six months and all creatures flourish. The wind thunders and fire originates from lightning.'

'Because of the root "*mih*", a cloud is known as *megha*.[558] The wise know that a cloud is *abhra* because water does not fall. Clouds are said to originate in three different ways. These three types of clouds are *agneya*, *brahmaja* and *pakshaja*. Having mentioned them, I will speak about their origin. *Agneya*[559] clouds are said to originate from heat and lead to smoke. They are established in their own

[557] One of Ganga's names.

[558] The root "*mih*" means to sprinkle and shower down water. Hence, *megha*. A cloud is also known as *abhra*. *Bhramsha* means to fall. Here, *abhra* is derived as negation of *bhramsha*. This is an unusual and contrived derivation. The standard derivation is that *abhra* is a bearer of water.

[559] From Agni.

qualities of chill and winds on foul days. They assume the forms of buffaloes, boards and intoxicated elephants. Assuming these forms, they roam around and pleasure themselves on earth. Life originates from clouds named *jimuta*.[560] They are devoid of the quality of lightning. With torrents of water, they hang downwards. These are silent clouds, with gigantic sizes. They are under the control of the *avaha* wind. They shower down with a range of one *krosha* or one and a half *kroshas*. They shower down on summits and slopes of mountains and fill them with water. Clouds called *brahmaja*[561] are born from Brahma's breath. They lead to the impregnation of cranes and bear those foetuses within them. They possess the quality of lightning and thunder in a pleasant tone. As a result of their continuous thunder, the limbs of the earth shiver and plants sprout. This is like a queen who has been instated in the kingdom, thus enjoying a new bloom of youth. Since they are associated with rain, they impart life to creatures. These clouds seek refuge with the second kind of wind, *pravaha*. They shower down within a range of one *yojana* or one and a half *yojanas*. The clouds named *pushkaravartakas* are born from wings.[562] They are full of rain, and it is said that their downpour originates in three kinds of ways. The mountains used to be extremely energetic. They increased in size and went wherever they willed. To ensure welfare of beings, Shakra severed their wings. The clouds named *pushkara* were born from the wings. Envious of water, they increased in size. Because of this reason, they are spoken of as *pushkaravartaka*. They assume many forms and thunder in a loud and terrible tone. At the end of a *kalpa*, they are the ones who create rain and control the *samvartaka* fire. This third kind of cloud is said to shower down at the end of an era. They assume many kinds of forms and fill up the earth. They bear

560 Derived from the word for life, that is, a nourisher of life.

561 Literally, born from Brahma.

562 *Paksha* means wing and these are *pakshaja* clouds. Usually, *pushkara* and *avarta* are classified as different types of clouds, the other two principal ones being *samvarta* and *drona*. But from a meteorological angle, there are several names. *Avarta* means to revolve, whirl around. Envious of water, *pushkara* clouds started to whirl around and became *pushkaravartaka* or *pushkaravarta*.

the wind in front and accomplish the end of the *kalpa*. The cosmic egg that was born from Prakriti was shattered. Brahma, the lord with the four faces who rules himself, was born from this. All the shells of the cosmic egg are described as clouds. Smoke welcomes all of them, without any distinction. The best among them is known as Parjanya. There are *diggaja*s in the four directions.[563] Elephants, mountains, clouds and serpents are distinct. But they belong to the same lineage and are said to have originated from water. Instructed to make the crops grow, Parjanya and the *diggaja*s shower down dew, born from their coolness, during Hemanta. They seek refuge with the sixth wind, named *pravaha*. This illustrious wind supports the divine and sacred Ganga, with water like *amrita*, when she courses through the sky. In her three flows, she is established along Svati's path.[564] *Diggaja*s receive this with their thick trunks and release it in the form of a drizzle. This is known as *nihara*.[565] To the south, there is the mountain known as Hemakuta. To the north of the Himalayas, stretching from the north to the south, there is an extensive city, known by the name of Pundra. The rain that descends there originates from snow. The wind known as *avaha* fetches an extremely large store of water and sprinkles this over the great Himalaya mountain. It showers down the remaining rain beyond the Himalayas and thereby ensures the flourishing of the region that is beyond. Two types of rain, for the development of two types of crops, have been described. Everything has been recounted about the development of clouds. It has been stated that the sun is the creator of rain. The sun is the foundation. It is the sun which ensures water in rain to flow. Presided over by Dhruva, the sun works to ensure rain. Presided over by Dhruva, the wind withdraws rain.'

'A planet emerges from the sun and roams through the entire circle of *nakshatra*s. After this, presided over by Dhruva, it enters Surya again. Therefore, understand the way Surya's chariot is established. The illustrious one rides on a golden chariot, with a single wheel, five spokes, three naves, eight bolts and with the rim

---

[563] There are four elephants that dwell in the four directions. These are known as *diggaja*s, the elephant (*gaja*) for a direction (*dik*).

[564] Svati *nakshatra* is Arcturus.

[565] Frost or heavy dew.

divided into six parts. The horses are tawny. Surya's radiant chariot moves on this wheel. The length and breadth of the chariot is said to be ten thousand *yojana*s. In size, the central shaft is twice the length of the seat. Brahma created this chariot with the objective that it should not be attached to anything else. It is divine and golden and is yoked to horses that are as fleet as the wind. In front of the wheel, the *chhanda*s are stationed in the form of horses. Its characteristics are similar to those of Varuna's chariot. On this divine chariot, Divakara moves through the sky. The different parts and limbs of Surya's chariot are thought of as the following. In the due order, the single wheel is *samvatsara* and the solar day is the nave. The *artava*s are the five spokes and the *ritu*s are described as the six parts of the rim. Such is the inner seat of the chariot and the two *ayana*s are the two pole-shafts. *Muhurta*s and *kalaa*s are beautiful bent trappings. *Kashtha*s are remembered as the nose and *kshana*s as the axle of the wheel. *Nimesha*s are the bottom of the chariot and *lava*s are described as the pole. Night is the fender and *dharma* is the standard that rises. The tips of the yoke and axle are described as *artha* and *kama*. In the form of horses, the seven *chhanda*s bear the burden of the chariot towards the left. These are *gayatri, trishtup, anushtup, jagati, pankti, brihati* and *ushnik* as the seventh. The wheel is fixed to the axle and the axle is anchored on Dhruva. Dhruva makes the axle rotate and as the axle rotates, so does the wheel. Urged by Dhruva, the axle moves, along with the wheel. Given the purpose, this was the way the chariot was constructed. Joined in this way, the radiant chariot achieves its purpose. Using this radiant chariot, he crosses over the firmament. Two reins are fixed at the ends of the yoke and axle.[566] Using the two reins attached to the yoke and the wheel, it moves around Dhruva. As they move through the sky, the reins of the chariot move in a circle. The ends of the chariot's yoke and axle are towards the south of Dhruva. As they revolve, Dhruva seizes them, as if protecting them. As they revolve, those two reins follow Dhruva. During *uttarayana*, the reins and the circle are shorter. During *dakshinayana*, the circle of revolution increases in size. The ends of the yoke and axle are fixed to the chariot with

---

[566] The word used is *rashmi*, which means rein, as well as ray.

the two reins. Dhruva seizes the two reins and makes Ravi move along. Established there, Dhruva tugs equally on these two reins and thus, Surya revolves within an inner circle. The distance between the quarterly points of the inner circle is described as eight thousand.[567] Thereafter, it is Dhruva who releases the reins and Surya revolves in an outer circle. As instructed, he moves faster along this circle.'

Chapter 23-1(23) (Description of Dhruva's movement)

Suta said, 'Devas, Adityas, sages, gandharvas, apsaras, gramanis, sarpas and rakshasas are established on that chariot. In the due order, they remain with Surya for two months each. In the months of Madhu and Madhava, the devas are Dhatri and Aryaman; the Prajapatis are Pulastya and Pulaha; the sarpas are Airavata, Vasuki, Kamsa and Bhima; the yakshas are said to be Rathakrit and Rathoujas; the gandharvas are Tumburu and Narada; the apsaras are Susthala and Punjikasthala; and the yatudhana rakshasas are Heti and Praheti.[568] They always reside with Surya in these months. In the months of Shuchi and Shukra, devas are Mitra and Varuna; the sages are cited as Atri and the famous Vasishtha; the apsaras are Sahajanya and Menakaa; the rakshasas are known as Pourusheya and Vadha; the gandharvas are Haha and Huhu; the yakshas are Rathasvana and Rathachitra; and the nagas are known as Nagasakshaka and Rambhaka. These are the ones who reside. There are other divinities who also reside in Surya. In the months of Nabhas and Nabhasya, the categories who reside in Bhaskara are Indra and Vivasvan as devas; Angiras and Bhrigu as sages; Elapatra and Shankapala as sarpas; Vishvavasu and Ugrasena as gandharvas; Shveta and Aruna as yakshas; the famous Pramlocha

---

[567] Yojanas is left implicit.

[568] The word Prajapati is used for a sage. The text doesn't always state which category an individual belongs to. We have added those for clarity.

and Anumlocha as *apsara*s; and Sarpa and Vyaghra as *yatudhana*s. In the months of autumn,[569] pure sages and *deva*s reside. *Deva*s are Parjanya and Pushan; the sages are Bharadvaja and Goutama; the *gandharva*s are Paravasu and Suruchi; the two *apsara*s, auspicious in signs, are Vishvachi and Ghritachi; the *naga*s are Airavata and the famous Dhananjaya; the commanders of *gramani*s[570] are Syenajit and Sushena; and the two *yatudhana*s are mentioned as Apas and Vata. These are the ones who always reside in Surya during Ashvina and Kartika. During the two months of Hemanta, *deva*s who reside in Divakara are Amsha and Bhaga; the sages are Kashyapa and Kratu; the serpents and *sarpa*s are Mahapadma and Karkotaka; the two *gandharva*s are Chitrasena and Urnayu; the two *apsara*s are Urvashi and Purvachitti; the commanders of *gramani*s are Tarksha and Arishtanemi; and the *yatudhana*s are said to be Vidyutsphurja and Shatayu. These are the ones who reside in Divakara during the months of Saha and Sahasya. In the months of Shishira, the species who reside are Tvashta and Vishnu as *deva*s; Jamadagnya and Vishvamitra as sages; Kambala and Ashvatara as the two *naga*s, sons of Kadru; Dhritarashtra and Suryavarcha as *gandharva*s; Tilottama and Rambha as *apsara*s; Brahmapeta and the famous Yajnapeta, the excellent *rakshasa*, as *rakshasa*s; and Ritajit and Satyajit are said to be the two *gandharva*s.[571] O excellent sages! These are the ones who reside in Surya in the months of Tapa and Tapasya. O *dvija*s! The lord Savitar, the cause of night and day, revolves and nourishes ancestors, *deva*s, humans and others. In the due order, these divinities reside for two months each. These seven categories[572] are proud of their positions in the twelve months. Their excellent energy contributes to Surya's energy. Using words they have themselves composed, the *rishi*s praise Ravi. *Gandharva*s and *apsara*s sing and dance and worship him. *Gramani*s, *yaksha*s and other beings gather

---

[569] That is, Ashvina and Kartika.
[570] That is, *yaksha*s.
[571] This should be *yaksha*s, not *gandharva*s. *Gandharva*s have already been mentioned.
[572] *Deva*s, *rishi*s, *naga*s, *gandharva*s, *apsara*s, *yaksha*s and *rakshasa*s.

his reins.[573] According to their strength, *sarpa*s and *yatudhana*s carry him. From sunrise to sunset, *valakhilya*s surround him and lead him. These divinities do this according to their valour, austerities, *dharma*, *yoga*, truth and strength. Their lord, Surya, scorches them with his energy. In this way, they reside in Divakara for two months each—*deva*s, *rishi*s, *gandharva*s, *pannaga*s, large numbers of *apsara*s, *gramani yaksha*s and the foremost *yatudhana*s. They heat, shower down, shine, blow and create. When they are described, they take away the auspicious *karma* of beings. They take away the auspicious deeds of humans who are wicked in their souls. Sometimes, they take away the wicked deeds of those who are virtuous in conduct. During the day, they follow Surya as he revolves. They shower, scorch and delight *praja*s. Until the Manus are destroyed, they protect all beings. During the *manvantara*s, these are their positions, and they are proud of these positions. This is true of past *manvantara*s, the current ones and future ones. Thus, the seven categories reside in Surya for fourteen *manvantara*s. All these categories dwell for fourteen *manvantara*s.'

'The sun releases heat during the summer and cold. He showers during the monsoon. He makes night and day. Depending on the season, he revolves and moves, satisfying *deva*s, ancestors and humans. Surya delights *deva*s with *amrita*. During the days of *shukla paksha*, he uses *sushumna*[574] to make the moon increase, until it becomes full. The Gods drink this during *krishna paksha*. As this is drunk during *krishna paksha*, the moon's digits decrease, until only one digit is left. At that time, its beams exude no more. Ancestors, *deva*s, *soumya*s and *kavya*s drink the nectar that is *amrita*.[575] Surya uses his rays to raise the water and release it again. Rain enables plants to grow. Mortals can satisfy their hunger through food and obtain drink. During *shukla paksha*, the Gods are satisfied with the nectar. During *krishna paksha*, ancestors are satisfied with the nectar. Mortals are constantly nourished with the food. Surya scorches and sustains them with his rays. When

---

[573] Alternatively, rays.
[574] One of the sun's rays.
[575] In this context, *soumya*s and *kavya*s are categories of ancestors.

Hari takes the water away, his rays are tawny.[576] His horses are tawny. When it is time for release, he releases it again. In this way, Savitar eternally nurtures mobile and immobile entities. Hari takes away with his tawny rays. His horses are tawny. Hari drinks up the water with one thousand tawny rays. After this, Hari releases again and his tawny steeds confound. In this way, Surya proceeds swiftly, astride his chariot with a single wheel. The horses proceed along the propitious path, resounding with the eternal sound of the *Veda*s. Yoked to seven horses, in the course of a day and night, the chariot with a single wheel traverses the earth, with its seven *dvipa*s and seven oceans. The *chhanda*s assume the form of horses and are yoked close to the wheel. They can assume any form they want and are beautiful and well-trained, travelling at the speed of thought. Those who know about the *brahman* say that the horses are tawny in complexion. In the course of a year, the horses circle eighty-three hundred times.[577] As the days pass, they traverse the inner circle, as well as the outer one. They were yoked at the start of the *kalpa* and will continue to bear the burden until the deluge arrives for creatures. Surrounded by the *valakhilya*s, they travel night and day. Using the foremost words they have composed, *maharshi*s praise the sun. Large numbers of *gandharva*s and *apsara*s serve him with singing and dancing. The lord of the day travels through the sky on horses that are swift.'

'Soma's chariot has three wheels, and the horses possess the complexion of the *kunda* flower. Ten horses are yoked, to the left and to the right, and he travels with these. He follows the path of the *nakshatra*s and his speed is supported by Dhruva. The increase and decrease in the beams are said to be similar to those of Surya. It should be known that the moon's chariot, with three wheels, has horses yoked on both sides. Along with the horses and the charioteer, the chariot originated from the womb of water. There are three wheels, each with one hundred spokes. The ten

---

[576] Hari is one of the sun's names and the word *hari* means tawny. There is thus a pun on words, with *harati* meaning to take away.

[577] This number is impossible to understand. Perhaps it is a typo and is meant to be 360.

horses are excellent and white. They are slim and divine. Without any obstructions, they travel at the speed of thought. Yoked only once to the chariot, they bear it until the yugas are over. White serpents are gathered around that chariot. The horses possess the same complexion, like that of a conch shell, and bear the chariot. Their names are Yajus, Chandamanas, Vrisha, Vaji, Nara, Haya, the famous horse Gavishnu, Hamsa, Vyoma and Mriga. These are all the names of the moon's ten horses. Instated in this way, the bear the divinity, the moon. Soma proceeds, surrounded by devas and ancestors. Towards the beginning of shukla paksha, Bhaskara is located on the other side of Soma. As the days pass, the moon is constantly filled. Devas constantly drink from the moon's body, which decays over a span of fifteen days. With a single ray, Bhaskara fills up the moon. Bit by bit, in the due order of days, sushumna is used for the filling up. Nourished by sushumna, the white digits increase. In this way, the digits decline during krishna paksha and are nourished during shukla paksha. Thus, Chandra[578] is nourished through Surya's energy. On pournamasi, the white disc is seen to be complete. In this way, from one day to another day, Soma is nourished during shukla paksha. From dvitiya to chaturdashi,[579] devas drink a lot of the juices, representing the essence of the water that is in the moon. They are delighted at drinking this water from the moon, which is a nectar that is like amrita. It is because of Surya's energy that this amrita is accumulated in the course of half a month. To partake of this amrita, on the single night of pournamasi, all the Gods, along with ancestors and rishis, worship Soma. At the beginning of krishna paksha, Soma faces Bhaskara. As devas and ancestors gradually drink its digits, they decay. Three thousand, three hundred, thirty-three and three devas drink from Soma. When they drink in this way, the dark digits of the moon increase. The white digits diminish, and the dark digits increase. As the days pass, the Gods drink in this way from the maker of the night.[580] Having drunk for half a month, the excellent

[578] The moon.
[579] Respectively, the second and fourteenth lunar days (tithis).
[580] The moon.

Gods depart at the time of *amavasya*. At the time of *amavasya*, the ancestors present themselves before the maker of the night. On the fifteenth day, a little is left of the digits. In the afternoon, the categories of ancestors resort to this last bit. For the duration of two *lava*s, they drink the remaining digits. At the time of *amavasya*, the *svadha* of *amrita* exudes through the beams.[581] Having drunk that *svadha* of *amrita* for a month, they depart. Using *sushumna*, Surya scorches Chandra and during *krishna paksha*, the Gods drink the nectar. The ancestors are of three types—*soumya*s, *barhishad*s and *agnishavtta*s. All those spoken of as *kavya*s are ancestors. *Dvija*s remember *kavya*s as *samvatsara*s or *panchabda*s.[582] *Soumya*s are known as *ritu*s and *barhishad*s are described as *masa*s.[583] O *dvija*s! The ancestors created as *agnishvatta*s are *artava*s. The ancestors drink the five digits. After fifteen digits have been drunk, there is one digit that is left and that is filled on *amavasya*.[584] At the start of a *paksha*, the increase and decrease in the sixteen digits of the moon is remembered. Thus, Surya is the cause behind the increase and decrease in the maker of the night.'

'I will next speak about the chariots of stars, planets and Svarbhanu.[585] The chariot of Soma's son[586] is sparkling and is full of the energy of water. Bhargava's[587] chariot is resplendent and energetic, resembling that of the sun. The ancillaries, flag and standard are also like that, and it thunders like a cloud. It is yoked to excellent horses that have many complexions and have originated from the earth. The ten immensely fortunate horses are Shveta, Pishanga, Saranga, Nila, Pita, Vilohita, Krishna, Harita, Prishata and Prishni. They are lean and are as fleet as the wind, or swans.

---

[581] *Svadha* is an exclamation made when oblations are offered to ancestors. Here, it stands for the oblations. Similarly, *svaha* is an exclamation made when oblations are offered to Gods.

[582] *Panchabda* means five years.

[583] As in, months.

[584] The moon has sixteen digits or *kalaa*s.

[585] Rahu.

[586] That is, Budha (Mercury).

[587] Bhargava is Shukra (Venus).

Bhouma's[588] excellent, golden and glorious chariot is yoked to eight horses. The red horses, born from the fire, can go everywhere and are not impeded. The prince is borne by these, straight, clockwise and anti-clockwise. The learned preceptor, Brihaspati,[589] is descended from the lineage of Angiras. He moves on a golden chariot, yoked to eight horses that are as fair as camphor. They are divine and possess the speed of the wind, or of swans. He remains in a *nakshatra* for a year and is thus placed in a *rashi*. Shanaishchara's[590] horses are strong and originated from space. He proceeds slowly, on a chariot that resembles black iron. Svarbhanu has eight black horses that possess the speed of thought. The horses are yoked once and bear a chariot that is full of darkness. Emerging from the sun, on *parva* days,[591] Rahu goes to the moon. Similarly, at the time of a lunar eclipse, he leaves the moon and goes to the sun. Ketu's chariot has eight horses that are as swift as the wind, or swans. They are strong and red, like donkeys. Their complexion is like the smoke when a straw is burnt. The mounts and chariots of the planets have thus been narrated. All of them are developed and are bound to Dhruva by wind in the form of rays. They scorch as they revolve. They revolve but are bound. They are developed because of wind in the form of rays, a wind that is invisible. Bound in this, the moon, the sun and the planets revolve in the firmament. As they revolve, all these categories of luminous bodies follow Dhruva. A boat is borne along in the water of a river. It moves, along with the water. In that way, these abodes of the divinities are borne along by wind in the form of rays. As they move in space, these categories of divinities cannot be seen. As long as the stars exist, the wind in the form of rays also exists. All of them are bound to Dhruva. They revolve and make others revolve. They move like the wheel of an oil press. They revolve and make others revolve. All the luminous bodies move in this way, tied by wind in the form of rays. This is like a circle of fire, a circle created by wind. The wind that bears the luminous bodies is known as *pravaha*. In this way,

---

[588] Bhouma is Mars.
[589] Jupiter, the preceptor of the Gods.
[590] Saturn's. The word Shanaishchara means one who moves slowly.
[591] At the time of a lunar eclipse.

the large numbers of luminous bodies move, bound to Dhruva. It should be known that in the firmament, Shishumara and Dhruva are made up of stars. If a sin is committed during the day, one is freed from it by looking at Dhruva at night. As long as the stars exist, they resort to Shishumara in the firmament, and such a person lives for that number of years and more. One should know that Shishumara's form is divided into parts. Uttanapada's son[592] is known as the upper part of the jaw. Yajna is known as the lower part of the jaw. Dharma constitutes the head. Narayana is the heart. Sadhyas and the two Ashvins are the two front legs. Varuna and Aryama constitute the posterior thighs. *Samvatsara* is the penis and Mitra is the anus. Agni, Mahendra, Maricha, Kashyapa and Dhruva are certainly in the tail. These four stars in Shishumara do not set.[593] *Nakshatra*s, the moon, the sun, the planets, and large numbers of stars are all fixed in the firmament. Some face forwards, some backwards. Some have retrograde movements. Dhruva presides over them, and they circle Dhruva. Dhruva is an excellent lord and is like a pivot in the firmament. After Agni, Indra and Kashyapa, Dhruva is remembered as the fourth. Located on the summit of Mount Meru, he alone makes them move. Those luminous bodies circle like a wheel. They are made to fall as if struck with a club. He glances towards Meru and performs its *pradakshina*.'

Chapter 24-1(24) (Placement of luminous bodies)

Suta said, 'Having heard this, the sages were again filled with doubts. Therefore, they again asked Romaharshana for an answer. "You have spoken in detail about the residences. What are the forms of *deva* abodes? What is the description of luminous

---

[592] That is, Dhruva. We are told later, rightly, that Dhruva is in the tail.
[593] Agni, Mahendra (the great Indra), Kashyapa and Dhruva. Today, other than Dhruva, it is impossible to identify the others. As will be clear, Maricha is not one of the four.

bodies? Please tell us everything about the determination of luminous bodies."'

Vayu continued, 'Hearing their words, Vayu controlled himself. To dispel their doubts, he uttered these excellent words.'

Suta said, 'Using their *jnana* and intelligence, the immensely wise ones have spoken about this. I will speak about the origin of the sun and the moon and about how the sun, the moon and the planets came to be remembered as abodes of *deva*s. After this, I will tell you about the origin of the three kinds of fire—the divine fire from the elements, the fire that originated from the water and the fire on earth. Brahma's birth is not manifest and his night was over. Nothing was manifest. Everything was enveloped by the darkness of the night. Everything was in the elements. All the specifics in the world had been destroyed. Bhagavan Svayambhu is the one who accomplishes the activities of the worlds. Wishing to manifest himself, he moved around like a firefly. At the start of the worlds, he saw Agni, with a refuge in earth and water. For the sake of illumination, the lord gathered it and divided it into three parts. The fire that purifies the world is spoken of as *parthiva* fire.[594] The fire that scorches in the sun is remembered as *shuchi*. The fire that originated from water is known as *vaidyuta*. I will speak about their characteristics. The fire that originated from a womb in the water is of three types—*vaidyuta*, *jathara* and *soura*.[595] Thus, Surya uses his rays to drink up water and blazes in the firmament. When it rains, there is *vaidyuta* fire and it is not pacified by water. The fire that is in the stomachs of humans is also not pacified by water. Thus, *vaidyuta*, *jathara* and *soura* fires have water as kindling. In some cases, water provides the energy. In some cases, water is the kindling. When fire is produced by rubbing *arani* sticks, that fire is pacified by water. The fire that purifies has flames. The *jathara* fire is described as one that lacks radiance. The fire that is in the solar disc is white and devoid of heat. It provides illumination. As the maker of the day heads towards setting, the radiance of the sun progressively diminishes by a quarter. The fire enters the night and

---

[594] Terrestrial fire, from *prithivi* (the earth).
[595] Respectively, fire in lightning, digestive fire and fire in the sun.

provides illumination only from a distance. When the sun rises
again, the heat of the terrestrial fire enters the sun, progressively
by a quarter. This is the fire that scorches. Illumination and heat
are characteristics of the energetic *soura* fire. The fires enter each
other and nourish each other. In the northern half of the earth,
as well as the southern half, when the sun rises and there is fire,
the night enters water. Therefore, water is warm during the day.
This is because, during the day, the night enters. When the sun
sets again, day enters the water. Therefore, during the night, the
water is seen as white and radiant. This is the due order in the
northern half of the earth and the southern half. Constantly, at
the time of sunrise and sunset, night and day enter the water.
Using his rays, Surya drinks up the water and heats. When mixed
with the terrestrial fire, this is known as the divine *shuchi*[596] fire.
Shuchi fire possesses one thousand rays and seems to be holding a
pot. With one thousand rays that spread out like arteries in every
direction, he drinks up water in all directions from rivers, oceans,
wells and canals, irrespective of whether the water is flowing or
stationary. Those one thousand rays exude cold, rain and heat.
Four hundred of those arteries have colourful forms and shower
down rain. The names of all these rays that release *amrita* as rain
are Chandanas, Sadhyas, Kutanas and Akutanas. There are three
hundred other rays that lead to cold. Those that lead to cold are
Drishya, Meghas, Yamyas and Hradinis. The names of the rays
that are limited in radiance are said to be Chandras. There are
three hundred rays that lead to heat. Their names are Shuklas,
Kuhakas and Vishvabhrits. The arteries are equally divided among
humans, ancestors and *devas*. Through the three types of rays,
he satisfies all those who belong to the three categories. Humans
obtain herbs, ancestors obtain *svadha* and the Gods obtain *amrita*.
During Vasanta and Grishma, he heats with three hundred rays.
During Varsha and Sharad, he showers down with four hundred
rays. During Hemanta and Shishira, he releases cold with three
hundred rays.'

[596] Meaning pure.

'Indra, Dhatri, Bhaga, Pushan, Mitra, Varuna, Aryama, Amshu, Vivasvat, Tvashta, Savitar and Vishnu.[597] It is Varuna in the month of Magha; Pushan in Phalguna; the divinity Amshu in the month of Chaitra; Dhatri heats in the month of Vaishakha; it is Indra in the month of Jyeshtha; in Ashadha, the sun is Savitar; in the month of Shravana, it is Vivasvat; in the month of Proshthapada, it is described as Bhaga; in the month of Ashvayuja, it is Parjanya;[598] in Kartika, the sun is Tvashta; it is Mitra in Margashirsha; and in Pousha, it is the eternal Vishnu. In working as Arka, Varuna has five thousand rays; Pushan has six thousand; the divinity Amshu has seven thousand; Dhatri has eight thousand; Shatakratu[599] has nine thousand; Savitar moves with ten thousand; Bhaga has eleven thousand; Mitra heats with seven thousand; Tvashta heats with eight thousand; Aryama moves with ten thousand; Parjanya[600] heats with nine thousand; and Vishnu scorches the earth with six thousand rays. During Vasanta, Surya is tawny; during Grishma, Arka is golden in complexion; during Varsha, the complexion is white; during Sharad, Bhaskara is pale; during Hemanta, his complexion is coppery; and during Shishira, Ravi is red. As a consequence of the seasons, there are described as Surya's hues. Surya provides strength to herbs, *svadha* to ancestors and *amrita* to the immortals. He bestows these three kinds of things to the three categories. In this way, the sun's one thousand rays accomplish tasks for the worlds. In exuding water, cold and heat, there are differences across the seasons. The resplendent and white disc is known as Surya. He is the foundation and origin of *nakshatra*s, planets and the moon. The moon, *nakshatra*s and planets should all be known as originating from Surya. Soma is the lord of *nakshatra*s. Divakara is the king of planets. The other five planets[601] should be known as lords, roaming around as they will. It is read that Chandra is described

---

[597] The sentence is left incomplete. These are the names of the twelve Adityas.

[598] Parjanya is being equated with Aryama.

[599] Performer of one hundred sacrifices, Indra's name.

[600] In an inconsistency, Parjanya is now equated with Vivasvat.

[601] Angaraka (Mangala), Budha, Shanaishchara, Shukra and Brihaspati.

as the fire in the sun and in water. I will describe the nature of the others properly. Understand. The commander of the army of the Gods is Skanda[602] and it is read that he is the planet Angaraka. Learned ones, who know about the *jnana* in the *Veda*s, speak of Narayana as Budha. The great planet Shanaishchara moves slowly and is the best among *dvija*s. He is himself Rudra Yama, the son of the sun and lord of the worlds. There are two radiant and large planets who are respectively the preceptors of *deva*s and *asura*s. They are Shukra and Brihaspati and both of them are Prajapati's son. There is no doubt that Aditya is the foundation of everything in the three worlds. The entire universe, with *deva*s, *asura*s and humans, originates from him. O Indras among *brahmana*s! There is radiance in the brilliant ones—Rudra, Upendra,[603] Indra, Chandra and the residents of heaven. All this energy in all the worlds belongs to him. He is in all *atman*s. He is the lord of all the worlds. He is the great divinity. He is Prajapati. Surya is the foundation of the three worlds. He is the supreme divinity. Everything is born from him, and everything dissolves into him. In ancient times, the existence and non-existence of the worlds flowed from Aditya. O *brahmana*s! It should be known that the radiance received in the universe was from the extremely radiant Ravi. Destruction happens into him, and rebirth occurs repeatedly. Without Aditya, there would have been no reckoning of all the measurement of time—*kshana*s, *muhurta*s, days, nights, fortnights, months, *samvatsara*s, seasons and *yuga*s. Without time, there would have been no *nigama* texts, no *diksha* and no process of *ahnika*.[604] If there is no division of seasons, how can there be flowers, roots and fruits? How can there be crops, sprouting, grass, or various types of herbs? All the activities of creatures, in heaven and on earth, will cease to exist. If Bhaskara does not heat and take up water, everything in the world will stop. He is time. He is fire. He is Prajapati in his twelve forms.[605] O best

[602] Kartikeya/Kumara.

[603] Indra's younger brother, Vishnu's name.

[604] *Nigama* texts are *Veda*s or ancillary texts, *diksha* is the process of initiation/consecration and *ahnika* means daily rites.

[605] The twelve Adityas in the twelve months.

among *dvija*s! Along with mobile and immobile entities, he heats
the three worlds. He is a mass of energy that destroys darkness in all
the worlds. Along with the wind, he resorts to a superior path and
heats everything in this world, above, below and sideways. This is
just like the radiance of a lamp suspended inside a house destroying
darkness, above, below and sideways. The king of planets, the
lord of the world, possesses one thousand rays. Using his rays,
Surya illuminates everything, in all directions. Among Ravi's one
thousand rays, there are said to be seven that are the foremost and
these are the origins of the planets. These are Sushumna, Harikesha,
Vishvakarma, Vishvashrava, Sampadvasu, Arvavasu and the last is
described as Svarat. Surya's ray of Sushumna nourishes the moon
when it decays. Sushumna is described as one that courses above
and sideways. Harikesha, which is in front, is described as the origin
of *nakshatra*s. Vishvakarma is the ray to the right, and it nourishes
Budha. Vishvashrava is at the back and the learned remember it
as Shukra's origin. The ray Sampadvasu is the origin of Lohita.[606]
The sixth ray, Arvavasu, is the origin of Brihaspati. The ray Svarat
nourishes Shanaishchara. In this way, planets, *nakshatra*s and stars
remain in the firmament because of Surya's powers. This is true of
everything in the universe.'

'The ones that do not decay are described as *nakshatra*s.[607]
Earlier, they used to fall down from their *kshetra*s. Since Surya's
rays fix them in their *kshetra*s, he is the creator of *nakshatra*s. Those
who have performed good deeds can cross over. *Taraka*s are those
that enable performers of good deeds to cross over the influence of
bad planets. Because of this crossing over, these white bodies are
*taraka*s.[608] The sun is known as Aditya because he constantly takes
away the energy and heat from everywhere in the firmament, earth
and night.[609] The root "*savana*" is conceived of in the sense of

[606] The red one, Mars.
[607] Derived from *na* + *kshiyante*, one that does not decay. This is not
a certain derivation. *Nakshatra*s are lunar mansions or asterisms. *Kshetra*
means field.
[608] *Taraka*s are stars, derived here from *tarana* (crossing over/saving).
[609] Derived from *adana* (taking away), an unusual derivation.

flowing. Since his energy makes the waters flow, he is thought of as Savitar. The root is said to convey the sense of carrying and causing delight. One thinks of the properties of whiteness, *amrita* and coolness. The divine orbs of Surya and Chandra are radiant in the sky. They are white and full of energy and water. They are auspicious, resembling round pots. The moon's disc is said to be full of dense water. Bhaskara's white disc is said to be full of dense energy. All the different divinities enter all these different positions. In different *manvantaras*, all of them seek refuge in *nakshatras*, Surya and the planets.[610] The abodes of the divinities are named after them. Surya enters the location known as Soura and Soma the one known as Soumya. Shukra enters the location of Shoukra, with six extremely radiant rays. Brihaspati enters the location known as Jaiva[611] and Lohita that of Louhita. The divinity Shanaishchara enters the location known as Shaanaishchara. Budha enters Boudha and Svarbhanu resorts to the location named after Svarbhanu. All the *nakshatras* enter locations meant for *nakshatras*. All these luminous abodes are meant for the performers of good deeds. When the beginning of the *kalpa* commenced, Svayambhu devised their conduct in these locations. They remain in these locations until the onset of the deluge. This is what happens with the locations of the divinities in all the *manvantaras*. They take pride and remain in these positions. Those who are past resided with past *devas*. Those in the future will reside with future *devas*. Those in the present, reside there with the current *devas*. In this *manvantara*, the planets are remembered as *vaitanikas*.[612] Aditi's son, Vivasvat, occupies the position of Surya in Vaivasvata *manvantara*. Dharma's son, named Tvishi, has the position of Soma. *Devas* are remembered as Vasus. The divinity Shukra is known as Bhargava, who performs sacrifices for *asuras*. The son of Angiras, extensive in energy, is remembered

---

[610] The names of the divinities who occupy these locations change from one *manvantara* to another.

[611] Jiva is another name for Brihaspati.

[612] A *vaitanika* is someone who has performed a sacrifice. By virtue of that good deed, they have become planets.

as the divinity who is the preceptor of *deva*s.[613] Tvishi's descendant
is remembered as the beautiful Budha. Shanaishchara is the
disfigured son of Samjna and Vivasvat.[614] The son born to Agni and
Vikeshi became the young lord of Lohita. The *nakshatra*s, also
named *riksha*s, are remembered as Daksha's daughters. Svarbhanu
is Simhika's son and this *asura* torments beings. Those who take
pride in the positions of Soma, *nakshatra*s, planets and Surya have
been described. The positions have been described and the divinities
who occupy these positions. The abode of Visvasvat, with the one
thousand rays, is white and full of fire. Tvishi's son has one thousand
beams, and his abode is white and full of water. Manojna's[615] abode
is dark and full of water, and he possesses five rays. Shukra's abode
is as white as a lotus and is full of water. He possesses sixteen rays.
Bhouma's abode of Lohita is full of water, and he possesses nine
rays. Brihaspati's large abode is green and full of water. He possesses
twelve rays. The dark abode of the one who moves slowly[616] is full
of water. He is said to possess eight rays. Svarbhanu's abode is dark
and he causes torment to all beings. It should be known that all the
*taraka*s are full of water and each of them possesses a single ray.
These are the refuges of those who have performed good deeds and
are described as being extremely white. They should be known to be
full of a dense mass of water. They were constructed at the beginning
of the *kalpa*. It is said that they possess illumination because of their
contact with Aditya's rays. Savitar's diameter is said to extend for
nine thousand *yojana*s. The dimension of the circumference is three
times that. The expanse of the moon is said to be double the expanse
of the sun. Svarbhanu can be either and extends below them.
Extracting the earth's shadow, he has been constructed in the shape
of a sphere. Svarbhanu possesses a third large abode that is full of
darkness. At the time of a lunar eclipse, it leaves the sun and goes to
the moon. At the time of a solar eclipse, it leaves the moon and goes

[613] That is, Brihaspati.
[614] He was disfigured because of a curse imposed by his stepmother,
when Samjna replaced herself with Chhaya.
[615] Budha's.
[616] Shanaishchara.

to the sun. It is known as Svarbhanu because it takes away the radiance of the firmament.[617] Bhargava's expanse has been determined as one-sixteenth that of Chandra's. This is the measurement, in *yojana*s, of the diameter and the circumference. Brihaspati's dimensions are known to be one-quarter smaller than those of Bhargava. Bhouma and Soura[618] possess dimensions that are one-quarter smaller than those of Brihaspati. In diameter and circumference, Budha is one-quarter smaller, compared to them. The dimensions and forms of *taraka*s and *nakshatra*s are similar to those of Budha. This is true of form, diameter and circumference. Those who know the truth know that *riksha*s are generally in conjunction with Chandra. The dimensions of *taraka*s and *nakshatra*s successively decline by five hundred, four hundred, three hundred and two hundred *yojana*s. The discs of *taraka*s are smaller than those of the preceding ones. However, among them, there is no *taraka* that is smaller than one and a half *yojana*s. There are three planets that are above and revolve extremely far away. These are Saturn, Jupiter and Mars and these are known to move slowly. The four giant planets that are below them move fast. These are Surya, Soma, Budha and Bhargava. In every direction, there are crores of *taraka*s and *riksha*s. Vidhatri laid down the rules for the movement of *riksha*s. Depending on the progress of *ayana*s, Surya moves above them, or below them. When Surya is on the path of *uttarayana*, on *parva* days, Chandra's movement is very fast. Since he is placed above and because of his movement, his beams cannot be seen. Similarly, when Surya is on the path of *dakshinayana*, Chandra resorts to the lower path. At the time of *pournamasi* and *amavasya*, Surya is always in line with the earth's horizon. He is not seen at the regular time and sets quickly. Similarly, when Surya follows the northern path, the maker of the night is seen on the southern path. At the time of *amavasya*, he is not seen. Since this is the movement and conjunction of the luminous bodies, at the time of the equinoctial points, Surya and Chandra's movement is such that they rise and set at the same time. But along the northern path, there are differences

---

[617] *Nudate* means to remove.
[618] Surya's son, Shanaischara.

in rising and setting. It should be known that during *pournamasi* and *amavasya*, they follow the circle set by luminous bodies. When the one with the rays moves along the path of *dakshinayana*, Surya moves below all the planets. Extending his expanse, the moon moves above this. The entire circle of *nakshatra*s moves above Soma. Budha moves above the *nakshatra*s, and Bhargava moves above Budha. When Bhargava is in retrograde motion, above it, Brihaspati is in retrograde motion. Otherwise, Shanaishchara is above Brihaspati and the circle of *saptarshi*s is above this. Dhruva is established above the seven *rishi*s. The intervening distance between *taraka*s and planets, placed one above the other, is two hundred thousand *yojana*s. On the basis of divine energy, the planets, Chandra and Surya are in the firmament. In their regular movements, they are constantly in conjunction with the *riksha*s. The planets, *nakshatra*s and Surya move above, below and straight. They come together and drift apart and simultaneously look at *praja*s. They face each other and come into conjunction with each other. The learned know that their conjunction does not mean that they get mixed up. This is the way the earth, luminous bodies, *dvipa*s, oceans, mountains, *varsha*s, rivers and those who reside in them are arranged. This is the way all the planets and *nakshatra*s originated.'

'Surya is Vivasvat, Aditi's son. Among all the planets, he is the first planet. During Chakshusha *manvantara*, he was born under Vishakha *nakshatra*. Tvishimat, Dharma's son, is the divinity who is Soma. He is the son of prosperity and his beams are cool. The maker of the night was born under Krittika *nakshatra*. After Surya, there is Shukra, Bhrigu's son, the possessor of sixteen rays. He is foremost among *taraka*s and planets and was born under Tishya[619] *nakshatra*. The planet Brihaspati is the son of Angiras and possesses twelve rays. The preceptor of the universe was born under Purva-Phalguni *nakshatra*. The planet who is Prajapati's son is red in his limbs and possesses nine rays. The *shruti* texts say that he was born under Purvashadha *nakshatra*. Shanaishchara, Surya's son, possesses seven rays and was born under Revati *nakshatra*. The planet Budha,

---

[619] The same as Pushya.

Soma's son, who rises with five rays, was born under Dhanishtha *nakshatra*. Shikhi,[620] Mrityu's son, destroys *prajas* and is full of darkness. The great planet, who destroys everything, was born under Ashlesha *nakshatra*. Daksha's daughters were born under *nakshatra*s that bear their own names. Rahu is full of energy and darkness and his disc is naturally dark. The planet who oppresses the sun and the moon was born under Bharani *nakshatra*. Bhargava and the other stars and planets must be understood. If the *nakshatra* at the time of birth is oppressed, there is a lack of qualities, and one is touched by that taint. Therefore, one must show respect to planets. Aditya is said to be the first among all the planets. Shukra is foremost among *tarakas* and planets, Ketu among those who emit smoke. Dhruva is the pivot, and the planets are divided in the four directions. Shravishtha[621] is the foremost among *nakshatra*s and the northern transit is the foremost among all transits. Among the five kinds of years, *samvatsara* is remembered as the first. Shishira is the foremost among *ritu*s and Magha among months.[622] *Shukla paksha* is foremost among *paksha*s and *pratipada*[623] first among *tithi*s. Between day and night, day is described as the best. Among *muhurta*s, the *muhurta* with Rudra as the divinity is the best.[624] O supreme ones! Among *kshana* and other measurements of time, those who know about time say that *nimesha* is the first. A period, consisting of the five kinds of years, starts with Dhanishtha and ends with Shravana. Depending on Bhanu's specific movements, it revolves like a wheel. Thus, those who know describe Divakara as the lord of time. He is the one who makes the four kinds of beings function and withdraw. The divinity Bhagavan Rudra himself is the one who urges this functioning. In this way, to accomplish the objective, the location of luminous bodies has been determined.

[620] Shikhi means the fiery and crested one. Here, it means Ketu.
[621] That is, Dhanishtha.
[622] These statements reflect precession of the equinoxes.
[623] The first day of the lunar fortnight. The other days follow in sequence, second and so on.
[624] Rudra *muhurta* is the *muhurta* at the time of sunrise, Brahma *muhurta* occurs before sunrise, followed by Samudra *muhurta*.

Ishvara created them for the conduct of the worlds. Briefly, ending with Shravana, they are fixed on Dhruva. They are established such that they are established in a circle all around him. Using his intelligence, Bhagavan arranged this at the beginning of the *kalpa*. They take pride in their locations, and he is in all the luminous bodies. Their origin is the consequence of Pradhana's transformation in this universal form. Using human eyes, no one is capable of enumerating the true nature of the coming and going of luminous bodies. Using intelligence and faith, learned and accomplished ones depend on *agama* texts, *anumana* and *pratakshya* to decide. O ones with excellent intelligence! O *brahmana*s! There are five methods to decide on the category of luminous bodies—the eyes, the sacred texts, water, images and calculations.'

Chapter 25-1(25) (Origin of the name Nilakantha)

Suta said, 'The immensely intelligent Vayu is engaged in the welfare of the worlds. Having said this, he performed *japa* with the chant that must be used when the illustrious Divakara reaches the mid-point. All the *rishi*s who had assembled there controlled themselves and stood there, hands joined in salutation. The one who goes everywhere[625] said, "O Nilakantha! You are the one who imparts life to beings. You must be worshipped at the end of every rite. I prostrate myself before you." There are sages who are controlled in their vows. They are the *valakhilya*s, who have cleansed their *atman*s. They are companions when travelling through the sky. There are eighty-eight thousand such *rishi*s, those who hold up their seed. They subsist on wind, leaves and water. Hearing this, they asked Vayu, "O excellent wind! You have spoken about Nilakantha. This is secret, sacred and auspicious. O supreme among those who know about the sacred! We wish to hear about this. O excellent one! Please tell us. O Prabhanjana! We wish to

---

[625] Vayu.

hear the truth about all this. How did Ambika's lord come to have
a blue throat?[626] O divinity! We wish to hear about this, especially
from your mouth. O Vayu! Everything that is spoken is urged by
you. The articulation of letters and the nature of speech is urged by
you. *Jnana* and enterprise are urged by you. It is when you fill up
that all the letters can be uttered. When you withdraw, there is no
speech, and it is impossible for those with bodies to utter sound. O
Anila! O one who goes everywhere! Letters originate from you. O
Samirana![627] Other than you, there is no other divinity who goes
everywhere. O Anila! From every direction, you witness the world
of the living. You know the divinity Vachaspati.[628] He is the lord
who leads all minds. Please tell us. Why was there disfigurement in
the region around his throat?" He heard the words spoken by sages
who had cleansed their *atman*s. The immensely energetic Vayu,
worshipped by the worlds, replied.'

Vayu said, 'Earlier, in *krita yuga*, there was a *brahmana* who
devoted himself to ascertaining the nature of the *Veda*s. His name
was Vasishtha and he had *dharma* in his *atman*. He was a son born
to Prajpati through his mental powers. He asked Kartikeya, whose
mount is an excellent peacock. He is the one who stole the collyrium
from the eyes of Mahishasura's women.[629] He is the great-souled
Mahasena,[630] whose voice rumbles like clouds. He is the one who
delights Uma's mind and is in disguise in the form of a boy. He is
the one who took life away from Krouncha.[631] He is the one who
delights Gouri's heart. "O noble one! What is this sparkling thing
that can be seen? It is like a mass of glistening collyrium. It can be
seen on the throat, as radiant as the moon, or the *kunda* flower.
How did this come to be? I am radiant and controlled and am a
devotee. Please tell such a person, when he is asking. This account is

---

[626] Ambika is Parvati. Nilakantha, Shiva's name, means one with a
blue throat. Uma is also Parvati's name, as is Gouri.

[627] Vayu's name.

[628] The lord of speech.

[629] That is, he made Mahishasura's wives widows. Mahishasura was
actually killed by Durga.

[630] Kartikeya's name is Mahasena.

[631] Kartikeya shattered Mount Krouncha with his spear.

full of the auspicious and the sacred. It destroys sins. O immensely fortunate one! To cause me pleasure, you should especially tell me about this." He heard the words spoken by the great-souled Vasishtha. The immensely energetic one, the one who destroys the army of the enemies of the Gods, replied.'

Skanda answered, 'O supreme among eloquent ones! I will tell you. Listen to my words. Earlier, when I was seated on Uma's lap, this is what I have heard. This was a conversation between the great-souled Sharva and Parvati. O great sage! To give you pleasure, I will describe this to you. The summit of Kailasa is beautiful. It is colourful, with many kinds of minerals. It resembles the rising sun and is as radiant as heated gold. The stairs are made of diamonds and crystals. There are colourful slabs near the feet of the mountain. It is divine and is full of gold. The many kinds of minerals give it colour. There are many kinds of trees and creepers and these yield diverse kinds of flowers and fruit. The place is full of *hamsa*s, *karandava*s and *chakravaka*s.[632] There are many sounds—the humming of bees, the cascade of waterfalls. The caverns resound with the calls of intoxicated peacocks and *kroundha*s.[633] It is full of large numbers of *apsara*s and adorned with handsome *kinnara*s. Many species of radiant *jivanjivaka*s[634] call. There are large numbers of cuckoos. It is frequented by *siddha*s and *charana*s. The excellent calls of cattle are like the rumbling of clouds. Scared and anxious on account of Vinayaka,[635] elephants leave their caves. There are the sounds of *veena*s and other musical instruments, delightful to sense like the ears. Many swings hang down and large numbers of women use these. From the swings and standards, there are the sounds of nets of bells. There are many sounds of lutes and flutes as if thirty peacocks are calling simultaneously. There is vocal music and the sound of musical instruments, plucked and struck. The caves are full of the sounds of swift sports and debates. Swans, pigeons and kings among cranes

---

[632] Respectively, swans, ducks and Brahminy ducks.
[633] *Krouncha* is a curlew or heron.
[634] *Jivanjivaka* (usually *jivajivaka*) is a pheasant.
[635] Ganesha.

happily sit there. Ganeshvara[636] plays there, exhibiting many kinds of bodily movements.'

'The great *yogi*, Bhutapati,[637] was there, surrounded by *bhutas*. Some had the faces of lions and tigers. They were terrible in speed, and some made fierce sounds. Others had the faces of deer, sheep, elephants and horses. Some had fierce faces, like cats. There were some with bodies resembling those of jackals. Some were short, others were tall. Some were extremely thin. Others possessed large stomachs that hung down. Some had short shanks. There were others with hanging lips. The shanks of others were like palm trees. Some had ears like the ears of cows. Some possessed a single ear. Some had large ears. Some possessed no ears. Some had many feet. Some possessed huge feet. Some had one foot. Some had no feet. Some had many eyes. Some possessed large eyes. Some had one eye. Some had no eyes. Some had a single fang. Some possessed large fangs. Some had many teeth. Some had no teeth. Some had one head. Some possessed large heads. Some had many heads. Some had no head. Some had a single tongue. Some possessed large tongues. Some had many tongues. Some had no tongue. Such were their forms. There was an extremely beautiful slab of rock, encrusted with gold and decorated with pure pearls, gems and jewels. Seated comfortably on this, the daughter of the king of the mountains[638] addressed the one who had destroyed Madana's limbs in these words.[639] "O Bhagavan! O lord of the past and the future! O one whose rule is marked by the sign of a bull![640] O Mahadeva! There is a radiance around your throat, and it resembles a cloud. It is not too dreadful and is auspicious. On your fair throat, it resembles a mass of blue clouds. O divinity! O one who destroyed Kama's limbs! What is this radiant thing on your throat? What is the cause

---

[636] *Gana*s are Shiva's companions and attendants. Ganeshvara (Ganapati) is any leader of *gana*s, but is a word specifically used for Ganesha.

[637] Lord of *bhuta*s, Shiva. *Bhuta*s are demons, or beings in general.

[638] Uma or Parvati.

[639] Shiva burnt down Madana/Kama, the god of love.

[640] Shiva is Vrishadhvaja, with a bull on his standard.

and reason for this? O Ishvara! Why is your throat blue? Please
tell me everything properly. I am curious about this." Hearing
Parvati's words, Shankara, Parvati's beloved, addressed her in these
auspicious words.'

Maheshvara said, 'Earlier, for the sake of *amrita*, Gods and
*danava*s churned the ocean of milk. Initially, a terrible poison
arose, as dazzling as the fire of destruction. O one with the
beautiful face! On seeing this, the faces of the large number
of Gods and *daitya*s became distressed. All of them went to
Brahma's presence. Seeing the large number of terrified Gods,
the immensely radiant Brahma asked, "O immensely fortunate
ones! Why are you scared and why are your minds anxious? I
have thought of prosperity with three kinds of characteristics for
you. O excellent Gods! Who has taken away that prosperity? All
of you are lords of the three worlds. You are devoid of fever.[641]
When you create *praja*s, there is no one who transgresses my
command. All of you travel around in *vimana*s and all of you can
easily go wherever you want. You are engaged and are capable of
constantly levying the adverse consequences of *karma* on *praja*s—
adhidaivika, *adhibhoutika* and *adhyatmika*. Why are you as
terrified as deer, as if lions have oppressed you? Why are you
miserable? Who has caused this lamentation? Where has this fear
arrived from? Quickly and properly, you should describe all this
to me." Hearing the words of Brahma, the *paramatman*, along
with the *rishi*s, the Gods, *daitya*s and *danava*s replied. "The Gods
and *asura*s churned the mass of milk. A terrible poison arose, with
the resplendence of the *samvartaka* fire. It is as dark as a serpent
or a bee. Its complexion is like that of a dark cloud. It manifested
itself, like death and destruction. Its radiance is like that of the
fire that arrives at the end of the *yuga*s. With a complexion like
that of the sun, it is blazing in every direction, as if it will devour
the three worlds. This kind of poison has arisen, and this poison

----

[641] Both physical and mental. The number three can be interpreted in
various ways. As stated in the text, there are more than three characteristics.
As stated earlier, there are eight kinds of *siddhi*s. The number three probably
refers to *prakamya*, *vashitvam* and *ishitvam*.

is like the fire of destruction. It has burnt down Janardana and made his fair and red limbs black. We saw Janardana's fair and red limbs turn black. At this, all of us were terrified and have sought refuge with you." The immensely energetic Brahma heard the words uttered by Gods and *asuras*, explaining what caused them fear. The grandfather of the worlds replied. "O *devas* and *rishis*, stores of austerities! All of you listen. This fierce poison arose when the large ocean was churned. It is like the fire of destruction, and it has been heard that this is *kalakuta*. As soon as it appeared, all the *devas*, lost their radiance. With the exception of Shankara, no one is capable of withstanding its force—not I, not Vishnu, nor the bulls among *devas*." The one who was born from a lotus, the one who was not born from a womb, but from the womb of a lotus, said this.'

'He remembered Oumkara and meditated on the radiance that exists in every direction. Brahma, supreme among those who know the *Veda*s, started his words of praise. "O Virupaksha![642] I prostrate myself before you. O one with divine sight! I bow down before you. O one who has Pinaka in his hand![643] I prostrate myself before you. O one with the *vajra* in his hand! I bow down before you. I prostrate myself before the lord of the three worlds. I bow down before the lord of *bhuta*s. I prostrate myself before the one who slays the enemies of the Gods, the one with Soma, Surya and fire in his eyes. I prostrate myself before the one who is Brahma, Rudra and Vishnu. I prostrate myself before the one mentioned in *samkhya* and *yoga*, the aggregate of the elements. I prostrate myself before the one who destroyed Manmatha's limbs, the one who made Kala show his back.[644] You are Rudra, whose seed is excellent. You are the compassionate lord of *deva*s. You are the one with matted hair. You are the cruel one. You are Shankara Hara. You are the one with the skull. You are the disfigured one. You are Shiva, the one who bestows boons. You are the one who destroyed

---

[642] One with malformed eyes, Shiva's name.

[643] Pinaka is the name of Shiva's weapon, interpreted as a bow, trident or staff.

[644] Manmatha is one of Kama's names. Shiva vanquished Kala (Death).

Tripura.[645] You are the one who destroyed the sacrifice.[646] You are
the lord of the *matrikas*.[647] You are the aged one. You are the pure
one. You are the free one. You are the strong one. You are the only
valiant one in the three worlds. You are Chandra. You are Varuna.
You are the foremost one. You are the fierce one. For *brahmanas*,
you are the one with many eyes. I prostrate myself before the one
who is *rajas* and *sattva*, the one whose origin is not manifest. You
are eternal. You are not eternal. I prostrate myself before the one
who is both eternal and not eternal. You are manifest. You are not
manifest. I prostrate myself before the one who is both manifest
and not manifest. You can be thought of. You cannot be thought
of. I prostrate myself before the one who can be thought of, who
is also the one who cannot be thought of. You are the one who
destroys the afflictions of the universe. You are the one who loves
Narayana. You are the one who loves Uma. You are Sharva. You
are the one who marked Nandi's face. You are *paksha*, *masa* and
half a *masa*. You are *ritu* and *samvatsara*. You possess many
forms. You are the one with the shaved head. You are the one
with the staff. You are the one with armour. I prostrate myself
before the one who holds a skull in his hand, the one who wears
the directions as his garment, the one with a tuft of hair on the
head. You possess a bow and a chariot. You are the self-controlled
brahmachari. You are *Rig Veda*, *Yajur Veda* and *Sama Veda*. You
are Purusha. You are Ishvara. I have worshipped you with this
stotram. You deserve to be praised. I prostrate myself before you."
O one with the beautiful face! In this way, Brahma praised me and
prostrated myself. He continued, "You know of my devotion and
that of *deva*s. You loosened your hair and released Ganga's waters.
You are subtle. Because of your *yoga*, you cannot be contemplated.
O Rudra! You are the lord whom no one can worship." In this
way, Bhagavan Brahma, creator of the worlds, first praised me. He
used many kinds of *stotram*s, originating from the *Veda*s and the
*Vedanga*s." At this, I addressed the grandfather in these significant
words. "O lord of the past, the present and the future! O protector

[645] Shiva destroyed a city of the demons, known as Tripura.
[646] An allusion to Daksha's sacrifice.
[647] Mother Goddesses.

of the worlds! O lord of the universe! O Brahma! O one excellent in vows! What task do I have to perform for you? Please tell me." On hearing these words, the lotus-eyed Brahma replied. "O lord of the past, the present and the future! O Ishvara! Hear the cause. O one with eyes like lotuses! The Gods and *asuras* churned the ocean of milk. O Bhagavan! A terrible poison arose. It is like a cloud. It resembles a dark cloud. Its radiance is like that of the *samvartaka* fire. On seeing this, all of us are terrified and our senses are agitated. O Mahadeva! Desiring the welfare of the worlds, please drink it. O lord! You are supreme among *devas*. You are capable of devouring it. O Mahadeva! Other than you, there is no one who is capable of withstanding its force." I heard the words spoken by Brahma Parameshthi.'

'O one with the beautiful face! I consented and accepted his words. I started to drink the poison, which was like Destroyer. I drank the extremely terrible poison, which had caused fear to the Gods. O one with the beautiful complexion! Instantly, my throat became black. It resembled the petals of a lotus, and it was as if an *uraga* had clung to my neck. It was as if Takshaka, king of the *nagas*, had arisen, with his flickering tongue." The immensely energetic Brahma, grandfather of the worlds, spoke. "O Mahadeva! O one excellent in vows! On your throat, it looks beautiful." O daughter of the supreme mountain! Hearing his words, I retained that terrible poison in my throat and became Nilakantha. O one with the beautiful face! O daughter of the king of mountains! While large numbers of Gods, *daityas*, *yakshas*, *gandharvas*, *bhutas*, *pishachas*, *uragas* and *rakshasas* looked on, I held that fierce and powerful poison of *kalakuta* in my throat. When the large number of Gods and *daityas* saw it being placed in this way, they were filled with great wonder. O one with the gait of an intoxicated elephant! At this, all the large number of Gods, *daityas*, *uragas* and *rakshasas* joined their hands in salutation and said, "O Isha! Your strength, energy and valour are wonderful. Your body and power of *yoga* are wonderful. O lord of *devas*! O one who destroyed Manmatha's body! Your Lordship is extremely wonderful. You are Vishnu. You are the one with four faces.[648] You are Death. You are the one who

---

[648] Brahma.

bestows boons. You are Surya. You are the maker of the night. You
are the one who makes the mobile and the immobile manifest. You
are fire. You are wind. You are earth. You are water. You are the
one who holds up everything, mobile and immobile. You are the
creator. You are the destroyer." Speaking these words, the Indras
among Gods lowered their heads and prostrated themselves. They
took the nectar with them and left on *vimana*s that possessed the
great speed of the wind, until all of them reached Meru.'

'This is a supreme and secret account. It is great and most
sacred among the sacred. This is the reason I am famous in the
three worlds under the name of Nilakantha. Svayambhu himself
recited this account, which destroys sins. This auspicious account
was sung by Brahma. If a person constantly retains it, I will narrate
the extremely great fruits he obtains. O one with beautiful hips!
O one with the beautiful loins! As soon as mobile or immobile
poisons[649] come into contact with his body, they are destroyed.
It pacifies the inauspicious. It dispels terrible nightmares. The
person is loved by women and becomes a king in assemblies. He is
victorious in debates and triumphs in battles. When he travels, he is
safe along the path. There is always prosperity in the home. O one
with the beautiful face! I will describe the destination obtained by
his body.[650] His beard becomes tawny. His throat becomes blue. His
hair is marked by the sign of the moon. He possesses three eyes and
holds a trident in his hand. He rides a bull and holds Pinaka. His
strength becomes like that of Nandi's. He is handsome and becomes
Nandi's equal in valour. Obeying my command, he travels in all the
worlds and the seven worlds. No one can obstruct his movements.
He is like the wind in the sky. With a strength that is like mine, he
remains till the onset of the deluge. O one with the beautiful hips!
I will speak about the destination obtained, in this world and in
the next one, by men who listen to this, full of devotion towards
me. *Brahmana*s obtain the *Veda*s, *kshatriya*s obtain the earth.
*Vaishya*s obtain gains, *shudra*s obtain happiness. The diseased are
freed of ailments. The imprisoned are freed of bonds. A pregnant

---

[649] Probably meaning liquid or solid.
[650] He becomes like Shiva.

woman has a son. A maiden obtains a virtuous husband. In this world and in the next world, a person who has lost his possessions gets them back. There are fruits obtained from properly donating one hundred thousand cows. If a mortal man listens to this divine account, he obtains those fruits. If a person constantly retains one quarter of a *shloka*, one-eighth of a *shloka*, one *shloka*, or half a *shloka*, he goes to Rudra's world. This is also what happens if a man unwaveringly devotes his mind to me and reads all of this in the presence of *deva*s and *brahmana*s. A devotee who is always full of faith goes to Rudra's world. O Devi! A man must devoutly read this, or have it read. There has been no *stotram* that is superior to this, nor will there be. *Yaksha*s, *pishacha*s, *bhuta*s and Vinayakas cannot cause impediments in a house where this praise is kept. O one with eyes like lotuses! Having stated the greatness of this praise, I am content. It destroys floods of sins. I have also told you about the auspicious fruits. The one with the four faces himself sang this.'

Suta concluded, 'Having narrated this account and its auspicious fruits to Devi, the one who has fixed the moon on his hair, the lord who loves Guha,[651] left for Kailasa on the back of the bull, along with Uma. I heard this account, which takes away sins, from Prajapati and have narrated it in your presence. After studying this entire account, along with its characteristics, the excellent *dvija*[652] left for Aditya's region.'

Chapter 26-1(26) (Origin of the *lingam*)

The *rishi*s said, 'The lord Mahadeva is great-souled. In detail and properly, we desire to hear about the qualities of his powers.'

Suta answered, 'In ancient times, after binding the immensely valiant Bali, the lord of three worlds, and conquering the three

---

[651] Kartikeya.
[652] It is not clear who this refers to. It might be Romaharshana. But it might be anyone from the line of narration described in Chapter 1.

worlds,[653] Vishnu spoke about this. The *daitya*s were destroyed and Shachi's consort was delighted. All the *deva*s arrived to meet the eternal lord.[654] The one whose *atman* is in the universe was near the ocean of milk. *Siddha*s, *brahmarshi*s, *yaksha*s, *gandharva*s, large numbers of *apsara*s, *naga*s, *devarshi*s and all the rivers and mountains approached the great-souled one and praised Purusha Hari. "You are the creator. You are the doer. O lord! You are the one who creates the worlds. It is through your favours that the three worlds have obtained a benefit that will not decay. All the *asura*s have been vanquished and Bali has been bound by you." The Gods, *siddha*s and supreme *rishi*s addressed Vishnu in this way.'

'Purushottama[655] replied to all the *deva*s. "O excellent Gods! Listen to the reason why I have become this. He is the creator of all beings. He is the lord Kala, he is the one who creates time. The worlds, along with Brahma and I, have been created through his *maya*. In the beginning, it is through his favours that I obtained *siddhi*. Earlier, the three worlds were devoured by darkness, and nothing was manifest. With all the beings inside my stomach, I was lying down alone. I possessed one thousand heads, one thousand eyes and one thousand feet. I held a conch shell, a *chakra* and a mace in my hands and was lying down on that pure water. At this time, in the distance, I saw some infinite radiance. Blazing in his own energy, he resembled one hundred suns. He possessed four faces and was a great *yogi*. He was a being who was golden in complexion. This divinity was clad in black antelope skin and was adorned with a *kamandalu*.[656] Within a *nimesha*, Purushottama[657] reached me. Brahma, worshipped by all the worlds, spoke to me. "Who are you? Where have you come from? Why are you here? O lord! Please tell me. I am the creator of the worlds. I am Svayambhu. My face is everywhere in the universe." Thus addressed by Brahma, I replied to him. "I am the creator of the worlds. Repeatedly, I am

---

[653] This is the story of Vishnu's *vamana* (dwarf) *avatara*.
[654] Meaning Vishnu.
[655] Vishnu.
[656] A sacred water-pot.
[657] The word meaning excellent Purusha, now a reference to Brahma.

also the destroyer." Desiring to vanquish each other, we spoke to each other in this way."

'O unblemished ones! At the time, we saw a blaze in the northern direction. On seeing this flame, we were amazed. That powerful energy was Sharva's radiance and we joined our hands in salutation. The radiance continued to increase in size. It was extremely wonderful. Brahma and I swiftly rushed towards that blaze. Penetrating the earth and the firmament, that fiery circle was established there. We saw a great radiance in the midst of that blaze. There was a greatly resplendent *lingam*. It was not quite manifest, and it was only one *pradesha*[658] in size. Right in the centre, it was not made of gold, silver, or rock. It could not be determined. It could not be thought of. Repeatedly, it was visible, and yet not visible. It was supreme and there were thousands of garlands of flames. It was extremely astounding and wonderful. There was great energy, and it was increasing tremendously. It was based inside a garland of flames and caused terror to all beings. It was very terrible in form and seemed to penetrate heaven and earth. At this, Brahma told me, "Swiftly proceed downwards. Let us ascertain the extremities of this great-souled one's *lingam*. Until the end is seen, I will proceed upwards." Having come to this agreement, we proceeded downwards and upwards. I proceeded downwards for one thousand years. However, I could not see the end and was terrified. In that way, Brahma proceeded upwards and could not find the end. Along with me, he returned to that great mass of water. We were both astounded and scared, confounded by the great-souled one's *maya*. Losing our senses, we remained there. We performed *dhyana* on Ishvara, whose face is on all sides. He is the lord without decay, responsible for the creation and destruction of the worlds.'

'We joined our hands in salutation before Sharva, who wields the trident. He is the one with an extremely terrible roar. He is fanged and is terrible in form. He is great and not manifest. We prostrated ourselves before him and said, "O lord of the worlds

---

[658] One *pradesha* equals eight *angula*s.

and *deva*s! O divinity! I prostrate myself before you. O great-souled Bhutapati! I prostrate myself before you. I prostrate myself before the eternal *yogi* who has obtained *siddhi*. I prostrate myself before the one in whom the entire universe is established. You are Parameshthi. You are the supreme *brahman*. You are the supreme and imperishable destination. You are the eldest. You are the lord who is Vamadeva, Rudra, Skanda and Shiva. You are the sacrifice. You are *vashatkara*.[659] You are Oumkara. You are *svahakara*. In all rites, you are *samskara*. You are *svadhakara*. You are the sacrifice. You are *vrata*s. You are *niyama*s. You are the *Veda*s. You are the worlds. You are *deva*s. You are Bhagavan, who is everything. You are the sound in the sky. You are responsible for the creation and destruction of beings. You are the smell in earth. You are taste in water. You are form in fire. You are Maheshvara. O lord of *deva*s! You are touch in the wind. You are the body of the moon. O lord of *deva*s! You are *jnana* in intelligence. You are the seed in Prakriti. You are the destroyer of all the worlds. You are Kala. You are the Destroyer, full of death. O lord! You are the one who sustains the three worlds. You are also the one who creates. With your eastern face, you assume the status of Indra.[660] With your southern face, you withdraw the worlds. There is no doubt that with your western face, you are Varuna. With your northern face, you assume the status of Soma, the excellent *deva*. O divinity! You are one and you are many. You are the cause behind the creation and destruction of the worlds. You are Adityas, Vasus, Rudras, Maruts, Ashvins, *sadhya*s, *vidyadhara*s, *naga*s, *charana*s, stores of austerities, *valakhilya*s, great-souled ones who have obtained *siddhi*s through austerities and those excellent in vows. O lord of *deva*s! All the others who are controlled in their *vrata*s have flowed from you. O

[659] *Vashatkara* is the exclamation 'vashat' made at the time of offering an oblation. *Svadha* is said at the time of offering oblations to the ancestors and *svaha* is said at the time of offering oblations to the Gods. The acts are *svadhakara* and *svahakara*. *Namaskara* is the act of bowing down/prostrating, while *samskara* is an act of cleansing/purification. *Vrata*s are vows, *niyama*s are rituals.

[660] Indra is the lord of the east, Yama of the south, Varuna of the west and Soma (or Kubera) of the north.

lord of *deva*s! Uma, Sita, Sinivali, Kuhu, Gayatri, Lakshmi, Kirti,[661] Dhriti,[662] Medha,[663] Lajja,[664] Kanti,[665] Vapus,[666] Svadha, Tushti,[667] Kriya,[668] Sarasvati, the Goddess of speech, Sandhya and Ratri[669] have flowed from you. You possess the strength of a million suns. I prostrate myself before you. You are as fair as one thousand moons. I prostrate myself before the one who wields *vajra* and Pinaka. I prostrate myself before the one who holds a bow and arrows in his hands. I prostrate myself before the one whose limbs are decorated with the mark of *bhasma*.[670] I prostrate myself before the one who destroyed Kama's body. I prostrate myself before the divinity Hiranyagarbha. I prostrate myself before the divinity whose garments are golden. I prostrate myself before the divinity whose womb is golden. I prostrate myself before the divinity whose navel is golden. I prostrate myself before the divinity whose seed is golden. I prostrate myself before the divinity whose one thousand eyes are wonderful. I prostrate myself before the divinity whose complexion is golden. I prostrate myself before the divinity whose hair is golden. I prostrate myself before the divinity whose valour is golden. I prostrate myself before the divinity who bestows gold. I prostrate myself before the divinity who is the lord of gold. I prostrate myself before the divinity whose roar is golden. I prostrate myself before the divinity who holds Pinaka in his hand. I prostrate myself before you, Shankara Nilakantha." Praised in this way, the immensely intelligent one manifested himself.'

'He is the lord of *deva*s, the womb of the universe. His radiance was like that of one crore suns. Full of compassion, the immensely radiant Mahadeva spoke. He seemed to devour the sky with his

[661] Fame. Personified forms of all these.
[662] Fortitude.
[663] Intellect.
[664] Modesty/shame.
[665] Loveliness.
[666] Beauty.
[667] Satisfaction.
[668] Rites.
[669] Night.
[670] Ashes.

one thousand mouths. His throat was like a conch shell and his stomach was excellent. He was decorated with many kinds of ornaments. His limbs were adorned with many colourful jewels. He wore diverse kinds of garlands and unguents. Bhagavan, with the Pinaka in his hand, the one who wields the trident, should be worshipped by all Gods. His sacred thread was formed by serpents. He is the one who grants Gods freedom from fear. His voice was like the roar of a large drum, resembling the thunder of a cloud. As he burst out laughing, the sound filled the entire universe. The loud sound of the great-souled one's voice scared us. Mahadeva said, "O best among Gods! I am pleased. You have witnessed great *yoga*. Be freed of all your fear. Earlier, you two eternal ones originated from my limbs. Brahma, the grandfather of the worlds, is my right hand. Vishnu, who is always unvanquished in battle, is my left hand. I am pleased with both of you. I will grant you the excellent boons you wish for." At this, delighted in our minds, we prostrated ourselves at the lord's feet. Mahadeva was stationed in front of us, pleased, and we spoke. "O divinity! O lord of Gods! If pleasure has been generated and if boons are to be bestowed on us, let us possess constant devotion towards you." The lord of *deva*s replied, "O immensely fortunate ones! It shall be that way. Create extensive *praja*s." Saying this, the lord, Bhagavan, vanished from the spot. I have thus spoken about the intelligent one's powers. This is supreme *jnana*. He is the one who is not manifest, known as Shiva. He is subtle and unthinkable. He can be seen with the insight of *jnana*. He is the lord of *deva*s, and we should prostrate ourselves before him. O Mahadeva! I prostrate myself before you. O Maheshvara! I bow down before you.'

Suta concluded, 'Hearing this, all the Gods returned to their own respective abodes, after prostrating themselves before the great-souled Shankara. If a person reads this praise of the great-souled Ishvara, he receives everything that he desires and is freed from all sins. Through Mahadeva's favours, Vishnu, whose power enters everywhere, said this about the eternal *brahman*. I have thus described everything about Maheshvara's strength.'

Chapter 27-1(27) (Entry into Daruvana and bathing in *Bhasma*)

The sages said, 'O Suta! O immensely intelligent one! Please speak to us yet again about the great-souled Mahadeva's greatness. We have curiosity about this. When a congregation of *devas* and *rishis* resided in Daruvana, to make the *maharshis* understand, why did he assume a disfigured attire? Knowing that it was Mahadeva, their minds were in a whirl. To seek his favours, they worshipped him, but Bhava was not pleased. Please tell us everything about that account and about what the lord of *devas* did. You are supreme among intelligent ones. Please tell us everything.'

Suta answered, 'O those who are attentive! I will speak about this account of *dharma*. Listen. O *brahmanas*! Formerly, in *krita yuga*, on the auspicious summit of Himalaya, there used to be a beautiful forest of *devadaru* trees.[671] It was full of many kinds of trees and creepers. Many sages were engaged in austerities there and these sages were devoted to their vows. Some of them subsisted by eating moss. Some of them lay down in the water. Some of them reached the space between the clouds, standing on the big toes of their feet. Some were *dantaulukhalinas*,[672] there were others who were *ashmakuttas*.[673] Some were in *virasana*.[674] Others practised the conduct of deer. Great in intelligence, they spent their times in these fierce austerities.'

'To show them his favours, the divinity arrived in that forest. Pale *bhasma* was smeared over his limbs. He was naked and all the signs were deformed. His hair was dishevelled and deformed. His teeth were horrible. His eager hands held a flaming torch. His eyes were red and tawny. His penis and testicles had the complexion

---

[671] *Devadaru* is a kind of pine. Since *vana* means forest, this was known as Daruvana.

[672] Those who use their teeth as mortars, that is, they eat raw grain that has not been ground.

[673] Those who eat raw grain after it has been ground on stone.

[674] Literally, posture of a hero. A seated position used by ascetics.

of red ochre.[675] His face possessed the complexion of burning coal but was adorned with tinges of white. Sometimes, he laughed in a terrible tone. Sometimes, he seemed surprised and sang. Sometimes, he engaged in dances of love.[676] Sometimes, he wept repeatedly. The wives[677] were confounded and quickly prevented him from dancing. He arrived at the hermitage and repeatedly begged for alms. He created a wife who was just like him in appearance. She was decorated with ornaments made of grass. His roar was like the bellowing of a bull. His roar was like the braying of a donkey. He started to deceive them and made all those with bodies laugh. The sages became angry at this, and the rage defiled them. Deluded by his *maya*, all of them approached, so as to curse him. "Since you bray like a donkey, you will become a donkey. Or you will become a *rakshasa*, *pishacha* or *danava*." Proportionate to their rage, as they willed, all of them cursed the divinity, the lord of the universe, with different kinds of curses. Despite their austerities, Shankara repulsed all of them. When there is the radiance of the sun, the stars located in the sky do not shine and illuminate. Shankara's energy was like that. The extremely great-souled Brahma is supreme and is the source of sacrifices. However, it has been heard that his prosperity was destroyed because of a *rishi*'s curse.[678] Vishnu is immensely valiant. However, because of Bhrigu's curse, he had to manifest himself ten times and was made eternally miserable. Earlier, because the *rishi* Goutama, who knew about *dharma*, was enraged, Indra's penis and testicles fell down on earth.[679] As a result of a curse, it was determined that the Vasus would have to reside in wombs.[680] As a result of a curse by the *rishis*, Nahusha

[675] *Gairika.*
[676] We have translated *shringara* as love.
[677] Of the sages.
[678] The sage Bhrigu thought that Brahma showed him disrespect and cursed him that he would not be worshipped. For similar reasons, Bhrigu cursed Vishnu that he would have to take ten *avatara*s on earth.
[679] When Indra seduced Goutama's wife, Ahalya.
[680] When the Vasus stole Vasishtha's cow, the sage cursed them that would be born on earth as mortals.

became a serpent.[681] Because of what a *brahmana* did, one could no longer drink from the ocean of milk.[682] Dharma was cursed by the great-souled Mandavya.[683] There are many other such hardships that occurred. But Virupaksha Mahadeva, lord of *deva*s, was not affected. Deluded in this way, they did not recognize Shankara.'

'"Therefore, all those *rishi*s spoke to each other. This is not the appropriate conduct decided for us, who are householders, or for those who are *brahmacharis* in the forest, or for those who reside in the forest.[684] Never has this been witnessed as *dharma* for mendicants.[685] O *dvija*s! He has confounded us and committed a great wrong. This is not *dharma* for those who are ascetics. Therefore, let his *lingam* fall. Speak in sweet tones and don at least one garment.[686] When you give up your *lingam*, you will be worshipped." Hearing the words of the *rishi*s, Bhagavan, who destroyed Bhaga's eyes,[687] replied in gentle words. It seemed as if Shankara was laughing. "O stores of austerities! My *lingam* cannot be made to forcibly fall by Brahma and the *deva*s, not to speak of others. O supreme *dvija*s! Hence, I will make the *lingam* fall." They answered, "You can remain in this hermitage, or go away." Thus addressed, Mahadeva acted so that his senses were delighted. While all of them looked on, the lord vanished from the spot. When Bhagavan vanished, Bhava transformed himself into a *lingam*. In the three worlds, no beings appeared and were not born. Everyone became anxious and there was no illumination. The sun

---

[681] Nahusha obtained the status of Indra, but made the sages carry his palanquin. In the process, his foot touched Agastya and he was cursed.

[682] This seems to be an extrapolated idea. Durvasa cursed Indra that he would lose his powers. (There are other reason for this curse too.) Hence, the ocean of milk was churned. Poison resulted and one couldn't drink from that ocean.

[683] When the punishment meted out was excessive, the sage Mandavya cursed Yama (Dharma) that he would be born on earth. He was born as Vidura.

[684] That is, those in *vanaprastha*.

[685] That is, those in *sannyasa*.

[686] This is addressed to Shiva.

[687] At the time of Daksha's sacrifice.

did not heat, and the fire lost its radiance. *Nakshatra*s and planets turned perverse. The *rishi*s were prosperous and sought to have offspring. But despite the time for menstruation arriving, there were no menses. Devoid of a sense of ownership and devoid of ego, they engaged in *dharma* again. But their power and valour was destroyed. They lost their energy. At the time, their minds were no longer fixed on *dharma*. All of them assembled together and went to Brahma's world. They went to Brahma's residence and saw the one who had originated from a lotus. All of them fell at his feet and narrated the incident concerning Shiva. "He was malformed and stupefying. His teeth were fierce. His eager hands held a flaming torch. His eyes were red and tawny. His penis and testicles were red, tinged with red ochre. Our daughters and daughters-in-law, especially daughters who are expecting, were present. Nevertheless, his wishes were perverse, and he wished to remain by their sides. Knowing that he was mad, we dishonoured him. We abused him and struck him, and his *lingam* was uprooted. To pacify his rage, we have sought refuge with you. O grandfather! We have not understood this act at all. Please tell us." Hearing the words of the *rishi*s, he meditated and got to know that this was Ishvara. Brahma controlled himself well and replied in these words. "This is the divinity Mahadeva, who should be known as Maheshvara. One cannot easily reach his supreme destination. He is the lord of *deva*s, *rishi*s and ancestors. After the end of one thousand *mahayuga*s, all those with bodies face dissolution. Assuming the form of Kala, Maheshvara destroys. Using his own energy, he is the one who creates all *praja*s. He alone is the wielder of the *chakra*, the one who bears the excellent Shrivatsa mark[688] on his chest. He is spoken of as a *yogi* in *krita yuga* and as *kratu* in *treta yuga*. He is *kalagni* in *dvapara yuga* and he is said to be Dharmaketu in *kali yuga*.[689] The learned know that Rudra has three forms. He is Agni with *tamas*, Brahma with *rajas* and Vishnu, who illuminates, with *sattva*. One form of his is remembered as

---

[688] The place where Shri (Lakshmi) resides. The twirl of hair on Vishnu's chest.

[689] *Kalagni* is the fire of destruction. Dharmaketu is one with *dharma* as his standard. It also happens to be one of Buddha's names.

one where he wears the directions as a garment. This is known as Shiva. The *brahman* and *yoga* reside in this form. This divinity is the lord of *devas*. He is the lord Ishana, who does not decay. O Indras among *brahmana*s! Restrain your anger and conquer your senses. Worship him in the form that you saw the great-souled one, as a *lingam*. Create an image in that form and seek refuge with the one who wields a trident in his hand. Thereafter, you will see the lord of *devas*. He cannot be seen by those who have not cleansed their *atman*s. When one sees him, all kinds of *ajnana* and all kinds of *adharma* are destroyed."[690] At this, they performed *pradakshina* of the infinitely energetic Brahma."'

'Bereft of sorrow, they remained in that forest of *devadaru* trees. As Brahma had said, they started the worship—on level ground, in colourful mountains, inside caves, along varied rivers and on sandy shores. One year passed and spring arrived. Assuming the very same form, the divinity arrived in the forest. There were many blossoming trees and creepers. That part of the ground was filled with the humming of large numbers of bees. It was full of charming sounds, from the calling of cuckoos. Mahesha entered the hermitage in the forest. All the sages controlled themselves and praised him. They used many kinds of garlands, incense and fragrances. Those immensely fortunate ones were with their wives, sons and attendants. Using gentle and eloquent words, they spoke to Girisha. "O lord of *devas*! In our ignorance, we did things in thoughts, words and deeds. You should pardon all those. O Shankara! Your conduct is wonderful, secret and deep. Even Brahma and the other *devas* do not know. We do not know how to welcome you. We do not know your movements. O Vishveshvara! O Mahadeva! You are who you are. I prostrate myself before you. Great-souled ones praise you, Maheshvara, lord of *devas*. I prostrate myself before Bhava, Bhavya, Bhavana and Udbhava.[691] I prostrate myself before the lord of *bhuta*s, who is infinite in strength and energy. You are the

---

[690] *Ajnana* is the opposite of *jnana* and *adharma* is the opposite of *dharma*.

[691] Respectively, the one who comes into being, the one who will come into being (or the excellent one), the cause, the source.

destroyer. You are tawny in your limbs. You are imperishable. You are the one who perishes. You support the waters of Ganga. O one with *guna*s in your *atman*! You are the foundation. O Tryambaka! O one with three eyes! O one who wields an excellent trident! I prostrate myself before Kandarpa.[692] I prostrate myself before the *paramatman*. O Shankara! O one with the mark of a bull! O lord of *gana*s! I prostrate myself before you. O one with a staff in your hand! O Kala! O one with a noose in your hand! I prostrate myself before you. In the *mantra*s of the *Veda*s, you are the foremost. You possess one hundred tongues. I prostrate myself before you. You are the past, the present and the future. You are the mobile and the immobile. O divinity! Everything in the universe has originated from your body. O Shambhu! Save me. O fortunate one! O Bhagavan! Be pleased. O Bhagavan! If a man does anything in ignorance, or if he does it knowingly, all that gets done through your *yoga* and *maya*." Delighted within their *atman*s, the sages praised him in this way. "With our austerities, we desire that we might be able to see you, as you were before. Let your *lingam* assume the natural form, as was the case before. I prostrate myself before the one who wears the directions as his garment. O eternal one! You are garlanded by bells that tinkle. O hideous one! O cruel one! O one with a horrible face! You have no form. You have an excellent form. Your form is the universe. I prostrate myself before you. O one with thorns around the hips! O Rudra! O *svahakara*! I prostrate myself before you. You are in the *atman*s of all those with life. The *guna*s are in your body. I prostrate myself before you. O one with a foul stench! O one with an excellent fragrance! O one with a trident in the hand! I prostrate myself before you. You are yourself the one with a blue crest. I prostrate myself before you. O one with a handsome throat! I prostrate myself before you. O Nilakantha! O divinity! O one who smears himself with ashes from funeral pyres! O one with the three *guna*s in your *atman*! I prostrate myself before the creator of the universe. O one who resides in a cremation ground! O one who has

---

[692] While Kandarpa is one of the names for Madana, the word can also be taken in the sense of time.

the form of a *preta*![693] You are Brahma. You are all the *deva*s. You are
all the Rudras! You are Nilalohita. You are the *atman* in all beings.
The *samkhya* texts speak of you as Purusha. Among mountains,
you are the great Meru. Among *nakshatra*s, you are Chandra.
Among *rishi*s, you are Vasishtha. Among *deva*s, you are Vasava.
Among all the *Veda*s, you are Oumkara. Among all the hymns from
the *Sama Veda*, you are Jyeshthasama.[694] O Parameshvara! Among
all those who reside in the forest, you are a lion. Among all village
animals, you are a bull. O Bhagavan! You are worshipped by the
worlds. You are everything, past, present and future. We see only
you there, just as Brahma had said. You are desire, anger, greed,
misery and insolence. We wish to restrain these. O Parameshvara!
Be pleased. O divinity! When the great destruction arrives, you press
your hand against your forehead. Therefore, you create a fire. The
flames from that fire engulf everything in the worlds. Therefore,
you are like a fire. There are many malformed fires. The fire that
arises from you burns down all those with life and all other entities,
mobile and immobile. O lord of Gods! When we are burnt, please
be our saviour. For the welfare of the worlds, you are the one who
sprinkles beings. O Maheshvara! O immensely fortunate one! O
lord! O one who casts an auspicious glance! O lord! Command us.
We will act in accordance with your words. You possess thousands
of crores of forms. O divinity! We are incapable of reaching your
limits. I prostrate myself before you."'

'At this, Bhagavan Isha addressed them in these words. "My
devotees are devoted to *bhasma*. The *bhasma* burns down their sins.
O *brahmana*s! Those who act in this way are controlled, devoted to
dhyana. Such people must not be abused. Such people must not be

[693] A *preta* is a ghost, the spirit of a dead person, or simply something
evil. A *bhuta* has the same meaning. Strictly speaking, there are differences
between *preta*, *bhuta* and *pishacha* (one who lives on flesh). A *preta* is the
spirit (not necessarily evil) of a dead person before the funeral rites have
been performed. A *bhuta* (not necessarily evil again) is the spirit of a dead
person who has had a violent death and for whom, proper funeral rites
have not been performed, and may not even be performed. A *pishacha*
(necessarily evil) is often created deliberately through evil powers.
[694] A special *suktam* from *Sama Veda*.

crossed. If a person desires welfare in this world, or the next one, he should not address them in disagreeable words. If a person is foolish in his mind and criticizes them, he criticizes Mahadeva. If a person constantly worships them, he worships Shankara. If you act in this auspicious way, you will obtain *siddhi* from me." Shiva told them about the supreme rites. They are unmatched and destroy great darkness. They got to know about these. All the fear, greed, delusion and worries were destroyed. They swiftly prostrated themselves and touched their heads on the ground. The *brahmana*s were delighted that Maheshvara had assumed his natural form. They used extremely pure and fragrant water, mixed with *kusha* grass and flowers. With water from large pots, they bathed Maheshvara. In melodious voices, they chanted many songs and uttered secret notes of *humkara*.[695] "I prostrate myself before the divinity who wears the directions as his garments. I prostrate myself before the one with tinkling bells. O Arddhanarishvara![696] O expounder of *samkhya* and *yoga*! O one with the dark clouds as a mount! O one with a garment made out of elephant hide! O one with an upper garment made out of antelope-skin! O one whose sacred thread is a serpent! Your wonderful earrings are colourful and beautifully crafted. You are ornamented in beautifully fashioned garments. Your garment is made out of the excellent hide of a lion. Your battle-axe is huge. I prostrate myself before Shankara." Desiring the welfare of the worlds, the excellent sages, devoted to the *dharma* of *varna*s, instated the *lingam* again. Delighted with the sages, Maheshvara replied to them. "O ones excellent in vows! I am pleased with your austerities. Ask for a boon." All the sages prostrated themselves before Maheshvara. They were great ascetics—Bhrigu, Angiras, Vasishtha, Vishvamitra, Atri, Goutama, Sukesha, Pulastya, Pulaha, Kratu, Marichi, Kashyapa and Samvarta. They prostrated themselves before Mahadeva and addressed him in these words. "O lord! Bathing in *bhasma*, being naked, *vamachara*,[697] contrary behaviour, worthiness of being

---

[695] *Humkara* means to utter the sound "hum", a sound believed to possess special powers.

[696] Lord who is half male and half female.

[697] Left-handed rituals.

served and unworthiness of being served—we desire to know
about these." Bhagavan replied, "I will now describe everything
about all these. I am Agni, along with Soma. Soma and Agni find a
refuge in me. The worlds find a refuge in fire, whether it has been
artificially kindled or not. There are many occasions when the fire
has burnt down the universe, with its mobile and immobile entities.
Everything can be accomplished through *bhasma*. It is sacred and
excellent. Energy exists in *bhasma* and creatures are sprinkled with
it. Fire rites must be performed in the three stages of life.[698] *Bhasma*
represents my energy, and a person is freed from all sins. Since
it shines[699] and possesses an auspicious fragrance, it is known as
bhasma. It is said that *bhasma* instantly destroys all sins. It should
be known that the ancestors survive on heat. *Deva*s originate from
Soma. Agni and Soma exist in everything in the universe, mobile
and immobile. I am the immensely energetic Agni. Soma is my
Ambika. I am myself Agni, Purusha. Soma is Prakriti. O immensely
fortunate ones! Therefore, *bhasma* is spoken of as my energy. I am
established by bearing my own energy on my body. Since then,
it has protected the worlds from all that is inauspicious. *Bhasma*
protects an expectant mother in a delivery chamber. If a person is
pure in his *atman,* has conquered his rage, has controlled his senses
and bathes in *bhasma*, he comes to my presence and does not return
from there.[700] This is the vow of *pashupata yoga*. Kapala[701] devised
this *yoga*. Earlier, this excellent *pashupata* vow was devised. All the
other *ashrama*s were created by Svayambhu later. This creation is
my creation, and it is full of shame, delusion and fear. *Deva*s and
sages are born naked. All the other humans in the world are also
born without garments. If the senses are not conquered, even those
covered with garments are naked. If the senses are conquered, it is
only then that the private parts are covered. A garment is not said
to be the reason. The supreme covering is forgiveness, fortitude,
lack of violence, non-attachment towards everything and treating

---

[698] Childhood, youth and old age, known as *tryayusha*.
[699] *Bhasati* means to shine.
[700] He is not born again.
[701] Kaapaala, a form of Bhairava.

honour and dishonour as equal. If a person smears his limbs with
pale *bhasma*, performs *dhyana* in his mind on Bhava and bathes
in *bhasma*, even if he has committed one thousand misdeeds, all
those are burnt down by *bhasma*, just as the energy of a fire burns
down a forest. Therefore, if a person constantly bathes himself with
bhasma thrice a day, he obtains the status of being a Ganapati. If a
person performs all the sacrifices, imbibes the *amrita* of performing
dhyana on Mahadeva and immerses all his sentiments in him, he
follows the northern path and obtains immortality.[702] Those who
resort to cremation grounds and follow the southern path obtain
anima, *mahima*, *laghima*, *prapti*, *garima* as the fifth, *prakamya*
as the sixth, *ishitvam*, *vashitvam* and immortality. Indra and the
other *deva*s are driven by desire and observe vows. All of them
are famous for their energy and obtain supreme prosperity. You
should get rid of arrogance and delusion and free yourselves from
attachment. Your natures should be devoid of the taints of *rajas* and
tamas. Know that what is regarded as contemptible is the excellent
pashupata vrata. Observe it. If a person purifies himself and reads
this, is faithful and conquers his senses, his *atman* is cleansed of all
sins and he goes to Rudra's world.'''

Chapter 28-1(28) (*Shraddha* at the time of *amavasya*)

The *rishi* asked, 'O Suta! Every month, at the time of *amavasya*,
King Pururava, Ila's son, used to go to heaven. Why was this
and how did he satisfy the ancestors?'

Suta replied, 'O Shamshapayani! I will describe his powers
and the connection between Ila's great-souled son and Aditya and
Soma. There is substance in the increase and decrease during *shukla
paksha* and *krishna paksha*. This has to do with the views about

---

[702] Northern path is being used as an expression for right-handed
and regular rituals, *dakshinachara*. Conversely, southern path means left-
handed *vamachara* rituals.

ancestors and the determination of ancestors. I will tell you about obtaining *amrita* from Soma and satisfying the ancestors and about seeing the ancestors, *kavya*s, *agnishavtta*s and *soumya*s. I will tell you everything about how Pururava satisfied the ancestors and the due order of *parva*s. When the sun and the moon are in conjunction with a *nakshatra* at the time of *amavasya*, for a single night, they reside in the same circle. At the time of every *amavasya*, he goes to see the maker of the day and the maker of the night, his maternal and paternal grandfather.[703] He goes there and waits for the right time, until Soma exudes for the sake of the ancestors. The learned Pururava, Ila's son, stays in heaven, desiring to worship Soma, along with the ancestors. He reflects on the duration of both *kuhu* and *sinivali* and worships *kuhu* when there are only two *lava*s left. He also worships *sinivali*. When there is only one digit left, he knows that it is *kuhu*. He waits for the right time, sees that it has arrived and worships. For satisfaction during an entire month, the nectar of *amrita* exudes from Soma. That nectar of *amrita* exudes for fifteen days.[704] During *krishna paksha*, his hands are scorched by the rays of the sun and he happily cools them with the instant honey that flows from Soma. In the fortnights, there are norms for offering oblations to the ancestors in heaven. Using the nectar of *amrita*, the Indra among kings offers oblations to the ancestors—*soumya*s, *barhishad*s, *kavya*s and *agnishvatta*s. The *ritu*s are said to be Agni. *Samvatsara* is held to be Agni. *Ritu*s originated from *samvatsara* and *artava*s were born from *ritu*s. *Artava*s are known as *arddha-masa*s and ancestors are the sons of *ritu*s. *Ritu*s are grandfathers. *Masa*s and *ayana*s are sons of the year. *Deva*s are great grandfathers. The five types of years are Brahma's sons. *Soumya*s are known to be born from Soma. *Kavya*s are known to be the sons of Kavi.[705] *Upahuta*s

---

[703] Pururava's father was Budha, the son of Chandra. Therefore, the moon (maker of the night) was Pururava's paternal grandfather. Pururava's mother was Ila, daughter of Vaivasvata Manu, the son of the sun (maker of the day). Therefore, the sun was Pururava's maternal great grandfather.

[704] These *shloka*s are very difficult to understand. We have tried to make them as clear as is possible.

[705] Kavi is Shukracharya's name.

are said to be *deva*s. *Somaja*s are said to be those who drink *soma*.
*Kavya*s are said to be those who drink *ghee*. There are said to be
three types of ancestors. These three types are *kavya*s, *barhishad*s
and *agnishvatta*s. Those who have been householders and have
performed sacrifices are certainly *ritu*s and *barhishad*s. Those
who have been householders but have not performed sacrifices are
*artava*s and *agnishvatta*s. The lords of *ashtaka*s[706] are *kavya*s. Now
learn about the five kinds of years. Of these, *samvatsara* is Agni
and Surya is *parivatsara*. Soma is said to be *idvatsara* and Vayu
is *anuvatsara*. Among them, Rudra is *vatsara*. These five kinds of
years make up a *yuga*. Every month, at the time of *amavasya*, there
are ancestors who drink nectar in heaven. These are described as
*kavya*s, *ushmapa*s and *divakirtya*s. As long as Pururava was there,
every month, he satisfied them with what exuded from Soma.
That nectar of *amrita* was offered to ancestors who drank *soma*.
Hence, it is known as *amrita*, *soumya*, nectar and honey. During
krishna paksha, the thirty-three *deva*s[707] progressively drink the
fifteen digits of the moon, which are the *chhanda*s in the form of
water. Having drunk the nectar of *amrita* for half a month, they
leave on *chaturdashi*. In this way, all the *deva*s drink the maker
of the night, who reaches *amavasya* with only the fifteenth digit
left. On *amavasya*, he is nourished by *sushumna*. For a duration of
two *lava*s, the ancestors drink the nectar of *amrita*. When Soma is
reduced as a result of being drunk, Surya uses *sushumna* to nourish
him and those who drink *soma*, drink again. When all the digits
are exhausted, Soma is nourished again. From one day to another,
in the due order, parts are nourished by *sushumna*. Digits diminish
during *krishna paksha* and are developed during *shukla paksha*. In
this way, Chandra's body is nourished through Surya's vigour. On
pournamasi, the white and complete disc is seen. This is what Soma
achieves during *shukla paksha* and *krishna paksha*. That is the
reason Soma is identified with the ancestors and is remembered as

[706] *Ashtaka* is the eighth lunar day, but during *krishna paksha,* the
dark lunar fortnight.
[707] *Deva*s are often mentioned as thirty-three, twelve Adityas, eleven
Rudras, eight Vasus and two Ashvins.

idavatsara. He passes through fifteen phases of exuding the nectar of *amrita*.'

'After this, I will speak about the *parva*s and the intervening periods between the *parva*s. Just as there are joints in sugarcane, in *arddhamasa*, there are joints within *shukla paksha* and *krishna paksha*. The difference between *amavasya* and *pournamasi* lies in these knots and joints. *Arddhamasa* consists of *dvitiya* and the other *parva*s.[708] The rite of *anvadhana*[709] is performed at the time of joints in the *parva*s. Among all the *parva*s and all the joints, *pratipada* is the first. At the beginning of *anumati*, a period of two *lava*s is known as *sayahna*.[710] Similarly, when it is *raka*, a period of two *lava*s is known as *aparahna*.[711] When *aparahna* has passed, the period of *sayahna* that occurs during *pratipada* of *krishna paksha* is included as part of *pournamasi*.[712] At the time of an opposite conjunction, when Surya is stationed two points below the horizon and the moon has duly risen two points above the horizon, this is known as *vyatipata*.[713] When *pournamasi* has passed, at the time of *vyatipata*, they look at each other. At such a time of *vyatipata*, they are like equals. Though Surya cannot be discerned at the time, one can count by considering his movements. This has been ordained as an instant period for undertaking *vashatkara*. When the moon is full and the *paksha* has been completed, the joint of the night is *purnima*. On the night of *pournamasi*, the maker of the night is radiant. On a day of *vyatipata*, the sun and the moon are both full and glance at each other. That *aparahna* is counted as part of *purnima*. The day preceding *purnima* is remembered under the name of *anumati*. This

---

[708] The word *parva* is often used for *amavasya* or *pournamasi*, or for days when there is a solar or lunar eclipse. But here, *parva* connotes a lunar day (*tithi*), *dvitiya* being the second and *pratipada* being the first.

[709] Placing kindling on the sacred fire.

[710] Literally, evening.

[711] Literally, late afternoon.

[712] Explaining the reconciliation between a lunar *tithi* and the solar day.

[713] *Vyatipata* is an inauspicious period that lasts for almost twenty-four hours during every lunar month. The text sounds obscure. The sun and the moon are on opposite sides of a solstice and their minutes of declination are the same, they being set apart by 180 degrees.

is because ancestors, along with *deva*s, approve of it.[714] There is a
night when the maker of the night is excessively radiant. Because
of the moon's radiance, the wise speak of this as *raka*.[715] When the
sun and the moon are in the same *nakshatra* and it is the fifteenth
night after *raka*, this is known as *amavasya*. After separating from
each other on *amavasya*, the sun and the moon look at each other
equally. This is spoken of as *darsha*.[716] Between *amavasya* and the
following day, this is a joint between *parva*s that lasts for two *lava*s.
The word *kuhu* has two *akshara*s, but the duration of the *parva* is
described as three.[717] When the moon is destroyed, the duration of
amavasya is until *madhyahna*[718] starts. Within half a day and night,
the moon reaches the sun. In the morning, along with Surya, he
goes to *samudra*.[719] When there is conjunction between the two, it is
always midday for Ravi. At the time of *pratipada* in *shukla paksha*,
Chandra is freed from the solar disc and there is space between the
two discs. This is the time of *darsha* and oblations must be offered,
along with *vashatkara*. That apart, the *parva* of *amavasya* should
be known as *ritumukha*.[720] During most of the day in the *parva*
of *amavasya*, the moon declines. During the day of *amavasya*, the
sun is seized. It is seized during the day of *amavasya* and declines
during the day. The one who is full of water[721] increases by a digit
during the days. Hence, those who know have given names to the
*tithi*s in accordance with this increase.[722] Surya and Chandra reveal

---

[714] From the root word, meaning approval/consent.

[715] From the root word, meaning cause of delight.

[716] *Darsha* is the day of the new moon. On that day, the moon can only
be seen by the sun, not by anyone else. The root means sight/appearance.

[717] The two *akshara*s in *kuhu* are *ku* and *hu*. It is extremely difficult to
make sense of some of these *shloka*s. *Kuhu* is the night of the new moon.
Perhaps what is meant is that *amavasya/darsha* (as a solar day), includes
the day and part of *sinivali* and part of *kuhu*.

[718] Midday.

[719] *Samudra* probably means the three *nakshatra*s of Ardra, Punarvasu
and Pushya. There is conjunction between the sun and the moon in these
*nakshatra*s.

[720] Beginning, that is, first day of a *ritu*.

[721] The moon.

[722] One digit on *pratipada*, two digits on *dvitiya* and so on.

themselves in this way. Gradually, the moon emerges from the solar disc. Except for a duration of two *lavas*, the moon touches the sun for a night and a day. That period of *darsha* is the time for offering oblations, along with *vashatkara*. This period concludes with *kuhu*, the sound made by a cuckoo.[723] The period after *amavasya* is said to be *kuhu*. When it is *sinivali*, the maker of the night diminishes by one unit. When the sun enters *amavasya*, this is known as *sinivali*. Barring *kuhu*, the duration of *anumati*, *raka* and *sinivali* is two *lavas*. *Kuhu* is separately described as *kuhu*. When there is conjunction between the sun and the moon in *vyatipata* of *purnima*, this is said to be *pratipada* and the duration of this *parva* is two units. The period between *kuhu* and *sinivali* is *samudra*. During this *parva*, when Soma is in the disc of Arka and the fire, its measure is one digit. In the nights of *shukla paksha*, these are the *parvas* and their joints. When Soma receives all its fifteen digits, this is *purnima*. At the time, the handsome moon is radiant, with a complete disc. The fifteen digits are progressively added. In addition to the fifteen digits, Soma possesses a sixteenth digit. Thereafter, Soma's decline occurs on the fifteenth day. Such are ancestors, *devas*, those who drink *soma*, those who enhance Soma, *artavas* and *ritus*. *Devas* think about their prosperity.'

'After this, I will describe ancestors who partake of monthly *shraddhas*. I will describe the nature of *shraddhas* and what is achieved through them. It is not possible to know about the movements of those who have died, or about their return, even through famous austerities. What need be said of eyesight? The ancestors in this world are remembered as ancestors of *devas*. These divinities are *soumyas*, *kavyas*, *ayajvanas* and *ayonijas*. All of these ancestors are divinities and *devas* speak through them. The ancestors of humans are different and are remembered as worldly ancestors. They are the father, the grandfather and the great-grandfather. Those who use hymns from the *Sama Veda* to perform sacrifices are known as *somavantas*. Those who offer oblations at sacrifices are described as *barhishads*. *Agnishvattas* are described

---

[723] The word *kuhu* also means the call of the cuckoo.

as those who offer oblations on behalf of those who are unworthy
of sacrifices. For them, *dharma* is said to be mixed with *adharma*.
Therefore, *dvija*s speak of them as *sayujyaga*s.[724] There are those
who are established in the *dharma* of *ashrama*s and are faithfully
engaged in rites, not suffering from exhaustion even at the end.
Until their bodies fall, they are engaged in seven kinds of tasks—
austerities, *brahmacharya,* sacrifices, having offspring, *shraddha*s,
learning and donations. They go to heaven and along with *deva*s,
ancestors, those with subtle bodies and those who drink *soma*,
enjoy themselves there, worshipped like ancestors. When water is
offered to them by relatives and others from the family, they become
content and partake of the monthly *shraddha*s. They are known
as *somaloukika*s and are ancestors of humans, partaking of the
monthly *shraddha*s. There are others. Because of their *karma*, they
are confined in the form of different species. They have deviated
from the *dharma* of *ashrama*s and are devoid of *svadha* and *svaha*.
These evil-souled ones become *preta*s in Yama's eternal abode and
their bodies are pierced. There, they face pain and grieve over their
own *karma*. They live for a long time there, but they are dried up.
They have beards and lack garments. They suffer from hunger and
thirst and run around, here and there. They desire rivers, ponds,
tanks and wells. They desire the food of others and are dragged
around, here and there. They are made to repeatedly fall down from
different places and face pain in Shalmala, Vaitarani, Kumbhipaka,
Karambhavaluka, Asipatravana and Shilasampeshana.[725] Because
of their own *karma*, they are flung down there. In those places, they
face miseries day and night. When they move to the other world,
they are established in these regions, meant for *preta*s. Using the
right hand, if their relatives place three *pinda*s[726] on *darbha* grass

---

[724] That is, those who have attained *sayujya*.

[725] These are the names of different hells, where a sinner faces hardships.
For example, Asipatravana is a place where the leaves of trees and bushes
are like swords. In Shalmala, there are silk cotton trees, full of thorns.
Karambhavaluka is covered with dry and hot sand. In Shilasampeshana,
the sinner is crushed with stones. In Kumbhipaka, he is cooked in a pot full
of boiling oil. Vaitarani is the name of a terrible river.

[726] Funeral cakes.

spread on the ground, uttering their names and *gotra*s, they are content. There are those who deviate, but do not reach those five places of hardship.[727] Thereafter, because of their own *karma*, they are born as immobile entities or inferior species. They are born in many kinds of forms as inferior species. In those species, they subsist on different kinds of food. The offerings given to them in the course of a *shraddha* become the food on which that respective creature subsists. At the due time, in the recommended vessels, this must be offered. The food offered is received, whatever be the nature of the creature now. This is just like cows being lost. A calf seeks out its mother. In that way, if food is offered at a *shraddha*, using *mantra*s, it reaches the ancestors. In this way, when *mantra*s are used to render faithfully, a *shraddha* is not futile. Having seen them with his divine sight, Kumara spoke about these things. He knows about the coming and going of *preta*s and about what they obtain through *shraddha*s. Such ancestors are described as *bahlika*s, *ushmapa*s and *divakirtya*s. *Krishna paksha* is their day and *shukla paksha* is night, when they sleep. In this way, *deva*s are ancestors and ancestors are *deva*s. *Ritu*s, *artava*s and *arddhamasa*s are remembered as the ancestors of each other. Thus, ancestors, *deva*s and ancestors of humans are pleased. They must be pleased through the rites of *shraddha* ceremonies. This subject of ancestors, those who drink *soma* and the nature of what constitutes an ancestor has been decisively described in the Purana. The meeting of Ila's son with Arka, Soma and the ancestors has also been described. He reaches and satisfies the ancestors with the nectar of *amrita*. The periods of *purnima, amavasya* and the places of hardship have also been briefly described to you. This is eternal creation. The universal nature of creation has only been partially described. It is impossible to enumerate it. A person who desires prosperity must possess faith. I have completed describing in detail, sequentially, Svayambhuva's creation. What will I describe to you next?'

---

[727] Apparently, six names have been given for hells. Since the number five is mentioned, Shilasampeshana may not be a separate hell.

Chapter 29-1(29) (Enumeration of *yugas*)

The *rishi* said, 'I wish to hear about the true nature of creation in the past Svayambhuva *manvantara* and about the four *yugas* in detail.'

Suta replied, 'In connection with the earth and other things, I have already spoken about the four *yugas*. But I will describe it. Listen. I will describe the true nature of the six aspects spoken about when talking about *yugas*—nature of a *yuga*, the difference between *yugas*, *dharma* of *yugas*, the bits that are *sandhyas* between *yugas*, the parts of a *yuga* and about how *yugas* are joined. I will speak about the enumeration of the four *yugas* in years, about how they are measured in the world in terms of human years. The duration known as a *nimesha* is known to be equal to the time taken to articulate an *akshara*. Fifteen *nimeshas* make up one *kashtha* and thirty *kashthas* are reckoned to make up one *kalaa*. One *muhurta* consists of thirty *kalaas* and there are thirty *muhurtas* in a day and night, divided equally. In the world of humans, Surya separates day from night. Hence, the day is for making efforts on tasks and the night has been thought of as a period for sleeping. A night and a day for ancestors constitutes a month for humans. *Krishna paksha* is the day for them. *Shukla paksha* is the night, when they sleep. Thirty human months are described as one month for the ancestors. In human terms, a little more than three hundred and sixty months constitute *samvatsara* for ancestors. In measuring, one hundred human years are reckoned to be three years and ten months for ancestors.[728] What is described as one year in the world of humans is one day and one night for *devas*. This has been determined certainly in the sacred texts. A day and a night for *devas* constitute one year and there are further sub-divisions. For *devas*, *uttarayana* is day and *dakshinayana* is night. Day and night for *devas* are further enumerated as follows. Thirty human years are said to be one month for *devas*. One hundred human years are known to be three months

---

[728] This should be three years and four months. The possibility of an intercalary month doesn't help decipher the figure.

and ten days for *devas*. These are described as measurements for
devas. Three hundred and sixty human years are said to be one
samvatsara for *devas*. Three thousand and thirty human years are
held to be one *vatsara* for *sapatarshis*. Nine thousand and ninety
human years are described as one *samvatsara* for Dhruva. Thirty-
six thousand human years are known to be one hundred years for
devas. These are described as the norms. Three hundred and sixty
thousand human years are known to be one thousand years for
devas. People who know about enumeration speak about such
numbers. The *rishis* have chanted about such measurements for
devas. The duration of *yugas* has been conceived in accordance with
measurements used for *devas*.'

'The wise have said that there are four *yugas* in Bharatavarsha.
These four are *krita*, *treta*, *dvapara* and *kali*. The first one is named
krita yuga, the next is *treta*. The next two are thought of as *dvapara*
and *kali*. *Krita yuga* is said to consist of four thousand years. *Sandhya*
has four hundred years. *Sandhyamsha* is of the same duration
and *sandhyamsha* is equal to *sandhya*. It is the same principle for
sandhya and *sandhyamsha* in the other three *yugas* too. Units of
measurement are thousands of years and hundreds of years. In the
due order, *treta yuga* has three thousand years and *dvapara* has two
thousand. *Sandhya* and *sandhyamsha* are equal and are respectively
three hundred years and two hundred years. O excellent *dvijas*! *Kali
yuga* lasts for one thousand years. *Sandhya* is equal to *sandhyamsha*
and both last for one hundred years. The duration of a *mahayuga*
is therefore described as twelve thousand years,[729] consisting of the
four—*krita*, *treta*, *dvapara* and *kali*. In human years, the duration
is seen to be the following. I will speak about the number of years
for *krita*. Listen. The duration of *krita yuga* is one million, four
hundred and forty thousand human years.[730] The duration of *treta
yuga* is one million and eighty thousand human years. The duration
of *dvapara* is seven hundred and twenty thousand human years.
The duration of *kali yuga* is three hundred and sixty thousand

[729] 400+4000+400+300+3000+300+200+2000+200+100+1000+100
= 12,000.
[730] 4000×360. And so on for the others.

human years. Without *sandhya* and *sandhyamsha*, the duration of
the four *yuga*s is three million and six hundred thousand human
years. With *sandhya* and *sandhyamsha*, the duration of the four
*yuga*s is four million, three hundred and twenty thousand human
years. The duration of the four *yuga*s, *krita*, *treta* and the others,
is said to be a little more than seventy-one in one *manvantara*.[731]
Understand the number of human years in a *manvantara*. Without
including the excess, this is three hundred and six million, seven
hundred and twenty thousand years. *Dvija*s who know about
enumeration have described this as the duration of a *manvantara*.
Time is measured in *manvantara*s, along with a measurement in
*yuga*s. The natural duration of *krita yuga* is four thousand years.
I will speak about the others, *treta*, *dvapara* and *kali*. However,
no one can simultaneously describe time in both kinds of ways.[732]
That is the reason, in the due order, I have not spoken about the
measurement of *yuga*s in both kinds of ways. I have been more
eager to describe the lineage of *rishi*s.'

   'At the beginning of *treta yuga*, Manu and the *saptarshi*s
spoke about the *dharma* of *shruti* and *smriti* texts, as instructed
by Brahma. The *saptarshi*s spoke about the characteristics of the
dharma of the *shruti* texts, in connection with taking a wife and
agnihotra, as described in *Rig Veda*, *Yajur Veda* and *Sama Veda*.
Svayambhuva Manu spoke about the *dharma* and good conduct of
the *smriti* texts, as has traditionally been passed down, with the good
conduct of *varna*s and *ashrama*s.[733] The *rishi*s achieved this through
truth, *brahmacharya*, learning and austerities. The *saptarshi*s and
Manu tormented themselves through austerities. Therefore, at the
beginning of *treta yuga*, *mantra*s, including the one that provides
salvation,[734] revealed themselves to them, without their thinking

---

[731] There are 71.4 *mahayuga*s in one *manvantara*. 4,320,000×71=
306,720,000.

[732] This sentence sounds strange. But probably means, there is no need
to use both *yuga* and *manvantara* simultaneously.

[733] The word used is *parampara*, which means to be passed down, in
an uninterrupted line of succession. Presumably, the allusion is to *Manu
Samhita*.

[734] Oumkara.

about it, or without their practicing rites. In the first *kalpa*, *siddhis* manifested themselves before *devas*. When those were destroyed, in thousands of past *kalpas*, other *siddhis* appeared and there were *mantras*. Those *mantras* again manifested themselves before them and the *saptarshis* uttered the *mantras* of the *Rig Veda*, the *Yajur Veda*, the *Sama Veda* and the *Atharva Veda*. Manu propounded the *dharma* of the *smriti* texts. In the beginning of *treta yuga*, the *Veda samhitas*[735] alone represented the ordinances of *dharma*. They remained when lifespans contracted in *dvapara yuga*. In *dvapara*, the *rishis* resorted to austerities and studying the *Vedas*. They are divine, without a beginning and without an end. Formerly, Svayambhu created them. From one *yuga* to another *yuga*, the *Vedas*, the *Vedangas*, *dharma*, *vratas* and the meanings and utterances of the *Vedas* remain constant. However, depending on the *yuga*, there are some changes. For *kshatriyas*, enterprise represents sacrifices, while for *vaishyas*, it is the offering of oblations that are sacrifices. For *shudras*, service represents sacrifices. For best among *dvijas*, *japa* constitutes sacrifices. In *treta yuga*, the *varnas* were protected by *dharma* in this way and rejoiced. They performed rites and had offspring. They were prosperous and happy. *Kshatriyas* followed *brahmanas*, *vaishyas* followed *kshatriyas*. *Shudras* followed *vaishyas*. They were devoted to each other. Their inclinations were auspicious and they followed the *dharma* of *varnas* and *ashramas*, in their mental resolutions, the words they spoke and in their own deeds. In *treta yuga*, all *karma* was always successful and bore fruits. In general, everyone in *treta yuga* possessed a long lifespan, intelligence, strength, beauty, freedom from disease, *dharma* and good conduct. Brahma established them in *varnas* and *ashramas*. However, subsequently, *prajas* became deluded and did not follow *dharma*. They opposed each other and approached Manu again.'

'Svayambhuva Prajapati saw the true nature of what had occurred. He meditated and had two sons through Shatarupa. They were Priyavrata and Uttanapada and they were the first lords of the earth. Since then, *rajans* have been born and they have wielded

---

[735] *Samhita* means collection, of *mantras* (hymns).

the rod.[736] These kings were known as *rajan*s because they brought delight to subjects. However, those who hid their sins could not be controlled by the lords of men. Therefore, Dharmaraja Vaivasvata Yama is described as the one who chastises them. The division into *varna*s is said to have happened during *treta yuga*. At that time, the *rishi*s, who were Brahma's sons, collected the *mantra*s. *Deva*s started the system of sacrifices. Along with Vishvabhuj[737] and the immensely energetic Indra of *deva*s, Shukra gathered all the means. In Svayambhuva *manvantara*, *deva*s had already started the system of sacrifices. Truthfulness, *japa*, austerities and donations are said to constitute *dharma* in *treta*. But one thousand such acts of *dharma* ended, and the *dharma* of violence was started. Those who were born were brave and immensely strong, with long lifespans. Those immensely fortunate ones used the rod. They were devoted to *dharma* and spoke about the *brahman*. Their eyes were like the petals of lotuses. They were broad in the chest, with well-formed joints. Those greatly spirited ones caused terror to lions. Their stride was like that of intoxicated elephants. They wielded large bows. In *treta yuga*, these were the *chakravarti*s. They possessed all the auspicious signs and resembled the circle of *nyagrodha* trees. The word *nyagrodha* means arms and therefore, *vyama* is spoken of as a *nyagrodha*.[738] If a person is such that his height measures a *vyama* and if his height and breadth are equal, he is known as one who resembles the circle of a *nyagrodha* tree. All *chakravarti*s possess seven jewels—a *chakra*, a chariot, a jewel, a wife, a treasure,[739] a horse and an elephant. The seven are also said to be—a *chakra*, a chariot, a jewel, a sword, an excellent shield as the fifth, a standard as *nidhi* and not killing beings, as the seventh. The seven are also described as—a wife, a priest, a commander, the

---

[736] *Rajan* is a king who delights the subjects (this is the etymology). Earlier, people naturally followed *dharma*. Now, kings were necessary to protect the virtuous and punish the wicked.

[737] The one who devours everything, Agni.

[738] *Vyama* is the distance between the tips of the fingers, when the arms are extended. It is a fathom and *nyagrodha* also means a fathom.

[739] *Nidhi*. Kubera possesses eight *nidhi*s.

maker of a chariot, a minister, a young elephant and the granting of life. These jewels are divine and were successfully obtained by those great-souled ones. For all *chakravartis*, fourteen such have been ordained. In all *manvantaras*, past and future, *chakravartis* are born on earth as portions of Vishnu. This is true of all *chakravartis* who have been born, past, present and future, in *treta yuga*, or elsewhere. There are four auspicious and wonderful objects that characterize all lords of the earth—an army, *dharma*, happiness and wealth. There are other objects that are equally obtained by kings, without any impediments—*artha*, *dharma*, *kama*, fame and victory. They surpass even sages in prosperity, *anima* and the other powers, lordship, capacity, learning and austerities. In strength and austerities, they surpass *devas*, *danavas* and humans. They are born in human bodies with such signs. The hair is soft. The forehead is lofty. The tongue sweeps clean. The lips and eyes possess the complexion of copper. Chests bear the Shrivatsa mark. The body hair stands up. Arms extend as far as the knees. The hands are coppery in complexion. Waists are thin. They resemble the circles of a *nyagrodha*. Shoulders and the passing of urine are like those of lions. The gait is like the stride of an elephant. The jaws are large. There are marks of a conch shell and a lotus on the soles of the feet and the palms. There were eighty-five thousand such radiant kings, who did not suffer from old age. In four places, the movements of *chakravartis* face no obstructions—the sky, the ocean, the nether regions and mountains. In *treta yuga*, *dharma* is said to consist of sacrifices, donations, austerities and truthfulness. Since then, *dharma* functioned on the basis of classification into *varnas* and *ashramas*. To establish norms, the policy of punishment came into being. All the subjects were happy and well-nourished. They did not suffer from disease and their minds were full. It is said that the single *Veda* came to assume four feet in *treta yuga*. At the time, humans lived for three thousand years. They had sons and grandsons and died in the due order.[740] This was the nature of *dharma* in *treta yuga*. Understand the nature of *sandhya* in *treta*.

---

[740] The young did not die before the old.

In *treta yuga*, the nature of *sandhya* was such that it was reduced by one-fourth. *Sandhya* was reduced by one-quarter and naturally, *sandhyamsha* was also reduced by one-fourth.'

Chapter 30-1(30) (Commencement of sacrifices)

Shamshapayani asked, 'In the beginning of *treta yuga*, how did sacrifices commence? In the course of the former Svayambhuva creation, how did they come about? Please tell me accurately. *Krita yuga* vanished, along with its *sandhya*. The time that existed was known as the onset of *treta yuga*. Plants were generated and the creation of rain had commenced. Conduct and subsistence in *garhasthya* and the other *ashrama*s had been established again. The classification and establishment of the *varna*s and *ashrama*s had taken place. After gathering together the necessary materials, how did sacrifices commence?'

Hearing this, Suta answered, 'O Shamshapayani! Listen. This is how sacrifices commenced at the beginning of *treta yuga*, in the former Svayambhuva creation. I will describe it in the due order. Along with its *sandhya*, *krita yuga* vanished. The period of time known as *treta yuga* arrived. Plants were generated and the creation of rain started. Conduct and subsistence in *garhasthya* and the other *ashrama*s were established. *Varna*s and *ashrama*s were established and the *mantra*s were collected together. *Mantra*s were invoked in rites, for this world and for the next world. Along with Vishvabhuk, the lord Indra started sacrifices. Along with all the *deva*s, all the required objects were collected. *Maharshi*s arrived at the horse sacrifice that started. The sacrifice was being performed with *pashu*s fit to be sacrificed and all those who arrived spoke to him. In connection with rites required for a sacrifice, *ritvija*s were eager to get on with the tasks. All those engaged in singing hymns from the *Sama Veda* started in melodious voices. Excellent *adhvaryu*s commenced deftly. Large numbers of *pashu*s worthy of being sacrificed had been obtained. *Brahmana*s who performed *agnihotra* rites were pouring oblations into the kindled fire. Divinities who preside over the senses had their shares in the sacrifice and in the due order, all those who partook of the sacrifice had been invited. All *devas* who existed at the beginning of the *kalpa* were worshipped. It was time for crushing the *soma* juice and all the *adhvaryus* and *maharshis* stood up. *Maharshis* glanced towards the large number of distressed *pashus*. They asked Indra, "What are the norms for this sacrifice? This is the *adharma* of the strong. Causing violence is *adharma*. O excellent God! Your sacrifice involves the killing of *pashus*. This is *adharma*. Violence towards *pashus* has started and this is destructive of *dharma*. This is not *dharma*, it is *adharma*. *Dharma* is not said to involve violence. If you desire to perform a sacrifice in accordance with the *agama* texts, follow the rules instructed for a sacrifice and the ordinances of *dharma*. O best among Gods! A sacrifice should be performed with seeds, so that there is no violence. The best seeds are those that have been kept for three years and have not yet sprouted. O immensely wise one! This is the *dharma* ordained by Virinchi[741] in ancient times." In this way, *rishis*, who had an insight into the truth, spoke to Vishvabhuk Indra.[742] A great debate ensued between Indra and the *maharshis*. They spoke about whether a sacrifice should be performed with mobile or immobile objects.'

'In the course of the debate, *maharshis*, who spoke the truth, were dejected. After having addressed their words to Indra, they asked Khechara Vasu.[743] "O immensely wise one! O king! How do you see the rites of a sacrifice? O Uttanapada's descendant! O lord! Please speak and dispel our doubt." Hearing their words, Vasu reflected on the strengths and weaknesses of their arguments. He remembered the sacred texts of the *Vedas* and spoke about the true nature of a sacrifice. The lord of the earth replied, "A sacrifice must be performed with whatever has been brought. A sacrifice can be performed with *pashus* fit to be sacrificed, or with seeds and fruits.

---

[741] Brahma.

[742] Vishvabhuk and Indra are equated here.

[743] Khechara means someone who travels in the sky. This means King Uparichara Vasu, who possessed the boon of travelling up, and through, the sky in his chariot. He was born in the Puru lineage.

Violence is a natural component of sacrifice. This is my view and that of the *agama* texts. *Maharshi*s have spoken about the signs of violence in *deva*s and *mantra*s. They practised long austerities and possessed insight about Oumkara and other *mantra*s that enable one to cross over. I have spoken about the truth cited there and therefore; you should also follow that. O *dvija*s! If the words uttered in the *mantra*s are accepted as proof, let the sacrifice continue. Otherwise, those words will be rendered false." When he replied in this way, those stores of austerities controlled themselves. They saw that this was inevitable and were no longer eloquent. As soon as he said this, the lord of men entered the nether regions. Vasu, who roamed around in the upper regions, henceforth roamed around in the nether regions. As a consequence of those words, he became a resident of the nether regions. Having desired to dispel doubts about *dharma*, the king moved to below the surface of the earth. Hence, even if one knows a lot, one should not try to dispel doubts with a single utterance. *Dharma* has many gates. It is subtle and its movement even more distant. Thus, no one is capable of definitively speaking about *dharma*, not even *deva*s and *rishi*s. Svayambhuva Manu is the only exception. *Maharshi*s have stated that non-violence is the gate to *dharma*. Following their own austerities, thousands of crores of *rishi*s have gone to heaven. Therefore, *maharshi*s do not praise either donations or sacrifices. Stores of austerities have donated roots and fruits that have been gleaned, vegetables and vessels for water. Thereby, they have been established in the world of heaven. The foundations of eternal *dharma* are lack of injury, lack of avarice, austerities, compassion towards beings, self-control, *brahmacharya*, truthfulness, pity, forgiveness and fortitude. These are difficult to achieve. It has been heard that unblemished *brahmana*s, *kshatriya*s and others have achieved success through austerities. There are kings like Priyavrata, Uttanapada, Dhruva, Medhatithi, Vasu, Sudhama, Viraja, Shankha, Pandyaja, Prachinabarhi, Parjanya, Havirdhana and others. There are many others who have gone to heaven through their own austerities. There are *rajarshi*s who possessed great spirits. Their fame is established. Hence, because of all these reasons, austerities are superior to sacrifices. In ancient times, Brahma used austerities to create the world and the universe.

Sacrifices do not follow, and austerities are described as the foundation. Objects and *mantra*s are intrinsic to sacrifices. Fasting is intrinsic to austerities. Through sacrifices, one obtains the status of being a *deva*. Through austerities, one obtains the status of being free from passions. The task of *brahmana*s is renunciation and non-attachment. Through such means, one conquers Prakriti. One obtains *jnana* and *kaivalya*.[744] These are described as the five destinations. In this way, in the former Svayambhuva *manvantara*, there was an extremely great debate between *deva*s and *rishi*s. The *rishi*s saw that he[745] was struck down by the strength of *dharma*. All of them ignored Vasu's words and returned to wherever they had come from. When the large number of sages had left, *deva*s completed the sacrifice. In this way, in the course of Svayambhuva *manvantara*, sacrifices commenced. Since then, sacrifices started and have been modified according to the *yuga*.'

Chapter 31-1(31) (Description of four *yuga*s)

Suta said, 'After this, I will again speak about the norms for *dvapara*. When *treta yuga* declines, it is the onset of *dvapara*. *Praja*s had accomplished *siddhi*s in the course of *treta yuga*. When it was the start of *dvapara yuga*, those vanished and were destroyed. In *dvapara*, they again appeared among subjects. However, there was confusion in *varna*s and disturbances in tasks. The conduct in *dvapara* is said to involve *rajas* and *tamas* and has sustenance of sacrifices, chastisement with the rod, intoxication, insolence, forgiveness and strength. In the beginning, there was *dharma* in *krita* and it continued during *treta*. But it was agitated during *dvapara* and destroyed during *kali yuga*. There will be perverse destruction of *varna*s and *ashrama*s will be mixed up. When this *yuga* commenced,

---

[744] *Kaivalya* is emancipation. The implied five destinations seem to be *kaivalya*, *jnana*, conquest of Prakriti, non-attachment (*vairagya*) and *sannyasa* (renunciation).

[745] Vasu.

the *shruti* and *smriti* texts were in opposition to each other. Because of the opposition between *shruti* and *smriti* texts, there is no certain determination. Since there is no certain determination, the true nature of *dharma* cannot be ascertained. There are differences about the true nature of *dharma*, even among men who are friends. They have different kinds of views and confuse each other. "This is *dharma*. This is not *dharma*. One cannot be certain." Since there is confusion about the causes, there is no certainty about tasks. These differences in points of view lead to confusion in insight. With such differences in insight, they cause disturbances to the sacred texts. It has been said that the single *Veda* had four parts in *treta yuga*. When lifespans contracted, they were classified again in *dvapara*. The *mantra*s recited by *rishi*s were again subject to divisions. However, the insight was confused. Therefore, in organizing *mantra*s and the Brahmana texts,[746] there were alterations in articulation of vowels and letters. This occurred when *maharshi*s read the *Rig*, *Yajur* and *Sama samhita*s. Sometimes, the differences are generally marginal. But sometimes, the differences are significant. This was the case with Brahmana texts, *kalpasutra*s,[747] *mantra*s, sayings and other texts. Some based themselves on these. But others did not believe them. They continued during *dvapara*. However, during *kali yuga*, one withdrew from them. There was only one *adhvaryu* text, but it was divided into two.[748] In general, opposite meanings are often taken and the sacred texts are disturbed. Many kinds of different schools cause confusion in the *adhvaryu* texts. In that way, the *Atharva Veda*, the *Rig Veda* and the *Sama Veda* were also subjected to alternative meanings. In *dvapara*, there was constant confusion and differing points of view. These divisions, counter divisions and numerous alternatives existed during *dvapara*. However, these were destroyed in *kali*. As a result of these being disturbed during *dvapara*, there was a lack of rain, death, disease and hardships.

---

[746] Brahmana texts have rules for sacrifices.

[747] The *kalpasutra*s are a part of *Vedanga* and indicate the norms to be followed in rites and rituals.

[748] Since *adhvaryu*s are chanted from *Yajur Veda*, this means *Yajur Veda*, divided into *Shukla Yajur Veda* and *Krishna Yajur Veda*.

Because of the miseries faced in thought, words and deeds, those who were born were no longer interested. As a consequence of indifference and miseries, they reflected on *moksha*. They reflected on *vairagya* but could see taints associated with *vairagya*. The taints associated with insight in *dvapara* led to the generation of ignorance. Ignorant ones also existed earlier, towards the beginning of Svayambhuva *manvantara*. But in *dvapara*, this produced those who were against the sacred texts. There were alternatives to *ayurveda*, Vedangas and *jyotisha* and alternatives to *arthashastra* and *hetushastra*.[749] Alternative commentaries and learning were developed for rites of the *kalpasutras*. There were separate divisions and schools for the sacred *smriti* texts. As *dvapara* continued, men resorted to different points of view. In ensuring subsistence, there were hardships in thoughts, words and deeds. In *dvapara*, for all beings, physical hardships became the most important. Greed was foremost in determining the conduct of traders. The truth was no longer certain. While sacred texts on the *Vedas* were composed, *dharma* was mixed up. *Varnas* and *ashramas* were destroyed and desire and anger were prevalent. In *dvapara*, attachment, avarice and slaying became prevalent. At the beginning of *dvapara*, Vyasa classified the *Vedas* into four parts. When *dvapara* came to an end, its *sandhya* was similar. The *dharma* that was established in *dvapara* was devoid of qualities. All the parts of *sandhya* were just like that. The last quarter of *sandhya* was similar.'

'Some parts were left during *dvapara*. Understand what will occur in *tishya*. The remnants of the *sandhyamsha* of *dvapara* will be prevalent in *kali*. Violence, envy, falsehood, illusion and the slaying of ascetics are natural in *tishya* and *prajas* will use these to obtain success. This is all they will do for the sake of *dharma* and *dharma* will decay. Despite praise expressed in thoughts, words and deeds, success will be not certain. There will be hunger and fear in *kali* and there will be constant diseases that lead to death. There will be the terrible fear of lack of rain and countries will be devastated.

---

[749] *Ayurveda* (literally, knowledge of life) is medical science, *arthashastra* is political economy (and governance), *hetushastra* means texts on logic.

In *tishya yuga*, people no longer accept the proof of the *smriti* texts.
In *kali yuga*, subjects die. Some die in the womb. Others die when
young. While some die when they are old, others die in childhood.
Sacrifices will be performed improperly. Studies won't be proper.
Deeds will be wicked and there will be evil *agama* texts. As a result
of the wicked deeds of *brahmana*s, fear will be generated among
*praja*s. Among men, there will be violence, illusion, jealousy, anger,
envy and lack of forgiveness. In *tishya*, all creatures will suffer from
attachment and greed. At the beginning of *kali yuga*, birth will be
associated with great agitation. At the time, the full lifespan for
men will be one thousand years. *Dvija*s will not perform sacrifices.
Nor will they study the *Veda*s. In due order, men, *kshatriya*s and
*vaishya*s, will be exterminated. *Shudra*s and *antyaja*s[750] will be
imprisoned, along with *brahmana*s. In sleeping, sitting and eating,
this is what will happen in the world at the time of *kali yuga*.[751]
Kings will generally be *shudra*s, who propagate heretical views.
The subjects who exist then will be devoid of qualities. Lifespans,
intelligence, strength, beauty and nobility of birth will be destroyed.
*Shudra*s will follow the conduct of *brahmana*s and *brahmana*s will
follow the conduct of *shudra*s. Thieves will follow the conduct of
kings and lords of the earth will follow the conduct of thieves. When
the end of the *mahayuga* arrives, servants will become masters.
Women will be evil in conduct and false. They will love liquor and
flesh. O excellent sage! They will become deceitful. O supreme
sage! When the end of the *mahayuga* arrives, wives will no longer
be faithful to a single husband. There will be a preponderance of
predatory beasts and cattle will be destroyed. When the end of the
mahayuga is imminent, the virtuous will withdraw from learning.
The great fruits of *dharma*, with donations as the foundation, will
be extremely rare. The observance of *dharma* will involve laxity in
the four *ashrama*s. In some places, the land will yield no fruits. In
others, it will yield a lot of fruits. The kings will not protect but will
enjoy shares in taxes. When the end of the *mahayuga* arrives, they

---

[750] *Antyaja* can loosely be translated as outcaste. Literally, it means
someone who is born in the extremities (of the main habitation).
[751] These are no longer differentiated, according to *varna*s.

will only be interested in protecting their own selves. Not protected by kings, *brahmana*s will earn a living through *shudra*s. At the end of the *mahayuga*, the best among *dvija*s will bow down before *shudra*s. When the end of the *mahayuga* presents itself, habitations will become marketplaces. *Dvija*s will sell auspicious objects and women will become harlots. Though there will be many mendicants in this *kali yuga*, excellent *dvija*s will sell the fruits of their austerities and sacrifices. At the time of the destruction of the *mahayuga*, it is said that the divinity[752] showers down in extraordinary ways. In this worst of *yuga*s, everyone will become a trader. When people sell merchandise, it will generally be through false weights. Everything will be full of those with evil conduct and behaviour, in the form of heretics and hunters. When the end of the *mahayuga* arrives, there will be few men and a lot of women. There will be many people who will beg from each other. When it is the end of the *mahayuga*, no one will repay a good turn. Everyone will be fraudulent and jealous. Everyone will be false and use harsh words. When it is the end of the *mahayuga*, the signs of this descent will be suspicion. The earth will be emptied of riches. Rulers, who are supposed to be protectors, will no longer be protectors. They will seize jewels that belong to others and oppress the wives of others. They will be evil-souled and full of desire. They will be inferior and will love to be rash. Their senses will be destroyed, and they will be crooked. They will wield spears and wear their hair loose. When it is the end of the *mahayuga*, those who are less than sixteen years of age will have children. When the end of the *mahayuga* presents itself, *shudra*s will practice *dharma*. Their teeth will be white, and they will subdue their senses. They will shave their heads and wear ochre garments. There will be those who will steal crops. Others will steal garments. Thieves will steal from thieves. When people seize objects, others will seize objects from them. *Jnana* and rites will vanish from the world and there will be no rites. Humans will suffer from insects, rats and snakes. Though people constantly desire those who can provide pacification of disease, such people will be very rare.

[752] Indra. Rains become unpredictable.

Countries will suffer from the inferior and people will reside near hermits. Overwhelmed by misery, the lifespan will be one hundred years. In *kali yuga*, all the *Veda*s will be seen, but will not be seen.[753] Oppressed only by *adharma*, sacrifices will suffer. Some will wear ochre garments, but not follow any texts. There will be *kapalika*s.[754] Others will sell the *Veda*s. Still others will sell *tirtha*s.[755] There will be other heretics who will act contrary to *varna*s and *ashrama*s. When *kali yuga* arrives, such people will be produced. *Shudra*s will become accomplished in studying the *Veda*s and in *dharma* and *artha*. Kings born as *shudra*s will perform horse sacrifices. They will kill women, children and cows and will kill each other. Subjects will try to obtain success by robbing each other. Utterances will be full of miserable accounts. Lifespans will be short. Because of diseases, lifespans will be limited. *Kali* is described as a being enveloped in *tamas*, with an addiction to *adharma*. There will be hatred and feticide will be practiced. Therefore, when *kali* arrives, lifespans, strength and beauty will decline. However, humans will obtain *siddhi* within a short period of time. O best among *dvija*s! At the end of the *mahayuga*, those who follow *dharma* will be blessed. There will be those without malice. They will practice the *dharma* spoken about in *shruti* and *smriti* texts. *Dharma* yields fruits when practised for an entire year in *treta*. Those fruits are said to be obtained when *dharma* is practised for a month in *dvapara*. According to capacity, if a wise person practices *dharma* for a day in *kali*, he obtains the same fruits. This is the status of *kali yuga*.'

'Now understand about *sandhyamsha*. From one *yuga* to another *yuga*, *siddhi*s diminish by three-quarters.[756] The nature of the *sandhya*s is just like that of the *yuga*s. The nature of the *sandhya*s is that their own portions are diminished by one-quarter. In this way, at the end of the *mahayuga*, the period of *sandhyamsha*

---

[753] Though they will be read, they will not be understood.

[754] Literally, those with skulls. The left hand holds a skull, used as a begging bowl for alms. The right hand holds a staff, with a skull at the top.

[755] *Tirtha* is a place of pilgrimage.

[756] If it was four quarters in *krita*, it becomes three quarters in *treta*, two quarters in *dvapara* and one quarter in *kali*.

arrives. To punish the wicked and slay the Bhrigus, he arises. His *gotra* is named Chandra and his name is said to be Pramati.[757] Earlier, in Svayambhuva *manvantara*, he was part of Madhava's portion. He roamed around the earth for a full twenty years. He gathered an army that consisted of horses, chariots and elephants. Hundreds and thousands of *brahmana*s picked up their weapons and surrounded him. He then killed all the *mleccha*s, along with all the kings who had been born as *shudra*s. The lord destroyed all the heretics. He killed all those who were not extremely devoted to *dharma*. The lord killed all those born from a mixture of *varna*s and those who earned a living through them, those from the north, those from the central region, those from the mountains, those from the east and those from the west, those who roamed around on the slopes of the Vindhyas, those from the south, along with Dravidas and those from Simhala, Gandharas, Paradas, Pahlavas, Yavanas, Shakas, Tusharas, Barbaras, Chinas, Shulikas, Daradas, Khasas, Lampakaras, Katakas and different types of Kiratas. The powerful one killed all those named *mleccha*s. Invisible to all beings, he roamed around the earth. He was born as the divinity from Madhava's portion. In his earlier birth, the valiant one was famous under the name of Pramati. In a former *kali yuga*, the lord was born in the *gotra* of Chandra. He emerged when he was thirty-two years old and for twenty years, killed all humans and all beings. Through these cruel deeds, he only left seeds on earth. There were the *vrishala*s,[758] generally prone to *adharma*. Through some means, he made them angry with each other and succeeded in destroying them. Along with his followers, he established a habitation between the Ganga and the Yamuna. In that past *kalpa*, along with his ordinary soldiers, he exterminated all the thousands of *mleccha* kings. When the end of the *mahayuga* arrives and it is the period of *sandhyamsha*, only a few subjects will be left, here and there. They will be overwhelmed by greed and will suffer from groups of evil planets. They will cause violence to each other and uproot

---

[757] Since the *gotra* is Chandra, this Pramati is the one who was the son of Nrideva. This Pramati was actually born in the Bhrigu lineage.

[758] While this means *shudra*, it also means outcast.

each other. When the end of the *mahayuga* presents itself, lacking a king, there will be anarchy. All the subjects will suffer fear from each other. They will be anxious and confused and will abandon their wives and homes. They will be negligent about their own lives and will be miserable, without any reason. With the *dharma* of the *shruti* and *smriti* texts destroyed, they will kill each other. There will be no ordinances and no defenders. There will be no affection and no shame. With *dharma* destroyed and their suffering, people will be reduced to a height of twenty-five *angula*s. With their senses afflicted by misery, they will abandon their sons and wives. They will suffer from a lack of rain. Grieving, they will have to give up the means of subsistence. Abandoning their own countries, they will reside in the frontier regions—rivers, oceans, marshy lands and mountains. Extremely miserable, they will subsist on flesh, roots and fruits. They will be clad in bark, leaves and hides. They will be devoid of rites and devoid of possessions. They will deviate from *varna*s and *ashrama*s and a terrible state of mixing will come about. The few subjects who are left will be reduced to such extremes. They will suffer from old age, disease, hunger, grief and indifference.'

'They will reflect on this state of indifference. After reflecting, they will arrive at a state of equanimity. From that equanimity, they will understand about the *atman*. From that understanding, they will develop *dharma* and good conduct. When *kali* is still left, they will themselves develop these palliatives. When the end of the *mahayuga* arrives, the delusion in their senses will change within a day and a night, as if they had been asleep. This will happen because of the strength of *krita*, which will come about. This is what will occur when the pure *krita yuga* arrives. The *praja*s who remained in *kali* will give birth in *krita yuga*. Staying invisible, the *siddha*s will remain and will roam around. They will be established there, along with the *saptarshi*s. In this world, they are described as seeds, for *brahmana*s, *kshatriya*s, *vaishya*s and *shudra*s. There will be no special difference between them and those born at the end of *kali*. The *saptarshi*s will speak about *dharma* to the others. In accordance with *varna*s and *ashrama*s, the rites will be divided into two groups of *shruti* and *smriti* texts and *praja*s will follow them. In *krita yuga*, *saptarshi*s will instruct about the *dharma* of *shruti* and *smriti* texts. At the end of the *mahayuga*, some of them will still remain, for the sake of establishing *dharma*. The sages and their rights are established in the *manvantara*s. This is just like grass being burnt by the heat of a forest conflagration. When there are the first rains, there is sprouting from the roots in forests. In this way, in this world, those in *krita yuga* originate from those in *kali*. Thus, one *yuga* leads to mutual offspring in another *yuga*. This continues without a break, until the *manvantara* itself is over. In due order, as the *yuga*s proceed, happiness, lifespans, strength, beauty, *dharma*, *artha* and *kama* are diminished by three quarters. Success in achieving *dharma* is also reduced in the *sandhyamsha*s of *yuga*s. O *dvija*s! I have thus described the transition between *yuga*s. There are means for all the four *yuga*s. When that cycle of four *yuga*s is multiplied one thousand times, this period is described as the duration of Brahma's day. All beings, upright and insentient, remain till the end of the *mahayuga*. This is described as the characteristic of all the *yuga*s. In the due order, when the cycle of four *yuga*s is multiplied by seventy-one, this is said to be the length of a *manvantara*. Whatever exists in a cycle of four *yuga*s, exists again in another such cycle, following the due order. There are differences between one cycle of creation and another cycle of creation. These are said to be thirty-five and are described as not more, nor less.[759] Like the *yuga*s, the *kalpa*s possess their own characteristics. There are also characteristics for all the *manvantara*s. Because of the nature of *yuga*s, the changes in *yuga*s have continued for a long time. They exist in that way, just as the world of the living goes through cycles of increase and decrease. In brief, these are said to be the signs of the *yuga*s and the past and future *manvantara*s in this world. If one *manvantara* is described, so are all the others. If one *kalpa* is known, so are all the others, including future ones. One should know this and not debate it. In all the *manvantara*s in this world, past and future, those who take pride in their positions and all their names and forms are identical. In this *manvantara*,

---

[759] The number thirty-five is unclear. Perhaps it means seven *rishi*s, seven ancestors, seven *deva*s, seven *asura*s and seven *yaksha*s, or something along those lines.

lords who are *deva*s are of eight types. According to need, all the *rishi*s and Manus are also equal. Such were the divisions of *varna*s and *ashrama*s in a former *yuga*. The lord always arranges for the nature of a *yuga*. The divisions of *varna*s and *ashrama*s in a *yuga*, *siddhi* in a *yuga* and everything related have been described. Now understand the nature of creation. In the due order, I will speak in detail about the nature of existence in a *yuga*.'

Chapter 32-1(32) (Lineage of *rishi*s)

Suta said, 'Hear about the *praja*s born in different *yuga*s— *asura*s, *sarpa*s, *gandharva*s, *pishacha*s, *yaksha*s and *rakshasa*s. Understand about the *yuga*s in which they are born and about how long they lived. *Pishacha*s, *asura*s, *gandharva*s, *yaksha*s, *rakshasa*s and *pannaga*s born in *krita yuga* were as broad as they were tall. The eight kinds born as divine species were ninety-six *angula*s tall, this being measured by their own fingers. Since they were nourished well, this was their natural measurement. There were humans who existed in the *sandhyamsha* of the *yuga*. Measured against *deva*s and *asura*s, they were forty-nine *angula*s shorter. *Deva*s and *asura*s were a full one hundred and fifty-eight *angula*s tall. That is how they are remembered by those born in *kali*. Measured by their own fingers, from head to foot, those born in *kali* are described as eighty-four *angula*s tall. In this way, humans become shorter by a portion in all the *yuga*s. This is true of all the *yuga*s, past and future. Using his own fingers, a man is described as eight *tala*s tall.[760] From head to foot, if a person is nine *tala*s tall and if his arms extend all the way up to his knees, he is worshipped even by the Gods. It should be known that from one *yuga* to another *yuga*, the heights of cows, horses, elephants, buffaloes and immobile entities increase

---

[760] *Tala* is the length of the inner palm, measured by the middle finger. Roughly, one *tala* = twelve *angula*s. Nine *tala*s is described as the length of divinities. So the average man is around 169 cm tall and for a divinity, this is 190 cm.

or decrease because of their own *karma*. The height of a humped
animal is seventy-six *angulas*. The height of an elephant is described
as a full one hundred and eight *angulas*. The height of a tree with
branches is described as nine hundred and sixty *angulas* and fifty
yavas.[761] Those who possess insight into the truth can see that the
signs of *devas* are such that their bodies are formed just like human
bodies. What is said to be more in *devas* is intelligence, not the
body. In that way, the bodies of humans are sometimes taller than
average. These are said to be the dimensions of *devas* and humans.
Pashus, birds, all immobile objects, cattle, goats, sheep, horses,
elephants and trees are all fit to be used in sacrificial rites. When
they are born in abodes of *devas*, they have corresponding forms.
Devas, auspicious in forms, can enjoy whatever they want. They are
happy enjoying mobile and immobile entities, depending on their
forms, structures and dimensions, as long as they are agreeable.'

'After this, I will speak about *shishtas*, *santas* and *sadhus*.[762]
The word *sat* means the *brahman*.[763] A person who is united with
the *brahman* is described as *santa*. A person who is not affected
by the ten material causes, possesses the eight signs and is neither
angered, nor delighted, is described as a person who has conquered
his *atman*.[764] *Brahmanas*, *kshatriyas* and *vaishyas* engage in general
dharma, as well as specific rites. Therefore, they are *dvijas*. A
person who follows *varnas* and *ashramas* roams around happily in
heaven. A person who follows the *dharma* of *shruti* and *smriti* texts
is described as one who possesses *jnana*, one who knows about

[761] Four *yavas* = one *angula*.

[762] *Shishtas* are those who are educated, *santas* are those who are
self-controlled, and *sadhus* are those who are virtuous. But the words are
almost synonymous.

[763] *Sat* means existence/truth, but also means the *brahman*.

[764] The ten material causes are the five senses of perception and five
organs of action. The eight signs can mean the eight *siddhis*, but probably
means *ashtanga yoga*. *Yoga* has eight elements—*yama* (restraint), *niyama*
(rituals), *asana* (posture), *pranayama* (breathing), *pratyahara* (withdrawal),
dharana (retention), *dhyana* (meditation) and *samadhi* (liberation/deep
meditation). That's the reason the expression *ashtanga* (eight-formed) *yoga*
is used.

dharma. To accomplish learning, if a *brahmachari* is engaged in his *guru*'s welfare, he is described as a *sadhu*. If a person in *garhasthya* follows the *sadhana* meant for householders, he is described as a *sadhu*. A *vaikhanasa* is described as a *sadhu* because he strives for *sadhana* and austerities in the forest. A mendicant who strives for the *sadhana* of *yoga* is described as a *sadhu*. These are described as *sadhu*s, since they follow the *dharma* of *ashrama*s and their respective *sadhana*s—in *brahmacharya*, *garhasthya*, *vanaprastha* and as a mendicant. *Deva*s, ancestors, sages and humans do not know whether this is *dharma* and that is not. There are differing points of view. The words *dharma* and *adharma* are often used in the sense of adherence to rites. Accomplished *karma* is described as *dharma* and unskilled *karma* as *adharma*. The root word "*dhri*" is said to convey a sense of nurturing. Anything that is not great and does not sustain is said to be *adharma*.[765] Instructed by an *acharya*,[766] *dharma* enables a person to achieve what is desired. An *acharya* also instructs that *adharma* leads to harmful fruits. A person is described as an *acharya* if he is aged, not greedy, self-controlled, devoid of arrogance, duly humble and upright. He himself follows and establishes good conduct. A person who searches out the sacred texts is said to be an *acharya*. *Dvija*s who know about *dharma* have said that *dharma* is of two types, following *shruti* texts and following *smriti* texts. The signs of *shruti* texts are two-fold—accepting a wife and *agnihotra*. The signs of *smriti* texts are described as *varna*s, *ashrama*s, good conduct, *yama* and *niyama*. On the basis of their learning, *saptarshi*s spoke about the *shruti* texts earlier. The *shruti* texts are the *Rig Veda*, the *Yajur Veda*, the *Sama Veda*, the Brahmana texts and the *Vedanga*s. Manu spoke about the good conduct of *smriti* texts in an earlier *manvantara*. Therefore, the *dharma* of the *smriti* texts is described as one that has a division according to *varna*s and *ashrama*s. These different kinds of *dharma* are known as the conduct of *shishta*s. The word "*shesha*" has the same meaning as "*shishta*".[767] Therefore, *shishta*s are described as

---

[765] Whatever sustains and holds up is *dharma*.
[766] Preceptor.
[767] Both words mean the remainder, those who were left.

those who are left. In the *manvantara*s, the *shishta*s remain in this world, established in *dharma*. These are Manu and the *saptarshi*s, the causes behind the extension of the worlds. Those who remain for the sake of establishing *dharma* are known as *shishta*s. I have already spoken about the *shishta*s, Manu and the others. From one *yuga* to another *yuga*, these *shishta*s follow *dharma* properly. Manu and the other *shishta*s repeatedly follow the three,[768] the policy of punishment, sacrifices, *varna*s and *ashrama*s. This virtuous conduct of *shishta*s was observed by the ancestors who came before them. There are eight characteristics of such good conduct—donations, truth, austerities, *jnana*, learning, sacrifices, departure[769] and compassion. This was followed by Manu and the *saptarshi*s in all the *manvantara*s and is described as *shishtachara*.[770] It should be known that if it has been heard, this is spoken of as *shrouta*, the *dharma* of the *shruti* texts. If it has been remembered, it is *smarta*, the *dharma* of the *smriti* texts. Sacrifices and the Vedas constitute *shrouta dharma*. *Smarta dharma* has *varna*s and *ashrama*s. I will speak about the parts and components of this *dharma*. When he is asked, if a person states exactly what has occurred, what he has exactly seen, this is a sign of truthfulness. Austerities take the form of *brahmacharya*, *japa*, silence and fasting. These are extremely terrible and difficult to practice. Sacrifices are described as arranging for the collection of *pashu*s, objects and oblations, the Rig, Yajur and Sama hymns and *dakshina* for *ritvija*s. Compassion is described as complete impartiality in outlook and a behaviour such that one regards all beings as one's own self, regardless of whether it causes benefit or harm to one's own self. If a person does not abuse when he is abused, does not strike back when he is struck and exhibits forbearance in thoughts, words and deeds, this is said to be forgiveness. Lack of greed occurs when a person does not appropriate the possessions of others, even when the owner is unable to protect and abandons his possessions out of fear. Refraining from sexual intercourse, thinking about it and conversing about

---

[768] The three Vedas.

[769] Probably meaning departure for the forest, or even death.

[770] Conduct of the *shishta*s, virtuous conduct.

it, is withdrawal described as *brahmacharya*. This is said to be an austerity without any weakness. If the senses do not indulge in falsehood, whether for one's own sake or others, this is a sign of self-control. If there is no attachment to the ten material senses and if a person exhibits the eight signs, without being enraged or without striking back, such a person is thought to be one who has conquered his *atman*. If a person gives a recipient a desired object that possesses qualities, earned through legitimate means, this is a trait of donating. Donations are of three types—inferior, medium and superior. The superior one is best, the inferior one is for accomplishing one's own selfish objectives. Out of compassion, if one divides one's possessions among all beings, this is a medium kind of donation. *Shruti* and *smriti* texts have laid down the principles of *dharma* for the *varna*s and the *ashrama*s. Virtuous *sadhu*s revere *dharma* that is not against *shishtachara*. Lack of hatred towards what is injurious, rejoicing at what is desired and withdrawal and indifference towards joy, torment and misery— these are the signs of *sannyasa*. Such a person casts aside all *karma*, regardless of whether it has been accomplished or has not been completed. Giving up the desired and undesirable is described as renunciation. In everything specific, the unmanifest exists. There are transformations in the sentient. Knowing about the distinction between the sentient and the insentient is described as *jnana*. These are said to be the signs and components of *dharma*. Earlier, in Svayambhuva *manvantara*, *rishi*s who knew about *dharma*, laid them down.'

'For a *manvantara*, I will now describe the principles for *chaturhotra* and *chaturvidya*.[771] In every *manvantara*, a different *shruti* text is recommended. Until the onset of the deluge, the *Rig*, *Yajur* and *Sama* texts, *deva*s, the Shatarudriya, the norms for oblations and the *stotram*s continue, as they always have, and are not abandoned. There are four kinds of *stotram*s—*dravya-stotram*, *guna-stotram* and *phala-stotram*, while *abhijanaka-stotram* is the

---

[771] *Chaturhotra* means the four kinds of officiating priests, mentioned earlier. *Chaturvidya* means the four *Veda*s.

fourth.[772] In all the *manvantara*s, there are *deva*s. Accordingly, Brahma has laid down the four kinds of *stotram*s for them. In this way, the large number of *mantra*s have four kinds of origin. The hymns of *Rig Veda*, *Yajur Veda*, *Sama Veda* and *Atharva Veda* are distinct. *Rishi*s tormented themselves through austerities that were fierce and extremely difficult to perform. Thereby, in an earlier *manvantara*, the *mantra*s manifested themselves before them. Lack of contentedness, fear, misery, lack of happiness and grief—these are the five.[773] As they wished, *rishi*s possessed insight about *taraka*. *Rishi*s possess the traits of being a *rishi*. I will describe the signs. In the past and the future, there are said to be five kinds of *rishi*s. Therefore, I will speak about *rishi*s and about how *rishi*s originated. There was a state of equilibrium among the *guna*s. Everything confronted dissolution. There was no division of the *Veda*s. Nothing could be discerned in the pervasive darkness. There was no intelligence. At the time, for the sake of consciousness, the one with consciousness[774] came into being, possessing both intelligence and consciousness. Both of them came into being simultaneously, like a fish and water. The *guna* of *sattva* came into being, presided over by consciousness. The action is consequent to the cause. This is how a material object comes to possess the characteristic of being an object and meaning comes to possess the characteristic of meaning something. When the time arrived, divisions arrived among the senses. In the due order, Mahat and the others manifested themselves. *Ahamkara* evolved from Mahat and the elements, and the senses resulted from this. There were differences between the elements and the elements evolved from each other. Through the cause, the effect instantly came about. This is just like sparks and particles simultaneously originating from a flaming torch. In that way,

[772] *Dravya-stotram* is praise of an object, or for an object. *Guna-stotram* is praise of a quality, or praise for a quality. *Phala-stotram* is praise of a fruit, or for a fruit. *Abhijanaka-stotram* is praise of a lineage, or for a lineage.

[773] The sentence is left dangling. Presumably, *mantra*s appeared to ward these off.

[774] Pradhana. We have taken liberties in the translation, so as to make the meaning clear. The *shloka*s are cryptic.

*kshetrajna*s evolved simultaneously from the cause. This is just like suddenly seeing a firefly in the darkness. Like the blazing firefly, there was an evolution from the unmanifest. There was a gigantic and embodied form. The learned lord stood there, at the door of the pavilion, beyond which, the great one existed. He is beyond darkness and one can think of his attributes. The *shruti* texts state, "The learned one is established there, beyond darkness." When this transformation occurred, intelligence manifested itself in four kinds of ways—*jnana*, non-attachment, prosperity and *dharma*. These are the four. These are known to be the means for a man to obtain success. A transformation in the great-souled one's body is said to have accomplished success. He is known as *kshetrajna* because he possesses knowledge about all the *kshetra*s. Since he was the first person to lie down, he is spoken of as Purusha.[775] Since he lay down in the midst of intelligence, he is spoken of as possessing understanding in his *atman*. The manifest and the unmanifest are encircled by the consciousness required for *siddhi*. In this way, *kshetrajna*, who possesses knowledge about the *kshetra*, transformed himself. Simultaneous with this transformation, the unmanifest himself became a *rishi* who exerted himself. Since he supremely exerted himself, he obtained the state of being a *paramarshi*.[776] The etymological root "*rish*" means to go and a person who approaches withdrawal at the outset is a *rishi*. Hence, it is said that the status of being a *rishi* manifested itself. They manifested themselves from Ishvara. They are sons born through Brahma's mental powers. When they originated, they surrounded Mahat. They were seen to be patient and great in all the qualities. Therefore, they are spoken of as *maharshi*s. They possess the insight of supreme intelligence. They are the sons of lords, born through mental powers and also born through the womb. These are *rishi*s who have obtained the status of being *rishi*s. They are beyond *ahamkara* and austerities. These *saptarshi*s possess insight about the true nature of *bhutadi*. The sons of *rishi*s are *rishika*s, born through the womb, from

---

[775] With the word derived from the first, the foremost.

[776] *Paramarshi* = *Parama rishi*, supreme *rishi*. While *parama* means supreme, the derivation of *arshayate* as exertion is suspect.

physical intercourse. Those *rishi*s are immensely energetic and possess knowledge about the *tanmatra*s and the truth. The *saptarshi*s possess insight into the supreme truth. The *rishika*s are the sons and the sons of the *rishi*s also know. They comprehend the truth and the specifics of that truth. Thus, the *saptarshi*s possess supreme insight into the *shruti* texts. They know about the one whose *atman* is not manifest, the *atman* in Mahat, the *atman* in *ahamkara*, the *atman* in the elements and the *atman* in the senses. This is spoken of as the five kinds of *jnana*. Hear about their names. Bhrigu, Marichi, Atri, Angiras, Pulaha, Kratu, Manu, Daksha, Vasishtha and Pulastya—these ten originated through Brahma's mental powers. They are themselves lords. Since they are supreme *rishi*s, they are described as *maharshi*s. Hear about the *rishi*s who were the sons of these lords. They are Kavya,[777] Brihaspati, Kashyapa, Chyavana, Utathya, Vamadeva, Apasya, Ushija, Kardama, Vishrava, Shakti, the *valakhilya*s and Arvata. They are known as *rishi*s because they obtained the status of being a *rishi* through their austerities. Hear about the *rishika*s, the sons of *rishi*s, born through the womb. They are Vatsara, Nagrihu, Bharadvaja, *rishi* Dirghatama, Brihaduktha, Sharadvata, Vajashrava, Shuchi, Vashyashva, Parashara, Dadhicha, Samshapa and King Vaishravana.[778] These are known as *rishika*s. Through truth, they obtained the status of being *rishi*s. They are described as lords, *rishi*s and *rishika*s. All of them composed all the *mantra*s. Understand. Bhrigu, Kavya, Prachetas, Richika, Atmavan, Ourva, Jamadagni, Vida, Sarasvata, Arshtishena, Yudhajit, Vitahavya, Suvarchas, Vainya, Prithu, Divodasa, Badhyashva, Gritsa and Shounaka—these nineteen, descended from the Bhrigu lineage, are those who composed *mantra*s.[779] There are thirty-three excellent ones who were descended from the lineage of Angiras—Angiras, Vaidyaga, Bharadvaja, Bashkali, Ritavaka, Garga, Shini, Sankriti, Purukutsa, Mandhata, Ambarisha, Yuvanashva, Pourakutsa, Trasadasyu, Dasyuman, Aharya, Ajamidha, Tukshaya, Kapi, Vrishadarbha, Virupashva, Kanva, Mudgala, Utathya,

---

[777] Shukracharya.
[778] Kubera.
[779] Some of these were kings.

Sanadvaja, Vajashrava, Ayasya, Chakravarti, Vamadeva, Asija, Brihaduktha, *rishi* Dirghatama and Kakshivan. All of them composed *mantra*s. Now hear about those descended from Kashyapa. There are five who spoke about the *brahman*—Kashyapa, Vatsara, Naidhruva, Raibhya and Devala. The *maharshi*s who descended from Atri's lineage and composed *mantra*s are Atri, Arvasana, Shyavashva, Gavishthira, Avihotra, *rishi* Dhiman and Purvatithi. Seven descended from Vasishtha's lineage are known as those who spoke about the *brahman*. They are Vasishtha, Shakti, Parashara, Indrapramati as the fourth, Bharadvasu as the fifth, Maitravaruni as the sixth and Kundina as the seventh. There are thirteen excellent ones from Kushika's lineage. They are known to have been devoted to *dharma* and are Vishvamitra, the son of Gadhi, Devarata, Udgala, the learned Madhucchanda, the *rishi*, Aghamarshana the second, Ashtaka, Lohita, Kata, Kola, Devashrava, Renu, Purana and Dhananjaya. There are three who are supreme in their deeds. Their limbs were full of the *brahman*. They are Agastya, Dridhayu and Vidhmavaha. Vaivasvata Manu and King Pururava, the son of Ila, are *kshatriya*s who are known to have acted so that they composed *mantra*s. There are three supreme *vaishya*s who are remembered as having composed *mantra*s— Bhalandana, Vatsa and Samkila. The *rishi*s who composed mantras were *brahmana*s, *kshatriya*s and *vaishya*s and their number is said to have been ninety.[780] Now hear about the sons of *rishi*s.'

Chapter 33-1(33) (Traits of *rishi*s)

S uta said, 'The sons of *rishika*s should also be known as the sons of *rishi*s. They propounded the Brahman texts. Hear about their names. There were *shrutarshi*s who knew about the *shruti* texts. I will briefly speak about the foremost ones. They were Bahvricha, Bhargava, Paila, Sankritya, Jajali, Sandhyasti,

---

[780] Including the three *vaishya*s, the number is ninety-three and not ninety.

Mathara, Yajnavalkya, Parashara, Upamanyu, Indrapramati, Manduki, Shakali, Bashkali, Shokapani, Naila, Paila,[781] Alaka, Pannaga and Pakshaganta. There were eighty-six such. Among these *dvija*s, the most important *shrutarshi*s were the Bahvrichas. They were Vaishampayana, Louhitya, Kanthakala, Avashavadha, Shyamapati, Palandu, Alambi and Kamalapati. The descendants and secondary descendants of these *shrutarshi*s numbered eighty-six. O *dvija*s! Jaimini, Bharadvaja, Kavya and Poushyanji, Hiranyanabha, Koushilya, Lougakshi, Kusumi, Langali, Shalihotra, Shaktiraja and Bhargava—these are spoken of as *dvijarshi*s who were Charaka *adhvaryu*s.[782] The *acharya* for the singing of *Sama Veda* hymns was King Pururava, Ila's son. Forty-six others and their disciples were *shrutarshi*s. Koushiti, Kankamudga, Kundaka, Parashara, Lobhalobha, with *dharma* in his *atman*, Brahmabala, Kranthala, Madagala and Markandeya, who knew about *dharma*, these nine[783] are known as *hotri*s who were *brahmachari*s. Subsequent Charaka *adhvaryu*s composed *mantra*s and Brahmana texts. They were Chalubhi, Sumati, Devavara, Anukrishna, Ayus, Anubhumi, Prita, Krishashva, Sumuli and Bashkali. These Charaka *adhvaryu*s were *adhvaryu*s who followed *brahmacharya* and they are revered. Madhyama *adhvaryu*s[784] were the learned Shuka, Vyasa's son, Louki, Bhurishrava, Somavi, Atunantakya, Dhoumya and Kashyapa. Among these, those who resided in the forest were Ilaka, Upanmanyu, Vida, Bhargava, Madhuka, Pinga, Shvetaketu, Prajadarpa, Kahoda, Yajnavalkya, Shounaka, Ananga and Niratala. There were women who spoke about the *brahman*. They knew about *dharma*. They are described as Aditi, mother of *deva*s; Jalapa and Manavi; the two auspicious and supreme *apsara*s, Urvashi and Vishvayosha; Mudgalaa; Atujiva; the illustrious Taraa; Pratimedhi; Margaa; Sujataa; Mahatapaa; Lopamudra, who knew

---

[781] A second Paila.

[782] *Dvijarshi* = *Dvija* + *rishi*. *Krishna Yajurveda* has a Charaka (Kathaka) recension.

[783] The text says ninety. We have corrected it to nine.

[784] This probably refers to the Madhyandina recension of *Shukla Yajurveda*.

about *dharma*; and Kōushitikaa. The *apsara*s were respected for their beauty. I have thus spoken about the most important sons of *rishi*s. These *rishi*s are remembered for having set up different schools of the Veda*s*. These *rishi*s and *rishika*s were lords. They composed *mantra*s. The sons of *rishi*s expounded on *kalpasutra*s and Brahmana texts. The *rishi*s and *rishika*s, along with their sons, were lords.'

'Understand the words used by those who possessed insight about *mantra*s. The deep sounds, which seem to blaze and instruct, are about *advaita*.[785] The signs and names speak about extreme direct perceptions. There is devotion towards the one who exists within all beings. Some speak about etymology. Other words express knowledge about the one who originated himself. There are also some *mantra*s, which are about different kinds of names. It is held that the words of the *rishi*s are about what they directly experienced. There is a lot about the many kinds of *nigama* texts and the declension of sounds. Such great sentences are remembered as words uttered by the *rishika*s. There are many doubts because parts of a sentence have not been clearly articulated. However, the words spoken by all the sons of the *rishi*s are about the supreme divinity. To talk about the cause, they used many examples and colourful words, leading to a loss in meaning. For all of them, human sentences were incapable of complete expression. In this way, the power of insight of the past *rishi*s is said to have got mixed up. Nevertheless, despite this fault of the species, they represent the best of what can be drawn out. This is the *jnana* of the past, the present and the future, medication for the miseries of birth. Despite the words getting mixed up, they perpetuated the strength of what was received from *guru*s. They were great and could go everywhere. They composed the *dharmashastra* texts. Those who were extremely great in excellent austerities are remembered as *rishi*s. They were Brihaspati, Shukra, Vyasa and Sarasvata. Vyasas, who composed sacred texts, are remembered as Vedavyasas. It is possible for the ones born later to be superior,

[785] Non-duality between the *jivatman* and the *brahman*. We have taken several liberties in these sections.

in intellect, to the ones born earlier. Those who were full of such prosperity are remembered as *rishi*s. When one thinks of a *rishi*, age is no yardstick of measurement. It can be seen that a man can be superior in intellect to a person who is older. Thus, in intelligence, strength and learning, a *rishi* is superior to an older person. A *mantra* from the *Rig Veda* is described as one where the same *pada* is used in the middle and all the *akshara*s are properly distributed.[786] A *mantra* from the *Yajur Veda* is described as one where the focus is not on *akshara*s and *pada*s, but on the rhythmic pauses, with an excess of *akshara*s at the end. A *mantra* from the *Sama Veda* has seven components—(1) *Hrimkara*;[787] (2) Pranava; (3) the song; (4) a hymn of praise as the fourth;[788] (5) response of the assistant *hotri*, as the fifth;[789] (6) *Upadrava* is said to be sixth;[790] (7) the conclusion is the seventh.[791] Excluding *Hrimkara* and Pranava, it is said to have five parts. "May your *dharma* be for the *brahman*." When this is said, it is described as a benediction. There can also be remorse, lamentation and responses to questions posed as a result of rage or hatred. All these kinds of learning are laid down as signs of a *mantra*. The signs of *Rig*, *Yajur* and *Sama mantra*s are said to be nine—(1) Form; (2) censure; (3) praise; (4) rebuking; (5) contentment; (6) questioning; (7) permission; (8) narration; and (9) benediction. These are held to be the different components. I will now speak about the twenty-four signs of differences among *mantra*s. (1) *Prashamsa*;[792] (2) *Stuti*;[793] (3)

---

[786] An *akshara* is a syllable, a bit with a single vowel sound. A *pada*, consisting of *akshara*s, is one quarter of the verse.

[787] The sound of *hrim*, a *bija mantra*.

[788] Known as *prastava*.

[789] Known as *pratihotra*.

[790] *Upadrava* is praise of the Sama hymn. This bit is best understood if one reads *Chandogya Upanishad* 2.8.2. A loose translation is the following. "When "ut" is said, that is uttered by the *udgatri*. When "prati" is heard, that is uttered by the assistant priest. When "upa" is heard, that is *upadrava*. When "ni" is heard, that is *nidhana*."

[791] Known as *nidhana*.

[792] Praise.

[793] Praise.

Akrosha;[794] (4) *Ninda;*[795] (5) *Paridevana;*[796] (6) *Abhishapa;*[797] (7) *Vishapa;*[798] (8) *Prashna;*[799] (9) *Prativacha;*[800] (10) *Ashis;*[801] (11) *Yajna;*[802] (12) *Akshepa;*[803] (13) *Arthakhyana;*[804] (14) *Samkatha;*[805] (15) *Viyoga;*[806] (16) *Abhiyoga;*[807] (17) *Katha;*[808] (18) *Samstha;*[809] (19) *Vara;*[810] (20) *Pratishedha;*[811] (21) *Upadesha;*[812] (22) *Namaskara;*[813] (23) *Spriha;*[814] and (24) *Vilapa.*[815] These are described as the twenty-four aspects of *mantras.* Earlier, *rishis* who knew the truth and knew about sacrifices, laid down ten components of a Brahmana text. (1) *Hetu;*[816] (2) *Nirvachana;*[817] (3) *Ninda;* (4) *Prashasti;*[818] (5) *Samshaya;*[819] (6) *Nidhi;*[820] (7) *Purakriti;*[821] (8) *Purakalpa;*[822]

[794] Rebuking.
[795] Censure.
[796] Lamentation.
[797] Curse.
[798] Revocation of a curse.
[799] Question.
[800] Reply.
[801] Benediction.
[802] Sacrifice.
[803] Reviling.
[804] Narration of meaning.
[805] Conversation.
[806] Separation.
[807] Application.
[808] Account.
[809] Establishment.
[810] Boon.
[811] Negation.
[812] Advice.
[813] Act of obeisance.
[814] Desire.
[815] Lamentation.
[816] Reason.
[817] Explanation.
[818] Praise.
[819] Doubt.
[820] Store.
[821] Earlier action.
[822] Earlier conception.

(9) *Vyavadharana-kalpana;*[823] and (10) *Upama.*[824] These have been laid down as the ten aspects of a Brahmana text. These have been laid down as the signs of Brahmana texts of all the branches. *Hetu* is said to be derived from a root that means "to kill". Thus, it destroys the arguments of others. Or, it can also be derived to mean that one goes towards the meaning of a word.[825] In that way, when one speaks of *nirvachana,* one means ascertaining and nurturing the meaning of a sentence. *Acharya*s speak of *ninda* when words of censure are used to find fault. The root meaning of *prashasti* or *prashamsa* is to praise the good qualities. "This is it." "This is not it." Such doubts about determination are *samshaya.* "This is what has been ordained." When there are such utterances, it is *vidhi.*[826] "So and so has said such and such." When learned people say this, it is *purakriti.* Something that can no longer be directly seen is spoken of as *purakalpa.* The word "*pura*" means something that belongs to the past. *Purakalpa* is about past conceptions, determined through *mantra*s, Brahmana texts, *kalpasutra*s and *nigama* texts, pure and vast in expanse. "It is like this, but it may also be like that." When one is uncertain in this way, it is *vyavadharana-kalpana.* "That is like this." Such a statement is *upama.* These are the ten features of a Brahmana text. At the outset, the learned have laid down that these are the signs of Brahmana texts. In addition, bit by bit, *dvija*s have composed commentaries on *mantra*s, their conceptions and the *vidhi* instructed for rites. The word *mantra* is derived from a root that means consultations and the word Brahmana is derived from *brahman.* Those who know about *sutra*s[827] say that a *sutra* must have a limited number of *akshara*s. It must not create doubts. It must possess substance and must face all directions. It must not be subject to any blemishes.'

---

[823] Special conceptions.

[824] Comparison.

[825] From '*hinoti*', meaning, to hasten.

[826] Meaning, rules.

[827] A *sutra* is a terse aphorism, with an allusion to a thread. It must be clear and capable of universal application. Facing all directions captures the comprehensive coverage.

Chapter 34-1(34) (Vyasa's *shishyas*)

Vayu said, 'Hearing what Suta had said, in reply, the *rishi*s said, "How were the *Veda*s classified? O immensely intelligent one! Please explain that to us again."'

Suta answered, 'This is an ancient account, from *dvapara yuga* of Svayambhuva *manvantara*. Brahma told Manu, "O immensely intelligent one! Protect the *Veda*s. O son! A change in the *yuga* has commenced and those born as *dvija*s are limited in vigour. In the due order, all of them have been enveloped by the taint of the *yuga*. It is evident that, subjugated by the *yuga*, all measurements have diminished. Out of all that was said in *krita yuga*, only one-thousandth part remains. Everything has been destroyed—lifespan, energy and strength. They have become limited. The rites of the *Veda*s must be performed. Otherwise, the *Veda*s will be destroyed. If the *Veda*s are destroyed, sacrifices will head towards destruction. When sacrifices are destroyed, the *Veda*s will also be destroyed, and everything will be destroyed. In the beginning, the *Veda*s had four feet and there were a hundred thousand *mantra*s. *Krishna Yajur Veda* possessed ten times the number. A sacrifice yields everything that is desired." Manu was engaged in the welfare of the worlds. Spoken to in this way, he signified his assent. The lord divided the single *Veda*, which possessed four feet, into four parts. O son![828] Following Brahma's words, he did this, with the welfare of the worlds in mind. I will tell you about the current conception of the *Veda*s. I will describe to you what was thought of in the past *manvantara*, on the basis of direct and indirect perception. O excellent ones! Listen.'

'In this *yuga*, there is Vyasa, the scorcher of enemies. He is Parashara's son and is known as Dvaipayana. He is Vishnu's eternal portion. In this *yuga*, urged by Brahma, he started to speak about the *Veda*s. For the sake of the *Veda*s, he gathered four *shishya*s— Jaimini, Sumantu, Vaishampayana and Paila as the

---

[828] The word used is *tata*. This means son but is used to address anyone who is junior or younger.

fourth. Lomaharshana was the fifth. O *dvijas*! Accepting him in the proper way, he made Paila hear *Rig Veda*. Vaishampayana was made the expounder of *Yajur Veda*. Jaimini was made to hear the meaning of *Sama Veda* and everything else that followed. It was the same for Sumantu, the excellent *rishi*, and *Atharva Veda*. The lord and illustrious master made me accept Itihasa, Purana and all the associated rules.[829] There was a single *Yajur Veda*, but he thought of it in four different parts. He thought of a sacrifice and four different kinds of officiating priests. There were *adhvaryus* for *Yajur Veda*, *hotris* for *Rig Veda*, *udgatris* for *Sama Veda* and *brahmanas* for *Atharva Veda*. Thus, for chanting the hymns of the *Rig Veda*, he thought of *hotris*. The lord of the world thought of *udgatris* for *Sama Veda* and *adhvaryus* for *Yajur Veda*. The *brahmanas* were meant to engage the king in tasks connected with *Atharva Veda*. He was accomplished in the meaning of the ancient accounts and composed Purana Samhita, with its accounts, subsidiary accounts, songs and the resultant rules in different *kalpas*. Whatever remained was added to *Yajur Veda* and sacrifices were added to this. It is the determination of the sacred texts that it is called *Yajur Veda* because of its association with *yajnas*. The feet uttered in *Yajur mantras* are uneven. Hence, they have to be sung by one hundred energetic *ritvijas*, who are accomplished in the *Vedas*. Used for a horse sacrifice, these nourish the sacrifice. Paila accepted *Rig Veda* and divided it into two. Having divided the compilation, the lord imparted it to two *shishyas*. Indrapramati was the first and Bashkala was the second. Bashkala, the excellent *dvija*, divided this into four compilations. He taught these to *shishyas* who were engaged in his welfare and in serving him. Bodhya was the first and Agnimatri was the second branch. Parashari was the third and Yajnavalkya was the last. Indrapramati, the excellent *rishi*, taught the compilation to the immensely fortunate and illustrious Mandukeya. Immensely illustrious, he in turn taught his son, Satyasrava, all of it. The lord Satyasrava taught his son Satyahita. O *dvijas*! Satyahita taught it to the great-souled Satyashriya, his son, who was devoted to *dharma*

---

[829] We have translated *kalpavakya* as associated rules.

and the truth. The immensely energetic Satyashriya had three
shishyas. They were learned and intent on receiving the sacred texts.
Shakalya was the first and Rathitara was a second. The third was
Bharadvaja, the son of Bashkala. They propounded the branches.
Shakalya, also known as Devamitra, was proud and insolent
because of his jnana. O dvijas! In the course of Janaka's sacrifice,
he came about his destruction.'

Shamshapayani[830] asked, 'How did the sage, who was proud
of his jnana, come about his destruction? What was the debate
that occurred at the time of Janaka's horse sacrifice? How did the
debate come about and who was it with? Please relate everything
that happened. It is known to you.'

Suta replied, 'On the occasion of Janaka's horse sacrifice, there
was a great assembly. Many thousands of rishis went there. They
wished to witness the sacrifice of rajarshi Janaka. On seeing all the
brahmanas who had arrived, a question arose in his mind. "Among
these, who is the best brahmana? How can I decide that?" Having
decided this, the lord of men thought of a means in his mind. He
brought one thousand cows, a large quantity of gold, villages,
jewels and female servants. The lord of men told the sages, "All of
you deserve the best of shares and I bow my head before you. The
wealth that has been brought here is for the best among you. O best
among dvijas! I have brought this wealth and this wealth is for that
person." The rishis, who possessed learning and forbearance, heard
Janaka's words. They saw that substantial collection of wealth.
They became greedy and wished to seize that wealth. Insolent about
their knowledge of the Vedas, they challenged each other. Their
minds were fixed on a sense of owning that wealth. One said, "This
is mine, not yours." Another said, "Why are you boasting?" In this
way, because of taints associated with wealth, they debated in many
kinds of ways. The immensely energetic ascetic, Yajnavalkya, was
present there. He was learned and wise and he was Brahma's son. He
knew about the brahman. He was born as part of Brahma's portion,
and he spoke these melodious words. "O shishya! O best among

those who know the *brahman*! Accept this wealth and take it home.
O child! There is no doubt that it belongs to me. In every kind of
debate, there is no one who is my equal. If any learned person is not
pleased with this, let him immediately challenge me." At this, that
ocean of *brahmana*s was agitated, like an ocean during a deluge.
Completely at ease, Yajnavalkya seemed to smile, as he spoke to
them. "O learned ones! You should not be angry and abuse me.
You speak the truth. Let us speak, according to our capacity. Let us
question each other." Thereafter, there were many kinds of debates
in the assembly. Many thousands of words were used, auspicious in
meaning. They resulted from subtle insight. These were ornamented
with knowledge about the world and knowledge about *adhyatma*.[831]
The king's examiners scrutinized them for truth and qualities. For
the sake of the wealth, there was a debate between those great-
souled ones. All the *rishi*s were on one side and Yajnavalkya was
on the other. The intelligent Yajnavalkya engaged with all the
sages. Each one was questioned individually and was unable to
respond. The immensely intelligent one, a mass of knowledge about
the *brahman*, defeated all the sages. Completely at ease, he then
spoke to Shakalya, who was the one who started the debate.[832] "O
Shakalya! Speak. What do you have to say? Why are you seated
there, as if you are meditating? The person who is performing the
sacrifice has offered a stake and I am taking it away." Made to
suffer in this way, his eyes turned coppery with rage. In the presence
of the sages, he addressed Yajnavalkya in harsh words. "You have
treated these excellent *dvija*s as if they are blades of grass. As a
result of your learning, you wish to seize this great accumulation of
wealth yourself." Addressed by Shakalya in this way, Yajnavalkya
spoke. "Know that the strength of those who are established in the
brahman lies in their learning and the extent to which they possess
insight about the truth. Desire has a connection with wealth. We

---

[831] Transcendental knowledge about the *paramatman*

[832] The debate between Yajnavalkya and Shakalya (named Vidagdha,
he was the son of Shakala) is described in 3.9 of *Brihadaranyaka Upanishad*.
That has the actual questions and answers. There, the last question asked
by Yajnavalkya was about the *brahman*.

desire it for that reason. We *brahmana*s are wealthy because we can
ask whatever questions we wish. We wish to ask questions, using
words that are full of meaning. The *rajarshi* has brought a stake
and I have taken that wealth away." Hearing these words, Shakalya
became senseless with rage. Yajnvalkya continued, desiring to ask
questions that were full of meaning. "Tell me now. What is the
question, full of meaning, that you wish to ask me?" Thereafter,
there was a debate between those two great ones who knew about
the *brahman*. Shakalya posed one thousand questions. While all the
*rishi*s heard, Yajnavalkya replied to all of them. Shakalya had no
more questions to ask and Yajnavalkya spoke to him. "O Shakalya!
I will ask you a single question. If you wish, answer me. For the
sake of the stake, reply. Otherwise, accept instant death here. What
is associated with subtle *jnana*, *samkhya* or *yoga*? Which is more
important, the path of *adhyatma*, or the path of *dhyana*?" The
intelligent Yajnavalkya urged him with this question. Shakalya did
not know the answer and died. This is how Shakalya's suffering
on account of the question is remembered. In this way, there was a
great debate for the wealth, among the *rishi*s, and between the *rishi*s
and Yajnavalkya. Announcing his own fame, Yajnavalkya took the
riches. Surrounded by his self-controlled *shishya*s, he went home.'

Chapter 35-1(35) (Description of Svayambhuva *manvantara*)

Suta said, 'Devamitra Shakalya was a great-souled bull among
*dvija*s. The intelligent one, supreme among those who knew the
*Veda*s, composed five *Samhitas*. He had five *shishya*s—Mudgala,
Gokhala, Khaliya and Sutapa. His child, Shaishireya, was the
fifth. He also propounded three other *Samhitas*—Shaka, Vaina
and Rathitara. As a fourth, the excellent *dvija* composed *nirukta*.
O excellent *dvija*s! He had four other *shishya*s—Paila, Ikshalaka,
the intelligent Shatabalaka and Gaja. Bharadvaja, Bashkala's son,
propounded three *Samhitas*. He had three great-souled *shishya*s,
who possessed the qualities. They were the intelligent Tvapanapa,

the intelligent Pannagari and the third was Arjava. They were
ascetics who were controlled in their vows. They were immensely
energetic and devoid of attachment. They were accomplished in
knowledge about the *Samhitas*. The Bahvrichas, who established
the *Samhitas*, have spoken about them. Vaishampayana's *shishya*
composed *Samhitas* for *Yajur Veda*. He expounded eighty-six such
and these *Samhitas* had auspicious hymns from the *Yajur Veda*.
He bestowed these on his *shishyas*. Following the ordinances, they
accepted them. But one among them, Yajnavalkya, the great ascetic,
was left out. There were eighty-six *shishyas* and each received an
alternative *Samhita*. Each one of them is said to have divided what
he received into three. As a result of this division into three, there
were new and auspicious divisions in the *Vedas*. These separate
differences pertained to the northern region, the central region and
the eastern region. Shyamayani was foremost among those from
the northern region. Asuri is remembered as the first to establish
the central part. Alambi was the first among those from the eastern
region. There were thus three regions. These are spoken of as
Charakas, *dvijas* who propounded the *Samhitas*.'

The *rishis* asked, 'What is the reason for them to be known
as Charaka *adhvaryus*?[833] Please tell us the truth. How were
the divisions brought about? How did they obtain the status
of Charakas?'

Suta answered, 'O excellent *brahmanas*! The *rishis* had
some tasks to perform. After reaching the slopes of Meru, they
consulted each other about this. "If any excellent *dvija* does not
reach this mountain within seven nights, he will have to perform
the penance for killing a *brahmana*. This is the rule we have
announced." At this, all those large numbers went there, with the
exception of Vaishampayana. Within seven nights, they reached
the place earmarked for the assembly. Because of the words of
the *brahmanas*, he[834] performed the penance for the killing of a
brahmana. Vaishampayana summoned his *shishyas* and said, "O

---

[833] Charakas are ascetics who wander around. The word is also used
specifically for a branch of *Krishna Yajur Veda*.
[834] Vaishampayana.

excellent *dvija*s! For my sake, perform the atonement required for
the killing of a *brahmana*. All of you gather together and speak
desirable and beneficial words to me." Yajnavalkya replied, "Let
the sages be. I will perform it alone. Through the strength and
power of my own austerities, I shall perform it." Thus addressed,
he became angry and expelled Yajnavalkya. He said, "Return
everything that you have studied." Thus addressed, the supreme
one, who knew about the *brahman*, returned the *Yajur Veda* to
his *guru*. He vomited the hymns out, along with blood, and they
assumed forms.'

'The *dvija* performed *dhyana* and worshipped Surya. The
expelled hymns on the *brahman* went and established themselves in
Surya. The hymns from the *Yajur Veda* went upwards and entered
the solar disc. Satisfied, Surya bestowed the hymns on the *brahman*
on him. Martanda[835] bestowed these on the intelligent Yajnavalkya,
who had assumed the form of a horse. *Brahmana*s use whatever
means possible to study those hymns from the *Yajur Veda*. However,
in the form of horses, they were given to the one who had assumed
the form of a horse. Those who perform penance for killing a
brahmana are described as Charakas because of what they do.[836]
Thus, Vaishampayana's *shishya*s are said to be Charakas. Those
Charakas came to be known as Vajins.[837] Listen. There are fifteen
excellent ones who came to be described as Vajins—Kanva,
Boudheya, Madhyandina, his son Vaidheya, Addhva, Bouddhaka,
Tapaniya, Vatsa, Javala, Kevala, Avati, Pundra, Vaineya and
Parashara.[838] They were Yajnavalkya's *shishya*s. The different
branches of the *Yajur Veda* are known to be one hundred and one.
Jaimini taught his son, Sumantu. Sumantu again taught his son,
Sutvan. Sutvan taught his son, Sukarman. Sukarman quickly studied
one thousand *Samhitas*. Sukarman, who was as radiant as the sun,
taught these to one thousand. But since they studied at a time when
one should not study, Shatakratu killed them. For the sake of his

---

[835] Surya.
[836] Based on *charana*, meaning performance or conduct.
[837] These Charakas are Yajnavalkya's *shishya*s. *Vajin* means a horse.
[838] There are only fourteen names.

disciples, he performed *prayopavesa*.[839] Seeing that he was angry, Shakra granted him a boon. "You will have two immensely energetic *shishya*s. They will be unmatched in radiance. Those two immensely wise ones will study one thousand *Samhitas*. O excellent *dvija*! The immensely fortunate Gods were angry with those."[840] Vasava spoke in this way to the prosperous and illustrious Sukarman. Seeing that the *dvija*'s rage had been pacified, the lord swiftly vanished. The intelligent and supreme *dvija*, Poushya, became his disciple. The second was Hiranyanabha Koushalya, a lord of men. Poushya taught five hundred *Samhitas*. His auspicious *shishya*s were named Poushyajins or Udichyasamagas.[841] Koushalya studied five hundred *Samhitas*. Hiranyanabha's disciples are described as Prachyasamagas.[842] Poushya's four disciples were Lougakshi, Kushumi, Kushidi and Langali. Understand the differences. The different Lougakshi schools were Nadayaniya, Tandiputra, the extremely learned one named Anovaina, who learnt it from Tandiputra, Sakoti's son Susaha and Sunaman. Kushumi had three *shishya*s—Ourasa, Parashara and the energetic Nabhirvitta. These are described as the three Kushumi schools. Sourishi and Shringiputra observed vows for a very long time. Ranayaniya and Soumitri were accomplished in the *Sama Veda*. Shringiputra, the great ascetic, propounded three *Samhitas*. Vaina, Prachinayoga and Surala were excellent *dvija*s. Kouthuma, Parashara's son, propounded six *Samhitas*. Asurayana and Vaishakhya were aged and devoted to the *Veda*s. The intelligent Patanjali was Prachinayoga's son. Kouthuma, Parashara's son, is said to have established six schools. Langali, also known as Shalihotra, propounded six *Samhitas*. The followers of Langali are said to be Halini, Jyamahini, Jaimini, Lomagayani, Kandu and Kohala as the sixth. These *shishya*s of Langali established *Samhitas*. Hiranyanabha had a single *shishya*, Prince Krita. This excellent

---

[839] While this means voluntary fasting to death, it is adopted by someone who has no worldly desires left. Sukarman did this.

[840] The ones who had been killed.

[841] The northern school. Samaga means to become accomplished in the *Sama Veda*.

[842] The eastern school.

human propounded twenty-four *Samhitas*. He spoke about them to
his *shishyas*. Listen. They were Radi, Radaviya, Panchama, Vahana,
Talaka, Manduka, Kalika, Rajika, Goutama, Ajabasta,
Somarajayana, Pushti, Parikrishta and Ulukhalaka. The younger
ones were Shali, Anguliya, Koushika, Shalimanjari, Paka, Shadhiya,
Kanini and Parasharya, with *dharma* in his soul.[843] These were the
ones who became Samagas. Among all those who were Samagas,
two are described as the best—Poushya and Krita. They propounded
alternate *Samhitas*. O *dvijas*! Sumantu divided the *Atharva Veda*
into two parts. He gave the black part to Kabandha. Just as he had
heard, the learned Kabandha divided it into two parts and gave one
to Pathya. He gave the second to Devadarsha and that lord divided
it into four. Devadarsha had four *shishyas* who were firm in their
vows. They were Moda, Brahmabala and Pippaladi. Shoulkayani,
who was established in austerities and knew about *dharma*, was the
fourth. Know the excellent threefold division of the Pathya school.
There were Jajali and Kumudadi and Shounaka is described as the
third. Shounaka divided it into two and gave one to Babhru. The
second *Samhita* was given to the intelligent one, known as
Saindhavayana. Saindhavayana, also known as Munjakesha, again
divided it into two parts. The alternative *Samhitas* of the excellent
Atharva Veda are Nakshatrakalpa, Vaitana, the third of Samhita-
vidhi, the fourth one of Angiras-kalpa and Shanti-kalpa as the fifth.
O excellent *rishis*! Along with me, Khadga divided the Puranas. For
the Puranas, these *shishyas* of mine are said to be firm in their
vows—Atreya, the intelligent Sumati, Kashyapa, Akritavrana,
Bharadvaja, Agnivarcha, Vasishtha, Mitrayu, Savarni, Somadatti,
Susharma and Shamshapayana. Three of them again composed
three different *Samhitas*. Kashyapa composed a *Samhita* and so did
Savarni and Shamshapayana. Mine is the fourth. These four are
original *Samhitas*. All of them have four parts and all of them
convey the same meaning. It is futile to think of alternative readings,
just as it is for branches of the *Vedas*. Other than the one by
Shamshapayana, all of them have four thousand *shlokas*. The first

---

[843] We only have twenty-two names in the list.

one is by Lomaharshana. The one by Kashyapa comes next.
Savarni's is the third and it is full of words that are straight in their
meaning. The other one, by Shamshapayana, is ornamented by the
trait of dispelling doubts in meaning. There are eight thousand and
six hundred *mantra*s in the *Rig Veda*, plus another thirty-five. The
*valakhilya*s chanted seven *suparna*s.[844] The number of hymns in the
Sama Veda is eight thousand and fourteen. Samagas sing these,
along with the Aranyakas, reciting "Soham".[845] The *chhanda*s
chanted by *adhvaryu*s are said to number twelve thousand. This is
the number of Brahmanas and *Yajur Veda* hymns thought of by
Vyasa. There are ordinary Aranyaka texts and there are ones with
*mantra*s. There are accounts that came later and the adjective
"former" is used for some. The *Yajur Veda* is said to also consist of
the Brahmanas and the Aranyakas, the ordinary ones, as well as
those with *mantra*s. Like a *haridru* plant,[846] there are appendices
and sub-appendices. There are very short verses in Taittiriya
Samhita. In the Vajasaneyaka school, the number of hymns in the
Rig Veda is enumerated as one thousand and nine hundred. The
number in the Brahmana segment is four times this. The total
number of hymns in the *Rig Veda* and the *Yajur Veda* is said to be
eight thousand, eight hundred and eighty. This includes hymns
about *Shukriya*[847] and the appendix by Yajnavalkya. Hear about
charanavidya[848] and its size. The number of hymns in the *Rig Veda*
is said to be six thousand and twenty-six. The number in the *Yajur
Veda* is said to be more than this. In other cases, the number of
hymns in the *Rig Veda* is eleven thousand and ten. It is also said that
the number of hymns in the *Rig Veda* is ten thousand one hundred
and ten. It is also said that there is proof that the number of *mantra*s
in the *Rig Veda* is one thousand. Such is the expanse of the *Rig*

[844] Here, *suparna* must clearly be understood as a group of hymns. For
example, the *Yajur Veda* has three *mantra*s that are recited together, and
these are known as *trisuparna*.

[845] 'I am he.' The text says *Sahoham*, or *Hoham*. This seems to be a
typo and we have changed it.

[846] Turmeric.

[847] Hymns from *Yajur Veda*, used when instating a new deity.

[848] One of the schools of *Atharva Veda*.

Veda and there are many different kinds of meanings. It has been determined that the number of hymns in the *Atharva Veda* is five thousand. It is also known to *rishi*s that the number is nine hundred and eighty. Apart from this, there is the Aranyaka, propounded by the Angirases. This is the enumeration of numbers, and such are the differences in the branches. Such were the ones who propounded, responsible for differences across the schools. In all *manvantara*s, there are such differences in the schools. Prajapati's *shruti* texts are eternal. However, such variations are remembered. This occurs because *deva*s are not eternal, and *mantra*s originate again and again. In *dvapara*, it is also said that the *shruti* texts were divided again. In this way, the illustrious and excellent *rishi* classified the *Veda*s. Handing these over to the *shishya*s, he left for the forest, to torment himself through austerities. His disciples, and the disciples of the disciples, created these differences across the schools. There are fourteen kinds of learning—the four *Veda*s, the *Vedanga*s, Mimamsa, the extensive Nyaya, Dharmashastra and Purana.[849] There are also the three of Ayurveda, Dhanurveda and Gandharva.[850] With the fourth of Arthashastra added, there are eighteen kinds of learning.'

'It should be known that the *brahmarshi*s were the first, followed by *devarshi*s. *Rajarshi*s came after them. For *rishi*s, there are three sources of origin. Those who speak about the *brahman* are born in three *gotra*s—Kashyapa, Vasishtha, Bhrigu, Angiras and Atri. Since they approach the *brahman*, they are spoken of as *brahmarshi*s. *Devarshi*s are the sons of Dharma, Pulastya, Kratu, Pulaha, Pratyusha, Deva and Kashyapa. Listen to their names. The two *devarshi*s, Nara and Narayana, are Dharma's sons. The *valakhilya*s are the sons of Kratu. Kardama is Pulaha's son. Kubera

---

[849] *Darshana* is more than a school of philosophical thought, since it also includes insight about *adhyatma*. Having said this, the six schools of *darshana* or philosophy are *nyaya, vaisheshika, samkhya, yoga, mimamsa* and *Vedanta*. *Vedanta* means the end of the *Veda*s and refers to the Brahmana, Aranyaka and Upanishad texts. As mentioned earlier, there are six *Vedanga*s.

[850] *Gandharva vidya* is about singing and dancing.

is the son of Pulastya and Dala is the son of Pratyusha. Two, Narada and Parvata, are Kashyapa's sons. They are known as *devarshi*s because they approach *devas*.[851] There are human kings, born in the lineage of Ila's son. Those in the lineages of Ikshvaku and Nabhaga are known to be *rajarshi*s. Since they approach *prajas* and cause them delight, they are known as *rajarshi*s. The unblemished *brahmarshi*s are described as those who are established in Brahma's world. The auspicious *devarshi*s are known to be established in the world of *devas*. It is the view that all the *rajarshi*s are established in Indra's world. Because of nobility of birth and austerities, *brahmarshi*s, divine *devarshi*s and *rajarshi*s are worthy of reciting *mantra*s. I will describe their traits. They possess knowledge about the past, the present and the future. They speak the truth. They are self-contented, and they can themselves ensure their understanding. They are famous for their austerities and know everything, while still in the womb. They are capable of reciting *mantra*s. They are prosperous and can go everywhere. *Rajarshi*s, *devas*, *dvija*s and humans, possess these qualities. Those who have achieved these qualities are thought of as *rishi*s. Those who possess seven qualities are described as *saptarshi*s. These seven are—a long lifespan; ability to compose *mantra*s; divine insight obtained from Ishvara; direct understanding about *dharma*; the establishment of a *gotra*; constant devotion towards the six tasks[852] and good conduct as a householder. They are impartial in attitude, even when the wicked act so as to cause them harm. Sometimes, they do not live in a village and survive on the basis of juices they prepare themselves. Some are intelligent householders. Others dwell inside forests. At the beginning of all the *yuga*s, *krita* and the others, they first act so as to establish *varna*s and *ashrama*s. At the time of the onset of *treta yuga*, all the *saptarshi*s again ensure the establishment of *varna*s and *ashrama*s. In their lineages, valiant ones are repeatedly born. The father gives birth to a son and the

---

[851] The text says *Veda*s. We have changed it to *devas*.

[852] The six tasks can be interpreted in different ways, the simplest being the six tasks allowed for a *brahmana*—teaching, studying, performing sacrifices, officiating at sacrifices, donating and receiving. But there are also other lists of six tasks, in *tantra* and in *yoga*.

son becomes a father. In this way, the lineage continues without a break, until it is the end of the *yuga*. The number of householders is said to be eighty-eight thousand. They resort to *pitriyana*, which is south of the sun. They accept wives and perform *agnihotra* rites. They are described as the cause of offspring. Many are householders. There are others who frequent cremation grounds. Eighty-eight thousand are also placed along the northern path. It is heard that *rishi*s who have held up their seed have reached heaven. At the end of the *yuga*, composers of *mantra*s and Brahmanas are born. This is what repeatedly happens in the course of *dvapara yuga*. The *rishi*s compose texts known as *kalpasutra*s and other sacred texts, full of knowledge. They ensure the performance of rites mentioned in the *Veda*s. This repeatedly occurred in the *dvapara yuga*s of Vaivasvata *manvantara*. *Maharshi*s classified the *Veda*s twenty-eight times.[853] In the first *dvapara*, Svayambhu himself classified the *Veda*s.[854] In the second *dvapara*, Prajapati was Vedavyasa. In the third, Ushanas was Vyasa and in the fourth, it was Brihaspati. Savitar was the fifth Vyasa, and the Lord Mrityu is described as the sixth. In the seventh, it was Indra and in the eighth, it is said to have been Vasishtha. Sarasvata was the ninth and Tridhama is described as the tenth. The eleventh was Trivarsha and after that, it was Sanadvaja. Antariksha was the thirteenth and Dharma was the fourteenth. Traiyaruni was the fifteenth and Dhananjaya was the sixteenth. Kritanjaya was the seventeenth and Rijisha is described as the eighteenth. After Rijisha, it was Bharadvaja. After Bharadvaja, it was Goutama. After Goutama, it was Uttama. After Uttama, it is said to have been Haryavana. After Haryavana, it is said to have been Vena Vajashrava. After Arvaka Vajashrava, it was Somamukhyayana. After that, it was Trinabindu. After Trinabindu, it was Tataja. After Tataja, it is said to have been Shakti. After Shakti, it was Parashara. After Parashara, it was Jatukarna and after Jatukarna, it is said to have been Dvaipayana.[855] There are twenty-eight ancient Vedavyases. In a future *dvapara*,

---

[853] This being the twenty-eighth *dvapara yuga* of Vaisvata *manvantara*.

[854] In an obvious typo (corrected), the text says seventh.

[855] There are problems of inconsistency with this list. Dvaipayana should have been the 28th, not the 30th.

when Dvaipayana belongs to the past, Droni,[856] the great ascetic, will be Vedavyasa and will establish branches in the future.'

'Brahma performed austerities and obtained the imperishable *brahman*. *Karma* is achieved through austerities and fame is achieved through *karma*. Truth is obtained through energy and imperishable bliss is obtained through truth. The immortal *brahman* pervades. The immortal *brahman* is spoken of as the seed. The eternal *brahman* is established in the single *akshara* of "OUM". It is spoken of as the *brahman* because of the attribute of greatness.[857] It is established in Pranava and is remembered as "*Bhuh Bhuvah Svah*" in *Rig Veda*, *Yajur Veda*, *Sama Veda* and *Atharva Veda*. I prostrate myself before the *brahman*. It is described as the cause behind the creation and dissolution of the universe. It is great, supreme and mysterious. I prostrate myself before that excellent *brahman*. It is fathomless and limitless. It is responsible for the delusion of the universe. For the sake of the *purusharatha*s, it assumes the form of illumination and enterprise. It is faith for those who possess the *jnana* of *samkhya* and destination for those who are in control of their *atman*s. This is the eternal and unmanifest *brahman*, the cause behind Prakriti. It is foremost. It is its own origin. It cannot be determined. It is praised as *sattva*. It cannot be divided. It is the seed. It does not decay. It has many forms. I always prostrate myself before the supreme *brahman*. I bow down. Since there were no *kriyas* in *krita yuga*, how can there be any question of not performing *kriyas* in *krita yuga*? Bhagavan said that he is everything—everything that is performed once; everything performed or not performed in the world; everything heard or worthy of being heard; good and evil; everything worthy of being known; everything worthy of being thought about; everything worthy of being touched; everything worthy of being eaten; everything worthy of being seen; anything heard or smelt; anything seen or known by Gods and *rishi*s; anything not seen; anyone who deserves to see; anything done by someone; anything thought by someone; anything done earlier; anything spoken by someone and whatever is being done by anyone anywhere. He is all

[856] Drona's son, Ashvatthama.
[857] From *brihat*, meaning extensive and great.

this. An act appears to be performed by an agent. But he is the one who gets it done. Non-attachment, excessive attachment, *jnana*, lack of *jnana*, love, hatred, *dharma*, *adharma*, happiness, unhappiness, death, immortality, above, sideways, below—the one who cannot be seen is the cause behind everything. He is Svayambhu. He is the eldest. He is Brahma Parameshthi. In every *treta yuga*, everyone repeatedly knows this. In every *dvapara*, what should be known is repeatedly classified. In the beginning of Vaivasvata *manvantara*, Brahma himself spoke about this. In the periods known as *yugas*, the *rishis* repeatedly return. Born from each other, they compile *Samhitas*. There are said to be eighty-eight thousand *shrutarshis*. Thus, this is the number of *Samhitas* that cycle again and again. There are those who resort to the southern path and there are those who frequent cremation grounds. From one *yuga* to another *yuga*, they repeatedly classify the branches. In every *dvapara*, s*hrutarshis* compile *Samhitas*. Depending on their *gotras*, there are branches, again and again. Until the end of the *yuga*, they are the composers of these branches. This should be known about the past and the future too. In all the past *manvantaras*, they were the ones who composed the past branches and this is what is going on in the present *manvantara* too. This is also what will occur in the future. The future flows from the present. Both the past and the future can be known from the present. This has been determined about the progressive nature of *manvantaras*, about *devas*, ancestors, *rishis* and Manus.'

'Along with the *mantras*, they proceed upwards and return again. For a period of ten *kalpas*, all the Gods repeatedly go to Janaloka. When the time set for them is over, they face destruction. They are bound to what is certain to happen. Because of their taints, they witness birth, preceded by ailments. Once they realize their defects, they can return from such conduct. In this way, they pass through ten *yugas*, meant for *devas*. From Janaloka, they go to Tapoloka and do not return from there. In this way, thousands of divine *yugas* have passed. They are destroyed, along with the *rishis*, and go to Brahma's world. No one is capable of describing this in detail, in the due order. This is because time has no beginning and it is impossible to enumerate it. Along with past *kalpas*, there have

been past *manvantara*s, ancestors, sages, *devas* and *rishi*s. Time
creates them and the *yuga*s proceed. This is the progressive nature
of *kalpa*s and *manvantara*s. In the past, there have been hundreds
of thousands of *praja*s. There is destruction at the end of a
manvantara and at the end of destruction, there is creation. Even if
a person speaks for one hundred years, he is incapable of describing
devas, *rishi*s, Manus and large numbers of ancestors in the due
order. Understand the enumeration of creation, expansion,
destruction and *manvantara*s in human years. Those who are skilled
in enumeration have described the duration of *manvantara*s. *Dvija*s
have computed that the duration of a *manvantara* is 306.72 million
years, without including the additional periods.[858] This is described
as the duration of a *manvantara*, expressed in human years. I will
now describe a Manu's *manvantara* in divine years. It is said to last
for eight hundred and fifty-two thousand divine years. Fourteen
times this number is said to be the duration until the onset of the
deluge. One thousand *mahayuga*s are described as the duration of
Brahma's day. At that time, all beings are burnt down by the rays of
the sun. With Brahma at the forefront, all *devas*, *rishi*s and *danava*s
enter the lord and divinity Narayana, supreme among Gods. At the
beginning of every *kalpa*, he is the one who repeatedly creates
beings. This is held to be the period for which *devas* and *rishi*s
remain. Understand the intervening periods between *manvantara*s.
O unblemished ones! I have already spoken to you about what is
known as a *mahayuga*. It is said to consist of four *yuga*s, *krita*, *treta*
and the others. Bhagavan, the lord, has said that the entitlement of
a Manu lasts for seventy-one *mahayuga*s, along with the extra
periods. I have thus described all the signs of *manvantara*s, past,
present and future. I have also told you about the creation of
Svayambhuva Manu. Let me now describe the intervening periods,
in the beginning and at the end, along with *rishi*s and *devas*. In the
ordained way, this is certain to occur. Before this *manvantara* comes
to an end, the lords of the three worlds, *saptarshi*s, *devas*, ancestors
and Manus realize that the *manvantara* has come to an end and the

---

[858] The additional period presumably refers to *sandhya*s and
*sandhyamsha*s. 306.72 million years.

intervening period has arrived. They understand that the duration
of their entitlement is over and their minds become anxious.
Anxious, all of them make up their minds to go to Maharloka.
When the *manvantara* is over and the period of preservation is also
over, *deva*s remain, till the onset of the next *krita yuga*. This is so
that the lords of the next *manvantara* can be born. When the
manvantara is complete and *kali yuga* is over, this is what happens
to *deva*s, ancestors, *rishi*s and Manus. When *krita yuga* sets in,
there are those who remain from the past *kali yuga*. The learned say
that the offspring of *krita* result from the preceding *kali*. In this
way, the start of a *manvantara* is based on the end of the preceding
manvantara. When the preceding *manvantara* has decayed, the
succeeding one sets in. At the start of *krita yuga*, there are virtuous
ones who remain. *Saptarshi*s and Manus remain there, waiting for
the right time. The ascetics remain, waiting for the next *manvantara*.
All of them wait for the next *manvantara*, for the sake of progeny.
When the rains start, the former ones ensure the functioning of the
successors. The opposite pairs of sentiments start to function. Herbs
start to grow. *Praja*s result here and there, without fixed habitations.
Means of subsistence start, but *dharma* does not exist. With the
mobile and the immobile destroyed, the world is devoid of happiness.
In villages and in cities, there are no *varna*s and *ashrama*s. There are
those who remained from the past *manvantara*, devoted to *dharma*.
These are *saptarshi*s and Manu, established there for the sake of
offspring. For the sake of *praja*s, those ascetics torment themselves
through extremely difficult austerities. As was the case earlier, those
who were destroyed are created afresh—*deva*s, *asura*s, large
numbers of ancestors, *rishi*s, humans, *sarpa*s, *bhuta*s, *pishacha*s,
*gandharva*s, *yaksha*s and *rakshasa*s. At the beginning of the
manvantara, those who remained, *saptarshi*s and Manu, instruct
them about virtuous conduct. Along with *deva*s, humans undertake
tasks. Following *brahmacharya*, they repay debts to *rishi*s. Having
offspring, they repay debts to ancestors. Performing sacrifices, they
repay debts to *deva*s. For a hundred thousand years, they follow the
dharma of *varna*s. After establishing the three *Veda*s, means of
subsistence, policy for punishment, *varna*s and *ashrama*s and

hermitages, they make up their minds to go to heaven. Thus, the former *devas* head towards heaven. Those former *devas* immerse themselves completely in *dharma*. When the former *manvantara* is over, all of them abandon their respective positions. Along with the *mantras*, they proceed upwards to Maharloka, free from ailments. With their minds having achieved *siddhi*, they withdraw from their entitlements. Self-controlled, they wait for the onset of the deluge. When the former *devas* go away, the places in the three worlds, meant for *devas*, become empty. Other *devas*, who resided in heaven, present themselves in this world. Full of austerities, they are the ones who occupy these positions. They possess truth, *brahmacharya* and learning. These are the *saptarshis* and Manu, along with *devas* and ancestors. With the former ones destroyed, these are the future ones, resulting from the earlier ones. They are the offspring. When there is the end of a *manvantara*, there is no break. In this way, preservation continues progressively in all the *manvantaras*, until the onset of the deluge. This is what happens at the intervening period of the past *manvantara*. Svayambhuva has spoken about the past and the future. Past *manvantaras* provide the basis for the future. In this way, offspring continue until the onset of the deluge, without a break. While the *manvantaras* continue, there are those who have proceeded to Maharloka.[859] From Maharloka, they go to Janaloka. Single-minded, from Janaloka, they go to Tapoloka. From Tapoloka, they proceed to Satyaloka. As a result of their sentiments and insight, they directly realize many things there. They remain in Satyaloka for an eternity. However, for some, there is a deviation in this permanence. At the time of secondary creation, because of their transformations, as the *manvantaras* proceed, they leave Satyaloka. They are united with material objects. But others, delinked from the material, enter the divinity Narayana. As a result of natural rules, the cycle of *manvantaras* continues for a long time. There is not a single instant when the cycle of increase and decrease does not go on in the world of the living. In this way, the *rishis* praised the Manus, who possessed

---

[859] These *shlokas* are difficult to understand, and we have taken liberties.

divine insight and had *dharma* in their *atman*s. They possessed
divine insight. This knowledge was obtained from what Vayu
composed, stated briefly and in detail. The account is about all the
*rajarshi*s, *surarshi*s, *brahmarshi*s, *uraga*s, the lords among Gods,
*saptarshi*s, ancestors and lords among *praja*s and about how these
cycles properly took place. There were noble ones who were born in
extensive lineages. They possessed learning and proper wisdom and
flourished because of this. Because of their deeds, radiance and
fame, those lords were sacred, renowned and worshipped. This
account is supreme and enables the attainment of heaven. It is
sacred and enables the listener to obtain sons. It is auspicious and
mysterious. It should be chanted on great *parva* days. It dispels
great misery and bestows peace and a long lifespan. This sacred
account is about Aja's famous offspring, lords of *praja*s, *devarshi*s
and foremost Manus. Narrated thus, may those lords of *praja*s
bestow success on me. In the due order, the *manvantara* of
Svayambhuva Manu has thus been described, progressively and in
detail. What will I describe next?'

Chapter 36-1(36) (Milking of the earth)

Shamshampayana said, 'In the due order, I wish to hear about
the other *manvantara*s, the lords of the *manvantara*s and about
Shakra, the chief among *deva*s.'

Suta replied, 'There are past *manvantara*s and future ones.
I will speak about them briefly, and in detail. Listen. The
past Manus are Svayambhuva Manu as the first. There are
Svarochisha Manu, Uttama, Tamasa, Raivata and Chakshusha
as the sixth. The remaining eight, including the future ones, are
Savarni, Rouchya, Bhoutya and Vaivasvata.[860] I will first speak
about the ones who came before Vaivasvata Manu. They were

---

[860] The current Manu is Vaivasvata. The names of the future Manus
are often given as Savarni, Daksha-Savarni, Brahma-Savarni, Dharma-
Savarni, Rudra-Savarni, Rouchya and Bhoutya.

sons born through mental powers. Listen. I have already spoken about the past Svayambhuva *manvantara*. After this, I will speak about the one of Svarochisha Manu. He was the second great-souled one and I will briefly talk about the creation of subjects. During Svarochisha *manvantara*, *deva*s were Tushitas. It is said that those learned ones consisted of two categories, Tushitas and Paravatas. During Svarochisha *manvantara*, the Tushitas were born as the sons of Kratu and Tushitaa. The Paravatas were born in Vasishtha's lineage. There were thus two categories, each numbering twelve. Born through wishes, there are said to have been twenty-four *deva*s. The Tushitas are described as Divasparsha, Jamitra, Gopada, Bhasura, Aja, Bhagavan, the immensely strong Dravina, the mighty-armed Aya, the valiant Mahouja, the famous Chikitvan, Amsha, the one who is read about and Rita as the twelfth. These sons of Kratu were drinkers of *soma*. The Paravatas of the past were the radiant Prachetas, Vishvadeva, Samanja, the famous Ajihma, Arimardana, Ayurdana, Mahamana, Divyamana, the immensely fortunate Ajeya, the immensely strong Yaviyana, Hotri and Yajvan. These were the *deva*s in Svarochisha *manvantara*. These were the twenty-four *deva*s who drank *soma* then. Their Indra was Vipashchit, famous in the worlds. The *saptarshi*s were Vashishtha's son, Urja; Kashyapa's son, Stamba; Bhargava's son, Prana; Rishabha, the son of Angiras; Poulastya's son, Datta; Atreya Nishchala, Atri's son; and Arvaviran, Pulaha's son. The nine sons of Svarochisha Manu are said to be Chaitra, Kimpurusha, Kritanta, Vibhrita, Ravi, Brihaduktha, Nava, Setu and Shruta. These sons extended the lord's lineage. For the second *manvantara*, the Purana enumerates these. *Saptarshi*s, Manu, *deva*s and ancestors—these four constitute the foundation of a *manvantara*. *Praja*s are their descendants. *Deva*s are sons of *rishi*s. Ancestors are sons of *deva*s. *Rishi*s are sons of *deva*s. This is the determination of sacred texts. *Kshatriya*s and *vaishya*s are born from Manu, while *dvija*s are born from *saptarshi*s. The *manvantara* has thus been described briefly, not in detail. The details of Svarochisha *manvantara* can be known from that of Svayambhuva *manvantara*. Even if one attempts for one hundred years, one is incapable of speaking about it in detail. This is because one would have to repeatedly speak about the many *prajas*, born from one lineage into another lineage.'

'In the third *manvantara* of Uttama Manu, there are said to have been five categories of *deva*s. I will describe them. Listen. They were Sudhamans, Vamshavartins, Pratardanas, Shivas and Satyas. Each of these groups are said to have twelve *deva*s. The twelve names of Sudhamans are described as Satya, Dhriti, Dama, Danta, Kshama, Kshaama, Dhvani, Shuchi, Isha, Urjja, Shreshtha and Suparna as the twelfth. The Vamshavartins are described as Sahasradhara, Vishvayu, two Samitaras, Brihad, Vasu, Vishvadha, Vishvakarma, Manasa, Virajasa, Jyoti and Vibhasa. The Pratardanas are described as Avadhya, Avarati, the lord Vasu, Dhishnya, Vibhavasu, Vitta, Kratu, Sudharman, Dhritadharman, Yashasvija, Rathormi and Ketuman. There were twelve Shivas—Hamsasvara, the generous Pratardana, Yashaskara, Sudana, Vasudana, Sumanjasa, Visha, Yama, Vahni, Yati, Suchitra and Sutapas. These are known as ones who had shares in sacrifices. Listen to the accurate statement of the names of Satyas. They were Dikpati, Vakpati, Vishva, Shambhu, Svamridika, Divi, Varchodhaman, Brihadvapu, Ashva, Sadashva, Kshema and Ananda. These were the twelve former Satyas and they had shares in sacrifices. These were *deva*s at the time of Uttama *manvantara*. The Indra of *deva*s was famous under the name of Sushanti. At the time of Prajapati Uttama, the sons of Angiras existed.[861] Vasishtha had seven famous sons, known as Vasishthas. All of them were *saptarshi*s during the *manvantara* of Uttama Manu. The great-souled Uttama Manu had thirteen sons—Aja, Parashu, Divya, Divyoushadhi, Naya, Devambuja, the unmatched Mahotsaha, Gaja, Vinita, Suketu, Sumitra, Sumati and Shruti. During the third *manvantara*, they established *kshatriya*s. The creations of Svarochisha and Uttama have been enumerated.'

'Now listen to what happened, progressively and in detail, during the *manvantara* of the fourth Manu, Tamasa. *Deva*s during the *manvantara* of this Manu were Pulastya's sons. Their categories are said to have been Satyas, Surupas, Sudhis and Haris. Each

---

[861] One can deduce that *deva*s of this *manvantara* were sons of Angiras. The sentence is left dangling.

of these categories had twenty-five *deva*s. In the course of this *manvantara*, senses are described as *deva*s. When senses manifest themselves, *rishi*s get to know. The senses establish proof, and the mind, the eighth, is at their head.[862] The powerful Shibi was Indra of *deva*s. O excellent ones! Hear about *saptarshi*s during that *manvantara*. They were Kavya, the son of Angiras; Prithu, the son of Kashyapa; Agni, the son of Atri; Jyotirdhama, the son of Bhrigu; Charaka, the son of Pulaha; Pivara, the son of Vasishtha; and Chaitra, the son of Pulastya. These were the *rishi*s of Tamasa *manvantara*. Tamasa Manu's sons were Janujangha, Shanti, Nara, Khyati, Shubha, Priyabhritya, Parikshit, Prasthala, Dridheshudhi, Krishashva and Kritabandhu.'

'I will describe the qualities of those described as *deva*s, during the fifth *manvantara* of Raivata.[863] Listen. They were Amitabhas, Bhutarayas, Vaikunthas and Sumedhas. They were the auspicious and excellent sons of Prajapati Vasishtha. In each of those four categories, there were fourteen radiant ones. The fourteen *deva*s described as Amitabhas during Raivata *manvantara* were Ugra, Prajna, Agnibhava, Prajyoti, Amrita, Sumati, Virava, Dhama, Nada, Shrava, Vritti, Rashi, Vada and Shabara. The names of Bhutarayas are known to have been Mati, Sumati, Rita, Satya, Edhana, Adhriti, Vidhriti, Dama, Niyama, Vrata, Vishnu, Saha, Dyutiman and Sushrava. Those described as Vaikunthas were Vrisha, Bhetta, Jaya, Bhima, Shuchi, Danta, Yasha, Dama, Natha, Vidvan, Ajeya, Krisha, Goura and Dhruva. Now understand about Sumedhas. They are described as Medha, Medhatithi, Satyamedha, Prishnimedha, Alpamedha, the lord Bhuyomedha, Diptimedha, Yashomedha, Sthiramedha, Sarvamedha, Sumedha, Pratimedha, Medhaja and Medhahanta. The virile and valiant Vibhu was their Indra. The *rishi*s of Raivata *manvantara* were Devabahu, the son of Pulastya; Sudhaman, the son of Kashyapa; Hiranyaroma, the son of Angiras; Vedashri, the son of Bhrigu; Urddhabahu, the son

---

[862] There are clearly errors in this part of the text. In no listing of the senses, can the mind be eighth.

[863] In an obvious typo, the text says Svarochisha. We have corrected it to Raivata.

of Vasishtha; Parjanya, the son of Pulaha and Satyanetra, the son
of Atri. During the fifth *manvantara*, the sons of Raivata were
Mahavirya, Susambhavya, Satyaka, Haraha, Shuchi, Balabandhu,
Niramitra, Kambu, Shringa and Dhritavrata. Svarochisha, Uttama,
Tamasa and Raivata—these four Manus are described as having
been descended from Priyavrata's lineage.'

'In the course of the sixth *manvantara* of Chakshusha,
there are said to have been five categories of *deva*s who resided
in heaven—Adyas, Prasutas, Bhavyas, Prithukas and the grand
Lekhas. All of them resided in heaven and they were named after
their mothers. They were the sons of Prajapati Aranya, Atri's son.
Each of these categories is said to have had eight *deva*s. The Adyas
are described as Antariksha, Vasu, Havya, Atithi, Priyavrata,
Shrota, Manta and Anumanta. The Prasutas are described as
Shyenabhadra, Shveta, the immensely illustrious Chakshu,
Sumanas, Prachetas, Vanenas, Suprachetas and the great-spirited
Muni. The Bhavyas were *deva*s remembered as Vijaya, Sujaya,
Mana, Syoda, Mati, Parimati, Vichetas and Priyanishchaya.
Now hear about the Prithukas. They were Ojishtha, the divinity
Shakuna, Vanadrishta, Satkrita, Satyadrishti, Jigishu, Vijaya and
the immensely fortunate Ajita. These were Prithukas who resided
in heaven. I will speak about the names of Lekhas. Listen. They
are described as Manojava, Praghasa, the immensely illustrious
Prachetas, Dhruva, Dhruvakshiti, the valiant Achyuta, Yuvanas
and Brihaspati. These are described as the Lekhas. The immensely
valiant Manojava was their Indra. The seven *rishi*s of Chakshusha
manvantara were Uttama, descended from Bhrigu; Havishman,
the son of Angiras; Sudhaman from the Kashyapa lineage; Viraja,
the son of Vasishtha; Atinama, the son of Pulastya; Sahishnu,
Pulaha's son; and Madhu, from Atri's lineage. The ten sons of
Chakshusha Manu were born through Nadvala.[864] They were
Uru, Puru, Shatadyumna, Tapasvi, Satyavak, Kriti, Agnishtuta,
Atiratra, Sudyumna as the ninth and Abhimanyu as the tenth. This
was the nature of the sixth *manvantara*. The current *manvantara*

[864] His wife.

of Vaivasvata has already been described, and I have progressively narrated, in detail, the *manvantara* of Chakshusha Manu.'

The *rishi*s asked, 'Whose heir was Chakshusa? Who was he born from? What was the lineage? Please tell us accurately about the ones who followed.'

Suta replied, 'O *dvija*s! Hear briefly about the Chakshusha creation. Prithu, Vena's valiant son, was born in this lineage. There are many other Prajapatis, such as Daksha, the son of Prachetas. Prajapati Atri accepted Uttanapada as an adopted son. Since the Prajapati was a king, the son also became one. For some reason, Svayambhuva Manu gave this son to Atri.[865] This was after Chakshusha *manvantara* started. O *dvija*s! With this as a preface, I will now speak about the sixth *manvantara*. Through the beautiful Sunrita, Uttanapada had four sons. Dharma's daughter was named Sunrita. She possessed excellent hips and was famous. Following *dharma*, she became Dhruva's auspicious mother. Possessing beautiful smiles, she was born through Dharma's wife, Lakshmi. Through Uttanapada, she gave birth to four sons—Dhruva, Kirtimanta, Ayushmanta and Vasu. She also had two sweet-smiling daughters—Svaraa and Manasvini. Their sons have already been described.[866] The valiant Dhruva tormented himself through austerities for ten thousand divine years. Desiring extensive fame, he fasted. He was Svayambhuva's grandson, and this occurred in the first *treta yuga*. Seeking immensely great fame, he sustained his *atman* in yoga. Pleased, Brahma bestowed on him the excellent status of being a luminous body. Until the onset of the deluge, he obtained this divine status of not being subject to rising and setting. On witnessing his excessive prosperity and greatness, Ushanas, the preceptor of *daitya*s and *asura*s,[867] chanted this *shloka*. "His austerities and valour are wonderful. His learning and great vows are wonderful. The *saptarshi*s are established there, with Dhruva

---

[865] *Harivamsha* also states this, but doesn't state the reason.

[866] This is not quite true. We have been told that Manasvini's son was Markandeya. But we haven't been told anything about Svaraa.

[867] Shukracharya.

above them. Heaven is attached to Dhruva.[868] He is the lord and master of the firmament." Through Bhumi, Dhruva had two sons, Srishti and Bhavya. They were kings. The lord Srishti told his own shadow, "Become a woman." Since he always spoke the truth, it instantly became a woman named Chhaya. Her body was divine and she was adorned in divine ornaments. Through Chhaya, Srishti had five unblemished sons—Prachinagarbha, Vrishabha, Vrika, Vrikala and Dhriti. Suvarcha, Prachinagarbha's wife, gave birth to a king named Udaradhi. In an earlier birth, this son had been Indra. The lord had obtained this status of being Indra by only eating once at the end of one thousand years. He had done this for an entire *manvantara*. Through Bhadra, Udaradhi had a son named Divanjaya. Through Varangi, Divanjaya's son was Ripu, who defeated his enemies. Through Brihati, Ripu's son was Chakshus, who possessed every kind of energy. His learned son was the Manu[869] who established *brahmana*s and *kshatriya*s. Pushkarini Varuni gave birth to Chakshusa Manu.'

The *rishi*s asked, 'O unblemished one! Why was Prajapati's daughter known as Varuni? You are accomplished. Please tell us the truth about this in detail.'

Suta answered, 'Aranya was the son of Udaka. He obtained the status of being Varuna. As a result of her brother's fame, she came to be known as Varuni. Through Nadvala, Manu had ten auspicious sons, who were extremely valiant. She was the daughter of Viraja Prajapati. They were Uru, Puru, Shatadyumna, Tapasvi, Satyavak, Kriti, Agnishtuta, Atiratra and Sudyumna as the ninth. Abhimanyu was the tenth. These were the sons of Manu and Nadvala. Through Agneyi, Uru had six sons who were immensely radiant—Anga, the famous Sumanas, Gaya, Shukra, Vraja and Ajina. Through Sunitha,

[868] The word uses the word Tridiva, meaning heaven. Tridiva is understood in either of two ways. It is the third layer, after *bhuloka* and *bhuvarloka*. It is also the place where the three (Brahma, Vishnu and Shiva) find pleasure.

[869] That is, Chakshusha Manu. His father was Chakshus and his mother was Pushkarini Varuni. Varuni is described as the daughter of Prajapati Virana. Here, her brother is Varuna.

Anga had a single son, Vena. Vena's crimes resulted in great rage. For the sake of offspring, the *rishi*s kneaded his right hand. When the hands were kneaded, the handsome Prithu was born. In this way, Prithu, famous for his manliness, was born. The *rishi*s said, "O *praja*s! Be happy. He will be your king. He has been born with armour and a bow and his energy seems to burn everything down. This lord of men will be the one who will grant you means of subsistence." Vena's son, Prithu, protected the worlds and was the ancestor of *kshatriya*s. The lord of the earth was the first one to be consecrated through a royal sacrifice. It was to praise him that the accomplished *suta*s and *magadha*s were born. The intelligent and great king milked the earth for crops. He provided a means of subsistence for subjects. In his act of milking the earth, *deva*s, a large number of *rishi*s, ancestors, *danava*s, *gandharva*s, a large number of *apsara*s, *sarpa*s, *punyajana*s,[870] mountains, trees and creepers were with him, with their own respective vessels. For the sake of sustaining life, she gave him the milk they wished for.'

Shamshapayana said, 'O one great in vows! Please narrate the story of Prithu's birth in detail. Earlier, how did the great-souled one milk the earth? In those ancient times, how were *deva*s, *naga*s, *brahmarshi*s, *yaksha*s, *rakshasa*s, *gandharva*s and *apsara*s with him? O Suta! What were the respective methods for them? In particular, what were their specific vessels? Who milked the milk? Which were the specific calves? Please tell us what is being asked. What was the specific type of milk? Please narrate everything in the due order. In those ancient times, for what reason was Vena's hand kneaded? Earlier, why were the *maharshi*s enraged? Please tell us that too.'

Suta replied, 'O *brahmana*s! I will tell you how Prithu originated from Vena. O excellent *dvija*s! Control yourselves and listen with single-minded attention. This story of the *brahman* should never be narrated to someone who is not pure, someone who is a sinner, someone who is not a *shishya*, someone who causes harm or to someone who does not observe *vrata*s. This sacred account is revered like the *Veda*s. It is blessed and bestows fame and a long

---

[870] *Saptajana* is a synonym. These were seven sages who were originally *rakshasa*s.

lifespan. It is a secret account, told by the *rishi*s. Listen to it now. It is about the origin of Prithu, Vena's son. After honouring *brahmanas*, if a mortal frees himself from jealousy and listens to it, or makes it heard, he does not have to grieve about what he has done and what he has not done. There was a king who protected *dharma*. This lord was Atri's equal and was born in Atri's lineage. This lord of subjects was named Anga. He had a son named Vena, excessively devoted to *adharma*. This lord of subjects was born as the son of Sunitha, Mrityu's daughter. Vena was the son of the daughter of Death and suffered from his maternal grandfather's taints. He pursued *kama* in this world and turned his back on *dharma*. A lord of the earth should establish rules of *dharma*. But he was addicted to *adharma* and transgressed the *Veda*s and the sacred texts. While he ruled, there was no studying and *vashatkara* in his kingdom. At the time, in great sacrifices, *deva*s did not drink *soma*. The cruel lord of subjects took a pledge. "There should be no sacrifices and no donations." His destruction presented itself. "I am the one to whom sacrifices should be performed. *Deva*s and *dvija*s should worship me through sacrifices. Sacrifices should be performed for me. It is to me that oblations should be offered." He transgressed all the ordinances. However, he has also performed a lot of donations. Therefore, with Marichi at the forefront, all the *maharshi*s spoke to him. "O king! We will consecrate ourselves for a sacrifice that will last for one hundred years. At the time, do not perform any act of *adharma*. That will not be eternal *dharma*. If that happens, there is no doubt that, as a lord of subjects, you will face destruction. Earlier, you took a pledge to protect the subjects." All the *brahmarshi*s spoke to him in this way. But the evil-minded Vena laughed. "Other than me, who possesses knowledge? Other than me, who else has created *dharma*? Who else should I listen to? In energy, austerities and truth, who else is my equal on earth? I am not evil-souled. Indeed, you do not know the truth about me. My power is such that, if I wish, I can burn down the entire earth, or flood it water, and all its *dharma*. I can create it and devour it. There is no need to think about this." The *maharshi*s sought to entreat Vena. However, he was so excessively ignoble that no one was capable of restraining him. They became angry. As the immensely strong one struggled, they seized him by the arms. Full of great rage, they kneaded his left hand. It has been heard that when he was kneaded, a being was initially born. This man was excessively short and dark. His senses were in a whirl. Scared, he stood there, hands joined in salutation. Seeing that he was agitated, they told him, "Sit down." Infinite in valour, he started the lineage of *nishadas*.[871] *Dhivaras* originated from Vena's sins. There were others who made their homes in the Vindhyas—Tamburas, Tuburas and Khashas. As a result of Vena's sins, it should be known that they are addicted to *adharma*.'

'After this, the *maharshis* kneaded Vena's right hand. Like a pair of *arani* sticks being rubbed, another being was born from this kneading. He was born from the large hand and blazed. Since he was born from the large palm, he became Prithu.[872] His body blazed as if he was the flaming fire. He was born holding the Ajagava bow,[873] which made a loud sound. For the sake of protection, he held radiant arrows and wore extremely resplendent armour. As soon as he was born, all the beings were delighted. They approached and the great king, Vena, went to heaven. This was because he had given birth to a virtuous and great-souled son, a *rajarshi*. The tiger among men was saved from the hell named *put*.[874] All the rivers and oceans gathered together every kind of jewel. For the sake of the consecration, all of them assembled, bringing their water with them. The illustrious grandfather arrived, along with all those from the Angiras lineage, the immortals and all mobile and immobile entities. Vena's son was consecrated as the lord of men. The immensely radiant one became a king of kings, a great protector of *prajas*. Along with the sons of Angiras, *devas* consecrated him as a great king. Vena's immensely fortunate son, the powerful Prithu, was the first *rajan*. His father had defeated enemies, but he

---

[871] *Nishadas* are hunters, residing in forests and mountains. The derivation is from '*nishida*', meaning, 'Sit down'. A *dhivara* is a fisherman.

[872] The word *prithu* means large.

[873] Typically, a bow made of horn.

[874] A son is known as *putra* because he saves (*trayate*) from the hell named *put*.

delighted subjects. That is the reason they loved him, and he came to be known as *rajan*.[875] When he advanced, the waters of the ocean were stupefied. Mountains crumbled and his standard was never shattered. The earth yielded crops and cooked food, without the ground being tilled. Cows were milked for whatever was desired and there was honey in every flower cup. At this time, he performed a sacrifice. Suta was born at the time, from *soma* juice, on the day when *soma* juice was extracted. Magadha was also born as the same time. When the Vishvadevas were present in the auspicious sacrificial ladle and there was the singing of hymns from the *Sama Veda*, he was born as Magadha, since all of them had assembled.[876] The oblations meant for Indra were mixed up with the oblations meant for Brihaspati. By chance, oblations were being offered to Indra, when Suta was born. As a result of this confusion, when he was born, there was the need for a rite of atonement. An oblation meant for the *guru* was surpassed by an oblation meant for the *shishya*.[877] An inferior overcame a superior and in this way, the birth occurred from a mixing of *varnas*. The father was a *kshatriya*, inferior in *varnas*, but the mother was a *brahmana*. Accordingly, a *suta* is described as one who follows the *dharma* of the superior and is his equal in *dharma*. However, since he is in the middle, his *dharma* is also to earn a living from the means of subsistence indicated for *kshatriyas*. He tends to chariots, elephants and horses and also performs the contemptible task of being a physician. To praise Prithu, the *maharshis* gathered them there. All the sages said, "This lord of the earth should be praised. This is a task appropriate for you and this lord of men is the recipient." At this, all the *sutas* and *magadhas* spoke to the *rishis*. "Through our deeds, we will please *devas* and *rishis*. However, we do not know about his deeds, or the signs of his fame. How will we praise him?" The energetic *dvijas* replied, "He will always be devoted to his tasks and will be truthful in speech. His senses will be controlled. He will possess

---

[875] From the root, meaning a king who delights subjects.

[876] From *samagata*, meaning to arrive, or come together.

[877] Brihaspati is the *guru* and Indra is the *shishya*. A *suta* is the child of mixed *varnas*, with a *kshatriya* father and a *brahmana* mother.

jnana and good conduct. He will be generous and undefeated in battles." Thus, the *rishi*s engaged them to praise his future deeds. Subsequently, the immensely strong Prithu performed these deeds. Accordingly, *suta*s and *magadha*s composed their songs. Prithu, the lord of *praja*s, was pleased with their praise. He bestowed the region of Anupa[878] on *suta*s and Magadha on *magadha*s. Since that time, *suta*s and *magadha*s have always praised lords of the earth. *Suta*s, *magadha*s and *bandi*s awake kings with words of benediction.'

'On seeing him, the *praja*s were extremely happy and the *maharshi*s said, "Vena's son, the lord of men, will provide a means of subsistence for you." At this, all the *praja*s rushed towards Vena's immensely fortunate son. "The *maharshi*s have said that you will provide a means of subsistence for us." When the *praja*s rushed towards him, he wished to ensure the welfare of the subjects. Therefore, the powerful one seized his bow and arrows and advanced in the direction of the earth. Scared of Vena's son, the earth assumed the form of a cow and fled from the spot. As she fled, Prithu seized his bow and followed her. Terrified of Vena's son, she went to Brahma's world and other worlds. But wherever she went, she saw Vena's son in front of her, with the raised bow in his hand. His sharp arrows blazed and his flaming energy did not decay. The great-souled one was great in his *yoga* and even the immortals found it impossible to assail him. Since she could not be saved anywhere, she sought refuge with Vena's son himself. The Goddess, who is always worshipped by the three worlds, joined her hands in salutation. She said, "O Vena's son! Can you not see that killing a woman is *adharma*? *Praja*s are nourished by me. How will you sustain them otherwise? O *rajan*! The worlds are established in me. I am the one who holds up the universe. O protector of the earth and *praja*s! Listen to my words. O lord of the earth! Because of me, the subjects who have been nourished should not be destroyed. Therefore, if you desire to do what is beneficial, you should not kill me. If one sets about it the right way, everything can be accomplished. O lord of men! If you kill me, you will be

[878] Literally, a place near water, or a marshy place.

incapable of protecting the *praja*s. I will merely vanish inside. O
immensely radiant one! Therefore, conquer your rage. It is said
that females, even if they belong to an inferior species, should not
be killed. O protector of the earth! You should remain established
in the truth and not give up *dharma*." The great-minded one heard
many such words uttered by her. With *dharma* in his soul, he
restrained his anger and spoke to the earth. "For the sake of a
single individual, or for one's own sake, if a person kills another,
that is a sin. It is a major sin to kill many for the sake of one. O
fortunate one! O auspicious one! However, if many live happily
if a single entity is killed, the killing of that entity is not a major
sin, or even a minor sin. O earth! I will kill you for the sake of
the subjects, unless, for the welfare of the universe, you decide
to act in accordance with my words now. If you turn your face
away from my instructions, I will quickly slay you with an arrow.
Establishing myself in that way, I will myself nurture the *praja*s.
O supreme among those who uphold *dharma*! Hence, you should
pay heed to my words. There is no doubt that you are capable
of constantly reviving the subjects. Assume the position of my
daughter. I will then restrain this arrow, terrible to behold, that
I have raised to kill you." Addressed in this way by Vena's son,
the virtuous earth replied, "O *rajan*! There is no doubt that I
will carry out everything you say. Show me a calf, so that my
milk of affection flows out. O supreme among those who uphold
dharma! Make me level everywhere, so that the flowing milk
spreads equally everywhere." At this, he cleared the mass of rocks
that were everywhere. The mountains had grown and Vena's son
used the tip of his bow to remove them. In the course of the past
manvantara, the earth had become uneven. All those uneven spots
now became naturally even. In the course of the earlier cycle of
creation, when the surface of the earth was uneven, there were no
divisions of cities and villages. There were no crops, or pens for
cattle. There was no agriculture, or paths for traders. This was
indeed the case in the former Chakshusha *manvantara*. All these
became possible only during Vaivasvata *manvantara*. There were
places where the ground became even, and all the subjects resided
in these places. Earlier, the food of *praja*s consisted of roots and

fruits. Accordingly, we have heard that they faced hardships. Since the time of Vena's son, everything became possible in the world.'

'The lord thought of Chakshusha Manu as a calf. He milked the earth for crops, which appeared on the surface of the earth. The auspicious subjects sustained themselves on this food. It is heard that the *rishi*s milked the earth again. Soma became the calf then and Brihaspati was the one who did the milking. All the different *chhanda*s, *gayatri* and the others, were the vessels. At the time, the milk was in the form of austerities and the eternal *brahman*. It is heard that with Purandara[879] at the forefront, the large number of *deva*s milked the earth, using a golden vessel. Maghavan was the calf and the lord Savitar was the one who did the milking. The milk was energy and honey and *deva*s subsisted on the basis of this. It is heard that the ancestors milked the earth again. Using a silver vessel, they swiftly satisfied themselves with *svadha*.[880] The powerful Vaivasvata Yama was the calf then and Antaka,[881] the powerful lord of the ancestors, was the one who did the milking. It is heard that the *asura*s milked the earth again. They used an iron vessel and obtained every kind of *maya*.[882] Virochana, Prahlada's immensely illustrious son, was the calf. Dvimurdha, Diti's son and the officiating priest of the *daitya*s, was the one who did the milking. They obtained *maya* as *payasam*[883] and all the *asura*s became accomplished in the use of *maya*. Subsisting on the basis of this, they obtained great valour and supreme strength. It is heard that when *naga*s did the milking, they used Takshaka as a calf. They milked the earth with a gourd as the vessel and the milk was poison. Vasuki, Kadru's valiant son, was the one who did the milking. O best among *dvija*s! *Naga*s and *sarpa*s subsisted on the basis of this. They became fierce and gigantic in size, with virulent poison. This was their food and they depended on this for their conduct and energy. *Yaksha* and *punyajana*s milked the earth again, using an

---

[879] Indra's name.
[880] *Svadha* was the milk.
[881] The Destroyer.
[882] *Maya* was the milk.
[883] *Payasam* is a dish made out sweetened milk and rice.

unannealed vessel. They made Vaishravana, who loves to disappear, the calf. Rajatanabha, Manidhara's father, was the one who did the milking. This son of a *yaksha* was controlled, immensely illustrious and greatly energetic. They sustained themselves on the basis of this and achieved their ultimate objective. *Rakshasas* and *pishacha*s milked the earth again. The *rakshasa* Brahmopeta was the calf and Kuberaka[884] was the one who did the milking. When the *rakshasas* did the milking, the powerful Sumali was the calf, and the milk was blood. The vessel for milking was a skull and the *rakshasa*s obtained the milk of becoming invisible. All the *rakshasa*s subsist on the basis of this milk. The large number of *gandharvas* and *apsara*s milked again, using a lotus as a vessel. They made Chitraratha the calf and the milk consisted of pure fragrances. The person who did the milking was Vasuruchi, Muni's auspicious son. He was the extremely strong king of the *gandharva*s, great-souled and like the sun in complexion. It is heard that the mountains milked the Goddess earth again. The herbs manifested themselves and many kinds of jewels. Himalaya was the calf, and the milking was done by Meru, the great mountain. The vessel was a mountain, and the mountains were established on the basis of this. It is heard that trees, and creepers milked the earth again. The vessel was the leaf of a *palasha* tree.[885] The milk was the technique of growing crops after they have been cut or burnt. The calf was a *plaksha* tree, and the milkman was the glorious *shala* tree.[886] The earth was milked for everything desired and made beings flourish. Vasundhara is Dhatri, Vidhatri and Dharani.[887] We have heard that Prithu milked her for the welfare of the worlds. She is the cause behind the establishment of the world, with its mobile and immobile entities.'

[884] Kubera (Vaishravana) has already been mentioned and this Kuberaka must be different from Kubera. There are typos in this part of the text.

[885] *Butea monosperma.*

[886] Tall tree.

[887] Vasundhara (or Vasudha), the one who holds riches (*vasu*), is the earth's name. Respectively, the one who nurtures, the one who creates and the one who supports.

Chapter 37-1(37) (Chakshusha creation)

Suta said, 'It is heard that Vasudha extends up to the frontiers of the ocean. Since she holds riches, she is known as Vasudha. Earlier, she was submerged in the fat of Madhu and Kaitabha. Therefore, those who know about the *brahman* and etymology, speak of her as Medini.[888] Thereafter, she became the daughter of Prithu, Vena's intelligent son. As a result of this, she came to obtain the name Prithivi. Prithu divided the earth and arranged for cities. The king established the garland of mines and habitations. She was inhabited by the four *varna*s and the intelligent one protected this. O excellent *dvija*s! Such was the power of the king who was Vena's son. All the large number of beings worshipped him and prostrated themselves before him. So did immensely fortunate *brahmana*s, accomplished in *Veda*s and *Vedanga*s. Prithu originated from the eternal *brahman* and deserved to be worshipped. Desiring great fame, immensely fortunate kings bowed down before him. Warriors desiring victory in battle also prostrated themselves before Prithu, Vena's son, the first *rajan*. Prithu was the first one who laid down principles for fighting and should be worshipped. Warriors advancing into battle chanted about King Prithu. Battles assume terrible forms. Those who wished to be famous, passing unscathed in battles, worshipped him. So did *vaishya*s and *rajarshi*s who adopted the occupations of *vaishya*s. They prostrated themselves before the immensely illustrious Prithu, who had ensured a means of subsistence. In the due order, I have described everything—the specific calves, those who did the milking, the vessels and the milk. In ancient times, the great-souled Brahma was the first one to milk the earth. He made Vayu the calf and the seeds on the surface of the ground were the milk. This occurred again in the course of Svayambhuva *manvantara*. Svayambhuva was made the calf, and all the different crops were the milk. After this, when Svarochisha *manvantara* arrived, with Svarochisha as a calf, Medini was milked,

---

[888] Medini is the one who is full of *meda* (fat). Madhu and Kaitabha were demons killed by Vishnu.

yielding crops. After this, during Uttama *manvantara*, the milking was done by the intelligent Devabhuja.[889] Uttama Manu was made the calf and all the crops constituted the milk. The earth was milked again, for a fifth time, during Tamasa *manvantara*, by Balabandhu. Tamasa Manu was made the calf. When the sixth *manvantara* of Charishtava arrived, the earth was milked by Purana, with Charishtava as a calf.[890] After this, Chakshusha *manvantara* arrived and Purana did the milking, with Chakshusha as the calf. When Chakshusha *manvantara* passed, Vaivasvata arrived. As I have described, in those earlier times, Vena's son did the milking. In this way, in ancient times, the earth was milked in past *manvantaras* by *deva*s and others, humans and other beings. It should be known that everything true of the past is also true of the future. During a *manvantara*, *deva*s are secure in heaven.'

'Now hear about Prithu's offspring. Prithu gave birth to two valiant sons—Antardhi and Pavana. Through Shikhandini, Antardhana[891] gave birth to Havirdhana. Through Agneyi, Havirdhana had six sons—Prachinabarhi, Shukla, Gaya, Krishna, Praja and Ajina. The illustrious Prachinabarhi was a great Prajapati. He possessed strength, learning, austerities and valour and was the single king on earth. Since the blades of the *kusha* grass always faced the east, he was known as Prachinabarhi.[892] After performing great austerities, the lord and Prajapati married Savarna, the ocean's daughter. Through Savarna, the ocean's daughter, Prachinabarhi had ten sons. All of them were named Prachetas and they were accomplished in *dhanurveda*. All of them followed identical *dharma* and tormented themselves through great austerities. They did this while lying down in the waters of the ocean for ten thousand years. As a consequent of their austerities, all the large trees covered the

[889] The text says Devanuja. We have corrected what seems to be a typo.
[890] There should actually be no such *manvantara*. This has probably been inserted to ensure a correspondence between the number of the *manvantara* and the number of times milking has been done, since Brahma did the first milking.
[891] The same as Antardhi.
[892] At all the sacrifices performed by Prachinabarhi, the blades of the *barhi* (*kusha*) grass faced the auspicious direction of the east (*prachi*).

earth. Since they were not protected, all the *prajas* were destroyed. As Chakshusha *manvantara* passed, this is what occurred. With the entire sky covered by trees, it was impossible for the wind to blow. *Prajas* could not do anything for ten thousand years. Engaged in austerities, all the Prachetas heard about this. Full of intolerance, they created wind and fire from their mouths. The wind uprooted the trees and dried them up. The terrible fire burnt them. Thus, all the trees were destroyed. When King Soma saw that all the trees had been destroyed, with a few remaining, he approached the Prachetas and spoke to them. "It is evident that the requirement has been accomplished. This is true. O kings! O all the sons of Prachinabarhi! For the sake of offspring in the world, cast aside your rage. When the wind and the fire are pacified, trees will grow on earth. This daughter of the trees, beautiful in complexion, is a jewel among men. Since I knew about the future, I nurtured her in my womb. Her name is Marisha. She has been created by the trees and is named accordingly.[893] She has been reared in Soma's womb and will be your wife. With half of your energy and half of my energy, the learned Prajapati, named Daksha, will be born through her. He is like the fire. As a result of your energy, the fire has generally burnt down the subjects. However, he will make *prajas* flourish again." The Prachetas accepted the words Soma spoke. They restrained their rage. From the trees, following *dharma*, they accepted Marisha as their wife. Using the powers of the mind, they made Marisha conceive. Through the ten Prachetas, Marisha gave birth to Prajapati Daksha, the valiant and immensely energetic one, born as Soma's portion. Initially, Daksha created *prajas* through his mental powers. Subsequently, he used physical intercourse. Using the powers of his mind, Daksha created mobile and immobile entities, bipeds and quadrupeds. Subsequently, he created women. He bestowed ten daughters on Dharma and thirteen on Kashyapa. Twenty-seven were given to the moon and they are like the eyes of time. Having bestowed these, he gave four to Arishtanemi, two to Bahuputra, two to Angiras and a single daughter to Krishashva. Offspring were born

---

[893] Marisha means a pot-herb, or the purple amaranth.

through them. This is what is chanted about the sixth *manvantara* of Chakshusha. The seventh Manu was Prajapati Vaivasvata. Since then, Vasus, *deva*s, birds, cows, *naga*s, Diti's offspring, *danava*s, *gandharva*s, *apsara*s and every other kind of species and *praja*, have originated through physical intercourse. Before this, it is said that creation happened through resolution, sight and touch.'

The *rishi* said, 'You have already spoken about the origin of *deva*s, *danava*s, auspicious *devarshi*s and the great-souled Daksha. You have also spoken about Daksha's origin from Prajapati's[894] breath of life. How was he again born through the great ascetics, the Prachetas? O Suta! We have a doubt about this, and you should explain this. He was the son of Soma's daughter. How did he become Soma's father-in-law?'

Suta answered, 'O excellent ones! Creation and withdrawal are a constant feature of beings. Rishis and learned people are not confused because of this. O *dvija*s! Daksha and all the others are repeatedly born, from one *yuga* to another *yuga*. They are destroyed again and the learned are not confused by this. O supreme *dvija*s! Thus, a person who is younger can become older than a person who lived before. Austerities are the most important and that is the reason for power.[895] If a person knows about this creation of mobile and immobile entities in the course of Chakshusha *manvantara*, he has offspring and a long lifespan. Crossing over, he obtains greatness in the world of heaven. Thus, I have briefly described the Chakshusha creation to you. In this way, the creations of six *manvantara*s have passed. O supreme *dvija*s! In the due order, the wise have succinctly spoken about these creations, starting with Svayambhuva and ending with Chakshusha. The details can be understood through that of Vaivasvata creation. All the other creations do not exceed, and do not fall short, of Vaivasvata. If a person desires freedom from disease, a long lifespan, expansion, *dharma*, *kama* and *artha*, he should read about the qualities of these, without any touch of envy. I will now describe, briefly and in detail, the creation of the great-souled Vaivasvata. Listen.'

---

[894] Meaning Brahma's.
[895] As a determinant of seniority.

Chapter 38-1(38) (Description of the *manvantara*)

Suta said, 'In the course of the seventh Vaivasvata *manvantara*, devas and supreme *rishi*s were born through Kashyapa, Marichi's son. The eight categories of *deva*s are described as Adityas, Vasus, Rudras, Sadhyas, Vishvadevas, Maruts, those descended from Bhrigu and those descended from Angiras. Adityas, Maruts and Rudras should be known as the sons of Kashyapa. The three categories of Sadhyas, Vasus and Vishvadevas are the sons of Dharma. *Deva*s known as Bhrigus are the sons of Bhrigu and those known as the Angirasas are the sons of Angiras. In Vaivasvata *manvantara*, it is held that these are the ones who are always easily born. After a long period of time has elapsed, they will also come about their destruction. This present auspicious creation is also known as that of Marichi's son. The present energetic Indra is named Mahabala. There are those who obtain the status of Indra in the past, the present and the future. In all the *manvantara*s, it should be known that they are similar in signs. They are lords of the past, the present and the future. All of them possess one thousand eyes and are Purandaras. All of them are Maghavans. All of them have crests and hold the *vajra* in their hands. All of them have performed one hundred sacrifices and possess one hundred qualities. Because of their *dharma*, energy, austerities, understanding, strength, learning and valour, they are established, subjugating all mobile and immobile entities in the three worlds. Like the powerful Vishnu, they are the lords of the past, the present and the future. I will describe all this to you. Listen. *Dvija*s say that there are three worlds—the past, the present and the future. *Bhuloka* is described as the past and *bhuvarloka* is described as the present. *Svarloka* is described as the future.[896] I will speak about the means. When meditating about the names of the worlds, Brahma first uttered the word "*bhuh*". That is

---

[896] The text uses the word *diva*, meaning heaven. For easier comprehension, we have replaced this with *svarloka*. *Bhuta* means the past, what has happened. *Bhavat* means the present, what is going on now. *Bhavya* means what will happen in the future.

the reason the first world came to be known as *bhuloka*. The root "*bhu*" is said to mean "to come into being", or "the appearance of the world". Since it became visible, it is known as *bhuloka*. This is the reason why *dvija*s speak of this as the first world. The second word that Brahma spoke was "*bhavat*". The word "*bhavat*" is used to refer to the period when something is currently produced. Based on the etymology, *bhuvarloka* is a world that is being produced. This is the reason why the second world of the firmament is referred to as *bhuvarloka*. After the second world originated, Brahma again uttered the word "*bhavya*". The word "*bhavya*" refers to a world of the future. The word "*bhavya*" is used to mean something that is yet to come. Hence, heaven is described as a world that is "*bhavya*". The earth is described as *bhuloka*, the firmament is *bhuvarloka* and heaven is described as the "*bhavya*" world. This is the determination of the three worlds. The three *vyahritis*[897] were uttered before the three worlds came into being. Those who know about etymology say that the word "*natha*" is associated with the idea of protecting. The *dvija*s describe those who are "*natha*"s of the three worlds of "*bhuta*", "*bhavat*" and "*bhavya*" as Indras. Indras are foremost among *deva*s and possess the qualities. In the *manvantara*s, *deva*s obtain shares of sacrifices. All the *yaksha*s, *gandharva*s, *rakshasa*s, *pishacha*s, *uraga*s and humans remember the greatness of Indras among *deva*s. Indras among *deva*s are preceptors, protectors, kings and ancestors. These excellent Gods follow *dharma* and protect *praja*s. In brief, these are said to be the signs of Indras among *deva*s. I will now speak about the *saptarshi*s who have resorted to heaven. They are the great ascetic, the intelligent Vishvamitra, descended from Koushika and Gadhi; the powerful Bhargava Jamadagni, Ourva's son; Brihaspati's son, the immensely illustrious Bharadvaja; the learned one named Sharadvat, devoted to *dharma* and descended from Utathya and Goutama; the illustrious Atri as the fifth, born as a portion of Svayambhu, with the *brahman* as his sheath; Vasishtha's son Vasuman, famous in the worlds, as the sixth; and Vatsara, born in Kashyapa's lineage and revered by the

---

[897] *Vyahriti* means the words *bhuh*, *bhuvah* and *svah*, uttered after OUM.

virtuous, as the seventh. These are described as the *saptarshi*s of the current *manvantara*. Vaivasvata Manu's nine sons were extremely devoted to *dharma*. They were Ikshvaku, Nriga, Dhrishta, Sharyati, Narishyanta, the famous Nabhaga, Dishta, Karusha, Prishadhra and Pamshu as the ninth.[898] The present *manvantara* is described to be the seventh. O *dvija*s! I have thus described the second *pada*, in the due order and in detail.[899] What will I describe next?'

Chapter 39-1(39) (Origin of *rishis*)

This is the start of the middle section of *Brahmanda Purana*.[900] Shamshapayana said, 'You have told us about the second *pada* of *anushanga*. Please described in detail what happens in the third *pada* of *upodghata*.'

Suta replied, 'I will describe in detail the third *pada* of *upodghata* and about everything that is said in this section, overall. O *brahmana*s! Listen to what I have to say. O *dvija*s! In the due order, hear in detail about the current creation of the great-souled Vaivasvata Manu. It has already been stated that it numbers seventy-one *mahayuga*s. Beginning with Manu and ending with the future, there are many kinds of accounts about large numbers of *deva*s, *rishi*s, *danava*s, ancestors, *gandharva*s, *yaksha*s, *rakshasa*s, *bhuta*s, giant *uraga*s, humans, animals, birds and immobile entities. After prostrating myself before Vivasvat, I will speak about the Vaivasvata creation. At the beginning of the *manvantara*, the ones who had started the last creation passed away. In the former Svayambhuva *manvantara*, there were *saptarshi*s and other *maharshi*s. Those who

[898] There are actually ten names and Vaivasvata Manu is sometimes stated to have ten sons, the names mentioned. The number can be reconciled by taking Dhrishta to be an adjective, meaning, insolent.

[899] Hence, this ends the second section of *anushanga pada*.

[900] As has been mentioned earlier, there are four parts in *Brahmanda Purana*—*prakriya pada, anushanga pada, upodghata pada* and *upasamhara pada*. *Upodghata pada* starts from here.

existed in Chakshusha *manvantara* also belonged to the past and Vaivasvata *manvantara* arrived. As a consequence of Maheshvara's curse, the great-souled and immensely energetic ones, Daksha and Bhrigu and the other *rishi*s, no longer existed. The seven *saptarshi*s were again born through mental powers. Svayambhu himself thought of them, as his sons. Those great-souled ones continued the process of creation by having offspring. In the due order, as was the case earlier, creation proceeded. I will describe the origin of those who were pure in *jnana* and *karma*. In the due order, I will describe everything accurately, briefly and in detail, explaining how the worlds were filled with mobile and immobile entities, the lineages and about how the ornamentation with planets and *nakshatra*s resulted.'

The *rishi*s asked, 'O excellent one! Through his mental powers, the *saptarshi*s had been born earlier. How did he again think of them as his sons? Please tell us that.'

Suta answered, 'In the course of the former Svayambhuva *manvantara*, there were those who had been thought of as *saptarshi*s. Thereafter, Vaivasvata *manvantara* arrived. Pierced by Bhava's curse, they no longer possessed the fruits of austerities. They did reach Janaloka once, but they had to return. In Janaloka, those *maharshi*s constantly spoke to each other. "The immensely fortunate Varuna will perform a sacrifice and at the time of Chakshusha *manvantara*, all of us will be born. All of us will be born as sons of the grandfather. That will be best for us." Cursed by Bhava in Svayambhuva *manvantara*, all of them said this. For the sake of creation, they returned from Janaloka and were born again during Chakshusha *manvantara*. The divinity Varuna, radiant in form, performed a great sacrifice. Desiring his earlier offspring, Brahma offered his seed as an oblation into the fire. We have heard that the *rishi*s had their second birth in the course of this long sacrifice. These eight sons of Brahma were Bhrigu, Angiras, Marichi, Pulastya, Pulaha, Kratu, Atri and Vasishtha.[901] All the *deva*s arrived at that extensive sacrifice. The various components of

[901] There are eight names, not seven. Names of the *saptarshi*s are not always consistent.

the sacrifice and *vashatkara* assumed personified forms. Thousands of hymns from *Sama Veda* and *Yajur Veda* assumed personified forms. The sacrifice was ornamented by hymns from the *Rig Veda* being chanted in the right order. The excellent hymns from *Yajur Veda* stood around in a circle, with Oumkara as the blazing mouth. To accomplish the objective of the sacrifice, all the *suktam*s, Brahmanas and *mantra*s were present. The excellent hymns of the *Sama Veda* stood around in a circle, Vishvavasu and other singers at the forefront, along with all the other *gandharva*s. Along with the ordained terrible rites, *Brahmaveda*[902] was present. As a result of the presence of the Angiras segments, it possessed two heads and two bodies. *Lakshmana, vistara, stobha, nirukta, svarabhakti, ashraya, vashatkara, nigraha* and *pragraha* were present.[903] Assuming a radiant form, Devi Ila was present and so were the directions and the lords of the directions. The wives, daughters and mothers of *deva*s were present. All of them arrived in embodied forms at the place where the divinity's sacrifice was taking place. Varuna himself assumed a handsome form. On seeing them, Svayambhu's semen fell down on the ground. There is no doubt that this occurred because it was ordained that the *brahmarshi*s would be born. Using his hands as a ladle, the grandfather held this and offered it as an oblation. As it oozed out, he used *mantra*s to offer it as an oblation. In this way, Prajapati created the aggregate of beings. When his energy flowed downwards, the *taijasa* world was created.[904] That liquid flow had traits of *tamas, sattva* and *rajas*. He held his own semen in the plate

[902] The personified form of *Atharva Veda*. *Atharva Veda* has two recensions. But the two heads/bodies probably refer to the two segments of benign/auspicious (known as *Atharvan*) and malign/inauspicious (known as *Angiras*).

[903] These are different components of proper recitation—*lakshmana* is sign; *vistara* is expansion; *stobha* is praise or pause; *nirukta* is etymology; *svarabhakti* is phonetic insertion of vowels; *ashraya* is an affix used for conjugation; *vashatkara* is the sound of *vashat*; *nigraha* is shortening the pronunciation; and *pragraha* is extending the pronunciation.

[904] With the three *guna*s of *sattva, rajas* and *tamas*, three kinds of *ahamkara* are created—*vaikarika, taijasa* and *tamasa, vaikarika* associated with *sattva* and *taijasa* with *rajas*.

meant for *ghee* and offered it as an oblation. When the semen was
offered as an oblation, the *maharshis* manifested themselves. As a
result of their own powers and own qualities, their bodies blazed.
He offered his semen into the fire once, as an oblation. Kavi emerged
from the flames.[905] Hiranyagarbha saw that he had split the flames
and had emerged. He said, "You will be Bhrigu."[906] Therefore, he
became Bhrigu. Mahadeva appeared and on seeing him, spoke to
Brahma. "O lord! Desiring that I should have a son, you should
consecrate him. He is the *deva* who has been born first. Let him be
my son." Svayambhu agreed to this and granted what Mahadeva
had said. Hence, Mahadeva bestowed on Bhrigu the status of being
his son. Thus, at Varuna's sacrifice, the lord obtained Bhrigu as
his son. The lord then offered a second oblation of semen into the
burning coal. The limbs of Angiras were formed by the burning
coal and he became Angiras because of this reason.[907] Witnessing
his origin, Vahni[908] spoke to Brahma. "I bore the semen. Therefore,
this second son should be mine. Thus addressed by Sadasaspati,[909]
Brahma agreed. Hence, Agni accepted Angiras and we have heard
that the descendants are known as Agneyas. Brahma, the creator of
the worlds, then divided the semen into six parts and offered these
as oblations. The *shruti* texts state that those born from Brahma
resulted. Marichi was the first and he arose from the rays.[910] Kratu
was born from the sacrifice. Therefore, he came to be known as
Kratu.[911] Atri was born and said, "I am the third." Therefore, he
is described as Atri.[912] The next was born with a mass of hair and
is described as Pulastya.[913] The next was born with long hair and

---

[905] Kavi is Shukra or Shukracharya and the word *shukra* also means
semen.

[906] Since *bhitva* means to split or divide. This is a contrived derivation,
as are some of the others.

[907] *Angara* means burning coal, specifically charcoal.

[908] Agni.

[909] Sadasaspati means the lord (president of an assembly). It has several
meanings and is also one of Rudra's names. Here, it means Agni.

[910] Marichi means ray/spark.

[911] Kratu means sacrifice.

[912] *Tritiya* means third.

[913] *Pula* means large/wide/extensive. The same root is used to derive
both Pulastya and Pulaha.

is described as Pulaha. After this, the self-controlled Vasuman was himself born, amidst wealth. Accordingly, those who know about the truth and known about the *brahman* describe him as Vasishtha.[914] These six *maharshis* are Brahma's sons, born through his mental powers. They extended the worlds and because of them, *prajas* flourished. Thus, these sons of Brahma are described as Prajapatis. It is from these *maharshis* that other ancestors resulted. They created categories of *devas*, famous in the seven worlds. There were seven categories who could not be vanquished[915] and they are famous in the seven worlds. They are famous as Marichas, Bhargavas, Angirasas, Poulastyas, Poulahas, Vasishthas and Atreyas. These categories are described as those who make the world of ancestors flourish. They have been briefly described. There are three other categories too— Amartas, Aprakashas and the famous Jyotishmantas.[916] Their king is the *deva* Yama, who has destroyed sins through *yama*. There are other Prajapatis. With single-minded attention, hear about them. They are Kashyapa, Kardama, Shesha, Vikranta, Sushrava, Bahuputra, Kumara, Vivasvat, Shuchivrata, Prachetas, Arishtanemi and Prajapati Bahula. In addition to these, there are many who are lords of *prajas*. Kushochayas and Valakhilyas originated as supreme *rishis*. They possessed the speed of thought and could go anywhere. They enjoyed every object of pleasure. There were others who were born from the *bhasma* and they are revered by large numbers of *brahmarshis*. There were categories of sages known as Vaikhanasas and they were devoted to austerities and learning. The two Ashvins, Nasatya and Dasra, revered for their beauty, were born.[917] It is known that Riksharajas were born from the movements of his eyes. Other Prajapatis were born from his ears. *Rishis* were born from the pores of his body-hair. Others originated from sweat and dirt

[914] Derived from *vasu* (wealth). Earlier, Vasuman has been described as Vasishtha's son.

[915] This means *rishis*.

[916] Respectively meaning immortals, those who are not manifest and the radiant ones. These are clearly classes of ancestors.

[917] The text says Nasta and Dvava. We have amended it. As stated in the text, this can be translated as those who originated from the nasal discharge.

on the body. *Ayanas*, *ritus*, *masas* and *arddha-masas* were created from the joints of his eyelashes. The years were his day and night. Luminous bodies were his terrible bile. Rudras emerged from his red blood. Gold is also said to have emerged from his blood. All this is said to be *taijasa*. *Pashus* are said to have emerged from the smoke. Rudras and Adityas emerged from the flames. *Devas* and humans emerged from the flames in the burning coal.'

'Brahma, the preceptor of the Gods, was praised by the Gods. They addressed him in these words. "You are the original cause of the worlds. You are Brahma, originating from the *brahman*. You are the one who grants every object of desire. All these lords of *prajas* will give birth to *prajas*. All of them are Prajapatis. All of them will perform austerities. Through your favours, the worlds will be sustained through their rites. They will extend your lineage and will eternally enhance your energy. All of them will become learned in the *Vedas* and will be lords of speech. Born from Prajapati, all of them will nurture the *Vedas* and *mantras*. Let them seek refuge in the truth of the *brahman*, the supreme austerity on earth. O lord! They, and all of us, have originated from you. O Brahma! The *brahmanas*, the worlds with their mobile and immobile entities, *devas* and Marichi and the other *rishis* are your offspring. We desire offspring. The immensely fortunate *devas* and *rishis* originated from the sacrifice. They originated from your lineage and are proud of the time and the place. They will establish the *prajas* in your form. These *dvijas* will establish the beginning and the end of the *yugas*." Reflecting on this a lot, the preceptor of the worlds replied. "There is no doubt that I have created them after thinking about it. You have been born in my lineage and so have the *maharshis*."'

'Among them, I will first describe the lineage of the great-souled Bhrigu, in the due order and in detail. He was the first Prajapati. Bhrigu had two unmatched wives. They were auspicious and were born in excellent lineages. The first was Hiranyakashipu's daughter, famous under the name of Divya. The other was Poulami, Puloma's daughter, the possessor of an excellent complexion. Through Divya, Bhrigu had a son who was supreme among those who know about the *brahman*. He was Shukra, supreme among wise ones and the preceptor of *devas* and *asuras*. He is a planet. He is always known as Ushanas and is also named Kavya. Through their mental powers, the ancestors known as Somapas had an illustrious daughter. She was named Gou and she was Shukra's wife, giving birth to four sons. They were Tvashta, Varatri, Shanda and Marka. Their energy was like that of the sun and their powers were thought to be equal to Brahma's. Varatri's sons were Rajata, Prithu, Rashmi and the learned Brihamgira. They were devoted to the *brahman* and performed sacrifices for *daityas*. They wished to destroy the *dharma* of sacrifices. Full of rage, they started to perform sacrifices.[918] When Indra saw that *dharma* was being destroyed, he went and spoke to Manu. "I desire to only make them perform sacrifices sanctioned by you." Hearing Indra's words, they left the spot. When they disappeared, Indra revived the consciousness of Manu's wife and freed her from the evil planet. He pursued them. Therefore, those sages made efforts to destroy Indra. Seeing that those wicked ones had returned, Indra laughed. Enraged, he burnt them down on the southern part of the sacrificial altar. Accompanied by wild dogs and jackals, they resisted him. Their heads were shattered and fell, date palms originating from these. In this way, in ancient times, Indra killed the sons of Varatri. Through Jayanti, Devayani was born as Shukra's daughter. Tvashta had a great son, Trishira Vishvarupa. This immensely illustrious one was born as the son of Yashodhara, Virochana's daughter. Vishvakarma is described as Vishvarupa's younger brother. Bhrigu had twelve sons; the *deva*s known as Bhrigus. They were Bhuvana, Bhavana, Antya, Antyayana, Kratu, Shuchi, Svamurdha, Vyaja, Vasuda, Prabhava and Avyaya. The twelfth one is described as Adhipati. These are the twelve *deva*s described as Bhrigu and they performed sacrifices. Divya gave birth to a daughter. She was the lord Kavya's younger sister. Poulami gave birth to a self-controlled *dvija* who was devoted to the *brahman*. While he was still inside the womb, in the eighth month, a cruel *rakshasa* devoured him. Since he was deprived in this way, he became Chyavana. However, since he

[918] There were different types of sacrifices. They wished to destroy *ijya*s, sacrifices performed to *deva*s.

retained consciousness, he was also Prachetana.[919] As a result of his
rage, Prachetana Chyavana burnt down these man-eaters. Through
Sukanya, this Bhargava[920] had two sons. They were Apravana and
Dadhicha, revered by the virtuous. Through Sarasvati, Dadhicha
had Sarasvata as a son. The immensely fortunate Richi, Nahusha's
daughter, was Apravana's wife. An immensely illustrious *rishi* was
born by shattering her thigh.[921] This was Ourva and his son was
Richika, who blazed like the fire in his energy. Through Satyavati,
Richika had Jamadagni as a son. In those earlier times, the Roudra
and Vaishnava *charu* prepared by Bhrigu's descendant was mixed
up.[922] When he was born, Jamadagni digested the Vaishnava fire
and came to be known as Jamadagni. Through Renuka, Jamadagni
had a son who was Shakra's equal in valour. This was the infinitely
energetic Rama, with both *brahmana* and *kshatriya* traits. Ourva's
son had one hundred sons and Jamadagni was the foremost.[923] Their
sons were thousands of Bhargavas. They mutually married other
rishi lineages and therefore, there are said to have been external

---

[919] *Chyavana* means being deprived, deprivation. *Chetana* means
consciousness.

[920] Meaning Chyavana.

[921] *Uru* means thigh and the name Ourva is derived from this. Here,
Ourva is described as the son of Apravana and Richi. Elsewhere (like the
Mahabharata), Ourva is described as the son of Chyavana and his wife
Arushi. The thigh was shattered when the Haihayas tried to execute the
pregnant Arushi.

[922] *Charu* is an oblation of rice, barley and pulses, cooked in butter and
milk. Roudra means a terrible *charu*, befitting a *kshatriya* and Satyavati
was the daughter of King Gadhi. Vaishnava *charu* means a peaceful *charu*,
befitting a *brahmana* and Richika was one. So that Satyavati and her
mother might both have sons, Richika prepared some *charu* and gave it
to her, one part meant for her, and one part meant for her mother. These
two were mixed up. Satyavati's mother gave birth to a *kshatriya* son with
brahmana traits. This was Vishvamitra. Satyavati would have given birth
to a *brahmana* son with *kshatriya* traits. Through Richika's favours,
this was passed down a generation and characterized Jamadagni's son,
Parashurama. Jamadagni's wife was Renuka. Here, the name Jamadagni is
derived from *janma* (birth) and Agni.

[923] The text says that Ourva's son was Jamadagni. We have changed it.

Bhargavas.[924] There were Vatsas, Vidhas, Arshtishenas, Yaskas, Vainyas, Shounakas and Mitreyus as the seventh. These families are also known as Bhargavas.'

'Now hear about the lineage of Angiras, Agni's intelligent son. Bharadvajas and Goutamas were born in this lineage. Among *devas* from the Angiras lineage, the greatly energetic Tvishimantas were foremost. Atharvan had three wives—Maricha's daughter, Surupa; Kardama's daughter, Svarat; and Manu's daughter, Pathya. Atharvan's descendants were born in this way, and they extended the lineage. Those who were born were great in their austerities and cleansed their *atman*s. Surupa's son was Brihaspati and Svarat gave birth to Goutama, Ayasya, Vamadeva, Utathya and Ushiti. Pathya's son was Dhrishni. Through mental powers, Samvarta was born as Dhrishni's son. Asasya's son was Kitava and Utathya's son was Sharadvat. Ushiti's son was Dirghatama and Vamadeva's son was Brihaduktha. Dhrishni's son was Sudhanva and Sudhanva's son was Rishabha. Rathakaras are remembered as *deva*s and they are famous as Ribhus.[925] Brihaspati's son was the famous and immensely illustrious Bharadvaja. Those younger to Brihaspati are described as Angirasas and *deva*s. Through Surupa's womb, Angiras had the sons—Adhari, Ayus, Danus, Daksha, Dama, Prana, Havishya, Havishnu, Rita and Satya. These were the ten. It should be known that there are fifteen lineages that are described as Angirasas—Ayasyas, Utathyas, Vamadevas, Ushitis, Bharadvajas, Samkritis, Gargas, Kanva-Rathitaras, Mudgalas, Vishnuvriddhas, Haritas, Kapis, Ruksha-Bharadvajas, Arshabhas and Kitavas. Through the lineages of other *rishi*s, there are those described as external Angirasas.'

'I will describe the different lineages of Marichi and there were excellent men in them. All mobile and immobile entities in the universe were born in this lineage. Inside water, desiring offspring, Marichi started to meditate. "Let me have a powerful son who possesses all the qualities and has offspring." The lord engaged in

[924] We have expanded the text, so as to make the meaning clear. External Bhargavas are presumably those born through such marriages.

[925] Rathakaras were carpenters and makers of chariots. They were descended from Sudhanva.

austerities and *yoga*. The lord struck the waters in this way by his
atman, and this gave birth to an unmatched son, named Arishtanemi.
He was a Prajapati. Since Marichi was engaged in austerities when
he produced this son, the son also performed austerities inside
water. For the sake of a son, he stationed himself within water and
meditated on virtuous speech. In this unmatched way, he remained
there for seven thousand years. This son was Kashyapa, who
was as learned as the sun and Brahma's equal in energy. In every
manvantara, he is born as a part of Brahma's portion. In connection
with Daksha's daughter, the lord became angry. At the time, he
drank *kashya, kashya* being a kind of liquor. He laughed harshly and
it is known that harshness in thoughts and deeds is said to be *kashya.*
*Brahmana*s say that *kashya* is liquor. Because he drank *kashya,* he
became Kashyapa. When words are used like a whip, those words
are said to be cruel. Since he was enraged when he was cursed by
Daksha, he became Kashyapa.[926] This is the reason he is referred to
as Kashyapa. Instructed by Parameshthi Brahma, Daksha, the son
of the Prachetas, bestowed his daughters on him. All of them were
mothers of the worlds and all of them spoke about the *brahman*. On
the occasion of Varuna's sacrifice, this is the sacred account of the
origin of *rishi*s. If a person knows this, he is auspicious and pure. He
obtains a long lifespan and eternal happiness. If a person hears this,
or nurtures it, he is freed from all sins.'

Chapter 40-1(40) (Prajapati's lineage)

S uta said, 'The creation of *praja*s during the sixth *manvantara*
of Chakshusha was withdrawn. Daksha was instructed by
Svayambhu himself to create *praja*s. He created all entities, mobile

---

[926] Kashyapa wanted to marry Daksha's daughters and became angry
when Daksha refused. Fanciful derivations are given of the name Kashyapa,
using puns. He drank *kashya*, a type of liquor. He used his words like
a whip (*kasha*). He harassed him (*karshita*) with words. Consequently,
Daksha cursed Kashyapa, but agreed, when Brahma asked him to do so.

and immobile. Initially, the lord created beings through his powers of the mind—*rishi*s, *deva*s, *gandharva*s, humans, *uraga*s, *rakshasa*s, *yaksha*s, *bhuta*s, *pishacha*s, birds, *pashu*s and *mriga*s. However, the *praja*s created through mental powers did not flourish. They were cursed by the intelligent Bhagavan Mahadeva. Therefore, he wished to create many kinds of *praja*s through physical intercourse. He married Asikni, the daughter of Virana Prajapati. She was an extremely great daughter, full of austerities. She was the one who nurtured the worlds. She held up everything in the universe— mobile and immobile. In this connection, two *shloka*s are chanted about Daksha, the son of the Prachetas. "In ancient times, Daksha married Asikni, Virana's daughter. But because of his insolence, to show him compassion, a million snakes followed Daksha. Whether the lord hid in rivers or mountains, they followed him. On seeing this, the *rishi*s said—the first Daksha will establish *praja*s, but the second Daksha will become a Prajapati." After some time passed, the one million snakes went away. Daksha, the son of the Prachetas, married Asikni, Virana's daughter. Virana's daughter gave birth to one thousand infinitely energetic sons. When the lord Daksha, the son of the Prachetas, saw that Asikni had given birth to these extremely energetic ones, he desired that *praja*s should flourish. However, *devarshi* Narada, Brahma's son, addressed them in disagreeable words. Those words led to their destruction. But in the process, he brought a curse on himself.[927] Parameshthi's son was born as Kashyapa's son. Born as Kashyapa's son through his mental powers, he was cursed again by Daksha. Therefore, he was born as Kashyapa's son, born through mental powers, a second time. This Narada had earlier been born as Parameshthi's son. Those descendants of trees[928] were famous as Haryashvas. They were

---

[927] These sons were the Haryashavas. When the Haryashvas were about to procreate, Narada told them that they should first ascertain whether there was enough space on earth to hold offspring. The Haryashvas went off to explore the earth and never returned. In that sense, they were destroyed. Narada was Parameshthi's (Brahma's) son, but he was reborn as Kashyapa's son. Narada did the same with a second round of Daksha's sons, the Shabalashvas, and was cursed again.

[928] Since Daksha was born through Marisha.

destroyed in the pursuit of *dharma*. There is no doubt that all this
was because of destiny. Enraged, the lord Daksha got ready to curse
him. Placing the *brahmarshi*s in front, Parmeshthi entreated him.
At this, Daksha arrived at an agreement with Parameshthi. "Let
Narada become your son,[929] through my daughter." Thereafter,
Daksha bestowed his beloved daughter on Parameshthi. Thus,
fearing the curse, *rishi* Narada was born again.'

Shamshapayana asked, 'Earlier, how were Prajapati's sons
destroyed by the divine *rishi*, Narada? I wish to hear the truth
about this.'

Suta replied, 'Daksha's sons, the Haryashvas, desired that
*praja*s should flourish. Narada approached those immensely valiant
ones and spoke to them. "You are behaving in a foolish way. You
do not know the space available for *praja*s on the surface of the
earth, inside, above or below. How can you create *praja*s?" Hearing
his words, they left in all the directions. Like rivers headed towards
the ocean, they have still not returned. When they were destroyed,
through Virana's daughter, the lord Daksha, son of the Prachetas,
again had one thousand sons. These sons, the Shabalashvas, again
desired that *praja*s should flourish. Narada made them hear the
words he had uttered earlier. All of them spoke to each other,
"What the *rishi* has himself told us is right. There is no doubt that
we should follow the footsteps of our brothers. Having ascertained
the dimensions of the earth, we will happily create *praja*s. That
illumination will set our minds at rest. We have been instructed
properly." Following that path, they too left in all the directions.
Desiring to determine the dimensions of the earth, they have not
returned, even today. Since then, if a brother is intent on searching
out his brother and leaves on this pursuit, he is swiftly destroyed.
A person who knows this should not undertake such a task. When
the Shabalashvas were destroyed, the lord Daksha became angry
and told Narada, "You will be destroyed and will have to reside
in a womb." When they were destroyed, the great-souled Daksha
had sixty famous daughters through Virana's daughter. Kashyapa,
Dharma, Soma, Bhagavan[930] and other *maharshi*s accepted these

[929] In the form of Kashyapa.
[930] Presumably meaning Shiva.

daughters as wives. If a person knows the entire truth about
Daksha's creation, he is blessed and obtains a long lifespan, fame
and offspring.'

Chapter 41-1(41) (Svayambhu's three *gunas*)

The *rishi*s said, 'At the time of Vaivasvata *manvantara*, please
tell us in detail about the origins of all the *deva*s, *danava*s
and *daitya*s.'

Suta replied, 'I will tell you about Dharma's lineage too. Listen.
Daksha, the son of Prachetas, bestowed ten of his daughters as
wives on Dharma—Arundhati, Vasu, Jamaa, Lambaa, Bhanu,
Marutvati, Samkalpaa, Muhurtaa, Sadhyaa and Vishvaa. Through
Sadhyaa, Dharma had the twelve Sadhyas as his sons. Those who
know about *deva*s say that these *deva*s are superior to all other
*deva*s. When Brahma wished to create *praja*s, he created these *deva*s
from his mouth. In all the *manvantara*s, they are described as those
with *mantra*s in their bodies. The names of *yajna*s for them are
Darsha, Pournamasi, Brihat, Rathantara, Vitti, Vivitti, Akuti, Kuti,
Vijnata, Vijnatri and Manoyajna.[931] There are the names of their
famous *yajna*s. As a result of Brahma's curse, they were again born
in Svayambhuva *manvanatra* as Jitas, in Svarochisha *manvantara* as
Tushitas, in Uttama *manvantara* as Satyas, in Tamasa *manvantara*
as Haris and in Raivata *manvantara* as Vaikunthas. In Chakshusa
manvantara, these Gods were easily born under the name of Sadhyas.
These immensely fortunate ones were Dharma's sons. These twelve
immortals were the Sadhyas. Earlier, they were born during
the *manvantara* of Chakshusha Manu. In the past Svarochisha
manvantara, they were the immensely energetic *deva*s, named
Tushitas. When there was a little bit of Chakshusha *manvantara* left,
these *deva*s, who had been Tushitas, spoke to each other. "We will
enter the immensely fortunate Sadhyaa. In the future *manvantara*,
this will be best for us." At the time of Chakshusha *manvantara*, they

[931] Since there are twelve Sadhyas, there should have been twelve
*yajna*s.

spoke to each other in this way. Thus, they were again born as the
sons of Dharma, Svayambhu's sons. Nara and Narayana were also
born, yet again. They had earlier been Vipashchit and Indra and had
also been Satya and Hari. In the former Svarochisha *manvantara*,
they had been the sons of the Tushitas. When the Tushitas became
Sadhyas, the names mentioned are Mana, Anumanta, Prana, Nara,
the valiant Apana, Viti, Naya, Haya, Hamsa, Narayana, Vibhu and
Prabhu. The twelve Sadhyas were born in this way. This was the
case in the former Svayambhuva *manvantara* and it happened again
at the time of Svarochisha *manvantara*. Listen to the subsequent
names of the Tushitas. They were Prana, Apana, Udana, Samana,
Vyana, Chakshu, Srotra, Rasa, Ghrana, Sparsha, Buddhi and
Manas. These are described as the former names of the Tushitas.'

'The Vasus were the sons of Vasu, and they are described
as being the younger brothers of the Sadhyas. They were Dhara,
Dhruva, Soma, Ayus, Anala,[932] Anila, Pratyusha and Prabhasa.
These are described as the eight Vasus. Dhara's sons were Dravina,
Hutahavya and Rajas. O son! Dhurva's son was Kala, who destroys
the worlds. The five sons of Soma[933] were the illustrious Varcha,
Budha, Grahabodhana, Dharormi and Kalila. The sons of Ayus were
Vaitandya, Shama, Shanta, Skanda and Sanatkumara, born with one
quarter of his energy. Through Svaha, Agni's son was Kumara, born
amidst a circle of brilliance. He had the younger brothers Shakha,
Vishakha and Naigameya. Anila's wife was Shivaa. Through her,
Anila had two sons—Manojava and Avijnatagati. Pratyusha's son
is known to be the *rishi* named Devala. Devala had two sons, who
were forgiving and learned. Brahma's sister was Bhuvana, who
spoke about the *brahman*. She achieved *siddhi* through *yoga*. It was
impossible for her to be attached to anything in the universe, and
she roamed around. She was the wife of Prabhasa, the eighth Vasu.
The lord and master of Prajapatis, Vishvakarma, was her son.'

'Vishvaa gave birth to ten famous Vishvadevas. They were Kratu,
Daksha, Shrava, Satya, Kala, Kama, Muni, Pururava, Mardravasa
and Rochamana as the tenth. These Gods, the auspicious sons of

---

[932] Agni.
[933] The text uses the word 'Chandra'.

Dharma, were born through Vishvaa. The Marutvantas are said
to have been born from Marutvati and the Bhanus from Bhanu.
The Muhurtas were born from Muhurtaa and Lambaa gave birth
to Ghosha. Samkalpaa gave birth to the learned Samkalpa. The
nine Vithis, with three resorting to the same path, were born from
Jamaa.[934] Every material object on earth was born from Arundhati.
This is described as the eternal creation of the learned Dharma.'

'O ones excellent in vows! I will describe the names of the *tithis*,
along with each *muhurta*. Listen as I speak. The division between
night and day is caused by the *nakshatras*. The *muhurtas* and all the
nakshatras divide night and day. In the space of a day and night,
there are said to be more than eighty-six *kalaas*.[935] Depending on
the specific movement of the sun, these always exist in every *ritu*.
Those who wish to determine *parvas*, use their knowledge of these
movements. When there is nothing specific about the time, it is
known that measurements are made on the basis of the sun. The
muhurtas till midday are Roudra, Sarpa, Maitra, Pitrya, Vasava,
Apya, Vaishadeva and Brahma. The *muhurtas* for the rest of the
day are Prajapatya, Aindra, Indragni, Nirriti, Varuna, Aryamna
and Bhaga. These are *muhurtas* of the day and are determined by
the sun. Their specific durations can be ascertained through the
shadow cast by a stake. In the due order, the fifteen *muhurtas* of
the night are said to be Ajaikapada, Ahirbudhnya, Pusha, the two
Ashvins, Yama, Agneya, the one known as Prajapatya, Soumya,
Aditya, Barhaspatya, Vaishnava, Savitra, Tvashtra and Vayavya.
This is the collection. The rising and setting of the moon can be
ascertained from the start of *nadikas*. The *muhurtas* are described as
the divinities of time. It is determined that all the planets should have
three positions. In the due order, these are known to be the southern,
the northern and in the middle. In truth, it has been determined
that the place known as Jaradgava is in the middle, Airavata is in

---

[934] *Vithi* is a division of the ecliptic, each *vithi* consisting of three
*nakshatra*s.

[935] As a measure of time, *kalaa* is variously defined. Here, one
muhurta is probably equal to three *kalaa*s, accounting for ninety *kalaa*s
in a day and night.

the north and Vaishvanara is in the south.[936] Ashvini, Krittika and Yamya[937] are known as Nagavithi. The word Gajavithi is used for Brahma, Soumya and Ardra.[938] It is held that Airavativithi consists of Pushya, Ashlesha and Aditya.[939] These three *vithi*s are said to constitute the northern path. Arshabhivithi is described as consisting of Purva Phalguni, Uttara Phalguni and Magha. The word Govithi is used for Hasta, Chitra and Svati. It is held that Jaradgavivithi consists of Jyeshtha, Vishakha and Anuradha. These three *vithi*s are said to constitute the middle path. The expression Ajavithi is used for Mula, Purvashadha and Uttarashadha. Margivithi consists of Shravana, Dhanishtha and Shatabhisha. Vaishvanarivithi consists of Purvabhadrapada, Uttarabhadrapada and Revati. These three *vithi*s are described as the southern path. Daksha bestowed twenty-eight[940] daughters on Soma. In *jyotisha*, all of them are described under the names of *nakshatra*s. Their children were infinite in radiance and energy.'

'Kashyapa accepted fourteen other immensely fortunate daughters as his wives. All of them were mothers of the worlds. They were Aditi, Diti, Danu, Kashthaa, Arishtaa, Anayu, Khashaa, Surabhi, Vinataa, Tamraa, Muni, Krodhavashaa and Kadru, the mother of *naga*s.[941] Hear about their children. O son! In Svayambhuva *manvantara*, there were twelve excellent Gods. They had the name of Vaikunthas and in Chakshusha *manvantara*, they were Sadhyas. Thereafter, Vaivasvata *manvantara* presented itself. When Aditi worshipped them, they spoke to each other. "Let us enter this immensely fortunate Aditi. In the course of this Vaivasvata *manvantara*, we will use *yoga* and half of our energy. We will become her sons. That will be best for us." All of them said

---

[936] Jaradgava, Airavata and Vaishvanara are the names of three of the nine *vithi*s.

[937] Bharani.

[938] Brahma means Rohini and Soumya means Mrigashira.

[939] Aditya means Punarvasu.

[940] Typically described as twenty-seven. The twenty-eigth *nakshatra*, Abhijit, is not a daughter.

[941] There are only thirteen names. The names vary across texts. Among obvious ones missing are Surasaa, Iraa, Vishvaa and Simhikaa.

this in the course of the current *manvantara*. Through Kashyapa, Marichi's son, the twelve Adityas were born again. In Vaivasvata *manvantara*, Shatakratu and Vishnu were born again as Nara and Narayana. Just as the sun rises and sets in this world, it is said that *deva*s also have origin and destruction. It is evident that they seek refuge in objects of the senses, like sound. They are attached to the eight *siddhi*s, starting with *anima*. Therefore, Gods are born again. It is said that their attachment to material objects is the reason for their being reborn. As a result of Brahma's curse, the ones known as Jayas were born as Jitas in Svayambhuva *manvantara*, as Tushitas in Svarochisha, again as Satyas in Uttama, as Haris in Tamasa, as Vaikunthas in Arishtava[942] and as Sadhyas in Chakshusha. These *deva*s were born again as Adityas in the seventh *manvantara*. They are described as Dhatri, Aryama, Mitra, Varuna, Amsha, Bhaga, Indra, Vivasvat, Pushan, Parjanya as the tenth, Tvashta and Vishnu. Vishnu was the youngest, but not the worst. These twelve Adityas were sons of the lord Kashyapa. Through Surabhi, Kashyapa had the eleven Rudras as his sons. This is because of Mahadeva's favours. The virtuous lady cleansed herself through austerities. They were Angaraka, Sarpa, Nirriti, Sadasatpati, Ajaikapada, Ahirbudhnya, the two kinds of Jvara,[943] Bhuvana, Ishvara, Mrityu and the famous Kapali. These *deva*s, the eleven Rudras, are the lords of the three worlds. As a result of her fierce and great austerities, Surabhi gave birth to them. In addition, two *devi*s were born to Surabhi as daughters. These were the extremely fortunate Rohini and the illustrious Gandharvi. Rohini gave birth to four daughters who were famous in the worlds. They were Surupa, Hamsakali, Bhadra and Kamadugdha. Kamadugdha gave birth to cows. Surupa had two sons. Hamsakali gave birth to buffaloes and Bhadra to the sheep species. Immensely fortunate and famous horses were born as Gandharvi's sons. These were Ucchaihshrava and others. They could travel through the sky and possessed the speed of thought. They were white, red, tawny, spotted,[944] green and white. It is said

---

[942] That is, Raivata.
[943] Mental and physical. But Jvara is counted as one in the list.
[944] Alternatively, dark grey.

that these horses, sons of Gandharvi, were mounts for *deva*s. Surabhi
next gave birth to a handsome buffalo that had the complexion of
the moon. He was born from a reservoir of *amrita*, had a hump,
was radiant and wore garlands. With Surabhi's permission, he was
given to Maheshvara, as a standard. The sons of Kashyapa, Rudras
and Adityas, have thus been described."

"Sadhyas, Vishvadevas and Vasus are said to be the sons of
Dharma. When kindling is offered, a single fire becomes many.
In that way, though the grandfather is one, he led to many forms.
Brahma, Antaka and Purusha are the same.[945] Svayambhu is one,
but is described as having assumed three bodies. These three are
described as Brahmi, Pourushi and the one known as Kala. When his
body is full of *rajas*, he creates *prajas*. It is held that the one known
as Kala is the one who destroys *prajas*. Pourushi, the body full of
sattva, is described as the preserver. Full of *rajas*, Brahma became
Kashyapa, Marichi's son. The one that is full of *tamas* is Antaka
and is born as Vishnu's portion.[946] It is said that Svayambhu's three
bodies are present in the three worlds. To accomplish different
objectives, he is established in these different aspects. He creates
prajas, shows favours to them, and destroys them. In this way,
Svayambhu is described as possessing three bodies—Prajapati,
Rudra and Vishnu. In the ancient *dharmashastras*, these three
bodies are described as *deva*s. There are those who are devoted
to *samkhya* and *yoga*. They possess power and nobility of birth.
They are sages who possess insight about the truth. With their
insight, they think of them as distinct. They are identical but are
also distinct. That is the reason different subjects think of them
differently. One says, "This is the supreme one." Another, with a
different view, says, "He is not this." Some say that Brahma is the
cause. Others say that it is Prajapati. Some say that Bhava is the
supreme truth. Others say that it is Vishnu. Attached to the pride
of their *jnana*, they are insensible. Considering the strength, time,
place, effects, tasks, causes and objectives, many different entities
are described as *deva*s. If a person praises one of them, he praises

---

[945] Identified here with Brahma, Shiva and Vishnu.
[946] This is a clear error/typo and should read Shiva.

them all. If a person abuses one of them, he abuses them all. A person who knows about *deva*s should not show hatred towards any. No one is capable of knowing about Ishvaras, who are established in their powers. Though one, he assumes three forms and confounds *praja*s. That is the reason people try to ascertain the difference between the three. Though they are inquisitive, their senses are attached, tainted and confused. They say, "This is the supreme one." Proud, another with different insight, says, "This is not he." They are just like *yatudhana*s and *pishacha*s, there being no difference. He is himself one, but is established in different forms. This is because of the *guna*s and these bodies confuse *praja*s. If a person worships anyone, he worships all three. Therefore, there is no difference between these three established *deva*s. Who is capable of knowing about one or different, numbers or lack of enumeration, coming and going or a limited number or numerous ones? He is the one who always creates, shows favours and devours. When there is separation from the *guna*s, he is conceived of as one. *Dvija*s speak of him in many ways— Rudra, Brahma, Indra, guardians of the world, *rishi*s, Manus and Narayana. But the *deva* is one. Prajapati, Rudra and Vishnu are his bodies. From one *manvantara* to another *manvantara*, these three bodies repeatedly cycle. There are other *kshetrajna*s who are born because of the lord's favours. They are born, equal to him in energy, fame, intelligence, learning and strength. Understand them. As a result of *rajas*, Kashyapa, Marichi's son, was born from Brahma's portion. As a result of *tamas*, Kala was born as his portion and is described as Rudra. As a result of *sattva*, Vishnu was born as his portion and is identified with a sacrifice. O *dvija*s! For the purpose of creation, Brahma's three bodies repeatedly cycle in *manvantara*s and in different periods of time. In all the *manvantara*s, *praja*s, mobile and immobile, are born once at the beginning of the *yuga* and remain until it is time for them to be withdrawn. When every *kalpa* ends, Rudra withdraws *praja*s. He becomes Kala, identified with a *yuga*. Rudra repeatedly withdraws again. When the end of the *kalpa* arrives, the sun has seven *samvartaka* rays. With these, the sun burns down the three worlds.'

'Vishnu always shows favours to *praja*s and protects them. Depending on the situation, he creates causes so that this can be done. At the beginning of Svayambhuva *manvantara*, he is known to have been born as Brahma's portion, from his Pourushi body that is said to consist of an excess of *sattva*. This lord and divinity were born first, through the mental powers of Akuti. When Svarochisha *manvantara* arrived, this *deva* was born again. Along with the other Tushitas, he was born as Ajita, the son of Tushitaa. In Uttama *manvantara*, the lord was born again, as Ajita, along with the excellent Gods known as Satyas, the sons of Satyaa. In that way, during Tamasa *manvantara*, the *deva* was born as Hari, along with the other Haris who were the sons of Harini. In Raivata *manvantara*,[947] the *deva* Hari was born again. He was named Vaikuntha and was born along with the others who were devoid of *rajas*. Vishnu was born as the son of Aditi and Kashyapa, Marichi's son. Vishnu Trivikrama conquered the three worlds in his three strides.[948] The lord returned these to Indra and the other *deva*s. Thus, in the past seven *manvantara*s, these bodies have been born seven times. In the past *manvantara*s, *praja*s were protected by them. This entire universe is created from him and dissolves into him again. All the immortals and lords of heaven are born as his portions and their energy, intelligence, learning and strength are enhanced. Anything possessing power, spirit, beauty and glory originates as a portion of Vishnu's energy. Understand this. Some men desire to believe that Vishnu's portion alone is born. One debates against another and cites examples to support his view. There is no difference between the three residents of heaven. Using their *yoga* and *maya*, portions of these Ishvaras are born and cause confusion. In describing their manifestations, there is nothing appropriate or inappropriate.[949] They are spoken of as anterior to *bhutadi*. Others say that they are in the midst of the elements. There are others who say that the three are attached to the elements. They test and show favours. They

---

[947] We have corrected the typo of Vaivasvata *manvantara*.

[948] In his *vamana* (dwarf) *avatara*.

[949] We have taken liberties in translating these *shloka*s, which aren't very clear.

themselves chastise the deceitful. They existed before me and their powers are supreme. Those who indicate the truth also say this about their rights. They are *devas*, born from *devas*, and make everything function. Their *karma* is great. These Ishvaras of the universe are the ones who are the real doers. Those who know about the *shruti* texts describe these four reasons.[950] The foolish do not know about the divisions between *devas*. In this connection, a *shloka* is cited about Yogeshvaras.[951] "Having obtained the strength of *yoga*, he wanders around everywhere. Having obtained material objects, he subsequently undertakes austerities. Like the sun withdraws the luminous bodies, he withdraws himself."'

Chapter 42-1(42) (Curse on Jayas)

Suta said, 'Desiring to create *praja*s, Brahma created *deva*s known as Jayas from his mouth. In all the *manvantara*s, they are described as possessing *mantra*s in their bodies. The twelve *yajna*s are Darsha, Pournamasi, Brihat, Saman, Rathantara, Chiti, Suchiti, Akuti, Kuti, Vijnata, Vijnatri and Manoyajna.[952] "Accept wives and perform *agnihotra* sacrifices." Having said this, the lord Brahma vanished from the spot. However, they didn't pay any heed to Parameshthi's words. But they did notice taints in the *karma* they followed. Therefore, they cast aside *karma* and the desire resulting from *karma*. They saw that the fruits of *karma* were subject to great decay and resorted to *yama*. Thus, they condemned existence and offspring and developed a sense of lack of ownership. Witnessing the taints, they desired to be freed from the cycle of birth. They cast aside *dharma*, *artha* and *kama*. Having flung those aside, they firmly established themselves in

---

[950] The number four hangs loose and may refer to the traits of power, omniscience, omnipresence and assuming *avatara*s. But this is speculative.

[951] Lords of *yoga*.

[952] In Chapter 41-1(41), the names were given slightly differently and only eleven were listed there.

supreme *jnana*. Getting to know about their intentions, Brahma became angry. Brahma spoke to the Gods who no longer exhibited enterprise. "I created you for the sake of *prajas*. There is no other reason for you to exist. I told you earlier that you should perform sacrifices and have offspring. However, you disregarded my words and have established yourselves in non-attachment. You hated your own births and did not welcome offspring. Desiring immortality, you did not practice *karma*. Therefore, you will have to take birth in this world seven times."[953] When they were cursed in this way by Brahma, the Jayas sought to placate him. "O lord! O great divinity! This has happened because of lack of *jnana*. Please pardon us." When they prostrated themselves and entreated him, Brahma spoke to them again. "The world must be enjoyed. Who deserves to be independent? Everything has originated from me. How can I be crossed? This is true of the establishment of beings, auspicious or otherwise. It should be known that everything that exists in the world, auspicious or inauspicious, is pervaded by me. Who in the world can cross me? Everything desired by beings, everything they think of and everything that they do is known to me. Everything in the universe, mobile and immobile, has been shackled by me. Who hopes to sever the bond and is interested in doing that? Even an insolent person has to bear this burden. It cannot but be otherwise. Without initiating *karma*, how can one wish to easily obtain *moksha*?" He spoke in this way to the *deva*s known as Jayas, whose senses were full of *adhyatma*. Prajapati looked at them and decided that they should certainly be punished. He said, "O Gods! Without fixing yourselves on me, you performed renunciation, though I had created an extensive course of action for you. Nevertheless, you will be born with divine sentiments, so that you can be happy. O excellent Gods! Your birth will occur easily, as you wish. In seven *manvantara*s, you will become *siddha*s. Starting with Svayambhuva *manvantara* and ending with Vaivasvata *manvantara*, you will be Gods." Thus, in this connection, Brahma sang an ancient *shloka*. "Full of

[953] In different *manvantara*s, as Yamas, Tushitas, Satyas, Haris, Vaikunthas, Sadhyas and Adityas.

rajas, the lord constantly resides in the three kinds of learning,[954] offspring full of the *brahman*, *shraddha* ceremonies, austerities, sacrifices and prompt donations. Nothing else is praised." Having uttered this *shloka*, full of meaning, he told the *devas* known as Jayas, "When Vaivasvata *manvantara* is over, you will return to my presence." After this, the divinity and Ishvara, who does not fear anything, vanished. Full of the strength of *yoga*, he assumed the form originally conceived.'

'In this way, in his rage, he cursed the twelve Ajitas. Those Gods became Jayas in the course of the Svayambhuva creation.[955] In Svarochisha *manvantara*, those *devas* were born as Tushitas. In Uttama *manvantara*, they were born as the sons of Uttama Manu and Satyaa. Thus, during Uttama *manvantara*, *devas* were known as Satyas. Those twelve Tushitas were then born as the sons of Harini. Those *devas* were named Haris and obtained shares in sacrifices. When Arishtava *manvantara*[956] arrived, the *devas* known as Haris were born as the sons of Vikunthaa and became superior Gods. In the fifth *manvantara*, these *devas* were known as Vaikunthas. When Chakshusha *manvantara* arrived, the Vaikuntha *devas* were again born as Sadhyas. When Chakshusha *manvantara* decayed and Vaivasvata *manvantara* presented itself, portions of the Sadhyas were again born as the sons of Aditi and Kashyapa, Marichi's son. In the current *manvantara*, those Gods are the twelve Adityas. They were born in the course of Chakshusha *manvantara*. Cursed by Svayambhu, the twelve immortals were born as Sadhyas. If a mortal person constantly listens to this account of the Jayas and is full of faith towards the Jayas, he overcomes impediments. This is the conduct of the seven sets of *devas*, their births and signs. I have completed that narration. What do you wish to hear now?'

---

[954] The three *Vedas*.

[955] Jayas are the same as Yamas. There is a play on words. Ajitas are those who are not vanquished, while Jayas are those who are vanquished. As a result of the curse, the unvanquished were vanquished.

[956] The same as Raivata *manvantara*.

Chapter 43-1(43) (Origin of Maruts)

The *rishi*s said, 'Please tell us in detail about the creation and destruction of *daitya*s, *danava*s, *gandharva*s, *uraga*s, *rakshasa*s, *sarpa*s, *bhuta*s, *pishacha*s, Vasus, birds and creepers.'

Thus addressed, Suta replied to the excellent *rishi*s.

Suta answered, 'Diti gave birth to two extremely strong sons and a daughter. Those two sons of Kashyapa are described as the ancestors of everyone. When *soma* juice was being extracted on the day of *atiratra*, at the time of a horse sacrifice, Kashyapa sat down on a separate seat, known by the name of *hiranyakashipu*.[957] While he was seated thus, the infant emerged from Diti's womb and seated himself on that seat. As a result of this act, he is described as Hiranyakashipu.'

The *rishi*s said, 'O lord! Please tell us in detail about the birth and powers of the great-souled *daitya*, named Hiranyakashipu.'

Suta answered, 'Kashyapa performed a horse sacrifice in the sacred region of Pushkara. The place was adorned by *rishi*s, *deva*s and *gandharva*s. The horse was released in the proper way and the accounts were being recited in proper fashion. Five golden seats were prepared. Three of these were for priests from his lineage. The other two had bundles of *kusha* grass, spread on planks. Four of them were for the main *ritvija*s and a golden seat was prepared for the *hotri*. The newly born infant sat down on this and chanted the narration in the right order, as if he was *maharshi* Kashyapa. Seeing his growth in this fashion, the *rishi*s gave him a name. As a result of this deed, he is described as Hiranyakashipu. Hiranyaksha was his younger brother.[958] Simhika was his younger sister, a queen who married Viprachitti and was Rahu's mother.'

'The *daitya* Hiranyakashipu performed supreme austerities. He remained for one hundred thousand divine years without food, his head hanging downwards. When Brahma was pleased, the

---

[957] Meaning, a golden mat.
[958] They were twins. In some accounts, Hiranyaksha is described as older.

daitya asked for boons—all the immortals and all beings would be unable to slay him, he would defeat *deva*s through his *yoga,* and he would obtain the status of all the *deva*s. "Please ensure that I possess prosperity, strength and energy. *Danava*s, *asura*s, *deva*s and *charana*s should come under my subjugation and all of them should eat only after I have eaten. Nothing wet or dry should be able to kill me and I should not be killed during night or day." Addressed in this way, Brahma agreed to grant him the boons. Brahma said, "O Diti's son! O son! You have asked for an extremely great boon. Nevertheless, know that it shall be exactly that way." Granting what was wished for, he vanished from the spot. Since then, with his greatness, the *daitya* pervaded everything in the universe, mobile and immobile. The destroyer of enemies could assume many different forms. He assumed the form of the sun and the moon and scorched the sky. He assumed the form of Vayu and always blew on earth. He was the cowherd, the shepherd and the tiller. He was the one who knew everything in all the worlds and became the expounder of *mantra*s. He was the leader, the protector and the person who ensured protection. He was the one who consecrated himself for performing sacrifices and also the person who performed the sacrifice. He was all the *deva*s and Gods, the drinkers of *soma.* Hear more about this. Everyone bowed down before him. He was the only one for whom sacrifices were performed. In ancient times, *daitya*s chanted this *shloka* about Hiranyakashipu. "In whichever direction King Hiranyakashipu glanced, in that direction, *deva*s and *maharshi*s prostrated themselves before him." In those ancient times, his death came about through Vishnu Narasimha. The lord assumed the form of *nara.*[959] Since he was born in the form of *nara,* those who know about the *Veda*s sing of him as Narasimha. With his austerities, the lord arose from the shores of the ocean. The lord and divinity's resplendent body consisted of all the *deva*s. He was immensely strong and is famous under the name of Sudarshana. In a wrestling match with the use of arms, he angrily used his nails

---

[959] *Nara* means man. *Simha* means lion. Narasimha is half-man and half-lion.

to tear apart the immensely strong Indra among *daitya*s. The nails were neither wet, nor dry.'[960]

'Hiranyaksha had five valiant sons who were extremely strong. They were Shambara, Shakuni, Kalanabha, Mahanabha and the extremely brave Surasantapana.[961] *Deva*s found it impossible to assail Hiranyaksha's sons. Their sons and grandsons are described in the classifications of *daitya*s. Hundreds and thousands of them were killed in the course of the Tarakamaya battle.[962] Hiranyakashipu had four extremely strong sons. Prahlada[963] was the eldest among them and Anuhrada came next. There were also Samhrada and Hrada. Hear about Hrada's sons. Understand that Hrada had two sons, Sunda and Nisunda. These two were extremely brave and killed *brahmana*s. Muka was also Hrada's heir. Maricha was Sunda's son, born through Tadakaa. In Dandaka, he was killed by the powerful Raghava.[964] In the encounter with Kirata, Savyasachi killed Muka.[965] The Nivatakavachas were born in the lineage of *daitya* Samhrada. Having been born, they cleansed themselves through great austerities. They were enemies of *deva*s. There were four who were leaders of *daitya*s—Jambha, Shatadundubhi, Daksha and the *asura* Chanda. These were the sons of Bashkala.[966] Now hear about Kalanemi's sons.[967] They were Bramajit, Kratujit, Devantaka and Narantaka. These were Kalanemi's sons. Now hear about Shambhu's[968] offspring. Shambhu's sons are described as

---

[960] Hiranyakashipu was killed in the evening, when it was neither day, nor night.

[961] The text says Sutasantapana. We have changed it to Surasantapana, meaning the one who scorched the Gods.

[962] A battle that took place between *deva*s and *asura*s over the abduction of Tara, Brihaspati's wife.

[963] Prahlada is also written as Prahrada.

[964] Rama.

[965] Savyasachi is Arjuna and Shiva appeared in the form of a hunter (Kirata).

[966] Bashkala was Anuhrada's son. There was also a Bashkala who was Hiranyakashipu's minister. There was more than one Bashkala.

[967] There was more than one Kalanemi. This is likely to be the Kalanemi who was Virochana's son and Virochana was the son of Prahlada.

[968] Shambhu was Virochana's son. These conflict with the statement that Virochana only had one son.

Rajaja and Goma. Virochana had one son, the powerful Bali. Bali had one hundred sons and all of them were kings. Among these, there were four who were foremost. They were valiant and extremely strong. The powerful king, Bana, possessing one thousand arms, was the best among them. The others were Kumbhagarta, Daya and Bhoja. There were Kunchi and others too. Bali is said to have had two daughters—Shakuni and Putanaa. Bali's sons and grandsons numbered hundreds of thousands. These groups were known as Baleyas, famous for their manliness and valour. Through Lohini, Bana had Indradhanva as a son.'

'When Diti's sons were killed, she pleased Kashyapa. Properly worshipped, Kashyapa was pleased with her and asked her to choose a boon. She asked for a boon. She repeatedly asked the illustrious one for this boon. Pleased at being asked to choose a boon, Diti spoke. The Goddess joined her hands in salutation and spoke to her husband, Kashyapa, Marichi's son. "I will earn this through my long period of austerities. I desire a son who will kill Shakra. I will perform austerities. You should grant me the conception. You should grant me a son who is worthy of killing Indra." Hearing her words, the immensely energetic Kashyapa, Marichi's son, was extremely miserable. He replied, "O one rich in austerities! It shall be that way. But you must remain pure during your pregnancy. You will give birth to a son who will kill Shakra in a battle. But this will only happen if you remain pure for one thousand years. You will give birth to a son who will be like Manmatha. He will be the best in the three worlds." This is what the immensely energetic one said at the time. Embracing her, the illustrious *rishi* returned to his own residence. When her husband had left, the Goddess Diti was filled with great joy. She went to Kushaplavana[969] and tormented herself through extremely terrible austerities. The lord Shakra heard about the conversation between the two of them. He went to Kushaplavana and addressed Diti in these words. "I will tend to you. Please grant me permission. I will bring kindling, flowers and fruits." She replied, "O child! As you wish, tend to me. Be attentive

[969] A hermitage to the east of Vishala. Here, some verses are identical to those in Valmiki Ramayana.

towards all your tasks and do what is best for you." Hearing the beneficial words spoken by his mother,[970] Shakra was delighted. Though his inner thoughts were tainted, he tended to her. Through the entire period of her vow, Shakra tended to her. Firm in his vows, he brought fruits, flowers and kindling. When it was time to remove her exhaustion, he massaged her body. Through the entire period, Shakra tended to Diti. There was only a short while remained for the vow to be over. Pleased, the Goddess spoke to Shakra. "O best among Gods! I am pleased with you. O son! Only ten years are left. O fortunate one! When those are over, you will be able to see your brother. O son! It is for your sake that I will rear him as someone who wishes for victory. O son! He will conquer the three worlds and you will be able to enjoy them with him. O son! Do I not know that your mind is full of devotion towards me?" As Diti spoke in this way to Shakra, the sun reached the mid-point of the sky. Placing her head on her knees, the Goddess went to sleep. With her hair hanging over her feet, the Goddess slept.[971] Everything below the navel is described as impure. Realizing that she had become impure, he thought this was the opportunity.'

'He witnessed the cause, and the resolution arose in his mind. Having seen the taint in the Goddess, he decided he could kill the foetus. Hence, Vrisha[972] entered Diti through her genital organs. Indra entered and saw the immensely energetic foetus inside the womb. He was scared and shattered the embryo, his enemy, into seven parts. He shattered the foetus with his *vajra*, which possessed one thousand joints. It repeatedly trembled and wept in a loud and terrible voice. Shakra repeatedly addressed the embryo, "Do not cry! Do not cry!"[973] He split the embryo into seven parts. Using his *vajra*, Indra split each of these into seven parts again. Meanwhile, Diti woke up. Diti exclaimed, "Do not kill it. Do not kill it."

[970] Since Shakra was Aditi's son, the word 'mother' is used in a broad sense.

[971] This was a double transgression. She slept during the day and her hair touched her feet.

[972] Indra.

[973] '*Ma roda! Ma roda!*' That is how they came to be known as Maruts.

To show respect for his mother's words, the wielder of the *vajra* fell at her feet. Still holding the *vajra*, Shakra joined his hands in salutation and told Diti, "O goddess! You were impure. You slept with your head on your feet. I found the opportunity and reached the foetus, who would have killed me in a battle. I shattered it into many fragments. You should pardon me." When the embryo was rendered futile, Diti was extremely miserable. She entreated the invincible and thousand-eyed one in these words. "The embryo has been rendered futile because of a crime I committed. O lord of *deva*s! O son! O immensely strong one! This is not your fault. There is no sin attached to the killing of an enemy. O lord! You need not be scared. I wish that you should do something agreeable for me. Otherwise, how will it be best for the foetus? Let my sons have places in the firmament. Let my seven sons roam on the shoulders of the wind. Let the seven, who have become forty-nine, be famous as Maruts. Let the first shoulder be on earth and the second in the sun. Let it be known that the third will be in the moon and the fourth in the large number of luminous bodies. Let the fifth be in the planets and the sixth in the circle of *saptarshi*s. Let the seventh be in Dhruva. These will be the seven shoulders of the wind. From time to time, my sons will roam around in these places. My sons will be lords of shoulders of the wind and roam around. The first shoulder of *avaha* will be on earth and will extend up to the clouds. The first category of my sons will roam around in this way. The second, *pravaha*, will extend from the clouds, up to the sun. It should be known that this second category will travel on the shoulders of the wind there. The third will be described as *udvaha* and will extend above the sun, to the point below the moon. This third category of my sons will travel on the shoulders of the wind there. The fourth category will be *samvaha*, above the moon and below the *nakshatra*s. O lord! This fourth category of my sons will roam around there. The fifth category of *vivaha* will extend from the *nakshatra*s, up to the *graha*s.[974] The fifth category of my sons

---

[974] The planets. *Graha* means anything that seizes. We have deliberately left this as *graha*s here, to indicate that *graha* need not always be equated with the physical presence of a planet. In *jyotisha*, the notion is more conceptual.

will roam around on the shoulders of the wind there. The sixth
will be *anuvaha*, above the *graha*s and up to the *rishi*s. The sixth
category of my sons will roam around on the shoulders of the wind
there. The seventh will be described as the one above the *rishi*s,
up to Dhruva. These sons will constitute *parivaha* and will remain
there, on the shoulders of the wind. From time to time, all my sons
will roam around in this way. As a consequence of what you did, let
them have the name of Maruts. O Shatakratu! In accordance with
the tasks that they do, these will be the separate names of my sons.
The names of the first category will be said to be Shakrajyoti, Satya,
Satyajyoti, Chitrajyoti, Jyotishmat, Sutapa and Chaitya. Now hear
about the second. They will be Ritajit, Satyajit, Sushena, Senajit,
Sutamitra, Amitra and Suramitra. This will be the second category.
Now understand the third. They will be Dhatu, Dhanada, Ugra,
Bhima, Varuna, Abhiyuktakshika and Sahvaya. I have spoken
about how the third category will be described. Listen. The fifth
category will be Idrik, Anyadrik, Sarit, Druma, Vrikshaka, Mita
and Samita.[975] The sixth category will be Idrik, Purusha, Nanyadrik,
Samachetana, Sammita, Samavritti and Pratiharta. These seven
categories, with each divided again into seven, have been described.
They will be known as both *daitya*s and *deva*s. All of them will
enter sacrifices and be praised by humans." These are the names
by which the forty-nine Maruts are enumerated. Diti spoke about
them to Shakra. Having given them names, Diti spoke to Shakra.
"My sons, who will travel on the shoulders of the wind, are your
brothers. O fortunate one! Let my sons travel with you and with the
*deva*s." Hearing her words, the thousand-eyed Purandara joined his
hands in salutation and said, "O mother! It will be that way. There
is no doubt that everything will happen exactly as you have stated
it. These great-souled sons will be revered by the worlds. Along
with *deva*s, your sons will obtain shares in sacrifices." Thus, all the
excellent Maruts, Indra's younger brothers, became *deva*s. All of
Diti's spirited sons are known as immortals. In the hermitage in the
forest, the mother and the son decided this. Delighted and bereft of

---

[975] The fourth category is missing, as is the seventh. There are clearly
problems with the text here.

anxiety, they went to heaven. If a person reads or hears about the auspicious birth of the Maruts, he becomes victorious in arguments and realizes his *atman*.'

Chapter 44-1(44) (Danu's lineage)

Suta said, 'Great and famous *asura*s were born in the lineage of Danu's sons. Viprachitti was foremost among them. Their valour was unthinkable. Having tormented themselves through austerities, all of them obtained boons. They were valiant and fixed on the truth. But they also used *maya* and were cruel. They were great in speed and strength. They were devoted to the *brahman* and tended to the sacrificial fire. Among all these, I will narrate the names of the most important. Understand. They were Dvimurdha, Shambara, Shankuratha, Vibhu, Shankukarna, Vipada, Gavishtha, Dundubhi, Ayomukha, Maghavan, Kapila, Vamana, Maya, Marichi, Asipa, Mahamaya, Ashira, Bhrishi, Vikshobha, Suketu, Ketuvirya, Shatahvaya, Indrajit, Dvivida, Bhadra, Devajit, Ekachakra, Mahabahu, Taraka, Mahabala, Vaishvanara, Puloman, Prapana, Mahashira, Svarbhanu, Vrishaparva, the great *asura* Purunda, Dhritarashtra, Surya, Chandra, Indratapana, Sukshma, Nichandra, Churnanabha, Mahagiri, Asiloma, Sukesha, Shatha, Mulakodara, Jambha, Gaganamurdha, Kumbhamana, Mahodaka, Pramada, Adma, Kupatha, the valiant Ashvagriva, Vaimriga, Virupaksha, Supatha, Halahala, Aksha, Hiranmaya, Shatagriva and Shambara.[976] Sharabha and Shvalabha are described as the sun and the moon of the *asura*s and were powerful against the Gods. These are described as the foremost sons in Danu's lineage. The numbers of sons and grandsons was infinite and it is impossible to enumerate them. Thus, *asura*s, *daitya*s and *danava*s have been described. *Daitya*s are described as those who drank *soma* juice and the sons of Danu as those who did not drink *soma* juice. There are other sons

---

[976] Clearly a second Shambara.

who are described, those who followed Danu's lineage. They are Ekaksha, Ashvaprabharishta, Pralamba, Naraka, Indrabadhana, Keshi, Purusha, Sheshavan, Uru, Garishtha, Gavaksha and the valiant Talaketu. They could not be killed by humans. These are described as those who followed the sons of Danu.'

'Those born as a result of union between *daitya*s and *danava*s were extremely terrible in valour. Through Simhika, Viprachitti's sons were known as Saimhikeyas. There were such fourteen great *asura*s—Shala, Shalabha, Savya, Sivya, Ilvala, Namuchi, Vatapi, Supunjika, Harakalpa, Kalanabha, Bhouma, Kanaka and the eldest among them, Rahu, the one who afflicts the sun and the moon. These sons of Simhika could not be assailed, even by *deva*s. They were born in a fierce lineage. All of them were cruel and killed *brahmana*s. There are said to have been ten thousand such categories of Saimhikeyas. They were killed by the strong Bhargava, Jamadagni's son. Svarbhanu's daughter was Prabhaa. Shachi was Puloman's daughter. Sadasya's daughter was Upadanavi and Vrishaparva's daughter was Sharmishtha. Vaishvanara had two daughters, Pulomaa and Kalikaa. Nahusha was the son of Prabhaa and Jayanta was Shachi's son.[977] Sharmishtha[978] gave birth to Puru and Upadanavi gave birth to Dushyanta. Vaishvanara's daughters were Pulomaa and Kalakaa.[979] Both these daughters married Maricha and had many offspring. Combined, they had sixty thousand sons and these were bulls among *danava*s. There were fourteen thousand others who resided in Hiranyapura. The Poulamas and Kalakeyas were *danava*s who were extremely strong. They could not be killed by *deva*s and were slain by Savyasachi.[980] Through Maya, Rambhaa gave birth to six extremely strong sons—Mayavi, Dundubhi, Putra, Mahisha, Kalika and Ajakarna. The daughter was Mandodari.[981] The creation of *daitya*s and *danava*s has thus been described. It is said that Anayusha had five extremely strong sons—Araru, Bala,

---

[977] Shachi was married to Indra.
[978] Married to Yayati.
[979] This is repetition, with Kalakaa instead of Kalikaa.
[980] Arjuna, described in Mahabharata.
[981] Married to Ravana.

Vritra, Vijvara and Vrisha. Araru's son was a great and cruel *asura*, named Dhundhu. As a result of Utanka's words, Kuvalashva killed him inside a cave.[982] Bala had two extremely valiant sons who were unmatched in energy. They were Nikumbha and Chakravarma, who used to be Karna in an earlier birth. Vijvara had two sons, Kalaka and Khara. Vrisha had four sons who were cruel in their deeds. They were Shraddhada, Yajnaha, Brahmaha and Pashuha.[983] Anayusha's sons have been described. Now hear about Vritra's. While Vritra was fighting against Indra, he had extremely terrible sons. These were extremely strong *rakshasa*s, known under the name of Bakas. Hundreds and thousands of them are described, as followers of the great Indra. All of them knew about the *brahman*. They were amiable and devoted to *dharma* and their forms were subtle. All of them reside inside *praja*s, surrounded by anger.[984] Krodhaa gave birth to unmatched sons who were excellent singers. They were Siddha, Purna, Vahvi, the valiant Purnamsha, Brahmachari, Shataguna and Suparna as the seventh. There were also Vishvavasu, Bhanu and Suchandra as the tenth. These sons of Krodhaa are described as the divine *gandharva*s.'[985]

Chapter 45-1(45) (Kashyapa's descendants)

Suta said, 'The *gandharva*s and *apsara*s were the children of Muni. They were Bhimasena, Ugrasena, Suparna, Varuna, Dhritarashtra, Goman, Suryavarcha, Patravan, Arkaparna, Prayuta, Bhima, the self-controlled and famous Chitraratha who conquered everything, Shalishira as the thirteenth, Parjanya as the fourteenth,

---

[982] Dhundhu was disturbing the sage Utanka's austerities. Usually, it is said that Dhundhu lived hidden under the desert, not a cave. Kuvalashva came to be known as Dhundhumara.

[983] Shraddhada should probably read Shraddhaha. The words would then respectively mean destroyers of *shraddha* ceremonies, sacrifices, *brahmana*s and animals.

[984] They dwell in the anger of subjects.

[985] The next chapter describes some as Muni's sons.

Kali as the fifteenth and Narada as the sixteenth. These divine
*gandharva*s are described as Muni's sons. They had twenty-four
younger sisters who were the *apsara*s. They were Aruna, Anapayaa,
Vimanushyaa, Varamvaraa, Mishrakeshi, Asiparnini, Alambushaa,
Marichi, Shuchikaa, Vidyutparnaa, Tilottamaa, Adrikaa,
Lakshmanaa, Kshemaa, the divine Rambhaa, Manobhavaa, Asitaa,
Subahu, Supriyaa, Subhujaa, Pundarikaa, Ajagandhaa, Sudati and
Surasa. There were also four sons who are described as excellent
and famous *gandharva*s—Subahu, Haha, Huhu and Tumburu.
*Gandharva*s and *apsara*s, Muni's children, have been described.
The *apsara*s of the world are described as Hamsaa, Sarasvati,
Sutaa, Kamalaa, Abhayaa, Sumukhi and Hamsapadi. There are
said to have been others[986]—Hamsa, Jyotishtoma, Madhyachara,
Daruna, Varutha, Varenya, the one described as Vasuruchi, Suruchi
as the eighth and Vishvavasu. Rishtaa gave birth to immensely
fortunate ones who were worshipped by *deva*s and *rishi*s. She gave
birth to three daughters, Arupaa, Subhagaa and Bhasi. Tumbaru's
auspicious daughters were Manuvanti and Sukeshi. It should be
known that there were ten *apsara*s who were *panchachuda*s.[987]
They are Menakaa, Sahajanya, Parnini, Punjikasthala, Kritasthala,
Ghritachi, Vishvachi, Purvachitti, the famous Pramlocha and
Anumlocha. These are the ten. Urvashi is said to be the eleventh.
As was appropriate for her lineage, she was unblemished in her
limbs. She was born from Narayana, who has no beginning and no
end. Menaa had a daughter named Menakaa, who was beautiful in
all her limbs. All these immensely fortunate ones are said to have
spoken about the *brahman*. It is said that there are fourteen other
auspicious categories of *apsara*s—Ahritis, Shobhavatis, Vegavatis,
Urjaas, Yuvatis, Sruks, Kurus, Barhis, Amritaas, Mudaas, Mrigus,
Ruks, Bhirus and Shobhayantis. These are the fourteen categories.
Ahritis were born through Brahma's mental powers. Shobhavatis
were daughters of the Maruts. Vegavatis were Rishtaa's daughters.
Urjaas originated from Agni. The extremely beautiful Yuvatis were
born from the rays of the sun. The auspicious Kurus were born

[986] Other *gandharva*s.
[987] Literally, those with five tufts or crests of hair.

from the moon's beams. The ones named Sruks originated from
a sacrifice. Barhis were born from *kusha* grass. The ones named
Amritaas are said to have originated from the *amrita* of water.
The ones named Mudaas originated from the wind and the ones
named Mrigus originated from the earth. The ones named Ruks
were born from lightning and the Bhirus were Mrityu's daughters.
Shobhayantis were Kama's daughters. These are described as the
fourteen categories. In this way, there were many thousands of
radiant *apsara* categories. They were wives and mothers of *deva*s
and *rishi*s. All these *apsara*s are identical. They are fragrant and
steady. With the exception of Hara, they use desire to affect everyone
in heaven. Since they could be touched by anyone in general, *deva*s
and *rishi*s were born from them. Thus, Narada and Parvata are
said to have been born through them. There was a third who was
younger, a daughter described as Arundhati. Despite being born in
this way, Narada and Parvata are *devarshi*s. Accordingly, Narada
and Parvata are said to have been revered.'

'Vinataa had two sons, Aruna and Garuda. *Gayatri* and the
other *chhanda*s, the *suparna*s and others that are used, those
inherent in hymns of the *Rig Veda*, originated with these birds.'[988]

'Kadru gave birth to thousands of *naga*s who hold up the earth.
Those great-souled ones have many hoods and travel through the
sky. There are many. Hear the names of the most important. Among
them, the most important *naga*s are Shesha, Vasuki and Takshaka.
There are also Akarna, Hastikarna, Pinjara, Aryaka, Airavata,
Mahapadma, Kambala, Ashvatara, Elapatra, Shankha, Karkotaka,
Dhananjaya, Mahakarna, Mahanila, Dhritarashtra, Balahaka,
Karavira, Pushpadamshtra, Sumukha, Durmukha, Sunamukha,
Dadhimukha, Kaliya, Alipindaka, Kapila, Ambarisha, Akrura,
Kapitthaka, Prahrada, Brahmana, Gandharva, Manishthaka,
Nahusha, Kararoma, Mani and others. These are known as the
Kadraveyas.'

'Hear about the sons of Khashaa. Khashaa gave birth to two
sons, Vikrita and Parushavrata. The elder was born at the time of the

---

[988] Suparna is a general name for birds and is specifically Garuda's
name. Here, *suparna* must also clearly be understood as a group of hymns.

evening *sandhya*, the younger at the time of the morning *sandhya*. The elder had one ear that was red. He possessed four arms and four feet. He trembled a bit and had two kinds of movement.[989] He had hair all over his body and his limbs were stout. His nose was excellent, and his stomach was large. His head was clear and his ears were large. He was immensely strong, and his hair was like *munja* grass. His mouth was short, but his tongue was long. He had many fangs and a large jaw. His feet and eyes were red and tawny. His eyebrows were thick, and his nose was long. He was a *guhyaka*,[990] with a white throat, large feet and a huge face. In this way, Khashaa gave birth to a son who was extremely terrible. The second, his younger brother, was born when Usha[991] was over. He had three heads, three feet and three hands and his eyes were black. His hair stood up, upright, and his beard was green. His body was as firm as a rock, but his body was short. However, his arms and body were gigantic in size and he had a loud roar. His mouth extended all the way up to his ears. He was strong, with a stout nose. His lips were thick, and he possessed eight fangs. A tongue protruded from his mouth and his ears were like cones. His dilated eyes were tawny. His hair was matted and he had two humps on his large shoulder. His chest was broad. His nose was thick and he was slender at the waist. His neck was red and wasn't thick. His penis and testicles hung down. She gave birth to such a younger son. As soon as they were born, they grew easily. Their bodies became instantly capable of exerting themselves. As soon as they were born, their limbs grew in size, and they started to tug at their mother. The elder one was cruel and pulled the mother. He said, "We are suffering from hunger. O mother! To save ourselves, we will devour you." However, the younger one tried to restrain him. He protected his own mother. He clasped the mother in his arms and spoke to the elder brother, trying to pacify him. At the time, their father appeared at the spot. He saw those two deformed

---

[989] He was amphibious.

[990] Often equated with *yaksha*s, semi-divine species, companions of Kubera.

[991] The break of day, the period just before dawn.

ones and spoke to Khashaa. On seeing the father, the two sons were scared and became one. Using their own *maya*, they merged into the mother's limbs again. At this, the *rishi* spoke to his wife. "What did they tell you? Tell me everything truthfully. This has happened because of your own transgression. A son or a daughter who is born, is just like the mother. If the mother possesses good conduct, a son will also have good conduct. The earth certainly possesses the complexion of the ground over which it flows. The good conduct, taints, beauty and qualities of the mother determine the son, though different offspring differ in fame." Having told Khashaa this, the unmatched and illustrious one summoned his sons. He pacified them and gave them names. Khashaa told him everything the sons had done regarding her. He debated what the mother had said and gave them names, using the etymological meanings of the words. The elder had said, "O mother! We will devour you", the word *bhaksha* being used in the sense of eating. Since he had used the word *bhaksha*, he became a *yaksha*.[992] The word *raksha* is used in the sense of protecting. The younger had said, "O mother! I will myself protect you." Therefore, this son came to have the name of *rakshasa*. In this way, their father foresaw the different kinds of acts they would engage in. He understood this from the way they had behaved towards their mother. His intelligence was refined, and he was surprised to see that they were hungry. Khashaa's husband instructed them that blood and fat would be their food. On seeing that they were hungry, their father bestowed this boon on them. "Your hands will always touch flows of blood. As you wish, your food will be flesh, blood and fat. You will roam around and eat in the night, devouring *dvija*s, *deva*s and others. You will be strong at night and weak during the day. Protect this mother of yours. That is the *dharma* that has been instructed." Telling his sons this, Kashyapa vanished from the spot.'

'When their father left, those two caused terrors to creation. They were ungrateful. They caused calamities and violence to life. They were immensely strong and great in spirit. They were gigantic

[992] This does not follow. The word *yaksha* is derived from honouring and worshipping.

in size and impossible to resist. They were accomplished in *maya* and became invisible. Therefore, they could vanish when they wanted. They were terrible and could assume whatever form they willed. Their nature was such that they did not suffer from diseases. Their conduct was appropriate to their forms. They wandered around, causing impediments. With a desire to devour *devas*, *rishis*, ancestors, *gandharvas*, *kinnaras*, *pishachas*, humans, *pannagas*, birds and animals, those two roamed around in the night. However, whenever they saw Indra's companions, they were agitated and didn't remain at the spot.'

'On one occasion, the *rakshasa* was wandering around alone in the night. He was searching for food and followed a sound. Two *pishachas*, Aja and Shanda, approached him. They were immensely brave and were the sons of Kapi. In their earlier lives, they had been *kushmandas*.[993] Their eyes were tawny, and their body-hair stood up. Their eyes were round, and they were extremely terrible. Their daughters were with them, and they were searching for an appropriate husband for them. Those two daughters could assume any form they wanted. They were hungry and along with the daughters, were searching for food. They saw the *rakshasa*, who could assume any form, in front of them. In this way, they suddenly came upon each other. They stood there, glancing at each other and wishing to seize each other. The fathers told the daughters, "Quickly bring him. Catch him and bring him alive. He is faltering at every step." Thus addressed, the daughters followed him and seized him. They seized him by the hand and brought him into the presence of their fathers. When he had been seized by the daughters, the two *pishachas* looked at the *rakshasa*. They asked him, "Who do you belong to? Who are you?" He told them everything. On hearing about his birth and deeds, Aja and Shanda bestowed their daughters on the *rakshasa*. They were satisfied at his deeds and therefore, bestowed the daughters, while they wept. Aja and Shanda followed the *pishacha* form of marriage and bestowed the daughters, announcing the wealth they possessed.

---

[993] A *kushmanda* is an evil spirit, sometimes described as Shiva's companion.

"This auspicious daughter is named Brahmadhana. *Brahmana*s are her food."[994] This is what Shanda said. "This daughter is named Jantudhana. There are freckles, resembling creatures, all over her limbs. She can seize all the wealth." This is what Aja announced as her wealth. The daughter named Jantudhana had masses of hair in all her limbs. She gave birth to a daughter named Yatudhanaa, who emitted loud roars. The daughter named Brahmadhana was red in complexion and had no hair. She gave birth to a daughter named Brahmadhanaa, who also emitted loud roars. In this way, those two daughters of *pishacha*s had offspring. I will describe the offspring they had. Listen. Yatudhanaa had ten sons—Heti, Praheti, Ugra, Pourusheya, Vadha, Vidyutsphurja, Vata, Aya, Vyaghra and Surya. Listen. Malyavan and Sumali were the sons of Praheti. Praheti had another prosperous son, famous under the name of Puloman. Another son was the immensely fierce Madhu, whose son was Lavana. He possessed the strength of great *yoga* and worshipped Mahadeva. Ugra had a valiant son, famous under the name of Vajraha. Pourusheya had five sons. They were immensely strong and fed on men. They were Krura, Vikrita, Rudhirada, Medasha and Vapasha. These are recounted as their names. Vadha's sons were Vighna and Shamana, evil in conduct. Vidyut's son was the *rakshasa* named Rasana, who was wicked in conduct.[995] Through his wife, Sphurja had the *brahma-rakshasa* Nikumbha as a son. Vata's son was Virodha and Aya's son was Janantaka. Vyaghra's son was Nirananda, who caused impediments at sacrifices. Sarpa's[996] sons were *rakshasa*s who were cruel *sarpa*s. The sons of Yatudhanaa have been described. Now hear about those of Brahmadhanaa. Brahmadhanaa had nine sons—Yajnapeta, Dhriti, Kshema, Brahmapeta, Yajnaha, Shvata, Ambika, Keli and Sarpa. These *brahma-rakshasa*s had extremely terrible sisters— Raktakarni, Mahajihva, Kshama and Ishtapaharini. In this way,

---

[994] There is probably an intended pun on *dhana* (wealth) and *adana* (food). *Brahmana*s are her *dhana* because *brahmana*s are her *adana*.

[995] Earlier, Vidyutsphurja was stated as one person. Now, Vidyut and Sphurja are stated as different individuals.

[996] Presumably, Sarpa is the same as Surya.

*brahma-rakshasa*s were born on earth. *Rakshasa*s have thus been described.'

'Now hear about *yaksha*s. The *yaksha* desired Kratusthalaa, a *panchachuda*. Desiring her, he traversed the path of searching all the celestial gardens—Vaibhraja, Surabhi, Chaitraratha, Vishoka, Sumana and Nandana, the excellent grove. Since his desire had been ignited, he followed many beautiful routes. Finally, he saw her in Nandana, along with all the other smiling *apsara*s. He thought of means of obtaining her but could not find a way. He was tainted by his own form and tainted by his deeds. "Since I am violent, all the beings hate me. How will I obtain this lady, who is beautiful in all her limbs?" Having thought of a means, he swiftly implemented it. The *guhyaka* assumed the form of Vasuruchi, a *gandharva*. From amidst the *apsara*s, he seized Kratusthalaa. Taking him to be Vasuruchi, she went along. While all the large number of *apsara*s looked on, for the sake of a son, the *yaksha* indulged in physical intercourse with her. Though he was seen, since he desired the *apsara*, he was not scared. The intercourse was successful and a son was born instantly. He immediately grew in size and blazed in his prosperity. He greeted his father with the words, "I am King Nabhi." The father replied, "You are Rajatanabha." He was born with his mother's beauty and his father's energy. As soon as he was born, he[997] returned to his own form. *Yaksha*s and *rakshasa*s return to their own forms when they are asleep, when they die, when they are angry, when they are scared and when they are delighted. Accordingly, the *guhyaka* smiled and spoke to the *apsara*. "O fortunate one! O one with the beautiful face! Along with your son, come to my home." Saying this, while she watched, he suddenly returned to his own form. All the other assembled *apsara*s were bewildered and fled. She followed those who were leaving. However, her son followed her and calmed her down. He took her and returned amidst the *gandharva*s and *apsara*s. The large number of *apsara*s saw how she had given birth to the *yaksha*'s son. They told Kratusthalaa, "You are the mother of *yaksha*s." Along with his son, the *yaksha* returned to his own

[997] The father.

abode. There is a *nyagrodha* tree named Rohina and *guhyaka*s lie down there. *Yaksha*s are said to reside in the *nyagrodha* named Rohina. The *yaksha* Rajatanabha is the grandfather of *guhyaka*s. He married the self-controlled Manivaraa, unmatched in her limbs. She was the fortunate daughter of Anuhrada, the *daitya*. Her son was Manibhadra, who was Shakra's equal in valour. Kratusthalaa had two auspicious daughters. They were named Punyajani and Devajani and these two sisters became his wives. Through Manibhadra, the auspicious Punyajani had twenty-four sons. They were Siddhartha, Suryateja, Sumana, Nandana, Manduka, Ruchaka, Manimanta, Vasu, Sarvanubhuta, Shankha, Pingaksha, Bhiru, Asoma, Durasoma, Padma, Chandraprabha, Meghavarna, Subhadra, Pradyota, Mahadyuti, Dyutimanta, Ketumanta, Darshaniya and Sudarshana. These sons were born through Punyajani. All of them were Manibhadra's sons and all of them were auspicious in signs. Their sons and grandsons were auspicious *yaksha*s and *punyajana*s. Through Manivaraa's son,[998] Devajani gave birth to auspicious sons—Purnabhadra, Haimavanta, Manimantra, Vivardhana, Kusu, Chara, Pishanga, Sthulakarna, Mahamuda, Shveta, Vimala, Pushpadanta, Jayavaha, Padmavarna, Suchandra, Paksha, Balaka, Kumudaksha, Sukamala, Vardhamana, Hita, Padmanabha, Sugandha, Suvira, Vijaya, Krita, Purnamasa, Hiranyaksha, Sarana and Manasa. These were the *yaksha*s who descended through Manivaraa's son and they are described as *guhyaka*s. They were beautiful in form, dressed in excellent garments. They wore garlands and were agreeable to behold. Their sons and grandsons numbered hundreds of thousands.'

'Khashaa had other sons. They were *rakshasa*s who could assume any form at will. I will describe the foremost among them. Listen. They were Lalavi, Krathana, Bhima, Sumali, Madhu, Visphurjana, Brihajjihva, Matanga, Dhumrita, Chandrarkabhikara, Budhna, Kapiloma, Prahasaka, Pidapara, Trinabha, Vakraksha, who roamed in the night, Trishira, Shatadamshtra, the *rakshasa* Tundakosha, Ashva, Akampana and Durmukha, who roamed in

---

[998] That is, Manibhadra.

the night. These were the categories and forms of the valiant and supreme *rakshasa*s. They roamed around in all the worlds and were like the Gods in their strides. She had seven other daughters. In the due order, hear about their names. They were Alambaa, Utkochaa, Utkrishtaa, Nirritaa, Kapilaa, Shivaa and the immensely fortunate Keshini. These are described as the seven sisters. The offspring they had led to the origin of groups. Through these auspicious ones, categories of *rakshasa*s evolved. They were impossible to withstand in battle and slew hordes of people. The group known as Alambeyas was cruel and so was the group known as Outkacheya. There were excellent *rakshasa*s known as Outkarshteyas and Shaiveyas. Similarly, there were the ones named Nairritas, those who followed Tryambaka. They originated in the course of creation of *praja*s and are supreme among Ganeshvaras. They are valiant, full of prowess. Nairritas are *deva-rakshasa*s. The one who has been appointed as their leader is famous under the name of Virupaka. Thus, hundreds of armies of these great-souled *gana*s originated. They generally follow Shankara, the lord of the universe. The great-souled king of *daitya*s, Kumbha, was gigantic in size. He gave birth to those who were immensely brave, immensely strong and immensely valiant. These were the extremely brave Kapileyas, known as *daitya-rakshasa*s. Through Keshini, the *yaksha* Kapila had others as sons. These were immensely strong and are known as *yaksha-rakshasa*s. Keshini had a daughter too, the inferior *rakshasi*[999] Nilaa. One of the Alambeyas was known as Surasika. His sons, through Nilaa, were known under the name of Nailas. They were terrible in valour and impossible to defeat. They travel everywhere on earth and in the worlds of *deva*s. There are many such creations and it is impossible to speak about them. The *rakshasi* named Vikacha was Nilaa's daughter. This daughter's sons were the Vikachas, great in spirit and valour. Virupaka had these sons, known as Nairritas, through her. These sons were extremely terrible. Hear about them, in the due order. They possessed cruel fangs. They were malformed, with large ears and large stomachs. They were Harakas, Bhishakas,

---

[999] Feminine of *rakshasa*.

Klamakas, Reravakas, Pishachas, Vahakas, Trasakas and others. These were *bhumi-rakshasa*s, foolish, but harsh in valour. They were innumerable. Assuming many forms, never seen before, they wandered around. Their strength and spirit were superior and it is said that they travelled in the sky. As they roam around in the sky, they can be seen somewhat, or hardly ever. In this way, hundreds and thousands of all these *bhumi-rakshasa*s pervaded the universe. There were many other minor *rakshasa*s. They had many forms and with many different kinds of movements, they covered many countries, in every direction. It is briefly stated that there were eight mothers of *rakshasa*s.[1000] These eight groups have been described in the due order. Some who were born were gentle, not acting without cause. Numbering hundreds of thousands, they roamed around in the world of mortals. They caused terror to beings and Putanaa is generally described as their mother.'

'In the world of humans, *grahas*[1001] are responsible for the deaths of children. These are Skandagrahas and others, Hasyas, Apakas, Trasakas and others.[1002] They are known as Koumaras and act in homes where there are children. There are specific Skandagrahas that use *maya*. There are *bhuta*s known as Putanas and their leaders wander around in the world. In this way, there are thousands of *gana*s who roam around on this earth. *Yaksha*s are described under the names of Punyajanas and Purnabhadras. *Yaksha*s and *rakshasa*s are descended from Pulastya and Agastya. The lord of Alaka[1003] is the king of all the Nairritas. Using their sight, *yaksha*s drink the blood, flesh and fat of men. *Rakshasa*s enter the body, while *pishacha*s oppress. Briefly, *deva*s possess all the auspicious signs. They are radiant and powerful. They are lords who can assume any form at will. They cannot be attacked. They are brave and are worshipped by all the worlds. They are subtle, energetic and pure.

[1000] Presumably, Khashaa, Alambaa, Utkochaa, Utkrishtaa, Nirritaa, Kapilaa, Shivaa and Keshini.

[1001] In this context, evil demons that seize.

[1002] Skandagrahas are evil planets, believed to affect children until they attain sixteen years of age.

[1003] Kubera, whose capital is Alaka.

They are worthy of being worshipped at sacrifices. They bestow boons and take part in sacrifices. These signs of *devas* also exist in *asuras*. However, *gandharvas* and *apsaras* are said to possess three-fourths of qualities *devas* possess. *Guhyakas* and *rakshasas* only possess three-fourths of qualities *gandharvas* possess. *Pishachas* only possess three-fourths of qualities *rakshasas* possess. In this way, starting with *devas* and *asuras*, each succeeding group is one-fourth less in prosperity, wealth, beauty, lifespan, strength, *dharma*, intelligence, austerities, learning and valour. Starting with *gandharvas* and ending with *pishachas*, there are four groups that belong to the species of *devas*.'[1004]

'O fortunate one! Now hear about the offspring in Krodhavashaa's lineage. Krodhaa gave birth to twelve daughters who were just like her own self. They became Pulaha's wives. Understand their names. They were famous as Mrigi, Mrigamandaa, Haribhadraa, Iravati, Bhutaa, Kapishaa, Damshtraa, Rishaa, Tiryaa, Shvetaa, Saramaa and Surasaa. Mrigi's sons were *harinas*, other small animals, rabbits, *nyankus*, *sharabhas*, *rurus* and *prishatas*.[1005] Mrigamandaa's children were bears, *gavayas*, buffaloes, camels, boars, rhinoceros and *gouramukhas*.[1006] Haribhadraa gave birth to *haris*, *golangulas*, *tarakshus*, *vanaras*, *kinnaras*, *mayus*, *kimpurushas*, lions, tigers, *nilas*, *dvipins*, *krodhitadharas*, *sarpas*, *ajagaras*, *graahas*, *marjaras*, *mushikas*, *mandukas*, *nakulas* and *valkakas*, who frequent forests.[1007] Through Pulahas, the excellent and auspicious one first gave birth to Hamsa. Thereafter, there were Ranachandra, Shatamukha, Darimukha, Harita, the terrible

---

[1004] Including *devas* and *asuras*.

[1005] *Harinas* are red deer, *nyankus* and *rurus* are antelopes and *prishatas* are spotted deer.

[1006] *Gavaya* is a wild ox. Here, *gouramukha* means a kind of buffalo.

[1007] *Hari* is a tawny monkey, *golangula* is a black monkey with a tail that resembles that of a cow, *tarakshu* is a hyena, *vanara* is a general term for a monkey, *mayu* is a specific type of *kinnara*, *nila* is a kind of dark blue ox, *dvipin* is a leopard, *krodhitadhara* (with a lower lip full of anger) is probably an adjective, *ajagara* is a python, *graaha* is a crocodile, *marjara* is a cat, *mushika* is a rat, *manduka* is a frog, *nakula* is a mongoose and *valkaka* is probably some animal with a golden hide.

Harivarma, who had auspicious signs, Prathita, Mathita, Harina and Langali. Shvetaa gave birth to ten brave ones, who were bulls among *vanaras*. They were Urddhvadrishti, Kritahara, Suvrata, Vinata, Budha, Parijata, Sujata, Haridasa, Gunakara and Kshemamurti. All of them were powerful kings. Their sons and grandsons were strong and impossible to withstand. *Devas, danavas*, humans, *yakshas, bhutas, pishachas, rakshasas* and serpents found it impossible to defeat them in battles. It has been laid down that their death will not come about through fire, weapons, poison or any other means. Their movements are unimpeded everywhere, on earth, in the sky, in the nether regions, in water and in the wind. They cannot be destroyed. There are innumerable spirited *vanaras* in various noble families—ten thousand crores, one thousand *arbudas*, one thousand *mahapadmas*, one hundred *mahapadmas*, ten *arbudas*, one hundred thousand crores, one thousand *niyutas*, *nikharvas*, tens of crores of *arbudas*, sixty crores, one hundred thousand *arbudas*, one hundred crores, ten *padmas* and nine *mahapadmas*.[1008] All of them were spirited and brave. They were immensely strong and could assume any form at will. They were attired in divine garments and ornaments. They were devoted to *brahmanas* and maintained sacrificial fires. They performed all the different sacrifices and gave away hundreds and thousands of *dakshina*. They were ornamented with crowns, earrings, necklaces and armlets. They were learned in the *Vedas* and the *Vedangas*. They were accomplished in the sacred texts of good policy. They could free themselves from weapons and also use these to destroy. They showed respect to divine *mantras* and were respected because they honoured divine *mantras*. They were capable, strong and brave and could strike with every kind of weapon. They were amiable and could assume divine forms. They did not suffer from old age or death. There were tens of thousands of lineages of these great-souled ones. It is said that Vishvakarma himself constructed their residences on the four flanks of Meru, in Hemakuta, Himalaya,

---

[1008] *Niyuta* is one million, crore is ten million, *arbuda* is 100 million, *nikharva* is 1000 million, *padma* is 1000 billion and *mahapadma* is one trillion.

Nila, Mount Shveta, Nishadha, Gandhamadana, in the seven *dvipa*s and inside caves in mountains. Those cities were of many types and were decorated with ramparts. They were beautiful in all the seasons and there were gardens everywhere. On the floors of their homes and on their beds, there were fragrant flowers that led to happiness. They were smeared with many kinds of unguents and divine ashes. Jewels were spread everywhere and in their minds, they achieved *siddhi*. *Vanara*s and *vanari*s[1009] were decorated with celestial ornaments. They drank honey and *madhvika* liquor[1010] and their food was mixed with nectar. Like large numbers of *deva*s in heaven, they observed rites and were happy. They were full of joy and were the chief sons of *deva*s and *gandharva*s. They were devoted to *dharma* and blessed with boons. They were immensely strong and fierce in battle. All of them were superior in spirits and devoted to *deva*s and *dvija*s. They did not fade and were fixed to the truth. They were eloquent and conversed on many kinds of subjects. They were forgiving and restrained in speech. They were devoted to good conduct. Brahma himself created them as ornaments of the forest. They were created to ensure devotion in the worlds and for the sake of Rama, a reservoir of qualities. This account about *avatara*s taken by monkeys destroys all sins. It is blessed, sacred and beautiful. It brings happiness and fame. I will describe it. Listen attentively.'

'Urddhvadrishti had a strong son, named Vyaghra. Vyaghra had five brothers and five sisters. He bestowed them on *vanara*s who had cleansed their *atman*s and were appropriate for them. The brother also found appropriate wives for his brothers. Sharabha, famous in the worlds, was born as Vyaghra's son. Sharabha's brothers were learned, honoured for their valour. They were kings of *vanara*s and established every kind of *dharma*. Sharabha had an immensely strong and intelligent son, named Shuka. His powerful son, born from the womb of Vyaghri, was named Riksha. He was an unassailable *chakravarti* and was revered by all those who were brave. He was greatly energetic and was the leader of all the groups of *vanara*s. He was accomplished about the methods for all the

---

[1009] Feminine of *vanara*.
[1010] Distilled from the *madhuka* tree.

weapons and always killed enemies. Since he was special in his qualities, Prajapati Viraja happily bestowed his daughter Virajaa, who was similar to him in qualities, on him, adorning her with gold. Riksha, leader of *vanara* groups, accepted her hand. The daughter possessed beautiful smiles. Her limbs were without blemish, and she was a sight to behold. On seeing that she was beautiful to behold, the great Indra had intercourse with her. She had a son, Vali, valiant and manly. The great Indra had this son through Virajaa, and he was the great Indra's equal in valour. In that way, in secret, Bhanu also had a son through her. Born through his portion, this was Sugriva, lord of groups of monkeys. Riksha, the leader of all the groups of monkeys, was extremely delighted when he saw that these two sons possessed strength, beauty and prosperity.[1011] He instated his eldest son Vali, who wore a golden garland. Vali was consecrated in this way and the powerful Sugriva was his follower. Like the lord of *devas* in heaven, he ruled over the kingdom. The great-souled one's wife was Sushena's daughter. Her name was Taraa, and she was immensely wise, with a face resembling the lord of the stars.[1012] She gave birth to a son, Angada, who wore bejeweled armlets.[1013] Through Mainda's eldest daughter, Angada had a son who was terrible in his valour. His name was Dhruva and he was immensely illustrious. Sugriva's wife was Rumaa, Panasa's auspicious daughter. She had three sons who were great in their deeds. The powerful Sugriva found beautiful wives for them and along with the *vanaras*, remained by Vali's side. Like an immortal, the fierce one remained with his brother for many years. Kesari obtained Kunjara's daughter as a wife. The immensely fortunate and pure one was named Anjana and she went to Pumsavana. She was proud of her youth and Vayu had intercourse with her. Through Vayu, who is the wind in the entire universe, she had Hanuman as a son. Kesari had other sons, famous in this world and in heaven. Hanuman was the eldest among them. Matiman

---

[1011] Born through his wife, they were the respective sons of Indra and Surya.

[1012] That is, the moon.

[1013] *Angada* means a bejeweled armlet.

was next. The others were Shrutiman, Ketuman and the intelligent Dhritiman. Along with their wives, all of Hanuman's brothers were properly established. Their father established them the way he was established and they had sons and grandsons. Hanuman was a *brahmachari* and was never united with a wife. No one in all the worlds was interested in fighting with him. In his speed and spread, he was like Vinata's son.'[1014]

'Agni's son was the powerful Nala, who was supremely difficult to defeat. This bull among *vanaras* was born in Kanakabindu's *kshetra*.[1015] There were other strong and immensely fortunate *vanaras*. The foremost among them, the leaders of groups of monkeys, should be known. They are Tara, Kusuma, Panasa, Gandhamadana, Rupashri, Vibhava, Gavaya, Vikata, Sara, Sushena, Sudhanu, Subandhu, Shatadundubhi, Vikacha, Kapila, Roudra, Pariyatra, Prabhanjana, Kunjara, Sharabha, Damshtri, Kalamurti, Mahasukha, Nanda, Kandarasena, Nala, Varuni, Chirava, Karava, Tamra, Chitrayodhi, Rathitara, Bhima, Shatabali, Kalachakra, Anala, Nala,[1016] Yakshasya, Gahana, Dhumra, Pancharatha, Parijata, Mahadipta, Sutapa, Balasagara, Shrutayu, Vijayakamkshi, Gurusevi, Yatharthaka, Dharmacheta, Suhotra, Shalihotra, Sarpaga, Pundra, Avaragatra, Charurupa, Shatrujit, Vikata, Kavata, Mainda, Bindukara, Asurantaka, Mantri, Bhimaratha, Sanga, Vibhranta, Charuhasavan, Kshanakshanamitahara, Dridhabhakti, Pramardana, Jajali, Panchamukuta, Balabandhu, Samahita, Payahkirti, Shubha, Kshetra, Binduketu, Sahasrapat, Navaksha, Harinetra, Jimuta, Balahaka, Gaja, Gavayanama, Subahu, Gunakara, Virabahu, Kriti, Kunda, Kritakritya, Shubhekshana, Dvivida, Kumuda, Bhasa, Sumukha, Suruvu, Vrika, Vikata, Kavaka, Javasena, Vrishakriti, Gavaksha, Naradeva, Suketu, Vimalanana, Sahasvara, Shubhakshetra, Pushpadhvamsa, Vilohita, Navachandra, Bahuguna, Saptahotra, Marichiman, Godhama, Dhanesha, Golangula and Netravan. I have accurately described the foremost monkeys. There are many names and I am incapable

---

[1014] That is, Garuda.
[1015] Agni had a son through Kanakabindu's wife.
[1016] Another Nala.

of describing all of them. Each of them possessed the strength of ten crores of elephants. Vali scorched his enemies and was established in Kishkindha. He was the king of all the armies of *vanara*s in the seven *dvipa*s.'

'Vali was immersed in *dhyana*. In an encounter, the immensely strong one caught Ravana by his left hand and placed him by his side.[1017] Within a *muhurta*, he swiftly went and touched the four directions—the southern ocean, the eastern ocean, the western ocean and the northern ocean. Vali's speed was like that of thought, or the wind, and he was not exhausted at all. The greatly valiant one defeated Ravana, who had made the worlds scream.[1018] When he was freed from Vali's arms, he was bewildered and lost his senses. Fierce in his valour, he placed him down at the foot of a tree and sprinkled his feet, palms and heads with extremely cool water. When he regained his senses, the lord of monkeys pretended to be greatly surprised. He spoke to the Indra among *rakshasa*s, who was terrible in battles. "O Indra and king of *rakshasa*s! You are like the great Indra in your valour. You have vanquished innumerable armies. In battles, you have defeated Yama and his advisers, Varuna, Kubera, the moon-god, the sun-god, large numbers of Maruts, Rudras, Adityas, Ashvins, Vasus, *daitya*s, Kalakeyas, extremely great and strong *danava*s, *siddha*s, *gandharva*s, *yaksha*s, *rakshasa*s, serpents, supreme birds, planets, *nakshatra*s, stars, insolent *bhuta*s and *pishacha*s who were extensive in strength and hundreds and thousands of human kings. With all these qualities, how did this happen to you? Your speed is equal to that of thought and the wind. You are capable of moving Meru. You are as invincible as the Destroyer. You are the destroyer of enemy cities and have made brave ones from all the worlds run away. Your strength is like that of the *vajra* and you have levelled mountains. You are

---

[1017] Vali was immersed in *dhyana*. Ravana first challenged Sugriva and then Vali to a fight. Defeating Ravana, Vali carried him around, under his armpit.

[1018] *Rava* means roar/howl and Ravana's name is derived from that. He made the worlds scream.

a *maharatha*[1019] and have agitated the seven oceans on seven
occasions. You are indifferent when you desire victory. You laugh
at the strongest of the strong. How have you been defeated by a
weakling like me, especially since I am a *vanara*? What is this curse
that has come over someone even the strong find to be invincible?
O bull among *brahmana rakshasas*![1020] Please tell me the reason for
this. I have granted you freedom from fear. Please trust me and do
not be scared." The powerful Dashagriva[1021] was anxious because of
his fear. Hearing Vali's words, he replied in words of conciliation.
"There is no doubt that I have defeated all the *deva*s and *asura*s in
battle. But never have I faced such a powerful person. Therefore,
casting aside all fear, I wish to be friends with you. O brave one!
You will never face me in a field of battle." Addressed in this
way, Vali spoke words signifying his assent. In those earlier times,
Ravana and Vali entered into an agreement. Delighted inside his
mind, Ravana left for Lanka, along with his forces. Vali defeated the
strong lord of *rakshasas* in Pushkara. He performed many sacrifices,
at which, food and drink were offered. Hundreds and thousands of
copious quantities of *dakshina* were offered. *Agnishtoma* sacrifices,
horse sacrifices, royal sacrifices, *nrimedha* sacrifices[1022] and every
kind of sacrifice were performed. Many kinds of donations were
always offered. *Deva*s and Indra of the *deva*s were propitiated in
many kinds of ways. *Brahmana*s were satisfied and for many years,
oblations were offered into the fire. Along with his younger brother,
Sugriva, he was happy. He ruled over the kingdom and the monkeys
had no reason for fear. He was devoted to *brahmana*s and followed
the *dharma* of the supreme *brahman*. He observed the ordinances
and performed rites. Accomplished in all the sacred texts, he enjoyed
himself for many years. At his sacrifices, the divine sage, Narada,
sang a chant. "In sacrifices, oblations, donations, speed and valour,
there is no one in the three worlds who is the equal of Vali, the
wearer of the golden garland."'

[1019] Great warrior.
[1020] Ravana was the son of a *brahmana*.
[1021] Ravana.
[1022] Where a man is sacrificed.

Shamshapayana said, 'How wonderful is the great power of the great Indra's powerful son. Vali performed one thousand sacrifices and was extremely difficult to defeat. You have said that Vali was an immensely wise *chakravarti*. Please tell us about Martanda. How did he come to be known as Martanda? O one excellent in vows! O lord! Please explain the exact etymological derivation to us.'

Suta replied, 'While *praja*s were being created, Prajapati himself gathered the energy from the beginning of the three worlds to the end, and placed it in Aditi's heart. Using his great *yoga*, he made it enter. Earlier, Bhagavan had created an egg inside her stomach. Inside the egg and inside the womb, the powerful foetus grew. When it grew excessively, *deva*s lost their energy.[1023] Scared, they spoke to Prajapati. "Knowing that you had created all of us, you have robbed us of our energy. Why have you done this to us? O lord! His strength and energy, fashioned by you, are excessive. Indeed, what will happen to us? Indeed, we will be eternally destroyed and so will all entities in the world, mobile and immobile. There is no doubt that all of them will be scorched soon. O supreme *brahmana*! You have placed energy and strength inside the egg. Withdraw it. Think, so that the best can be ensured for us. The learning, energy and power are easily consuming everything." Thinking about this, Bhagavan Prajapati took it out. He placed strength inside the egg, and an infant grew inside the egg. It is said that the energy and strength inside the egg became the infant. When it was taken out, it resembled a dead lump. Prajapati saw this and divided the egg into two parts. He placed the two fragments side by side. Inside one, he saw the foetus, weak in strength, but full of energy. He raised it up and placed it in Aditi's lap. He said, "Born from you, this is Aditya. Since the egg was dead, he will be known as Martanda."[1024] The learned know Savitar by this name. The great grandfather arranged from greater energy inside it. It is held that the two shells of the egg possessed supreme energy. The lord separated them and placed them in Iravati's navel.[1025] Desiring that she might

---

[1023] One deduces that Adityas were also inside the womb.

[1024] From *mrita* (dead) *anda* (egg).

[1025] Iravati being Krodhavashaa's daughter.

give birth, he made them enter her stomach. Iravati gave birth to four elephants who are revered by the worlds. They are supreme in strength and are kings of elephants. *Deva*s mount them. They are Airavana, Kumuda, Anjana and Vamana. I will subsequently speak about them in detail. In this world, he is foremost because of his excessive and infinite energy. Using his rays, the illustrious Savitar provides direct illumination. O *dvija*s! The world beyond Lokaloka is devoid of illumination. There is a lot of proof that everything on the outside is enveloped in darkness. O excellent *dvija*s! I have heard all this accurately from the illustrious Vyasa, Parashara's great-souled son. Sanatkumara spoke about this earlier and Vayu also spoke about this earlier. In many kinds of ways, others have also separately spoken about this. Everything can be achieved if one listens to the sacred Puranas. They are like *amrita*. Even if he is born as other species, he roams around without any fear. If the story of Martanda's birth is recounted in a house, or is heard, it should be known that there is no one who is his equal. His children never die before their time.'

'Riksha was a strong *vanara* and his sister was Rikshaa. Through Prajapati, her son was the immensely wise and famous Riksharaja,[1026] Jambavat, who defeated valiant ones. Through Vyaghri, he had a daughter named Jambavati, who had eyes like a lotus. Her father bestowed her on Vaasudeva. Riksharaja had other immensely strong sons. They were Jayanta, Sarvajna, Mrigarat, Sankriti, Jaya, Marjara, Balihahu, Lakshanajna, Shutarthakrit, Bhoja, Rakshasajit, Pishacha, Vanagochara, Sharabha, Shalabha, Vyaghra and Simha. Their sons and grandsons numbered hundreds of thousands. As a result of their qualities, Rikshas were worshipped by *deva*s and *danava*s. Marjara had immensely strong sons, the Marjaras.[1027] There were hundreds of thousands and all of them were full of valour. They were immensely energetic and were the *acharya*s of *sharabha*s and predatory creatures. They ate *prishata*s, rats and birds. They were dexterous in jumping around and made all living creatures suffer. They inhabited villages, parts of forests,

---

[1026] King of bears (*riksha*).
[1027] *Marjara* is a cat.

hollows, caves, homes, basements of houses and residences inside houses. They were skilled and moved around in many kinds of ways and could be seen in villages. There were others that naturally reside in forests and roamed around there. They moved around during the day, at night and at the time of the *sandhyas*. Some had the complexion of blue clouds, others were brown and red, with eyes that squinted. Some were dark in complexion, others were tawny, smoky and coloured. Talons and teeth were their weapons. They were terrible and their cries were like those of peacocks. Saramaa had two brave sons who were impossible to withstand. These are described as Shyama and Shabala, Yama's followers. Their sons were unassailable, and these had sons and grandsons. It is said that among *sarameyas*,[1028] this lineage is always learned. At the moment, those belonging to this species are terrible in form and immensely strong. The cause distress to men from every kind of *jati*.[1029] They are attached to residing in villages. If a person hears about the birth of creatures with curved teeth, or makes it heard, he has no fear from creatures with curved teeth, from thieves, or from any other source. It was been determined that such a person will die instantly.[1030] He will not be imprisoned. He will not be born in a mixed *varna*. In the stage of *vanaprastha*, he will obtain *dharma*, craved by sages. He will be endowed with divine wealth and strength. He will not deviate from *jnana* and will be born as a *deva*. It is said that there are eleven species of *vanaras*—*dvipins*, *sharabhas*, *simhas*, *vyaghras*, *nilas*, *shalyakas*, *rikshas*, *marjaras*, *lohasas*, *vanaras* and *mayus*.[1031] The leader of all these is the powerful King Vali. In conflicts between *devas* and *asuras*, he always prided himself on being a killer of terrible and strong *asuras*, who could withstand blows. The great-souled Brahma, who holds up the worlds had already thought of this and had created this species, who destroyed those who were

---

[1028] Saramaa's son is a *sarameya*, that is, a dog.

[1029] Lineage into which one has been born.

[1030] Without suffering.

[1031] *Simha* is a lion, *vyaghra* is a tiger, *shalyaka* is a porcupine and *lohasa* is a kind of *vanara*.

excessive in strength, as the great Indra's aides. The monkeys have thus been spoken about.'

'Now hear about Iravati's children. Bhouvana[1032] brought together the two parts of the shell from Surya's egg. He held them in his hand and chanted the *rathantara* hymn. While he was chanting this *Sama* hymn, Bhouvana immediately went to Iravati and handed these over, so that she might have sons. Airavata is said to be Iravati's son. He was born first and is the king of elephants. He is the mount of the king of *devas*. He is white in complexion and has four tusks. The elephant known as Airavata is handsome. His base is like a single mass of collyrium, and the elephant has a golden tinge. Bali's mount is the elephant Bhadra, with six tusks. The she-elephant, Abhramu,[1033] gave birth to four sons—Anjana, Supratika, Vamana and Padma. These powerful elephants, born through Abhraumu, became *diggajas*. Anjana is Yama's mount and had four sons—Bhadra, Mriga, Manda and Samkirna. The gentle Supratika is an elephant who belongs to the lord of the waters.[1034] Padma is an elephant who is slow and fair. He belongs to Ailavila.[1035] The dark animal is an elephant who bears Pavaka.[1036] He had eight sons, known as Padma, Uttama, Padmagulma, Agaja, Vatagaja, Gaja, Chapala and Arishta. Their descendants were fierce elephants. These elephants resemble tawny clouds and their hair and nails are white. In the due order, I will describe other elephants born from *Sama* hymns. The famous Kapila and Pundarika were born from *rathantara*. It has been heard that the ones names Supratika and Pramardana were also born from this. They are brave, with stout heads and tusks. Their hair and nails are pure. Elephants born in this lineage are described as strong and auspicious. Pushpadanta was born from Brihatsaman and he has six tusks. His sons are the tusked Padmapucchavan and Tamraparna, who move around in herds. There were others born in this lineage, beautiful to behold,

---

[1032] Also known as Bhoumana, Vishvakarma, architect of the gods.
[1033] Airavata's wife.
[1034] Varuna.
[1035] Kubera.
[1036] Agni's mount, Vamana.

with trunks that hang down. Their skins, tongues and trunks are dark. The faces are large and extended. Vamadeva, Ajana, Shyama and Saman were born from Vamana. Vamana's wife was Anganaa and her sons were Nilavan and Lakshana. The elephants born in this lineage are bulky. They are fierce and their heads and necks are handsome. They are spirited, with broad chests and firm feet. When Supratika's deformity went away, he attained the same form as Saman. He had three sons—Prahari, Sampati and Prithu. Elephants born in this lineage are tall, with long trunks. The hair on the head is neatly parted and they are gentle at the time of sexual intercourse. Through Anjanavati, Anjana had Anjanaa as a son. He had two sons, described as Pramathi and Purusha. The elephants born in her lineage have gigantic heads that are neatly divided between the two sides. They are handsome and resemble pleasant clouds. They are well-built and the complexion is like the outside of a lotus. They are brave and never miserable, with large faces. Born through *Sama* hymns, Kumudadyuti gave birth to Kumuda, the son of Chandramas. Born through Pingalaa, Kumuda's sons were Mahapadma and Urmimali. It should be known that elephants born in this lineage love to fight. They resemble mountains and clouds. They are excellent, strong and extremely intelligent. For victory in battles between *devas* and *asuras*, the Gods accepted these. When the objective behind the creation of these elephants was achieved, they were released in different directions. The gods gave these directions to many such species of elephants. Lomapada was given the region of Anga and he classified elephants.[1037] An elephant with two tasks is called *dvirada*.[1038] Since it uses its trunk like a hand, it is called *hasti*.[1039] Since it restrains, it is *varana*.[1040]

[1037] Lomapada was the king of Anga. There is a text known as *gajashastra* (manual on training of elephants), authored by Palakapya. This has references to the kingdom of Anga, though it wasn't necessarily composed in Anga.

[1038] Two (*dvi*) tusks/teeth (*rada*).

[1039] *Hasta* means hand.

[1040] *Varana* means to ward off.

Since it has tusks, it is *danti*.[1041] Since it roars, it is *gaja*.[1042] Since it roams around in groves, it is *kunjara*.[1043] It is *naga* because there is no place that cannot be reached by it.[1044] It is *matanga* because it is intoxicated.[1045] Since it uses two to drink,[1046] it is described as *dvipa*. It is *samaja* because it originated from *Sama* hymns. These are the different kinds of classification. The tongues withdraw from the usual function of speaking because of Agni's curse.[1047] Elephants do not know how strong they are and their scrotums are hidden. Both of these remain hidden because Gods cursed elephants. Many kinds of spirited elephants originated when *diggajas*[1048] united with the daughters of *deva*s, *danava*s, *gandharva*s, *pishacha*s, *uraga*s and *rakshasa*s. Names are decided on the basis of habitat and birth. It should be known that Abhramu is the king of these elephants. The desolate region from the Koushiki river to the ocean, and to the north of Ganga, is known as the habitat of Anjana elephants, with a single tusk. The region to the north of Vindhya and south of Ganga and the region of Karusha, divided by Ganga, is the habitat of Supratika. The region on the other side of Utkala and to the west of Kaveri is described as the forest where Vamana, Ekasuka's son, resides. The region on the other side of Louhitya[1049] and to the west of Sindhu, extending up to the mountains, is described as Padma's forest.'

'It should be known that Bhutaa gave birth to *bhuta*s, Rudra's followers. They are stout, lean, tall, short, dwarfs, upright, with long ears, with hanging lips, with long tongues, with small stomachs, with one eye, malformed, with long hips, with stout calves, dark,

---

[1041] *Danta* means tusk/tooth.

[1042] From *garjana* (roar/trumpet).

[1043] *Kunja* is a grove.

[1044] From *na* (no) + *gamyam* (to be reached).

[1045] *Matta* means mad/intoxicated.

[1046] The two hollows in the trunk.

[1047] When Agni hid from the sage Bhrigu, the elephant revealed the hiding-place and was cursed.

[1048] The text uses the word *dignaga*, which means the same thing as *diggaja*.

[1049] Brahmaputra.

fair, blue, with white faces, with red faces, tawny, speckled, smoky in complexion, with red noses, with hair like *munja* grass, with hair that stands up, with snakes as sacred threads, with many heads, without feet, with a single head, with no head, fierce, hideously formed, with two tongues, with shaved heads, with matted hair, hump-backed, crooked like dwarves, residents of excellent ponds, oceans, rivers and banks, with a single ear, with gigantic ears, with ears like cones, without ears, with curved fangs, with nails, without teeth, without tongues, with a single hand, with two hands, with three hands, without hands, with a single foot, with two feet, with many feet, infused with great *yoga*, immensely spirited, with excellent minds, immensely strong, capable of going anywhere, without impediments, with knowledge of the *brahman*, capable of assuming any form at will, terrible, cruel, worthy, believers that both nectar and liquor are worthy, with deep teeth, with large tongues, without hair, with deformed faces, with skulls, with bows, holders of bludgeons, holders of swords and spears, with no garments, with colourful garments and with colourful garlands and unguents. Some eat with their hands, some eat with their mouths and some eat with their heads. Some eat food-grains, others eat flesh. Some drink liquor, others drink *soma*. Some are terrible and wander around during *sandhya*. Some are amiable and roam around during the day. Some are harsh to the touch and roam around at night. Those who roam around at night are terrible. The minds of all these are devoted to the supreme divinity, Bhava. All of them hold up their seed and do not have wives or sons. In this way, there are hundreds and thousands of *bhutas*, who perform *yoga* with the *atman*. All of them are Bhava's companions and are described as *bhutas*.'

'*Kushmandas* are repeatedly born as the sons of Kapishaa. It is said that *pishachas* are born in couples and their complexion is tawny. All these tawny *pishachas* live on flesh. There are sixteen couples in the lineage now.[1050] I will describe the names and forms in the lineage. They are Chagala and Chagalaa; Vakra and Vakramukhi; Dushpura and Puranaa; Shuchimukha and Shuchi;

[1050] One male and one female. The male is mentioned first. As stated, there are the names of 18 couples. This is also true of the categories.

Vipada and Vipadi; Angaraka and Jvalaa; Kumbhapatra and
Kumbhi; Pratunda and Pratundika; Upavira and Viraa; Ulukhala
and Ulukhali; Akarmaka and Karmaki; Kushanda and Kushandika;
Panipatra and Panipatri; Pamshu and Pamshumati; Nitunda and
Nitundi; Nipuna and Nipuni; Balada and Keshanadi; and Praskanda
and Skandika. These are described as the sixteen *pishacha* couples
and they belong to sixteen categories—Ajamukhas, Vakramukhas,
Puranas, Skandinas, Vipadas, Angarikas, Kumbhapatras,
Pratundakas, Upaviras, Ulukhalikas, Akarmakas, Kushandikas,
Pamshus, Panipatras, Naitundas, Nipunas, Suchimukhas and
Uccheshanadas. These are the sixteen. These are described as the
noble *kushmanda*s. Male and female *pishacha*s were born in these
lineages. They are horrible and malformed. There is an infinite
number of sons and grandsons. Understand the signs of *pishacha*s
next. Ajamukha *pishacha*s have hair all over their bodies. Their
eyes are round and they have cruel fangs and nails. Their limbs
are crooked and they are harsh in speech. Kushandika *pishacha*s
have no ears and hair. They wear no garments. Their skins are
their garments. They love to eat and always eat flesh. Vakramukha
*pishacha*s have crooked limbs, hands and feet. It should be known
that they move in a crooked way and can assume any form at will.
Naitunda *pishacha*s have round stomachs and noses that are like
snouts. Their bodies, heads and hands are short. They eat sesamum
and love blood. Akarmaka *pishacha*s have forms that resemble
monkeys. They are voluble and move by leaping around. They
reside on trees and love cooked food. Their arms are upraised,
and their body hair stands up. Their eyes bulge out and they live
anywhere. Pamshu *pishacha*s release dust from their limbs. Their
bodies are dry, and they resemble bees. Their garments are made
out of bark and they wield spears. Upavira *pishacha*s always reside
in cremation grounds. The eyes of Ulukhala *pishacha*s do not
move. They have large and lolling tongues. Their ornaments are
made out of mortars. They hold jewels and are deceitful. Panipatra
*pishacha*s subsist on offerings that are made. Their heads are large,
like those of elephants and camels. Their calves are thick and
curved. Kumbhapatra *pishacha*s eat food that is not visible. Their
body-hair is subtle and tawny. When they roam around, they are

sometimes seen, and sometimes unseen. Nipuna *pishacha*s roam around, without any followers. Their mouths extend all the way up to their ears. Their eyebrows hang down and their noses are thick. Purana *pishacha*s love homes that are empty. They are short and stout. Their hands and feet cover their noses. Their eyes look downwards, towards the ground. Balada *pishacha*s[1051] frequent delivery-chambers. Their hands and feet are turned backwards. They move backwards and are as swift as the wind. Vipadaka *pishacha*s survive on the blood from battlegrounds. They are naked and have no fixed abode. They have elongated penises, testicles and calves. Other than Skandina *pishacha*s, there are others that survive on leftovers.[1052] Thus, sixteen different species of *pishacha*s have been described. Brahma saw these kinds of *pishacha*s and was filled with compassion. Since they were limited in intelligence, he was filled with pity and granted them a boon. They can vanish amidst *praja*s and can assume any form at will. They can roam around at the time of both the *sandhya*s. He gave them abodes and means of subsistence—broken houses; empty houses; houses with limited water; destroyed habitations; houses inhabited by wicked people; houses not cleaned and smeared; houses where there are no *samskara*s; royal roads; paths; pleasure-groves;[1053] quadrangles; doors of mansions; entries and exits; roads; rivers; *tirtha*s; trees in chaityas;[1054] and trunk roads. All these places have been earmarked for *pishacha*s. The Gods have determined that they can survive on people who follow *adharma*. They can subsist on those who mix up *varna*s and *ashrama*s, fraudulent artisans, thieves, those who commit breach of trust and many others who earn through illegitimate means. At the junctions of *parva*s, when rites are started, the following are said to be oblations that must be continuously offered to *pishacha*s—honey, flesh, cooked food mixed with curds, crushed

---

[1051] Probably the same as Suchimukhas.

[1052] That is, Uccheshanadas.

[1053] Alternatively, *nishkuta* can be taken as a hollow in a tree.

[1054] The word *chaitya* has several meanings—sacrificial shed, temple, altar, sanctuary and a tree that grows along the road.

sesamum, *sura*, *asava*,[1055] incense, turmeric, *krisara*,[1056] edible food made out of sesamum and molasses, black garments, fragrances and flowers. After granting *pishacha*s these, Brahma made Girisha, the wielder of the trident, lord of all *bhuta*s and *pishacha*s.'

'The beautiful Damshtraa gave birth to sons who were lions and tigers. Her sons were also leopards and other predatory creatures that eat meat. Listen to all the offspring that Rishaa had. She had five daughters. Hear about their names. They were Minaa, Aminaa, Vritta, Parivritta and Anuvritta. Hear about their offspring. Minaa's children were *makara*s with one thousand teeth,[1057] *pathina*s, whales and *rohita*s.[1058] The lineage is extensive. Aminaa gave birth to four kinds of *graaha*s—*madgura*, *shanku*s, *ugra*s and *shishumara*s.[1059] Vritta gave birth to many kinds of turtles that roam around in the water. She also gave birth to many kinds of conch-shells. Anuvritta gave birth to many kinds of frogs and bivalve shells. Parivrittaa's offspring were different types of oysters, cowries, conch shells, gallinules and leeches. The five branches of Rishaa's lineage have thus been described. Tiryaa's lineage extended in many kinds of ways. All creatures born from sweat originated through her. O *dvija*s! Worms are born when the body is moistened through sweat. Creatures known as *ushana*s are born from the sweat and dirt in human bodies. There are many kinds of ants and insects with many feet. There are many kinds of conch shells, rocks and spikes. In this way, there are many kinds of creatures on earth that are born from sweat. There are also those born from water heated by the sun and from rain. There are also creatures born from the bodies of deer and other animals. There are flies and creatures born in slimy

---

[1055] *Sura* is a general term for liquor. *Asava* is made through distillation, not mere fermentation.

[1056] *Krisara* is a dish made out of sesamum and grain.

[1057] *Makara* is a mythical aquatic creature but can loosely be translated as crocodile or shark.

[1058] *Pathina* is a scale-less and large river fish, *rohita* is *rohu*.

[1059] *Graaha* is anything that seizes, the word often equated with crocodile/alligator. *Madgura* is the *magara* alligator, *shanku* is the skate fish, *ugra* is also some variety of skate fish and *shishumara* (in this context) is the estuarine crocodile.

regions, partridges and white ants. There are many such lineages, dark and blue, born from dirt. There are creatures born from water and creatures born from sweat. There are insects born from the water near *kasha* grass. There are those with many feet, born from hollow cane. They are described as those that live in bark, those that live in hair and those that live in slime.[1060] These are described as the species that originate from water and sweat. There are worms that are born from beans, black gram and pulses. There are creatures born from the fruits of *bilva*, rose-apple, mango and areca nut. They originate in lentils, jackfruit and paddy. There are those hidden within dry hollows. There are many other species that do not live for a long time. There are creatures born from horses and from poison. If cow dung is kept for many days, there are creatures born from it. O *brahmanas*! Worms are always born from wood. Scorpions are born from sweat and from dry cow dung. There are creatures born from cows, buffaloes and other animals. They are born from fish. In particular, there are many that are born from heaps of food. There are many that are born from different types of elephants. There are others that are subtle, belonging to the species of leeches. They are subtle ones, born from pigeons, ospreys and parrots. There are many kinds of other species that are born from flies. These generally reside in leftover food, stagnant water and mud. There are different kinds of gnats and bees. There are seven types of white ants that are born from cows. Predatory creatures that bore through jewels are mentioned. Entities born without placenta have thus been described. Different kinds of centipedes[1061] are born from excrement. I have thus briefly enumerated the species born from sweat. They are said to have been born in this way because they are under the subjugation of their past *karma*.'

'There are other species born from Nirritaa and from evil portents. Some *bhutas* are born from wombs, others are said to originate naturally. In general, *devas* are known to originate naturally. Some *devas* are born from wombs, other *devas* are born through some other reason. Saramaa had two sons—Dullolaka and

---

[1060] Respectively, *simhala*, *romala* and *picchila*.
[1061] We have translated *shataveri* as centipede.

Laloha. The four types, *srimara*s[1062] and others, should be known
as their children. Dullola[1063] had eight sons— Shyama, Shabala,
Lohita, Anjana, Krishna, Dhumra, Aruna and Kadruka.[1064] Surasaa
gave birth to one hundred *sarpa*s, each possessing more than one
hood. Takshaka is the king of *sarpa*s and Vasuki that of *naga*s. This
line of Krodhavashaa's descendants possesses an excess of *tamas*.
These were Pulaha's descendants.'

'Now hear about Tamraa's creation.[1065] Tamraa gave birth to
six famous daughters—Gridhri, Bhasi, Shuki, Krounchi, Shyeni
and Dhritarashtrikaa. Through Aruna, Gridhri gave birth to two
valiant and extremely strong sons. They were Sampati and Jatayu,
the excellent birds. Through Vijayaa, Sampati's sons were Dvirasya
and Prasaha. In those earlier times, Jatayu's sons were herons,
vultures and *karnika*s.[1066] Bhasi, Shuki, Krounchi, Shyeni and
Dhritarashtri[1067] were Garuda's wives. I will tell you about their
offspring. Through Shuki, Garuda had six famous sons—Sukha,
Sunetra, Vishikha, Surupa, Surasa and Bala. In those ancient times,
the great-souled sons and grandsons of Garuda numbered fourteen
thousand, and they fed on *pannaga*s. The lineage flourished because
of the offspring the sons and grandsons had. In the due order, I
will speak about the regions they pervaded—all of Shalmala-
dvipa; Mount Devakuta; Manimanta, the king of mountains with
one thousand peaks; Parnamala; the mountain Sukesha, with one
hundred peaks; Kourara, with five peaks and Mount Hemakuta.
Their speed was like that of a terrible wind, and they were as radiant
as rubies. Garuda's great-souled descendants pervaded the summits
of mountains. Bhasi's sons are described as bearded vultures, owls,
crows, cocks, peacocks, sparrows, pigeons, partridges, herons,
*vardhinasa*s,[1068] hawks, curlews, storks and *saras* cranes. There

[1062] Kind of animal that is found in marshy places, similar to deer.
[1063] The same as Dullolaka.
[1064] These are colours, respectively, dark, speckled, red, dark black
(like collyrium), blue black, smoky, pinkish red and tawny.
[1065] This is abrupt. This is the Tamraa who was Kashyapa's wife.
[1066] Some unidentified bird that must have been similar.
[1067] The same as Dhritarashtrikaa.
[1068] A large bird of prey.

were other birds of prey too. The beautiful Dhritarashtri gave birth to swans, ducks, *chakravaka* birds and all the other types of aquatic birds. O supreme *dvija*s! It is known that Shyeni had an infinite number of sons and grandsons. I have spoken about Garuda's descendants.'

'Now hear about Iraa's[1069] offspring. Iraa gave birth to three daughters who had eyes like lotuses. They were the mothers of *vanaspati*s, *vriksha*s and creepers. Their names were Lataa, Alataa and Virudhaa. Lataa gave birth to *vanaspati*s, which have fruits, but no visible flowers. Alataa gave birth to *vriksha*s, which have both flowers and fruits. Virudhaa's offspring are creepers, winding plants, lantanas, hollow grass[1070] and other kinds of grass. This ends the account of the lineage.'

'I have described Kashyapa's descendants, mobile and immobile. The entire universe is covered by their sons and grandsons. I have partially described the nature of this creation. I have briefly described the creation of *praja*s by Marichi's son. Even if one tries for one hundred years, it is impossible to describe it in detail. Aditi was devoted to *dharma* and Diti was strong. Surabhi was devoted to austerities and Danu was devoted to *maya*. Muni loved fragrances and Krodhaa was devoted to studying. Arishtaa loved singing and Khashaa is said to have been devoted to cruelty. Kadru was prone to rage and Krodhaa was devoted to purity. Vinataa loved mounts and Tamraa loved killing. Iraa was compassionate and Anayu loved to eat. Such was the conduct of all the mothers of the worlds. The sons of Lord Kashyapa were similar to their mothers in *dharma*, good conduct, intelligence, forgiveness, strength, beauty, excess of *sattva*, *rajas* and *tamas*, devotion to *dharma*, devotion to *adharma* and nobility of birth. They were *deva*s, *asura*s, *gandharva*s, *yaksha*s, *rakshasa*s, *pannaga*s, *pishacha*s, *pashu*s, *mriga*s, birds and creepers. They were born through Daksha's daughters, who were women. Therefore, *deva*s and others know about human nature. *Deva*s and all the others originated through women. Hence, in all the *manvantara*s, humans are the best. Humans strive for *dharma*, *artha*, *kama* and

---

[1069] Married to Kashyapa.
[1070] Such as bamboos.

moksha. Gods and *asura*s belong to species where nourishment flows downwards. That is the reason, to accomplish their tasks, they are repeatedly born as humans. Such is the power of lineage, and this has been enumerated in detail—Gods, *asura*s, *gandharva*s, *apsara*s, *yaksha*s, *rakshasa*s, *pishacha*s, birds, *uraga*s, flying creatures, predatory creatures, crested creatures, all the herbs, works, insects, flying insects, inferior creatures, aquatic creatures, *pashu*s and handsome *brahmana*s, who possess auspicious signs. If a person constantly hears it and accepts it, without any jealousy, he is blessed and prosperous. He obtains a long lifespan. This brings benefit and happiness. If a person controls himself and reads this account in an assembly of great-souled *brahmana*s, he obtains offspring, wealth, everything that he loves and an auspicious end after death.'

Chapter 46-1(46) (Lineage of *rishi*s)

S uta said, 'In this way, the great-souled Kashyapa created *praja*s. All the mobile and immobile entities were established. Prajapati instated the foremost among them in positions of lordship. In the due order, he instructed them about their kingdoms. Soma was instated in the kingdom of *dvija*s, creepers, *nakshatra*s, planets, sacrifices and austerities. Brihaspati became the lord over the universe of Angirasas. Kavya was instated in the kingdom of those of the Bhrigu lineage. Vishnu became the lord of Adityas and Pavaka the lord of Vasus. Daksha became the lord of Prajapatis and Vasava of Maruts. Prahlada, Diti's descendant, became the king of *daitya*s. Narayana became the lord of Sadhyas and Vrishadhvaja of Rudras. Viprachitti was instructed to become the king of *danava*s. Varuna became the lord of waters and Vaishravana was instated in the kingdom of *yaksha*s, *rakshasa*s, kings and wealth. Vaivasvata Yama was instated in the kingdom of the ancestors. Girisha, wielder of the trident, became the lord of all *bhuta*s and *pishacha*s. Himalaya became the lord of mountains and the ocean of rivers. Chitraratha became the lord of all the *gandharva*s. Ucchaihshrava was instated

as the king of all horses. The tiger became the king of *mrigas*[1071]
and the bull of all animals with humps. Garuda, supreme among
those who fly, became the lord of all birds. Vayu, supreme among
strong ones, became the lord of fragrances, winds, invisible entities
and all those who are similar in strength. Shesha became the lord
of all those with fangs and Vasuki of *nagas*. Takshaka became the
lord of reptiles, *sarpas* and *pannagas*. Parjanya, foremost among the
Adityas, was instated as the lord of oceans, rivers, clouds and rain.
Kamadeva became the lord of all the different groups of *apsaras*.
Samvatsara became the lord of *ritus*, *masas*, *artavas*, *pakshas*,[1072]
vipakshas, *muhurtas*, *parvas*, measurements like *kalas* and
kashthas, progress of *ayanas*, calculations and conjunctions. Viraja
Prajapati's famous son, named Sudhanva, was instated as the king
over the eastern direction. In that way, Kardama Prajapati's son,
named Shankhapada, was instated as the king over the southern
direction. The great-souled Ketumanta, the undecaying son of
Rajas, was instated as the king over the western direction. In that
way, Hiranyaroma, the invincible son of Prajapati Parjanya, was
instated as the king over the northern direction. Vaivasvata Manu
was made the lord of humans. Following *dharma*, they ruled over
their respective dominions and the entire earth, with its seven *dvipas*
and habitations. Earlier, in Svayambhuva *manvantara*, there were
those who had been consecrated as kings by Brahma. These became
Manus. There were kings who belonged to past *manvantaras*. When
there was a new *manvantara*, others were instated. For the past and
future *manvantaras*, all these lords are described. Prithu, supreme
among men, was consecrated through a royal sacrifice, following
the rites instructed in the *Vedas*. He was a powerful king of kings.'

'In this way, Kashyapa, the immensely fortunate lord and master
of *prajas*, had sons. He wished to have sons who would carry forward
his own *gotra*. Therefore, he performed supreme austerities. He
thought, "Let me have two sons who will carry forward my *gotra*."

[1071] The natural translation of *shardula* is tiger, but the word also
means a lion.

[1072] In an obvious typo, the text says *yakshas* instead of *pakshas*.
Vipakshas are intervening periods between *pakshas*.

To this end, the great-souled Kashyapa meditated. Thereafter, from Brahma's portions, two greatly energetic sons manifested themselves. They were Vatsara and Asita and both of them spoke about the *brahman*. Vatsara gave birth to Nidhruva and the extremely illustrious Rebhya. Raibhya is known as Rebhya's son. Hear about those of Nidhruva. Through Sukanya, Chyavana had Sumedhaa as a daughter. She was Nidhruva's wife and the mother of *kundapayins*.[1073] Through Ekaparnaa, Asita had the prosperous and extremely illustrious Devala, who was devoted to the *brahman* and supreme among Shandilyas, as a son. Three lineages descended from Kashyapa—Nidhruvas, Raibhyas and Shandilyas. The *deva* who wields the *vajra* and other *devas* are also his sons. They were born as sons of Lord Manu after eleven *mahayugas* had passed and *dvapara yuga* commenced. Marutta's son was Narishyanta and Narishyanta's son was Dama.[1074] Dama's son was Rajyavardhana. Rajyavardhana's sons were Sudhriti, Nara and Kevala. Kevala's sons were Bandhumat and Vegavat. Vegavat's son was Budha and Budha's son was Trinavindu, lord of the earth. He became king at the onset of the third *treta yuga*. Through Alambushaa,[1075] he had a daughter named Ilavilaa. Vishrava, who extended the Poulastya lineage, was born through her.[1076] Brihaspati, extensive in deeds, is described as the *acharya* of *devas*. His daughter was unmatched and was named Devavarnini. Vishrava married Devavarnini, Pushpotkataa and Vakaa, the daughter of Malyavat, and Kaikasi, who in turn, was the daughter of Malin. Hear about their offspring.'

'Devavarnini gave birth to the eldest, Vaishravana. As a result of divine determination, he was noble, full of learning. He possessed the beauty of a *rakshasa* and the strength of an *asura*. He possessed three feet and an extremely large body. His head was stout and his jaw was huge. He possessed eight teeth and a green beard. His complexion was red and his ears were like spikes. His

---

[1073] Those who drink from pits in the ground or from water-pots.
[1074] There is a sudden break. Marutta was descended from Vaivasvata Manu.
[1075] An *apsara*.
[1076] Vishrava was the son of Pulastya and Ilavila (Idivila or Idavira).

arms and forearms were short. His complexion was tawny and he was extremely terrible. However, he was intelligent from birth and possessed *jnana* about transformations. As soon as he saw him, his father himself said, "This is Kubera." The word "*ku*" is used to abuse, and "*bera*" means body.[1077] Since his body was ugly, he came to be known as Kubera. He was Vishrava's son and there was also a resemblance to Vishrava. Therefore, he also came to be known under the name of Vaishravana. Through Riddhi, Kubera gave birth to the famous Nalakubara.'

'Kaikasi gave birth to Ravana, Kumbhakarna, the daughter Shurpanakhi and Vibhishana as the fourth. Dashagriva[1078] had ears like spikes. He was tawny and the hair on his head was red. He possessed four feet and twenty hands. He was gigantic in size and immensely strong. His complexion was like that of excellent collyrium. He had curved teeth and his throat was red. He possessed the energy, beauty and strength of a *rakshasa*. As a result of his spirit and intelligence, Ravana defeated *yakshas* and *rakshasas*. Ravana was terrible and cruel and drove others away. In an earlier birth, Ravana had been Hiranyakashipu. The *rakshasa* had been a king for thirteen *mahayugas*. O *dvijas*! Measured in terms of human autumns, Ravana ruled for fifty-six million, one hundred and sixty thousand years.[1079] He was so terrible that he caused sleepless nights to *devas* and *rishis*. In the twenty-fourth *treta yuga*, the good merits of Ravana's austerities were exhausted. When he encountered Rama, Dasharatha's son, he and his followers were destroyed. Pushpotkataa's sons were Mahodara, Prahasta, Mahaparshva and Khara. Pushpokataa's daughter was Kumbhinasi. Vakaa's sons were described as Trishira, Dushana and the *rakshasa* Vidyujjihva. Vakaa is also said to have had a daughter named Anupalikaa. These were the ten cruel *rakshasas* descended from Pulastya.[1080]

[1077] *Ku* means bad, ugly.

[1078] Ravana.

[1079] 4,320,000 X 13 = 56,160,000.

[1080] Ravana, Kumbhakarna, Mahodara, Prahasta, Mahaparshva, Khara, Trishira, Dushana and Vidyujjihva make up nine. Therefore, Vibhishana is part of the ten.

They caused terror to people and were impossible for *deva*s to counter. All of them were brave and obtained boons. They had sons and grandsons. There were all these *yaksha*s and *rakshasa*s, descended from Pulastya. There were also cruel *brahma-rakshasa*s, descended from Agastya and Vishvamitra. These were devoted to studying the *Veda*s and observed austerities and vows. Poulastya Aidavida Savyapingala was their king.[1081] Among all the groups of *rakshasa*s, there were three that performed sacrifices—*yatudhana*s, *brahmadhana*s and *varta*s. They roamed around during the day. The wise say that there are four groups that roam around at night—Poulastya, Nairritas, Agastyas and Koushikas.[1082] It is thus said that there are seven species of *rakshasa*s. I will describe their forms and innate nature. They are tawny and their eyes are round. They are gigantic in size, with large stomachs. They possess eight curved teeth and ears like spikes. Their body-hair stands up. Their gaping mouths extend all the way up to the ears. Their smoky hair is like *munja* grass and stands up. Their heads are stout, with a white tinge. Their forearms and thighs are short. Their faces are coppery, and the tongues and lips hang down. The eyebrows are long, and the noses are thick. The limbs are blue, and the throats are red. The eyes are terrible and sombre. Their voices are loud and horrible. Their calves are knotted and malformed. Their noses are stout and peaked. Their bodies are as firm as stone. Right from birth, they are terrible and cruel. Generally, they find it difficult to accomplish tasks. They wear earrings, armlets, bracelets and crowns, with headdresses. They wear many kinds of ornaments and colourful garlands, fragrances and unguents. They are said to eat cooked food, flesh and humans. The learned say that such is the *dharma* and form of *rakshasa*s. In battles, no one can equal their strength, intelligence and use of *maya*.'

'Pulaha's sons were all the *mriga*s, predatory creatures, those with curved fangs, *bhuta*s, *sarpa*s, *pishacha*s, *srimara*s, elephants, *vanara*s, *kinnara*s, *mayu*s and *kimpurusha*s. These

[1081] Kubera, Idavida's son, descended from Pulastya. Savyapingala (tawny on the left) is Kubera's name.
[1082] Koushikas are the ones who were descended from Vishvamitra.

were the descendants of Krodhavashaa and I have already spoken about them.'

'In this Vaivasvata *manvantara*, it is said that Kratu did not have offspring. He did not have wives or sons. Nor did he release his semen.'

'I will now describe the lineage of Atri, the third Prajapati.[1083] He had ten beautiful wives, devoted to their husband. These ten were the daughters of Bhadrashva and the *apsara* Ghritachi. They were Bhadraa, Shudraa, Madraa, Shalabhaa, Maladaa, Balaa and Halaa. Other than these, there are said to have been Gochapalaa, Tamarasaa and Ratnakutaa. Among those in this lineage was the one named Prabhakara. Through Madraa, he had the illustrious Soma as a son. When Surya was struck by Svarbhanu,[1084] it started to fall down from the firmament to earth. The word was enveloped by darkness and it was Prabhakara who provided the illumination. The sun, which was falling, was told, "May all be well with you."[1085] As a result of the *brahmarshi*'s words, the sun did not fall down to earth from the firmament. Atri's is the best among *gotra*s, with great and famous ascetics. Through the practice of sacrifices, it is he who ensured that Gods would not be killed. He had sons who were just like his own self. The lord cleansed himself through extremely great austerities and had those ten sons. They were *rishi*s who were accomplished in the *Veda*s and are known as Svastyatreyas. There were especially two who were extremely energetic and devoted to the *brahman*. The revered Datta[1086] was the eldest and Durvasa was his younger brother. The youngest was a daughter, Abalaa, who spoke about the *brahman*. In this connection, those who know the Puranas recite a *shloka*. "Atri's great-souled son is serene in his *atman* and is without blemish. Dattatreya represents Vishnu's body." Those who know the Puranas say this. There are four from this *gotra* who are famous

---

[1083] After Pulastya and Pulaha, Kratu is not being counted since he did not have children.

[1084] Rahu.

[1085] Atri said this.

[1086] Dattatreya.

on earth—Shyavashva, Mudgala, Vagbhutaka and Gavisthira.
There are also another four in Atri's lineage who were immensely
energetic—Kashyapa, Narada, Parvata and Arundhati. Arundhati
was born through mental powers. Now hear about Arundhati's
descendants.[1087] Narada bestowed Arundhati on Vasishtha. As
a result of Daksha's curse, the immensely energetic Narada held
up his seed.[1088] In ancient times, there was the Tarakamaya battle
between *devas* and *asuras*. The entire world suffered from drought
and everyone, including the Gods, were anxious. The intelligent
Vasishtha performed austerities and revived *prajas*. Many kinds of
fruits, roots and herbs resulted. As a result of his compassion, he
revived them and revived the herbs. Through Arundhati, Vasishtha
had Shakti as a son. Through Adrishyanti, Shakti had Parasara as
a son and he was like his own body. Through Kali, Parasara gave
birth to Lord Krishna Dvaipayana. Through Arani, Dvaipayana
had Shuka, who possessed qualities, as a son. Through Pivari,
Shuka had six children—Bhurishrava, Prabhu, Shambhu, Krishna,
Goura as the fifth and the daughter Kirtimati, who was firm in
her vows and the mother of *yoga*. She was the wife of Anuha
and Brahmadatta's mother. There are said to be eight great-souled
ones who were born in Parashara's lineage—Shveta, Krishna,
Poura, Shyamadhumra, Chandin, Ushmada, Darika and Nila.
These were the Parasharas. After this, hear about the descendants
of Indrapramati. Through Kapinjali Ghritachi, Vasishtha had
Kuni as a son and he was also known as Indrapramati. Through
Prithu's daughter, he had Vasu as a son. Upamanyu was Vasu's son
and this is how Oupamanyus originated. These Mitra-Varunas[1089]
are also described as Kundineyas. There are other Vasishthas

[1087] There are apparent inconsistencies, reconciled because of multiple
births. Sandhya was born through Brahma's mental powers and was
subsequently reborn as Arundhati, the sage Medhatithi's daughter.
According to another account, Arundhati was Narada's sister. Therefore,
a brother could bestow a sister in marriage. According to yet another
account, Narada had a daughter named Arundhati. Daksha cursed Narada
because Narada led his sons astray.

[1088] Text missing

[1089] Vasishtha was descended from Mitra-Varuna.

known as Ekarsheyas. These are described as the eleven Vasishtha lineages.'[1090]

'Thus, the eight famous sons born through Brahma's mental powers have been described. They were extremely fortunate brothers who established lineages. Full of large numbers of *deva*s and *rishi*s, they held up the three worlds. They had hundreds and thousands of sons and grandsons. Like the sun with its rays, they pervaded the three worlds.'

Chapter 47-1(47) (Rites for ancestors)

The *rishi*s asked, 'Bhavani was earlier Sati, Daksha's daughter. How was she born for a second time as Umaa? She was the daughter of the king of the mountains himself, through Menaa, the daughter of the ancestors. Menaa was the daughter of the ancestors, born through their mental powers. Who were they? Their daughter's son was Mainaka and their daughter's daughters were Umaa, Ekaparnaa, Ekapatalaa and Ganga, the best among rivers. Who was the oldest among them? Please instruct us about everything that you have been instructed about. I[1091] wish to hear about the auspicious and supreme *shraddha* rites. Who are described as their sons? Whose fathers were they? How did they originate? What is their nature? The ancestors are like divinities for *deva*s. Are they in heaven? I wish to know about the excellent creation of ancestors. What do we offer the ancestors, so that they are pleased? What is said to be the reason for their not being visible? Which ancestors are in heaven and which ancestors are in hell? When three *pinda*s are offered, the names of the father, the father's father and the great-grandfather are mentioned. At the time of *shraddha*s, when the names are mentioned and these are offered, how do they reach the ancestors? If they happen to be in hell, how can one bestow the

---

[1090] Eight from Parashara, those through Upamanyu, those through Kundi (Kuni) and the Ekarsheyas.

[1091] The statement is in the singular.

fruits on them? On the daughter's side, what are the names of the ancestors? We have heard that, in heaven, *deva*s also worship the ancestors. This has been heard many times and I wish to hear about this in detail. You should explain all this clearly.'

Suta replied, 'In accordance with my wisdom and in accordance with what I have heard, I will describe this. In all the *manvantara*s, the ancestors are born as the sons of *deva*s. In the due order, the past and the future become older and younger.[1092] In the former *manvantara*s, past ancestors existed, along with *deva*s. I will certainly describe to you the ones who exist now. Shraddhadeva Manu[1093] started the system of *shraddha* rites. Thinking that they would worship him, the Lord Brahma created *deva*s. However, desiring fruits, they abandoned him and started to worship themselves. At this, Brahma cursed them, "You will be foolish and will lose your senses. Hence, you will not know anything. In the worlds, you will be deluded." All of them prostrated themselves and entreated the grandfather. To show a favour to the worlds, the lord spoke again. "You have committed a transgression. Perform *prayashchitta*. If you ask your sons, you will obtain *jnana* from them." Desiring to perform *prayashchitta*, they asked their own sons. They controlled themselves and asked about the rites that needed to be understood. Controlling themselves, the sons, who knew about *dharma*, instructed them about many things, concerning *prayashchitta* in thoughts, words and deeds. The residents of heaven regained their senses. Delighted, they spoke to the sons. "Since you have kindled understanding in us, you have become our fathers. You have bestowed *dharma*, *jnana* and non-attachment on us. What boon will we grant you?" Brahma spoke. "You are truthful in speech. Hence, what you have said must come true. It cannot but be otherwise. You have said that your own sons will become your fathers. Therefore, they will become ancestors. Grant them this boon." These were the words of Parameshthi Brahma. Accordingly, the sons obtained the status of fathers, and the fathers obtained the status of sons. Hence, those sons became ancestors, and it is

---

[1092] The former fathers are born as the future sons of the present sons.
[1093] The God of funeral ceremonies, Yama.

said that this is how they obtained the status of being fathers. It is said that this is how sons became fathers and fathers became sons. For the sake of nourishment of ancestors, Brahma spoke to them again. "In the course of a *shraddha* ceremony directed at ancestors, if a person performs harmful acts, the fruits will not be able to nourish ancestors. Nourished by you, they will constantly flourish. Soma will be nourished through *shraddha* ceremonies and will nourish the worlds, along with all the mountains, forests, mobile and immobile entities. For the sake of nourishment, humans will undertake *shraddha* ceremonies and the ancestors will always bestow nourishment on *prajas*. In the course of a *shraddha*, when three *pindas* are offered, mentioning the name and the *gotra*, the fathers and great grandfathers will be present everywhere. Through the offerings rendered at *shraddhas*, they will nourish *prajas*." In earlier times, these were the instructions issued by Parameshthi Brahma. Success in donations, studying and austerities is obtained through this. There is no doubt that ancestors bestow *jnana* on you. Thus, ancestors are *devas* and *devas* are ancestors. *Devas* and ancestors are mutually ancestors and *devas* to each other.'

The sages heard Brahma's words, as recounted by Suta, who had cleansed his *atman*. In response, they asked Suta again.

The *rishi*s asked, 'What are the different groups of ancestors[1094] and when did these groups come into being? The ancestors are supreme divinities and are nourished by Soma and *devas*.'

Suta replied, 'I will tell you about the excellent creation of ancestors. Earlier, Shamyu[1095] asked his father, Brihaspati, about this. Brihaspati, who knew about every kind of jnana and meaning, was seated. Full of humility, his son, Shamyu, asked him this question. "Who are the ancestors? How many are there? What are their names? How did they originate? How did they obtain the status of being ancestors? Earlier, how did ancestors constantly nourish sacrifices? At *shraddhas*, why are rites first performed for these great-souled ones? What should be offered at *shraddhas*? What are the

---

[1094] The text says groups of sages. It should read, groups of ancestors and we have corrected the statement.

[1095] Brihaspati's eldest son.

great fruits from these offerings? Where do the fruits of *shraddha*s become eternal, in *tirtha*s or in rivers? By performing a *shraddha* ceremony, how does an excellent *dvija* obtain everything? What is the time for performing a *shraddha*? What are the rites that must be followed? O illustrious one! I wish to learn about this accurately and in detail. In the due order, you should explain to me what I have mentioned." In this way, the immensely intelligent Brihaspati was properly asked. Supreme among those who could answer questions, in the due order, he answered the question. Brihaspati answered, "O son! I will tell you what you have asked me about. This is an excellent and serious question, asked with proper humility. O son! At the time, nothing existed—the sky, the firmament, the earth, *nakshatra*s, directions, the sun, the moon, night, or day. The universe was enveloped in darkness. Brahma alone existed, engaged in tormenting himself through extremely difficult austerities." Shamyu spoke to his father again. He[1096] was supreme among those who knew about the *brahman*, having bathed himself in all the vows of the *Veda*s. He was supreme among those who possessed every kind of *jnana*. "Prajapati is the lord of all beings. What kind of austerities did he perform?" Brihaspati answered, "Among all kinds of austerities, *yoga* is the supreme austerity. Using *dhyana*, the illustrious one created the worlds, *jnana*, past and future worlds, all the *Veda*s, *yoga* and *amrita*. Brahma, the eye of the worlds, created all this. There were radiant worlds, named Santanakas. There are divinities known as Vairajas. They are like Gods of the Gods who are in heaven. Brahma is full of eternal *yoga*. Earlier, using his *yoga* and austerities, the lord created these divinities. These are immensely spirited and immensely energetic, known as Adidevas.[1097] They yield everything that is desired and should be worshipped by *deva*s, *danava*s and humans. They are described as possessing seven groups, worshipped by the three worlds. Three of these are without forms and four possess forms. The three at the top are conceived as those who do not have forms. The four that are below possess forms that are subtle. *Deva*s come after this, and the earth comes

---

[1096] Brihaspati.
[1097] Original *deva*s, before the *deva*s.

after them. This is the progressive order of the worlds. They shower down on the worlds and Parjanya originates from them. Food results from the rain and the worlds originate. In this way, they nourish Soma and nourish food. Revered by the worlds, they are known as the ancestors of the worlds. They possess the speed of thought and *svadha* is their food. They have cleansed themselves of every kind of desire. They have cast aside avarice, delusion and fear. Bereft of sorrows, they are assured. Having abandoned *yoga* too, they have obtained worlds that are beautiful to behold. They are divine, sacred, bereft of sins and great-souled. They are reborn at the end of one thousand *mahayugas* and speak about the *brahman*. Those without form regain their *yoga* again and obtain *moksha*.[1098] Through the great strength of their *yoga*, they abandon everything, manifest and unmanifest. They vanish, like a meteor in the sky, or an instant flash of lightning. Through the great strength of their *yoga*, they cast aside the bonds of the body. Like rivers that proceed to the ocean, they no longer possess names. One should carefully undertake sacrifices and worship these preceptors through rites. The ancestors are pleased with *shraddhas*. Using their *yoga*, they nourish Soma. On the basis of their *yoga*, the three worlds are nourished and obtain life. Therefore, one should always make efforts to resort to *yoga* and render offerings to them at *shraddhas*. *Yoga* is the strength of ancestors. Soma functions because of *yoga*. One can feed one hundred thousand *brahmanas*, or anyone who comes. If one person who knows *mantras* is fed, it is like feeding all of them. Hear about this. If a single person who knows *mantras* arrives and is fed, that is sufficient. If a single *snataka* is pleased, it is like all of them being pleased.[1099] Feeding a single *acharya* of *yoga* is equivalent to feeding one thousand who know about *mantras*, or one hundred *snatakas*. One is then saved from great fear. *Yoga* is superior to one thousand lives in *garhasthya*, one hundred in *vanaprastha* and one thousand in *brahmacharya*. Prajapati said, 'A non-believer, a person who follows *adharma*, a narrow person or a thief, cannot be saved,

---

[1098] Some are reborn, while others attain *moksha*.

[1099] A *snataka* is an individual who has completed the *brahmacharya* stage of studying and is ready to enter the next stage of life.

other than by donating to a *yogi*.' A tiller is content when the
rains are good. Like that, when a son or a grandson feeds a person
engaged in *dhyana*, the ancestors are content. If a person engaged
in *dhyana* is not available, a *brahmachari* must be fed. If such an
indifferent person is not available, a person engaged in *garhasthya*
must be fed. Brahma's instructions are that a person engaged in
dhyana and *yoga* is superior to a person who stands on one foot
for one hundred years, subsisting only on air. This is described
as the original group of infinitely energetic ancestors. This group
exists forever, purifying all the worlds. After this, I will speak
about all the other groups. In the due order, I will speak about
what is conceived, regarding the establishment of their lineage.'"

Chapter 48-1(48) (Rites for ancestors continued)

Brihaspati said, 'Among all the victorious groups of ancestors
in heaven, seven are described as the best. Four possess forms
and three do not have forms. I will describe their worlds and the
nature of their creation. Listen. I will describe their daughters and
the sons of their daughters. There are those who reside in radiant
worlds named Santanakas. These groups of ancestors are without
form and are the sons of Prajapati. O best among *dvija*s! They are
resplendent and are known as Vairajas.[1100] O son! These are the
ancestors who enhance the *yoga* of *yogi*s. Through the strength
of their *yoga*, they constantly nourish *yogi*s. They are nourished
through *shraddha*s and nourish Soma. Nourished in this way, Soma
nourishes the worlds. They had a daughter named Menaa, born
through mental powers. She was the wife of the great mountain,
Himalaya, and had a son named Mainaka. He is supreme among
mountains and Mount Krouncha is another son. Through the king
of mountains, Himalaya had three daughters. They were Aparnaa
and Ekaparnaa and the third was Ekapatalaa. Ekaparnaa sought

[1100] The word *viraja* means shining/resplendent. Vairajas are thus the
first group of ancestors and their daughter was Menaa.

refuge under a *nyagrodha* tree and Ekapatalaa sought refuge under a *patala* tree.[1101] Aparnaa was without a habitation. Thus, they undertook austerities that were difficult for even *deva*s and *danava*s to perform. They did this for one hundred thousand years. As food, Ekaparnaa only had a single leaf. Ekapatalaa had only a single *patala* flower. These two only ate once, when the cycle of one thousand years was complete. However, the other one did not eat at all, though her mother sought to restrain her. Miserable on account of her motherly affection, she restrained her and said, "U! Ma!"[1102] She spoke in this way to Devi Aparnaa, who performed this extremely difficult task. Consequently, the immensely fortunate one became famous in the three worlds under the name of Umaa. Based on her deeds, that is the derivation of her name. Such was the power of the austerities undertaken by the three maidens that, as long as the earth, with its mobile and immobile entities remains, they will be remembered. Despite the austerities, the bodies of the three were sustained through the strength of their *yoga*. All of them were extremely fortunate and for them, youth was permanent. All of them spoke about the *brahman* and all of them practiced *brahmacharya*. Umaa, with the beautiful complexion, was the eldest and the best among them. She was full of the great strength of *yoga* and offered herself to Mahadeva. She adopted Ushanas, Bhrigu's son, as her adopted son. The virtuous Ekaparnaa, devoted to her husband, became Asita's wife. Himalaya bestowed her on the intelligent preceptor of *yoga*. Full of *jnana*, she gave birth to Devala, who was devoted to the *brahman*. Ekapatalaa was the third of the daughters. She presented herself before Jaigishavya, Shatashalaka's son. Her two sons, born without a womb, are said to be Shankha and Likhita. These were the auspicious and immensely fortunate daughters of Himalaya.'

'The eldest was Rudrani and her own qualities were supreme. Umaa and Shankara were extremely pleased with each other

---

[1101] *Patala* is the trumpet flower. The word *parnaa* means leaf. Ekaparnaa means a single leaf, Ekapatalaa means a single *patala* flower and Aparnaa means even without a leaf.

[1102] The letter 'U' is just an exclamation, while '*ma*' means 'do not'.

and attached to each other. Knowing this, Vritra's slayer[1103] was
scared. He was afraid that any child who resulted from physical
intercourse between them would render him incapable. Therefore,
Indra sent Havyavahana to their presence. "O Hutashana![1104]
Act so that there is an impediment in the path of their physical
intercourse. You can go everywhere, and no sin will attach to you."
Thus addressed, Vahni did as he had been told. The divinity left
Umaa and discharged the semen on the ground. Enraged, Umaa
immediately cursed Agni. Her voice choking in rage, she addressed
Vahni in these words. "O Hutashana! You interrupted our act of
intercourse before we were satisfied. You performed an act you
should not have. Therefore, you are evil-minded. A conception has
resulted from Rudra's extremely radiant semen. You must bear it
in your womb. That is your punishment." As a result of Rudrani's
curse, the conception was transferred inside Hutashana's womb. O
dvija! He bore this for many years. He then approached Ganga and
said, "O supreme among rivers! Listen. Since I have been forced
to bear this conception, I am suffering from great distress. O one
who flows downwards! For the sake of my welfare, please bear this
foetus. Through my favours, you will have a son who will be the
bestower of boons." Thus addressed, the great river was extremely
delighted and agreed. Though her senses were scorched, she bore
that foetus. As a consequence, the great river suffered from a great
hardship. Suffering, she cast aside the foetus, which blazed like
a fire. Through Rudra, Agni and Ganga, a son was born and he
was red in complexion. He was extremely energetic and powerful,
resembling one hundred suns. The immensely fortunate Kumara,
Jahnavi's son,[1105] was born in this way. At the time of his birth, the
sky was covered by *vimana*s and vehicles that could fly. In the sky,
the drums of *deva*s were sounded in melodious tones. *Siddha*s and
*charana*s, who roam around in the sky, showered down flowers.
Here and there and everywhere, the best among *gandharva*s sang.
All the *yaksha*s, *vidyadhara*s, *siddha*s, *kinnara*s, thousands of

---

[1103] Indra.
[1104] The one who devours oblations, Agni. Vahni is also Agni's name.
[1105] Jahnavi is Ganga's name.

giant *naga*s, and the best among birds presented themselves before
Shankara's immensely fortunate son, born through Agni. His
power struck *daitya*s, *vanara*s and *rakshasa*s. With the exception
of Arundhati, the wives of the *saptarshi*s, who were on their way
to have their ablutions, went to see the *deva* born through Agni.
They surrounded the lord who was Rudra's son. He resembled the
rising sun. Full of great love, they acted as if they were his mothers.
Simultaneously, Jahnavi's son was suckled by all these *devi*s. So that
he might suckle, the handsome one created six faces and he is known
as Shanmukha.[1106] When he was born, the large number of *danava*s
could not withstand the power of *deva*s and relieved themselves.
That is the reason he came to be known as Skanda.[1107] In earlier
times, he was reared by the Krittikas.[1108] Hence, the destroyer of
*asura*s came to be known as Kartikeya. When the enemy of *daitya*s
yawned, his own unvanquished spear emerged from within his
mouth, amidst a blazing garland of flames. The powerful Vishnu,
who enters everywhere, created two handsome birds, a peacock
and a cock, from Garuda and handed these over to Skanda, so
that he might play. Vayu gave him a flag. Sarasvati gave him a
large *veena*, which made a loud sound. Svayambhu gave him a goat
and Shambhu gave him a sheep. O *brahmana*! Through the force
of his *maya*, he brought down Mount Krouncha.[1109] He shattered
and brought down the supreme Tarakasura. The powerful enemy
of *daitya*s, the lord who was Agni's son, was consecrated as the
commander by Indra, Upendra and the immensely fortunate *deva*s.
Therefore, one reads about the leader of Gods as the *senapati*[1110]
of *deva*s. Skanda, the lord who is the lord of all the worlds, creates

[1106] The one with six faces. Across texts, stories of Kartikeya's birth
aren't consistent.

[1107] This is a most unusual derivation. The usual explanation is that he
came to be known as Skanda because the semen oozed out (*skanna*).

[1108] The Pleiades. Kartikeya/Kumara/Skanda was reared by the
Krittikas. They adopted him as their son.

[1109] In usual accounts, he shattered it with his spear.

[1110] Commander of armies, general.

carnage among enemies of *deva*s.[1111] He was surrounded by many kinds of *pramatha*s[1112] and *deva*s, large numbers of *bhuta*s, many kinds of *matrika*s and large numbers of *vinayaka*s.'

'There are worlds named Somapadas. Marichi's sons reside there, in the firmament, and are worshipped by *deva*s. It is heard that the ancestors named Barhishads, drinkers of *soma*, reside there.[1113] Born through mental powers, their daughter was the river named Acchodaa. She flows from a divine lake named Acchoda. Her fathers have never been seen by her. She did not know her own fathers and chose another father, thus committing a transgression against the ancestors. Aila's son, Amavasu, was travelling through the sky and she chose him. He was instated in a *vimana* in the sky and was with the *apsara* Adrikaa. As a result of her transgression, she could no longer travel through the sky. Since she sought another father, she deviated from *yoga* and fell down. As she was dislodged from the firmament and fell down, she saw three *vimana*s, as small as a *trasarenu*.[1114] Her ancestors were stationed in these. They were extremely subtle and not very clear. They seemed to be inside a fire, and yet not inside a fire. She was falling down, with her head facing downwards. Suffering, she exclaimed, "Please save me." They said, "Do not be scared," thus stabilizing her. Miserable, she tried to placate them through her words. The ancestors spoke to their daughter, who had deviated because of her act of transgression. "O one with the beautiful smiles! You have deviated and are falling down because of your sinful conduct. Depending on one's *karma*, *deva*s make one suffer the consequences in this body and in this world. That is the way the fruits of *karma* are always reaped. For *deva*s, fruits of *karma* result instantly. For humans, they materialize after death. O daughter! Hence, you will reap the fruits of your

[1111] Since the word *skandana* means suppression/purge, there is a play on words.

[1112] Those who strike, Shiva's followers.

[1113] Barhishads are the second group of ancestors, and their daughter was Acchodaa.

[1114] *Trasarenu* is very small in size. *Anu* is often translated as atom and three *anu*s constitute one *trasarenu*.

austerities after death." Thus addressed, she again sought to placate the ancestors. They thought about this and driven by compassion, showed her their favours. Witnessing what was certain to occur, the ancestors, drinkers of *soma*, spoke to her. "You will be born on earth in the world of humans and will become the daughter of the great-souled king, Amavasu. O beautiful one! When you have become his daughter, you will obtain the worlds again. In the twenty-eighth *dvapara yuga*, you will be born as a fish. You will become the daughter of King Amavasu and Adrikaa.[1115] You will give birth to the *rishi* who will be Parashara's heir. The *brahmarshi* will divide the single *Veda* into four parts. Through Mahabhisha Shantanu,[1116] you will have two sons who will extend their fame. You will give birth to Vichitravirya, who will know about *dharma*. You will also give birth to King Chitrangada, who will possess every kind of spirit and strength. Once you have given birth to them, you will regain these worlds again. As a result of the transgression you have committed towards the ancestors, you are condemned to this abhorred birth. However, you will be the daughter of the king and Adrikaa. Having become their daughter, you will regain these worlds again." Thus addressed, Satyavati was born as the daughter of a *dasha*. She was Adrikaa's daughter and was also the daughter of a fish. She was born through Amavasu. She was born through Adrikaa, in the form of a fish, at the confluence of Ganga and Yamuna. Since it was the king's semen, she was the king's daughter too.'

'The worlds known as Virajas are in the firmament and the group of ancestors known as Agnishvattas, as radiant as the sun, desire these.[1117] Groups of *danavas*, *yakshas*, *rakshasas*, *gandharvas*, *kinnaras*, *bhutas*, *sarpas* and *pishachas*, who desire fruits, worship

[1115] This was Satyavati, the mother of Vedavyasa, through the sage Parashara. Adrikaa was an *apsara*, cursed to become a fish. Amavasu is the same as Uparichara Vasu. Satyavati was born through a fish and initially, bore the smell of fish and was the adopted daughter of a fisherman (*dasha*). Satyavati was subsequently married to King Shantanu.

[1116] Mahabhisha was Shantanu's name in a former life.

[1117] These are the third group of ancestors, and their daughter was Pivari.

them. They are described as the sons of Prajapati Pulaha. Their daughter, born through mental powers, is famous under the name of Pivari. She was a *yogini*, the wife of a *yogi* and the mother of a *yogi*. O supreme among *dvijas*! In the twenty-eighth *dvapara yuga*, Vyasa, the glorious and great *yogi*, will be born. He will be full of *yoga*. Resembling a smoke without fire, the one named Shuka will be born through Vyasa and Arani. The great ascetic will be born in Parshara's lineage. Through Pivari, daughter of the ancestors, he will have five sons, complete in their learning and conduct about *yoga*. They will be Krishna, Goura, Prabhu, Shambhu and Bhurishruta. He will also have a daughter, Kirtimati. She will be a *yogini* and the mother of a *yogi*. She will be Brahmadatta's mother and Anuha's queen. This great sage[1118] will be free and will pervade everything. He will follow the path lit by the rays of the sun, a path from which there is no return. Three groups of ancestors have been spoken about.'

'O best among *dvijas*! I will speak about the other four. Understand. These have radiant forms. The Kavyas are the sons of Kavi Agni and Svadha.[1119] These ancestors reside in the world of *devas*. They are radiant and dazzling in illumination. To obtain success in everything desired, *dvijas* worship them. Born through mental powers, their daughter is said to be Yogotpatti. Sanatkumara bestowed her on Shukra as a wife. She was known as Ekashringaa and extended the deeds of the Bhrigus.'

'In ancient times, the sons of Angiras were nurtured by the Sadhyas. They reside in the firmament, where the rays of the sun envelop all the worlds. These are the ancestors, radiant in heaven, described as Upahutas. Seven groups of *kshatriyas*,[1120] who desire fruits, worship them. Born through mental powers, their daughter is famous under the name of Yashoda. It is held that this queen was the mother of the great-souled Khatvanga. At his sacrifice, *maharshis* sang a chant, when they witnessed the birth of the great-

---

[1118] Brahmadatta.

[1119] This is the fourth group of ancestors, and their daughter was Yogotpatti or Ekashringaa.

[1120] With one descended from each of the *saptarshis*.

souled Shandilya from the fire. "Dilipa is the one performing the sacrifice. If men control themselves and witness it, they will conquer heaven. He is great-souled and follows the vow of truth."[1121]

'The ancestors named Ajyapas are the sons of Prajapati Kardama. These were sons who were thus born in Pulaha's lineage. They reside in worlds that revolve. They can travel through the sky, as they will. In *shraddha* ceremonies, desiring fruits, groups of *vaishya*s worship them. Born through mental powers, their daughter is famous under the name of Virajaa. This virtuous lady was Nahusha's wife and Yayati's mother.'[1122]

'The ancestors named Sukalas are sons of the great-souled Vasishtha, Hiranyagarbha's son. *Shudra*s worship them. In the firmament, there are worlds named Manasa. They reside there. Born through mental powers, their daughter is Narmada, supreme among rivers. She purifies creatures and flows along Dakshinapatha. She married Purukutsa and was the mother of Trasadasyu.'[1123]

'As the lord of a *manvantara*, Manu approaches them. Thus, at the start of every *manvantara*, he initiates *shraddha* rites. O excellent *dvija*s! Hence, full of faith and following one's own *dharma*, offerings must be made to the ancestors in the due order. All the vessels used must be made out of silver or embellished with silver. If offerings are made at a *shraddha*, uttering "*svadha*" first, the ancestors are pleased. If the first *soma* libation at an *agnishtoma* sacrifice is offered to ancestors, one obtains the fruits of a horse sacrifice. If *soma* is offered to Agni and the sun, the ancestors are pleased. In turn, the ancestors please him and his lineage. The ancestors grant him the desired nourishment and the desired offspring. There is no doubt that he obtains nourishment and offspring and goes to heaven. Among all rites for *deva*s, rites for the ancestors are special. It is said

---

[1121] This is the fifth group of ancestors and their daughter was Yashoda. Yashoda was the mother of Khatvanga, also known as Dilipa. Evidently, Shandilya was born at King Dilipa's sacrifice.

[1122] This is the sixth group of ancestors and their daughter was Virajaa. There are different accounts of Kardama Prajapati's birth. In one account, he is Pulaha's son, explaining the reference to Pulaha's lineage.

[1123] This is the seventh group of ancestors, with Narmada as a daughter.

that the ancestors must be worshipped before *deva*s. The path of *yoga* followed by ancestors and the abodes of ancestors are subtle. They cannot be seen through the physical eye. But using austerities, *brahmana*s are successful in seeing them. These are the ancestors, their worlds, their daughters and the sons of their daughters. It is said that a person performing a sacrifice must worship them. Four are with form and three are without form. *Deva*s also make careful attempts to honour them through *shraddha*s. All of them, including Indra, are attentive in their minds and faithfully join their hands in salutation. Vishvadevas, Sikatas, Prishnijas, Shringins, Krishnas and Shvetambujas worship them, following the proper rites.[1124] So do excellent Vatarasanas, Divakrityas, clouds, Maruts and Brahma and the other residents of heaven. So do all the *rishi*s, Atri, Bhrigu, Angiras and the others. So do *yaksha*s, *naga*s, birds, *kinnara*s and *rakshasa*s. Desiring fruits, all of them constantly worship the ancestors. Thus, these great-souled ones are properly worshipped at *shraddha*s. Hundreds and thousands of times, they bestow everything that is desired. One can thereby abandon the three worlds and *samsara* and the fear of old age and death. One can obtain *moksha*, *yoga*, prosperity, a subtle body, the lack of a body, every kind of non-attachment and everything infinite. The ancestors bestow this. Prosperity is described as *yoga* and *yoga* is said to be prosperity. Without the prosperity of *yoga*, how can one obtain *moksha*? This is like a person without wings trying to travel through the sky, just as a bird travels through the sky. Among every kind of *dharma*, the eternal *dharma* of *moksha* is the best. Through the favours of ancestors, great-souled ones obtain this. The ancestors bestow crores of pearls, lapis lazuli, garments, horses, elephants, jewels; thousands of *vimana*s bedecked with pearls and lapis lazuli, yoked to swans and peacocks, with nets of tinkling bells and ever-lasting flowers and fruits, served by large numbers of *apsara*s and full of everything desired; offspring, nourishment, memory, intelligence, kingdoms and freedom from disease. When they are pleased, the ancestors bestow all these on humans.'

[1124] These are different groups of divinities.

Chapter 49-1(49) (Description of kindling)

Brihaspati said, 'For ancestors, it is said that a silver vessel, or a vessel embellished with silver, must be used. The mention of silver, seeing it, donating it, ensures eternal residence in heaven. Silver is the best donation. It is said that by donating this, a virtuous son saves his ancestors. Earlier, when the earth was milked, a silver vessel was used to milk *svadha*. O son! Whether it is *svadha* or something else desired, such a donation brings eternal benefit. The presence of black antelope-skin, seeing it, or donating it, destroys *rakshasa*s, has the radiance of the *brahman* and saves *pashu*s and sons. Brahma's eternal injunction is that the best purifying articles for *shraddha* rites are a gold or silver vessel, the first day in the month of Ashvina,[1125] the eighth *muhurta* of the day, sesamum and the presence of a *tridandi*.[1126] This enhances lifespan, deeds, offspring, prosperity, wisdom and descendants. The south-eastern direction must be earmarked for the construction of the sacrificial altar. It must be in the form of a well-constructed square, with each side measuring one *aratni*. I will speak about the norms for the location, as instructed by the ancestors. This leads to blessings and enhances lifespan, freedom from disease, strength and complexion. Three pits must be dug there and there must be three poles, made of *khadira* wood.[1127] The lengths of each of these poles must only be one *aratni* and they must be embellished with silver. The depth of the pits must be one *vitasti* and the radius on each side must be of four *angula*s. The pits must face the south-east. They must be firm and free of grass. The person performing the *shraddha* must be pure. He must clean himself and be pure. The person performing the *shraddha* must purify himself with the milk of a goat, the milk of a cow or water. Eternal satisfaction is obtained if the *tarpana*[1128]

[1125] *Douhitra* has been translated in this way.

[1126] A mendicant carries a rod with three staffs tied together. Thus, he is a *tridandi,* and the word is used as a metaphor for controlling thoughts, words and deeds.

[1127] *Khadira* is a kind of tree.

[1128] Literally, rendering satisfaction.

is done with water. If a person controls himself and does this, he obtains everything that he desires, in this world and in the next one. In this way, he should control himself, bathe thrice a day and worship the ancestors. If one does this properly and uses the indicated *mantra*s, one obtains the fruits of a horse sacrifice. The pits, with a radius of four *angula*s, must be constructed on the day of *amavasya*. If the sacrifice is performed twenty-one times, the three worlds are sustained. The performer obtains nourishment, prosperity and a long lifespan, and so do his children. He obtains radiance and prosperity in heaven and in the course of time, obtains *moksha*. It purifies, destroys sins and yields the fruits of a horse sacrifice. If the worship is carried out by *dvija*s who have cleansed themselves, the fruits obtained are those of a horse sacrifice.'

'I will speak about the immortal *mantra*s devised by Brahma. At the beginning and the end of a *shraddha* ceremony, one must always recite this thrice and perform *japa* with it. "I prostrate myself before *deva*s, ancestors and great *yogi*s. *Namah* eternally to Svaha and Svadha." When the *pinda*s are offered, one must also control oneself and perform *japa*. The *pinda*s proceed swiftly to the ancestors and *rakshasa*s run away. With this *mantra*, the ancestors save in the three periods of time.[1129] Those who speak about the *brahman* must control themselves and always read this at the time of a *shraddha*. A person who desires a kingdom must control himself and always perform *japa* with this *mantra*. This enhances energy, valour, wealth, spirit, blessings, lifespan and intelligence. If a person follows the *niyama*s and performs *japa* with this, the ancestors are pleased. I will now state the *saptarchisha mantra*.[1130] This is auspicious and bestows everything wished for. "With form and without form, the ancestors blaze in their energy. I constantly prostrate myself before them. They are engaged in *dhyana*, with eyes of *yoga*. They are the leaders of Indra and the others, the ten, Marichi and other others,[1131] and the *saptarshi*s. I prostrate myself

---

[1129] The past, present and future.

[1130] Literally, with seven rays. There are seven verses in the *mantra* and seven groups of ancestors.

[1131] The ten sons born through Brahma's mental powers.

before the ancestors, who bestow what is wished for. They are the leaders of Manu and the others, of the sun and the moon. In all the rites concerning the ancestors, I prostrate myself before them. I join my hands in salutation and always prostrate myself before the ancestors of *nakshatras*, *grahas*, Vayu, Agni, heaven and earth. They are leaders of *devarshis* and are worshipped by all the worlds. They are the saviours of all beings. I prostrate myself before those grandfathers. I join my hands in salutation and always prostrate myself before Prajapati, cows, Vahni, Soma, Yama and the lords of *yoga*. I prostrate myself before the seven groups of ancestors, in the seven worlds. I prostrate myself before Svayambhu Brahma, who possesses the insight of *yoga*." This is said to be the *saptarchisha mantra*, used by large numbers of *brahmarshis*. It is sacred, supreme and glorious and destroys disease. If a man follows these rules, he obtains three boons—food, lifespan and sons. The ancestors bestow these on earth. A person must be faithful and full of great devotion. He must conquer his senses. He must control himself and constantly perform *japa* with the *saptarchisha mantra*. He then becomes the single emperor over the earth, with its seven *dvipas* and oceans.'

'Anything cooked in the food for eating, or anything eaten outside the house, must never be eaten without offering it first. After this, in the due order, I will describe the vessels used for oblations. Associated fruits are spoken about. As I describe them, listen. If a vessel made of *palasha* leaves is used, one obtains the radiance of the *brahman*. If one thinks about wealth, one should use a vessel made out of *ashvattha* leaves.[1132] If one desires constant lordship over all creatures, it said that one made of *plaksha* leaves must be used. *Nyagrodha* must be used for nourishment, offspring, intelligence, wisdom, fortitude and memory. For fame and destruction of *rakshasas*, it is said that a vessel made of *kashmari*[1133] leaves must be used. For excellent good fortune in the world, *madhuka*[1134] is mentioned. If one does it in a vessel made of *phalgu*[1135] leaves,

[1132] The holy fig tree.
[1133] The plant *Gmelina arborea*, also known as *gambhari*.
[1134] *Bassia latifolia*.
[1135] The Redwood fig tree.

everything desired is obtained. *Arka*[1136] is used for supreme radiance and special illumination. *Bilva*[1137] is used for constant prosperity and intelligence and a long lifespan. Vessels made from any kind of corn or grain yield fields, pleasure-groves and ponds. For Parjanaya to shower down, a vessel made of bamboo must be used. The best of food must be offered in these excellent vessels. If one does this, one obtains the fruits of every kind of sacrifice. If a person is constantly devoted to offering garlands made of flowers and excellent fragrances to the ancestors and is engaged in the rites, he shines like the sun. If a person makes efforts to offer *guggula*[1138] to the ancestors, along with honey and curds, he obtains the fruits of an *agnishtoma* sacrifice. If a person devotedly offers excellent incense and fragrances to the ancestors, he obtains great peace, both in this world and in the next one. One must always be attentive in rendering offerings to the ancestors. If a person controls himself and constantly offers a lamp to the ancestors, he obtains unmatched and auspicious vision as an objective. He obtains the radiance of energy, fame, beauty and strength on earth and is radiant in heaven. He is surrounded by *apsara*s and rejoices in an excellent *vimana*. A person must control and purify himself and worship the ancestors with fragrances, flowers, incense, *japa*, oblations, roots, fruits and prostration. After this, he must worship *dvija*s with food and donations of wealth. At the time of a *shraddha*, the grandfathers assume the form of the wind and enter the bodies of foremost *dvija*s. That is the reason I am telling you this. Excellent *dvija*s must be honoured with donations of garments, jewels, cows and villages. They must be offered food and drinks. When *dvija*s are worshipped, the ancestors are pleased. Therefore, in the proper way, one must always make efforts to worship *dvija*s. A *dvija* must perform the act of *ullekhana*[1139] with both hands, with the left hand over the right one. In the course of a *shraddha* ceremony, the act of *prokshana*[1140] must be done with a great deal of attention. An intelligent person will

---

[1136] The sun-plant.
[1137] Wood-apple.
[1138] A fragrant gum resin.
[1139] The act of etching the names on the ground.
[1140] Sprinkling of water, done with *darbha* grass.

gather *darbha* grass, *pinda*s, foodstuffs, different kinds of flowers, fragrances, donations and ornaments and offer them progressively. Collyrium must be crushed properly. Following the due procedure, oil for bathing must be offered thrice, using the tips of a bunch of *darbha* grass. While offering to the ancestors, one must kneel on the ground, and the sacred thread must be worn over the right shoulder. This must be done while offering excellent collyrium and garments. A *dvija* will do the acts of *khandana*,[1141] *prokshana* and *ullekhana* once for the ancestors of *deva*s and thrice for other ancestors. For all the ancestors, a single *pavitra*[1142] must be worn on the hand. A mirror must be shown over antelope-skin and *pinda*s must be offered while chanting *chaila mantra*.[1143] Three *pinda*s must always be placed on the ground, mixed with *ghee* and sesamum. While doing this, a person devoted to his ancestors must kneel down on the ground, with the sacred thread placed over his left shoulder. He must invoke his father, grandfather, great grandfather and the other ancestors. Carefully, using *pitri-tirtha*,[1144] the *pinda*s must be sprinkled with water, in a counter clockwise direction. Some men desire to separately offer food and other edible items to their maternal grandfathers. Using the thumb, the three *pinda*s must be offered in the due order. This enhances nourishment. In the due order, the *pinda*s must carefully be offered, between the knees. With the left hand placed over the right, as the water flows, the *mantra* must be recited. Extremely attentively, using the hands, the first *pinda* must be released towards the south, reciting, "*Namah vah pitarah shoshaya*".[1145] Attentive in all acts of *dharma*, the left hand

[1141] Breaking/cutting.

[1142] A ring of *kusha* grass, worn on the fourth finger.

[1143] Since *chaila* means *kusha* grass, this is a *mantra* chanted while wearing the *pavitra*, or for *kusha* grass in general. In particular, this can also be *gayatri mantra*.

[1144] The region between the right thumb and the right index finger.

[1145] This is part of a broader *mantra* from *Shukla Yajur Veda*, 2.32. 'ॐ नमो वः पितरो रसाय, नमो वः पितरः शोषाय, नमो वः पितरो जीवाय, नमो वः पितरः स्वधायै [OUM! Prostrations to the ancestors for juice, prostrations to the ancestors for ardour, prostrations to the ancestors for life, prostrations to the ancestors for *svadha*]'. *Soumya* means amiable. In these sections, there are some typos in the text.

must be placed over the right, and one should recite, "*Namah vah pitarah soumyah*". The etching on the ground must be sprinkled with water from the vessel. A new piece of thread must be offered, made of silk, jute or cotton. Woven silk, velvet and *kousheya* silk must be avoided. In the sacrifice, one should avoid sprinkling water with a piece of cloth that has not been washed. The ancestors are not pleased with these and if these are offered, harm results.'

'*Trikakuda* collyrium is always the best.[1146] The best is oil from black sesamum that has been carefully preserved, sandalwood, aloe, *tamala*, *ushira*, a lotus, incense, *guggula*, white *turushka* and white flowers.[1147] Lotuses and water lilies are the best. All wildflowers with fragrance and form are excellent. Flowers with hollow tubes and the yellow amaranth are also excellent. However, there are flowers that must always be avoided at *shraddhas*, for example, those without a smell, or with a pungent smell. If a person desires nourishment, such flowers must always be avoided. It is instructed that the invited *dvija*s must always sit facing the north. In the indicated way, the person performing the rite must sit facing the south. Facing them, he must carefully spread the *pinda*s over the *darbha* grass. If these norms are followed, it is as if the grandfathers are directly worshipped. For a seat, the best *kusha* grass is one where the leaves are green, thick, soft and smooth. Near the root, the branches must be blue. The length must be one *aratni* and water from *pitri-tirtha* must be used for consecration. This is also the case with *shyamaka*, *nivara* and *durva* grass. Earlier, Prajapati, the best among those who are famous, became a horse. His hair fell down on the ground and became *kusha* grass. That is the reason *kusha* grass is always revered at the time of a *shraddha*. A person who desires prosperity must always offer *pinda*s on *kusha* grass. His offspring then obtain nourishment, radiance, intelligence, fame and beauty. They will always be beautiful and will cleanse themselves of sins. For the sake of offering a *pinda*, one must sit facing the south and

[1146] Collyrium that comes from a mountain with three peaks. This was the name of a specific mountain.
[1147] *Tamala* is a tree with a dark bark, *ushira* is a kind of grass and *turushka* is a kind of incense.

the *darbha* grass must be spread only once. The tips of the blades must face the south-east. I will now speak about the rites. The man performing the rite should not be dejected, angry or distracted. His mind should be controlled, only focused on the act of performing the *shraddha*. "I will destroy everything with an impurity. I have destroyed all the *asuras* and *danavas*. I have slain all the *rakshasas*, *yakshas*, large numbers of *pishachas* and *yatudhanas*." Using this *mantra*, a person should control himself and patiently etch out the altar properly. Desiring auspicious intelligence, he must fling it towards the north, in the direction of the *dvijas*.[1148] Thus, all the *asuras* avoid a person who recites the *mantra* to the ancestors in the indicated way. If the *mantra* is chanted in a region, *rakshasas* avoid that region.'

'A virtuous person should not see, touch or give food that is impure in any kind of way. If a man does not wear the *pavitra* on his hand, he does not obtain the fruits of the rite. These rites must always be observed in the performance. If a person always does this, the grandfathers bestow whatever he wishes for. If the *shraddha* is always performed in this controlled way, the ancestors are delighted in their minds and *rakshasas* are dejected. In a *shraddha*, one must always avoid *shudras*, milk from sheep, *balvaja*,[1149] sand, *virana*,[1150] anything excessively pungent and *laddu* sweetmeats. Grass unworthy of a sacrifice must be avoided. One should avoid applying collyrium to the eyes, using oil while bathing, use of fragrances and wearing sewn garments. If the rite is performed with *kusha* grass that has grown after being cut, one obtains the fruits of a horse sacrifice. For offering flowers, fragrances and ornaments, the following *mantra* is cited. "The *kusha* grass must be one that has regrown. The *barhi* grass must be one that has regrown. In this way, ancestors are *devas* and *devas* again become ancestors." One must carefully kindle *dakshinagni* and offer oblations into it. For success in all other rites that involve oblations, ordinary fires

---

[1148] The sentence is unclear, the suggestion being that the *darbha* grass is flung towards the north.

[1149] A coarse grass, *Eleusine Indica*.

[1150] The fragrant grass, *Andropogon Muricatus*.

can be used. It is recommended that the kindling must be placed within the blazing flames. With a controlled mind, the fire must be kindled in every direction. For offering oblations, in the due order, there are three *mantra*s. "I prostrate myself before Agni, who bears the *kavya*. Svadha. I prostrate myself before Angiras." "I prostrate myself before Soma, honoured by the ancestors. Svadha. I prostrate myself before Angiras." "I prostrate myself before Vaivasvata Yama. Svadha. This is certain." The offering to Agni must always be made to the south, that to Soma to the north and that to Vaivasvata in the intervening direction. Offering of gifts, exclamations of "Svadha", etching, offering of oblations, *japa*, showing obeisance, special acts of *prokshana*, application of collyrium, application of oil for bathing and the offering of *pinda*s—all these must be done when the fire blazes with a lot of *ghee* and kindling. When oblations are offered by *dvija*s into a kindled fire, one obtains the fruits of a horse sacrifice. One must always make efforts to carry out the indicated rites.'

'In particular, the fire must be kindled with a lot of *ghee* and kindling. Oblations must be offered into a fire that blazes without smoke. The rite then becomes successful. If oblations are offered into a fire that does not blaze properly, or lacks kindling, the person performing the rite becomes blind, in this world and in the next one. That is what we have heard. If there is insufficient kindling, if the fire is harsh, if there aren't flames in every direction, if there are flames with smoke that curls in an anti-clockwise direction, the rite is unsuccessful. If the fire emits a foul smell, in particular if it is blue or black, or if the fire burns downwards, towards the ground, one should note that this indicates defeat. The fire must have flames that curl towards the top, resembling glossy *ghee*. The fire must be gentle, curling in a clockwise direction. There will then be success. The person performing the rite will be constantly honoured by groups of men and women. For eternal benefit, ancestors and the fire must be worshipped in this way. For a *shraddha*, the leaves, fruits and kindling of *bilva* and *udumbara* are extremely sacred. They are especially worthy of being used. O best among *dvija*s! They are pure and sanctify birth and deeds. For fruits in a *shraddha* rite, I have already indicated the vessels. In that way, in the due order, one should know everything about kindling. Controlling

his mind, he should ask, "May I perform the rite in the fire?" The
excellent *dvija*s will grant him permission and say, "Please do so."
He should then take *ghee* in a vessel and offer oblations into the fire.
The following trees are particularly praised for kindling—*palasha,
plaksha, nyagrodha, ashvattha, vikankata, udumbara, bilva* and
chandana.[1151] These are fit for sacrifices. So are *sarala, devadaru,
shala* and *khadira*. There are some thorny trees from villages that
are fit for sacrifices. Following the words of the ancestors, these
can be used for worship and kindling. There are said to be fruits
if oblations are rendered into a fire that uses *shataphala*[1152] as
kindling. I will tell you about the fruits from such rites. Listen. The
fruits are eternal, like those of a horse sacrifice, and one obtains
everything wished for. However, there are trees that are condemned
for *shraddha* rites—*shleshmantaka, naktamala, kapittha, shalmali,
nipa* and *vibhitaka*.[1153] *Chirabilva, kola, tinduka, balvaja* and
kovidara must always be avoided in *shraddha* rites.[1154] Large trees,
with birds residing in them, should be avoided. One should also
avoid all the other trees not worthy of sacrifices. In rites connected
with a sacrifice, it is said that the *mantra* "*svadha*" must be used for
ancestors and "*svaha*" for *deva*s.'

Chapter 50-1(50) (Continuation of *shraddha* rites)

Suta said, '*Deva*s and Gods are always said to be dependent on each
other. They restrain each other. In the *Atharva Veda*, Brihaspati
mentioned this rule. Ancestors must be worshipped first and *deva*s

---

[1151] Vikankata is *Flacourtia Sapida*, a tree from which sacrificial ladles
were made, *chandana* is sandalwood, *sarala* is pine, *devadaru* is cedar,
shala is the *sal* tree and *khadira* is the catechu tree.

[1152] Pomegranate.

[1153] *Shleshmantaka* (*shleshmataka*) is *Cordia myxa*, *naktamala* is
the Indian beech, *kapittha* is wood apple, *nipa* is *Ixora bandhucca* and
vibhitaka is *Terminalia bellirica*.

[1154] *Chirabilva* is *Holoptelea integrifolia*, *kola* is *Ziziphus jujube*,
tinduka is the ebony tree and *kovidara* is the orchid tree.

thereafter. *Deva*s also carefully worship ancestors. Daksha had a daughter, famous under the name of Vishvaa. She gave birth to ten sons who knew about *dharma*, famous as Vishvas.[1155] They are famous in the three worlds and are revered by all the worlds. All those great-souled ones performed great and fierce austerities. They did this on the beautiful slopes of Himalaya, frequented by large numbers of *deva*s and *rishi*s. Pleased at the purity of their minds, the ancestors spoke to them. "We are pleased. Ask for the boon you desire. What will we do for you?" When the ancestors said this, Brahma, the greatly energetic creator of the three worlds, whom they had also pleased, said, "I am pleased at your austerities. What do you wish for? What will I do for you?" Thus addressed by Brahma, the creator of the universe, all the Vishvas collectively replied to Brahma, the creator of the worlds. "Please let us have a share in *shraddha* rites. That is our desired boon." Brahma, worshipped by the Gods, told them, "It shall be in accordance with your desired boon." The ancestors added, "There is no doubt that it will be this way. Anything seen there will be enjoyed with us. You will eat at *shraddha*s meant for us, undertaken by humans. We are speaking the truth. You will first be worshipped with garlands, fragrances and food. You will be offered first. We will be offered thereafter. The act of *visarjana*[1156] will first be done for us. That for *deva*s will follow. In all rites concerning *bhuta*s, *deva*s and ancestors, in acts of *shraddha* and hospitality, these two rules must be followed.[1157] If this is done, everything will be done properly. Everything be complete." Along with the large number of ancestors, this is the boon Brahma granted them. The divinity who shows favours and compassion acted as he had spoken.'

'It is said in the *Veda*s that there are five major sacrifices for men.[1158] A man must always undertake these five great

---

[1155] That is, Vishvadevas.

[1156] Literally, sending away or dismissal. The end of the worship.

[1157] The order of worship and release.

[1158] Usually stated as offerings to *deva*s, ancestors, *rishi*s, humans and animals/birds.

yajnas. Hear about the regions earmarked for those who perform these. These regions are without fear and without dust. There is no grief there, nor any failed enterprise. These are Brahma's regions, worshipped by all the worlds, and those are obtained. *Shudra*s must also perform these five sacrifices, but without the use of *mantra*s. If a person eats without undertaking these, he suffers eternally from a debt. If a person cooks for himself alone and eats, he is evil-souled and suffers from a debt. Therefore, a learned person always undertakes the five great sacrifices. The offerings should be laid out in the north-east, or near a water body. The offerings must be prepared well and flung high up into the air. Cow's urine, dung, a thread and the offering must be placed inside an excellent horn and flung up. That *naivedya*[1159] in the form of a *pinda* is for any ancestor who may still be alive. Following the rules, the offering of food and other edible items must be made. Some wish that *naivedya* must attentively be offered to those who are alive too. The great-souled ancestors are *deva*s of the *deva*s. Some *acharya*s desire that *brahmana*s must always be worshipped first, with the offering of *pinda*s taking place thereafter. Brihaspati, accomplished in the meaning of *dharma*, has said that this is not the case. The *pinda*s must be offered first. *Brahmana*s must be fed thereafter. The great-souled ancestors have *yoga* in their *atman*s. They originated from *yoga*. Immersed in their *yoga*, the ancestors nourish Soma. Therefore, one must attentively offer pure *pinda*s to those who practice *yoga*. This is a direct offering of oblations to the ancestors. If a person based in *yoga* accepts it, it is as if one thousand *brahmana*s have accepted it. Like a boat saves in the water, this act saves the person undertaking the rite and others who eat. A terrible punishment unleashed by *deva*s instantly descends on a place where the wicked are honoured and the virtuous shown disrespect. Ignoring a person devoted to *dharma*, if a foolish person is fed first, the performer is destroyed. If a man desires enjoyment, the first *pinda* must always be offered into the fire. Along with *mantra*s,

---

[1159] Offering of food.

a person desiring offspring must carefully offer the *pinda* in the middle. For excellent beauty, the *pinda* must always be offered to cows.[1160] For wisdom, fame and deeds, it must be left in the water. A person desiring a long lifespan must offer it to crows. A person desiring tenderness must offer it to cocks. These are instructed as the fruits of disposal of the *pinda*s. It can be flung up into the sky, or placed in the water, in a southern direction. Ancestors reside in the sky, or in the southern direction. One *brahmana* will say, "Take the tips out from the *pinda*s." When other *brahmana*s signify their assent, he can do as desired. All the flowers, fruits, edible items and food will be taken out from the tips of the *pinda*s and offered as an oblation into the fire. Once the edible items, food, drink, roots and fruits have been offered as an oblation into the fire, the rest of the *pinda* can be placed in a southern direction. After offerings to Vaivasvata and Soma, after rendering the *pinda*s as *naivedya* and after performing the water-rites, the *brahmana*s will subsequently be fed. According to capacity, he will feed *brahmana*s in the due order. He will satisfy them with succulent food that is gentle, warm and fragrant. He will control himself and attentively stand there, his hands joined in salutation. To obtain what he desires, a man will be faithful. The grandfathers bestow the qualities of superiority, gratefulness, generosity, refined speech, austerities, sacrifices and donations. I will progressively describe the auspicious and ordained rites, once the *dvija*s have eaten. Listen. A person devoted to his ancestors will sprinkle the ground, as has been instructed earlier. In accordance with the indicated rites, he will then scatter the food. Reciting "*svadha*", in the recommended way, he will then give *brahmana*s copious quantities of *dakshina*. He will then honour the excellent *dvija*s and ask, "What is to be done with the rest of the food?" Having obtained their permission,[1161] a controlled person will join his hands in salutation, follow them[1162] and release them.'

[1160] These sections are about disposal of *pinda*s.

[1161] To eat.

[1162] As they depart, he will follow them up to the door.

Chapter 51-1(51) (Description of sacred places)

Brihasapati said, 'If they are worshipped even once, the undecaying ancestors are pleased. They are great-souled and possess *yoga* in their *atman*s. They are immensely energetic and cleansed of sins. There are many desired places on earth that yield the world of heaven after death and in the course of time, show their favours by bestowing *moksha*. I will speak about those auspicious rivers and lakes, *tirtha*s, sacred spots, mountains and hermitages.'

'Amarakantaka is always sacred in the three worlds. This is the sacred and excellent mountain, frequented by *siddha*s and *charana*s. In ancient times, for billions and millions of thousands of years, the illustrious Angiras tormented himself there, through extremely difficult austerities. Death cannot access that place, nor can *asura*s and *rakshasa*s. As long as the earth sustains, there is no fear there, nor any adversity. With the energy of austerities, that excellent mountain is radiant. The *samvartaka* fire is always present on Mount Malyavan. The *kusha* that is to the south of Narmada is said to be soft and fragrant, serene, golden in complexion and beautiful to behold. Earlier, for an *agnihotra* sacrifice, the immensely energetic and illustrious Angiras spread out excellent *kusha* grass and saw a staircase ascend to heaven. A wise person should offer *pinda*s on the *darbha* grass in Mount Amarakantaka at least once. I will describe the fruits. This enhances the delight of the ancestors and the *shraddha* becomes eternal. The ancestors always go to that *kshetra* and vanish. At the time of *parva*s, a sacred lake of flames is seen there. The river there is *vishalyakarani*, which removes stakes from living beings. On the peak of the lordly Malyavan, on the other half of the region of Kalinga, on that excellent mountain, there is a waterbody, with an eddy that stretches south-east. O best among *rishi*s! For granting *siddhi*, this is said to be the supreme *kshetra* on earth. *Deva*s and *daitya*s honour this place and Ushanas chanted a *shloka* about it. "In this world, men, devoted to their ancestors, who reach Amarakantaka and satisfy their ancestors through a *shraddha* are blessed." There is no doubt that *siddhi* can

be obtained with a little bit of austerities. Even if a person worships
*deva*s once in Amarakantaka, he goes to heaven.'

'Mount Mahendra is sacred and beautiful and is frequented by
Shakra. If one climbs it, one is purified. A *shraddha* there bestows
great fruits. When one reaches the summit of Vailata, divine sight
starts to function. He becomes unassailable to creatures and roams
around like a *deva* on earth. If a person bathes and donates in
Sapta-Godavari[1163] or in the hermitage in Gokarna, he obtains
the fruits of a horse sacrifice. If a man bathes at the spot, he is
sanctified and is cleansed of his sins. Maheshvara Rudra, lord of
*deva*s, tormented himself through austerities there. For the sake of
non-believers, *deva*s have hidden proof in Gokarna. If a person who
is not a *brahmana* reads the *savitri mantra* there, he is destroyed.
The abode of *deva*s and *rishi*s is on the summit and is frequented by
*siddha*s and *charana*s. If a person follows *niyama*s and climbs it, he
goes to heaven. The place is adorned with beautiful trees and divine
sandalwood trees. Water fragrant with sandalwood continuously
flows there. The river named Tamraparni flows from that spot. From
the great grove of sandalwood trees, it flows towards the southern
ocean. There are oyster shells there and they produce pearls. The
river known as Tamraparni bears them down to the great ocean.
If devotees bring water mixed with shells and pearls, they are freed
from physical and mental ailments and go to Amaravati. The shells
and pearls result from the sandalwood. If these are used, even by
a person who has committed a sin, the ancestors are saved. This is
stated in the *shruti* texts.'

'O excellent *dvija*s! A person who casts off his body in the
following places instantly goes to Amaravati—Chandratirtha
Kumari, the eternal source of the Kaveri and the *tirtha*s on Shriparvata,
Mount Vaikrita and Mount Oushira, where, because of *palasha*,
khadira, *bilva*, *plaksha*, *ashvattha* and trees without thorns on one
side, the region is known to be divided into two. Rites undertaken
in a *tirtha* on Shriparvata and Mount Vaikrita have eternal power
and are successful. Even if the rites are performed imperfectly,

---

[1163] In East Godavari district.

they become perfect. The sacred and supreme river, Narmada, is the daughter of the ancestors. A *shraddha* rite undertaken there, becomes ever lasting. The sacred forest of Mathara is frequented by *siddha*s and *charana*s. They disappear there, in that great mountain. In the sacred Mount Vindhya, there is a waterfall that differentiates between those who follow *dharma* and those who follow *adharma*. Sinners cannot see that flow, but the virtuous can see the flow. This is how the sins of some evil doers become apparent. Lake Matanga in Kailasa destroys sins. Birds, that can travel as they will, bathe there and go to heaven. *Shraddha*s performed in the following places are pure and always remain infinite—the *tirtha* of Sourparaka;[1164] Mount Palamanjara; Pandukupa, on the shores of the ocean; the sparkling banks of Pindaraka, free from sins; Shrivriksha; Chitrakuta; the eternal Jambumarga; and the sacred mountain of Asita, the intelligent *acharya* of yoga. At these places, the *sankalpa* becomes eternal.[1165] At Pushkara, the *shraddha* becomes ever lasting and austerities yield great fruits. That is also the determination for Prabhasa, near the great ocean. In Devika,[1166] there is a well named Vrisha, frequented by *siddha*s. The water that emerges from there always has the sound of a cow mooing. It is devoid of all sins and lords of *yoga* always resort to that place. I will speak about the fruits of a *shraddha* offering rendered there. The *shraddha* performed there is eternal. The ancestors are pleased and everything desired is obtained. There is a Jataveda rock there, representing eternal Agni himself. *Shraddha*s and fire-rites performed there always become eternal. A person who enters the fire there, finds delight in the vault of heaven. There is a place the fire becomes serene and is revived again. Anything offered there become ever lasting. There is a *tirtha* named after ten horse sacrifices and another *tirtha* named after five horse sacrifices. There is no doubt that sacrifices performed there yield the desired fruits. The famous *tirtha* named Hayashira instantly bestows boons. A *shraddha* performed there is ever lasting

---

[1164] This is the same as Surparaka, probably identified with Sopara (Nala Sopara) in Maharashtra.

[1165] *Sankalpa* is the resolution undertaken before any rite.

[1166] Probably a tributary of Iravati (Ravi).

and the donor enjoys himself in heaven. *Shraddha*s and donations in the place known as Sunda-Upasunda destroy sins. *Shraddha*s, *japa*, oblations and austerities are said to be eternal there. The ancestors are always satisfied in the auspicious *tirtha* of Ajatunga. On *parva* days, the shadows of the residents of heaven are always seen there. On earth, there is a place where Viraja trees grow. Anything given there becomes eternal. That place is bereft of all sins and the lords of *yoga* always frequent it. I will speak about the fruits of *shraddha*s and donations there. The ancestors are always directly worshipped there. In this world, such a person becomes controlled. After death, he obtains greatness in heaven. In general, the region of Madrava is sacred and there is a lake named after Shiva there. The sacred lake of Vyasa is there and so is the divine lake of Brahma. Mount Urjanta is sacred, and lords of *yoga* make their abodes there. The sacred hermitage of the great-souled Vasishtha is there.'

'*Tirtha*s named after the *Rig Veda*, the *Yajur Veda*, the *Sama Veda*, the *Atharva Veda*, *kapota*s,[1167] flowers and the fifth *Veda* were created by Svayambhu himself. A *dvija* who goes there and seeks refuge in the fire, is freed. *Shraddha*s, *japa*, oblations and austerities become infinite. Pundarika is a great *tirtha* and the fruits obtained resemble a white lotus. O immensely wise one! Brahma-*tirtha* yields fruits that are equal to the fruits obtained from all sacrifices. The fruits are eternal at the confluence of the Sindhu with the ocean and in Panchanada.[1168] Viraja is sacred and so is Mount Madrava. *Shraddha*s must be offered in Saptanada[1169] and especially in Manasa. They must be performed in Mahakuta and in the mountains Ananta and Trikakuda. At the time of *sandhya*, a great marvel is witnessed in Mahanadi. This cannot be seen by a person who lacks faith. Nor can it be seen by a person who is not firm in his vows. There, a person who desires eternal benefits must always perform *shraddha* in the evening to the ancestors, invoking them one at a time. There, it becomes evident whether

---

[1167] *Kapota* is a pigeon. This is a reference to *kapota tirtha*, described in detail in *Brahma Purana*.

[1168] Land of five (*pancha*) rivers (*nada*), identified with Punjab.

[1169] Seven rivers.

a man has cleansed his *atman* or not, whether he has controlled his speech or not. The *tirtha* is named Svargamargaprada[1170] and it yields instant boons. The *saptarshi*s abandoned their bark garments there and went to heaven. Even today, those bark garments can be seen in the water. If a man bathes in that excellent *tirtha*, he obtains heaven. The place is famous as Nandi's abode and is frequented by *siddha*s. Nandhishvara's image is there, but it cannot be seen by those who are devoid of good conduct. When the sun rises, golden sacrificial posts can be seen in the rays. Those who perform *pradakshina* are delighted and go to heaven. In particular, among all the *tirtha*s, Kurukshetra is special. This is the sacred spot of the great-souled Sanatkumara, the lord of *yoga*. It is said that if sesamum is offered to the ancestors there, the fruits are always eternal. It is said that the *shraddha* performed by Dharmaraja[1171] there, was eternal. Following the due order and rites, a *shraddha* must be offered on *amavasya*. In particular, if a man worships the ancestors in Sannihita in Kurukshetra,[1172] such a son is freed of his debts. A person who desires eternal benefits must offer a *shraddha* along the banks of Sarasvati, in Vinashana, in Plaksha-Prasravana, in Vyasa-*tirtha*, along the banks of Drishadvati, in Triplaksha, the grove of Omkara, in Shakravatara, along the banks of Ganga, in the excellent mountain of Mainaka and at the source of Yamuna.[1173] All sins are destroyed by the waters, which are seen to be extremely hot, or extremely cold. Yama's sister[1174] is Martanda's auspicious daughter and nourishes. As has been stated by the ancestors earlier, *shraddha*s there are eternal.'

[1170] Bestowing the path to heaven.

[1171] Yudhishthira.

[1172] Sannihita Sarovara in Kurukshetra, where the seven sacred rivers assemble.

[1173] Vinashana is where Sarasvati vanishes in the desert. *Plaksha* is a fig tree and the Sarasvati originated from the Shivalik hills in the Himalayas from below a fig-tree. This fountain at the foot of the fig tree is called Plaksha-Prasravana. Plaksha is sometimes also identified with Paonta Sahib in Himachal Pradesh. Vyasa-*tirtha* is in Thaneshvara.

[1174] Yamuna.

'If a person bathes in the lake known as Brahmatunda, he instantly becomes a *brahmana*. *Shraddha*s, *japa*, oblations and austerities performed there are eternal. The great ascetic, Vasishtha, became like a pillar there and did not move around. Even today, trees can be seen there, with jewels in their leaves. A pair of scales can be seen there, differentiating *dharma* from *adharma*. *Brahmana*s weigh and measure the excellent fruits of *tirtha*s there. The *yogini*, famous as Gandhakali,[1175] was the daughter of the ancestors. She gave birth to the intelligent and great sage Vyasa, who classified the *Veda*s into four. He was born in Parashara's lineage and was born as one-fourth of Brahma's portion. She gave birth to the great-souled and great *yogi*. There is a lake named Acchodaka and the river Acchodaa flows from there.[1176] Because of a certain determined reason, she had to be born again as a fish. Her sacred hermitage is there, frequented by those who have performed virtuous deeds. It is said that if a *shraddha* is performed there once, its benefits are eternal. If something is given at the river, it simultaneously fixes the mind in *yoga*. Kuberatunga and Vyasa-*tirtha* destroy sins. A *shraddha* offered at Brahmavedi is said to be infinite.[1177] It is always frequented by *siddha*s and is seen by those who have cleansed their *atman*s. Nanda is to the north-east of the altar. It is Anirvatana.[1178] It is a *kshetra* that bestows *siddhi* and is frequented by the Gods. Having reached there, a person does not return.'

'The intelligent Mahadeva placed his foot in Mahalaya. He did this to show compassion to beings and to show proof to non-believers. A *shraddha* performed at Viraja is ever lasting and so is one at Mahalaya. Those who perform *shraddha*s in Nanda, Viraja and Mahalaya save themselves and save ten generations of predecessors and ten generations of successors. A person who does so in Kakahrada becomes a *jatismara*.[1179] He becomes infinitely

[1175] Satyavati.
[1176] Referred to earlier as Svacchoda and Svacchodaa,
[1177] Kurukshetra is often called Brahma's altar (Brahmavedi) or the northern altar (Uttaravedi).
[1178] A place from where one does not return to *samsara*.
[1179] A person who remembers his past life.

energetic, with a golden complexion. The sacred lake of Koumara is protected by *naga*s and serpents. If a man bathes in Kumara-*tirtha*, he goes to heaven. There is a divine temple in Umatunga. If a person performs the extremely difficult austerity of standing on one leg and fasting there, he blazes in radiance for a *yuga*. If a person desires eternal benefit, he should perform a *shraddha* in Umatunga, Bhrigutunga, Brahmatunga or Mahalaya. In every part of Shalagrama, a *shraddha* never decays. It is rare to see a person who has not cleansed his *atman* there. There are specific instructions for those who are virtuous and for those who are wicked. There is Brahma's sacred Devahrada. The pure king of *naga*s accepts *pinda*s from the virtuous there, but he never accepts from those who are wicked. The serpents are extremely radiant, and it is impossible for them to eat the cooked food. There are two *tirtha*s where *dharma* can be directly seen. These are Shandilya's *karavati*[1180] and Vamana's cave. If one goes there, one becomes purified. A *shraddha* performed is eternal. Anything in the nature of *japa*, oblations, austerities and *dhyana* are performed well. If a person bases himself in *brahmacharya* and devotion towards his *guru*, he lives for one hundred years. There are these and other excellent rivers. Bathing there, frees the bather from sins. Kumaradhara can be seen there and it destroys sins. Vyasa's seat of *dhyana* can be seen there, even today. The mountain is located towards the north-east of Kantipura.[1181] There is a sacred pond there, protected by a large number of *kinnara*s. If a *brahmana* bathes there, he attains all his desires, for an eternity. Unseen to all beings, he roams the earth, like a *deva*. There is Kashyapa's great *tirtha*, known as Kalasarpi. If a person desires eternal and undecaying benefit, a *shraddha* must be performed there.'

'There is a waterfall in Devadaru-vana that provides proof. It can be seen that the sins of persons who perform good deeds are washed away. It is said that the benefits are eternal and everlasting at Prayaga on the Bhagirathi. This is also true of Kalanjara in Dasharna, Naimisha and Kurujangala. One should make efforts

[1180] Probably meaning a fig tree.
[1181] In Nepal.

to undertake a *shraddha* in the city of Varanasi. The lord of *yoga* is always present there. Anything given there becomes eternal. If one goes to these sacred *chaitya*s and performs *shraddha*s there, they become eternal. Anything in the nature of *japa*, oblations and *dhyana* is performed well. In Louhitya, Vaitarani, Svargavedi and the shores of the ocean, if her names are uttered, Devi can be seen. Brahma's lake is there in Dharmaprishtha in Gaya. A *shraddha* offered at Gridhravata in Gaya bestows great fruits. For five *yojana*s all around, snow falls there. There is the sacred hermitage of Bharata, located in what is said to be the most sacred of regions. All the men can see Matanga's forest there. As a proof for the worlds, he established everything connected with *dharma*. The forest of Dandaka is sacred and is frequented by those who have performed virtuous deeds. It is said that the *tirtha* of Vishalya is there. On the pair of scales there, in accordance with many sacred texts, there is immediate proof of people who have committed sins. Their side goes down.[1182] A *shraddha* performed in *tritiya*, at the foot of Niradha's circle, or in the great lake of Koushiki, yields great fruits. The intelligent Mahadeva placed his foot on the slopes of Munda. For many *yuga*s, he tormented himself through extremely difficult austerities. Within a short period of time, a man devoted to *dharma* casts off his sins there, like a snake casting off its old skin. This causes delight to *siddha*s and sinners find it terrifying. It is protected by extremely large and extremely terrible *uraga*s with flickering tongues. The *tirtha* named Kanakanandi is famous in the world. It is on the north of Munda's slopes and is frequented by large numbers of *brahmarshi*s. If men bathe there, they go to heaven in their physical bodies. It is said that a *shraddha* offered there is always eternal. Having bathed there, a man's body is freed from the three kinds of debt. One must perform *shraddha* after bathing in Lake Manasa.'

'On the banks of Sarasvati, there is a great temple to *deva*s. If one climbs that and performs *japa*, one obtains *siddhi* and after that, goes to heaven. If one goes to the north of Manasa, one

---

[1182] Is heavier on the pair of scales.

obtains excellent *siddhi*. If one bathes in that best of lakes, one
witnesses a great wonder. The immensely fortunate Goddess Ganga
has three flows. Having been dislodged from heaven, the virtuous
one flows from Vishnu's feet and is radiant in the firmament there.
One can see a gate in the sky, resembling the sun. It is sacred,
made out of molten gold, and is like a large gate that leads to
heaven. The river flows from there and adorns all the oceans. She
purifies all beings, especially those who know about *dharma*. The
auspicious Chandrabhaga and Sindhu emerge from Manasa. The
divine Sindhu, supreme among rivers, flows to the western ocean.
The mountain named Himalaya is decorated with many kinds of
minerals. Its length stretches for many thousands of *yojanas*. It is
full of *siddhas* and *charanas* and is frequented by large numbers
of *devas* and *rishis*. There is a beautiful pond there, known by the
name of Sushumna. If a person bathes in that flow, he lives for ten
thousand years. A *shraddha* offered there brings great benefits and
is infinite. A *shraddha* performed there always saves ten generations
of predecessors and ten generations of successors. Every place in the
Himalayas is sacred. Every place around the Ganga is sacred. All
the oceans and all the rivers, flowing into the oceans from different
directions, are sacred. A learned person must undertake a *shraddha*
in such and similar other places. Through bathing, oblations and
donations, a person is purified. The rites of a *shraddha* must always
be performed on the summits of mountains, along the ridges, in
caverns, caves and secluded spots on the slopes, in waterfalls, along
the banks of rivers, sources of rivers, the confluences of rivers
with great oceans, the pens of cows, confluences of rivers, forests,
in fragrant spots that have been cleaned and smeared, in places
smeared with cow dung and in vacant houses. A person who desires
to obtain everything should attentively perform a *shraddha* in such
places, having proceeded in a south-eastern direction. Such an
intelligent person attains the *brahman* and obtains *siddhi*. That is a
place earmarked for those in the three *varnas*, those who follow the
varnas and the *ashramas*. To attain this, they must cast aside rage
and worship the ancestors. A brave person must control himself
and full of faith, travel to the *tirthas*. Even a sinner is purified.
What need be said of a person who has performed virtuous deeds?

Such a person is not born as inferior species, nor is he reborn in a wicked region. A *brahmana* obtains heaven. He obtains means of attaining *moksha*. There are five kinds of people who do not obtain benefit from visiting a *tirtha*—a person who lacks faith, a sinner, a non-believer, a person whose doubts have not been dispelled and a person who argues about causes.'

'One obtains supreme *siddhi* from the *tirtha* that is the *guru*. This is the best of *tirtha*s. *Dhyana* is a supreme *tirtha*. The eternal *tirtha* of Brahma is greater than that. *Dhyana* is superior to fasting. The withdrawal of the senses is required. By bringing *prana* and *apana* under control, one repeatedly binds the *prana* that is connected with fasting. Restraint of the intelligence and the mind is the best among all kinds of withdrawal. It should be known that there is no doubt about *pratyahara* being a mode for *moksha*. The mind is the most terrible of the senses and causes a transformation in intelligence and the others. Fasting enables them to decay. It should be known that fasting is the best kind of austerity. If intelligence and the mind are restrained, no intelligence about anything else originates. All taints decay and all the senses also decay. Like a fire without kindling, this withdrawal leads to the purification of the *atman*. The *kshetrajna* can then engage with causes, *guna*s and everything manifest and unmanifest. Thus, a person who knows about *yoga* engages in *yoga*. He has no destination or abode. There is nothing, manifest or unmanifest. There is nothing, existent or non-existent. There is no cause or effect and he is based in nothing.'

Chapter 52-1(52) (Norms for purification)

Brihaspati said, 'After this, I will speak about the fruits of all kinds of donations, things that are fit for *shraddha* rites and articles that are to be avoided. *Agnishtoma* must be performed in a place where there is snowfall, or the snow must be gathered. This is sacred and brings supreme benefit and a long lifespan. A *shraddha* must not be performed at night, since Rahu is seen elsewhere at the time. As soon as Rahu is seen, one must quickly gather all one's possessions to undertake the rite. One must perform it when there is an eclipse. Otherwise, one will suffer, like a cow sinking into mud. If a person performs it at the time of an eclipse, like a boat on the ocean, this will carry him across all sins. In sacrifices to the Vishvadevas and Soma, the meat of a rhinoceros is the supreme oblation. We use the flesh of a hornless rhinoceros to destroy all jealousy. Tvashta performed a sacrifice for the great-souled lord of *devas*. When Shachi's husband was drinking the *soma*, a little fell in the middle, on the ground. *Shyamaka* originated from this and is used to satisfy the unvanquished ancestors. Sprays of the juice stuck to his nostrils and became sugarcane. Therefore, sugarcane pacifies phlegm and is cool, mild and sweet. To accomplish all desires, rites for ancestors should be undertaken with *shyamaka* and sugarcane. If one renders the first offering with these, one swiftly attains *siddhi*. It is said that for the purpose of a sacrifice, *shyamaka* has two names. Since it has been created by *devas*, it is described as *akshata*. *Prasatika, priyangu, mudga, harita* and others possess qualities that are similar to those of *shyamaka*.[1183] Black gram, sesamum, barley and *shali*[1184] are excellent.'

'In *shraddha* rites, *mahayava, nishpava, madhulika* and black rice mixed with iron must be avoided.[1185] One must make efforts to avoid *rajamasha*. But *mashura* is sacred and *kusumbha* is Shri's abode.[1186] The following articles and others are excellent and sweet—when it rains constantly, *vrishaka* and *vasaka; bilva, amalaka, mridvika, panasa, amrata* and *dadima; tavashomlayata, kshoudra, kharjura* and *amra* fruit; *kasheru, kovidara, talakanda* and *visa; tamala, shatakanda, madvasuchanta* and *kandiki; kaleya, kalashaka, bhuripurna* and *suvarchala; mamsaksha; duvishaka* and *bubuchetamkara; kaphalaka, kana, draksha, lakucha* and *chocha; alavu, grivaka, vira, karkandhu* and *madhusahvaya; vaikankata,*

[1183] *Prasatika* is a kind of rice with small grains. In this context, *harita* probably means green gram.

[1184] *Shali* is a fine rice.

[1185] *Mahayava* must mean barley with large grains, *nishpava* is a kind of pulse and *madhulika* is a variety of wheat.

[1186] *Rajamasha* is a kind of bean (*rajma*). *Kusumbha* is safflower.

nalikera, shringaja and *pakarushaka; pippali, maricha, patola* and the *brihati* fruit; the fragrant flesh of large animals and everything astringent.[1187] *Nagara* can be given and so can *dirghamulaka*.[1188] Bamboo shoots, succulent *sarjaka* and *bhustrina* can be offered.[1189] The following objects must always be avoided in *shraddha* rites— garlic, carrot, onion and round radish. *Karambha*[1190] and other objects that are devoid of taste and smell must be avoided. I will tell you the reason. Earlier, there was a battle between *deva*s and *asura*s and Bali was defeated by the Gods. When his limbs were pierced by arrows, drops of blood fell down. Garlic and all the other things originated from these. In that way, red juices and salt from barren lands must be avoided in *shraddha* rites. This is also true of women who are going through their monthly periods. One should avoid foul-smelling and frothy water, water that has overflowed, water that does not satisfy a cow and water collected during the night. A person who knows will avoid the milk from sheep, deer, camels, all animals that have a single hoof, buffaloes and yaks. After this, I will speak about the spots that must be carefully avoided, about

---

[1187] *Vrishaka* is a kind of plant, *vasaka* is a medicinal plant, *amalaka* is a kind of myrobalan, *mridvika* is another name for grapes (*draksha*), *panasa* is jackfruit, *amrata* is hog-plum, *dadima* is pomegranate, *tavashomlayata* cannot be pinned down, *kshoudra* is a kind of honey, *kharjura* is date, *amra* is mango, *kasheru* is a kind of grass with a bulbous root, *talakanda* is the sprout of a palm, *visa* (*ativisa*) is a medicinal plant, *tamala* is the Indian bay leaf, *shatakanda* cannot be identified, *madvasuchanta* cannot be identified, *kandiki* is a kind of tuber, *kaleya* is a kind of wood, *kalashaka* is a pot-herb, *bhuripurna* cannot be identified, *suvarchala* is the common sunflower, *mamsaksha* probably refers to a flesh derivative or the fleshy part of a fruit, *duvishaka* cannot be identified, *bubuchetamkara* cannot be identified, *kaphalaka* should probably be *kapalaka* (a type of cucumber), *kana* is the ear of a corn, *lakucha* is breadfruit, *chocha* is cinnamon, *alavu* is gourd, *grivaka* cannot be identified, *vira* is a medicinal plant, *karkandhu* is jujube, *madhusahvaya* cannot be identified, *vaikankata* cannot be identified, *narikera* is coconut, *shringaja* is aloe, *pakarushaka* cannot be identified, *pippali* is long pepper, *maricha* is pepper, *patola* is pumpkin and *brihati* is brinjal.

[1188] Respectively, dry ginger and radish.

[1189] *Sarjaka* is buttermilk and *bhustrina* is a fragrant grass.

[1190] Flour or meal mixed with curds.

those who must not see a *shraddha* and everything about purity and impurity. One should devoutly perform a *shraddha*, subsisting on wild roots and fruits. If a person does this, he attains the status of a king and eternal heaven. In *shraddha* rites, one must avoid grounds with harmful noise, spots that are narrow, a place pervaded by animals or undesirable in any other way and ground that has a foul stench. Rivers that extend all the way up to the sea and doors, to the south or the east, must be avoided. For twelve *yojana*s on every side, the region known as Trishanku must be avoided. The region named Trishanku has Mahanadi on the north and Mount Venkata on the south. This must be avoided in all *shraddha* rites. One must make efforts to avoid regions like Karaskara, Kalinga, regions to the north of Sindhu and places where the *dharma* of *ashrama*s has been destroyed. *Nagna*s[1191] and others must not present themselves at *shraddha* rites and witness them. If they see them, those do not reach fathers and grandfathers.'

Shamyu said, 'O illustrious one! Please tell me properly about *nagna*s and others. I am asking you.'

Brihaspati answered, 'For all beings, the three[1192] are stated to be a covering. Those who are deluded and discard them are *nagna*s and other people. When virtue is destroyed, there is no support and a person becomes a *vrishala*. There is no doubt that a *brahmana*, *kshatriya* or *vaishya* becomes a *vrishala* if he gives up virtue and seeks *moksha* through some other path, or if he does not see that virtue, *Veda*s and *ashrama*s are proper. Earlier, in a battle between *deva*s and *asura*s, the *asura*s were defeated. O son! Consequently, they created and gave birth to heretics, those who have no texts and listen to the aged,[1193] Shakyas, *ajivaka*s and *karpata*s. Those who do not follow *dharma* are *nagna*s and similar people. *Nagna*s and

---

[1191] While *nagna* means naked, this specifically means naked mendicants.

[1192] The three *Veda*s.

[1193] We have translated *vriddhashravika* in this way. Since Vriddhashrava means Indra, this can also stand for Indra's worshippers. *Nirgrantha* has been taken as an adjective, without texts. Shakyas are Buddhists, while *ajivika*s (*ajivika*s) are a sect of religious mendicants. *Karpata*s are a heretical sect.

other people are a *dvija* who wears matted hair in vain, a *dvija* who
shaves his head in vain, a *dvija* who is naked in vain, a *dvija* who
observes vows in vain and a *dvija* who performs *japa* in vain. There
are also those who abandon the eternal *dharma* of the lineage or
earn subsistence through their wives. Because of what they do, they
are described as those who follow wicked paths. If a *shraddha* is seen
by such a person, it goes to *danava*s. One must avoid it being seen
by a person who has killed a *brahmana*, an ingrate, a non-believer,
a person who violates his *guru*'s bed, a bandit or a cruel person.
All those who have fallen and have committed cruel deeds must be
shunned. If a person speaks when *deva*s and *rishi*s are debating, or
if he criticizes *deva*s, *brahmana*s and knowledge handed down, a
shraddha seen by him goes to *asura*s and *yatudhana*s. It is said that
krita yuga is for *brahmana*s, *treta yuga* is for *kshatriya*s, *dvapara
yuga* is for *vaishya*s and *kali yuga* is for *shudra*s. The ancestors
were worshipped in *krita yuga* and the Gods in *treta yuga*. Battles
were always worshipped in *dvapara yuga* and heretics in *kali yuga*.
A person dishonoured, a person cast aside, a cock, a village pig and
a dog—if any of these see a *shraddha*, they destroy it. Anything
seen by a dog or a pig is like an ailment that has been going on
for a long time. Anything that has fallen down or is faded should
never be seen. Food seen by them does not deserve to be *havya* or
kavya. It must be abandoned. However, in times of a calamity,
it can be cleansed by a superior object. If oblations have initially
been seen by them, they have been destroyed and must be cast
aside. When they have been touched by them, it is recommended
that they be purified through *prokshana*. Alternatively, the same
objective can be accomplished by covering with white mustard or
black sesamum. One should make efforts so that such objects are
seen by the *guru*, the sun, the fire and other articles that purify.
The following must be avoided in a *shraddha* rite—food that falls
down when one is astride a seat; food that is kicked by the feet; any
food seen by a polluted creature; food that is stale or tainted in any
other way; food that is burnt or has been licked by the fire; food
that is full of sand, worms, stones and hair; oilcakes and sesamum
that have been pounded; cooked food to which salt has directly
been added; anything seen or defiled by a dog or polluted in some

other way and the garment of an *avadhuta*.[1194] There are some who pride themselves on being learned by opposing the *Veda*s. They do not perform sacrifices. Like dust, they destroy a sacrifice. In a *shraddha*, one should avoid the consumption of curds mixed with vegetables, herbs, brinjals and anything that causes terror. Salt from the Sindhu and that originating in Manasa are extremely sacred and must directly be flung into the fire. Using one's hands, one must make efforts to place this in the fire. It is said that using *brahma-tirtha*,[1195] cow dung must be touched to the head. *Prokshana* must be used for articles, and they must be purified again. Stones, roots, fruits, sugarcane, ropes and hides are purified by placing them in water, or sprinkling them with water. Anything made of wickerwork can also be purified in the afore-mentioned way. Articles made of ivory, bone, wood and horn are purified by scraping them. It is recommended that anything made of clay must be burnt again. Jewels, pearls and coral are purified by using a conch shell. Everything made of hair or wool is purified by using powdered white mustard or sesamum.'

'It is said that all bipeds are purified through clay and water. The method of purification is that of washing from head to toe with water. It is said that cotton is purified with ash and fruits; flowers and leaves are purified by immersing them in water. There are different methods of purifying the ground—washing, smearing, scraping, smearing, dousing with water, burning, digging and making a cow walk over it. These are said to be the means of purification. The ground in a village is purified by the wind that is raised when cows traverse it. It is recommended that earth should be used for the purification of men and quadrupeds. Such are the excellent methods of purification that have been instructed. I will speak about what has not been instructed. Listen attentively. In the morning, one should leave the house and proceed in a south-western direction, for a distance travelled by an arrow. When releasing excrement, the

---

[1194] An *avadhuta* is an ascetic who has renounced all worldly attachments. However, it also has the nuance of someone who has been cast off from society and has been excluded by it.

[1195] The line at the base of the right thumb is known as *brahma-tirtha*.

head must be covered. The head must never be touched with the hand. In a secluded spot, the ground must be covered with white grass, wood, leaves or pieces of bamboo, so that it cannot be seen. He should face the north during the day and the south during the night. He should not speak and should gather some water and earth. He must pick up the *kamandalu* in his right hand and with his left hand, use clay to clean his anus thrice. After this, slowly and in the due order, the earth must be applied to the left hand ten times. Thereafter, earth must be applied on both hands seven times. After using earth to clean the feet, he must follow the norms and perform *achamana*.[1196] The three handfuls of water stand for the divinities of the sun, the fire and the wind. One must always take care to have two *kamandalu*s, without holes. The first one will be used to clean oneself and the feet. The second is used for *achamana* and rites for *deva*s. If a person eats tainted food, it is recommended that he should fast for three nights. If he causes harm to a *brahmana*, it is said that he must perform the hardship of *prayashchitta*. If he touches a dog or *shvapaka*,[1197] he must torment himself through hardships. If he touches human bones, to purify himself, he must fast. If the bones have fat in them, the fasting must be for three nights. Otherwise, it can be for one night. Karaskaras, Kalingas, Andhras and Shabaras are wicked regions. So are men who reside to the north of Sindhu, or further north. These places are populated by men who are sinners. They are shunned by the virtuous and by *brahmana*s accomplished in the *Veda*s. If a deluded person goes there, out of attachment or delusion, he will lose his prosperity and the sins will not be destroyed by drinking sanctified water or by going to Mount Yugandhara. If a person goes to an impure region, he accumulates every kind of sin. He can be freed from his sins by climbing Bhrigutunga, going to the sacred Sarasvati, going to the waters of the beautiful river Ganga or the Goddess Mahanadi, other rivers that flow from Himalaya and are worshipped by *rishi*s and by

---

[1196] Rinsing and cleaning the mouth with water.

[1197] *Shvapaka*s are sometimes equated with *chandala*s. *Shva* means dog and *paka* means to cook. Thus, *shvapaka* means someone who cooks dogs (eats dogs) or cooks for dogs (lives with dogs).

going to all the *tirtha*s in lakes, rivers and waterfalls. He then enjoys heaven for an eternity. If there is a death or birth in the family, it is said that a *brahmana* is impure for ten nights. It is twelve days for a *kshatriya*, half a month for a *vaishya* and one month for a *shudra*. For all the *varnas*, a woman going through her monthly period is purified in four nights. Purification is recommended if one touches a woman going through her period, a woman in the delivery-chamber, a dog, an *antyaja*, a naked person and those who have carried dead bodies. A *dvija* will be purified if he bathes with his clothes on and smears himself with clay twelve times. After sexual intercourse or vomiting, the purification is identical. A man must perform the act of purification after washing his hands with water and mud. After bathing, he must wash his hands with water and mud again. This smearing with clay must be done thrice, ending with twelve times. For all kinds of rites, this is always the recommended means of purification. Each foot must be smeared with clay and washed thrice. This is the means of purification for a forest. I will now speak about what is done in a village. For purification of hands and others, the clay must be applied fifteen times. Excess clay can be applied and the clay must be washed with water. When clay is no longer visible, the entire purification must be completed with water. If a person does not cover his neck and head and goes to a road where there are shops, he becomes impure. If he does not wash his feet, he remains impure even after performing *achamana*. After washing, the vessel must be set aside and *achamana* performed. The purification must also be undertaken for other objects. Flowers, grass and oblations are sprinkled with water. Objects brought by others must be placed down and the purification performed. For a *shraddha*, nothing must be touched until *prokshana* has been performed. Any object must be brought from the north and released in the south.'

'The performer of a *shraddha* must always undertake the rite in a secluded spot. In anything connected with *deva*s and ancestors, one is polluted if one touches leftovers. In such cases, the southern altar must be touched with the right hand and rendering offerings to *deva*s and ancestors with both hands. *Achamana* must be performed if there is nocturnal emission, after passing urine and

excrement, after spitting, after bathing with oil, after eating, after
wearing a garment, after touching leftovers, after washing the feet,
after speaking to a person who has touched leftovers, eating when
one is supposed to be controlled, in all cases of doubt when one has
loosened the tuft of hair on the head, on touching the sacred thread
without reason, on touching a camel or sheep, after seeing a person
one should not speak with, on touching the teeth with the tongue,
on making a sound with the fingers and on seeing a fallen person.
If a person is deluded and performs *achamana* while standing, he
remains impure. He must sit down in a pure spot, control himself
and face the north or the east. He must wash the feet first. He must
place his hands on his knees and touch water. He must control
himself and controlled and pleased, he must drink water thrice. He
must rinse his mouth twice and perform the purification once. After
this, he must touch water to the back, the head, the hands and the
feet. Purified in this way, anything resolved occurs. When *achamana*
is performed in this way, the *Veda*s, sacrifices, austerities, donations
and observance of *vrata*s bear fruits. A person who is deluded and
undertakes rites without *achamana* is a non-believer.[1198] There is
no doubt that all his rites are in vain. One should not associate
with impure words or intelligence. Nor should one touch anything
condemned. It should be known that some things are pure, unless
they have been rendered tainted and impure by a calamity. These
are thoughts, words, fire, time, etchings, announcements of rites
and eternal *jnana*. Out of delusion, if a person mixes up the rites,
there is no doubt that the fruits go to *pishacha*s and *yatudhana*s. If
the purification is performed without faith, the fruits go to those
born as *mleccha*s. If a sinner does not perform sacrifices, he is born
as an inferior species. However, even then, if the man performs
rites of purification, he resides in heaven and obtains *moksha*.
*Deva*s desire and this has been stated by *deva*s themselves. The
Gods always avoid those who are terrible and impure. Those who
perform auspicious rites follow the rules and undertake purification
thrice. O *dvija*s! If a person is intelligent and extremely devoted to

---

[1198] In these sections, the text seems to be corrupted and liberties have
been taken.

*brahmana*s; if he is full of purity; if he is controlled and devoted to ancestors; and if he has compassion, the *deva*s grant him whatever his mind desires, even if he wishes for what is best in the three worlds. The ancestors enhance his prosperity.'

Chapter 53-1(53) (Test of a *brahmana*)

The *rishi*s said, 'O Suta! You are blessed. You have described to us the rites for a *shraddha*. We have heard the rites for a *shraddha*, as described by the *rishi*s. It has specifically been described to us in great detail. O immensely wise one! What are the views of the *rishi* about anything else in the *Vedas*?'

Suta replied, 'O *brahmana*s! I will describe in detail the views of the immensely fortunate *rishi* about *shraddha*s. Listen. I have spoken about *shraddha*s earlier and about the rules to be followed for *shraddha*s. I will now speak about what is left, the testing of *brahmana*s. *Brahmana*s should not be tested always, but they should be for this case of this excellent and sacred rite. We have heard that *deva*s and ancestors have always spoken about such testing. Anyone seen to possess taints must be excluded from the rites. If one knows this, one must make efforts to avoid him and not reside with him. For the sake of a *shraddha*, a learned person should not test an unknown *dvija*. There are *siddha*s who roam around on this earth, in the form of *brahmana*s. Therefore, when an *atithi*[1199] arrives, one should join one's hands in salutation and welcome him. He must be worshipped with *arghya*, *padya*, food and oil for a bath. Assuming many different kinds of forms, *deva*s and lords of *yoga* always roam around the earth, up to the ocean. They do this so that *praja*s may be engaged with *dharma*. Therefore, a man must always be controlled, worshipping an *atithi*. I will describe the dishes and their fruits. If milk is offered, one obtains the fruits of an *aghishtoma*

[1199] *Atithi* means *a-tithi* and is therefore not any guest, but a guest who arrives uninvited and is unexpected.

sacrifice. In the case of *payasam*, the fruits are of *uktha*.[1200] With *ghee*, the fruits are of a *sodashi* sacrifice.[1201] With honey, the fruits are those of *atiratra*. If a man faithfully feeds *brahmana*s everything they wish for, he accomplishes every objective. If one treats all *brahmana*s as *atithi*s, the fruits obtained are always those obtained from every kind of sacrifice. For a *shraddha* or a rite connected with *deva*s, if a person shows disrespect towards an *atithi*, *deva*s drive him away and destroy his wealth. To show favours to the worlds, *deva*s and ancestors enter a *dvija* in invisible form and eat what the *brahmana* eats. If the guest is not worshipped, he burns down. If he is honoured, he bestows everything wished for. Therefore, using everything one possesses, one must always worship an *atithi*. For a virtuous person, whether he is in *garhasthya* or *vanaprastha*, an *atithi* who arrives is always known to be equal to a *valakhilya* or a mendicant. An *abhyagata* is someone who has been invited for food. However, an *atithi* arrives when there is no fire.[1202] An *atithi* is said to be someone without a *tithi*. This is said to be the derivation of *atithi*. The following cannot be an *atithi*—a person without *vrata*s, a narrow-minded person, a person devoid of learning, a person who does not possess specialized knowledge, a person who does not have offspring, a person not devoted to *deva*s and a person who commits sins. If a host desires the fruits of a sacrifice, he must honour and donate to a person who is thirsty, exhausted, has travelled a lot and is hungry. O *brahmana*! A hungry person must never be told, "There is nothing." He must always be honoured. After welcoming him, things must be given to him.'

'At a *shraddha*, one must always feed the following—a person who is not suffering from a wound; a person who finds subsistence difficult but is not a beggar; and an intelligent person who is always devoted to solitude. Only an evil-souled person will say, "I will not give to him." Even if he has one hundred births, such a person will not be freed of his sins. If a man happily feeds *brahmana*s in the

---

[1200] Rite where *Sama Veda* is recited.

[1201] A kind of *soma* sacrifice.

[1202] The *atithi* is unexpected, no fire has been lit for cooking food. An *abhyagata* is expected.

same *pankti*,[1203] irrespective of whether they have been invited or not, that *pankti* destroys his sins. Otherwise, he is a sinner and all his good merits of *ishta* and *purta*[1204] are seized and destroyed. A mendicant must be before all *brahmana*s. After the *yogi*, a person who knows will seat an excellent *brahmana* who has studied the five—the *Veda*s and Itihasa.[1205] A person who has studied three *Veda*s will be after that and a person who has studied two *Veda*s after that. A person who has studied one *Veda* will be after that and an *upadhyaya*[1206] after that. I will speak about the numbers of those who purify. Listen. In the due order, all this has been instructed earlier—a person who knows the six *Vedanga*s; a *yogi*; a person who practices *dhyana*; a person who knows all the *tantra*s; and a person who is a wanderer. These five are known to purify a *pankti*. A person who knows about the rules for a *shraddha* also purifies. So does a person who is accomplished in at least one out of the fourteen kinds of learning.[1207] All those who enhance honour purify the *pankti*. There are undoubtedly those who know *trisuparna*, those who maintain five fires,[1208] those who chant *Sama* hymns, *brahmana*s who follow the norms and constantly wander around for twelve years, those who know *Trinachiketa*,[1209] those who know the three *Veda*s, *brahmana*s who constantly study *dharma* and *brahmana*s who are accomplished in the great texts composed by Brihaspati. O *brahmana*s! All of these are said to purify *pankti*s.'

'If a *dvija* is invited to a *shraddha*, but has intercourse with a woman, his ancestors lie down on that semen for a month. Donations must be made to a person devoted to *dhyana*, an intelligent person

---

[1203] Row. When sitting down to eat, different *varna*s are meant to sit in different rows.

[1204] *Ishta* is religious rites, *purta* is civic works.

[1205] Itihasa is known as the fifth *Veda*.

[1206] An ordinary teacher, inferior to an *acharya*.

[1207] Four *Veda*s, Six *Vedanga*s, *arthashastra*, *dhanurveda*, *ayurveda* and Itihasa-Purana. The list isn't consistent. Sometimes, *nitishastra*, *dharmashastra* and *gandharva-veda* are added.

[1208] Performing austerities with four fires on four sides and the sun overhead.

[1209] *Trinachiketa* is a part of the *Yajur Veda*.

and a compassionate person. In *shraddha* rites, a mendicant
or a *valakhilya* must be fed. If the hospitality is for a person in
vanaprastha, worship alone ensures contentment. A person in
garhasthya must be fed, after worshipping the Vishvadevas. *Rishis*
are satisfied if a person in *vanaprastha* is honoured. *Valakhilyas*
are satisfied if Purandara is honoured. Worshipping mendicants
is like worshipping Brahma himself. A fifth *ashrama*, consisting
of a mixture of the four, is not pure. In a *shraddha*, or in a rite
involving *deva*s, only the four *ashrama*s should be worshipped.
Those who are outside the four *ashrama*s must not be welcomed
at a *shraddha*. Those who are outside the four *ashrama*s must
remain there, subsisting only on air. A person who torments himself
through austerities, but does not belong to an ashrama, should not
be invited. There are those who defile a *pankti*—a person who
professes to be learned and speaks about *moksha*, even though he
is not a mendicant; a person engaged in fierce austerities; a person
who argues about many things in colourful ways and those who
criticize *dvija*s. There are all the others who defile *pankti*s—those
prone to excessive fasting; those who follow *samkhya* but are non-
believers and criticize the *Veda*s and those who criticize *dhyana*.
There are those who shave their heads unnecessarily, those who
wear matted hair unnecessarily, *karpata*s, those who are not
compassionate, those who do not follow good conduct and those
who eat anything. They must be shunned. The following must not be
fed *havya* or *kavya*—artisans, those not distressed at not following
good conduct, those cast out by the worlds, singers and those who
earn subsistence by selling the *Veda*s. Anyone who associates with
these becomes dark in complexion. All those who eat with *shudra*s
also defile *pankti*s.'

'*Brahmana*s must always avoid livelihood through ploughing,
agriculture, trade, animal husbandry, serving someone who is not
a *guru* and serving the enemy. One must always avoid those who
make false resolutions and have wicked conduct. In a *shraddha*
rite, one should shun a person who bears false witness, a person
who indulges in calumny, a person who shows his insolence, a
person who commits minor sins, especially one who commits major
sins, a person who employs someone else to study the *Veda*s, a

person who does not donate, or is greedy and deluded about the fruits or a person who sells the *Veda*s. There can be no substitute to studying the *Veda*s. A person who employs someone else is a sinner. In such cases, an expounder of the *Veda*s is deprived of the fruits. A donor is deprived of the fruits. A person who employs a servant to teach, or is taught by such a servant, does not deserve to be invited to a *shraddha*. Nor does a *brahmana* who engages in buying and selling. Buying and selling are condemned means of earning subsistence. These are means of livelihood for a *vaishya* and are sins for a *brahmana*. If a person pays someone to study the *Veda*s, or if another person earns a living through the *Veda*s, both of these do not deserve to be invited to a *shraddha*. They are like the husband of a *putrika*.[1210] A person who approaches his wife in vain,[1211] or a person who performs a sacrifice in vain, should not be invited for a *shraddha*. Nor should a *dvija* who earns a living through lending money, or a person whose wife is attached to someone else, or a person who is attached to someone else's wife. A person addicted to *artha* or *kama* should not be fed at a *shraddha*. Nor should a person who is against the dharma of *varna*s and *ashrama*s, or against all the rites. Thieves and those who perform sacrifices for everyone pollute the *pankti*. If a *dvija* eats like a pig, if he eats from his palm, or if he speaks while eating, the ancestors do not accept the offering. The leftovers from a *shraddha* should not be given to women or *shudra*s. Out of delusion, if a person does this, the food does not go to the ancestors. Therefore, the leftovers from a *shraddha* rite must not be given away. Other than curds and *ghee*, anything that is leftover should be given to the son and not to anyone else. In particular, food and other leftovers must be disposed of in this way. Satisfied with flowers, roots and fruits, the ancestors finally leave. The ancestors partake of the food as long as the heat has not left it. The ancestors partake of the food as long as the eating takes place silently. Donations, receiving, oblations,

---

[1210] A *putrika* is a daughter who is regarded as a son. After marriage, she lives in her father's household. Her son is regarded as her father's son and becomes the heir.

[1211] With offspring not as the intended motive.

eating, offerings and rendering of *padya* through the thumb must
be done in such a way that these do not reach *asura*s. This is true
of everything, especially donations. One must sit down on one's
knees and perform *achamana*. In *shraddha* rites, those with shaved
heads, those with matted hair and those with ochre garments must
be shunned. Those who always base themselves on good conduct,
those with *jnana*, those engaged in *dhyana*, those devoted to *deva*s
and great-souled ones—the sight of such people purifies. Offerings
must be made to those who have tufts of hair on their heads, those
whose garments are red with mineral dyes and those who are
*tridandi*s. All the lords of *yoga* constantly pervade the three worlds.
They see everything that goes on in the universe. They have the
manifest and the unmanifest under their control and base everything
on the supreme. Those great-souled ones have perceived existence
and non-existence, cause and effect. Those great-souled ones have
created every kind of *jnana*, about *moksha* and everything else.
Therefore, if a person is constantly devoted to them, he obtains
excellent fruits. If a person knows the hymns of the *Rig Veda*, he
knows the *Veda*s. If he knows the hymns of the *Yajur Veda*, he
understands a sacrifice. If he knows the hymns of the *Sama Veda*, he
comprehends the *brahman*. If a person knows the mind, he knows
all the *Veda*s.'

Chapter 54-1(54) (Praise of donations)

Brihaspati said, 'After this, I will speak about the fruits of
donations. This saves all beings, brings happiness and
is the path to heaven. Everything that is best in the world and
everything that is loved by a person—if a person seeks to abide by
the commands of the ancestors, all this must be given to them. A
person who donates food obtains, for eternity, a divine *vimana*, as
radiant as the sun and made out of gold, served by celestial *apsara*s.
Without being restricted, if a person offers dishes at a *shraddha*
rite, he obtains a long lifespan, radiance, prosperity, beauty and
the auspicious. At the time of a *shraddha*, if a person who knows

about sacrifices gives the sacred thread for a sacrifice, he obtains the fruits of donating the *brahman*, something that purifies all *brahmana*s. At the time of a *shraddha*, if a person donates an over-flowing *kamandalu* to *brahmana*s, honey, milk, *ghee* and curds present themselves before the donor. At the time of a *shraddha*, if a person gives a *kamandalu* marked with the sign of a *chakra*, he obtains a cow that is easily milked, yielding divine milk. At the time of a *shraddha* rite, if a person gives two pieces of footwear filled with cotton, he obtains a beautiful vehicle, and his feet are happy. If a person honours a *brahmana* and gives him a fan made out of palm leaf, he obtains every kind of gentle and fragrant flower. By giving a *brahmana* a pair of footwear at the time of a *shraddha*, a learned person obtains a new and divine vehicle, yoked to horses. At the time of a *shraddha*, if a person gives an umbrella garlanded with flowers, it transforms itself into an excellent mansion that follows him wherever he goes. At the time of a *shraddha*, if a learned person gives a mendicant a habitation that is full of jewels, a bed and food, he obtains greatness in the vault of heaven. He obtains pearls, lapis lazuli, garments, many kinds of jewels and millions and billions of divine vehicles. For eternity, he obtains a divine *vimana* with the complexion of the sun and the moon, sacred and extremely great. It can travel through the sky and is full of everything desired. It is surrounded by *apsara*s and can travel anywhere it wishes, at the speed of thought. Praised in every direction, he resides in that supreme *vimana*, surrounded by divine flowers. The learned say that this is what happens with excellent donations. At a *shraddha*, one must offer shining vessels made out of gold. Succulent tastes, food and good fortune will then present themselves. At a *shraddha*, if a person gives *dvija*s sesamum and sugarcane, he obtains friends in this world and good fortune with women. At the time of feeding on the occasion of a *shraddha*, if a person donates agreeable metal vessels, he becomes the recipient of everything desired, beauty and wealth.[1212] At the time of a *shraddha* rite, if a person gives silver or gold, as a result of that

---

[1212] There is a pun on the word *patra*, which means vessel, as well as recipient.

donation, he obtains everything desired, radiance and wealth.
At the time of a *shraddha*, if a man donates a cow that has had
only one calf, one that fills a pot when it is milked, cattle and
nourishment present themselves before him. When it is winter, if a
man makes efforts to donate a fire with a lot of wood, he obtains
radiance and good fortune and his body blazes like the fire. When
it is the onset of winter, if a person gives kindling to *dvija*s, he is
always victorious in battles and when reborn, obtains prosperity.
At a *shraddha*, worthy recipients must be honoured and welcomed
with fragrant garlands and fragrances. If one gives great-souled
ones fragrant garlands, many kinds of happiness result. Young
women, devoted to their husbands, present themselves before the
donor. At a *shraddha*, if a person donates beds, seats, vehicles,
land and mounts, he obtains the fruits of a horse sacrifice. At
the time of a *shraddha*, if a *brahmana* full of qualities presents
himself and a person gives him whatever he desires, the donor
obtains memory and intelligence. At a *shraddha*, if a person is
welcoming and donates vessels filled with *ghee*, he obtains the
fruits of donating a cow that has had only one calf and when
milked, yields an entire pot.'

'At a *shraddha*, if a person gives whatever is wished for,[1213]
he obtains the fruits of a *pundarika* sacrifice. If a person donates
a grove full of flowers and fruits, he obtains the fruits of a *gosava*
sacrifice. If he donates wells, gardens, ponds, fields, cow-pens and
houses, he enjoys himself in heaven, for as long as the moon and
stars exist. At a *shraddha*, if a person donates couches studded with
jewels and decorated with them, his ancestors are satisfied and he
enjoys the world of heaven. In this world, if a person donates
food, chariots and excellent vehicles, he is honoured in the eight
directions and his wealth and grain increase. After following the
norms and feeding *brahmana*s, they must be given garments made
out of leaves, silk and wool, bedspreads and blankets, antelope-
skins, gold, coloured woollen garments and the hair of deer. A man
who is full of faith obtains the fruits of a horse sacrifice. He obtains
many beautiful wives, sons, servants and attendants. All creatures

[1213] By the recipient naturally.

in the world remain under his control and he does not suffer from ailments. At a *shraddha*, if a person gives garments and girdles made out of wool, silk and cotton, he obtains all the excellent and extensive desires that are in his mind. His adversity is destroyed, like darkness when the sun rises. Like the moon amidst *nakshatra*s, he is radiant in an excellent *vimana*. In every rite associated with *deva*s, *deva*s have praised garments. In the absence of garments, rites connected with sacrifices, donations and austerities do not exist. Therefore, at the time of a *shraddha*, garments must always be given. A man who donates these at a *shraddha*, obtains everything. Therefore, at a *shraddha*, one must always be attentive and make efforts to donate these. Consequently, a donor obtains everything that he desires, a kingdom and heaven. He enjoys the fruits of a sacrifice, prosperous with everything that is desired. If a person donates well-prepared food and edible items, usually mild, like a *svastika*,[1214] along with sugar, *krisara*, honey, *ghee*, milk and *payasam*, he obtains the fruits of an *agnishtoma* sacrifice. At a *shraddha*, if a man gives many kinds of food and curds and products of milk, without mixing them, he does not grieve during the monsoon, or when Magha *nakshatra* is in the ascendant. *Brahmana*s must be fed *ghee* and *ghee* must be sprinkled on the ground. At a *shraddha*, if a person donates this when there is the shadow of the elephant,[1215] he does not grieve. If a person gives many kinds of food items, like cooked rice, *payasam*, *ghee*, honey, roots and fruits, he obtains joy in this world and in the world hereafter. Sugar mixed with milk yields extensive and eternal benefits. With vegetables, meat-juices, *saktu*,[1216] parched corn, *apupas*,[1217] *kulmasha*[1218] and curried dishes, delight is obtained for a year. Pleasant curds and fried food must be used to honour and feed them. If this is done at a *shraddha*, a person obtains

---

[1214] In this context, *svastika* is a kind of cake.

[1215] This is known as *gajacchaya*, that is, when there is an eclipse, or when the sun and the moon are in Hasta *nakshatra*.

[1216] Pounded ground meal, colloquially known as *sattu*.

[1217] A sweet cake.

[1218] An inferior grain.

the Padma *nidhi*.[1219] At a *shraddha*, if a person uses new crops and makes efforts to honour and feed, he enjoys all the objects of pleasure and is honoured when he goes to heaven. An *atithi* must be fed excellent food items in the form of *bhokhsya*, *peya*, *lehya* and *choshya*.[1220] Before feeding, he must join his hands in salutation and offer the best of seats. If he does this, he obtains the excellent fruits of every kind of *yajna* and *kratu*. One must quickly and happily offer a hungry person warm and cooked food. Having honoured the person, it must attentively and faithfully offered, along with mild dishes. A person who offers such cooked food will obtain a *vimana* that resembles the rising sun, always served by crores of maidens. There is no other donation that is superior to the donation of cooked food. It is through food that beings are born, live and obtain their powers. There is nothing superior to donating life. The worlds are established in food. Therefore, by giving food, one obtains the fruits of donating the worlds. It is said that Prajapati himself is food and thus, everything is in it. Hence, there has been no donation that is equal to that of donating food, nor will there ever be. A man devoted to his ancestors will swiftly obtain all jewels, mounts, women and everything else on earth. If a person joins his hands in salutation and offers shelter to *atithi*s, *deva*s wait for him, offering thousands of different kinds of divine hospitality. A person who donates everything, becomes the sole emperor on earth. However, even if one makes three, or two, types of donations, one is happy. Donations are supreme *dharma* and are honoured and worshipped by the virtuous. There is no doubt that lordship over the three worlds is established in donations. A person who is not a king obtains a kingdom. A person without wealth obtains excellent wealth. A man devoted to his ancestors, with a diminished lifespan, obtains a lifespan.'

[1219] One of Kubera's treasures.

[1220] The word *bhokshya* is being used in the sense of *charvya*. The four types of food are those that are chewed (*charvya*), sucked (*choshya* or *chushya*), licked (*lehya*) and drunk (*peya*).

Chapter 55-1(55) (Right *tithi*s for *shraddha*s)

B rihaspati said, 'After this, I will speak about the revered rites for *shraddha*s. These are of three types—*kamya, naimittika* and *nitya*. The three *ashtaka shraddha*s are performed in *krishna paksha* for sons and wives.[1221] The first is the best, when Akhandala[1222] is the divinity. Prajapati is the divinity for the second and the Vishvadevas are the divinity for the third. The rites for the first must always be performed with *apupa*s, those for the second always with meat. The rites for the third must be performed with vegetables. These are the rules about articles used. As recommended, these are the *nitya shraddha*s desired by ancestors. There is a fourth kind that must specially be performed. A learned person must use all his possessions to undertake these *nitya shraddha*s. He swiftly obtains benefit and delight, in this world and in the next one. At the time of *parva*s, the ancestors are the divinities. At the time of *tithi*s, *deva*s are the divinities. At the end of the month, if ancestors are not worshipped in this way through *ashtaka*s, they become like cows that have fallen down. There is no doubt that all his wishes become futile, in this world and in the next one. There is benefit for those who worship. Non-believers head downwards. Those who give, proceed towards *deva*s. Those who do not give, proceed towards inferior species. Those who worship, obtain everything in full measure— nourishment, offspring, memory, intelligence, sons and prosperity. If it is performed on *pratipada*, wealth is obtained, and anything obtained is not destroyed. If it is performed on *dvitiya*, he becomes lord over bipeds. A person who desires the best performs it on *tritiya* and obtains the destruction of enemies and sins. If a person undertakes it on *chaturthi*, he can see weaknesses in enemies. If he performs it on *panchami*, he obtains great prosperity.

[1221] *Ashtaka* is the eighth lunar day, but during *krishna paksha*. The three singled out are those in the months of Margashirsha, Pousha and Magha. When the three *ashtaka*s are performed in a single month, the three relevant days are the seventh, eighth and ninth lunar *tithi*s in the month of Magha.
[1222] Indra.

If he undertakes the *shraddha* on *shashthi*, he is worshipped, even if he does not make efforts. A man must always undertake a *shraddha* on *saptami*. In that case, he becomes a great lord and the leader of *gana*s. If a man undertakes it on *ashtami*, he obtains complete prosperity. A man who desires prosperity and women must perform the *shraddha* on *navami*. A man who undertakes it on *dashami* obtains Brahma's prosperity. If a man always offers gifts on *ekadashi*, he obtains supreme prosperity. He obtains the *Veda*s and a status of equality with all the *brahmana*s. If he does it on *dvadashi*, he obtains victory, a kingdom, a long lifespan, riches, increase in progeny, animals, intelligence, independence and excellent nourishment. If he undertakes it on *trayodashi*, he obtains a long lifespan and prosperity. If a young person has died in the house, or if a person has been killed through the use of weapons, donations must be undertaken on *chaturdashi*. One must always make efforts to be pure and perform *shraddha* on *amavasya*. He then obtains everything that he desires and infinite heaven. For all twins born under unfavourable stars, *shraddha* must be performed on *amavasya*. One then obtains everything that is desired. If one performs *shraddha* when Magha *nakshatra* is in the ascendant, one obtains every object of desire. At that time, it is as if the ancestors are directly worshipped. This is because the ancestors are the divinities for Magha and the fruits are described as ever lasting.'

Chapter 56-1(56) (*Shraddhas* under specific *nakshatras*)[1223]

Brihaspati said, 'Yama spoke about *shraddha*s to Shashabindu.[1224] Hear about the desirable acts under separate *nakshatras*. If a man always ignites the fire and performs a *shraddha* at the conjunction of Krittika, he is extremely firm in his vows and obtains

---

[1223] This chapter is a paraphrase of sections from Anushasana Parva of Mahabharata.
[1224] Famous king.

radiance in heaven. One who desires offspring should do it under Rohini. One who desires energy should do it under Soumya.[1225] If a man performs a *shraddha* under Ardra, he generally becomes the perpetrator of cruel deeds. A human who performs a *shraddha* under Punarvasu, obtains fields and daughters. A man who desires nourishment should perform a *shraddha* under Tishya.[1226] A person who worships the ancestors under Ashlesha obtains brave sons. A person who performs a *shraddha* under Magha becomes the best in his class. A man who worships the ancestors under Purva Phalguni obtains good fortune. Uttara Phalguni leads to offspring, with the person becoming generous, with good conduct. Worshipping the ancestors under Hasta leads to his becoming the foremost in an assembly. If he performs it under Chitra, he obtains handsome sons. If a he does it under Svati, he earns gains through trade. A man who desires sons should wish to perform *shraddha* under Vishakha. If a man does it under Anuradha, he becomes an emperor. If he always does it under Jyeshtha, he becomes a lord and is always the best. Desiring the cure of disease, one should wish to do it under Mula. Under Purva Ashadha, one obtains great fame. If a man does it under Uttara Ashadha, he is devoid of sorrow. If he does it under Shravana, he obtains the supreme destination in this world. If he does it under Dhanishtha, he obtains a share in a kingdom and copious wealth. If one desires *siddhi* and wishes to conquer the worlds and obtain the *Vedas* and *Vedangas*, one should undertake a *shraddha* under Varuna's *nakshatra*.[1227] If one does it under Purva Proshthapada,[1228] one obtains many kinds of means of subsistence. If one does it under Uttara Proshthapada, one obtains thousands of cattle. If one does it under Revati, one obtains many kinds of articles hidden in wells. If one does it under Ashvayuja,[1229] one obtains horses. Under Bharani, one becomes supreme among virtuous people. Having heard about these rites for *shraddha*s, Shashabindu

---

[1225] Mrigashira.
[1226] That is, Pushya.
[1227] Shatabhisha.
[1228] The same as Bhadrapada.
[1229] Ashvini.

acted accordingly. With his strength, he conquered the entire earth effortlessly and ruled over it.'

Chapter 57-1(57) (Testing a *brahmana*)

Shamyu asked, 'O supreme among eloquent ones! When offered to ancestors, what gives the greatest satisfaction? What gives benefits for a long time? What is conceived as infinite?'

Brihaspati replied, 'Those who know about *shraddha*s also know about oblations for the rites of *shraddha*s. Hear accurately from me about all their fruits. If sesamum, *vrihi*, barley, *masha*, roots, fruits and water are offered in a *shraddha*, the grandfathers are satisfied for a month. Fish pleases them for two months and venison pleases for three months. Rabbits please for four months and the flesh of birds for five months. The meat of a boar pleases for six months and that of a goat for seven months. If it is a mountain-goat, the pleasure lasts for eight months. With the flesh of a *ruru* antelope, the grandfathers are pleased for nine months. With the flesh of a *gavaya*, they are pleased for ten months. If the flesh of sheep is offered, the satisfaction lasts for eleven months. O *dvijas*! If the milk of cows is offered at a *shraddha*, the satisfaction lasts for an entire year. With the flesh of a rhinoceros, the satisfaction obtained by ancestors is infinite. At the time of *gajacchaya*, if payasam, honey and *ghee* are offered, the satisfaction is imperishable. With the meat of a black goat, the satisfaction is eternal. In this connection, those who know about ancient accounts recite a chant the ancestors sung. I will describe this to you accurately. Listen. "Will there not be someone in our lineage who will render offerings to us on *trayodashi*? Will we not be offered the completely red meat of a goat during the monsoon, or when Magha *nakshatra* is in the ascendant? Many sons should be sought so that at least one goes to Gaya. There should be one who has a *gouri*[1230] as wife, one who releases a blue bull."'

[1230] A girl less than eight years old.

Shamyu asked, 'O father! What are the fruits of Gaya and the others? I am asking you. Please tell me. Please tell me about all the sacred fruits obtained by donors.'

Brihaspati answered, "In Gaya, shraddha, japa, oblations and austerities are eternal. O son! The ancestors reside there and hence, these are described as ever-lasting. When the son born through a gouri attains twenty-one years of age, he should perform a great rite. The fruits of this are described as great. I will speak about the fruits of releasing a bull. Listen. A person who releases a bull purifies ten preceding generations and ten succeeding generations. After vrishotsarga,[1231] he should descend into the water of a river and touch the water. This is said to bring eternal benefit to the ancestors. If the bull touches the water with its tail or its limbs, there is no doubt that everything becomes eternal for the ancestors. If the bull touches the ground with its horns or hooves, or scratches the ground, this becomes an eternal channel of honey for the ancestors. The shruti texts say that the satisfaction obtained by ancestors through the release of a bull is equal to that obtained from digging a pond measuring one thousand nalvas[1232] on every side. At the time of a shraddha rite, if a person offers molasses mixed with sesamum, honey, or something mixed with honey, everything becomes eternal. Humans must always donate, without testing a brahmana. However, it has been heard that the testing must be done in rites connected with devas and ancestors. Dvijas who have performed all the vratas of the Vedas and have bathed, sanctify the panktis. Those who are accomplished in languages, those engaged in studying vyakarana, those who have studied the Puranas and dharmashastras, those who know Trinachiketa, those who maintain the five fires, those who know the suparnas, those who know the six Vedangas, the son of a brahmana who is like a God, those who know chhanda, those who know Jyeshthasama, those who have bathed in all the sacred tirthas and performed vratas there, those who have immersed themselves in avabhritha after all the sacrifices, those who are always devoted to the truth, those who are always devoted to their own dharma and

---

[1231] Offering a bull, setting the bull free at the time of a shraddha.
[1232] A nalva is a measure of distance, equal to 400 hastas or cubits.

those devoid of anger and avarice—these are the ones who should be invited to a *shraddha*. They purify *pankti*s and anything given to them becomes eternal. *Brahmana*s devoted to *yoga* and *vrata*s are worthy of being invited to *shraddha*s. Through this, the trinity of Brahma, Vishnu and Maheshvara are worshipped. If a man worships them, along with the ancestors, he obtains the worlds. The first among every kind of *dharma* is said to be the *dharma* of *yoga*. This is the most sacred among everything sacred. This is the most auspicious among everything auspicious.'

'I will describe those who do not deserve to be seated in a *pankti*. Listen. A fraudulent person, a drunkard, a person who keeps animals, a person banished, one who works as a servant in a village, one who earns a living through usury, a shop-keeper, a trader, a person who burns houses, a seller of poison, a *vrishala*, a person who performs sacrifices in a village, a *kandaprishtha*,[1233] a pimp, an alcoholic,[1234] a seller of *soma*, a person who has travelled beyond the ocean, a servant, a back-biter, a person who commits perjury, a person who argues with his father, a person who keeps the wife's lover in the house, a person who has been cursed, a thief, a person who makes his living through artisanship, an eulogist, a cook, a person who criticizes friends, a person who possesses one eye, a lame person, a non-believer, a person who has discarded the *Veda*s, a mad person, an eunuch, a person who has killed a foetus, a person who has violated his *guru*'s bed, a person who subsists as a physician, a glutton, a person who has intercourse with another person's wife and a person who sells the *vrata*s and *niyama*s of *brahmana*s—all these must be avoided. Anything given to a non-believer, or to one who violates vows, is lost. Anything given to a trader brings no benefit, in this world or in the next one. At a *shraddha*, nothing deserves to be given to the following—a person who appropriates something left in trust, an ingrate, a person devoid of the *Veda*s, a drummer, an artisan and a person devoid of *dharma*. A trader who buys and sells what should not be traded,

---

[1233] A *kandaprishtha* is a *brahmana* who earns a living by making arrows, or is the husband of a courtesan.

[1234] Two different words are used for drunkard, *madyapa* and *madhupa*.

and a person who praises him, can be invited elsewhere, but not for a *shraddha*. O *dvija*! When a widow marries and has a son, donating to this person is like offering oblations on ashes. Giving to a one-eyed person destroys the merits of sixty donations. Giving to a eunuch destroys one hundred merits. Giving to a person suffering from white leprosy destroys five hundred merits. If one gives to a person suffering from wicked ailments, one thousand such fruits are destroyed. Such a foolish donor is dislodged from the fruits.'

'If one eats with the head covered, if one eats while facing the south, if one eats while wearing shoes, if one donates without showing honour—Brahma has devised that all these become shares for the Indra among *asura*s. A dog or the slayer of a *brahmana* must never be seen. Therefore, rice mixed with sesamum must be scattered all around. Sesamum seeds, all around, are said to ward off *rakshasa*s and dogs. A *shraddha* is destroyed by the glance of a pig, the beating of the wings of a cock, the touch of a woman who is going through her period and if anything is offered in rage. If anything is offered on the banks of a river, in a beautiful lake or river, or in a secluded spot, the grandfathers are pleased. When offering, the right knee must touch the ground and one should not speak. Surrounded in the proper way, one must follow the norms and wear the ring of *darbha* grass on the hand. One must begin the task of worshipping the ancestors after pleasing the ancestors. One must first take the permission of the *dvija*s and following the rules, perform the fire-rites. The offerings to ancestors must be laid down on the ground, offered to the sun, or placed on a bed of *darbha* grass. In the proper way, *shraddha* rites must be performed in the forenoon of *shukla paksha*. It is performed in the afternoon in *krishna paksha*. Rohina *muhurta* must not be crossed.[1235] The ancestors are great-souled. They are immensely energetic and are great *yogi*s. In this way, depending on the time and the place, they must always be worshipped. A man devoted to the ancestors obtains *yoga*, which is so very difficult to obtain.

[1235] Rohina *muhurta* is the best time for performing *shraddha*s. It is in the forenoon, before midday. It is sometimes described as the ninth *muhurta* of the day.

Through *dhyana*, one proceeds towards *moksha*, transcending both auspicious and inauspicious *karma*. Sacrifices are said to be the cause for deluding the world.[1236] Brahma concealed this in the cavity of his heart. Kashyapa, the great-souled *yogi*, supreme among those who knew about *yoga*, revealed this *amrita* from within the cavity. Sanatkumara spoke about this great destination of the *brahman*. This is a great secret, even to *deva*s and devoted *rishi*s. By making efforts of devotion towards ancestors, learned men obtain this. In brief, a person devoted to the ancestors, a person who places the ancestors at the forefront, obtains everything, without making a great deal of effort. There is no doubt about this. Everything given at *shraddha*s bestows great fruits. *Shraddha*s in *tirtha*s and caves yield eternal benefits. One obtains heaven. All these have been spoken about. Having heard about the rites of *shraddha*s, if a man does not act accordingly, he is a non-believer. He is submerged in a terrible hell and is enveloped in darkness. This should not be condemned, especially by *yogi*s. If a person condemns this, or censures *yogi*s who are immersed in *dhyana*, desiring *moksha*, such a person circles around as a worm. There is no doubt that a person who listens to such censure also proceeds to a terrible hell. That hell is terrible to behold and is enveloped by darkness everywhere. If a man censures the lords of *yoga*, he never goes to heaven. If a man listens to the censure of lords of *yoga*, who have controlled their *atman*s, there is no doubt that he is submerged in hell for a long period of time. He is cooked in Kumbhipaka and his tongue is repeatedly sliced off. Like stones flung into the ocean, such men suffer. In thoughts, words and deeds, one must avoid hatred towards those who are engaged in *yoga*. Otherwise, there is no doubt that one reaps the fruits, in this world and after death. An accomplished person does not necessarily obtain the *paramatman*. Because of his own *karma*, he roams around in the three worlds. Because of aberrations, a person accomplished in the *Rig*, *Yajur* and *Sama Veda*s can also suffer. Prakriti is beyond transformations. A person accomplished in the three *Veda*s must go beyond the *guna*s. He must be accomplished

[1236] They are not the real objective.

in the three *guna*s. A person accomplished in the twenty-four[1237] is truly accomplished. A person who has merely studied is not necessarily accomplished. A person who has understood all this correctly crosses over to the other side and remains there, until the onset of the deluge. A *dvija* who does not follow the path of *yoga* through *pratyahara* is not accomplished in everything. He does not know how to cross over to the other side. One should know what there is to be known. A person who knows *yoga* obtains what there is to be known. A person is not said to know what should be known merely because he is said to be accomplished in the *Veda*s. There are those who know what is to be known. Having known, they remain established in this. These are said to be the ones who truly know the *Veda*s. The others are merely accomplished in the *Veda*s. There is no doubt that a person who is devoted to the ancestors obtains sacrifices, *Veda*s, everything desired, austerities of different kinds, a long lifespan and offspring. If a person controls himself and faithfully reads about the *shraddha* rites, he obtains all these and the fruits of *tirtha*s and donations. He sanctifies the *pankti* and is foremost among *dvija*s. Those who seek refuge with such *dvija*s obtain everything that they desire. If a person constantly listens to this, if a *dvija* makes others hear it, if he is free from jealousy and has conquered anger, if he is devoid of avarice and delusion, he obtains the fruits of *tirtha*s and other things and of donations and other things. There is no doubt that he obtains the mode for *moksha* and the best method for attaining heaven. If a person always acts accordingly, he obtains nourishment in this world and the next one. If a person controls himself and attentively reads these rites in assemblies, at the intervening periods between *parva*s, he obtains offspring. Subsequently, he comes full of energy and is radiant in the worlds of the residents of heaven. I prostrate myself before Svayambhu, who spoke about these rites. I always prostrate myself before the great lords of *yoga*.'

[1237] The five senses, the five objects of the senses, the five organs of action, the five elements, mind, intelligence, ego and consciousness. The twenty-four *tattva*s (principles) of *samkhya*.

Chapter 58-1(58) (Rites of a *shraddha*)

Brihaspati said, 'Thus, the ancestors are *deva*s and are divinities even for *deva*s. There are seven categories of non-decaying ancestors who are always established in their abodes. All those great-souled ones are the sons of Prajapati. The first category enhances *yoga* in *yogi*s. The second category is for *deva*s and the third category is for *danava*s and others. It should be known that the others who remain are for the *varna*s. *Deva*s worship those who are established in every kind of *jnana*. The four *ashrama*s worship them in the due order. Following the *agama* texts, all the *varna*s worship the four categories. Those of mixed *varna*s and *mleccha*s also worship them. The ancestors are delighted with those who worship the ancestors devoutly. Desiring nourishment and desiring offspring, the ancestors are worshipped. The grandfathers bestow nourishment, offspring and heaven. The rites for ancestors are superior to the rites for *deva*s. It is said in the *smriti* texts that ancestors must be worshipped before *deva*s. Men do not know the subtle movements of ancestors, who used the path of *yoga*, even if one is successful in austerities. What need be said about eyesight? A silver vessel, or one embellished with silver, must always be used. For *deva*s and ancestors, this is said to be excellent and purifying. Mentioning the name and the *gotra*, the relatives must offer three *pinda*s. The rule is that these must be spread out on the ground, or on a mat of *kusha* grass, with the sacrificial thread over the right shoulder. Wherever the *pinda*s are placed, the ancestors are pleased. This offering of food transforms into food the person has. This is just like a calf lost in a cow-pen seeking out its own mother. In that way, the *mantra* conveys the food to wherever the being may happen to be. With the name and the *gotra* mentioned, the *mantra* conveys the offered food to them. Consequently, even when they take one hundred births, the satisfaction follows them. This is how Brahma Parameshthi's power abides. Desiring eternal worlds, the ancestors were his first creation. O unblemished one! I have thus spoken about ancestors, worlds, the daughters of ancestors, the sons of those daughters and those who perform the rite. O son! In the due order, I have spoken to you about the ancestors.'

Shamyu said, 'O father! You have spoken about the divine creation of ancestors, the worlds, their daughters and the sons of the daughters, and I have heard. You have described donations, purification, fruits, what is imperishable and *dvijas*. Everything has been stated. From today, I will accurately undertake everything that has been stated.'

Brihaspati answered, 'Earlier, the lord Angiras spoke about this to the *rishis*. So that their doubts might be dispelled, all the *rishis* questioned him in an assembly of men. Formerly, there was a sacrifice that lasted for one thousand years. Brahma, the lord of all *devas*, bathed and consecrated himself as the one who would preside over that sacrifice. Five thousand years have passed since then. In those ancient times, *rishis* who knew about the *brahman* chanted a *shloka*. "Earlier, Brahma, the *paramatman*, consecrated himself for the sacrifice. Desiring the eternal, he offered cooked food there to the ancestors." Parameshthi Brahma did this for the welfare of the worlds.'

Suta concluded, 'In this way, earlier, Brihaspati was questioned by his intelligent son. He spoke about the creation of ancestors, and I have repeated that.'

Chapter 59-1(59) (Bhrigu and Parashurama)

Vasishtha said, 'O king![1238] The great-souled and infinitely energetic Jamadagni conducted himself in this way for some years. O tiger among kings! Rama was supreme among those who upheld every kind of *dharma*. He knew the truth about the *Vedas* and *Vedangas*. He was accomplished in all the sacred texts. Full of humility, the immensely intelligent one served his parents. Through his own acts and conduct, he enhanced the delight of others.

[1238] This section about Parashurama, related by Vasishtha, begins abruptly. As we will discover much later, the king in question is Sagara.

O king! In this way, some years passed. Rama, supreme among intelligent ones, served his parents. O king! Urged by destiny, on one occasion, the greatly energetic one wished to go to his grandfather's[1239] house and got ready. The bull among the Bhrigu lineage massaged the feet of his parents with his head. He joined his hands in salutation and spoke these humble words. "O father! O mother! There are some words, full of meaning, that I wish to submit before you now. I wish to tell you about this and you should hear. My mind has been anxious for a long time, and I am eager to see my grandfather. Therefore, with your permission, I will now leave for his side. My grandmother is also eager to see me. Desiring this, she has affectionately summoned me through the mouths of many. Seeing one's grandfather and grandmother brings joy. I seek your permission to go to their side." They heard his words, which were uttered with a great deal of respect. Their eyes filled with tears of great joy. They embraced the immensely fortunate one and lovingly inhaled the fragrance of his head. O son! Both of them congratulated him and offered their benedictions. "O son! Leave happily for your grandfather's house. On seeing you, your grandfather and grandmother will be delighted. Having gone there, follow the norms and serve them. O child! For some time, reside happily in that house. But do not remain there for a very long period of time. O immensely fortunate one! You have our permission. Go there safely and see them. We are incapable of subsisting for even an instant without seeing our son. Therefore, you should not remain in your grandfather's house for a very long period of time. O son! With his permission, if you go to your great grandfather's house, take his permission and quickly return from there." Having been thus addressed, the immensely intelligent circumambulated them and prostrated himself. Taking the permission of his parents, he went to his grandfather's house.'

'Rama went and entered the hermitage of the great-souled Richika, the noble descendant of the Bhrigu lineage. The place was adorned by the sage and his *shishyas*. The loud and extensive

---

[1239] That is, Richika's. Richika's wife was Satyavati. Richika's father was Ourva. Ourva's father was Chyavana.

sounds of recitation echoed in every direction. It was full of every kind of agreeable creature, the natural enmity of creatures pacified. He entered the beautiful hermitage. Richika was seated on a seat. O Indra among kings! Rama saw his grandfather in front of him. Like a sacrificial fire, he blazed in his austerities. Like *dakshina* serving a sacrifice, he was being served by Satyavati. O king! The two of them saw that Rama was approaching their presence. They examined him for a very long time, the way one looks at a person whom one has never seen before. "Who is this, blazing amidst a heap of austerities? He is being worshipped by all the auspicious signs. He is a child, but seems to be strong, serious and humble." They thought in this way, their minds full of joy and curiosity. Full of humility, Rama gradually approached them. The intelligent one stated his own name and *gotra*. Full of joy, he touched the feet of his grandparents with his head and hands and greeted them. With delight in their minds, they raised up the excellent one. They greeted him separately and pronounced their blessings. With tears of joy flowing from their eyes, they embraced him and made him sit on their laps. They glanced at his face, which was like a lotus, and were filled with great happiness. When the extender of the lineage was happily seated, the couple asked him about his welfare. "O child! Are your parents fine? What about your brothers? We hope you can subsist easily, without a great deal of effort." O king! As asked, he told them everything about himself, his parents and his brothers, and about their activities. O great king! Because of the qualities of their affection, Rama was delighted and resided in the house of his father's parents. He caused delight in the minds of all creatures. Devoted to serving them, he resided there for some months. O king! The great-souled and noble descendant of the Bhrigu lineage then sought their permission. He wished to visit the abode and hermitage of his grandfather's *guru*.[1240] Full of joy, they congratulated him and uttered their blessings. As instructed by them, he proceeded towards Ourva's hermitage.'

[1240] That is, the grandfather's father, Ourva.

'In the due way, he prostrated himself before the great ascetic who was Chyavana's son. Having received the permission, he went to the hermitage of the descendant of the Bhrigu lineage and was delighted. He went to the hermitage of the foremost sage, the Bhargava. It was surrounded by other hermitages, those of sages who were serene in their minds. He saw him, surrounded by them in all directions. There was cool and gentle shade, with the qualities of all the seasons. There were trees full of flowers and fruits and he was delighted. There were sounds of the calls of many kinds of birds and it was pleasant to the ears. Every direction echoed with many kinds of chants about the *brahman*. In every direction, there were *mantra*s, oblations, offerings of *ghee*, smoke and fragrances. The fragrance of the floods of *ghee* wafted everywhere in the forest. O king! On all sides, the place was ornamented with kindling, *kusha*, staffs, girdles and deer-skins, brought there by the sons of sages. It was ornamented by the daughters of sages roaming around in every direction. They held vessels full of flowers and water in their hands. The shade extended up to the outer limits of the cottages. Without any hesitation and without any fear, herds of does rested there, along with their fawns. Herds of excellent *rishya* deer[1241] looked on, chewing the cud. Peacocks and peahens called in melodious tones, starting the *tandava* dance. Heaps of *nivara* grain were scattered around there, left to dry in the shade, near the spot where the sounds of the deer could be heard. But they did not eat up even a single grain. At the right time, the sacrificial fire was kindled and *atithi*s who came were honoured. Thinking about what is there in the *agama* texts, there was extensive practice of the *chhanda*s. All the *smriti* texts were read and there was discussion about the meaning of the *shruti* texts. Sacrifices to *deva*s and ancestors commenced. The place was agreeable to all creatures. There were many people who were ascetics. Those who were cowards did not frequent that place. The sacred spot enhanced austerities and brought happiness to all beings. It brought joy to stores of austerities and was like another Brahma's world. The fragrance of flowers wafted everywhere and

---

[1241] The white-footed antelope.

there was the buzzing of honeybees. Many kinds of breezes blew in the air there. He saw that excellent hermitage, which possessed such qualities. He entered humbly, like a performer of good deeds entering the abode of the immortals.'

'Rama entered and approached his own great-grandfather. O king! He saw him there, surrounded by hundreds of sages and *shishya*s. He was seated in the middle of the altar, on a mat of *kusha* grass, intent on explaining. He had a white beard and matted hair. He was adorned with a sacred thread meant for *brahmana*s, made from *kusha* grass. His right leg was on his left thigh and his left knee was on his right thigh.[1242] The bull among rishis was covered in a *yogapatta*.[1243] The right hand, with the palm shining like a lotus, was in *vyakhana mudra*.[1244] The radiant left hand was placed on the *yogapatta*. In words that were full of subtle meaning, he was explaining the Aranyaka texts and the best among sages heard the store of austerities. O great king! Rama saw his great-souled great grandfather and approached slowly. O king! When they noticed him approach from a distance, all the sages were affected by his power and were filled with doubt. Bhrigu, immeasurable in his *atman*, was content at his arrival.[1245] O lord of the earth! He stopped the conversation and looked at him. Rama approached, his head lowered in humility. He greeted him in the proper way, like Upendra greeting the creator. In the proper way, he humbly greeted

[1242] He was seated cross-legged, probably in *padmasana* (the lotus posture).

[1243] A piece of cloth spread over the back and the legs.

[1244] A *mudra* is a symbolic and mystical positioning of the fingers and the thumb. In *vyakhana mudra*, used for explanation, the index finger is bent to touch the tip of the thumb and the other three fingers are held straight.

[1245] The line of descent becomes confused in the text. Parashurama's great grandfather was Ourva. But the text mentions Bhrigu. Bhrigu's son was Chyavana and Chyavana's son was Ourva. The word Bhrigu can be interpreted to mean anyone from Bhrigu's lineage, except that Bhrigu's wife, Khyati, is also mentioned. The only possible explanation is that sections are missing. Parashurama first went to see Ourva and then went to see Bhrigu.

Khyati. In the due order of age, Rama then greeted the sages. All of them were delighted and pronounced their blessings. Taking their permission, the intelligent one sat down on the ground. When Rama was blessed, greeted and seated, Bhrigu looked at him and asked him questions about his welfare. "O child! Is all well with you? Are your parents well? What about your brothers and your father's parents? Why have you come here, to my presence, now? Have you been instructed to do so, or did you come on your own?" As is proper, Rama answered everything that had been asked by the great-souled one. He spoke about his father, mother and great-souled brothers. O king! He told him that he had seen that both his father's parents were well. Affectionately asked, he happily told Bhrigu about everything else. He reported everything else, about what he desired. O king! Bhrigu heard everything that Rama said. On seeing him, he was especially delighted and congratulated him.'

'O king! Rama remained in that hermitage for some days, seeking to bring pleasure through everything he did. O king! On one occasion, the supreme among excellent sages told Rama, "O child! Come." He summoned him and took him aside to a secluded spot. Bhrigu was seated. He joined his hands in salutation and approached him. Pleased in the core of his heart, Rama stood before him. Pleased in his mind, Bhrigu pronounced his blessings and greeted him. He glanced affectionately at Rama, who was not at all filled with doubt. "O child! Listen to the words that I am about to speak to you now. This is for your welfare, for our welfare and for the welfare of all the worlds. O son! Follow my command and go to the great mountain, Himalaya. Leave this hermitage now. Make up your mind to perform austerities. O immensely fortunate one! Having gone there, construct an auspicious hermitage. Practice *niyamas* and austerities and worship Mahadeva. With your unmatched devotion, within a short period of time, please him. You will obtain great benefits from him. There is no need to think about this. As a result of your devotion, Shankara will swiftly be pleased. He will then satisfy every desire that exists in your mind. Shankara is affectionate towards his devotees. O son! When the lord of the universe is pleased, as a boon, ask him for all the weapons that you desire. This is for your welfare and to accomplish an extremely difficult task for the *deva*s. This difficult task can only be accomplished with a lot of weapons. Therefore, you must worship Shankara, the divinity who is the lord of *deva*s. If you are full of great devotion, you will obtain what you wish for.'

Chapter 60-1(60) (Parashurama's austerities)

Vasishtha said, 'Having been thus addressed by Bhrigu, he agreed and prostrated himself. Rama took his permission and made up his mind to go. In the proper way, he circumambulated Bhrigu and Khyati and prostrated himself. They greeted him, embraced him and pronounced their blessings. He bowed down to all the sages and took their permission. Having decided to undertake austerities, he emerged from the hermitage. He followed the path his senior had instructed him about. The great-souled Rama went to the Himalaya, supreme among mountains. He passed over many kinds of countries, mountains, rivers and groves. He went past the residences of the best among sages. Here and there, along the path, he resided in the abodes of the sages. He dwelt in *tirtha*s and the best of *kshetra*s and proceeded slowly. He saw and passed over many beautiful countries. He then reached the supreme and excellent Himalaya. He went to that supreme among mountains, with many kinds of trees and creepers. He saw large summits, which seemed to be etched against the sky. The regions were beautiful, adorned with many kinds of colourful minerals. The mountain was adorned with sparkling jewels and herbs. In some places, the wind caused dry trees to rub against each other and caused fires. The wind fanned the flames and caused new fires that burnt down. In some places, the spreading rays of the sun touched *arkopalas*[1246] and created fires. The ice on the rocks melted and this caused the forest conflagrations to be pacified. The golden rays of the sun spread through crystal and collyrium that sparkled like the moon. That light spread and the rays touched each other. In some places,

---

[1246] *Arkopala* is a sunstone, identified as a crystal or ruby. It acts like a lens or magnifying glass.

there was shade. In other places, it seemed to blaze. Young ascetics
frequented the valleys and the slopes of the mountains. There were
some radiant groves, wet with snow, inhabited by large numbers of
siddhas. Lit by the rays of the sun, there were golden rocks, resorted to
by large numbers of yakshas. Since the extremities were illuminated,
it was as if the yakshas were entering the fire. In some places, the
caves were filled with the afflicted calls of herds of deer. Attacked by
hyenas, they emerged from the mouths of caves and leapt down. In
some places, the shining slopes of rocks and the trunks of trees were
marked, when leaders of herds of boar and tigers had fought against
each other. In some places, the rocks and the slopes had been broken
up by the hooves of gavayas, pursued by she-elephants, who took
them to be their cubs. There were places where rocks and clumps of
the forest were crushed, where crazy and intoxicated male elephants
in rut had fought, desiring to have intercourse with she-elephants. In
some places, the rocks were marked by the paw marks of lions, as
enraged by the trumpeting, they had chased elephants. Suddenly, lions
leapt down and shattered the temples with their nails. In some places,
the forest was filled with shrieks of elephants attacked in this way.
In some places, the boulders and caves seemed to be shattered by the
deep and terrible roars of maned lions, as they were forcibly dragged
away by creatures with eight feet.[1247] In some places, the rocks were
seen to be broken. This was because many angry hunters had engaged
with the leaders of herds of bear and had fought against them. In
some places, she-elephants sported in the groves in the mountain. In
other places, intoxicated male elephants pursued the she-elephants
through the groves. The breath from the mouths of sleeping lions
filled hundreds of caves. Not scared of this grave danger, deer roamed
around in those secluded spots. Herds of yak sported, moving around
slowly. They were scared that their tails and hair would get caught in
the thorny bushes. Many kinnaris[1248] filled the caves in the mountains.
As they kept tala,[1249] all the directions echoed with the sound. Here
and there, the divinities of the forest moved around. Their feet were

---

[1247] Sharabhas.
[1248] Feminine of kinnara.
[1249] As in the measurement of time in music.

wet with the juices of lac and this left marks on the ground. Flocks of peacocks and peahens called in melodious tones. They spread their feathers and danced around in every direction. The breeze blew and fanned the body of the forest, causing delight. Consequently, flowers were showered down on the land and in the water. Right up to the end of the forest, the place was filled with the calls of excited male cuckoos, as they tasted the juices of the best among seasons.[1250] The many flowers intoxicated the bees and their buzzing was like singing. The calls of many kinds of birds seemed to render the forest deaf. The ground was wet with the honey from the best of flowers. Right up to the end of the forest, the wind had scattered them around and had covered the ground. In every direction, waterfalls cascaded down from great heights, descending with a large roar on uneven rocks, and seeming to deafen everyone. On every side, there was an extensive canopy and shade, caused by the large branches of trees—*patala* trees, *kadamba, nimba, hintala, sarja, bandhuka, tinduka, kapittha, panasa, ashoka*, mango, *inguda, ashana, naga, champaka, punnaga, kovidara, priyangu, priyala, nipa, bakula, bandhuka, aksha, tamalaka*, grapes, *madhuka, amalaka, jambu, kankola, jati, bilva, arjuna, karanja, bijapuraka, pichula, ambashtha, kanaka, vaikankata, shami, dhava, putrajiva, abhaya, arishta, loha, udumbara* and *pippala*.[1251] There

---

[1250] That is, spring.

[1251] *Kadamba* is *stephegyne parvifolia, nimba* is *azadirachta indica, hintala* is a variety of palm, *sarja* is another name for the sala tree, *bandhuka* (also known as *bandhujiva*) is *Pentapetes Phoenicia, tinduka* is ebony, *ashoka* is *Saraca Indica, inguda* is a medicinal tree, *ashana* is *Pentaptera tomentosa, naga* (*nagakeshara, nageshvara*) is a flowering tree, *champaka* is a tree with yellow and fragrant flowers, *punnaga* is nutmeg, *priyala* is a vine, *bakula* is a flowering tree, *bandhuka* (*bandhujiva*) is the shrub *Pentapetes Phoenicia, aksha* is *rudraksha, tamalaka* is the *tamala* tree, *madhuka* is *Bassia Latifolia, kankola* is the *ashoka* tree, *jati* is a kind of jasmine, *arjuna* is a tall tree, *karanja* (*karanjaka*) is the Pongame oil tree, *bijapuraka* is lemon, *pichula* is *Tamarix Indica, ambashtha* is an unidentified medicinal plant, *kanaka* is a medicinal plant, *vaikankata* (*vikantaka*) is the Indian plum, *shami* is the name of a tree believed to contain fire, *dhava* is the axlewood tree, *putrajiva* (*putranjiva*) is a kind of herb, *abhaya* is a kind of myrobalan, *arishta* is a medicinal plant, *loha* is aloe and *pippala* is a holy fig tree.

were many other beautiful trees in every direction. They extended continuously for a long distance and covered the place with shade. They were so dense that the rays of the sun could not reach the ground. There were many ripe fruits and surviving on these, the monkeys were well-nourished and strong. Here and there, hundreds of streams of water flowed from between the rocks. Many of them gushed out suddenly. O king! Hundreds of rivers flowed over the uneven terrain, great in force. There were large lakes, filled with lotuses and water lilies. In every direction, these lakes were adorned with flocks of many kinds of birds. He reached the Indra among mountains, a mountain with ice covering the peaks.'

'The best of the Bhrigu lineage was delighted and started to climb. The great-minded Rama entered the dense forest there. O king! He wandered around and approached a large tree that grew in a solitary spot. As he wandered around, from every direction, the does looked at him. As they glanced at him with suspicious eyes, he was over-joyed at their charming glances. There, the breeze bore along the delightful fragrances of the forest. As the breeze fanned him, he was happy and looked at the extensive beauty of the forest. With subtle discrimination, Bhargava roamed around the various spots. He looked and debated the existence of different kinds of minerals and opposite sentiments.[1252] "How wonderful. Brahma has consecrated this as the king over all mountains and Himalaya has a share in sacrifices. I have now reached this place. It is abundantly clear that this is the emperor of mountains. Because of the sweet sound that whistles through the hollow bamboo, he has made this forest sweet. These heaps of snow are clinging to its hips. It appears as if this radiant mountain has covered itself with a white piece of cloth from every side. On top of these heaps of dense snow, the mountain seems to have covered itself with an upper garment of many hues, made out of sandalwood, aloe, camphor, musk and kumkuma. The decorations on the limbs are evident and can be seen, resembling those of a sensual person. Gigantic elephants have been struck by lions and large pearls have been dislodged from their

[1252] Like hot and cold.

temples, illuminating the mountain on every side. The summits are ornamented with many trees, creepers, winding plants and flowers. It is ornamented by a canopy of thick and continuous clouds. The limbs of the mountain are decorated with many kinds of minerals. It is adorned with every kind of jewel. The radiant Kailasa adorns it, like a radiant and white umbrella. In every direction, it is surrounded by those with faces like elephants and horses.[1253] The mountain's residence is a cave and the large entrance is illuminated by jewels. He is seated on a throne, in the centre of that isolated cave. There are trees in all directions, acting like guards with canes in their hands. Like an emperor, the great king can be seen by people, but cannot be approached by them. Yaks roam around here and there and seem to fan him with their whisks. Peacocks and others dance and *kinnara*s sing his praise. There are many radiant beings who are serving him. It is evident that this Indra among mountains has been instated in a position of kingship. With his prosperity and energy, he transcends and covers the entire earth." O great king! There was a large lake with sparkling water. It was beautiful, adorned with clumps of *kumuda*s, *utpala*s, *pankaja*s and *kalhara*s.[1254] They were red and yellow, white and blue. From every direction, the place was decorated with many other aquatic trees. There were hundreds of swans, cranes, gallinules, *jivanjivaka*s, *chakravaka*s, ospreys and bees. A gentle breeze blew from all sides. Here and there, schools of *saphari*[1255] and other fish swam. Because of the internal waves, it seemed as if the lake was dancing. The best of the Bhrigu lineage reached that excellent lake. All along the banks, many kinds of birds called in melodious tones.'

'He constructed a large and auspicious hermitage along the bank. Rama, supreme among intelligent ones, made up his mind to undertake austerities there. He controlled himself and controlled his senses, subsisting on vegetables, roots and fruits. He fixed his mind and *atman* on the lord of *deva*s and performed austerities.

[1253] These are semi-divine species.

[1254] *Kumuda* is a lotus that blooms during the night, *utpala* is a blue lotus, *pankaja* is a lotus and *kalhara* is the white water lily.

[1255] A small silvery-white fish.

Full of great devotion, he traversed along the path indicated by
Bhrigu. O king! Single-minded in attention, he worshipped the lord
of *deva*s. He had no habitation during the monsoon. During the
winter, he remained in the water. During summer, he performed
austerities for a long time, in the centre of five fires.[1256] He
conquered *kama* and the other enemies and dispelled the six waves
of distress.[1257] He used his intelligence to conquer the opposite
pairs of sentiments and the torment of austerities did not make
him anxious. He controlled himself and purified his body through
yama and *niyama*. He controlled the breath of life in his body
through *pranayama*. The great sage conquered everything and
seated himself in *padmasana*. He was silent and his mind did not
waver. He controlled his vision and devoted himself to *pratyahara*.
He practiced *dharana* and steadily fixed his mind and *atman*. He
performed *dhyana* on the divinity who is the lord of *deva*s and saw
Parameshvara. Since he had become a *maitra*[1258] internally, all his
impediments were removed. He thought of the lord of *deva*s and
saw the *guru* of the universe in his *dhyana*. He performed *dhyana*
on that consciousness, his body and senses remaining immobile.
He remained in that state for some time, like a lamp in a place
where there is no wind. He performed *japa* on the divinity who is
the lord of *deva*s, using his own intelligence to perform *dhyana* on
him. He worshipped the one whose *atman* is immeasurable, the
Ishvara who is in all existence. This was Ishvara in his *nishkala*
aspect,[1259] without blemishes. This was an unthinkable and supreme
refulgence, the supreme form that *yogi*s meditate on. This was
eternal and always pure. This was serene and beyond the senses.
This was unmatched. It did not move and consisted only of bliss. It
pervaded everything, mobile and immobile. O tiger among kings!

[1256] With four fires on four sides and the sun overhead.
[1257] The six vices or enemies are *kama* (desire), *krodha* (anger), *lobha*
(avarice), *moha* (delusion), *mada* (arrogance) and *matsarya* (jealousy). The
six waves of distress are hunger, thirst, decay, death, grief and delusion.
[1258] The word *maitra* is being used in the sense of a perfect *brahmana*.
[1259] Without form. *Sakala* means with a form.

Bhargava thought of this form of the lord of *deva*s for a very long time, with the sentiment, "I am He".'

Chapter 61-1(61) (Parashurama's austerities continued)

Vasishtha said, 'There were *rishi*s who had cleansed their sins through austerities—Bhrigu, Atri, Kratu, Jabali, Vamadeva and Mrikandu. They were senior in *jnana*, *karma* and age. They were great, praised for their vows. O king! All of them were told about the great-souled one's supreme austerities. Hearing this, all of them were filled with curiosity and went there to see. Those sages, revered by the seniors, went there to see. They went to the hermitage where Rama was tormenting himself through austerities. They resided in sacred *kshetra*s and arrived from a great distance. His fierce austerities and *jnana* were the best in the worlds. Having praised this, all of them returned to their own hermitages.'

'O excellent king! As Rama continued in this way, Bhagavan Shiva became extremely pleased in his mind. Bhagavan Shankara wished to test the extent to which he was devoted to him. O king! He assumed the form of a hunter who hunts animals and approached him. His body was like a mass of broken collyrium. His eyes were large and red. He was young and held a bow and arrows. He was tall and his body was as firm as the *vajra*. His jaw, arms and shoulders were raised. The hair on his head and his beard were tawny. He smelt of flesh and fat. He was one who caused violence to all beings. As a result of coming into contact with thorny bushes, there were scars and wounds on his body. He was repeatedly chewing on a piece of meat, from which, blood dripped. As a result of the burden of two carcasses, his shoulders were bent. As he swiftly advanced, the force of his thighs brushed against the trees. Resembling a mountain with feet, he arrived at the spot. He arrived at the shores of the lake, full of flowering trees. He laid down that burden of flesh at the root of a tree. For some time, he seated himself under the shade of the tree.'

'Seated near the shore of the lake, he saw the descendant of
the Bhrigu lineage. After this, he got up quickly and approached
him. He joined his hands in salutation and greeted Rama. He spoke
to the tiger of the Bhrigu lineage in a deep voice that seemed to
thunder like the clouds and seemed to emerge from inside a cave.
"I am Toshapravarsha.[1260] I reside in this great forest. I am the
lord of this region, along with all its creatures, trees and creepers.
I move around, impartial towards all creatures and eat their flesh.
I am impartial towards all beings. I do not have parents or anyone
else. I do not pay the least bit of attention to anything that cannot
be eaten or cannot be drunk. I do not pay any specific attention
to what should be done and what should not be done. No one
should come here, reside here, or approach this place. With my
strength, I do not even allow Shakra. There is no doubt about this.
Everyone knows that this region depends on me. Therefore, without
my permission, no one can come here. This is my account. I have
told you everything. Now you tell me the truth about yourself,
especially about your conduct. Who are you? Why have you come
here? Why have you stationed yourself here? Will you get up and
go somewhere else? What do you wish to do?" Thus addressed, the
immensely radiant Rama smiled. He remained silent for a while,
with his face lowered. "Who is this unassailable person, with a
voice that thunders like the clouds? He spoke words that were full
of deep meaning, clearly articulated in *padas* and *aksharas*.[1261] Why
does his body create this great suspicion in me? His body is that
of someone inferior, resembling beautiful arrows." As he thought
this, auspicious portents were seen. They appeared on his body,[1262]
indicating that his desired objective would be accomplished. In his
mind, the bull among the Bhrigu lineage thought about this in many
kinds of ways. He addressed the hunter in gentle words, with well-
crafted *aksharas*. "O fortunate one! I am Jamadagni's son. I am a
Bhargava, known by the name of Rama. Following the instructions

[1260] Literally, one who showers down contentment.
[1261] *Padas* are combinations of words, *askharas* are syllables.
[1262] There are both auspicious and inauspicious portents that appear
on the body, such as the throbbing of the limbs.

of my *guru*, I have come here now, to perform austerities. Full of devotion and observing *niyama*s, my austerities are for the lord of all the worlds. I have worshipped him for a long time. He is the lord of everything. He is every kind of refuge. He is the one who grants freedom from fear. He is the three-eyed Shankara, who crushes sin, affectionate towards his devotees. Through my austerities, I will satisfy the omniscient one, the destroyer of Tripura. I have been practicing *niyama*s in this hermitage, on the shores of the lake. Bhagavan is compassionate towards his devotees. Until Hara shows himself to me, I will remain here. That is my view. That being the case, you should decide to go somewhere else. Otherwise, the *niyama*s I have set for myself will be impaired. I am an *atithi* who has come from some other country to the place where you reside. I am also an ascetic and a sage. Hence, I should be devotedly honoured. If I reside near you, only sin will accrue to me. Residing near me will only cause you unhappiness. Therefore, do not roam around, or do other things, within the limits of my hermitage. Move away and be happy, in this world and in the next one." Hearing the words of the bull among the Bhrigu lineage, his eyes turned coppery-red with rage. He replied to the one whose eyes were also coppery-red with rage. "O *brahmana*! Why do you condemn the prospect of my residing near you so much? You are behaving like an ungrateful person now. Have I caused any harm to you, or to anyone else in the world? Who reprimands an innocent and controlled person? O bull among *brahmana*s! O one with a long life! If my presence, my sight, residing with me and conversing with me are to be condemned, you should move away from this hermitage immediately. I am hungry. Why should I abandon my own residence? As you have asked me, how can I give up my own residence? I will not go far away, especially from this spot. You should go somewhere else. Or, if you so wish, remain here. Under no circumstances, can I move from this place." O king! Hearing his words, the extender of the Bhrigu lineage became slightly angry and replied in these words. "Hunters are exceedingly cruel and cause fear to all beings. They are always engaged in deceitful acts and are shamed by all creatures. Born into such a lineage, you are a sinner. You cause violence to all living beings. O evil-minded one! That being the case, why should you not be shunned by virtuous people? Accordingly, you should know that you are inferior in class. You should quickly go somewhere else. There is no need to think about this. You desire to protect your body. That is the reason you do not approach thorns and similar things. You cannot tolerate pain. In that way, life is loved by all those with bodies. Just like you, anyone who is struck feels pain. There is no violation of this. Non-violence towards all beings is eternal *dharma*. Since you act against this, you are always reviled by virtuous people. To sustain your own life, you kill all those with bodies. How can virtuous people converse with you? O worst among men! Therefore, you should swiftly leave this place. Otherwise, because of what I do inadvertently, there may be harm to you. If you do not leave this place on your own, I will have to use force. It is evident that if you do not use your own intelligence, I will have to do something to make you move. Your remaining here will not be beneficial for you, even for half an instant. How can a person who hates *dharma* and constantly acts against it, obtain peace?"'

'In the form of the hunter, the wielder of Pinaka was delighted on hearing Rama's words. However, he replied, seemingly in rage. "I think that everything undertaken by you is futile. Are you the first person to possess *jnana*? Where is this Shambhu from? What are these austerities? O foolish one! Why are you now facing these hardships of austerities? It is certain that your efforts are in vain. Shankara will not be satisfied with this. Shambhu is satisfied with conduct that is contrary to the behaviour of the worlds. O extremely evil-minded one! Other than you, which intelligent mortal will engage in austerities in this way? There is no doubt that it is better for me to leave this place now. You are associated with Shambhu, who is not worshipped according to the rites. You are his worshipper. You are engaged in worshipping him, as if he is the only person in this world. You are the appropriate worshipper for someone like him. There is no need to think about this. Parameshthi Brahma is the grandfather of the worlds. Shambhu severed his head and suffered from the sin of killing a *brahmana*. O *brahmana*! Thereby, Shambhu incurred the sin of killing a *brahmana*. You have been instructed.

That being the case, how could you have acted in this way? I now think that your qualities are the same as those of Rudra's. O sage! That is the reason you have obtained *siddhi* within a short period of time. In general, a person who kills his mother is shunned by all the worlds. That is the reason you are engaged in austerities in this desolate forest.[1263] Killing a *guru*, killing a woman and killing a *brahmana* are grave sins and impurities. That is the reason you are engaged in austerities. But austerities will not destroy the sin. It is indeed true that *prayashchitta* is recommended for sins. However, there is no salvation for those who kill their mothers. The view of the worlds is that non-violence is a sign of *dharma*. O Rama! If that is the case, why did you kill your mother with your own hand? You have committed the terrible sin of killing your mother, censured by all the worlds. After that, you willingly profess yourself to be devoted to *dharma* and criticize others. I see that you are smiling, not knowing about the intolerable sin you have yourself committed. Instead, considering yourself to be adequate, you point out the sins of others. If I abandon my own *dharma* and roam around without any fear, it is then that you should reprimand me, not because of what you have wilfully determined in your own mind. I kill creatures only to sustain my mother, my father, my sons and others. I regard that as my own *dharma*. From one day to another day, I bring meat to my family and follow my own *dharma*. This is the means of subsistence the creator has ordained for me in earlier times. With this meat, I constantly nourish my parents. Had I killed more than necessary, I would have committed a sin. We cannot be criticized for killing what is required for subsistence. Think about this and then criticize me or praise me. In ancient times, virtuous and wicked *karma* has been ordained. In every possible way, that is what one should do. Use your own intelligence to reflect on the difference between you and me. In every possible sentiment, I am engaged in nurturing my friends. But you abandoned your aged father and killed your mother. You then proclaim yourself to be someone

---

[1263] To test obedience, Jamadagni asked Parashurama to kill his mother, Renuka. After Parashurama did this, Renuka was brought back to life.

who follows *dharma* and have come here, to engage in austerities. Those who know about the foundations and those who are clear in their insight, do not wag their tongues and utter such words. I know accurately everything about your conduct. O extender of the Bhrigu lineage! Therefore, enough of these austerities. They are futile. If you desire happiness, cast aside these austerities, which cause hardships to the body. O Rama! Go somewhere else, where people do not know about you.'"

Chapter 62-1(62) (Parashurama's austerities continued)

Vasishtha said, 'O protector of the earth! Rama, supreme among intelligent ones, was addressed in this way. He was surprised and examined this in his mind. He then spoke the following words. Rama said, "O immensely fortunate one! Who are you? Please tell me. You are no ordinary man. Your body seems to possess Indra's characteristics. Your words are full of wonderful meanings and *pada*s. They possess the quality of being profound. Hearing your extremely wonderful words, I take you to be omniscient. Are you Indra, Vahni, Yama, Dhatri, Varuna, the lord of riches, Ishana, Tapana,[1264] Brahma, Vayu, Soma, Guru[1265] or Guha? You should be the foremost among one of these. Yet, I can see the class that you have been born into and that causes a doubt in my mind. It is heard that Bhagavan Vishnu Purushottma is adept in the use of *maya*. You have come to me in this form. Please tell me who you are. Are you the omniscient Parameshvara, the lord of the universe? Are you the *paramatman*, from whom, all *atman*s originate? Are you the eternal one, who brings bliss to the *atman*? Are you Bhagavan Shiva, who pervades the universe and roams around as he pleases? Given this body, you cannot be anyone else. There is no one else in the world who possesses such a powerful body. The words that

[1264] Surya.
[1265] Brihaspati.

have emerged from your lips are excellent and extensive in meaning. I think Hara has assumed this form, driven by affection towards his devotee. I suspect that he has directly manifested himself in front of me, so as to test me. A mere hunter will not possess a form like this. Therefore, I prostrate myself before you. Show me your beautiful and excellent form. Reveal your body, full of great qualities, to me. Show me your favours. I have many doubts in my mind. Let those be destroyed. In every kind of way, show me your form now and destroy the delusion in my intelligence. Destroy it by merely resorting to your own form. O immensely fortunate one! Prostrating my head, I am beseeching you. I have clasped my hands in salutation. Who are you? Reveal yourself to me." Having said this, the extremely fortunate descendant of the Bhrigu lineage wished to know. Therefore, he seated himself on the ground and immersed himself in *dhyana*. He was seated in *padmasana*. He was silent and controlled his words, body and mind. He controlled the movement of his *prana*. Pervasive in intelligence, he remained in this state for a very long time. He controlled the aggregate of his senses and fixed his mind in his heart. Using the sight of *dhyana*, he thought of the lord of *devas*, the preceptor of the universe. As he used this sight to search within his *atman*, he saw the lord of the universe. The one who is compassionate towards his devotees had assumed the form of a hunter of animals. At this, Bhargava swiftly got up and opened his eyes. He saw the divinity standing in front of him, in that body.'

'He is the refuge. He is affectionate towards his devotees. O great king! He had shown him that favour and had manifested himself in front of him. On seeing this, Rama was filled with respect. All over his limbs, the body-hair stood up. There were tears of joy in his eyes. Full of devotion towards him, the immensely intelligent one fell on the ground, at his feet. His words choked as a result of the respect, and he spoke in faltering words. O king! He said, "O Sharva! O Shankara! Be my refuge." At this, satisfied at his devotion, Shambhu assumed his own form. Rama had prostrated himself on the ground and he raised him up. With his own hands, the creator of the universe raised up the extender of the Bhrigu lineage. He joined his hands in salutation and praised the divinity, the lord

of *deva*s, standing in front of him. Rama said, "I prostrate myself
before the lord of *deva*s, Shankara, whose form is primordial. I
prostrate myself before Sharva, the serene one. I prostrate myself
before the eternal one. I bow down. I prostrate myself before the
one who is blue in the throat, the one with the form of Nilalohita. I
prostrate myself before the lord of beings. I prostrate myself before
the abode of beings. Your forms are manifest and not manifest.
You are Mahadeva Midha. You are Shiva, with many forms. I
prostrate myself before the one with three eyes. I bow down. O
Sharva! Be my refuge. O lord of the universe! I am your devotee.
You are the refuge for those who have no other refuge. O divinity!
O Shankara! I have behaved badly towards you and have used
harsh words. O Bhagavan! I did that in my ignorance, and you
should pardon me. Your form cannot be known to anyone else,
even virtuous ones. What need be said about a mere man? O lord of
everything! Other than you yourself, no one is capable of knowing
you properly. O Shankara! Therefore, be pleased with me in every
possible way. I have no destination other than you. I prostrate
myself before you. I prostrate myself repeatedly. I bow down." In
this way, he joined his hands, with cupped palms, and worshipped
the one who stood in front of him. Bhagavan, who permeates the
universe, was pleased in his *atman*. Bhagavan replied, "O son! I
am pleased with your present austerities. O excellent Bhargava!
Your devotion is without blemish. I shall give you everything that
you ask for. You are extremely devoted to me. There is no need
to think about this. I know everything that is circulating in your
heart now. Therefore, without any hesitation, act in accordance
with whatever I tell you. O child! Right now, you do not possess
the power to sustain terrible weapons. Therefore, you must again
undertake terrible austerities. In due order, travel everywhere on
earth and in all the *tirtha*s. Bathe there and purify your body. After
that, you will obtain all the weapons." O king! Having said this,
while Rama looked on, the lord and divinity, who determines the
destiny of the earth, disappeared instantly from the spot, in that
body. When the lord of the universe vanished, Rama prostrated
himself before Shankara. He made up his mind to travel the earth
and bathe in all the *tirtha*s.'

'In the due order, he therefore travelled around the entire earth. Following the norms, with a controlled *atman*, he bathed in all the *tirtha*s. Following the norms, in *tirtha*s, the foremost *kshetra*s and temples to *deva*s, he attentively satisfied ancestors and *deva*s. He performed the rites of fasting, austerities, oblations, *japa* and bathing. He followed the norms, did this in the *tirtha*s and travelled the earth. In the due order, he did this in the *tirtha*s and travelled around the earth. O king! As he slowly performed *pradakshina*, his body was rendered pure. Obeying Shambhu's instructions, Bhargava circumambulated the earth. After this, he again returned to the spot where he had resided earlier. O king! Having gone there, he remained there and with *niyama*s and austerities, devoutly worshipped the divinity, Uma's consort.'

'O king! At the time, there was a battle between *deva*s and *asura*s which went on for a very long time. It made the body-hair stand up. The extremely strong *asura*s defeated *deva*s in that battle. Without any fear, they robbed the immortals of all their prosperity. Vasava and all the other *deva*s were defeated in that battle. Robbed of their prosperity by the enemy, they went and sought refuge with Shankara. They pleased the protector of the universe. Prostrating themselves, they chanted victorious praises. The Gods prayed that the divinity who wields Pinaka might slay the *asura*s. O king! At this, the one who bestows boons pledged to *deva*s that the *danava*s would be killed. Shambhu spoke to Mahodara.[1266] "On the southern slope of the Himalayas, there is a great ascetic named Rama. He is the son of a sage and is extremely energetic. Following my instructions, he is performing austerities. Go there now and tell him about my command. O Mahodara! Quickly bring the one who is performing austerities here." Thus addressed, Mahodara agreed. He prostrated himself before Isha and with the speed of the wind, went to the place where Rama was. He arrived at the spot and saw Rama, the great sage. He humbly addressed the one who was performing austerities in these words. "O noble Bhargava! Shambhu desires to see you. I have come here because of his command. Therefore, come to the

---

[1266] One of Shiva's *gana*s.

presence of his lotus feet." Hearing his words, Bhargava got up
swiftly. He happily accepted the command on his head and replied
in words of assent. Mahodara quickly brought Rama to Shambhu's
presence. They swiftly reached Kailasa, supreme among mountains.
The best of the Bhargava lineage saw Shankara, affectionate towards
his devotees, along with all the *bhuta*s and Indra and the other
immortals. He was being praised by Narada and the other sages,
stores of austerities. Beautiful *gandharva*s sang and large numbers
of *apsara*s danced. Attired in a garment made out of elephant-hide,
the lord of *deva*s was being worshipped. He was three-eyed and
had the moon on his crest. All his limbs were smeared with ashes.
He had a mass of tawny and matted hair and he was decorated in
ornaments made out of *naga*s. His arms and lips were long. His
amiable and pleased face resembled a lotus. O king! In an assembly
of Gods, he was seated on a golden slab.'

'Joining his hands in salutation, the noble Bhargava slowly
approached the lord of *deva*s. On seeing the one with the handsome
throat, all the body-hair on his body stood up. With his body wet with
tears of joy, he approached Hara's presence. He spoke reverential
words, full of devotion, and his words choked because of his joy. In
*akshara*s composed in *vyala*,[1267] he said, "I prostrate myself before
the lord of *deva*s." He fell down and touched the feet of Tripura's
destroyer with his head. In the midst of the large number of *deva*s,
Shiva was pleased. With a delighted face that resembled a lotus,
he raised Rama, as *deva*s looked on. He smiled and affectionately
addressed him in sweet words. "These Gods have been attacked by
large numbers of *daitya*s and have been dislodged from their own
positions. They are unable to kill them and have approached me.
O Rama! Therefore, wishing to do something agreeable for *deva*s,
follow my command. Slay all the large numbers of *daitya*s. It is my
view that you are capable." With his hands joined in salutation,
Rama prostrated himself before Sharva. While all the *deva*s heard,
he replied in these humble words. "O lord! You are in all *atman*s
and are omniscient. What is not known to you? Nevertheless, please
listen to the words I submit. Shakra and all the other immortals are

---

[1267] Here, *vyala* means a specific type of *chhanda*.

incapable of killing the enemy. How can I do that alone? O lord of *devas*! I do not know about weapons. I am not skilled in fighting. Without weapons, how can I kill all the enemies of the Gods?" Thus addressed, the lord of *devas* gave the great-souled one his brilliant energy, which was full of all of Shiva's weapons and was as radiant as the fire of destruction. He gave him his own *parashu*,[1268] which was capable of subduing all weapons. While all the Gods heard, pleased in his *atman*, he spoke to Rama. "Through my favours, you will slay all the enemies of the Gods. O amiable one! You will possess a power that all enemies will find impossible to resist. With this weapon alone, go and fight with the enemies. In the right way, you yourself will come to acquire the skills of fighting." Addressed in this way, Rama prostrated himself before Shambhu. He accepted and raised up Shiva's *parashu*, meant for the enemies of the Gods. Rama, born from a portion of Vishnu's energy, was radiant. Combined with devotion towards Rudra, he dazzled like the sun at midday. He took the permission of the three-eyed one. Along with all the *devas*, he proceeded, having made up his mind to fight and kill the *asuras*. Thereafter, there was a battle between *devas* and *asuras* again. O king! It was extremely terrible, meant to obtain victory over the three worlds. In that battle, the mighty-armed Rama was extremely terrible. He used the *parashu* to angrily kill the great *asuras*. With blows that were as powerful as a strike of the *vajra*, he killed thousands of *daityas*. Like a second Destroyer, Rama angrily strode around in that battle. He killed all the *daityas* and delighted all the *devas*. In an instant, Rama, supreme among those who strike, destroyed them. All the *daityas* and *danavas* were killed by Rama. All those who were not killed saw Rama and were filled with fear. All the large numbers of *asuras* were either killed, or ran away. Having taken Rama's permission, the Gods returned to heaven again. Having killed Diti's descendants, Rama also took the permission of the immortals. He returned to his own hermitage and devoted his mind to austerities. The immensely intelligent one created Shambhu's image, in the form of a hunter of animals. He controlled himself and in that hermitage, devoutly worshipped it. In

---

[1268] *Parashu* is a battle-axe. Hence, Rama became Parashurama.

the proper way, he used fragrances, flowers, *naivedya*, praises and *stotram*s. He was full of devotion and obtained supreme joy.'

Chapter 63-1(63) (Bhargava's conduct)

Vasishtha said, 'As a result of his devotion and his *yoga*, the lord of the universe was pleased in his *atman*. Along with the large number of Maruts, he came there and showed himself. He saw the three-eyed divinity, Chandrashekhara,[1269] the lord of *deva*s. His mount was an excellent bull. Shambhu was with one crore *bhuta*s. His eyes dilating in joy, he respectfully stood up. Bhargava devoutly prostrated himself on the ground, in front of Sharva. He then stood up and bowed down before the lord of *deva*s again. Joining his hands in salutation, Rama praised the lord of the universe. Rama said, "O divinity! O lord of *deva*s! I prostrate myself before you. O Parameshvara! I prostrate myself before you. O lord of the universe! I prostrate myself before you. O destroyer of Tripura! I prostrate myself before you. O one who presides over everything! I prostrate myself before you. O one who is affectionate towards devotees! I prostrate myself before you. O lord of all *bhuta*s! I prostrate myself before you. O Vrishabhadhvaja![1270] I prostrate myself before you. O lord of all lords! I prostrate myself before you. O ocean of compassion! I prostrate myself before you. O abode of everyone! I prostrate myself before you. O Nilalohita! I prostrate myself before you. O one who destroys all the numerous enemies of the Gods! O one with the trident! I prostrate myself before you. O Kapalin![1271] O one who protects all the worlds! I prostrate myself before one. O one who always resides in a cremation-ground! O one who resides in Kailasa! I prostrate myself before you. I prostrate myself before the one who holds the noose, the one who swallowed the poison *kalakuta*. O one whose might is worshipped by the immortals! O

[1269] With the moon on the crest, Shiva's name.

[1270] The same as Vrishadhvaja, with the bull on the banner.

[1271] Shiva's name, one with a skull.

powerful one! O self-originating one! O witness to the *karma* of beings in the entire universe! O Shambhu! I prostrate myself before you. O one with the foam of the three flows[1272] and the moon on the crest! I prostrate myself before you. O one with Indras among serpents as your necklace! O Shiva! O *paramatman*! O one whose body is covered with *bhasma*! O one with the sun, the moon and the fire as eyes! I prostrate myself before you. O Kapardin![1273] O one who crushed the *asura* Andhaka! I prostrate myself before you. O destroyer of Tripura! O destroyer of Daksha's sacrifice! I prostrate myself before you. O one whose broad chest is dyed with the saffron from Girijaa's[1274] breasts! O great Mahadeva! O one who wears the hide of an elephant as a garment! I prostrate myself before you. O one whose form *yogis* perform *dhyana* on! O Shiva, whose energy is unthinkable! O one who resides in the centre of the pericarp of the lotus that is in the heart of your own devotees! O one whose form is the essence of the determinations of all *agama* texts! I prostrate myself before you. O one who kindles understanding in all the Indras among *yogis*! O one whose *atman* is *amrita*! I prostrate myself before you. O Shankara! O one whose greatness pervades everything. O *paramatman*! O Sharva! O serene one! O *brahman*! O one with the universe as your form! I prostrate myself before you. O one who lacks a beginning, a middle and an end! O eternal one! O one whose form is not manifest! O one whose own form is both manifest and not manifest! O one whose *atman* is both subtle and not subtle! I prostrate myself before you. O one who can be known through *Vedanta*! O one whose form is the *vijnana* in the universe! I prostrate myself before you. O one whose feet are worshipped by arrays of the heads of Gods and *asuras*, resembling flowers! I prostrate myself before you. O one with the handsome throat! O creator of the universe! O maker of the worlds! I prostrate myself before you. I bow down. You possess the *guna* of *rajas* in your *atman*. You are the one who determines the creation of the universe. O one with a form as Hiranyagarbha!

[1272] That is, Ganga.

[1273] Shiva's name, one with matted hair.

[1274] Girijaa is the daughter of the mountain, Parvati.

O Hara! O one who existed before the universe! O *atman* of the universe! O cause behind the establishment and expansion of the worlds! I prostrate myself before you. O one whose form is that of *sattva jnana*! O supreme one! O one who exists in every *atman*! O transformation in the form of *tamas guna*! O one who destroys the universe! O one who assumes the form of Rudra at the end of a *kalpa*! O one who knows about *para* and *apara*![1275] I prostrate myself before you. O one without transformations! O eternal one! O one with cause and effect in your *atman*! I prostrate myself before you. O one who kindles understanding in those who lack intelligence! O one who causes transformations in intelligence and the other senses! O one whose *maya* causes differences and makes *deva*s like Vasus, Adityas, Maruts, Sadhyas, Rudras and Ashvins have different points of view! I prostrate myself before you. I bow down before you. You are without transformation. You are without birth. You are eternal. You are subtle in form. There is no match for you. No one knows you, not even *yogi*s who are always free of blemishes. You are impossible to know. Brahma and the others do not know you properly. Indeed, it is because of that and their *karma* that they roam around in worldly existence for a long time, until they approach your feet. You are the one who destroys lack of *jnana*. Until then, whether a person is learned or lacking in senses, he wanders around in *samsara*. If a person fixes his intelligence at your lotus feet, he alone is skilled. He alone is accomplished. He alone is a sage. He alone is learned. Your virtuous existence exists in the three *Veda*s. But it is extremely subtle and mysterious, even to those who are learned. How can a foolish person like me comprehend it? Your greatness is beyond the approach of words. How can I praise it now? Since I am dumb in intelligence, enough of this attempt to praise you. However, though I am ignorant, I have praised you devoutly. O lord of *deva*s! Be pleased. Indeed, you are affectionate towards your devotees." In this way, Rama faithfully extolled Shankara and he seemed to smile, as he replied in words that rumbled like the clouds.'

[1275] The words *para* and *apara*, superior and inferior, can be interpreted in different ways, one being *para-brahman* and *shabda-brahman*.

'Bhagavan answered, "O Rama! I am extremely pleased at your bravery and good conduct, your austerities and your devotion towards me, in particular, your *stotram*. Therefore, ask for a boon, whatever exists in your heart. I will give you everything. All shall be given to you." Thus addressed by the lord of *deva*s, the extender of the Bhrigu lineage prostrated himself. O king! He joined his hands in salutation and spoke these words. "O divinity! If you are pleased with me and I am worthy of being given a boon, I wish for all the *astras*[1276] from you. There shouldn't be anyone who is superior to me in *astra*, *shastra*, or the sacred texts. Through your favours, let no one in the worlds be able to defeat me in battle." O king! Shambhu agreed to this. Extremely pleased, in the due order, he gave Rama all the *astra*s and *shastra*s, along with their *mantra*s. He gave him all the *astra*s, with the four types, application, withdrawal and so on. With a pleased face, Rama faced Shankara and accepted these. He also received an excellent chariot with an excellent standard, unimpeded in speed and yoked to white horses. Shankara gave Rama two quivers, full of an inexhaustible supply of arrows. He received a divine bow with a firm bowstring, Vijaya. It did not decay and could not be shattered. He received extremely expensive and colourful armour that could not be penetrated by any weapon. O lord of men! He bestowed unmatched bravery on him and the boon of being invincible in battle. He obtained the strength to nurture his breath of life for as long as he wished. He gave him a *bija mantra*[1277] named after him and fame in all the worlds. He also granted Bhargava great power in his austerities. O king! As was appropriate, he gave Rama devotion towards himself. Thereafter, in that body, along with all the *bhuta*s and immortals, Chandrashekhara Shambhu swiftly disappeared. Having obtained

---

[1276] *Astra* and *shastra* are both weapons and the words are often used synonymously. However, an *astra* is a weapon that is hurled or released, while a *shastra* is held in the hand. The word *astra* is often used, as in this case, for divine weapons. Such *astra*s had *mantra*s, for invoking, release and withdrawal. The four types probably mean invoking, release, withdrawal and countering.

[1277] This was named after Parashurama.

everything that he wished for, Rama was successful. When Sharva had left and was no longer visible, he spoke to Mahodara. "O Mahodara! For my sake, you should protect all these—the chariot, bow and other things. When I have a task to perform, I will remember you. You will then return everything, the chariot, bow and other things, to me." Having agreed to this, Mahodara left the noble Bhargava.'

'Successful in his objective, he wished to go and see his *gurus*. As he proceeded, he came to a cave in a forest in the Himalayas. Urged by his pre-determined *karma*, Rama entered that cave. There, he saw a fleeing child, evidently alive with a great deal of effort. As he was being pursued by a tiger, the *brahmana*'s son seemed to be very frightened and was crying. On seeing him, his heart was overcome by compassion, and he was anxious to save him. Shouting "Stay", "Stay" to the tiger, he pursued it. The extender of the Bhrigu lineage pursued it speedily, for a long time. The extremely terrible tiger reached an extremely terrible forest. Pursued by the tiger, the *dvija*'s son fled inside a cave. He fell down there, scared that he would have to give up his life. Rama's eyes were red with rage, and he wished to save the *brahmana*'s son. He picked up a blade of grass and used a *mantra* to invoke an *astra* on the *kusha*. Meanwhile, the powerful hyena[1278] dashed towards the *dvija* who had fallen. It saw him and roared, making the space between heaven and earth tremble. As the tiger was about to strike with its talons, he burnt it down with the fire of the *astra*. He quickly freed the *dvija*, who had not been wounded at all. With its body burnt down by the *brahmana*'s fire, the sinner assumed the form of a *gandharva* in the sky and addressed Rama affectionately. "Earlier, as a result of the curse of a *brahmana*, I had become a hyena. You have now freed me from the curse and I will go to heaven." Saying this, he left quickly and Rama was astounded.'

'Full of compassion, he picked up the *dvija*'s son, who had fallen down. He addressed the *dvija*'s son in these words. "Do not be scared." O king! He gently massaged his limbs and brought life

---

[1278] In the text, the tiger becomes a hyena, and the hyena again becomes a tiger.

back into him. Raised up by Rama, he opened his eyes. He looked around and saw the best of the Bhrigu lineage in front of him. He saw the tiger, which had been burnt into ashes, and was amazed. Having lost his fear, he asked, "Who are you? How have you come here? Who reduced this one, who was about to kill me, to ashes? This was a hyena, terrible in form. It seemed to be like another Death itself. O immensely intelligent one! My mind is still numb with fear. Though it has been killed, it still appears to me that it is present in all the directions. I think that you are everything to me— my father, my mother, my well-wisher, and my *guru*. When I faced a great calamity, you gave my life back to me. There is a supreme sage named Shanta. He is a great ascetic. I am his son. Desiring to visit *tirtha*s, I went to Shalagrama. From there, I left for Mount Gandhamadana. I wished to see Badarikashrama, frequented by large numbers of many kinds of sages. Desiring to go there, I lost my way on Mount Himalaya. I entered a beautiful and dense forest, a region not favourable for people. I headed eastwards, for a distance of only one *krosha*. Such was destiny that I came under its subjugation. Suffering from fear, I started to run. I fell on the ground and have now been raised up by you. You were full of love and pity, the way a father behaves towards his son. This is my account. I have told you everything." O Indra among kings! Asked by him, Rama told him everything about his own account, in the due order. Full of affection, they conversed with each other. However, he did not wish to stay there for a long time and wished to leave. Following him, Rama also emerged from the mouth of the cave. Having emerged, he[1279] happily left for the residence of his parents. Though he had been brought down on the ground by a tiger, he was without a wound. Rama killed the tiger and protected him. O Indra among kings! Therefore, the *brahmana*'s son became famous on earth under the name of Akritavrana.[1280] Since then, he followed Rama, like a shadow on the ground, when there is light. O lord of the earth! Under every possible situation, he remained his great friend.'

[1279] Rama.
[1280] Meaning, someone who has not been wounded.

'Followed by him, he went to Bhrigu's presence. He saw Khyati and humbly greeted her. They were delighted and affectionately greeted him, pronouncing their benedictions. Wishing to bring them pleasure, he resided there for a few days. Then, having taken their permission, he went to the hermitage of the great sage, Chyavana. He was surrounded by a large number of *shishya*s and he greeted him. He[1281] was controlled inside and his mind was serene. The great-minded one also honoured his wife, Sukanya. Full of delight, they too greeted Rama. He then wished to go and see Ourva, the store of austerities, in his hermitage. The intelligent one honoured him and was greeted back in return. O king! Wishing to give him pleasure, he resided there for a few days. Released by him, full of joy, he slowly proceeded towards Richika's house. The handsome Bhargava reached the place, along with Akritavrana. Separately, he prostrated himself at the feet of the parents of his father and greeted them. O king! Delighted, they greeted him back and uttered their blessings. Asked by them, generous in intelligence, he told them everything about his conduct. O Indra among kings! In the due order, he told them everything that had transpired. He remained there for a few days. Then, full of supreme joy, he took their leave and went to the residence of his parents. O king! He reached the excellent hermitage of his parents. In the right way, the descendant of the Bhrigu lineage paid his respects at their feet. He prostrated himself at their feet and they lovingly raised him up. They embraced him and sprinkled him with tears of joy that flowed from their eyes. They pronounced their blessings, seated him on their laps and repeatedly looked at his face. They touched his limbs and were filled with great delight. They asked, "O Rama! What have you done for such a long time? O son! Where have you come from? Who has come with you? Who is he and how has he come here with you? O child! Both of you tell us everything that has happened."'

[1281] Chyavana.

Chapter 64-1(64) (Kartavirya Arjuna arrives)

Vasishtha said, 'O king! Asked by them, Rama joined his hands in salutation. He told them everything that he had done. Following the instructions of the *guru* of the lineage,[1282] he had undertaken austerities. Following Shambhu's command, in the due order, he had visited the *tirtha*s. Following his command and for the immortals, he had killed the *daitya*s. Through Hara's favours, he had met Akritavrana. Rama told his parents everything that he had done, causing them delight. In detail, they heard everything that he had done. O king! Both of them were filled with great joy. O great king! Thus, the descendant of the Bhrigu lineage served his parents. In particular, he showed no differentiation among his brothers.'

'At this time, on a certain occasion, the lord of Haihaya went there on a hunt, with the four kinds of forces.[1283] At the time, the sky was tinged red, as if with *bandhuka* flowers. In every direction, the red rays of the sun robbed the large number of stars of their brilliance. A gentle breeze blew and stirred the grove of *ketaki* flowers.[1284] In the morning, it touched the lotuses in the lake and bore their fragrance. Birds had built their nests in trees along the banks of the Narmada. They called in melodious tones, bringing pleasure to the ears and the mind. The *tirtha*s along the banks of the Narmada dispelled sins. Groups of sages descended in the waters and chanted about the eternal *brahman*. They performed their daily rites and returned to the banks of the river. Having performed their tasks, the best of sages returned to their hermitages. Each brave wife was eagerly performing the household tasks. In accordance with the rites meant for sages, they were milking the cows for oblations. The sons of sages carried the milk to the proper places. They had been born in lineages that performed *agnihotra* rites. Everything brought happiness to all beings. Lotuses bloomed and bees buzzed. In every direction, birds left their habitations in nests. There

---

[1282] That is, Bhrigu.
[1283] Chariots, elephants, horses and infantry.
[1284] *Ketaki* is the fragrant crew pine or caldera.

were those who were moving slowly on crazy elephants, horses and chariots. The slow breeze that blew in the forest at the time brought delight to their bodies. People proceeded to the end of the hermitage, carrying flowers and water. There were many who wore deer skins as garments, accomplished in studying. *Mantras* were chanted in the proper way, in high and low pitches. As these were chanted, oblations were offered into the fire. Everywhere, rites were performed in accordance with the utterance of *mantras*. The energy of the sun resembled the flames of a blazing fire and scorched the darkness, driving it away in every direction and spreading everywhere on earth. When the sun rose, the darkness of the night was destroyed. The stars vanished and the quarters sparkled.'

'The king, the lord of Haihaya, completed his morning rites and emerged for the hunt. He left the city, and his priest was with him. All his forces were also with him, horses, chariots and elephants. The prosperous one was with his advisers and kings who were friends. He made the surface of the earth bend under the burden of his great army. O king! The roar of chariots echoed in all the directions. The stride from the waves of his army raised dust and covered the sky, as if was crowded with hundreds of *vimanas*. With his large army, he entered the terrible forest in the Vindhyas. In every direction, the excellent king created great agitation. The king surrounded the forest with his own soldiers. He killed many kinds of fierce animals with his sharp arrows. The warriors drew their bows all the way back up to the ears and shot sharp arrows. The bodies of some tigers were pierced and they fell down on the ground. The infantry used the terrible force of swords to slice the bodies of some. Drenched with blood, some herds of boar fell down on the ground. Terrible spears were released, and these spears shattered the heads. Heaps of deer fell and covered the earth, like mountains. All the limbs of lions, bears, *sharabha*s and others were pierced by iron arrows. Drenched with blood, they covered the earth in every direction. Some birds were brought down with bludgeons. Some animals were pursued by hunting dogs. Others started to run away. Some shrieked in afflicted tones. They were scared and feared for their lives. The forest was extremely agitated, as if the end of the *yuga* had arrived. With their weapons, the soldiers killed many animals—boars, lions, tigers, porcupines, species of rabbits, yaks, *ruru* antelopes, jackals, *gavaya*s, bears, many wolves, spotted antelopes, leopards, red rhinos, deer of many different colours and all the *nyanku* antelopes. Some were cubs being suckled. Some were aged. There were many couples too. These were killed with sharp weapons, even those that should not be killed with weapons. In this way, there was incessant and terrible violence, with animals being killed. After this, the king's soldiers were filled with great exhaustion.'

'The sun reached midday. Scorched by the heat and suffering from thirst, along with the soldiers, the king reached the Narmada. With his forces and mounts, he descended into the water. Suffering from hunger and thirst, the king immersed himself in the auspicious water. He bathed and drank the extremely cool and pleasant water. He ate the tasty and white shoots of lotuses. Along with his army, the king descended into the water and sported there. The bank was adorned with clumps of trees, and he rested there. When the one with the sharp rays was elongated,[1285] the king and his followers and soldiers emerged from the forest and caves in the Vindhyas, intending to return to the city. As he proceeded, on the banks of the Narmada, he saw the hermitage of the great-souled Jamadagni, auspicious in conduct. The lord of the earth made the soldiers withdraw, some distance away. With a few attendants, he went to the hermitage. Along with his priest, he went to that beautiful hermitage. The king approached the tiger among sages and lowered his head in salutation. Jamadagni greeted the excellent king and uttered his blessings. In the proper way, he honoured him with *arghya*, *padya* and *asana*. The sage arranged for whatever honours were possible. In front of the great sage, the supreme king seated himself on a sparkling seat, while the sage seated himself on a seat made of *kusha* grass. The excellent and supreme sage asked him about the welfare of his sons, friends, relatives and others. After remaining there for some time, he invited the king to be his *atithi*. The king was extremely happy and spoke to Jamadagni. "O *maharshi*! Please grant me permission. Let me go to my own city.

[1285] The sun was setting.

O great sage! I have all my forces and mounts with me. You reside in the forest and survive on forest-fare. You will not be able to extend hospitality to us. Or perhaps, because of the strength of your austerities, you may be able to perform the act of hospitality. Even then, you should grant me permission to go to the city. O supreme sage! Otherwise, all this excessive number of soldiers will cause suffering to the ascetics and impair their observance of *niyamas*." Thus addressed, the sage told him, "Remain here for a while. I will provide the hospitality for you and your followers." He summoned his *dogdhri*.'[1286]

'He said, "This is my *atithi*. He has come here. Hence, you should do everything to honour him properly now." Thus, addressed by the sage, the *dogdhri* did everything for the hospitality. To show respect for the words of the sage, it was instantly milked for everything worthy of the king. The hermitage of the noble Bhargava became as radiant as the residence of the king of the Gods. As a result of the powers of the cow, it assumed a form that is impossible to think of. There were different kinds of prosperity, impossible to accomplish. There were large numbers of mansions on all sides. Their radiant and sparkling tops seemed to touch the full moon and the white clouds. They were large and lofty, encrusted with many blazing jewels and coloured with gold. The mansions were made out of bronze, brass, copper, gold, silver, mortar, bricks, plaster, wood and mud and mixtures of these. There were many separate mansions, pleasing to the eyes and the mind. There were expensive and dazzling platforms, radiant with jewels and gold. There were steps that led up, with places to sit down and rest. These were adorned with sloping beams, doors, gates, bolts, thresholds, terraces and courtyards. The upper parts and balconies of the mansions were beautiful. There were sparkling archways and extensive quadrangles. Divine jewels and celestial pictures decorated the pillars and walls. There were superior and inferior jewels. Golden thrones and seats were studded with excellent jewels. There were many kinds of food,

---

[1286] *Dogdhri* is a cow that can be milked. This was a *kamadhenu*, a cow that could be milked for anything desired.

edible items and drinks, in many vessels, in several places. All the habitations were full of every kind of prosperity, worthy of immortals. It was pleasing to the mind and the eyes. With the beautiful women, the hermitage came to resemble a city.'

Chapter 65-1(65) (Kartavirya Arjuna spends the night)

Vasishta said, 'Using its power, the noble sage's cow created a grand city that resembled that of Indra of the immortals. After creating the homes, it created large numbers of appropriate men and women. The bodies of the women were decorated with many kinds of ornaments, flowers, fragrances and silk garments. They cast sidelong glances and were generous in expressing sentiments of love. Their acts, beauty and comeliness were wonderful, and they possessed all the qualities. The teeth within their quivering lips spread clusters of beams and illuminated their faces, which vanquished lotuses and the moon. Their sweet words were full of the *asava* of prime youth. Because of the love, their sidelong glances caused churning. Their pleased hearts spread the radiance of affection. They were adorned with *shringara*, as if with flowers from a *kalpa-taru*.[1287] Their adornments of good fortune, youth, beauty, desire and sweet form were comparable to those of celestial women. Their waists bent from the burden of two breasts that were like heated golden pots. The weight of bearing their heavy hips seemed to lead to exhaustion, with the sweat assuming the form of red lac on their feet, as they touched the ground. They were decorated with armlets, necklaces, bejewelled bangles, golden necklaces and sparkling earrings on their ears. The garlands kissed the tips of their mass of hair. There was the tinkling sound of girdles and anklets. They teased with fake anger, assurances, great jests,

---

[1287] *Kalpa-taru* is a tree that grants whatever one wishes for. Here, *shringara* means ornaments/garments, in preparation for bouts of love.

beautiful conversation and fake censure and ire. Through their
sentiments, they were skilled in disturbing the king and all those
who were dear to him. When they spoke, the sounds of the voices
were sweet, as if they emerged from the song of a *gandharva*, or
from his plucking a musical string. Their fingers and palms were
accomplished in playing the *veena*. They were eager to make both
serious and light conversation. The women were intoxicating and
excessively eloquent in conversing, agitating the minds of those
who desired them. They were skilled in modes of love and did not
lack in prosperity, generosity, beauty, qualities and good conduct.
There were many such, eager to perform household tasks, but also
intent on serving them. All around, the houses were also filled with
numerous male attendants, possessing appropriate good qualities,
beauty, splendour and radiance. There were royal roads, shops
full of merchandise, mansions, flights of stairs, temples to *deva*s
and quadrangles. On every side, these were filled with citizens who
possessed all the qualities and had satisfied all their desires. There
were innumerable groups of unmatched mansions, filled with many
colourful and radiant jewels. There was a lot of appropriate housing
for chariots, horses, elephants, camels, cows and goats. There were
separate residences for the Indra among men, vassal kings, riders,
foot-soldiers, generals, leaders, *brahmana*s and others, charioteers
of chariots and *magadha*s and *bandi*s. There were many large
streets, markets and colourful squares, where articles were being
bought and sold. There were sparkling houses for courtesans, filled
with extremely expensive utensils and constructed well. There were
lofty turrets, blazing with expensive jewels. There was housing for
dogs and vultures, residences for travellers and halls for dancing.
There were colourful flags and banners and white canopies were
spread above the pavilions. There were many beautiful lakes, ponds
and wells, full of water and fragrant with the pollen of many kinds
of *kalhara*s, *pankaja*s, *kumuda*s and *utpala*s. They were full of
*chakravaka*s, swans, ospreys, cranes and storks. Groves of trees
extended right up to the banks of the water—mango, *priyala*,
panasa, *amra*, *madhuka*, *jambu*, *plaksha*, *nagakeshara*, *ketaki*,
punnaga and *champaka*. The trees were full of birds. There were

trees like *mandara, kunda, karavira*, beautiful *yuthika* and *yati* and
these had many kinds of flowers and fruit.[1288] All around, one could
see groves meant for pleasure and they were so adorned as to cause
wonder in the world. The gentle and fragrant breeze that blew was
representative of all seasons but seemed to reprimand summer. O
Indra among men! The city was evidently full of prosperity and
every kind of object of pleasure, causing joy to Gods and *asuras*.
Having immediately created it, full of good fortune and objects of
pleasure, the cow used for oblations swiftly went and informed the
sage about this. The supreme sage thus got to know that the cow
used for the *dvija*'s oblations had devised what was necessary for
the king's hospitality.'

'He summoned a *shishya* who possessed all the qualities
and quickly sent him to the king. Having quickly gone there,
the son of a sage humbly spoke to the lord of the earth. "The
instructor of our lineage has said that arrangements have been
made for a king's hospitality. Please accept it quickly." Taking
the permission of the excellent sage, the king entered the excellent
city and was honoured there, along with his entire army. The
cow used for the sage's oblations was capable and had arranged
for habitations with every kind of object of pleasure. The noble
king entered and saw the city, which was capable of confounding
all the worlds. He was himself patient and generous. His face
filled with pleasure. But along with his army, he was extremely
surprised at what he saw. His form was beautiful, and he was a
worthy recipient. Therefore, as he proceeded, they eyes of large
numbers of divine women seemed to drink him in. The lord of
Haihaya proceeded along the royal road and was delighted,
like Shakra when he entered Kubera's abode, along with a large
number of immortals. As he proceeded along the royal road, all
the women of the city sprinkled him with water, mixed with the
fragrance of sandalwood. From the tops of the mansions, they
showered down flowers, parched grain and garlands. The hands

[1288] *Mandara* is the coral tree, *karavira* is oleander and *kunda, yuthika*
and *yati* are types of jasmine.

of the women of the city resembled lotuses and they eagerly welcomed and honoured him with these showers of parched grain. At the time, the fragrance of lotuses and white flowers caused delight and groups of bees seemed to sing. The men and women of the city scattered jewels and pearls along the route. As he was showered in this way, the lord of the earth was radiant. He resembled Mount Mandara, with the one with the cool beams spreading its beams all around. This reflected the glory and generosity of a *brahmana*'s austerities, and it was impossible for people to conceive it. It was rarer still for them to desire this prosperity. O king! As he witnessed the prosperity of the city, the lord of the earth praised it in thoughts and words. The lord of Haihaya thought, "This is extremely rare on earth. All the delightful prosperity of a *kshatriya* cannot match this and is not even one hundredth part of a *brahmana*'s prosperity and powers, unthinkable even for the Gods." As he proceeded with his priest, ministers and others, he observed the affluence and prosperity of the citizens in the centre of the city. As he proceeded, being honoured by the citizens of the city, he rejoiced when an attendant pointed out a colourful mansion. "O king! The noble sage has decided that this is appropriate, given the respect due to you. Along with your followers, please accept this." Effortlessly, the king retreated and advanced in the direction of the house that had been designed for him. In every direction of the road, the delighted citizens assembled, their cupped hands bearing many kinds of gifts. At every step, he was greeted with sounds of "Victory". Along the road, the sounds of the trumpets seemed to make a person deaf. Gradually, the king passed through three chambers and was reverentially greeted by the guards. They kept the large number of ordinary people away. His advisers held him by the hand and made him enter the residence. There, the women of the city greeted him with a lamp, curds, a mirror, fragrances, flowers, *durva* grass, *akshata* and other objects. As he went inside the royal residence, they playfully delighted the king with many kinds of honours. Along with them, he quickly entered the residence, which was radiant with many kinds of jewels and beautiful nets.

The generous and illustrious one ascended a seat made out of excellent gold, with a thin piece of cloth spread over it. The king seated himself comfortably inside the house. The women of the city quickly brought him many kinds of gifts. Musical instruments were sounded. Ornaments, fragrances, flowers, decorations and the best of gifts were offered. It was the end of the day and in accordance with his own views, he lord of Haihaya completed the daily rites. He spent the rest of the day in many kinds of sports and pleasure. Seeing that the end of the day had arrived, along with all his ministers, advisers and followers, the king completed all the rites that were appropriate for the close of day. He then immediately went to an assembly, where the lamps held in the hands of servants completely dispelled the darkness. Worshipped by his priest, ministers, vassal kings and hundreds of leaders, he sat down on the seat there. In that assembly, the king was delighted with many kinds of objects, like Indra of the Gods, tended to by large numbers of *devas*. For a long period of time, he was amused by the playing of musical instruments. He witnessed the dancing, the jesting and the narration of accounts. The jesting, sporting and dalliances of large numbers of courtesans made him content. Till midnight, the lord of the earth amused himself in this way, with many kinds of luxury and amusement. After this, the king made all his brave and valiant companions leave for their own residences. These were appropriate to their greatness and qualities. The lord of the earth left for the residence that had been earmarked for him and entered it. It was appropriate for him, with extremely expensive garments, garlands, ornaments and other things. He was delighted. The king's soldiers had many kinds of food, drinks, excellent edible items, honey, flesh, milk, *ghee* and other things. With all these delightful objects of pleasure, in the city, the followers of the Indra among men were over-joyed, like large numbers of *devas* in heaven. The king's followers were happy at many kinds of objects. They told each other, "What will we achieve with our houses, wealth and other articles? Let all of us reside here." The king performed all the rites for the night. He lay down on the excellent bed, in the residence earmarked

for him. It was radiant and auspicious, illuminated with heaps of
jewels. The Indra among men slept happily, for a long time.'

Chapter 66-1(66)
(Kartavirya Arjuna seizes the cow)

Vasishtha said, 'When night was over, sutas, magadhas and
bandis approached the sleeping king and sang loudly and
eagerly, so as to wake him up. There were sounds of veenas and
flutes, mixed with the clapping of hands and keeping of tala.[1289]
Everything was extremely pleasant to the ears. The tones were sweet
and praiseworthy. The tones were gentle and the murcchana[1290]
was clear in the composition. The song sung was agreeable, with
high pitches and low pitches. The sutas and magadhas spoke to
the great-souled sleeping king. Desiring to wake him up, they
used many kinds of soft words. "O Indra among kings! Behold.
As the radiance of your lotus face increased, the moon has been
vanquished and is setting. O lord! Wishing to see your lotus face
and exceedingly eager, the sun has shattered the darkness and has
approached Mount Udaya.[1291] O king! O jewel on the crests of all
those who belong to chandra vamsha! O immensely intelligent one!
Enough of sleep. Please get up now." Hearing their words, the lord
of the earth woke up, just as the one with eyes like a lotus[1292] wakes
up in the ocean of milk, from his couch on Shesha. With the sleep
gone from his eyes, he arose and lovingly performed the daily rites.
He performed everything properly, leaving nothing out. With divine
garlands, fragrances and ornaments, he worshipped his desired
divinity and the cow. He touched durva grass, collyrium, a mirror
and auspicious signs. He made donations to those who desired them
and bowed down before cows and brahmanas. He emerged from

[1289] The beating of time in music.
[1290] Modulation, the rise and fall of sounds along the musical scale.
[1291] The sun rises from behind Mount Udaya and sets behind Mount Asta.
[1292] Vishnu.

the city and worshipped the sun. All the ministers, vassal kings and leaders approached him. O king! Joining their hands in salutation, they prostrated themselves before the excellent king. Surrounded by them, he approached the store of austerities. Wearing a crown that was as radiant as the sun, he prostrated himself at his feet. The bull among sages greeted the king and pronounced his benedictions. The lord of the earth addressed him in humble and conciliatory words. When he was seated, pleased in his mind, the *maharshi* addressed him in these words. "O king! I hope that the night that has passed was pleasant for you. O Indra among kings! We live in the forest and survive on forest-fare. Following the *dharma* of animals, we are only capable of maintaining ourselves in some form or other. Inhabitants of the city find it extremely difficult to remain in the forest. O Indra among kings! Anything one is not used to, is extremely difficult to tolerate. You and your followers had to go through the difficulty of residing in a forest. Indeed, the fact that you have done it, even once, enhances your honour." Showing his pleasure first, the sage addressed the king in this way. As if he was smiling, he replied. "O *brahmana*! Why are you saying this? We have witnessed your greatness. The entire world is astounded at this greatness. O great sage! The consciousness of my soldiers has been struck by the prosperity that resulted from your powers and they do not wish to leave this place. O lord! It is through the power of austerities like this that the worlds are always supported. Indeed, the radiance of a *brahmana* is unthinkable. O lord! It is not surprising that you should be able to do this through your austerities. Indeed, it is certain that, in the due order, you can bring about the three states of the worlds.[1293] We have clearly witnessed the great success of your austerities, revered by people. O *brahmana*! I seek your permission. I will go to my city." Kartavirya lovingly said this. The sage honoured him properly and signified words of assent. Permitted by the sage, he emerged from the hermitage. Surrounded by his soldiers, he left for the city.'

[1293] Creation, preservation and destruction.

'As he was proceeding along the road, the lord of the earth thought about this in his mind. "How wonderful is the success obtained through austerities, causing amazement in the worlds. Through those, he has obtained such an excellent cow, which can be milked for everything desired. What can I accomplish through my entire kingdom, or through *yoga*? They are but a trifle. The cow, a jewel among cows, is with the excellent sage. Indeed, through that, one can even generate the prosperity of heaven. Indra's prosperity and position are worshipped by the three worlds. But I think it is evident it is not worth one sixteenth of the portion this cow is worth." While the lord of the earth was thinking this, from behind, his minister, Chandragupta, joined his hands in salutation and spoke to him. "O tiger among kings! Why are you returning to the city? Even if you protect the kingdom and the city, what fruits do you gain from that? O lord! O king! Until the jewel among cows is bound in your residence, there will be no prosperity in your kingdom. It will be empty. I have witnessed another wonder. O king! Listen to that. There are agreeable houses, filled with charming women. There are many kinds of mansions and imperishable wealth, not seen before. In an instant, I have seen all that vanish within the cow. O excellent king! All those have now been reduced to the hermitage. If the cow possesses such powers, what is impossible to obtain? You are a being who deserves all jewels. Therefore, it is your duty to accept that cow. If you approve of this, do what will ensure the subsistence of all those who depend on you." The king replied, "I do not wish to know about this. This is unworthy. The property of a *brahmana* should not be taken away. My mind is scared." When the king said this, the priest, Garga, supreme among intelligent ones, spoke, seeming to censure. "O king! The property of a *brahmana* must never be taken away. In this world, there is nothing as indigestible as a *brahmana*'s possessions. O Haihaya! Poison not only harms the intended victim, but also the person who has used it. A *brahmana*'s property is like *arani* and the fire that arises from it burns down the entire lineage, right up to the roots. In this world, the property of a *brahmana* is like indigestible poison and there is no antidote. O lord of the earth! It is bitter in consequence and leads to the fruit of sons and grandsons being destroyed. Deluded by prosperity, the minds of lords always turn foolish. When the eye is tempted by greed, what can such a person not do? O excellent king! Other than you, who knows the consequences of taking something, without it being given? The mind should think of giving things to brahmanas, instead of taking away from them. O mighty-armed one! You should not commit an act that will be condemned by virtuous people. You should not do anything that will lead to a loss of your fame in the worlds. You have been born in a great lineage, of those who are generous and mighty-armed. You should not come under the subjugation of this act and destroy the fame now. Alas! There are some who earn a subsistence from you, but wish to submerge their master in an ocean of hardship. Their elevation is because of your favours. But they are eager to submerge you. Desiring prosperity, a man loses his senses and does what is unthinkable. A king who follows the recommendations of these mad followers suffers instantly. This ignorant minister will take the king along an unwise path. Along with himself, this evil-minded one will make the king submerge, like a boat made out of iron. O tiger among kings! Therefore, you should not follow the path indicated by this foolish one. You should follow the path indicated by me, not by this extremely evil-minded one." He was speaking words that were beneficial for his master. However, the minister insulted him and spoke to the king again. "This one is a brahmana. He only looks at what will be beneficial for his own varna.[1294] Dvijas are incapable of knowing about a king's great tasks. King should use their own intelligence to decide on royal tasks. A brahmana is not interested in any task that does not involve receiving food and gifts. A brahmana must never be disrespected and must always be worshipped. He must be given gifts. There is nothing more that can be accomplished by him. O king! Therefore, accept that cow as your own and leave for your own city thereafter. Otherwise, give up the kingdom. Go to the forest and perform austerities. O lord of the earth! Forgiving is the quality of brahmanas. The rod is the quality of kshatriyas. If you seize it forcibly, there may be adharma.

[1294] Since Jamadagni was also a brahmana.

O king! If you think there is a sin associated with forcible seizure, give the *rishi* a price, in the form of cows, horses and other things. Then accept the cow. You are worthy of having a share in jewels. Hence, your task is to make that cow your own. Why will practitioners of austerities be interested in accumulating jewels? O king! The strength of a store of austerities is in being serene. Moreover, he is pleased with you. Therefore, if you ask him for the cow, come what may, he will give it to you. Alternatively, give him cattle, gold and whatever else he wants. Collect a great deal of wealth and give it to him, in return for the cow. A king who desires great prosperity does not ignore a great jewel. This is what my intelligence tells me. What do you think?" The king replied, "Go to the *brahmana* and make special efforts to placate him. O minister! Give him what he wishes for and bring the cow from him." Thus addressed by the king, the minister was urged by destiny. He withdrew and quickly went to Jamadagni's hermitage.'

'After the king had left, along with Akritavrana, Rama left for the forest, to collect kindling. With the army, the minister reached the hermitage. He prostrated himself before the tiger among sages and addressed him in these words. Chandragupta said, "O *brahmana*! The king has ordered the following. On earth, kings deserve to enjoy jewels. This cow is a jewel. It is supreme among *dogdhri*s on earth. Therefore, accept the appropriate price for the cow—jewels and gold. You should give this cow, a jewel among cows, to me." Jamadagni replied, "This cow is used for oblations. Under no circumstance, will I give it away. The king is generous. How can he desire a *brahmana*'s possession?" The minister said, "The king deserves to own a jewel. That is the reason he desires it. I will give you ten thousand cows. You should give him the cow in return." Jamadagni replied, "I have not been born as someone who engages in buying and selling. This cow easily gives me what I need for oblations and I am not interested in giving it away." The minister said, "O *brahmana*! Give it in exchange for half the kingdom, or everything the king possesses. If you give this single cow, it will be best for you." Jamadagni replied, "O evil-minded one! As long as I am alive, I will not give this cow to anyone, not even to Vasava, not even if his *guru*[1295] asks me to. On the basis of

---

[1295] Brihaspati.

your words, why will I give it to the king?" The minister said, "As a well-wisher, of your own will, you should give the cow to the king. If it is seized by force, what will you do?" Jamadagni replied, "The king gives to *brahmanas*. If he seizes it, what can a *brahmana* like me do, except surrender it voluntarily?" Thus addressed, the evil-minded minister was enraged. He started to take away the sage's milk-yielding cow by force.'

Chapter 67-1(67) (Jamadagni is killed)

Vasishtha said, 'Full of rage, Jamadagni spoke to him again. "A man who knows should not take away a *brahmana*'s possessions. O evil-minded one! If you take my cow away by force, you will incur a sin. I know that your lifespan has come to an end. Otherwise, you would not have acted in this way. You wish to take this away by force. But you will never be able to do that. If the cow itself decides to engage, the king will be destroyed. Instead of giving to them, the property of ascetic *brahmanas* is being seized. Except Arjuna, who has lived for one hundred years, will any other person, who wishes to remain alive, act in this way?" Addressed thus, goaded by time, the minister became angry. He tied the cow firmly with a noose and started to forcibly drag it away. Jamadagni was also urged by his inevitable *karma* and became filled with rage. As the milk-yielding cow was being dragged away, he resisted this with all his strength. "As long as I am alive, I will seek to free this cow." Extremely angry, the great sage firmly clung to the cow's neck with his hands." The extremely ruthless Chandragupta was filled with great rage. He asked his own soldiers to take him away. In this world, the *rishi* was amongst those who were most unassailable. However, following their leader's command, the king's servants surrounded him from all sides and seized him. They struck him with rods, whips, poles and fists. They struck him and dragged him far away from the cow. Though he was struck and suffered, he was full of forgiveness. Not being prone to rage is the great treasure of virtuous people. Because of his own austerities, he was capable

of striking them and protecting himself. But he thought that the
entire world would be destroyed because of this. Therefore, he
controlled his anger. Earlier, he used to be prone to great rage.
However, on his mother's account, Rama had placated him. Since
then, the ascetic was always serene. He was struck severely, and the
joints of his limbs were shattered. Losing his senses, the immensely
energetic one fell on the ground. When the sage fell, the evil-souled
one was scared. He instructed the servants to quickly take the cow
away, with force. O king! Along with the calf, they firmly tied
the cow with nooses. Striking it with whips, they started to drag
it away. They struck it with whips and rods. Struck in this way,
the milk-yielding cow became extremely angry. Suffering from the
blows, it was filled with great rage. It tugged at the firm nooses and
freed itself. When it freed itself from the firm nooses, the soldiers
surrounded it from all sides. Making the sound of *humkara*, it
rushed towards them angrily, on every side. In every direction, it
struck them with its horns, hooves and the tip of its tail. Full of
intolerance, it drove away the king's minister and the soldiers. In
this way, the milk-yielding cow made all the servants flee. While
all the beings watched, it rose up into the sky. The hopes of all
those cruel ones were shattered. Their limbs were mangled. They
seized and bound the calf and started to drag it away. The servants
seized the calf, without the milk-yielding cow. The sinner[1296]
swiftly arrived in the king's presence. Having approached the
king, he prostrated himself and praised him. Terrified, he told him
everything that had happened.'

Chapter 68-1(68) (Parashurama's vow)

Vasishtha said, 'The king heard everything, about Jamadagni
being killed and so on. His mind became extremely anxious
and he thought about many things. "In the eyes of both the worlds,

---

[1296] Chandragupta.

I have been extremely cruel. I have taken away a *brahmana*'s property. I have also killed him. Both are extremely contemptible. Alas! Ignorantly, I did not listen to what the *brahmana* said. I was deluded and lost my sense of shame. Hence, I did not accept his words." His heart shattered, he thought this. Followed by his soldiers, he returned to his own city. Along with his attendants, the king returned to the city.'

'O king! Renuka suddenly emerged from the hermitage. She saw her husband lying down on the ground, immobile. All his limbs were wounded and covered with blood. Since he had lost his senses, she thought that her husband had been killed. As if struck by a bolt of lightning, she lost her senses and fell down on the ground. After a long time, she arose from the ground, miserable. She fell down again and lamented in loud tones. Covered with the dust of the ground, she lamented a lot. She was miserable. Her eyes filled with tears and she was immersed in an ocean of grief. "Alas! O protector! O beloved! O one who knew about *dharma*! O one who was an ocean of the *amrita* of being compassionate! Alas! Shame on such excessive serenity. No one should desire something like this. You suddenly emerged from the hermitage and have got me submerged in this ocean of hardship. O one who bestows honours! Flinging me into this fathomless ocean, where have you gone? Friendship of the virtuous is with *saptapada*.[1297] But I have failed to do that with you. You have departed alone, though you should have taken me with you. O husband! On seeing the state, you are in now, my heart should have been shattered. O immensely fortune one! But those of women are hard and it has not happened." She repeatedly lamented and wept in this way. Overwhelmed by great grief, she shrieked, "O Rama! O Rama!" Meanwhile, having gathered kindling, Rama returned from the forest. He returned to the hermitage, along with Akritavrana. On the way, he had seen many evil portents and was scared. Having seen them, his heart was anxious, and the lord returned to the hermitage quickly.'

[1297] *Saptapada* means seven steps. Taking seven steps together is a pledge of friendship, usually around a fire. *Saptapada* is also performed in the course of a marriage, with a pledge to be together for seven lives.

'On seeing him arrive, she was greatly afflicted again and wept. A new round of grief overwhelmed Renuka and she wept. O king! Suffering as a result of the separation from her husband, in front of Rama, she beat her stomach with both her hands. Along the road, Rama had already got to know everything about the incident. Now he saw his mother, suffering from grief, like a female osprey. He was miserable. Though he was overwhelmed by grief and sorrow, the intelligent one resorted to his fortitude. His eyes filled with tears, and he stood there, his face facing the ground. Akritavrana saw Rama in that state and spoke to him. "O tiger of the Bhrigu lineage! What is this? This is not worthy of you. O immensely fortunate one! Those like you never grieve excessively in this way. Those who are great and possess fortitude, do not grieve over a loss. Grief dries up all the senses. Abandon this grief. O mighty-armed one! It is not worthy of someone like you. Indeed, sorrow alone destroys all objectives, in this world and in the next one. How can you have time for grief? Control your heart. You possess the wealth of fortitude. Comfort your mother. She has lost her senses because she has become a widow and is weeping. An object that has gone never returns. Therefore, cast aside everything that is in the past. Think of what needs to be done." Rama was grieving and was comforted in this way. Gradually, he pacified himself. Overwhelmed by sorrow and grief, Renuka wept repeatedly. She struck her stomach with her hands twenty-one times. His eyes full of tears, Rama approached her. He comforted his mother and said, "Enough of weeping." She was suffering from grief and sorrow on account of her husband. He said, "You have struck your chest[1298] twenty-one times. Therefore, I will exterminate all the kshatriyas that number of times. I will slay them, everywhere on earth. I am speaking the truth. Hence, cast aside this grief now and resort to your fortitude. Indeed, anything that has gone, belongs to the past and does not exist now." Renuka, suffering from great grief, was addressed in this way. With a great deal of effort, she resorted to her fortitude and replied in words of assent.'

[1298] Here, the text says, *vaksha* (chest). Earlier, it said, *udara* (stomach).

'O king! With his brothers, the mighty-armed Rama followed the norms and started the arrangements for cremating his father's body in the fire. Renuka's body was overwhelmed by grief, on account of her husband. Firm in her vows, she summoned all her sons and addressed them in these words. Renuka said, "O sons! Your father, auspicious in conduct, has proceeded to heaven. I desire to follow your father. You should grant me leave to do so. It is impossible to tolerate the sorrow of widowhood. How will I bear it? If I remain without my husband, I will be reprimanded. Therefore, I will follow my beloved husband. That way, I will constantly be with him, in the other world. When I enter this blazing fire, within a short while, I will be my husband's beloved *atithi*, in the world of the ancestors. O sons! Your task is to agree with me. If you wish to do what brings me pleasure, you should not say anything against this." Firm in her resolution, Renuka addressed them in these words. She made up her mind to follow her husband and enter the fire. Meanwhile, an invisible voice was heard from the sky. In an extremely grave tone, it addressed Renuka and her sons. "O Renuka! Along with your sons, listen attentively to these words. O fortunate one! Do not be rash. I will speak what will be dear to you. Anyone who desires his welfare, should not act in a rash way. If a person does not die and lives, he witnesses everything auspicious. Therefore, resort to the treasure of your fortitude and wait for the right time. O one with the sweet smiles! There is a cause hidden inside you. Within a short while, your husband will regain his senses. O beautiful one! When he gets back his life, you will obtain what you desire. You will obtain many auspicious things, which will last for many nights." Hearing these words, Renuka resorted to her fortitude. Showing due respect to these words, the sons were filled with joy. They took their father's body inside the hermitage again. They placed the sage in a place where there was no wind and seated themselves, all around him. Though their minds were not filled with joy, they sat there. They saw many great and auspicious portents. The minds of those bulls among sages were somewhat assured because of this. They sat there with their mother, desiring that their father might come back to life.'

'O king! At this time, because of the power of destiny, the sage who established the Bhrigu lineage[1299] arrived there. The intelligent one arrived there, following his own will. He was the one who composed the *mantra*s of *Atharva Veda*. He was himself accomplished in the *Veda*s and *Vedanga*s. He was wise about the meanings of all the sacred texts. He was worshipped by all the Gods. He possessed knowledge of *mritasanjivini*, which is extremely difficult for even sages to know. He used this to bring back *danava*s, killed by *deva*s, back from the dead. He composed the sacred text known as Ushanas. When kings used this, they obtained the fruit of getting their kingdoms back. He composed that and even now, all kings survive on the basis of that. The great sage reached the hermitage and entered. He saw all of them in that state, overwhelmed by grief. They were delighted to see Bhrigu, the ancestor of their lineage. They arose, honoured him and gave him an excellent seat. The great sage greeted them and pronounced his benedictions over all of them. He asked them what had happened, and they reported everything. Hearing this, Bhrigu, who knew *mantra*s, quickly gathered some water. He used his knowledge, recited the *mritasanjivini mantra* and sprinkled water. "If my sacrifices, austerities and vigour have been auspicious, because of those, let him come back to life. Let him arise, as if he has been asleep." Bhrigu, the performer of virtuous deeds, uttered these auspicious words. Like another Guru,[1300] Richika's son arose. On seeing Bhrigu, his own forefather, stationed there, he worshipped him. O lord of men! He devoutly prostrated himself. He joined his hands in salutation and spoke. Jamadagni said, "I am blessed. I have accomplished my objective, and my birth has been successful. I have now seen your feet, worshipped by Gods and *asura*s. O one who bestows honours! What will I do to serve you now? Through the water from your lotus feet, purify your own lineage." Rama had brought *arghya*. Saying this, full of joy,

---

[1299] That is, Bhrigu himself. Usually, knowledge of *mritasanjivini* is attributed to Bhrigu's son, Shukracharya. The sacred text for kings is known as *Shukra-Niti*.

[1300] Brihaspati.

he offered it at his feet and devoutly lowered his shoulders. Along with his family members, the great-minded one sprinkled the water on his head. After honouring Bhrigu, he humbly questioned him. "O illustrious one! Why did the evil king commit this sin? I followed the norms and treated him properly, like an *atithi*. O immensely wise one! I took him to be virtuous. Why did he act in this evil-minded way?" The intelligent Bhrigu, lord of every kind of learning, was asked in this way. O lord of the earth! He thought about this for some time and discerning the reason, spoke. Bhrigu said, "O son! O immensely fortunate one! Hear about the seed behind this act. O omniscient one! O unblemished one! This is why he committed a sin towards you. Earlier, for the destruction of the lord of the earth, Vasishtha had cursed him.[1301] 'O foolish one! Because of a crime you commit against a *dvija*, your valour will be destroyed.' When the sage said that, how could it be otherwise? This immensely valiant Rama will strike that unassailable bull among kings. O mighty-armed one! He will kill him. He has already taken that pledge. 'O mother! Suffering from great grief, you have struck your stomach twenty-one times. Therefore, I will exterminate *kshatriya*s from this earth, twenty-one times.' You, his father, may constantly try to restrain him. O one who bestows honours! Since destiny is strong, this is bound to happen. The immensely fortunate king served the aged. The immensely intelligent one obtained understanding from Dattatreya, born as Hari's portion. The great-souled one is directly his devotee too. Hence, as a result of killing him, there will be a sin." O great king! Bhrigu, Brahma's son, said this. In the course of what was bound to happen in the future, the learned one returned to wherever he had come from.'

[1301] Apava Vasishtha's hermitage was burnt down by Kartavirya Arjuna, using a fire. Consequently, Apava Vasishtha cursed him. This story is narrated in the Mahabharata. Since Vasishtha is the name of a lineage, rather than that of one individual, Apava Vasishtha need not be the same as the Vasishtha who is narrating.

Chapter 69-1(69) (Brahma's advice)

Sagara asked, 'O Brahma's son! O immensely fortunate one!
Please tell me what Bhargava did. Enraged by what the king had
done, what did the immensely valiant one do?'

Vasishtha replied, 'The immensely fortunate Bhrigu departed.
Devoted to his father, the angry Rama repeatedly sighed and spoke
these words. Parashurama said, "Behold the folly of the king, who
has walked along a perverse path. Kartavirya, who is learned, tried
to kill a *brahmana*. I think that destiny is powerful. As a result of
its powers, all those with bodies are deluded and commit auspicious
and inauspicious deeds. All the *rishi*s have heard the pledge I took. I
will avenge the enmity towards my father by killing Kartavirya. Even
if Indra and all the other Gods and *danava*s seek to protect him, I
will kill the king. It cannot but be otherwise." The extremely great-
souled Rama uttered these bold words. Hearing them, Jamadagni
spoke to his son. Jamadagni said, "O Rama! Listen. I will tell you
about the eternal *dharma* of the virtuous. Hearing this, all humans
are driven to acts of *dharma*. Immensely fortunate and virtuous ones
wish to obtain *moksha* from *samsara*. Even if they are struck and
criticized, they never become angry. Immensely fortunate and self-
controlled ascetics possess the treasure of forgiveness. Those who act
virtuously in this way, always obtain imperishable worlds. Even if the
wicked strike with rods and words, despite being struck, if a person
is not agitated, he is described as virtuous. If a person strikes back
when he is struck, he is not virtuous. He is a sinner. We are virtuous
*brahmana*s. We should forgive. O son! In killing that lord of men,
there will be an extremely great sin. Therefore, I am trying to restrain
you now. Forgive and undertake austerities." O son of a king! His
father instructed him in this way. Understanding, Rama, the scorcher
of enemies, replied to his father, who always followed the conduct of
being forgiving. Parashurama replied, "O father! O immensely wise
one! Listen to what I am submitting now. For extremely great-souled
and virtuous people, you have instructed about peacefulness. That
peacefulness is for the virtuous, the distressed and those who can be
regarded as *guru*s and lords. However, one should not use peaceful

methods against those who are wicked in conduct. That does not lead to happiness. Hence, my task is to kill Kartavirya. O revered one! Please grant me permission to act in accordance with the enmity inside me." Jamadagni said, "O Rama! O immensely fortunate one! Listen attentively to my words. You will act in accordance with what is inevitable. It cannot but be otherwise. O son! Leave this place. Go to Brahma and ask him about what is beneficial and what is not. There is no doubt that you should act in accordance with what the lord instructs you." Thus addressed, the immensely intelligent one bowed down before his father.'

'He went to Brahma's world, impossible for ordinary people to reach. He saw Brahma's world, constructed with molten gold. All the ramparts and pillars were of gold, embedded with jewels. He saw the immensely energetic Brahma seated there. He was astride a beautiful bejewelled throne, decorated with gems. He was surrounded by Indras among *siddha*s and Indras among sages, immersed in *dhyana*. He was smiling happily, looking at the dancing *vidyadharis*.[1302] The lord was the one who bestowed the fruits of austerities, the creator of the worlds. In complete control of his mind, he was meditating on the *brahman*. To the group of devotees on every side, he was speaking about secret *yoga*. The descendant of the Bhrigu lineage saw the non-decaying one and devoutly prostrated himself. On seeing Rama, who had bent down, he greeted him and pronounced his benedictions. After enquiring about his welfare, he asked, "O child! Why have you come here?" Questioned by Vidhatri, Rama told him everything, from the beginning, about the conducts of Kartavirya and his own great-souled father. O one who bestows honours! He heard everything and ascertained the objective. Thereafter, he spoke to Rama, who was devoted to *dharma*, about what would lead to a happy consequence. "O child! In your rage, you have taken a pledge that will be extremely difficult to carry out. O young *brahmana*! Because of Bhagavan's favours, this creation became possible. O son! Following his command, with a great deal of effort, I created the universe. You have taken an oath that will lead to its destruction.

[1302] *Vidyadhara* is a learned, semi-divine species, *vidyadhari* is the feminine.

You desire to exterminate kings from the earth twenty-one times. That is because of the sin of a single king and because your father suffered. The eternal creation of *brahmana*s, *kshatriya*s, *vaishya*s and *shudra*s repeatedly originates from Hari and dissolves into him. Therefore, the pledge that you have already taken must fail. But there is a way whereby your task may easily meet with success. Go to Shiva's world and obtain Shiva's permission. There are many kings on earth who are Shankara's servants. Without the command of Lord Mahesha, who can kill them? They wear radiant armour on their limbs. They possess spears that are impossible to assail. Make efforts and seek methods to obtain the auspicious seed of victory. If one starts with the right method, everything one attempts can be accomplished. From your *guru*, Hara, accept the *kavacha* of Shri Krishna *mantra*.[1303] Without Shiva's strength, it is extremely difficult to vanquish Vishnu's energy. The *kavacha* named *trailokya-vijaya*[1304] is extremely wonderful. Inform Shankara about everything accurately and obtain what is extremely difficult to get. He is compassionate and affectionate towards those who are distressed. Pleased with you qualities, there is no doubt that he will also give the divine *pashupata* weapon.'"

Chapter 70-1(70)
(Parashurama receives the weapons)

Vasishtha said, 'Hearing Brahma's words, he prostrated himself before the *guru* of the universe. With an over-joyed mind, he went to Shiva's world. It was one hundred thousand *yojana*s above Brahma's world and could not be discerned or described. It was greater than the greatest and only *yogi*s could reach it. Vaikuntha's world was to its right and Gouri's world was to its

---

[1303] In general, *kavacha* means armour. More specifically, it is an amulet, over which, *mantra*s have been pronounced. Or the *mantra* itself is a *kavacha*.

[1304] Literally, conquest of the three worlds.

left. It was above all the worlds and Dhruv's world was above it. Because of the energy of his austerities, Rama went to Shiva's world and saw it. It was unmatched and was full of many kinds of curious objects. Indras among *yogi*s and *siddha*s who followed the auspicious Pashupata vow resided there. There were serene people, devoid of jealousy, who had earned good merits through crores of *kalpa*s of austerities. It was full of foremost trees like *parijata*.[1305] It was adorned with *kamadhenu*s. Using *yoga*, the *yogi* Shankara had created it, following his own will. Even the preceptor of artisans, Vishvakarma, had not seen it. There were hundreds of divine lakes, radiant with rubies. It was adorned and extremely beautiful, equipped with bejeweled altars. It was surrounded by ramparts, decorated with gold and jewels. It was extremely lofty, rising up to touch the sky. It was clear, with the hue of milk. There were four gates, adorned with bejeweled altars. There were red flights of stairs and bejeweled pillars and steps that led down into the water. It was decorated with many colourful paintings and was extremely charming. There was a beautiful residence in the centre, adorned with a principal gate.[1306] Rama, with *dharma* in his soul, saw it and was filled with wonder. He saw two gatekeepers stationed there and they were extremely terrible. Their teeth were extremely cruel. Their eyes were red and malformed. They were extremely strong and valiant and resembled mountains that had been burnt. Their limbs were smeared with ashes, and they were attired in garments made out of tiger-skin. They blazed with the energy of the *brahman* and held tridents and spears. On seeing them, his mind was slightly scared. Humbly, he said something. "I prostrate myself before you two lords. I have come here to see Shankara. Please ascertain Ishvara's command. Having obtained his permission, you should allow me to enter." Having heard his words, those two went and obtained Shiva's permission. Obtaining the permission, Ishvara's two companions permitted him to enter. Having obtained the permission, he happily entered the inner quarters. There, the *dvija* saw an extremely beautiful assembly-hall, full of large numbers

---

[1305] One of the five trees in heaven, the coral tree.

[1306] *Simhadvara*, lion-gate, the main gate.

of *siddha*s. Seeing this, filled with many kinds of fragrances, the
lord was filled with wonder. He saw the serene three-eyed Shiva
Chandrashekhara there. His hand was adorned with a trident and
his garment was an excellent tiger-skin. His limbs were smeared
with ashes and his sacred thread was made out of a *naga*. He was
delighted within his own *atman* and had accomplished all his desires.
His radiance was equal to that of one crore suns. He had five faces
and ten arms. This was an image that showed favours to devotees.
Using *tarka-mudra*,[1307] he was speaking about *yoga* and *jnana* to the
*siddha*s. He was being happily praised by the Indras among *yogi*s
and groups of *pramatha*s. He was surrounded by *bhairava*s and
*yogini*s and groups of Rudras. On seeing him, Rama was filled with
great delight. He lowered his head and prostrated himself. Kartikeya
was to his left and Ganeshvara to his right. Nandishvara, Mahakala
and Virabhadra were in front. He saw Durgaa, with one-hundred
arms, seated on his lap and prostrated himself before her too.'

'The learned lord started to praise him in faltering words. "I
prostrate myself before the lord Shiva Ishana. You are the one
who does not decay and pervades. You are fierce, with serpents
as ornaments. You wear a radiant garland of human skulls. You
are the creator of all the worlds, the one who undertakes creation,
preservation and destruction. You are the eldest one, assuming
the form of Brahma and the others. I know you as an ocean of
compassion. The *Veda*s are incapable of praising you. You cannot
be reached through speech or thoughts. You cannot be obtained
through *jnana* or intelligence. You are without form. I prostrate
myself before you. Shakra and the other large number of Gods,
*rishi*s, humans and *asura*s do not know the truth about you. I
prostrate myself before the one who is greater than the greatest.
All the worlds, with their mobile and immobile objects, are created
from your portion. The dissolve again into you. I prostrate myself
before the one who pervades the universe. The fire that results
from the slightest bit of your anger burns down everything, from

[1307] Literally, this means the posture adopted for debating and arguing.
The tip of the thumb touches the index finger. The other fingers are close
together and are held out straight. *Tarka-mudra* specifically refers to the
position of the hands, rather than the overall posture. It is also known as
jnana-mudra.

the upper worlds to the nether regions. I prostrate myself before
the supreme Hara. Your eight forms deserve to be worshipped by
the universe—as earth, wind, fire, water, space, the person who
performs a sacrifice, the moon and the sun. I prostrate myself before
the one who is the sacrifice. You assume the form of Kala. You are
the original creator of the universe. You are the preserver. In your
large and fierce form, you pervade the universe. At the end, you
assume the form of Rudra and destroy again. I seek refuge in your
form as Kala." Saying this, the delighted Bhargava eagerly fell down
at his feet. Playfully, the ocean of compassion raised him up with
his left hand and placed his other hand on his head. He greeted him
and uttered his blessings. Affectionately, he placed him in front of
Ganesha. The eyes of the one who fulfils every wish were wet with
compassion. He glanced at his wife Umaa and spoke. Shiva said,
"O *brahmana* boy! Who are you? Whose lineage have you been
born in? For what purpose have you come here? Please tell us. I am
pleased with your sentiments of devotion. I will grant you whatever
is in your mind." Hara is the one who removes the afflictions of the
universe. Lovingly, he spoke to the great-souled Bhrigu.'

'He bent down again before the lord and *guru* of the Gods,
the ocean of compassion, and spoke quickly. Parashurama said, "O
lord! I have been born in the Bhrigu lineage and am Jamadagni's
son. O one worshipped by the universe! My name is Rama and
I have sought refuge with you. O protector! I have come to your
presence to accomplish a certain task. O lord of the universe!
Please ensure the success of my desire. King Kartavirya arrived on
a hunt. O divinity! My father, Jamadagni, treated him as an *atithi*.
As a result of his greed and strength, the king, evil in intelligence,
brought him down. Seeing that he was dead, the cow went away
to the world of cows. The king felt no grief at the death of my
innocent father. He left for his own city. Thereafter, my mother
wept bitterly. Our great ancestor, Bhrigu, who knows about the
affairs of the world, got to know about this. O Mahadeva! He
arrived there and I too returned from the forest. He knows about
*mantra*s. Along with me, he comforted my mother and brothers,
who were grieving a lot. He also revived my father. Before Bhrigu
arrived, I became enraged at my mother's sorrow. O divinity! To
comfort my mother, I took a pledge. My mother had struck herself

twenty-one times. Therefore, I resolved to exterminate *kshatriyas*
from earth that number of times. O divinity! O lord of the universe!
Please ensure that this is done. Mahadeva is the protector. That is
the reason I have come to your presence." Hearing these words,
Mahadeva glanced towards Durgaa's face. He lowered his face and
thought for a while. Meanwhile, Durgaa was surprised and laughed
a lot. O great king! She spoke to Bhargava, whose mind was fixed
on enmity. "You are the son of a *dvija* and an ascetic. O great
brahmana boy! In your rage and rashness, you wish to eliminate
kings from earth twenty-one times. Without any weapons, you wish
to kill the lord Arjuna, who possesses one thousand arms. Through
the playful furrowing of his eyebrows, even Ravana was rebuffed.
In ancient times, Shri Hari gave him a *kavacha* and a spear that
possesses excessive energy. How do you desire to kill him? The
Lord Shankara is an ocean of compassion and can act to counter
these. O son! Other than Ishvara Shankara, no one else is capable of
performing this virtuous task." Shambhu, ocean of compassion, thus
obtained Devi's permission. The lord addressed Jamadagni's son in
these compassionate words. Shiva said, "O *brahmana*! From today,
you will become like Skanda to me. O immensely intelligent one! I
will give you a *mantra* and a divine *kavacha*. Through this favour,
you will be able to playfully kill Kartavirya. You will also empty the
earth of kings twenty-one times." Saying this, Shankara gave him
a *mantra* that is extremely difficult to obtain. He also gave him the
extremely wonderful *kavacha* named *Trailokya-vijaya*, the noose
of *naga*s, the Pashupata weapon, Brahmastra, which is extremely
difficult to obtain, Narayanastra, Agneyastra, Vayavyastra,
Varunastra, Gandharvastra, Garudastra, the extremely wonderful
Jrimbhanastra, a club, a spear, a battle-axe, a trident, an excellent
staff and all the aggregate of *shastra*s and *astras*.[1308] He was
delighted and prostrated himself before the serene Shiva, Durgaa,
Skanda and Ganeshvara. Circumambulating them, Rama went to

[1308] *Trailokya-vijaya* is a weapon that allows the possessor to conquer
the three worlds. These are divine weapons, named after Brahma, Narayana,
Agni, Vayu, Varuna, the *gandharva*s and Garuda. Pashupata is Shiva's own
weapon. Jrimbhanastra makes the opponent yawn and go to sleep.

the supreme *tirtha* of Pushkara and consecrated the *mantra* stated by Shiva and the excellent *kavacha*. The descendant of the Bhrigu lineage accomplished everything he had set out to do. He killed Kartavirya, his soldiers and his family. Delighted, the descendant of the Bhrigu lineage returned to his own father's house.'

Chapter 71-1(71) (Trailokya-vijaya *mantra*)

S agara said, 'O best among sages! O lord! I have heard everything that you have spoken about. Please tell me about the *Trailokya-vijaya kavacha*, that bestows victory everywhere.'

Vashishta replied, 'O child! Listen. I will tell you about this exceedingly wonderful *kavacha* and about the *mantra* that brings eternal *siddhi* to *sadhakas*, bestowing happiness. At the end of the *pada*, one must utter, "To Gopijana-Vallabha".[1309] The great *mantra* has ten *aksharas* and must end with "*svaha*". It bestows objects of pleasure and emancipation. The *rishi* is Sadashiva and the *chhanda* is said to be *pankti*.[1310] The divinity is Krishna and it is recited and used to obtain everything. The *rishi* for *Trailokya-*

[1309] *Gopa* is a cowherd. *Gopi* is the feminine. Gopijana-Vallabha is the one loved by *gopis*, that is, Krishna. Since Krishna and Rama were later *avataras*, there is a chronological issue. It is possible that these sections, especially those on Krishna, were added to the text subsequently. Not only is there a reference to Krishna, Radhaa is also mentioned.

[1310] Each *mantra* has a *rishi* who composed it and a divinity to whom it is addressed. The *pankti chhanda* has ten *aksharas* in every *pada*. The text leads to confusion between a *mantra* to Krishna and the *Trailokya-vijaya kavacha*. The Krishna *mantra*, in *pankti chhanda*, is simply—Gopijana-Vallabhaya Svaha, 'To the one loved by Gopis, Svaha.' The rest can be taken to be *Trailokya-vijaya*, composed in *jagati*. However, the classic *jagati chhanda* should have twelve *aksharas* in every *pada*. As stated in the text, this has sixteen *aksharas* and is actually *ashti chhanda*. *Anga-nyasa* is the mental appropriation (*nyasa*) of different limbs of the body (*anga*) to different divinities. *Kara-nyasa* is similarly done to different parts of the hand (*kara*). In this *mantra*, *anga-nyasa* acts as the *kavacha*. In addition, the *kavacha* is worn as an amulet.

vijaya kavacha is Prajapati. The *chhanda* is *jagati* and the divinity is Rajeshvara himself. It is said that it should be used to conquer the three worlds.'

'"Let Pranava protect my head. I always prostrate myself before Shri Krishna. Let him always protect my forehead. To Krishna. *Svaha*. Let Krishna protect the pupils of my eyes. To Krishna. *Svaha*. Let him always protect my eyebrows. To Hari. *Namah*. Let him always protect my nose. OUM. To Govinda. *Svaha*. Let this always protect my cheek. I prostrate myself before Gopala. Let the *kalpa-taru* protect my ears. *Kleem*.[1311] To Krishna. *Namah*. Let him always protect my two lips. *Shreem*. To Krishna. *Namah*. Let him protect my rows of teeth. OUM. To the lord of *gopi*s. *Svaha*. Let these three *akshara*s of "Shri Krishna" protect the gaps between my teeth. Let him always protect my tongue. OUM. To Shri Krishna. *Svaha*. Let him always protect my palate. To Rameshvara. *Svaha*. Let him always protect my throat. To Radhikaa's lord. *Svaha*. Let him always protect my neck. To the lord of all the *gopi*s. *Namah*. Let him always protect my shoulders. OUM. To the lord of *gopa*s. *Svaha*. Let him protect my back. To the one who assumed a boy's form. *Namah*. *Svaha*. Let this always protect my stomach. To Mukunda. *Namah*. *Hreem*. *Shreem*. *Kleem*. To Krishna. *Svaha*. Let him always protect my hands. OUM. To Vishnu. *Namah*. *Svaha*. Let him protect my two arms. OUM. *Hreem*. To Bhagavan. *Svaha*. Let him protect my row of nails. To Narayana. *Namah*. Let him protect the gaps between my nails. OUM. *Hreem*. *Shreem*. To Padmanabha. Let him always protect my navel. OUM. To the lord of everything. *Svaha*. Let him always protect my hair. *Namah*. To Krishna. *Svaha*. Let him always protect my *brahmarandhra*.[1312] OUM. To Madhava. *Svaha*. Let him always protect my forehead. OUM. *Hreem*. *Shrem*. To the lord of *rasika*s.[1313] Let him always protect my waist. *Namah*.

[1311] These are *bija-mantra*s, each with a single *akshara*—क्लीम्, श्रीम्, ह्रीम्. Each of these has three *varna*s and each of these *varna*s possesses mystical significance.

[1312] *Brahmarandhra* is the centre of the brain and *sahasrara chakra* is located inside *brahmarandhra*.

[1313] A *rasika* is a graceful person, a person who possesses taste.

To the lord of all *gopis*. Let him always protect my thighs. OUM.
Namah. To the destroyer of *daityas*. *Svaha*. Let him protect my
knees. To Yashoda's delight. *Namah*. Let him protect my calves. To
the one who loves the pleasure of *rasa*.[1314] *Svaha*. Let him protect
my modesty. To Vrindaa's[1315] beloved. *Svaha*. Let him protect all
my limbs. Whole-heartedly, let Krishna always protect me in the
east. Let the lord of Goloka himself protect me in the south-east. Let
the one who is the form of the complete *brahman* always protect
me in the south. Let Krishna protect me in the south-west. Let Hari
protect me in the west. Let Govinda protect me in the north-west.
Let the lord of *rasikas* protect me in the north. Let the one who
sports in Vrindavana always protect me in the north-east. Let the
lord of Vrindaa's life always protect me in an upwards direction. Let
the one who destroyed the immensely strong Bani always protect
me in a downward direction. Let Nrisimha always protect me in
the water, on land and in the sky. Let Madhava himself protect me
when I am asleep and when I am awake. Let the unattached lord,
present in all *atmans*, protect me in all directions." O lord of the
earth! This is said to destroy every kind of sin. This is the *kavacha*
named *Trailokya-vijaya*.'

'I have heard it from the mouth of Shiva Paramesha. It
should never be revealed to anyone. After worshipping the *guru*,
the *kavacha* must be worn in the proper way, around the neck,
or on the right hand. There is no doubt that a person who does
this, becomes like Vishnu himself. If a person is such a *sadhaka*, the
Goddesses of speech and wealth also reside with him. If a person
succeeds in wearing such a *kavacha*, there is no doubt that he is like
a *jivanmukta*.[1316] It has been determined that he obtains fruits equal
to those obtained through crores of years of worship. Thousands of
royal sacrifices, hundreds of horse sacrifices, all the great donations
and *pradakshina* of the earth do not earn even one-sixteenth of the
merits obtained through *Trailokya-vijaya*. Vows, fasting, *niyamas*,

1314 The festival and dance of *gopas* and *gopis*.
1315 Vrindaa is Radhikaa's name, but can also be interpreted as a
multitude.
1316 A person who has been emancipated, though he is alive.

studying, teaching and bathing in all the *tirtha*s do not earn even a fraction of the merits. Becoming a *siddha*, becoming immortal and obtaining the status of Sri Hari's servant—there is no doubt that all these are obtained if one successfully wears the *kavacha*. If a person performs *japa* one million times, he becomes successful in wearing the *kavacha*. If a person wears the *kavacha* successfully, there is no doubt that he is victorious. O lord of the earth! O child! A kingdom can be given away. A head can be given away. The breath of life can be given away. But even in a calamity, this *kavacha* must never be given away. For the sake of saving you, I have revealed this. O one who brings radiance to your lineage! Follow my command and understand. Wear this *kavacha* and become a *chakravarti*.'

Chapter 72-1(72) (The stag and the doe)

Sagara asked, 'O Brahma's son! O immensely fortunate one! You have done a great favour to me. You have revealed this unblemished *kavacha* to me. Ourva showed me his favours and I obtained all the weapons through him.[1317] O lord! I have now become a recipient of your compassion. How was the brave King Kartavirya destroyed by Rama, Indra among Bhargavas? Please describe this to me in detail. The king was the recipient of favours from Datta,[1318] while Rama obtained favours from Shiva. O *guru*! How did those two valiant ones face each other in the battle?'

Vasishtha replied, 'O king! Listen. I will tell you about the conduct of King Kartavirya and the great-souled Rama. This destroys sins. Rama received the *kavacha* and the *mantra* from his *guru*'s mouth. Full of supreme devotion, he followed the *sadhana*. He slept on the ground, bathed thrice a day and observed the *sandhya* rites. Attentive, Rama resided in Pushkara for one hundred years. O king! Generally, Akritavrana gathered kindling, flowers, *kusha* and other objects from the forest, brought them and gave them to Bhargava.

[1317] The sage Ourva was King Sagara's teacher.
[1318] Dattatreya.

Rama, supreme among intelligent ones, was always engaged in *dhyana*. He worshipped Lord Krishna, who destroys all sins. Rama performed sacrifices to the lord of the universe. One hundred years passed in this way and he was always engaged in *dhyana*.'

'O great king! On one occasion, to bathe, Rama went to the centre of the great Pushkara and witnessed a great wonder there. A stag came there, along with a doe, and they were running. They were chased by a hunter on a hunt. He[1319] was scorched by the heat and was suffering greatly. O immensely fortunate one! He was thirsty and was eager to drink some water. As Rama watched, he arrived at the shore of the lake. He was followed by the scared doe, the possessor of darting eyes. Scared in their minds, both of them drank the water there. At that time, the hunter arrived there, with a bow and arrows in his hands. He saw Rama, the descendant of the Bhargava lineage, stationed there. Akritavrana was also there, but he was looking far away. He[1320] was scared of the descendant of the Bhrigu lineage and thought. "This Rama is immensely valiant and destroys the wicked. While he is watching, how can I kill the stag and the doe?" O excellent king! Filled with such thoughts, the hunter remained there. On account of Rama, his mind was scared. Rama saw the scared stag and doe drink water. The intelligent one debated, "Where is the reason for fear here? There is no roar from a tiger and no hunter can be seen. What is the reason for their fear and why are their eyes darting? Perhaps the deer species has been created with such darting eyes. That is the reason they are glancing with darting eyes, even while they are drinking water. There is no other reason here. Why are they distressed and filled with fear? It can be discerned that their limbs are suffering and they are trembling." In the centre of Lake Pushkara, the intelligent one thought in this way. Along with a *shishya*,[1321] Rama was stationed there. As long as they were there, those two drank water and sought refuge under the shade of a tree. Seeing the great-souled Rama, they happily conversed with each other. The doe said, "O beloved! As long as Rama is stationed

---

[1319] The stag, not the hunter.
[1320] The hunter.
[1321] Akritavrana.

here, let us also remain here. In the presence of this brave one, we need not suffer from any fear. Even if the hunter arrives here and seeks to strike us, the mere glance of the sage will reduce him to ashes." Hearing the doe's words, the stag looked at Rama and was satisfied. Full of delight, it spoke to its own beloved. "O immensely fortunate one! O beautiful one! It is exactly as you have said. I also know about the powers of the extremely great-souled Rama. The person who can be seen by his side is his *shishya*, Akritavrana. That immensely fortunate one had also been terrified and afflicted, as a result of the fear of a tiger. O immensely fortunate one! This Rama is Jamadagni's youngest son. He saw that his father had suffered at the hands of Kartavirya. Extremely angry, he has taken a pledge to kill the king. To accomplish that task, he had earlier gone to Brahma's world. Instructed by Brahma, he had gone to Shiva's world. Having taken Shiva's permission, he had approached Shiva's presence. He had told him everything about the conduct of the king and his own father. Full of compassion, Mahadeva had greeted the descendant of the Bhrigu lineage and had given him Krishna's *mantra* and the impenetrable *kavacha*. He had also given him his own Pashupata weapon and the collection of other *astra*s. Having affectionately given him the weapons, he had lovingly released him. O fortunate one! Intent on undertaking *sadhana* with the *mantra*, he has come here. The intelligent one, with *dharma* in his soul, constantly performs *japa* with Krishna's *kavacha*. While the extremely great-souled one has been doing this, one hundred years have passed. O fortunate one! However, in performing *sadhana* with the *mantra*, he has still not obtained *siddhi*. There is a reason for this. O one with the liquid eyes! It is held that there are three types of *bhakti*—superior, middling and inferior. Uttama *bhakti* is that of Shiva, Narada, the great-souled Shuka, *rajarshi* Ambarisha, Rantideva, Maruti,[1322] Bali, Vibhishana, the great-souled Prahlada, the *gopi*s and Uddhava. O one with the auspicious eyes! Middling *bhakti* is that of Vasishtha and other lords among sages and Manu and others. Inferior *bhakti* is shown by ordinary people. Though he constantly practices *yama*, Rama is only devoted to the middling

---

[1322] Hanuman.

kind of *bhakti*. Since he has not served the lord of *gopi*s in this way, he has not obtained *siddhi*." At being told this by its beloved, the doe was delighted in its mind and immediately asked about the characteristics of *bhakti* that gives rise to love.'

'The doe asked, "O virtuous one! O beloved! O immensely fortunate one! O dear ones! Your words are out of this world. How did you come to acquire this kind of *jnana*? Please tell me about that now." The stag replied, "O beloved! O immensely fortunate one! Listen. Such *jnana* results from meritorious deeds. On seeing Bhargava today, those good merits have been generated in me. This Bhargava is auspicious in his *atman*. He is devoted to Krishna and has conquered his senses. He always serves his *guru* and lovingly performs the *nitya* and *naimittika* rites. O beautiful one! That is the reason why, on seeing him today, the *jnana* has been generated in me. Concerning all beings in the three worlds, this indicates the nature of auspiciousness and inauspiciousness. Thus, I got to know about the great-souled Rama's conduct today. If one hears about it, one obtains the auspicious and sins are destroyed. Whatever he will do, also comes under the purview of that *jnana*. There is *bhakti* that is known as superior. Without it, even with the *mantra* and the *kavacha*, one will not obtain *siddhi* in millions and millions of years. O fortunate one! When Bhargava receives Agastya's favours, he will obtain the *stotram* known as Krishna-*premamrita*.[1323] That bestows superior *bhakti*. Knowing this, he will obtain *siddhi* for the *mantra* and the *kavacha*. The sage knows the truth about this. He is full of compassion and grants freedom from fear. He will instruct him about the truth of that *jnana*, which brings happiness. The immensely intelligent one will get to know about the *stotram* known as Krishna-*premamrita*. All its units are made out of Shri Krishna's conduct. Having thus obtained *siddhi* with the *kavacha*, he will kill the king who is the lord of the Haihayas, along with his sons, advisers, well-wishers, soldiers and mounts. O beloved! He will eliminate kings from the earth twenty-one times." O king! Having told the doe this, the stag stopped. He also came to know about the reasons why he had become a deer.'

[1323] Full of the *amrita* of love towards Krishna.

Chapter 73-1(73) (Parashurama visits Agastya)

Sagara said, 'O sage! O one who knows about the supreme truth!
So one who knows about the purport of *dhyana* and *jnana* and
about those whose minds are immersed in *bhakti* towards Bhagavan!
Please show me your favours. O immensely fortunate one! You are
praised because you narrate virtuous accounts. Having heard all
this about Bhargava's conduct from the mouth of the stag, about
the past, present and future and about Narayana's account, what
did the doe ask again? O lord! Please tell me about that in detail.'

Vasishtha replied, 'O king! Listen. I will narrate the stag's great
account. Since it knew about the truth, it described everything
the doe asked. Having heard about the great-souled Bhargava's
conduct, the doe lovingly again asked its beloved about the true
meaning of *jnana*. The doe said, "This is praiseworthy. This is
laudable. O immensely fortunate one! There is no doubt that you
have been successful. Through seeing him, *jnana* that is beyond
the senses has been generated in you. Therefore, tell me everything
about the reasons behind you and me. O lord! As a result of what
karma have we obtained birth as inferior species?" Hearing the
words spoken by its beloved, the stag described its own conduct
and that of the doe.'

'The stag said, "O beloved! O immensely fortunate one! Hear
about the reasons why we have become deer. O immensely fortunate
one! In *samsara*, it is nature that is the cause behind existence. For
a living being, the nature of virtuous and wicked *karma* determines
the appearance of memory. Earlier, in the country of Dravida, I was
born in a family of *brahmana*s, possessing many kinds of prosperity.
My *gotra* was Koushika. My father was named Shivadatta and he
was accomplished in all the sacred texts. Four of us were born as his
sons and we were excellent *dvija*s. The eldest was Rama. Dharma
was younger to him and Prithu was younger to Dharma. O beloved!
I was born as the fourth and was known by the name of Suri. In
the due order, the immensely illustrious Shivadatta performed our
sacred thread ceremonies. He taught us the *Veda*s and *Vedanga*s,
along with all their mysteries. There, all four of us were engaged in

studying the Vedas. Devoted to *jnana*, we were engaged in serving our *guru*. We went to the forest and brought back flowers, water, kindling, *kusha* grass and clay. Having brought these back, we gave to our father and studied. On one occasion, all of us reached a mountain in the forest. O one with bewitching eyes! It was named Oudbhida and it was on the banks of River Kritamala. It was dawn and all of us bathed in the great river. Pleased in our minds, we offered *arghya*, performed *japa* and climbed that excellent mountain. There were *shala, tamala, priyaka, panasa, kovidara, sarala, arjuna, puga, kharjura, narikela, jambu, sahakara, katphala* and *brihati* trees.[1324] There were many other kinds of trees and these trees existed for the sake of others. They possessed pleasant shade and were full of the delighted calls of many kinds of birds. The caves were frequented by tigers, lions, bears, rhinoceroses, musk-deer, gigantic elephants, *sharabhas* and others. There were *mallika*,[1325] *patala, kunda, karnikara, kadamba* and other flowers. The wind carried their fragrances far away. Groups of many kinds of jewels were strewn around, blue, yellow, white and red. The peaks seemed to playfully etch against the sky. From inside crevices, waterfalls descended from lofty tops, with a loud roar. The place was frequented by many kinds of predatory beasts, small animals and birds. We brothers saw these curious objects and were delighted. It was as if we no longer remembered ourselves and got separated from each other. Meanwhile, a doe arrived there, very thirsty. O beloved! It desired to drink water from the top of a waterfall. As it was drinking water, roaming around as it willed, an extremely terrible tiger arrived there. It seized the doe, which was afflicted by fear. On seeing that it had been seized, I fled in fear. I fell down from above and as I died, I remembered the doe. Having died, the doe was born as you. Since I remembered the doe, I was born as a stag. O fortunate one! Though I have been born, I do not know where my elder brothers have gone. I have remembered this, about your conduct and mine.

[1324] *Priyaka* is the same as *priyangu*, *puga* is areca nut, *narikela* is coconut, *sahakara* is the same as mango, *katphala* is the bayberry tree and *brihati* is a medicinal plant.
[1325] A kind of jasmine.

O fortunate one! I will tell you not only about the past, but the future too. Listen. There was a hunter who closely followed us from the rear. Since he feared Rama, he maintained his distance. He has now been devoured by a lion. Following destiny, he has given up his life. He has gone to heaven.[1326] We have drunk water from the centre of Pushkara. In addition, we have seen this Bhargava, who is Vishnu's form himself. Hence, the sins we committed across many births have been destroyed. We will see Agastya. We will hear the *stotram* that bestows the right destination. We will go to the auspicious worlds and nowhere else. After going there, no one grieves." The stag, handsome to behold, spoke in this way to its beloved and stopped. It looked at Rama, was pleased in its mind and no longer suffered.'

'Along with his *shishya*, Bhargava heard what the stag had said. O Indra among kings! He was amazed. With Akritavrana, he made up his mind to go to Agastya's hermitage. He bathed and performed the daily rites. Very happy, he departed. As he travelled along the path, Rama saw the dead hunter, killed by a lion. The great-souled one was astounded. He travelled half a *yojana* in the direction of the smaller Pushkara. He happily performed his midday ablutions and *sandhya* rites. He reflected and decided that the stag had spoken about what was beneficial for him. The stag and doe followed him at the rear. They too drank water in Pushkara and sprinkled their bodies with water. As Bhargava looked at them, they also headed in the direction of Agastya's hermitage. Having performed his *sandhya* rites, Rama reached Kumbhaja's hermitage.[1327] The great-minded one was worried that Pushkara was in bad shape.[1328] As he proceeded, he touched the water and purified himself at the *tirtha*s of Vishnupada and the sacrificial pit of *naga*s, established by *saptarshi*s. O king! He went and sought refuge in Agastya's hermitage, the place at which Sarasvati, Brahma's daughter, arrived, to fill three wells, so that Vidhatri could perform *agnihotra*. There

---

[1326] Since he did not kill the stag and doe.

[1327] Agastya was born from a pot (kumbha) and is therefore known as Kumbhaja.

[1328] It was probably drying up.

were many sages who resided along its sacred and auspicious banks.
Bhargava saw the great wonder of Kumbhaja's hermitage. It was
populated by deer and lions together, tranquil in their minds. It was
full of trees like *kutaja, arjuna, nimba, paribhadra, dhava, inguda,
khadira, asana, kharjura* and *badari*.[1329] With Akritavrana, Rama
entered. He saw the sage Kumbhaja seated, serene in his mind.
Meditating on the eternal *brahman*, he resembled a placid lake. The
cottage for his residence was made out of tender leaves and he wore
a deer skin. He was seated on a mat of *vrishi*, over which, a piece of
silk cloth has been spread.[1330] O great king! He prostrated himself
and recited his own name. "I am Rama, Jamadagni's son. I have
come here to see you. O one who purifies the world! Know this
from my act of prostration. I bow down." When Rama said this,
he opened his eyes slowly. He looked at him and uttering words of
welcome, he instructed him to take a seat. The bull among sages
asked a *shishya* to bring *madhuparka*.[1331] Offering this, he asked
about his welfare and that of his family and about his austerities.
Thus asked, Rama replied to the one who had originated from a pot.
"O lord! Now that I have seen you, all is well with me. However,
a doubt has been generated in me. Through your words, which are
like *amrita*, please dispel it. O lord! In the centre of Pushkara, I saw
a stag. It recounted everything about me, the past and the future.
Hearing that, I was filled with wonder and have come and sought
refuge with you. O lord! Please save me. Show me your compassion,
so that I can be successful with the great mantra. O *guru*! Shiva
gave me Krishna's *kavacha*. Please ensure success in that too. I have
been striving for more than one hundred years. However, I have
not obtained *siddhi*. Therefore, please show me your compassion
and tell me about it." O great king! Hearing the question asked by
the extremely great-souled Rama, he meditated for a while and, in
his heart, understood what the stag had said. He also knew that

[1329] *Kutaja* is a kind of coral tree, *paribhadra* is another name for
devadaru, *asana* is the Indian laurel and *badari* is the jujube tree.
[1330] *Vrishi* is an ascetic's seat, made out of *kusha* grass.
[1331] *Madhuparka* is a mixture of honey and water, customarily offered
to a guest.

the stag and doe had come to his own hermitage, to hear about Krishna's *stotram*, which was like *amrita*. The sage reflected on the reasons and comforted Bhargava with his own words, which were like *amrita*.'

Chapter 74-1(74) (Krishnamrita *stotram*)

Vasishta said, 'Agastya, born from a pot, got to know about all the reasons. Pleased in his mind, he spoke to Bhargava Rama. Agastya said, "O Rama! O immensely fortunate one! Listen. I will speak words that will be beneficial for you. You will thereby swiftly gain *siddhi* in the *mantra*. O immensely wise one! You have already got to know about the three signs of *bhakti*. If a man strives with these, he quickly obtains success. Once, desiring to see Ananta, I reached Patala, adorned by the Indras among kings of *naga*s. O immensely fortunate one! There, full of great joy, I saw the siddhas in every direction— Sanaka and the others, Narada, Goutama, Jajali, Kratu, Ribhu, Hamsa, Aruni, Valmiki, Shakti and Asuri. O *dvija*! There were other great *siddha*s, Vatsyayana being the foremost. For the sake of *jnana*, they were seated near the lord of hooded ones and were worshipping him. O immensely fortunate one! To happily hear about Vishnu's accounts, this earth, who sustains beings, was also seated there, in her own form, along with the Indras among *naga*s and great-souled *siddha*s, who were bowing down before him. She was seated in front of him, always listening to the accounts attentively. Whenever the earth asked Shesha, who holds up the earth, something, he showed her his favours and answered, while all the *rishi*s heard. O child! I heard about the auspicious Krishna-*premamrita stotram* there. I will describe it to you. That is the reason you have come here. The earth had just heard about the conduct of Varaha *avatara*, one that destroys sins. It bestows happiness and emancipation and is responsible for *jnana* and *vijnana*. O child! Having heard everything, the earth was delighted and prostrated herself before the one who holds up the earth. Wishing to know about Krishna's conduct, she asked again.

The earth said, 'He ornamented the lives of all men who resided in Nanda's Vraja.[1332] In his pastimes, the divinity, Krishna, assumed a body there. He has many names, indicating his diverse victories. Without any delay, I wish to hear about the most important names. O Vasuki![1333] Please tell me about Vasudeva's names. In the three worlds, there is nothing more meritorious.' Shesha replied, 'O earth! O one with the beautiful hips! O Goddess! I will tell you one hundred and eight names. Listen. They bestow emancipation on people. They represent the pinnacle of everything auspicious. They bestow the eight kinds of *siddhi*, *anima* and others. They destroy crores of major sins and yield fruits equal to those obtained by visiting all the *tirtha*s. They destroy sins and bestow the fruits of every kind of *japa* and *yajna*. If one recites Krishna's names once, the fruits are the same as those obtained by chanting the sacred names of the three[1334] one thousand times. Hence, this *stotram* is the most sacred and destroys sins. O dear one! For these one hundred and eight names, I am the *rishi*. The *chhanda* is *anushtup*.[1335] The divinity is *yoga*. It brings pleasure to Krishna.'"

" '(1) Shri Krishna;[1336] (2) Kamalanatha;[1337] (3) Vasudeva; (4) Sanatana;[1338] (5) Vasudevatmaja;[1339] (6) Punya;[1340] (7) Lila-manusha-vigraha;[1341] (8) Shrivatsa-Koustubha-dhara;[1342] (9) Yashoda-

---

[1332] Vraja is a place where cows reside. This is the region where Krishna resided, during his childhood.

[1333] Ananta and Vasuki are not the same. They are brothers. This should really read Ananta/Shesha.

[1334] Presumably meaning Brahma, Vishnu and Shiva.

[1335] With eight *akshara*s in every *pada*.

[1336] The numbering doesn't exist in the text. We have added it. Though we have explained the names, a proper understanding requires familiarity with Krishna's life-story.

[1337] Lord of Kamalaa (Lakshmi).

[1338] Eternal one.

[1339] Vasudeva's son.

[1340] Sacred one.

[1341] One who has playfully assumed a human body.

[1342] One who wears Shrivatsa and the Koustubha jewel. Shrivatsa is the curl of hair on Krishna/Vishnu's chest, the place where Shri resides.

vatsala;[1343] (10) Hari; (11) Chaturbhujatta-chakra-asi-gada-shankhadyudayudha;[1344] (12) Devaki-nandana;[1345] (13) Shrisha;[1346] (14) Nandagopa-priyatmaja;[1347] (15) Yamuna-vega-samhari;[1348] (16) Balabhadra-priyanuja:[1349] (17) Putana-jivitahara;[1350] (18) Shakatasura-bhanjana;[1351] (19) Nanda-Vraja-janananandin;[1352] (20) Sacchidananda-vigraha;[1353] (21) Navanita-viliptanga;[1354] (22) Navanita-nata;[1355] (23) Anagha;[1356] (24) Navanita-lavahari;[1357] (25) Muchukunda-prasadakrit;[1358] (26) Shodasha-stri-sahasresha;[1359] (27) Tribhangi;[1360] (28) Madhurakriti;[1361] (29) Shuka-vagamritabdhindu;[1362] (30) Govinda; (31) Govindampati;[1363] (32) Vatsa-palana-sanchari;[1364] (33) Dhenukasura-mardana;[1365] (34) Trinikrita-Trinavarta;[1366] (35) Yamalarjuna-bhanjana;[1367]

[1343] Loved by Yashoda.
[1344] One who has raised the weapons of *chakra*, a sword, a mace and a conch-shell in his four hands.
[1345] Devaki's delight.
[1346] Shri's lord.
[1347] Nandagopa's beloved son.
[1348] One who restrained Yamuna's powerful flow.
[1349] Balabhadra's beloved younger brother.
[1350] One who took away Putana's life.
[1351] One who destroyed the *asura* in the form of a cart.
[1352] One who delights the people of Nanda's Vraja.
[1353] One whose form consists of truth, consciousness and bliss.
[1354] One whose limbs are smeared with butter.
[1355] One who dances for butter.
[1356] Sinless one.
[1357] One who takes away a *lava* of butter.
[1358] One who showed favours to Muchukunda.
[1359] Lord of 16,000 women.
[1360] One in *tribhanga* form, with three parts of the body (neck, wrists, knees) bent.
[1361] With a sweet form.
[1362] The moon that rises from the ocean of *amrita* that is Shuka's speech.
[1363] Lord of those who know about cows.
[1364] One who moves around, protecting calves.
[1365] One who crushed Dhenukasura.
[1366] One who reduced Trinavarta to a blade of grass.
[1367] One who broke the two *arjuna* trees.

(36) Uttala-talabheta;[1368] (37) Tamala-shyamalakriti;[1369] (38)
Gopa-gopishvara;[1370] (39) Yogi; (40) Surya-koti-samaprabha;[1371]
(41) Ilapati;[1372] (42) Paramjyoti;[1373] (43) Yadavendra;[1374]
(44) Yadudvaha;[1375] (45) Vanamali;[1376] (46) Pitavasa;[1377] (47)
Parijatapaharaka;[1378] (48) Govardhanachaloddharta;[1379] (49)
Gopala; (50) Sarva-palaka;[1380] (51) Aja;[1381] (52) Niranjana;[1382]
(53) Kamajanaka;[1383] (54) Kanjalochana;[1384] (55) Madhuha;[1385]
(56) Mathuranatha;[1386] (57) Dvarakanatha;[1387] (58) Bali;[1388] (59)
Vrindavananta-sanchari;[1389]   (60)   Tulasi-dama-bhushana;[1390]
(61) Syamantaka-manerharta;[1391] (62) Nara-Narayanatmaka;[1392]
(63) Kubjakrishtambara-dhara;[1393] (64) Mayi;[1394] (65) Parama-
purusha;[1395]   (66)   Mushtikasura-Chanura-mallayuddha-

[1368] One who broke the tall palm tree.
[1369] With a form that is as dark as a *tamala* tree.
[1370] Lord of *gopa*s and *gopi*s.
[1371] As radiant as one crore suns.
[1372] Lord of the earth (Ilaa).
[1373] Supreme radiance.
[1374] Indra among Yadavas.
[1375] One who extended the Yadu lineage.
[1376] With a garland of wild flowers.
[1377] With yellow garments.
[1378] One who took away the *parijata* tree.
[1379] One who raised up Mount Govardhana.
[1380] One who protects everything/everyone.
[1381] Without birth.
[1382] Without blemish.
[1383] Kama's (Pradyumna's) father.
[1384] With eyes like a lotus.
[1385] Destroyer of Madhu.
[1386] Lord of Mathura.
[1387] Lord of Dvaraka.
[1388] Strong one.
[1389] One who roams around in the outskirts of Vrindavana.
[1390] Decorated with a garland of *tulasi* (the holy basil).
[1391] One who took away the Syamantaka jewel.
[1392] With Nara and Narayana in his *atman*.
[1393] One who was attracted by Kubja and wore her garments.
[1394] Possessor of *maya*.
[1395] Supreme being.

visharada;[1396] (67) Samsara-vairi;[1397] (68) Kamsari;[1398] (69) Murari;[1399] (70) Narakantaka;[1400] (71) Anadi-brahmachari;[1401] (72) Krishnavyasana-karshaka;[1402] (73) Shishupala-shirashchetta;[1403] (74) Duryodhana-kulantakrit;[1404] (75) Vidurakrura-varada;[1405] (76) Vishvarupa-pradarshaka;[1406] (77) Satyavak;[1407] (78) Satya-sankalpa;[1408] (79) Satyabhama-rata;[1409] (80) Jayi;[1410] (81) Subhadra-purvaja;[1411] (82) Vishnu;[1412] (83) Bhishma-mukti-pradayaka;[1413] (84) Jagadguru;[1414] (85) Jagannatha;[1415] (86) Venu-vadya-visharada;[1416] (87) Vrishabhasura-vidhvamsi;[1417] (88) Bakari;[1418] (89) Bana-bahukrit;[1419] (90) Yudhishthira-pratishthata;[1420] (91) Barhi-barhavatamsaka;[1421] (92) Parthasarathi;[1422] (93) Avyakta;[1423]

[1396] Skilled in wrestling with Mushtikasura and Chanura.
[1397] Enemy of *samsara*.
[1398] Kamsa's enemy.
[1399] Mura's enemy.
[1400] Destroyer of Naraka.
[1401] A *brahmachari* who has no beginning.
[1402] One who destroyed Krishnaa's (Droupadi's) hardships.
[1403] One who severed Shishupala's head.
[1404] One who ended Duryodhana's lineage.
[1405] One who bestowed boons on Vidura and Akrura.
[1406] One who revealed the universal form.
[1407] Truthful in speech.
[1408] Truthful in resolution.
[1409] Devoted to Satyabhama.
[1410] Victorious one.
[1411] Subhadra's elder brother.
[1412] One who enters everywhere.
[1413] One who bestowed emancipation on Bhishma.
[1414] *Guru* of the universe.
[1415] Lord of the universe.
[1416] One skilled in playing the flute.
[1417] One who destroyed Vrishabha (in the form of a bull) *asura*.
[1418] Baka's enemy.
[1419] One who severed Bana's arms.
[1420] One who established Yudhishthira.
[1421] Adorned with peacock feathers.
[1422] Partha's (Arjuna's) charioteer.
[1423] Not manifest.

(94) Gitamrita-mahodadhi;[1424] (95) Kaliyaphani-manikya-ranjita shri-padambuja;[1425] (96) Damodara;[1426] (97) Yajnabhokta;[1427] (98) Danavendra-vinashana;[1428] (99) Narayana; (100) Param *brahman*;[1429] (101) Pannagashana-vahana;[1430] (102) Jalakrida-samasakta-gopi-vastrapaharaka;[1431] (103) Punyashloka;[1432] (104) Tirthapada;[1433] (105) Vedavedya;[1434] (106) Dayanidhi;[1435] (107) Sarva-tirthatmaka;[1436] and (108) Sarva-graha-rupi.[1437] He is greater than the greatest and these are the divinity Krishna's one hundred and eight names. In earlier times, after hearing the *amrita* of *Gita*, Krishna,[1438] Krishna's devotee, composed this *stotram*, which brings pleasure to Krishna. I heard it. It is named Krishna-*premamrita* and it bestows supreme bliss. It destroys great calamities and miseries. It greatly enhances the lifespan. In a birth, one may undertake donations, vows, austerities and visiting *tirtha*s. Hearing this, or reading it, bestows qualities that are crores and crores of times greater. It bestows sons on those who have no sons. It provides a goal to those who have no destination. It brings wealth to the poor and victory to those who desire victory. It bestows nourishment on children and families of cows. It enhances auspiciousness. For children, it pacifies children's diseases and evil planets. It brings peace. At the end, it brings the memory of Krishna. It dispels the

[1424] The great ocean of *amrita* of Bhagavat Gita.

[1425] One whose beautiful lotus feet are embellished by rubies from Kaliya's hood.

[1426] With a rope around the stomach.

[1427] One with a share in a sacrifice.

[1428] Destroyer of Indras among *danava*s.

[1429] Supreme *brahman*.

[1430] With the devourer of *pannaga*s (Garuda) as a mount.

[1431] In the course of sporting in the water, the one who stole the garments of *gopi*s.

[1432] With great fame.

[1433] One whose feet are a *tirtha*.

[1434] One realized through the *Veda*s.

[1435] Store of compassion.

[1436] With all the *tirtha*s in his *atman*.

[1437] One who takes the form of all the planets.

[1438] Krishna Dvaipayana Vedavyasa.

three kinds of worldly hardship. O fortunate one! It accomplishes
what has not been obtained. One should use it for one's own *japa*.
"To Krishna. To the Indra among Yadavas. To the *yogi* who is
in *jnana-mudra*. To the lord. To Rukmini's lord. To the one who
knows *Vedanta*. I prostrate myself." O great Goddess! Day and
night, one should perform *japa* with this *mantra*. All the planets
will be favourable. He will be loved by everyone. He will be
surrounded by sons and grandsons. He will be prosperous, with
every kind of success. After enjoying all the objects of pleasure, he
will obtain *sayujya* with Krishna.' The illustrious Ananta, the lord
who assumed the form known as Samkarshana, the one who holds
up the world, said this. The one who holds up the entire universe,
the one who bestows honours, said this and stopped. Sanaka and
all the others were there, around him. They honoured him, having
been submerged in an ocean of delight. They honoured the lord of
serpents and spoke to him. The *rishi*s said, 'I prostrate myself. O
one who sanctifies the entire universe! I bow down. If a devotee
seeks refuge with you, you destroy his afflictions. You hold up the
earth. You are an ocean of compassion. O Shesha! O lord of the
universe! I prostrate myself before you. You made us drink the
amrita about Krishna. O lord! You have cleansed us of our sins.
O lord! Those like you are full of compassion towards those who
are distressed. You uplift those who bow down before you.' In this
way, they prostrated themselves at the feet of the lord of serpents,
with their minds fixed on what bestows every kind of wish. All of
us performed *pradakshina* of the one who holds up the earth and
returned to our own respective residences. O Rama! This *stotram*
is an ocean of the *amrita* of love. It is full of Krishna, Radhaa's
beloved, and bestows *siddhi*. O Rama! O immensely fortunate one!
This *stotram* is extremely difficult to obtain. It has been heard from
the illustrious Shesha himself, when he spoke about it. There are
all kinds of groups of *mantra*s, *stotram*s and *kavacha*s in the three
worlds. If one practices this, one obtains success in all of those."
O great king! In this way, he told him about Krishna-*premamrita*
stotram. As soon as the sage stopped speaking, a divine vehicle
arrived there. It was followed by four *siddha*s, who could assume

any form they willed and travel at the speed of thought. The stag and doe bowed down at Agastya's feet and took his leave. They happily leapt up and ascended. They assumed divine forms, with the conch-shell, *chakra* and other marks. While all beings and Bhargava and Agastya watched, they went to Vishnu's world, revered by all *deva*s.'

This ends Volume 1 of Brahmanda Purana.

Acknowledgements

The corpus of the Puranas is huge—in scope and size. The Mahabharata is believed to contain 1,00,000 *shloka*s. The Critical Edition of the Mahabharata, edited and published by the Bhandarkar Oriental Research Institute, Pune, doesn't quite contain that many *shloka*s. But this still gives us some idea of the size of the epic. To comprehend what 1,00,000 shlokas mean in a standard word count, the ten-volume unabridged translation I did of the Mahabharata (published by Penguin) amounts to a staggering 2.5 million words. After composing the Mahabharata, Krishna Dvaipayana Vedavyasa composed the eighteen *mahapuranas*, or major Puranas. Or so it is believed. (There are *upapuranas*, or minor Puranas too.) Collectively, these eighteen Puranas amount to 4,00,000 *shloka*s, meaning a disconcerting and daunting number of 10 million words.

After translating the Bhagavat Gita, the Mahabharata, the *Harivamsha* (1,60,000 words) and the Valmiki Ramayana (5,00,000 words), it was but natural to turn one's attention towards translating the Puranas, that is, the major Puranas. This is the daunting Purana Project, so to speak. (All these translations have been, and will be, published by Penguin Random House India.) As the most popular and most read Purana, the *Bhagavata Purana* was the first to be translated (three volumes, 5,00,000 words). The *Markandeya Purana*, another popular Purana (one volume, 1,75,000 words), came next. This was followed by the *Brahma Purana* (two volumes, 3,90,000 words), the *Vishnu Purana* (one volume, 175,000 words) and the *Shiva Purana* (three volumes, 6,75,000 words). The

Brahmanda Purana (two volumes, 3,76,000 words) is the sixth in the series. With eighteen Puranas, the number six is a threshold, in the sense that one-third of the Purana Project has been completed. But this is in terms of the number of Puranas, not in terms of the number of *shloka*s, since the *Padma Purana* and the *Skanda Purana* are huge. That these translations were well-received was encouragement along the intimidating journey of translating the remaining Puranas and I am indebted to the reviewers of these various translations. Two obvious points that are sometimes missed: First, the quality of the texts, on the basis of which these translations are being done, varies from one Purana to another. If a Purana has been read a lot, such as the *Bhagavata Purana*, *Markandeya Purana* or *Vishnu Purana*, the text tends to be clean, not characterized by typos. Clearly, the *Brahmanda Purana* isn't one of these and there are typos in the text. Second, the structure of the text varies, depending on the subject. The *Shiva Purana* was a difficult Purana to translate and, as the reader will discover, so is *Brahmanda Purana*.

As I have traversed the route of the Purana Project, my wife, Suparna Banerjee Debroy, has been a constant source of support and encouragement, providing the conducive environment for the translation work to continue unimpeded. The journey of translating hasn't been an intimidating one only for me. Penguin Random House India must also have thought about it several times, before going ahead with the Purana translations. Most people have some idea about the Ramayana and the Mahabharata, but the Puranas are typically rendered in such dumbed down versions that the readership for unabridged translations had to be created. However, Penguin also believed in the Purana Project, which still stretches into some interminable horizon in the future, more than one and a half decades down the line. For both author and publisher, this is a long-term commitment. But six have been completed and *Kurma Purana* (one volume) is next in the line. I am indebted to Penguin Random House India, in particular, Meru Gokhale, Moutushi Mukherjee and Yash Daiv. The exceptional editing has ensured that the final product is superior to what I delivered. These Purana translations have been brought alive by the wonderful illustrations by Shamanthi Rajasingham and *Brahmanda Purana* is no different. I also thank the cover designers.

Murli Manohar Joshi is much more than a politician and a former member of Parliament and union minister. Though his subject is physics, his interest in Sanskrit and the Sanskrit legacy runs deep. Ever since the days of the Mahabharata translation, he has taken a keen and avuncular interest in the progress of the translations. With the threshold of six crossed, I can think of no better person to dedicate the *Brahmanda Purana* to.

12 December 2023   Bibek Debroy

Scan QR code to access the
Penguin Random House India website